SCHOLAE ACADEMICAE

SCHOLAE ACADEMICAE

SOME ACCOUNT OF

Studies at the English Universities
in the Eighteenth Century

CHRISTOPHER WORDSWORTH

Reprints of Economic Classics

AUGUSTUS M. KELLEY PUBLISHERS
New York 1969

Published by

FRANK CASS AND COMPANY LIMITED

67 Great Russell Street, London WC1

Published in the United States by
Augustus M. Kelley, Publishers
New York, New York 10010

First edition   1877
New impression   1968

SBN 678 05085 6

Library of Congress Catalog Card No. 79–93271

378,42
W925a

74-5502

Printed in Holland by
N.V. Grafische Industrie Haarlem

PREFACE.

No one who has any experience of the working and life of Cambridge can be ignorant how completely we have been removed from Cambridge of half a century ago, or that we have lost almost the last glimpse of what our University, even forty years since, was like.

Not only has she changed, as all that lives must change, but one after another the men of advanced years or of clear memory (such as Dr Gilbert Ainslie, Francis Martin, Sedgwick, Shilleto and Dr Cookson) have passed away, leaving no such memoranda as Gunning or Pryme left, at least none which are at present generally accessible, to tell us what were the methods and processes of University Study through which were educated the minds which have done much to make our University and our Country what they are.

In this quick transition of our academical methods, customs, and institutions, the difficulty becomes intense when we set ourselves to attempt to picture either of our Universities (for the like holds good of *Oxford*[1]) at a period removed still further from us by two or three generations.

---

[1] It is as well here (as elsewhere) to apprise the Reader that in the names of persons or colleges mentioned in this volume the *italic type* has been reserved (except where no confusion was anticipated, *e.g.* on pp. 140—142, or in a reprint) for those which belong to *Oxford* or some foreign seminary.

Though I am conscious how unworthy my work is of the Universities, to the knowledge of whose history I desire even remotely to contribute, I have endeavoured to collect in this volume some of the materials which are requisite for a faithful account of Cambridge and *Oxford* in the Eighteenth Century. These lay scattered and isolated, partly in memoirs and miscellaneous publications, and I have taken some pains to bring to light some of the secrets of University history and of literary lore which have lain dormant in manuscripts, known perhaps to a few, and read, it may be, by fewer.

The Table of Contents and the Index will enable the curious to use the volume as a book of reference.

The following method of arrangement has been adopted:

Six chapters (II—VII) are devoted to the history and method of the old Cambridge test and examination for the first degree in Arts, and of mathematics, the study predominant; after which a place is given (ch. VIII) to the '*trivials*' (grammar, logic and rhetoric), which under the more ancient *régime* led the undergraduate on his four years' march. Classics and Moral Philosophy, the subsidiary studies of the old *Tripos* (X, XI), close this portion of the work.

The elements of professional education are next considered, viz. Law (ch. XI), with which Oxford has taught us to associate modern history, thereby encouraging us to give a place to the complete equipment of a man of the world (XII).

Oriental Studies (XIII) supply so much of the special education of a Divine as can be well divorced from the topic of Religious Life, which is not here under our consideration. The elementary methods of the Physician's education are described in five chapters (XIV—XVIII) on physics, anatomy, chemistry, mineralogy and botany.

Special qualification for the second degree in Arts, though barely recognized at Cambridge, was more fully developed at Oxford (XIX); but its antient '*quadrivial*' subjects were either neglected, studied independently as music (XX), or anticipated in the course of astronomy, &c. (XXI).

The concluding chapter (XXII) is miscellaneous and supplementary; while the nine *Appendices* contain documents relating chiefly to old courses and schemes of study, methods of examination and disputations, honorary degrees, Cambridge University Calendars, and the University Press. A collection of undergraduates' letters will probably interest several readers as they have beguiled me in transcribing them.

In producing the present publication I have been enabled, by the generosity of the Syndics of the Cambridge University Press, to complete the second of three works on *University Life and Studies in England during the Eighteenth Century*, which were announced in the Preface to a book on *Social Life*, published by Messrs Deighton, Bell and Co. in 1874, in compliance with the provision for the Le Bas Essay prize.

That the day is not far distant when the materials which I have collected and published already will be worked up and turned to good account by one who is well qualified for the task, I have good reason to hope.

For the present I will record my thanks to the Rev. Professor John E. B. Mayor of S. John's, and to Mr H. Jackson of Trinity, who with great patience and kindness have suggested improvements and corrections while the sheets have been passing through the press: to Mr H. Bradshaw of King's, the University Librarian, and to the past and present Librarians of Gonville and Caius College; to the Rev. H. R. Luard, the University Registrary, to Professor T. M^{c}K. Hughes, Mr J.

W. L. Glaisher, and the Rev. Ri. Appleton of Trinity, to the Rev. T. G. Bonney of S. John's, to Mr R. L. Bensly of Gonville and Caius, and to Mr J. D. Hamilton Dickson and the Rev. Arthur Lloyd of Peterhouse, as well as to the Rev. Professor J. R. T. Eaton of *Merton,* the Rev. Professor T. Fowler of *Lincoln,* and the Worshipful Walter G. F. Phillimore of *All Souls* College, *Oxon.,* for criticizing or supplementing certain sections or passages; to the Rev. H. G. Jebb, rector of Chetwynd, and to Mr F. Madan, fellow of *Brasenose* College, as well as to Professor John E. B. Mayor, the Rev. W. G. Searle of Queens', and Mr J. W. Clark of Trinity, for their liberality in communicating papers or MS. collections in their possession.

My obligations to books are, I hope, sufficiently expressed in the text and notes of this work, unless it be to Mr Thompson Cooper's *New Biographical Dictionary* (1873), a work of most agreeable comprehensiveness.

CONTENTS.

[1] See also pp. 264, 265.   [2] See pp. 266—268.

[3] See also p. 264.

APPENDICES.

[1] The ground or excuse for printing this 17th century document in the present collection will be found stated below on p. 273.

---

[1] This tract, or one with the same full title, is ascribed in Watt's *Bibl. Brit.* 985 i. to W. Wotton, D.D., author of *Reflexions on Antient and Modern Learning*, who graduated B.A. at Catharine-hall in 1679, and subsequently gained a fellowship at S. John's and a prebend at Salisbury.

CORRIGENDA.

Page	line	from the	for	read
14	13	top	*second*	*third*
99	4	,,	the bishop's son	prebendary of Salisbury
129	12	,,	Bates, W. Emm. and King's,	Bates, W. Emm. and Queens'.
251	6	,,	Plane Spherical	Plane and Spherical

UNIVERSITY STUDIES.

CHAPTER I.

GENERAL INTRODUCTION. LIBRARIES AND LECTURES.

> 'Books were there
> Right many, and in seeming fair.
> But who knows what therein might be
> 'Twixt board and board of oaken tree?'
>   *The Ring given to Venus.*—W. Morris.

THE eighteenth century is hardly far enough removed from us to be canonized among 'the good old times,' and the tradition of abuses which have been since reformed or partially reformed, is sufficiently strong an *advocatus diaboli* to deter us even from beatifying it.

Nevertheless, if we search into its records, we shall, I believe, find no lack of interest in them, though in form (with the exception of such books as Boswell's *Johnson*) they are apt to be almost repulsive.

Considering the two great shocks which England had sustained in the preceding sixty years, the last century, or at least the reign of Queen Anne, might be said to have opened hopefully.

Politically there was not sufficient cause for either Jacobite or Whig to despair for the future ; the star of the national army and navy was in the ascendant, and our commercial prospects had markedly improved even before the Revolution. The

Church was improved in temporalities by the Queen, in respect both of her fabrics and of her poverty-stricken clergy : the
Lower House of Convocation was making efforts to revive ecclesiastical discipline, and to repress immorality. The venerable
Society for Promoting Christian Knowledge had originated in
1699 : a branch of it was already doing missionary work in the
plantations of Maryland, and received a charter in 1701 as the
Society for the Propagation of the Gospel. Hammond and
Jeremy Taylor were dead, but Lake and Ken both lived, and
the works of all of them were keeping alive a secret, but a very
clear and strong, flame in the hearts of some of our men and
women.

In the province of literature, which more nearly concerns
our present subject, matters were even more hopeful, except in
the department of amusement, where Steele and Addison had
not yet produced their wares as a set-off against the pernicious
artificial comedy, nor had the *Spectator* as yet drawn the attention of the public to the charms of Shakespeare and Milton.

Clarendon's *History of the Rebellion,* destined to become a
source of twofold advantage to his own university, came out
in 1702—4 ; while Burnet's 'romance,' as the staunch Churchmen called it, had reached its second volume.

Sir Isaac Newton had published his *Principia* in 1687, and
John Locke his *Essay* in 1689 :—which two works were to
mould the mind of Cambridge for the coming century.

John Ray had published his important works, and was alive
until 1705, two years before the birth of Linnaeus. Robert
Boyle had died at the end of 1691.

Among the 'heads' at Oxford the most noted was John Mill,
principal of S. Edmund Hall. To him Richard Bentley addressed an Epistle in 1690, and after publishing Boyle Lectures
and Dissertations on Phalaris, was installed master of Trinity
College, Cambridge, Feb. 1, 1699—1700. To his activity, as
much as to the writings of Newton and Locke, we may attribute the revival of Cambridge studies since the Revolution.

When Zachary Conrad von Uffenbach visited the English
Universities in the summer of 1710, few things seem to have
impressed him so much as the wretched state in which most of
the college libraries were kept.

The great exception, it is hardly necessary to say, was the noble library of Trinity College.

But even here the librarian knew little of his charge, while at the smaller colleges the condition of things was most deplorable. In 'Tschies Colledge,' (*Käse Collegium*) as his servant called the enlarged foundation of Gonville, the librarian was not to be found, and all the books that were to be seen were in a miserable attic haunted by pigeons[1], and so dusty that the German was forced to take off his ruffles[2].

So of the other colleges, with a few exceptions. In one he noticed that the illuminated initials had been snipt recklessly out of a manuscript of Aulus Gellius. But, alas! 'Pembrocks-Colledge' is not the only place at Cambridge where this barbarity has been committed; nor is the Vatican the only library where the keeper has turned a dishonest penny by selling the paintings from the vellum. We can sympathize with Uffenbach's blunt *abeat in malam crucem talis Bibliothecarius*[3]! But what should we think now-a-days if Bodley's librarian employed his time as Hudson did in disturbing the readers with a noisy '*he! he! he!*' or in making a profit from the sale of duplicates? We should not then be surprised to find that the under-librarians, ill-paid and well-worked like master Crab and Tom Hearne, looked anxiously lest they should lose the expected

[1] In T. Baker's *Act at Oxford* (1704) one of the characters talks of putting up his horses in the College library at Balliol on that festive occasion.

[2] Uffenbach, *Reisen* iii. 13 &c. (Ulm, 1754).

[3] *Ibid.* iii. 59, 60; cp. 37. 'A great bibliographer relates with glee how by a present of some splendidly bound modern books he obtained possession of the chief treasures of a certain cathedral library. In that library you yet may turn over volume after volume out of which the illuminations have been sliced by the penknives of visitors. In that library you still see *strata* as it were of collections—plenteous ore in one generation from folios to broadsheets, in the next *tenuis argilla*. . . .

Small blame to chapters cut down to four or five clergymen.'— *Quarterly Rev.* cclix. 249, 250. In Peterhouse library the gilding &c. of some of the initials of Fust and Schaeffer's Latin Bible (Mentz, 1462) has been scratched and mutilated in days when even choristers were allowed free access to the room, which was in sad disorder when Uffenbach visited it, Aug. 7, 1710. One of the offenders (a freshman or a junior soph) has left not only his name but the date of his indenture in the burnished gold—[Jacques] 'Spearman, 1732'.

Dr. W. Stanley, ex-master of C.C.C.C., printed (at Bowyer's) in 1722, at his own expense, a catalogue of the Parker MSS. which Nasmith improved in 1774.

douceur. When such days return we may expect to see, as Uffenbach saw them, the country folk staring in amazement at the Bodleian 'like a cow at a new gate[1].'

With Mr W. Dunn Macray's *Annals of the Bodleian Library, Oxford* before us, we cannot complain that there is lack of information about the past history of that institution. Something of the same kind on a smaller scale has been contributed in behalf of the Cambridge University Library by Mr Bradshaw; and it is to be hoped that he will not allow this to remain in so inaccessible a place as the pages of the *University Gazette*[2] of 1869. In 1870 Mr Luard edited for the university a *Chronological List of the Graces, Documents,* &c. which concern the Library.

In Isaac Casaubon's time (1613) the Bodleian collection was meagre, but was more conveniently open for readers than those of Paris. Its appearance in 1691 is described by Mrs Alicia D'Anvers in *Academia:* or the *Humours of the university of* Oxford *in Burlesque Verse* (pp. 20—23). Its arrangement had varied little from what it was about 1675 when David Loggan sketched it for his *Oxonia Illustrata*, the duodecimos on the lower shelves, the folios with chains at the top[3].

But in the more important respect of its contents it was in Hearne's time (1714) double what it had been when Casaubon was at Oxford a century before, *i. e.* at the latter date its manuscripts were 5916, and printed books 30169.

Uffenbach spent about two months at Oxford in the autumn of 1710, and some of his impressions of the Bodleian have been translated by Mr Macray from the *Commercium Epistolare*. A no less curious account, to which I have already made allusion, is contained in his German diary[4], of which professor Mayor's summary is tarrying in the press. Uffenbach seems to have little higher opinion of 'bookseller' Hudson and Crabb than

---

[1] *Ibid.* III. 88, ' wie eine Kuh ein neu Thor ansahen.' Cp. 157.

[2] Nos. IX—XV. pp. 69, 77, 85, 93, 101, 109, 117.

[3] Cp. the *Guardian*, No. LX. (1713). The books in libraries down to the beginning of last century had no titles on the back: they were arranged in the shelves with their fore-edge outward, and on it was written the name or class-mark. At Peterhouse a catalogue of each shelf was written on the oaken panel at its end.

[4] *Reisen* III. 87—179.

Hearne himself had, but he commends the latter, and notices his great share (and Crabb's) in the new catalogue which came out eventually in 1738 (2 vols.) with no mention of him whatever. Uffenbach includes all three officials in the charge of over-anxiety for fees : but it must be admitted that they were miserably under-paid. After the foreigner had got formal admission as a reader he made his first regular visit, which he describes after the following sort :—I asked the way to the *Baroccian* mss.; Mr Crabb told me that he would bring me any ms. I required; I told him that I wished to go through the principal mss. by the catalogue and make notes of each. At last he agreed to go up with me if I would give him a good present. So I was fain to open my purse and give him a guinea. I preferred giving the profit to him, *diesem armen Teufel,* rather than to the head-librarian *Hudson;* for first I must have given him more, and next I should have seen less; for he does not always stay to the end: whereas Mr *Crabb* is poking about the whole time. Next morning I wished to return to the *Baroccian* mss.; but as Mr *Crabb* was occupied with strangers and had much besides to do, I turned over the register of donations.

It was probably most unfortunate for the library that Hearne, its most devoted worker, was excluded on some paltry charge of Jacobitism in 1715. Between 1730 and 1740 we learn[1] that many days passed without there being a single reader in Bodley, and rarely above two books *per diem* were consulted, whereas about 1648-50 the average was above a dozen. In 1787 complaints were formally lodged against the librarian for neglect and incivility by Dr T. Beddoes (*Pemb.*) the chemistry reader. New rules were drawn up, and matters began to improve[2] about 1789. In 1794 we find the curators

---

[1] Macray, 152. The advantage which undergraduates enjoyed of easy access to the Bodleian and other libraries on their tutors' introduction is insisted on by prof. Bentham (*Divinity Lectures,* p. 37) in 1774, and by Philalethes in answer (p. 7) to V. Knox's misstatements, 6 Feb. 1790. Gibbon, as a gentleman-commoner, had a key of Magdalen library in 1752 (*Misc.*

Works I. 53). It was not until 1829 that B.A.s were allowed to have books out of the Cambridge library, after a two years' struggle for the privilege. In 1833 some rules were printed relating to the admission of undergraduates, and in 1834 it was ordered that they should ring a bell before entering the library.

[2] Macray's *Annals,* 75, 152.

in consultation with the librarians of the colleges respecting scarce books[1], &c.

Uffenbach had visited the Cambridge public library a fortnight before he went to Oxford. In those days, when the present Catalogue-room was still the Senate-house, our collection of books was, as he saw it, contained in 'two mean rooms of moderate size. In the first on the left-hand side are the printed books, but very ill arranged, in utter confusion. The catalogue is only alphabetical, and lately compiled on the basis of the Bodleian catalogue. It is also local, indicating where the books are to be sought. In the second room, which is half empty, there were some more printed books, and then the MSS., of which, however, we could see nothing well, because the librarian, Dr *Laughton* (or as they pronounce it, *Laffton*), was absent; which vexed me not a little, as Dr Ferrari highly extolled his great learning and courtesy. *Rara avis in his terris.*

'We met here however by accident the librarian of *St John's* library, Mr Baker, a very friendly and learned man, by whose help we saw several other things; for otherwise the maid, who had opened the door and was with us, would have been able to shew us but little.' He describes the Codex Bezæ, some Anglo-Saxon MSS., which he saw, and an untidy drawer of miscellaneous coins. The under library-keeper, who was there, gave him a leaf of an imperfect codex of Josephus written with thick ink, as a curiosity to take away[2]!

We cannot but look with envy upon the donation-book and enriched catalogues of the Bodleian. Although the *Gough* and *Douce* collections did not come in until the present century (1809, and 1834), yet Ri. *Rawlinson's* (including Hearne's curious papers) was acquired in 1755, and the (original) *Godwyn* collection was imported in 1770. But beside these, numerous smaller legacies, &c. came pouring in from Locke, Hody, Narcissus Marsh, South, and Grabe (1704—24), Tanner (1736), J. Walker (1754), and Browne Willis in 1760: —not to mention many other less eminent donors. Mean-

---

[1] Macray's *Annals*, p. 200.

[2] *Reisen* III. p. 20 (prof. Mayor's version, p. 140). Also pp. 33—40, 70—75, 81. Baker, Ferrari and Newcome enriched St John's library in 1740, '44, '65.

while Cambridge came off very poorly, whether because she did not make such graceful speeches to her benefactors, or because the inexorable care with which Bodley kept the books within his walls pleased book-collectors better than the excessively accommodating open-handedness[1] wherewith we lent, and practically *gave away* our treasures,—or from whatever cause, I cannot say. Since Holdsworth's books in 1649 and Hackett's in 1670 Cambridge acquired no considerable collections with one grand exception[2], and her treatment of that one was not very encouraging to future donors.

In September, 1710, Sherlock received an announcement from Lord Townshend that King George I. was about to present to the University (whether out of regard to whiggish[3] rationality or ignorance, the party wits could not agree) the valuable library of the late Bishop Moore of Ely, which he had purchased for 6000 guineas.   This collection exceeded the number of thirty thousand volumes (including 1790 MSS.), and was more than double of the existing stock of our University Library.

In the course of fifteen years a new Senate-house[4] was built in order to set free the present catalogue-room for the reception of this noble gift; but, as Mr Bradshaw says, it

---

[1] The *convenience* of our system was appreciated by the learned Oxonian, Humphrey Wanley, in 1699. He testifies thus (Ellis' *Letters of Lit. Men*, 289): 'The truth is, the Cambridge gentlemen are extremely courteous and obliging, and, excepting those of Bennet College [where they were bound by sterner laws than the Bodleian], I can borrow what books I please.'   The *inconvenient* part of the Oxford conservative system is much relieved by the use of the 'camera,' and the liberty which the curators now have to lend out MSS. and rare books when really wanted; while the peril attending our Cambridge liberty has been diminished of late years by a wholesale draughting-off of the rarer books into surveillance.

[2] We might mention also the Worts' benefaction (1709), of which a contemporary account is given by Reneu to Strype in an appendix to this volume: but it was not until a century later that this part of the fund was applied to this object.   It is now worth about a thousand pounds annually to the library.

[3] It is curious that in 1718, the year of Bentley's degradation, Philip Brooke (Joh.) the librarian was admonished for neglect in July and resigned under a charge of *want of loyalty* in December, and the V.-C. (Gooch) was inhibited by the proctor Towers on the same plea for his leniency in dealing with him.

[4] An account of expenses of building the senate-house, 1722—32, is in Caius Coll. Library, MS. 621, No. 10. Also for further completion, 1767—9, *ibid.* MS. 604 (=339 *red*), No. 53 ; MS. 602 (=278 *red*), No. 6; and MS. 621, No. 16.

was 'upwards of five and thirty years before the new library was ready for use, and during that time the pillage was so unlimited that the only wonder is that we have any valuable books left.' When at last the arrangement was completed (July, 1752) the MSS. were bundled into shelves with no care or order[1], though a respectable inventory was made of them.

At the same period (1748) no less than 902 volumes were reported as missing from the old library, so that our loss was not only from Bishop Moore's collection. Yet in that very year the new 'Orders for the publick library' gave readers freedom of access to the books. Indeed it was not until 1809 that any special restriction was put upon the borrowing of MSS. The result was that at the review of the library in 1772 a large number of rare books were not forthcoming. Graduates were convicted of stealing books in 1731 and 1736; and in 1846 J. Dearle was transported for the same offence.

[1] The following extracts from T. Baker's letters to J. Strype in 1715 and the following years, may be thought interesting.

Univ. Camb. MS. Add. 10, No. 95. 'Cambr. Oct. 6th [1715] You see our university flourisheth, by the King's Royall bounty. It is indeed a noble gift, I wish we may finde as noble a Repository to lodge it in, wch is much talkt of, and I hope will be effected. In the mean while I doubt it will be some time before I can have the turning of the MSS: otherwise I should hope to have somewhat to impart.'

No. 96. 'Cambridge, Oct. 16. As to a new Library, I have nothing certain to inform. The Law Schools have been spoke of, but as there is hardly roome enough, so they that think of that, seem neither to consult the honor of the Donor, or of the university. The great design wch is likewise spoke of, is a new Building to front ye present Schools on either side the Regent walks, with an Arch in the middle. For this money is wanting, and yet if it were begun, I should hope, such a public work would hardly stick

for want of encouragement! In the mean while that wing of the Library is spoke of for the MSS: in the part of wch the present MSS. are lodg'd already, and the printed Books remov'd.'

No. 98. (18 Feb. 1715—16.) Baker regrets that he is still unable to get at the books.

No. 99. [28 June, 1716.] 'We seem to have come to a resolution, to fit up the Law Schools for the Bp of Ely's Books, but as the execution will be slow, so I am sure that there will want roome for a great part of them.'

No. 100. 'Cambridge, Nov. 9, 1716. 'When the Bp of Ely's Books are opened (wch I doubt they will not be in hast) I shall hope to meet with somewhat worth imparting.'

No. 107. 28 Sept. 1717. 'not one book yet put up; nor one class towards receiving them, and when all is finisht will be a very unequal Repository to so noble a gift.' And the King expected to visit Cambridge.

No. 117. 8 Mar. 1717—18. 'One part ... almost finisht, tho' it will not hold much above half the Books.'

In 1766 it was agreed to print a catalogue of the printed books, but no trace even of a commencement of the work is known to exist. It was not until 1794 that Nasmith undertook to make a fuller list of the MSS. on the basis of the then existing one. About this time the library hours were from 10 a.m. to 2 p.m.

In 1740 vols xxiv—xlii. of Baker's MSS. were acquired, and the Askew classical MSS. in 1786. Donations are recorded from Mr Worthington (1725), Archd. Lewis (1727), Duke of Newcastle (1759), King Charles III. of Spain (1764), Duke of Marlborough (1782), Earl of Hardwicke (1798), and Sir R. Worsley (1799) for small presents, such as Oxford received in abundance.

From the nature of the terms of admission into the Cambridge library[1] it is impossible to measure the use made of it at any period as was done in the case of the Bodleian, but one of the causes which probably deterred some from frequenting that building in the more studious months, was not wanting here. The severity of cold in winter of which Mr Macray speaks had power to dishearten even the enthusiastic Thomas Baker, whose health was not good[2]. It was not until 1790 and 1795 that fire-places were put into our library, and warming apparatus was recommended in 1823, and 1854—6. About 1797 Marshall, the library-keeper, became perfectly crippled with rheumatism, and his assistants could not stay above three years in the library, which 'was so extremely damp that few persons could pass any length of time in it with impunity[3].'

But to return to Uffenbach's visit to England in 1710. The absence of librarians and others for the vacation at Cambridge obliged him to betake himself to other occupations, which he recounts in a no less interesting way. But even in term-time when he reached Oxford it was unfortunate that

[1] In answer to K. Charles' *quaere* in Aug. 1675 the Cambridge heads declared that 'No University members under the Degree of Masters of Arts have admittance to the use of the publick Library, and those upon no other caution but their Matriculation oath, taken at their admission into the University. If any strangers be permitted the use of the Library, it is by licence given them from the V. Chancellor.' (Dyer *Priv.* I. 370.)

[2] MS. Add. 10, No. 62 (19 April, 1712).

[3] Gunning *Reminisc.* Vol. II. ch. iii.

when the visitor wanted to go to the Ashmolean museum, the under-librarian had gone off to the Oxford races (*Sept.* 18), whither Uffenbach himself went in a barge to see the 'Smoak-race[1],' horse races, &c. Still more must we regret that he visited the universities in the long vacation, both for the credit of the country and for the knowledge which we might have gained of the manners of the time:—for though he attended a music party and met some of the celebrities of the day at the *Greek's Coffeehouse* and elsewhere, yet many of the senior members of the University were not in residence; and of undergraduate-life we hear next to nothing, and that little not from personal observation.

Soon after his arrival in Cambridge,—that wretched town which he described as about the size of Höchst near Frankfurt, —Uffenbach was astonished to hear from his cicerone, the Italian Ferrari, that there were no classes or lectures (*collegia*) in the summer, and in winter only three or four, and those generally delivered to the walls (*die sie vor die Wände thun*). It is possible that he had heard an account of what were at Oxford actually called *Wall-lectures*[2]—the *sex sollemnes lectiones* of the statutes, 'read *pro forma* in empty school' (1773) as a qualification for the degree of M.A., and the 'ordinaries' for D.D., which were performed in a slovenly way and to the bare walls, unless some tiresome visitor came in and shamed the student into a more serious exhibition of his proficiency. Ferrari, a foreigner, was not a good person to explain to another the manners and customs of Cambridge, which both in name and thing differed widely from those of the seminaries with which they were familiar. Suffice it to say that if they had made enquiry in term-time they would have found Roger Cotes of Trinity, Daniel Waterland of Magdalene,

---

[1] Probably a *smock-race:* see *The Scouring of the White Horse* (by the author of 'Tom Brown'), which illustrates the sports of Thames-country. Compare also Uffenbach's account of the contest 'der das garstigste Gesicht dazu macht' with 'grinning through horse-collars.' Also Hearne's account (*Diary*, 20 Sept. 1720) of a race be-tween two running footmen who wore even less covering than the athletes of the present day—*braccatos, immò ne braccatos quidem,* as an Oxford proctor called them.

[2] [Bliss'] *Oxoniana* I. 62. Cp. *Consideration on the Public Exercises,* Oxon. 1773. *p. x.*

Nicholas Sanderson of Christ's, Chr. Anstey (the elder) and J. Newcome of St John's, and I know not who beside[1], with well-filled lecture-rooms in 1710.   And if they failed to find in his college auditorium their friend Richard Laughton of Clare, the popular 'pupil-monger,' it would be only because then, as in the preceding year, he was proctor, and in his own person (as we shall see below) fulfilling the office of moderator in the schools for the University at large, where he was encouraging the senior sophs and questionists to adopt the Newtonian philosophy in the exercises for their bachelor's degree.

I have shewn already in my *University Life* (pp. 83—87) that at the *close* of the eighteenth century a large number of professors at each University did not pretend to lecture. But though this was doubtless a bad state of things, and would have sounded still more deplorable to a foreigner who was ignorant of our English system of college tutors and lecturers; still this would not prove that even at the dead time, a century after Uffenbach's visit, all teaching-life was extinct at our Universities.

There was always a supply of *college tutors* who, like R. Laughton of Clare, fulfilled their duty scrupulously, and consequently made their colleges popular with careful parents and aspiring students. Nor indeed, as I have previously shewn, was the common neglect by any means universal among the *professors*. In a small society it sometimes happened (as indeed it may now) that some precocious freshman[2] read faster than his tutor did in lectures with the bulk of the men of his year, and in the lack of the new intercollegiate system was excused attendance. But [Waterland's] *Advice to a Young Student* (a thoroughly practical and popular guide, which had a 'run' in MS. and print for at least thirty years) is only one among several witnesses which might be produced to prove that students relied upon their college tutors for initiation in each subject which they took up. Even Gibbon, when it was represented that he had generalized too much from his own

---

[1] William Whiston of Clare, Lucasian professor, published *Praelectiones Physico-Mathematicae*, Cantabrigiae *in Scholis publicis habitae* up to that time, and was silenced only in the autumn of that year.

[2] e.g. *Sir J. Fenn*, Caius, 1757; *Sir W. Jones, Univ.* 1764; *H. Gunning*, Chr. 1785.

brief and deplorable experience at Magdalen College, Oxford, whither he went in his fifteenth year in 1752, and remained but fourteen months, diversifying that short period by 'schemes' or excursions to Bath, to Buckinghamshire, and four to London,—even Gibbon was able to mention the names of John Burton (D.D. 1752), who before his time had been a most painstaking tutor of Corpus Christi, Oxon. for fifteen years, and of Sir William Scott, M.A. 1767 (afterwards Camden Reader of History, and celebrated as a judge under the name of Lord Stowell), who after his time migrating from Corpus Christi became a good and popular tutor at University College, Oxon. One of his own tutors at Magdalen (for Gibbon had the misfortune tc change his instructor) was T. Waldgrave or Waldegrave (D.D. 1747), whom he describes as 'a good, sober man, but indolent;' and who frequently walked with his pupil to the top of Heddington-hill and 'freely conversed on a variety of subjects[1],' though the lad was pleased to neglect his Terence lectures which others attended for an hour every morning. In Gibbon's second term his tutor went out of residence and was succeeded by a careless man as it appears. But at that very time George Horne was a fellow of the college; about the time Gibbon should have taken his degree Ri. Chandler, learned in inscriptions, came into residence, and at least two years before he *wrote* his 'Autobiography[2]' Martin Joseph Routh had edited the Euthydemus and Gorgias of Plato, and was already deep in theological research. Forty years earlier E. Holdsworth, a Wykehamist well versed in Virgil, had been a successful tutor at Magdalen (1711-15) until he chose rather to leave his demyship and the certainty of a fellowship than to take the oaths of allegiance[3].

But, as we see, Gibbon had generalized unduly from the condition of the 'monks of Magdalen' (where no 'commoners' were admitted) in 1752 to the normal condition of that and all 'the other colleges of Oxford and Cambridge.' In answer

[1] Had he known his former pupil's theological difficulties, Waldegrave would in 1753 have striven to dispel them. (See Gibbon's *Misc. Works*, Vol. II. Letter xi.)

[2] Gibbon seems to have commenced his 'Autobiography' after he went to Lausanne in 1782. It was *published* posthumously by Ld Sheffield in 1796.

[3] Nichols' *Lit. Anecd.* III. 67 *n.*

to this assumption Dr Parr in note 84 to his *Spital Sermon* (Easter Tuesday 1800)[1] has merely to array, with occasional comments, some three hundred and fifty names of eminent men of letters and science who had resided in the universities in his own time.

The following list of certain subjects on which there were lectures at different periods in the colleges is taken at random from biographies &c., and is of course a mere specimen.

1710.   *St John's*, Camb., for freshmen.   *M.* Hierocles[2], *Tu., Th., Sat.,* Logic.   In a later term, Algebra: for junior sophs, Ethics: senior sophs, Tacquet's Euclid[3], Rohault's Physics.

1737.   *St John's*, Camb.   Logic.

1738.   *Ch. Ch. Oxon.*   Puffendorf.

1747.   *Trin. Coll.* Camb.   Cicero de Officiis.

1752.   *Magd. Oxon.*   Terence for freshmen daily.

1755.   *Trin. Coll.* Camb.   Puffendorf, Clarke on the Attributes, Locke, Duncan's Logic.   Daily early lectures in hall, with a weekly *viva voce* examination conducted in Latin.

1766.   *Trinity Hall*, Camb.   Cicero de Officiis.

1767.   *Peterhouse*, Camb.   Newton's Principia, Greek Testament.

1770[4].   *Christ's Coll.*, Camb.   Classics and Locke alternate mornings.   Two evenings, Greek Testament, one a Greek or Latin book.

1772.   *Jesus*, Camb.   Algebra, and Duncan's Logic.   These,

[1] Sydney Smith in the 1st no. of the *Edinburgh Review* compared Parr's sermon, with its abnormal notes, to the wig which its author wore:—'while it trespasses little on the orthodox magnitude of perukes in the anterior parts, it scorns even episcopal limits behind, and swells out into boundless convexity of frizz, the μέγα θαῦμα of barbers, and the terror of the literary world.'

[2] *i. e.* the work of Hierocles the Neo-Platonist, edited by P. Needham, *Camb.* 1709.

[3] Cambridge editions of Tacquet's Euclid in 1702—3, 1710, by Whiston (then Lucasian professor), with select Theorems of Archimedes and practical corollaries.

[4] This date and place are conjectural —from the *Monthly Magazine*, 1797, i. p. 360 *a.* For the year 1772 one authority mentions only two subjects at Jesus Coll., another mentions three others as well, and that for freshmen only; which shews that we must not take the rest of my list as exhaustive.

with classical books, Euclid and Arithmetic, were the freshmen's lectures at all colleges, the Logic, however, not being universally taught.

1780. *Cath. Hall,* Camb. Moral Philosophy.

1785. *Christ's Coll.,* Camb. Euclid, I—VI., Maclaurin's Algebra, Classics, Locke, Moral Philosophy, Grotius and Logic and (?) Chemistry. (Gunning's *Reminisc.,* I. 11.)

1793. *Trinity College,* Camb. A junior soph, Euclid, XI.

It will be observed that our first and fullest list (Ambrose Bonwicke's at St John's, in 1710-13), just coincides with the time of which Uffenbach conceived so gloomy an impression. A glance at Waterland's Scheme, which will be found in the *second appendix* to this present volume, will give us a still clearer and more encouraging view of Cambridge College-lectures between 1710 and 1740.

I have mentioned the weekly examination at Trinity, conducted in the Latin language. *Yearly* college examinations were the exception in that century, but some account of those established at St John's, Cambridge, in Dr Powell's days, will be found in *another appendix.* Under Dr Postlethwaite yearly examinations of freshmen and junior sophs were instituted at Trinity in 1790. Bp Monk, when head-lecturer in 1818, extended the college examination to students of the third year[1]. We find, moreover, that throughout the century candidates for degrees were examined sometimes nominally, sometimes thoroughly, by the fellows of their own colleges before they were allowed to pass to the public examination of the schools or senate-house. Examples of college tutors examining their pupils privately to see whether they made proper progress are not wanting[2].

One of Gibbon's reflexions on his experience of Magd. Coll., Oxon. in 1752, is—'A tradition prevailed that some of our predecessors had spoken Latin declamations in the hall; but of

---

[1] *Life of Bentley,* II. 424.

[2] Gunning *Reminisc.* I. ch. i. In chapter ii. the same author says it was the custom of his college (Christ's) 'for the undergraduates to send in to the Dean once a week a Latin theme' besides their lectures. This was just two years before Gibbon *wrote* his 'Autobiography.'

this ancient custom no vestige remained: the obvious methods of public exercises and examinations were totally unknown.'

If he referred to the order of gentlemen-commoners alone, we may make reply, as Evelyn testifies (*anno* 1637), that at Balliol they 'were no more exempted from exercise than the meanest Scholars there' and Erasmus Phillips of Pembroke, nearer his own time, had in 1721 to take an essay to the Master, and to declaim in hall. But it is also true that in 1774 (fourteen years before Gibbon's Memoir was written) the fellow-commoners of St John's, Cambridge, were obliged to attend the examination:—in 1790, in *all* the colleges of Oxford, a more rigorous discipline was enforced upon noblemen and gentlemen-commoners than the amendments of V. Knox proposed, and in *several* the heirs of the first families of the kingdom submitted to the same exercises and the same severity of discipline with the lowest members of the society. In 1802, S. M. Phillipps, a fellow-commoner of Sidney, was 8th wrangler. Nevertheless, it must be admitted that even in later times, students of this rank were *in some instances* allowed to be idle or even encouraged in idleness. Indeed, the *university* as distinct from their college examinations appear scarcely to have reached them, and it is even asserted that Felix Vaughan, of Jesus College (who was also a good classical scholar), was the first fellow-commoner whose name appeared on the *tripos*. He was eleventh senior optime in 1790, being two places below John Tweddell. James Scarlett (Lord Abinger, Exchequer Baron) of Trinity, who took his degree in that same year, though not in honours, is said by Peacock (*Statutes*, p. 71 *n.*) to have been the first fellow-commoner who in later times appeared in the *schools*.

In 1750 however Gray mentions (*Letter to* Wharton, III. 78) the election to a fellowship at Pembroke, Camb., of E. Delaval, a fellow-commoner 'who has taken a degree in an exemplary manner, and is very sensible and knowing.'

Also T. Gisborne, fellow-commoner of St John's, B.A. 1780, was sixth wrangler and senior medallist.

But if Gibbon's remarks related to all ranks of students impartially, the following pages must serve to limit the scope of his censure.

CHAPTER II.

THE TRIPOS.

'Cry you mercy, I took you for a joint-stool.'
K. Lear, Act iii. Sc. 6.

BEFORE entering upon the details of the university exercises and examinations, we ought to try to divest ourselves of a modern opinion, that study exists for examinations rather than examinations for study. Indeed, to apply the measure of their prevalence and efficiency to the education of past generations, would be to commit an anachronism.

We might look in vain for any public examination to justify the learning and research which in the seventeenth century made English students famous :—whose efforts were fostered, rather by the encouragement of tutors and friends, than by the disputations in the schools. Examinations in our modern acceptation there were none. As books became cheaper, the quicker and the more diligent students discovered that they could acquire knowledge for themselves where previous generations had been dependent on the oral teaching. Then arose the necessity of examination, and as this has come to be more scientifically conducted, and its results to be more public, and at last in a sense marketable, there has been a fresh demand for oral instruction.

Again, the increased use of paper and of printing[1], which has

---

[1] There was a paper duty in England from 1694 to 1861 (Haydn, *Dict. of Dates*). About 1770 the mathematical part of the senate-house examination was demonstrated on paper by the candidates, but the questions were

done much to improve and facilitate the art of examining, has in a great measure changed the character of the tripos itself.

The Cambridge tripos is a development of the eighteenth century, and its growth may be fairly taken as a sign of the vitality of Cambridge.

The ground in which it was nursed was the new senate-house, which was in course of preparation in the years 1722-30. The *name* of 'the mathematical tripos' was indeed unknown : for not only was it not exclusively mathematical until the intro-duction of the Previous Examination, nor was it called so until there was a classical tripos from which to distinguish it; but the very name of *tripos* by no means implied an examination.

The history of its name is scarcely less remarkable than the development of the examination to which in process of time it came to be applied.

In the ceremonies which were performed on Ash-Wednesday, in the middle of the sixteenth century, at the admission of questionists to be bachelors of arts, an important function was executed by a certain 'ould bachilour' who was appointed as first champion on the side of the examining and honour-holding university. He had to 'sit upon a stoole before Mr Proctours' and to dispute first with the 'eldest son' (the foremost of the questionists) and afterwards with 'the father' (a graduate representing the paternal or tutorial piety of the hall or college coming to the rescue of the young combatant) on the two questions thrown down as a challenge by the eldest son. At this period, the only 'tripos' was *the three-legged stool.*

When we next catch full sight of these proceedings a century later, soon after the Restoration of K. Charles II., we find the 'ould bachilour,' if not recognised already as a licensed buffoon, yet needing to be exhorted by the Senior Proctor 'to be witty but modest withall.' Whether it was the contempt for cere-monies which was rife in England in the Reformation period, or the example of the royal patron of *Ignoramus* (who would,

dictated orally by the moderator who sat at a table with them. At certain times they were engaged by themselves with a problem paper, of which they must have obtained a MS. copy. Before the year 1801 the problem papers (but not the other questions) began to be printed. I do not remember to have seen one above eighty years old.

it may be supposed, have thoroughly enjoyed the incongruities of a noisy Commemoration), or from these and other influences, the university Quadragesimal ceremonies, though not entirely stript of their religious character, (private prayer being substituted for Mass and the *de profundis*,) had lost their dignity. We find in the second year of K. Charles I. (May, 1626) the Heads[1] protesting against this degeneracy. Not only had the 'eldest son' or questionist, whom we may consider as the principal, handed over the conduct of his case to the 'father' whose client he was, but the serious exposition of the argument on the part of the university had now, by custom, fallen into the hands of the first and second regent Master of Arts, while 'the bachelor,' their junior counsel, was apt, in spite of the protests of disciplinarians, to open the case against the petitioner in a speech more remarkable for personalities than for artisprudence. For upwards of a century we find the university authorities scandalized by this functionary and falling foul of him. Accordingly there was some appropriateness in the change of language which (apparently some time between 1560 and 1620) recognised him no longer as the 'old bachelor answering' but as 'the tripos[2]' (or 'Mr Tripos' *quasi dicerent* 'Mr Three-legged stool') according to the figure whereby important personages are sometimes referred to as 'the Chair,' 'the Woolsack,' or 'the Bench.'

We find the name Tripos or Tripus applied to the B.A. speaking at the 'prior' and 'latter' *acts* of Comitia Minora or Bachelors' Commencement, both colloquially and in academical documents, for a period of more than a century[3]. Possibly

---

[1] Cooper, *Annals*, III. 185, says 8th *May*.—Dyer, *Privil.* I. 293, gives the date as 1⁰ *Mai*.

[2] When writing *Univ. Life*, p. 41 *n.*1, I was inclined to think that in Hearne's day *Tripos* had come to be used as an equivalent for *Praevaricator* or *Varier*, the corresponding of disputant at the Major Commencement. A comparison with p. 231 in that volume makes me conclude that this was no exception to the ordinary distinction of the terms, but that Mr Law or Lawes (no other than the author of the *Serious Call*, as

Mr Leslie Stephen has pointed out) was 'tripos' at the later act, 'in comitiis posterioribus' of the Bachelors' Commencement—only he seems to have been something more than an ould bachilour—a young M.A. J. Byrom, who mentions the degradation of 'one Law,' a M.A. and fellow of Emmanuel, to be a soph, says that his speech was 'at the Trypos.'

[3] *e. gr.* 1620, 1626, 1665, 1667, 1702, 1740. See references in *Univ. Life*, pp. 218, 220, 228—231.

because of the capabilities which it afforded for puns and allusions classical to the Delphic Oracle, mathematical to trilaterals, and personal to any one who in some way or another could be likened to the fylfot which *quocumque ieceris stabit*.

But this use of the title was not destined to continue. In the course of the period (a hundred and twenty years or more) which has been indicated as assigning the name *Tripos* to a personage, we find frequent references to the humorous *orations* delivered in the schools by those who filled this office. These at first were known as *Tripos-Speeches* (1713, 1740), but in process of time *shared*, if they did not finally *appropriate*, their composers' title.

When it was that Mr Tripos ceased to take part in the arguments of the Sophs' schools I cannot exactly determine. I should conjecture that the custom was not allowed long to survive the opening of the senate-house in 1730 and the improvement which took place in university examination between that date and 1750. For many years it had been usual to circulate copies of Latin verses (*carmina comitialia*[1]) bearing reference to the formal 'questions' under disputation. Among other disputants the two Messieurs Tripos of the year were expected to produce each his two sets, which composition custom has continued; and at the present time these *verses* (still known as *Tripos-verses*, though the writer is never called the Tripos) are the only reliques of the disputations which, so far as the Arts faculty is concerned, have been entirely superseded by the Previous Examination and improved examination for the degree. These papers of verses about the middle of the last century afforded the single opportunity still conceded to the Triposes for giving vent to their wit and humour, and these broadsheets came (like the speeches of their predecessors) to usurp the title of their composers.

About the year 1747-8 the moderators began the custom of printing honour-lists on the back of the two yearly triposes (*i.e.* sheets of tripos-verses) so that instead of the first Mr Tripos and his speech upon one of two questions at the former Act on Ash-Wednesday, and a second Mr Tripos and his speech more or less humorous upon one of two other questions at the latter Act

---

[1] Such verses were published as early as the 16th century.

of the Bachelors' Commencement in Lent, there were, in the middle of the last century and subsequently, two sets of Latin verses more or less humorous, composed by two nominees of the Proctors, upon two questions, and at the back a list of *Baccalaurei quibus sua reservatur senioritas Comitiis Prioribus* who had done more than *satisfy* the moderators by their disputations in the schools during the previous year and in their subsequent examination, *viva voce* and on paper, in the senate-house. Their names in the year 1753 and subsequently were further distinguished as 'wranglers' and 'senior optimes.' Secondly two other sets of verses[1] backed by a list of *Baccalaurei quibus sua reservatur senioritas Comitiis Posterioribus* or junior optimes and οἱ πολλοί. Since 1859 the two papers (prior and posterior) have been combined; and the lists (known as tripos-lists) are circulated entire at the June Commencement. Such interest as is now attached to them belongs rather to the verses than to the lists of the several triposes (for the name has now at last come to signify degree examinations) which have been circulated already severally. But in times when there was but one examination in the Arts faculty (viz. before the classical tripos was established in 1824, distinct from or rather in addition to the mathematical and philosophical senate-house examination) the honour-list printed with the verses on the paper must have been a more precious document; and in common parlance an honour-man's name was said to stand in such and such a place *in the tripos* of the year, *i.e.* upon the back of the tripos-verses. And lastly, as the honour-list was considered as representing the examination itself, so the name has come

---

[1] It was customary, at least about the close of the last century, for the classical medallists to make Latin speeches or declamations in the law school after the distribution of verses on the second tripos day. They may have had some licence of speech given them as Mr Tripos had in earlier days. At all events, in 1790 Tweddell took that occasion to reflect upon the medals examination, in which he was *only* second medallist (Wrangham, who had written audacious tripos-verses in the previous year, being judged first). Gunning, *Reminisc.* I. vii. (cp. II. iii.) says 'on the first Tripos day.' This I think must be an oversight, for according to his own edition of *Wall's Ceremonies*, pp. 86, 90, the candidates for the Chancellor's Medals sent in their names the day after the first tripos, and the successful ones declaimed on the *second* tripos day.

in the last stage to be transferred[1] from the list to the examination, the result of which is published in that list.

Thus step by step we have traced the word TRIPOS passing in signification Proteus-like from a thing of wood (*olim truncus*) to a man, from a man to a speech, from a speech to two sets of verses, from verses to a sheet of coarse foolscap-paper, from a paper to a list of names, and from a list of names to a system of examination.

[1] However, as early as 1713 J. Byrom of Trinity applies the term to an *occasion* and not to a *person* or paper, when speaking of Law's Jacobite speech he says it was delivered ' at the Trypos, a public meeting of the university.'

CHAPTER III.

THE SOPHS' SCHOOLS IN THE EARLY PART OF THE CENTURY.

'Bona noua, Mater Academia, bona noua.'
Bedell Buck's *Book* (1665).

IN the sixteenth and seventeenth centuries many students may have got their first degree in Arts with little examination or none at all[1]. Each was called upon to answer one question in 'Aristotle's Priorums' and to be able to walk through the Respondent's Stall! In 1555 and 1665 we read of all candidates being required to keep the Lenten exercise of 'sitting in xl^{ma}' (quadragesima), which ceremony is also described in *D'Ewes'* diary (1619), *p.* 67. 'It was the custom for the Bachelor commencers to sit in the Schools during the whole of Lent, "except they bought it out," and to defend themselves against all opponents.' But it must have depended entirely upon the Regents whether any student was called upon to dispute; and the arguments and questions which *were* uttered seem to have been often frivolous and undignified. At Oxford the proceeding seems to have been conducted in a still more unseemly manner. Just before Laud's cancellariate a number of 'necessary regents' in addition to the 'masters of the schools' had to be called in to aid the proctors in quelling the fights and in checking the potations and lounging which disgraced the schools of that university[2].

---

[1] Some account of the early process for degrees is given in my *Univ. Life,* pp. 209, 213, 214, 217, 219. The *insignia doctoralia* (in spite of Bentley's eloquent exposition in his *Terence*) have not been used since 1843.

[2] See *Oxford Univ. Commission* Report (1852), p. 57.

From the answers of Heads and Presidents, Aug. 9, 1675, to the enquiries sent by Monmouth the Chancellor on the King's command, it appears that it was then possible to receive a degree after putting in 'cautions for the performance' of the statutable exercises, and then forfeiting the payment, and that this was not seldom done at Cambridge[1].

One very curious thing which we must notice is, that the 'acts' in the 'Schools' as distinct from the examination in the senate-house were by no means exclusively mathematical. In Puritan times[2] the mathematics were, comparatively speaking, neglected at Cambridge (though Ptolemy, Apollonius' Conics and Euclid were generally read), and in the latter half of the following century, after the mathematical revivals about 1645 and 1708, metaphysical and moral questions began to monopolize the 'Schools.'

The year 1680 brought one of the most important innovations, *viz., the appointment of moderators.* Up to that time the *proctors* had presided in the sophs' schools *ex officio.* Thus provision was made that the disputations should be conducted by persons chosen especially for their scientific qualifications and judgment. The advantage of the new office seems to have been at once recognised, for in 1684 the moderators were appointed to take a prominent part in the *examination* of those who had passed through their disputations[3].

An account of the ordeal passed by a candidate for the B.A. degree at the close of the seventeenth century is given in the *Diary* of Abraham de la Pryme. A summary of this is given in the *Autobiographic Recollections* (p. 55) of his descendant, Professor G. Pryme. The following fuller and more accurate edition was put forth by the professor's son Charles de la Pryme for the Surtees Society, 1869—70, *vol.* 54. *p.* 32.

'1694. *January.* This month it was that we sat for our degree of bachelors of arts. We sat three days in the colledge [St John's] and were examin'd by two fellows thereof in retorick, logicks, ethicks, physicks, and astronomy; then we were sent to the publick schools, then to be examined again three more days

[1] Dyer, *Privil.* i. 369.
[2] Seth Ward (Sid. *Camb.*; Prof. Savil, Pres. Trin. *Oxon.*) *Vindiciae*
Academiarum, 1654, c. 8.
[3] See Monk's *Bentley*, i. p. 11.

by any one that would. Then when the day came of our being
cap'd by the Vice-Chancellor, wee were all call'd up in our
soph's gowns and our new square caps and lamb-skin hoods on.
[Till 1769 *undergraduates* wore round caps.] There we were
presented, four by four, by our father to the Vice-Chancellor,
saying out a sort of formal presentation speech to him. Then
we had the oaths of the dutys we are to observe in the university read to us, as also that relating to the Articles of the Church
of England, and another of allegiance, which we all swore to.
Then we every one register'd our own names in the university
book, and after that one by one, we kneel'd down before the
Vice-Chancellor's knees, and he took hold of both our hands
with his saying to this effect, "*Admitto te*," &c. " I admitt
you to be batchellour of arts, upon condition that you answer
to your questions; rise and give God thanks." Upon that as
he has done with them one by one they rise up, and, going to a
long table hard by, kneel down there and says some short
prayer or other as they please[1].

'About six days after this (which is the end of that day's
work, we being now almost batchellors) we go all of us to the
schools, there to answer to our questions, which our father
always tells us what we shall answer before we come there, for
fear of his putting us to a stand, so that he must be either
necessitated to stop us of our degrees, or else punish us a good
round summ of monny. But we all of us answer'd without any
hesitation; we were just thirty-three of us, and then having
made us an excellent speech, he (I mean our father) walk'd
home before us in triumph, so that now wee are become com-
pleat battchellors, praised be God!

'I observed that all these papers of statutes were thus imperfect at bottom, which makes one believe that they were very
much infected with Jacobitism.' (This refers I suppose to the
forms of the Oath of Allegiance.)

---

[1] Each having done 'his obeisance
to Mr V. C.' kneels at the upper table
and 'giveth God thanks in his Private
Prayers &c.' *Bedell* Buck's *Book* 1665.
Perhaps this was the origin of the
ceremony of the Esquire Bedells di-
recting the questionists to the South
side of the Senate-House (*Wall—Gunning* 1828, p. 78). Buck mentions that
'they which are admitted *ad practi-
candum in Medicina vel Chirurgia* do
never kneel at the Table; neither do
they which are incorporated.'

It was Bentley's boast[1] that about 1708-10 by the example of Trinity College, 'the whole youth of the University took a new spring of industry...mathematicks was brought to that height that the questions disputed in the Schools were quite of another set than were ever heard there before.'

Of the good part taken by Ri. Laughton, Whiston and Nic. Sanderson, in adding life to the mathematical teaching and exercises in our university, we shall have occasion to speak hereafter.

It was at this period that John Byrom, scholar of Trinity, was looking forward to 'change this tattered blue gown for a black one and a lambskin, and have the honourable title of Bachelor of Arts.'   Previous to that time he had read Plutarch, Locke's *Essay*, Grew's *Cosmologia Sacra* (prescribed by his father as an antidote), Ray's *Wisdom of God in the Creation*, Whear's *Method of Reading Histories*, his tutor's ms. Chronology, lectures in Geometry, the *Tatler*, *British Apollo*, and had composed themes, and declamations, besides reading French, Italian, Spanish and Hebrew.   Writing from Cambridge to John Stansfield, 21 Dec. 1711, he had previously been 'busy in preparing to defend my questions, though I might have spared my pains; for my first opponent was a sottish and the second a beauish fellow, neither of them conjurers at disputing; the third lad put me to my defence a little more tightly, but urged nothing that was unanswerable; so I came off very gloriously, though I wish I had had better antagonists, for I think I could have maintained those questions well enough.   I most of all mistrusted my want of courage to speak before such a mixed assembly of lads, Bachelors, Masters of Arts, &c., but I was well enough when once up.   When I came down I was overjoyed that I had done the last of my school exercises in order to my degree.'   A Trinity man had been stopped that week for insufficiency[2].

Three or four years later the royal addition to our University Library led to a rearrangement of our public buildings, and it is very likely that the temporary disestablishment of the

---

[1] Ri. Bentley *to* T. Bateman, Xt.mas Day [1712]. *Corresp.* no. CLXVI. p. 449.

[2] *Chetham Soc.* 1854, pp. 15—17. Byrom's *Memoirs*, I.

old senate-house and Physick, Law and Greek schools may
have contributed to the degeneracy and disorder of the academical proceedings for the B.A. degree between 1715 and 1730.
In July of the latter year the present senate-house was inaugurated, and in December of the following year an attempt was
made by Dr Mawson, V.-C., to improve the exercises of the
sophs and questionists which had grown disorderly and irregular, partly (it may be) through the perpetuation in 1721 of a
grace which had been passed on an emergency in 1684, whereby
the examinations, declamations, &c. were not held at one
regular time for all. The publication of Johnson's *Quaestiones*
points also to some temporary revival about 1730.

In 1739, which, to judge from Gray's *Correspondence*, might
be considered as the midst of one of the dark ages of Cambridge, in the decline of Bentley and Baker, there was light
enough for some to see the need of revising or reviving the
oath taken at degrees[1]. On Feb. 25, 1747-8, the form, involving a declaration on the part of the candidate, that according to the best of his knowledge he had performed the statutable and customary exercises, was adopted[2]. It is from this
time that the honour-lists printed in the *Camb. Univ. Calendar*
date. Dr Paris (who had been on the Oaths' Syndicate of
1739) was now Vice-chancellor, and exerted his influence
to revive some of the exercises which had been disused for
several years. Among these were the declamations to be made
by bachelors for the degree of M.A. This revival was unpopular with the bachelors; and Chr. Anstey, junior, a fellow of
King's, afterwards author of the *New Bath Guide*, took occasion
to ridicule the authorities in two Latin declamations[3], April and
June, 1748, which provoked his suspension. A few months later
the Duke of Newcastle was elected Chancellor of Cambridge,
and it appears from the ephemeral literature which sprang up
about the reforms ushering in his cancellariate, that there

---

[1] Cooper's *Annals*, iv. 242.

[2] *Ibid.* 258.

[3] One of them was a mere rhapsody
of adverbs in the fashion of the Oxonian humorist Tom Brown. It appears that Anstey considered the en-
forcement of the regulation in his own
case as an infringement of the privileges of King's Coll. (Cooper's *Annals*
iv. 261, and *Cole* ap. Mayor's *Bonwicke*,
p. 258.)

were some tokens of revived studiousness among undergraduates[1].

It was at this time that Richard Cumberland (the dramatic
writer and essayist), was an undergraduate at Trinity. He had
received the elements of a sound and elegant scholarship at
Bury under Kinsman, and at Westminster in the days of
Nichols and Vincent Bourne, while his early holidays had
been spent in playing battledore-and-shuttlecock in the lodge
with master Gooch, the son of his grandfather's antagonist, in
beating such undergraduates as he could get to run short races
in the walks, and in listening to Bentley's learned conversation
with his visitors. When he matriculated at the age of fourteen he was put into rooms in the turret-staircase, in close
proximity to the 'Judges' Chambers,' where he had been born,
and under the wing of his grandfather's successor, Dr Smith,
and of his tutor, old Dr Morgan, who (being troubled by the
gout, and, it may be, by his pupil's inattention at his lectures
on *De Officiis*) left him to his own resources until he took
the living of Gainford.   Cumberland was then handed over to
Dr P. Young (Bp. of Norwich), then professor of Oratory, who
paid him still less attention, and in his third year to James
Backhouse the efficient Westminster tutor. He had not read
the first proposition of Euclid when his name appeared among
the 'opponents' for the 'act' which was to open the schools for
that year. His tutor begged him off, and after some encouragement from the master (cousin of Roger Cotes, and founder of
the Smith's prizes), he set to work and mastered 'the several
branches of mechanics, hydrostatics, optics and astronomy' in
the best treatises of the day, allowing himself only six hours'
sleep, and dieting himself with milk and cold bathing. Having
acquired the habit of making his notes, working his propositions, and even *thinking*, in the Latin language, he no longer
felt that terror which he had experienced before, though now
he was called upon to keep not a mere 'opponency' but an 'act'
itself, and though his first antagonist was 'a North-country
black-bearded philosopher, who at an advanced age had been

---

[1] [Green's] *Academic*, 1750, pp.23—26, mentioned in *Univ. Society*, pp. 72,
619, 624.

admitted at Saint John's to qualify for holy orders (even at that time a finished mathematician and a private lecturer in those studies).' 'After I had concluded my thesis which precedes the disputation' (says Cumberland in his *Memoirs*[1]), 'when he ascended his seat under the rostrum of the moderator......I waited his attack amid the hum and murmur of the assembly. His argument was purely mathematical, and so enveloped in the terms of his art, as made it somewhat difficult for me to discover where his syllogism pointed without those aids and delineations, which our process did not allow of; I availed myself of my privilege to call for a repetition of it, when at once I caught the fallacy and pursued it with advantage, keeping the clue firm in hand till I completely traced him through all the windings of his labyrinth. The same success attended me through the remaining seven arguments, which fell off in strength and subtlety, and his defence became sullen and morose, his Latinity very harsh, inelegant, and embarrassed, till I saw him descend with no very pleasant countenance, whilst it appeared evident to me that my whole audience were not displeased with the unexpected turn which our controversy had taken. He ought in course to have been succeeded by a second and third opponent, but our disputation had already been prolonged beyond the time commonly allotted, and the schools were broken up by the Moderator with a compliment addressed to me in terms much out of the usual course on such occasions.'...

'Four times I went through these scholastic exercises in the course of the year, keeping two acts and as many first opponencies. In one of the latter, where I was pitched against an ingenious student of my own college, I contrived to form certain arguments, which by a scale of deductions so artfully drawn, and involving consequences, which by mathematical gradations (the premises being once granted) led to such unforeseen confutation, that even my tutor, Mr Backhouse, to whom I previously imparted them, was effectually trapped, and could as little parry them, as the gentleman who kept the act, or the Moderator who filled the chair.'

His second act was, like the former, for a time delayed; for

[1] pp. 75, 76.

the junior moderator[1] made an unsuccessful attempt to compel him to comply with the custom of the schools by bringing forward one metaphysical in the place of a third mathematical question.

In due course of time the senate-house examination came on, to supplement, rectify, or confirm the impressions given by the disputations in the. schools. Cumberland says that it 'was hardly ever' his 'lot during that examination to enjoy any respite.' He 'seemed an object singled out as every man's mark, and was kept perpetually at the table under the process of question and answer[2].'

By the time he was convalescent from a fever induced by the exertions of his tardy application to mathematics, he learnt that his name would appear tenth at the back of the first tripos verses, viz. among the wranglers and senior optimes, for we have no formal distinction between them till three years later.

The next glimpse that we get of the schools is in the year 1752, which, with the account of Fenn, ten years later, does not differ materially from Cumberland's account, except in some curious details which were peculiar to the several occasions, although they add to our general view of the proceedings, shewing as they do what accidents might diversify the public exercises and examinations.

In the former, which is W. Chafin's (of Emmanuel) account of one of the preliminary *acts* kept in 1752, the writer says, ' I was keeping an act as respondent under Mr Eliot [Lawr. Elliot, Magd.] the moderator; and [W.] Craven [4th wrangler, afterwards Arabic prof. and master] of St John's was my second opponent. I had gone through all the syllogisms of my first, who was [W.] Disney [Trin., senior wrangler, and only four years later prof. of Hebrew], tolerably well; one of the questions was a mathematical one from Newton's *Principia,* and Mr Craven brought an argument against me fraught with fluxions; of which I knew very little and was therefore at a nonplus, and

---

[1] Cumberland, who bears testimony to the generosity of this moderator, calls him the Reverend Mr Ray, fellow of *Corpus Christi*...afterwards domestic chaplain to the Abp. of Canterbury. In the Univ. Calendar he appears as *Thomas Wray*, M.A. *Chr.*

[2] *Ibid.* p. 79.

should in one minute have been exposed, had not at that instant the esquire bedell entered the schools and demanded the book which the moderator carries with him, and is the badge of his office. A convocation was that afternoon held in the senate-house, and on some demur that happened, it was found requisite to inspect this book, which was immediately delivered, and the moderator's authority stopped for that day, and we were all dismissed; and it was the happiest and most grateful moment of my life, for I was saved from imminent disgrace, and it was the last exercise that I had to keep in the schools[1].'

Our next extract relates not to the acts in the schools but to the 'preliminary canter' in college and the Senate-house examination.

Sir John Fenn (editor of the *Paston Letters*) took his degree at Cambridge (Caius) in 1761, sixty-seven years after A. de la Pryme. Having read the Cambridge books on Arithmetic, Algebra, and Geometry in his school-days, he received permission from the tutor, J. Davy, to absent himself from lectures when he pleased. In his *Early Thoughts*, &c. he says :—

'The week we took our degree of Bachelor of Arts we sat in the little combination-room of the College for three days to be examined by such of the fellows as chose to send for us to their rooms.

'I sat my three days with the other questionists (or candidates for degrees) but was never once sent for during the whole time. I believe the fellows, not having lately applied themselves to the studies of Mathematics and Natural Philosophy, did not choose to examine those who were in the habit of those studies; but be that as it may, I was the only one of the candidates not sent for[2].

'On the following Monday, Tuesday, and Wednesday, we

[1] *Gent. Mag.* Jan. 1818, p. 11. Being invalided by small-pox at the time of the tripos, Chafin received an 'honorary senior optime.' *Baker-Mayor*, II. 1090.

[2] There was no other honour-man of his year in that college. Perhaps the fellows wished only to make sure that no one who would disgrace their college should be presented for the university competition.

sat in the Senate-house for public examination; during this time I was officially examined by the Proctors and Moderators, and had the honor of being taken out for examination by Mr [W.] Abbott, the celebrated mathematical tutor of St John's College, by the eminent professor of mathematics Mr [E.] Waring, of Magdalene, and by Mr [J.] Jebb of Peterhouse, a man thoroughly versed in the academical studies, afterwards famous for his various writings and opinions unfavorable to the Established Church, of which he was sometime a member, but afterwards deserting it, resigned his preferment, and practised as a physician.   On the Friday following, the 23rd of January, 1761, I was admitted to my degree and had the honor of being placed high [5th] in the list of wranglers.'

J. Wilson of Peterhouse, afterward judge of the Common Pleas, was senior, T. Zouch of Trin. was third.   Fenn was elected to an honorary fellowship at Caius, but did not reside there much after taking his degree.

We learn from the *Gentleman's Magazine* of 1766 (29 Jan.), that the sophs were to deliver copies of their 'theses' to be read at their disputations to the moderators, and that the best were to be printed by the university.   At this time, by the efforts of Waring, Jebb, Law and Watson, our schools grew into a flourishing condition, which they retained until they quietly withered away in the fresh growth of the Mathematical and Classical Triposes.

CHAPTER IV.

ACTS OR DISPUTATIONS IN THE SCHOOLS IN THE LATTER PART OF THE CENTURY.

> ' See Gray, so used to melt the tender eyes,
> Stretch'd on the orbit of a *circle* dies!
> And Goldsmith, whom deserted Auburn haled,
> See on a pointed *triangle* impaled!
> And to encrease their torment, while they're rackt
> Two undergraduate Devils keep an *act:*
> Who stun their ears with Segments and Equations.
> Moons horizontal, Tangents, and Vibrations,
> And all the jargon of *your* schools they're pat in;
> Bating they speak a little better Latin.'
>
> *The Academick Dream* (1774), p. 14.

IN the early part of the eighteenth century the examination for degrees was not in all cases adequate to the measure of knowledge or to the capacity of the candidates.

In 1731, just after the new senate-house was in use, the exercises of sophisters and questionists were ordered to be performed in the Lent term on the same days and in the same form as in the terms after Easter and Michaelmas. Lent term 'for many years had been a time of disorder by reason of divers undue Liberties taken by the younger Scholars, an Evil that had been much complained of; and all Exercise had either been neglected or performed in a trifling ludicrous manner[1].'

[1] Masters' *Hist. of C. C. C. Camb.*, p. 196.

Fifty years later we find this *trifling* (so far as the degree of B.A. was concerned) confined only to the 'huddling,' which was done (as will be seen in due course) *after* a fair, though not fully statutable, modicum of solemn exercises and examinations.

It might have been inferred from the condition of Oxford that *Cambridge* needed Jebb's agitation in 1774-6 to arouse hostile authorities to improve the time-honoured academical exercises. However, such was not the case; and it is satisfactory to know that this great reformer had little fault to find with the existing trial of the Sophs' year. He felt the need of inquiry into the work of undergraduates in the earlier part of their course alone; and for this the personal reminiscences of Cumberland and Paley are his justification. As it was, in Jebb's time (1772) the ordeal was not despicable nor despised, and idle men were apt to think themselves driven to take refuge in the ranks of the fellow-commoners (at that period not liable to examination); or else to declare their intention of proceeding in Civil Law as *harry-sophs*[1].

From such authorities as are mentioned in the foot-notes[2], we are able to gather a fairly complete and, in some respects, a minute account of the exercise required at Cambridge from Senior Sophs and Questionists in the last year of qualification for the degree of Bachelor of Arts, during the period which lies between the years 1772 and 1827.

The first and very important ordeal through which all candidates had to pass were the

ACTS AND OPPONENCIES,

or public exercises of the Schools, conducted in Latin under the superintendence of the two *Moderators*, who were usually senior or second wranglers of past time, and to whom also fell the

[1] See my *Univ. Life*, pp. 556, 643, 644.

[2] *Jebb's Works* (1772—87), II. 284—300.
Gunning's Reminisc. s. ann. 1786, 1787.
Camb. Univ. Calendar, 1802. Introd.

(copied largely from *Jebb*).
Gradus ad Cantab. 1803, 1824.
[J. M. F. Wright's] *Alma Mater*, 1827 (relating to 1818).
Facetiae Cantabrigienses. 1836.
Dr Whewell, 'Of a Liberal Education.' 1845.

chief responsibility of the public examinations of the senate-house, which constituted the final trial[1].

In the student's third year, after the Senate-house examinations of those lucky wights who were his seniors in university-standing by a twelve-month, the Moderators having received a list of the students aspiring to honours at the next examination from the tutors of the several colleges (King's[2] excepted) by the hand of a Proctor's servant, with appropriate marks (such as *reading, non-reading*[3], *hard-reading man*, &c.)—send notice on the second and subsequent Mondays in Lent Term to five students to 'keep their act' on the five first days beginning with that-day-fortnight. The Moderator's man (who expects a fee of six-pence for his trouble, as well as eighteen-pence at the time of the act, and other fees from the three opponents) delivers the notice in the following form:

Respondeat *Gunning*, Coll. *Christ.*
5[to] die *Februarii* 1787.   *T. Jones*, Mod[r].

The 'Respondent' or 'Act,' as he now may call himself, is ready in the course of an hour or so to wait upon the Moderator with three copies of three subjects on which he purposes to argue (having selected them, perhaps, from the numerous examples in *Johnson's Quaestiones Philosophicae in Vsum Juvent. Acad.*[4])—in the following form:

---

[1] The last *act* for a B.A. degree at Cambridge was performed in 1839. They must have been discontinued, as Mr H. Sidgwick has observed to me, by the independent action of the moderators of the time (T. Gaskin, Jes., and Joseph Bowstead, Pemb.), for these exercises were commended as a guide to the moderators in the report of the Examination Syndicate in the previous year, confirmed May 30, 1838. Moderators have been appointed annually since 1680. Up to that time the Proctors held the responsibility of moderating, and in 1709—10 Ri. Laughton, Clar. being proctor, chose to preside.

[2] Jebb adds 'Trinity-Hall.'

[3] R. H. C. writing in the *Monthly Magazine* in 1797, p. 266, asserts that the so-called *non-reading men* were generally studious, only they read other subjects than mathematics.

[4] Not that he would have found anything so modern as *Paley* there.—Tho. Johnson, of Eton, King's, and Magd. Colleges. His *Quaestiones* were printed at Cambridge (pp. 1—54, 8vo.) *typis Acad.* 1732. The demand for such a manual, giving reference to authorities on certain stock 'questions,' may be taken as a proof of the good effect of Dr Mawson's reformation of the Lent disputations when he was V. C. in 1730, 1731.

Q. S.[1]

Recte statuit Newtonus in 2da sectione Libri I.
Recte statuit Newtonus in 3^{ia} sectione Libri I.
Recte statuit Paleius de Utilitate.

Except in such cases as that of Paley himself who, when a Senior Soph in 1762, proposed to *deny* the eternity of Hell Torments and the Justice of Capital Punishment[2], (though, even in his case, the objection to this was not raised by the Moderators —Jebb and Watson—themselves), but was induced to compromise the matter by *affirming* the former question which he had proposed to deny, so leaving the negative to the three opponents, who were always expected to espouse the Worse Cause founded on some fallacy[3];—the Moderator generally accepted the theses brought to him, and 'at his leisure' (says the garrulous Calendar of 1802, quoting Jebb, 1772) transcribes into his book the questions, together with the names of the Respondent, and of three other students whom, from enquiry of their tutors, he thinks suitable to oppose his arguments. To each of them he sends a copy of the questions with their own names and the words *opponentium primus, secundus,* or *tertius,* denoting the order in which the three are to dispute.

In earlier times there was *Disputationum Academicarum Formulae* by R. F. 8vo and 16mo 1638.

[1] I suppose these initials meant *Quaestiones sunt:* cp. Wesley's *Guide to Syllogism,* p. 109.

[2] Jebb's specimen, 1772, was

'Q. S.

Planetae primariae retinentur in orbitis suis vi gravitatis, et motu projectili.

Iridis primariae et secundariae phaenomena solvi possunt ex principiis opticis.

Non licet magistratui eivem morti tradere nisi ob crimen homicidii.
—— Resp. Jan. 10mo.'

In Johnson's *Quaestiones (Metaphysicae),* 1732, reference is made to the following authorities on the question:

'Utr. *Aeternitas Poenarum contradicit divinis Attributis?* Origin of Evil in Ap. § 2. Burnet *de Statu Mortuorum* XI. p. 290. Tillotson's, Fiddes's and Lupton's *Sermons on Hell Torments.* S. Colliber's *Impartial Enquiry,* p. 103, and his *Essay on Nat. and Revealed Religion,* 142. Swinden's *Appendix to Treatise on Hell.* Episcopii *Respons. ad Quaest.* p. 67. Whitby's *Appendix to* II. *Thess.* Rymer's *Revealed Religion,* VII. Nicholls's *Conference,* III. 309. Scott's *Chr. Life,* v. § 5. 91. Bates' *Existence of God,* XII. Abp. Dawes's *Serm.* v. 73. Fabricius *de Veritate Rel. Christ.* 720.'

[3] *Facetiae Cantab.* p. 120. Watson's *Autobiog. Anecdotes,* I. 31. Wesley's *Guide to Syllogism,* Appendix on *Academical Disputation,* p. 97.

The first Respondent of the year, under the overwhelming responsibility which has devolved upon him—that of 'opening the Schools'—takes out a *dormiat*[1] from the dean of his college, enabling him to sit up late at night to study, without thought of having to rise early to the chapel service. He then sets to work to practise and prepare himself for the coming encounter. In the course of the fortnight he asks the three opponents to take wine with him, partly perhaps to secure personal good-will, when the wordy encounter comes on, partly, it appears, to arrange the sham-fight beforehand[2].

In 1782 'Jemmy' Wood (the future senior wrangler and Master of St John's) was the worse for one of these act's-wines, and subsequently and consequently more sober *act's-breakfasts*[3] were substituted for them.

Soon after the beginning of this century it became usual for the three opponents to return the compliment in the form of 'tea and turn-out[4].' From the last of these festive gatherings, the Respondent retired early to give the Opponents fair opportunity of comparing their proposed arguments and making sure to avoid repetitions[5].

When the fateful day arrives, the Moderator of the week, pre-

---

[1] Cp. Gunning's *Reminisc.* i. iii., and my *Univ. Life*, p. 590.

[2] This, however, was a comparatively late refinement. 'The Rev. Reginald Bligh, A.B.' in the advertisement (1781) at the end of his second frantic attack upon Plumptre and Milner for not giving him a fellowship at Queens' when he was one place above the 'wooden-spoon,' accuses G. Law of having 'bribed his opponent to shew him his Arguments, and *teach* him to take them off.'

Not only were there stock subjects to which it was usual to resort, but even the line of argument was provided either by references to standard *loci classici* such as are indicated in Johnson's *Quaestiones*, or even by traditional 'strings' (as they were called at Oxford), which no doubt were preserved after the manner of Tom Brown's

'vulguses,' or sold by poor students, or such characters as Jemmy Gordon. At least, it is recorded of T. Robinson, of Trinity, 7th wrangler in [Bp. Pretyman] Tomline's year 1772, as something exceptional that '*he always made his own arguments when he kept an opponency*' (Life by E. T. Vaughan, pp. 28, 29).

[3] *Gradus ad Cantab.* ed. 1, 1803, *s. v.*

[4] *Id.* ed. 2, 1824, *s. v.*

[5] Gunning *Reminisc.* s. a. 1787. *Alma Mater*, ii. 37. In *Symonds D'Ewes'* time (1619) the Respondent treated the combatants *after* the disputation. So also after his act in the College Chapel of St John's, he entertained the fellows and fellow-commoners with sackpossets in the 'parlour' or Combination-room. (*Diary*, ed. Halliwell, 67, 68.)

ceded by the Proctor's man (or 'bull-dog') carrying the quarto volume of Statutes[1], enters the Philosophical Schools at 3 *p.m.*, (1 *p.m.* in 1818), and, ascending his chair[2] at the side of the room, says *Ascendat Dominus Respondens*.

The Respondent accordingly mounts the rostrum on the opposite side of the Schools, and reads a Latin thesis on whichever of his three subjects he prefers. This is usually 'the *moral* question[3]'—'Recte statuit Paleius de Utilitate' in our supposed case:—if not from Paley, it is generally taken from the writings of Locke, Hume, Butler, Clarke, or Hartley. The thesis takes about ten minutes. Then the Moderator says, *Ascendat Opponentium primus*, and the first Opponent enters the box below the Moderator's chair, and facing the Respondent. He opposes the thesis in eight arguments of syllogistical form, the Respondent attempting to 'take off' or reply to each in turn, the entire discussion being carried on in Latin more or less debased. The Moderator, who has been acting all the while as umpire, when the disputation has begun to slide into free debate, says to the Opponent, *Probes aliter*[4], whenever an argument has been disposed of. At last he dismisses the first Opponent with some such compliment as *Domine Opponens, bene disputasti*—(*optime*

[1] See above, p. 30.

[2] Until 1669 the professor's original gothic stone chair with those of the opponent and respondent stood in the Divinity School at Oxford. *See* Wood *ap.* Warton's *Bathurst*, p. 91. The wooden ones in the Cambridge Schools still remain.

[3] As early as 1710-11 it needed all the influence of an enthusiastic proctor and moderator (Ri. Laughton of Clare) to induce a soph (Sir W. Browne of Pet.) to keep his acts in *mathematical* questions (*Nichols' Lit. Anecd.* III. 328). But by the middle of the century the Cambridge examination was so far crystallizing into *the mathematical* tripos that a questionist (R. Cumberland) was enabled by academical authority in 1750 to resist the demands of a moderator who had required him to produce *one* metaphysical question, he

having already distinguished himself in mathematical argument.

[4] Gunning *Reminisc.* II. x. The forms of syllogisms, &c. commonly in use may be found in Mr C. Wesley's *Guide to Syllogism* 1832, pp. 99-106, and in *Notes and Queries*, 1st S. VI. p. 55. Gil. Wakefield (*Memoirs*, 1804, II. 75 *n.*) tells of 'a *Moderator* in the Astronomical Schools at Cambridge, very ill qualified for his office, who was incapable of settling the debate between a resolute opponent and his respondent; and to pacify the former was accustomed to terminate the controversy by a look of complacency on the opponent and this conciliatory decision: *Domine opponens! hoc fortasse verum esse possit in quibusdam casibus, sed non in hoc casu. Probes aliter.*' ['Probo,' I take it, is a misprint, and *rerum* for verum.]

disputasti, or *optime quidem disputasti*), and his place is taken
by the second Opponent, who has to array five arguments
against the Respondent, and in his turn makes way for *Dominus
Opponentium tertius,* of whom but *three* are required. The
Respondent has to do his best to 'take them off,' as with his
first Opponent; and when his task is done, he is examined by
the Moderator as to his mathematical knowledge, that he may
be the better *classed* for the coming Senate-house examination:
and at last is dismissed with *Tu autem, domine Respondens,
satis et optime quidem, et in Thesi et in Disputationibus, tuo
officio functus es* (in which case he may have good hopes of
turning out a wrangler); or even *summo ingenii acumine disputasti,* which may suggest very high expectations indeed; or with
the more guarded praises of *satis et bene,* or simply *bene,* or *satis,
disputasti.* Such compliments gave rise to the classification of
students as senior and junior *Optimes.*

In general *optime quidem* was the highest praise expected
even by future wranglers; but in 1790 W Lax of Trinity introduced a fashion of giving high-flown compliments as moderator.
He also extended the length of the Acts to two hours, which
duration *custom* seems to have continued—so at least it was in
1820. In the eighteenth century an hour and ten minutes was
the usual time. Was this a Jewish mode of reckoning a disputation *per tres horas consecutivas*[1]?

'The distinguished men of the year appear *eight* times in this
manner in the schools,—twice as Acts (or Respondents), and
twice in each grade of Opponency. One act and three opponencies are kept before the Commencement (the beginning of July),
and the other moiety in[2] the October term. The οἱ πολλοί
(generally *non-reading men*) have less to do, some of them not
appearing more than once or twice, except in the farce of
huddling, which will be described below : and on some of them
occasionally a *Descendas*[3] is inflicted, or an order to quit the

---

[1] Cp. Gunning's *Reminisc.* 1. v. and
Jebb's account (1772), 'the Moderator
appearing a *little before two.*' The
change of the usual dinner-hour (see
my *Univ. Life,* p. 657; Gil. Wakefield's
Mem. ch. vii.) was the cause of this
alteration, which was effected by a

grace, Feb. 14, 1792, providing that
the exercises should take place from
3 to 5 p.m.

[2] In the *Calendar* 'before' was an
erratum.

[3] *Facetiae Cantab.* p. 54. *Alma Mater*
II. 129, and my *Univ. Life,* p. 588.

box for incompetency. This, however, is not very frequent: whenever it does happen, the stigma is indelibly fixed on the unfortunate object[1].'

I have ventured to expand an 'argument' of three 'conditional syllogisms' from the last page of Mr C. Wesley's *Guide to Syllogism.*

'Quaestio tertia est : *Recte statuit* Paleius *de Virtute.*'

The Respondent, having read his Latin thesis founded upon Paley's *Moral Philosophy,* is confronted by the first Opponent, who begins the attack at the Moderator's bidding. 'Ascendat Dominus Opponentium primus.'

Op. 'Si Dei voluntas sit virtutis regula, cadit quaestio. Sed Dei voluntas est virtutis regula. Ergo cadit quaestio.'
Resp. 'Concedo antecedentem, et nego consequentiam[2].'
Op. 'Probo consequentiam :—Si Dei voluntas ideò nos astringat quia praemia poenaeque vitae futurae ex Dei arbitrio pendent, valet consequentia. Sed Dei voluntas nos astringit propter haece praemia et poenas quae ex arbitrio Ejus pendeant. Ergo valet consequentia.'
Resp. 'Concedo antecedentem, et nego consequentiam.'
Op. 'Iterum probo consequentiam :—Si igitur posito quod angelorum malorum princeps summo rerum imperio potitus esset, voluntas ejus nos pari jure astringeret, valent consequentia et argumentum. Sed posito quod Sathanas summo rerum arbitrio potitus esset, voluntas ejus nos pari jure astringeret. Ergo valent consequentia et argumentum.'
Resp. 'Ut alia taceam, Deus homines felices vult ; angelorum malorum princeps, miseros ; huic ut resistamus, Illi ut

Even in the bachelors' schools the Moderator in Nov. 1733 had to admonish T. Ferrand, a fellow of Trin., with '*Modeste te geras.*' (Byrom's *Diary.*)
[1] *Univ. Calendar* for 1802. *Introd.* p. xvi.
[2] The *consequentia* (= συλλογισμός, *collectio, conclusio.* See also *Ar. Rhet.* II. xxi. *Cic. Acad. Post.* II. 8, 9, 30) is the connexion between the *antecedent* and *consequent* (consequens) of such a conditional syllogism. The argument given in the text seems exactly to fit the syllogistic form, 'Si A sit B cadit quaestio,' &c. &c., which forms the subject of an inquiry by 'M.' in *Notes and Queries,* 1st S. VI. 55 b. By later logicians the word *minor* is used instead of *antecedens.* In earlier times the *consequens* was also called *assertio,* and the *consequentia* called loosely *consequens.*

obediamus, ratio et natura suadent. Priusquam angelorum malorum princeps hominum felicitatem velle possit, naturam suam se exuat necesse est.'

Mod. (*to Opponent*) 'Probes aliter,' &c., &c., to n_1 arguments; viz., in the last century, *eight*.

If ever a mathematical question was chosen instead of the 'moral' one, a very small stock of Latin would suffice. An argument on the 9th Section of Newton, and another on the truth of the Differential and Integral Calculi, are given by Mr C. Wesley. In the latter the Opponent begins with

'Si inter limites $x = a$, $x = b$, $\int \frac{dx}{x}$ fiat hoc loco $\frac{a}{b}$, cadit quaestio.' And the Respondent's final reply consists of *six lines of algebraical symbols pure and simple*, and then the conclusion—

'Ergo valor fractionis $\frac{a^n - b^n}{n}$, cum $n = 0$, non evanescit, sed fit hoc loco $\frac{a}{b}$, ideoque nulla discrepantia existit.'

Though about 1830 men were called upon to defend all three of the questions on their papers against a limited number of 'arguments'; it is easy to see why at the end of the previous century the third or 'moral' question was the popular one, and, as a general rule, the only one discussed. However, we have seen above, p 29, that in 1753 an act was kept in Newton with fluxions. In 1772 there does not seem to have been any general rule as to which question the respondent should choose. It may be that the grace of 19 *Mar.* 1779 may have given the first impetus to the study of Moral Philosophy, which about that time became the favourite subject for the acts.

As to the Latinity of the schools, several typical anecdotes are current. W. Farish of Magdalene (afterwards professor of Chemistry[1]), who was moderator in 1783 and later years, usually figures in them.

---

[1] W. Farish was vicar of S. Giles, Cambridge, where he was well known for his mechanical contrivances. He put up over the pulpit in the old church a paraboloid sounding-board, which was likened to a tin coal-scuttle bonnet. While it enabled all the congregation in that most irregularly built

The faithful dog of some *dominus opponentium tertius* having followed his master into the schools, felt no doubt complimented when the astonished moderator in his own canine Latin exclaimed:

Verte canem ex!

Another choice phrase of Farish's was *facimus tam bene sine quam cum*[1]. Yet again; a *poll-man* running into the Schools in haste having neglected to put on a small item of his academical habit, which was *de rigueur* on these occasions, was thus reminded:

*Domine Opponentium Tertie, non habes quod debes.—Ubi sunt tui...*eh! eh! *Anglicè* Bands?

He is said to have answered thus, hesitatingly,

Domine Moderator, sunt in meo...Anglicè Pocket.

The following anecdote will give a notion of a certain class of arguments which were occasionally brought forward in this century, when the disputations were on their last legs, and the establishment of the Classical Tripos had given courage to clever men who had no special capacity for mathematics. I have heard it from Mr Shilleto, of Peterhouse, who (I had hoped) would have revised this account. He was then a scholar of Trinity keeping a second opponency under Francis Martin, who was then moderator (late bursar of Trinity, seventh wrangler in 1824).

edifice to hear the weak voice of the preacher, it conducted not a few whispers to his ear. His house (which Dr Whewell was about to occupy when Dr Wordsworth resigned the mastership of Trinity in 1841, and is now inhabited by E. Wayman, Esq.) in the neighbourhood of the School of Pythagoras has still the grooves whereby a partition was run up at pleasure through the ceiling of one floor to the room above, or *vice versa*. One evening having almost sat-out his dining-room fire in some dynamical calculation, being suddenly seized with a desire to make himself more snug, he let down the division from above, forgetful of his guests on the upper floor, who awoke from their first sleep to find themselves bewitched into a double-bedded room. Such was his absence of mind that on one occasion he gave 'the measles' to his congregation in place of 'the Blessing.' His brother was author of *Toleration of Marriage*.

[1] *Alma Mater* I. 198. Jacob Bryant records the following elegancy of a *College* Moderator of the same period (about 1789), '*Domine opponens non video vim tuum argumentum.*' Nichols' *Lit. Anecd.* VIII. 541.

The question to be disputed was a trite and favourite subject[1], *Recte statuit Paleius de Suicidiis.* This last word is no doubt a barbarism, though to most English ears unequivocal, and sanctioned by time-honoured use in the Philosophical Schools. The Opponent aforesaid being called upon for an argument began thus : *Non recte judicat Dominus Respondens de suicidio, ut ego quidem censeo, ergo cadit quaestio : si* sues *enim omnino non* caedemus, *unde quaeso* pernam, hillas, sumen, *unde inquam* petasonem *sumus habituri ? Est profecto judaicum et, ut ita dicam'*—'*Erras, Domine Opponens !'* interrupts the Moderator, '*non enim de* suibus caesis *loquitur Respondens, sed de aliquo qui* ultro sibi necem consciverit.' (All this while the Respondent, good mathematician and Johnian though he was, being unacquainted with the terms of Latin pork-butchery, was puzzling his brain to think how he could 'take off' an argument which he could not well understand.) '*Quid est ergo* suicidium' (continues the Opponent) '*ut latinè nos loquamur, nisi* suum caesio ?'

Mr Martin, who had won Bell's and Craven Scholarships, and might (it was thought) have been senior classic, if he had been a candidate for honours in that new Tripos, enjoyed the joke, which would have been thrown away on Professor Farish had *he* been the moderator.

Jebb's opinion of the worth of these acts in 1772 is interesting and satisfactory, as coming from a rigid disciplinarian and a radical reformer as times went. He says, 'These exercises are improving ; are generally well attended ; and consequently are often performed with great spirit. But many persons of good judgment, observing, with pain, the ·unclassical Latin, generally uttered by the student upon these occasions, have maintained that the knowledge of that language is not promoted by the present method of disputation ; and have delivered it as their opinion, that these exercises should be held in English in order to their absolute perfection.'

[1] Cp. *Alma Mater* ii. 36. In earlier times the only authority to which T. Johnson referred 'the academic youth' in 1732 on the *Quaestio* 'Utrum Suicidium sit illicitum ?' was *Adams on Self-Murder.*

Forty-seven years later the Senate-house examination had so far left the disputations in the rear, that Whewell said[1] these had no immediate effect upon a man's place in the tripos, yet although the syllogisms were 'such as would make Aristotle stare, and the Latin would make every classical hair in your head stand on end,' still it was, he thought, 'an exercise well adapted to try the clearness and soundness of the mathematical ideas of the men, though they are of course embarrassed by talking in an unknown tongue.'

[1] Whewell's *Writings and Letters* (Todhunter) ii. 35, 36.

CHAPTER V.

THE SENATE-HOUSE EXAMINATION.

We'll send *Mark Antony* to the Senate house,
And he shall say you are not well to day.
Julius Cæsar, Act II. Sc. 2.

THE candidates having been in the three terms beneath the scrutiny of two *pairs* of Moderators[1], at least in the capacity of opponent, have arrived at the dignity of *Questionists* by about the middle of January, six weeks before the First Tripos[2]. is published. They breakfast with the 'Father' of their college[3] at 7 o'clock on the morning of Plough-Monday (ominous name to modern academical ears for the Monday after Epiphany!) se'nnight. Then (though they are not yet formally admitted *ad respondendum Quaestioni*) the B.A. examination begins: the *Admission* of Bachelors taking place on the following Friday, five weeks before 'the *First Tripos* comes out'; this is the expression of the *Univ. Calendar*, but it does not mean the first publication of the honour list.

The examiners have already made a preliminary assortment

---

[1] *Univ. Calendar*, 1802. Introd. xvi., xvii.

[2] As at the present day, the printing and publishing of the *Tripos Paper* with its *Verses* was by no means contemporaneous with the settlement and proclamation of the honour *list*.

[3] By *Statutum Acad. Eliz.* cap. L. § 28, the usual expense of breakfasts and dinners at the time of the disputation is to be lightened and diminished by the Master and the majority of the Fellows.

of the examinees, into '*classes*' of six, eight, or ten, according to the notes made by the moderators at their acts (the persons in each class being arranged alphabetically), and half-a-dozen of these classes (eight, or so, in all) have been published at Deighton's, or elsewhere[1], on the previous Thursday.

Those who were placed by the Moderators in the 1st or 2nd classes were allowed on even a slight pretext to claim an *aegrotat Senior Optime*[2]—'a *Nervous Fever*, the *Scald of a Tea-kettle*, or a *Bruise of the Hand*, frequently put a period to the expectation of their friends[3]' in the case of some who, having done well in disputation beyond their hopes, in greater discretion than valour thought good to retire with a vague honour degree, without being subjected to further examination. This was called '*gulphing it*[4].'

The following account of the Senate-house Examinations is quoted [with the exception of remarks enclosed in *square brackets*] from John Jebb's account (1772), and the revision of it adopted in the Introduction to 'the *Cambridge University Calendar* for the year 1802,' and was true up to 1827.

'On the *Monday* morning, a little before *eight* o'clock, the Students, generally about a *Hundred*, enter the Senate-House, preceded by a Master of Arts, who on this occasion is styled the *Father* of the College to which he belongs. On two pillars at the entrance of the Senate-House are hung the *Classes;* and a Paper denoting the hours of examination of those who are thought most competent to contend for *Honors.*

'Immediately after the University clock has struck *eight,* the names are called over, and the *Absentees*, being marked, are subject to certain fines. The classes to be examined are called out, and proceed to their appointed tables, where they find pens, ink, and paper provided in great abundance. In this manner, with the utmost order and regularity, more than *two thirds* of the young men are set to work within less than five minutes after the clock has struck eight. There are *three* chief tables, at which *six examiners* preside. At the first, the *Senior Moderator* of the present year and the *Junior Moderator* of the

---

[1] *Univ.Calendar* for 1802, pp. xvii. lx.

[2] A list of *Proctor's Optimes* and *aegrotats*, omitted in the Camb. *Calen-*

dar, will be found in an *Appendix.*

[3] *Univ. Calend.* p. xliii.

[4] *Alma Mater*, 1827, ii. 60.

preceding year[1]. At the second, the *Junior Moderator* of the
present, and the *Senior Moderator* of the preceding year. At
the third, the *Two Moderators* of the year previous to the *two*
last, or *Two Examiners* appointed by the Senate. The two
first tables are chiefly allotted to the *six* first classes; the third
or largest to the οἱ πολλοί. The young men hear the Propositions or Questions delivered by the Examiners [from books in
their hands][2]; they instantly apply themselves; demonstrate,
prove, work out, and write down, fairly and legibly (otherwise
their labour is of little avail) the answers required. All is
silent; nothing heard save the voice of the Examiners; or the
gentle request of some one who may wish a repetition of the
enunciation. [The examination was conducted in English even
before the year 1770.] It requires every person to use the
utmost dispatch; for as soon as ever the Examiners perceive
any one to have finished his paper and subscribed his name to
it, another Question is immediately given. A smattering demonstration will weigh little in the scale of merit; every thing
must be fully, clearly, and scientifically brought to a true conclusion. And though a person may compose his papers amidst
hurry and embarrassment, he ought ever to recollect that his
papers are all inspected, by the united abilities of *six* examiners,
with coolness, impartiality, and circumspection. The Examiners
are not seated (1802)[3], but keep moving round the tables, both
to judge how matters proceed, and to deliver their Questions at
proper intervals. The examination, which embraces *Arithmetic,
Algebra, Fluxions,* the Doctrine of *Infinitesimals* and *Increments,
Geometry, Trigonometry, Mechanics, Hydrostatics, Optics,* and
Astronomy, in all their various gradations, is varied according
to circumstances: no one can anticipate a question; for in the
course of five minutes he may be dragged from *Euclid* to
Newton; from the humble arithmetic of *Bonnycastle,* to the
abstruse analytics of *Waring.* While this examination is pro-

[1] Previous to 1779 the two Moderators of the year were the only *regular*
examiners. At that date those of the
preceding year were given equal and
final authority with them. In 1791
they had been deputed to examine the
Poll-men especially.

[2] *Alma Mater.*

[3] In Jebb's time (1772) the Moderators sat at the same table with the
candidates.

ceeding at the three tables between the hours of *eight* and *nine,* printed Problems...are delivered to each person of the *first* and *second* classes; these he takes with him to any window he pleases, where there are pens, ink, and paper prepared for his operations. It is needless to add that every person now uses his utmost exertion, and solves as many Problems as his abilities and time will allow.'

In Jebb's time the examination by the *Moderators* was the least important; when not engaged with *them,* any student was liable to be taken aside for an hour and a half together by the *Father* of some other college, to undergo a scrutiny in every part of mathematics and philosophy which he professed to have read. In like manner any M.A., or a doctor in any faculty, might subject him to the same ordeal. All such examiners were expected to give an account of their impressions;—Fathers to Fathers, and other graduates 'to every person who shall make the inquiry.'

This plan was not always very satisfactory. John Frere (Caius), of Roydon, (M.P., F.R.S., F.S.A. &c., elder brother of Lady Fenn, the writer of *Cobwebs to Catch Flies* and other delightful productions of 'Mrs Teachwell' and 'Mrs Lovechild'), was expected by many to beat Paley in 1763. 'He had already acquired singular fame in the schools, as well from the fluency of his language and his dexterity in repelling the arguments of an antagonist, as from a confidence in his own abilities, and an overbearing manner, which, till he very happily apologized for it in the thesis to his second act, had excited a general disgust... Mr Frere's tutor, who was one of the examiners, requested of Mr Paley on the morning of the first day, that in case any other gentleman offered to examine him he would say that he was engaged as he wished to examine him himself, though he never made good his intimation. He afterwards applied to the Moderators for permission to look over the Problems given to the first class (which consisted of Paley, Frere, Hutton and Hall, all of whom had distinguished themselves in the schools and gained the highest mark of excellency in the Moderator's book), together with the solutions which each individual had returned; a request which, as implying a suspicion of undue partiality, was instantly and peremptorily refused. Mr Paley's tutor, on the other hand, though not a member of the Senate, by anxiously enquiring of one of the Moderators how his pupil had acquitted himself, was enabled to correct a mistake which had arisen from two sets of papers having been delivered without names, and the inferior set attributed to Mr Paley.   When on being first called upon for examination, the first class came to the bottom of the stairs, which led up to the gallery where the Moderators were seated, Mr Paley, after some hesitation amongst the whole party, ascended first, Mr Frere followed, then Mr Hutton, and lastly Mr Hall.   On the subsequent days of examination the same order was observed, a circumstance which appears singular, as their names were afterwards so arranged in the honour list.   As soon as Mr Paley was announced to be senior wrangler, one of the fellows of Caius accused the Moderators of partiality in giving him the precedence of Mr Frere; but that gentleman, on hearing the altercation, came forward and ingenuously acknowledged that Mr Paley was his superior.'   He had been promised a handsome estate[1] if he had been senior.

'The Moderators and Fathers[2] meet at breakfast and at dinner. From the variety of reports, taken in connection with their own examination, the former are enabled about the close of the second day (1772) so far to settle the comparative merits of the candidates as to agree upon the names of four-and-twenty, who to them appear most deserving of being distinguished by marks of academical approbation.'   [These were the Wranglers and *Senior* Optimes.   These together numbered only 12 in 1765; in 1759—60 they reached about 30; with those exceptions the aggregate numbers in each year from 1747-8 to 1776 never exceeded 28 nor fell short of 18: but the exact number four-and-twenty was adhered to only four times in those twenty-nine years.   The four honorary patronage degrees and occasional *aegrotats* (which *then* were classed) may have altered the numbers somewhat; but the numerical limit must have been found to be absurd.   From the year 1777 there is hardly any sign of an attempt to control the number of the names on the 'first tripos paper.'   In 1824 (the year of the institution of the Classical

---

[1] £1000. *Bp.* Watson's *Anecd.* i. 30.

[2] Jebb's account is here resumed.

Tripos) there were 59, thirty-one being wranglers, and twenty-eight senior optimes: there were only seven junior optimes that year.

Another statement of Jebb's, that 'in the latter list, or that of Junior Optimes, the number twelve is almost constantly adhered to,' applies with truth to a period of nineteen years (1758-76). There were two considerable exceptions; 1760, when there were as many as 18 junior optimes, and the very year in which he wrote (1772), when there were as few as *six*.

The sketch of the examination questions given on pages 46, 50, refers to the year 1802. Jebb's account of them, thirty years earlier, when there were only two days and a half employed, is as follows :]

'The examination is varied according to the abilities of the students. The moderator generally begins with proposing some questions from the six books of Euclid, plain (sic) trigonometry, and the first rules of algebra. If any person fails in answer, the question goes to the next. From the elements of mathematics, a transition is made to the four branches of philosophy, viz. mechanics, hydrostatics, apparent astronomy, and optics, as explained in the works of Maclaurin, Cotes, Helsham, Hamilton, Rutherforth, Keill, Long, Ferguson, and Smith. If the moderator finds the set of questionists, under examination, capable of answering him, he proceeds to the eleventh and twelfth books of Euclid, conic sections, spherical trigonometry, the higher parts of algebra, and Sir Isaac Newton's Principia; more particularly those sections which treat of the motion of bodies in eccentric and revolving orbits; the mutual action of spheres, composed of particles attracting each other, according to various laws; the theory of pulses propagated through elastic mediums; and the stupendous fabric of the world.'

'The subject-matter of the *problems* of those days was generally the extraction of roots, the arithmetic of surds, the invention of divisers, the resolution of quadratic, cubic, and bi-quadratic equations; together with the doctrine of fluxions, and its application to the solution of questions "*de maximis et minimis*," to the finding of areas, to the rectification of curves, the investigation of the centre of gravity and oscillation, and to the circumstances of bodies, agitated, according to various laws, by centripetal forces, as unfolded and exemplified in the fluxional treatises of Lyons, Saunderson, Simpson, Emerson, Maclaurin, and Newton.'

The first problem paper of 1802 contained fifteen questions, of which the following are specimens:

1. Given the three angles of a plane triangle, and the radius of its inscribed circle, to determine its sides.

7. The distance of a small rectilinear object from the eye being given, compare its apparent magnitude when viewed through a cylindrical body of water with that perceived by the naked eye.

8. Find the fluents of the quantities $\dfrac{d\dot{x}}{x \cdot a^2 - x^2}$ and $\dfrac{h\dot{y}}{y \cdot \overline{a+y}|^{\frac{2}{3}}}$.

15. From what point in the periphery of an ellipse may an elastic body be so projected as to return to the same point, after three successive reflections to the curve, having in its course described a parallelogram?

'At *nine* o'clock the doors of the Senate-house are opened. Each man bundles up his papers, writes his name on the out-side sheet, delivers them to the examiners, and retires (only *half-an-hour* being allowed) to breakfast. [Many of the candidates, as we have seen, had already breakfasted with the Father of their college. But Gunning took his at 9 o'clock with a friend in Trinity, throughout the examination in 1786.]

'At *half-past nine* all return again to the Senate-house; the roll is called over; particular classes are summoned up to the tables [though not to the same tables and examiners which each had attended during their first session] and examined as before 'till *eleven*, when the Senate-house is again cleared.......'

The following are some of the specimens of miscellaneous questions dictated by the moderators in 1802:

Trisect a right angle.

Investigate the rule for the extraction of the square root.

Required the value of ,583 of a pound.

Assign the physical cause of the blue appearance of the sky on a clear day, and its redness at sun-set.

Clear the equation $x^3 - \dfrac{px^2}{m} + \dfrac{qx}{n} - r = 0$ of fractions.

Compare the centripetal with the force of gravity.

Given the altitude of the mercury in the barometer at the top and bottom of a mountain, to find its height.

Prove the Binomial Theorem by the method of increments.

Given a beam, and the weight that will break it, to find the length of a similar beam, which being similarly situated will break by its own weight.

Find the fluxion of x^x when it is a minimum.

'Some of the lower classes are mostly employed in demonstrating Euclid, or solving Arithmetical and Algebraical Questions....... The examination being thus continued 'till *eleven*, an adjournment of *two* hours take place. At *one* o'clock the whole return. Problems are then given to the 3rd, 4th, 5th, and 6th classes, while the Table Examinations proceed nearly as before.'

The *third* and *fourth* classes had twenty problems in the afternoon—among others,

1. Inscribe the greatest cylinder in a given sphere.

3. Given the declination of the sun, and the latitude of the place, to find the duration of twilight.

11. Let the roots of the equation $x^3 - px^2 + qx - r = 0$ be a, b, and c, to transform it into another whose roots are a^2, b^2, c^2.

17. If half the earth were taken off by the impulse of a comet, what change would be produced in the moon's orbit?

The *fifth* and *sixth* classes had fifteen problems, *e.g.*

2. Every section of the sphere is a circle.—Required a proof.

6. Inscribe the greatest rectangle in a given circle.

[Summation of simple series to n terms and *ad infinitum*, some very simple equations with one unknown quantity].

15. How far must a body fall internally to acquire the vel. in a circle, the force varying $\dfrac{1}{D^2}$?

'At *three* o'clock the Senate-house is again cleared for *half-an-hour;* during which time the Proctors treat the Fathers and Compounders with tea and coffee[1]. On the return, the examinations are resumed, and continue till *five* o'clock, when the Senate-house Examinations break up for the day.

'At *seven* o'clock in the evening [6 p.m. in 1818] the first *four* classes...go' to the Senior Moderator's room [or the Combination-room of his college], where they continue till *nine* [or ten, 1818] to solve Problems; and are treated with fruit and wine. [The number of students admitted to the evening problem-papers became gradually less and less exclusive[2]. In 1788 only those in the first *two* classes were admitted except under exceptional causes; in 1802 we find *four* classes, and in 1818 *six* (i.e. *all* the candidates for honours). The entertainment provided became more formal in corresponding ratio. In 1788 the students helped themselves to wine and dessert at a sideboard, and in 1818 they were all given *tea* before beginning their twenty-four problems. At the *earlier* date it was considered rather severe to be required to extract the square and cube roots *as far as three places of decimals!* I give two specimens of those set fourteen years later (1802).

15. Construct the equation $a^2y^2 - x^2y - a^3 = 0$.

16. Compare the time of descent to the center in the logarithmic spiral with the periodic time in a circle, whose radius is equal to the distance from which the body is projected downward.

The work of *Examination Tuesday* was similar to that of the Monday, and so was that of the Wednesday until the year 1779, when it was determined to give more prominence to the examination in 'Natural Religion, Moral Philosophy, and Locke' which was at that time very superficial, consisting as it did at best of an occasional question or two in Locke, Butler's *Analogy,* or Clarke's *Attributes,* thrown in by the Moderator after he had

---

[1] They were relieved from giving more elaborate entertainments by a grace of March 26, 1784.

[2] However in Gil. Wakefield's time (*Memoir* I. 109) 'the *three* first classes went to the *Moderator's* room at *Clare* Hall, in the evening, to solve *problems.* Similar examinations in the Moderators' rooms in the evenings of Monday and Tuesday for the first *six* classes are mentioned as late as 1828 in Wall-Gunning's *Ceremonies*, p. 71.

exhausted his mathematical stock. By grace of Mar. 19, 1779, the examination was continued till 5 p. m. on a fourth day, Thursday; and all Wednesday was devoted to the moral subjects[1]. At the same time the Moderators of the previous year were added to the regular official staff of examiners, and (by a grace of March 20) the system of *brackets* ('classes quam minimas') introduced.

In 1808 a fifth day was added to the examinations; and in 1827 an encroachment was made on the Friday and Saturday of the preceding week, leaving the Wednesday free. Other changes were made in 1832, 1838, and other years, until in 1868 we find no acts and opponencies (the last was kept in 1839), no *viva voce* examination, no previous classification (the old 'classes' were abolished in 1838), but *the four days* and *the five days* with a respite of ten days between.

But from about 1780 until 1808 there were only four days (but *longer* days) spent in the senate-house. And here we will resume the course of the examination in the words of the Narrative of the Sixth Calendar of the University of Cambridge.]

'*Examination Wednesday.* The hours of attendance are the *same* this day as the former. The examinations are confined solely to *Logic, Moral Philosophy*, and points relative to *Natural* and *Revealed Religion.* The authors chiefly respected are *Locke, Paley, Clarke, Butler*, &c.[2] Wednesday, comparatively speaking, is considered a day of leisure, though all are full employed at stated periods as usual. [Howbeit, Gunning and many others found the time hang heavy on their hands, and solaced

---

[1] There is a tradition that in 1804 J. B. Hollingworth of Peterhouse (afterwards Norrisian Professor and Archdeacon of Huntingdon) won his B.A. degree by his knowledge of Locke. This however was considered extraordinary, and he was placed no higher than next but one to the 'wooden-spoon.' On the other hand James Blackburn of Trinity got his place as 14th senior optime in 1790 by solving *one* very hard problem. In consequence of a dispute with his tutor he would attempt nothing but that. Gunning

Reminisc. i. ch. vi.

[2] When Jebb wrote 1772-5 there was no special day for 'philosophy,' but after the other subjects 'the Moderator sometimes asks a few questions in Locke's *Essay on the Human Understanding*, Butler's *Analogy*, or Clarke's *Attributes.* But as the highest academical distinctions are invariably given to the best proficient in mathematics and natural philosophy, a very superficial knowledge in morality and metaphysics will suffice.' (ii. 292.)

themselves with *teetotum* 'below stairs[1],' perhaps while waiting
for their class to be called up for their one hour's examination.]
Answers to the respective Questions are seldom given *viva voce*,
but are required to be *written* down fully and legibly. It is
expected in the examinations of this day, all persons, whether
they be candidates for Honors or not, acquit themselves with
respectability in the solution of the several Questions which the
examiners may think proper to propose. The few subsequent
Questions will give an idea of this day's examination.

For what purpose does Locke recommend the study of
Geometry and Mathematics?

Give the reasons which Gisborne urges against Paley's Principles of Moral Philosophy.

What is Paley's opinion on Subscription to Articles of
Religion?

Define simple and mixed modes: and shew wherein Identity
consists.

How is Enthusiasm to be discovered?

'The examinations of this day conclude, as usual, at *five*
o'clock; but the fatigue of the Examiners is by no means diminished; for during the whole of this, as on the preceding
nights, they have a multitude of Papers to inspect, and to affix
to each it's degree of merit; according to which a new arrangement of the classes is made out called the *Brackets*.

'*Examination Thursday*....At *eight* o'clock the new Classifi-
cations or *Brackets* [an invention of the year 1779], which are
arranged according to the order of merit, each containing the
names of the candidates placed alphabetically, are hung upon
the pillars [in the Senate-House. Should the Examiners wish
to intimate that there is a *magnum intervallum* between two
Brackets, they insert between them a number of lines propor-
tionable to that interval. A 'bracket' *may* include only *one*
name; seldom more than ten are so classed together. In 1802
there were fifteen brackets in all: the names of two men afterwards in the fourth (final) class were unnoticed in the Brackets].
Upon the exhibition of the *Brackets*, disappointment or satisfaction is visible in the countenances of the Examined; some

[1] The Moderators sat in the gallery about 1763.

think their merits are placed too low, while others rejoice in the *Bracket* assigned them. It seldom happens that a person either *rises* or *falls* from a *Bracket;* his ultimate station being fixed somewhere within its limits. Each *Bracket* is examined [much as the *Classes* were on the preceding days], and when any one evidently appears to have distinguished himself above the rest [of those associated in his own bracket], his proper place is determined, and the Examiners give him no further trouble; and in this manner the rest are arranged. Should any one however be dissatisfied, as frequently happens, he has the power of *challenging* (often a dangerous experiment) any that he pleases to a fresh examination; in which case the Moderators call to their assistance the Proctors and some Masters of Arts; who, after the most impartial and sometimes laborious scrutiny, determine the point at issue, and give judgment accordingly. [Isaac Milner[1] of Queens' was often thus called in to arbitrate: if he was hearing a *challenge* of some stupid men in the 5th or 6th classes he would call out to the Moderator at the other end of the room, *In rebus fuliginosis versatus sum:*—so translating his favourite expression '*Sooty fellows!*'

Fresh editions and revisions of the Brackets are published at 9 and 11 *a. m.*, and 3 and 5 *p. m.*, according to the course of the examination, liberty being given to any man to *challenge* the bracket immediately above his own on each occasion, until] 'at *five* o'clock the examinations are finished.

'The Proctors, Moderators, and Examiners retire to a room under the Public Library to prepare the list of Honors, and determine the situation of every person that has been examined. Thousands of the papers are frequently again produced, and their real character subjected to the keen criticism of an aggregate tribunal of *eight* learned men. The whole business is sometimes settled without much difficulty in a few hours; sometimes not before two or three o'clock the next morning[2]. [The name of the Senior Wrangler was generally published at midnight.] At this meeting it is determined whether all are to have their degrees *passed;* sometimes two or three are found deficient, in which case they are *plucked,* i. e. turned over to

---

[1] A ferocious charge of unfairness was hurled at him by Reg. Bligh of his college in two pamphlets, 1780-81.

[2] See *W. Gooch's* letters in Appendix.

Ash Wednesday (*Dunce's Day*), or 'till such time as they have qualified themselves for their degree. It is scarcely necessary to add, that so little is required of these low men, that all compassion on the defeat of their hopes, is totally out of the question.

[At the end of the century[1] 'two books of Euclid's *Geometry*, Simple and Quadratic Equations, and the early parts of Paley's *Moral Philosophy* were deemed amply sufficient. Yet in the year 1800 three students failed to pass even this test.' In 1774 a Syndicate was appointed to consider the case of such idle men '*secordia torpentibus*' as well as that of those who 'read too high.']

'In consequence of the insufficiency of many of the Questionists in 1799, Mr Palmer [Joh.], Senior Moderator, signified that for the future no degree should pass, unless the Candidate should have a competent knowledge of the *first* book of *Euclid*, *Arithmetic*, *Vulgar* and *Decimal Fractions*, *Simple* and *Quadratic Equations*, and *Locke* and *Paley*. This regulation was communicated to the Fathers in the Senate-House, January 18, 1799, and agreed to.

'Such being the case, it is esteemed a reproach, both to the Father and the College, to send any men without being qualified, at least to bear an examination such as that above prescribed; for all Societies, some time previous to *Examination Monday*, try the merits of their own men, before they permit them to undergo the Senate-House Examination. A select number (*thirty at least*, Stat. Acad.) of those who have most distinguished themselves, are recommended to the Proctors for their approbation; and if no reason appears to the contrary, their names are set down according to merit, and classed in three divisions, viz. *Wranglers*, *Senior Optimes*, and *Junior Optimes*; which constitute the three orders of *Honor*. The rest are arranged according to merit, but not having obtained any Honor, are styled the οἱ πολλοί, or multitude. [The position of '*Captain of the Poll*' was one of distinction. The lowest honor, or *last* Junior Optime, obtains the appellation of the *Wooden Spoon*. The last *three*, *four*, &c. of the οἱ πολλοί, who

---

[1] G. Pryme's *Recoll.* p. 92.

are *hard run* for their degrees, are arranged *alphabetically*, and usually obtain some distinctive title; such as the *Alphabet, Elegant Extracts, Rear Guard, Invincibles,* [*Constant Quantities,* and *Martyrs*], &c., or sometimes their titles are deduced from their number and concurring circumstances of the day, as *The Twelve Judges* or *Apostles, The Consulate, The Executive Directory* or *Septemvirate;* &c. [if there was but one, he was called *Bion,* who carried all his learning about him without the slightest inconvenience. If there were two, they were dubbed the *Scipios; Damon and Pythias; Hercules and Atlas; Castor and Pollux.* If three, they were ad libitum *the Three Graces;* or *Three Furies; the Magi;* or *Noah, Daniel,* and *Job.* If seven, they were *the Seven Wise Men;* or *the Seven Wonders of the World.* If nine, they were the unfortunate *Suitors of the Muses.* If twelve, they became the *Apostles.* If thirteen, either they deserved a round dozen, or, like the Americans, should bear thirteen stripes on their *coat and arms*[1]], &c.

' In the list of Honors, *four*[2] additional names used to be inserted at the discretion of the Vice-Chancellor, the two Proctors, and the Senior Regent. Whether from abuse in bestowing these Honors, or the insignificance attached to the characters of those who have accepted this Cobweb Plumage, none at present [1802] are hardy enough to offer, and none so ridiculous as to accept them....'

[These were known as *Proctor's Senior Optimes*[3] or 'gratuitous Honorati' (Gil. Wakefield). In earlier times the number was not thus limited, nor the names always put at the foot of the Senior Optimes, but ' distributed *ad libitum* in various parts of the lists.' Tim. Lowten, a good classic, with considerable interest as a Johnian, seems thus to have been placed next the senior wrangler in 1761, and above T. Zouch of Trinity, who was properly second wrangler. Thus also in 1680, Ri. Bentley was hustled down from his proper place as third wrangler to

---

[1] *Oxf. and Camb. Nuts to Crack,* p. 247.

[2] Wrangham's *Memoirs* of *Zouch,* p. xxxi. See my *University Life,* p. 210.

[3] When we read of M. Robinson that in 1650 Dr Arrowsmith, master of St John's, ' *by the proctor's indulgence had sent him unsought the seniority of all his year,'* we have a plain proof of the lack of any formal examination at that time.

sixth. In like manner in 1776 four names[1] were placed between the senior wrangler and Gil. Wakefield of Jesus. Wakefield thought this was an artifice of the V. C., Ri. Farmer, and the senior proctor W. Bennet, both Emmanuel men, to make the interval seem greater between him and their senior wrangler (Archdeacon) John Oldershaw. Wakefield's editor, however, (1804) thinks that it was done with the purpose rather of giving Bp H. W. Majendie a lift. About 1710 Ri. Laughton, Proctor and Moderator, used 'a promise of the senior optime of the year' to induce (Sir) Wm. Browne, then a student of Peterhouse, to keep his acts on *mathematical* questions[2].

Gunning, in his edition of *Wall's Ceremonies*, p. 72, *n.* (1828) says, that 'some years since a Person thus nominated claimed to be a Candidate for the Classical Medal. His claim was disallowed ; and in consequence of the discussion which took place on the subject, this absurd practice was shortly afterwards discontinued.' However, our Appendix will shew some instances of honorary senior optimes winning the medal.]

'Those who take the degree of Bachelor of Arts at any other than this time, are called Bye-Term Men ; they are arranged *alphabetically* in classes according to their supposed acquirements, either as *Baccalaurei ad Baptistam* [if admitted *ad respondendum quaestioni* after Ash Wednesday] or *ad Diem Cinerum* [if on or before that day, which was called *Dunce's Day*]; and inserted in the list of seniority among the οἱ πολλοί, [i. e. they, or any of them, may be placed before or after any one or other of the classes of the 'Poll.' They pay heavier fees to the junior proctor and marshall.]

---

[1] The tripos for 1776 commenced thus—

    J. Oldershaw, *Emm.*
    G. Isted, Trin.
    H. W. Majendie, Chr.
    Ri. Relhan, Trin.

    Nic. Simons, Chr.
    Gil. Wakefield, *Jes.*
See below, Appendix on honorary degrees.

    [2] Nichols' *Lit. Anecd.* III. 328.

CHAPTER VI.

THE ADMISSION OF QUESTIONISTS. HUDDLING.

Haec alii sex
Vel plures uno conclamant ore Sophistae.
JUVENAL VII. 166, 167.

IT is unnecessary to go through all the details of the admission
of the Questionists on Friday (afterwards *Saturday*) morning as
detailed by Mr Raworth in the Calendar of 1802. Suffice it to
say that the class-lists of the Questionists are hung on the
pillars at 8 *a.m.* At 10 a Bedell calls up the Houses to hear
the Moderator's Latin speech, and admit their *Supplicats* which
are approved, and carried to the Scrutators in the non-regent-
house to be placeted. The Questionists come down from the
gallery of the senate-house ; and at a given signal the *hoodling*
begins, *i.e.* each man's bed-maker puts his rabbit's-fur hood
over his head. The School-keeper gives all men so distinguished a copy of the following oath:

'Iurabis quod nihil ex iis omnibus sciens uolens praeter-
misisti, quae per leges aut probatas consuetudines huius
Academiae, ad hunc gradum quem ambis adipiscendum, aut
peragenda, aut persoluenda, requiruntur, nisi quatenus per
gratiam ab Academia concessam tecum dispensatum fuerit.
Iurabis etiam quod Cancellario, et Pro-cancellario nostro comi-
ter obtemperabis, et quod statuta nostra, ordinationes, et consuetudines approbatas, obseruabis. Denique iurabis quod com-

positionem inter Academiam et collegium Regale factam sciens uolens, non uiolabis. Ita te Deus adiuuet et sancta Dei Euangelia.'

The 'Fathers' present their 'Sons' to the Vice-Chancellor as 'tam moribus quam doctrina[1]...idoneos ad respondendum quaestioni.' The Vice-Chancellor admits them authoritatively, *ad respondendum quaestioni* (after they have taken the oath aforesaid with those of Supremacy and Allegiance), thereby licensing them, somewhat tardily, to undergo examination. This doubtless was a remnant of the ancient custom of admitting questionists to be examined in 'Aristotle's *Priorums*[2]' by the 'Proctors, Posers, and other Regents.' About the year 1555 (*Bedell Stokys' Book*) it was the custom for the Father to add his conclusion upon the answer of his 'chyldren,' and if he shewed signs of making any lengthy strictures upon them, the Bedell was expected to 'knock hym out,' *i.e.* to drown his remarks by hammering on the schools door[3]! This part of the proceedings was not more seemlily conducted in the 18th century. For as the Questionists were *admitted* they went to the *Sophs' schools*[4] under the Univ. Library: the Father, Moderator, or some other Regent ascended the moderator's

---

[1] 'A scholar that was to take his degree of B.A., was asked by the Dean, who was to present him to the congregation, with what conscience he could swear him, who had spent his university career so unprofitably, to be fit for that degree *both in learning and in manners?* The scholar answered him, that he might well swear him to be fit '*tam moribus quam doctrina*,' for so the oath runs in Latin.' *Reprint* by Halliwell, *from a 17th cent. Jest-Book.*

[2] See my *Univ. Life,* pp. 208, 217.

[3] One taking an ordinary degree in a bye-term, *ad diem Cinerum,* or *ad Baptistam,* answered his question in the Senate-House. *Ceremonies.* Wall-Gunning, 1828, p. 166.

[4] ap. *Notes and Queries,* 2 S. viii. Most of the candidates had gone through some more serious acts and opponencies in the schools already and only made up the deficit in the statutable number by this fiction, but by some abuse of authority *fellow-commoners* were admitted (1772) with no other performance than this which they despatched in the space of ten minutes 'reading in that time two theses, and answering sixteen arguments against six questions: hearing also two theses, and proposing at least eight arguments against six questions in his turn. From the precipitation with which the candidate reads his theses, answers and proposes arguments, the whole of the ceremony is very expressively denominated, "huddling for a degree."' Jebb's *Works* II. 298, 299. At last they spoke such gibberish as *I-us think-us that-us.*

pulpit and made a pair of them occupy the respondent's and opponent's boxes. The mock Respondent then said simply ' *Recte statuit Newtonus,*' to which the mock Opponent as simply answered ' *Recte non statuit Newtonus.*' This was a disputation, and it was repeated as many times as the statutes required. The parties then changed their sides, and each maintained the contrary of his first assertion. 'I remember (adds the late Prof. *A. De Morgan*) thinking it was capital practice for the House of Commons.' By the side of this the specimen syllogism given in the *Gradus ad Cantabrigiam*, 1803, (s.v. *Huddling*),

> Asinus meus habet aures
> Et tu habes aures.
> Ergo: Tu es asinus meus—

was quite rational. 'This, which Sir Thomas More says, was "the form of arguing used by yonge children in grammer schooles" in his time, would be thought very good *huddling* for old boys at the University.' (1803).

According to the Cambridge *Ceremonies* (Wall-Gunning, 1828, p. 163), the huddling was performed in the case of candidates for an ordinary degree, who had not kept all their statutable exercises, before their *supplicats* were presented to the Caput. They were got through in the Sophs' school in presence of the Fathers of their colleges, a B.A., and a Soph. They were also examined by the moderators in their rooms. A young gentleman who was not conspicuous for mathematics was asked by the mock moderator in the mock Latin for which the schools were so famous, *Domine respondens, quid fecisti in Academia triennium commorans? Anne circulum quadrasti?* To which he made answer, shewing his trencher cap with its angles considerably the worse for rough usage, *Minime, Domine eruditissime; sed quadratum omnino circulavi*[1].

On account of the shortness of the Lent Term, permission was granted in 1684 (Dec. 16), to make the work lighter by the passing of two graces[2], allowing inceptors in arts to make their disputations with an M.A. any day in term-time in the Logic, Philosophy, or Law schools, from 7 to 9, or 9 to 11 a.m., and 1 to 3, or 3 to 5 p.m., in the presence of the Proctor (or a

---

[1] *Notes and Queries*, 2 S. viii. 191.   [2] *Dyer Priv. Camb.* i. 265, 266.

regent his deputy) and at least six B.A.'s, and to hold disputations or declamations of inceptors and questionists, *even out of term*, at the Proctors' pleasure, provided that the questions were duly posted on the doors and a Moderator present, as well as twelve Sophs at the Sophs' disputations, and six B.A.'s at the Bachelors' declamations. That day, thirty-seven years later, Dec. 16, 1721, these *exceptional* graces were made *perpetual*.

But we find Bentley's opponent, Serjeant Miller, complaining as early as 1717, that 'when the Students come to take the degree of B.A., among other things they swear[1] that they have learned rhetoric in the first year of their coming to the University; in the second and third, logic; and in the fourth year, philosophy; and that they have performed several other exercises, which through the multitude of scholars and the want of time appointed for them if they are performed at all, they are, the greatest part of them, in the manner which they call *huddling*—which is in a slighter manner than the usual mootings are in the inns of court.'

It appears that the licence granted by the graces[2] of Dec. 16, in 1684 and 1721 had brought the more ancient Lenten disputations into contempt, so that just ten years after the latter date (*i.e.* on Dec. 16, 1731) it was ordered by a grace that the exercises of Questionists and Sophisters should be performed in *that* term as regularly as they were after Easter and Michaelmas! All exercises had for some time been 'neglected or performed in a trifling and ludicrous manner[3].' There is no appearance of any cessation of these mock exercises up to the year 1840[4].

The question asked by the Moderator was usually something ridiculous, and the answer quite immaterial. The commonest question was *Quid est nomen?* and the answer *Nescio.* About 1830 it was customary to ask a student whether he had

---

[1] There is no reason to suppose that the students knew the statute well enough to understand that all this was implied in their oath. In the 18th cent. teachers in Rhetoric, Logic, and Ethics, &c. were appointed at Peterhouse every year. There were Logic and Locke lectures and examinations at Trinity between chapel and breakfast in 1755. *Univ. Life*, p. 117.

[2] Dyer *Privil. Camb.* I. 265-6, 269.

[3] Masters' *Hist. C. C. C. C.* 196. Cooper's *Annals* IV. 211.

[4] The 'classes' continued till 1839, the 'acts' till 1840.

been to the opponents' tea-party, and his expected answer again *Nescio*[1]. If any fun could be made of the student's name the opportunity was not lost. For example, Joshua *King*, [afterwards president] of Queens', senior wrangler in 1819, was asked *Quid est* Rex? He answered boldly *Socius Reginalis*. J. *Brasse* (sixth wrangler) was accosted in 1811 with *Quid est aes*? (then pronounced *ease*). *Nescio, nisi finis examinationis* was his reply. E. *Hogg* was attacked [1806] with *Tu es porcus*: to which he retorted (the moderating M.A. being a Johnian) *Sed non e grege porcorum*.

It should be remembered that these jests were allowed only after the business of examinations was over. When a man was asked *in the Senate-house* to *give a definition of Happiness*, and answered 'an exemption from *Payne*'—that being the name of an examiner—he was justly 'plucked' for want of discrimination in time and place[2]. The art of playing upon names was carried to great perfection, and more opportunely, by the late registrary, Jos. Romilly, at matriculations.

A good specimen of his wit is found in his remark to a freshman (1834) who was asked how he spelt his name—one of no uncommon sound—and replied ' *W, double O, double D.*' 'I trust, Sir, that the simplicity of your character will make amends for the *duplicity* of your name[3]?'

---

[1] Cp. *Whewell's Writings and Letters* (Todhunter) ii. 5.

[2] *Facetiae Cantab.* 103, 142, 85. *Alma Mater* ii. 103. Another man ventured in the little-go of 1847 to emphasize his translation of Livy's ' horrida palus '—*that horrid Marsh*, this being the examiner's name.

' The real disputations,' says De Morgan (*Budget of Paradoxes*, 305), ' were very severe exercises. I was badgered for two hours [1826] with arguments given and answered in Latin—or what we called Latin—against Newton's first section, Lagrange's Derived Functions, and Locke on innate Principles. And though I *took off*

every thing, and was pronounced by the moderator to have disputed *magno honore*, I never had such a strain of thought in my life. For the inferior opponents were made as sharp as their betters by their tutors, who kept lists of queer objections drawn from all quarters.'

[3] Cp.

' One can think of the pun
He would make just for fun;
One can think of his ever kind look
And the pains he would take
To prevent a mistake
As Jex put his name in the book.'

*Narrative of Mr Jex Jex of Corpus,
By A. C. D. Barde* (1864) p. 14.

CHAPTER VII.

THE MATHEMATICKS.

'There is figures in all things.'
K. Henry V. Act VI. Sc. 7.

A UNIVERSITY speech made probably in the year 1654 by Isaac Barrow[1] (who a few years later had the singular fortune to be predecessor of Newton as Lucasian professor, of Bentley as master of Trinity, and of Porson as Greek professor) will give the reader a notion of the progress of Cambridge mathematics previous to the appearance of Newton.

'Nempe *Euclidis, Archimedis, Ptolemaei, Diophanti,* horrida olim nomina iam multi e uobis non tremulis auribus excipiunt. Quid memorem iam uos didicisse *arithmeticae* ope, facili et instantanea opera uel *arenarum* enormes numeros accurate computare' &c.—After referring to astronomical studies, he continues—'Sane de horribili monstro, quod *Algebram* nuncupant, domito et profligato multi e uobis fortes uiri triumpharunt: permulti ausi sunt *Opticem* directo obtutu inspicere; alii subtiliorem *Dioptrices* et utilissimam doctrinam irrefracto ingenii radio penetrare. Nec uobis hodie adeo mirabile est, *Catoptrices* principia et leges *Mechanicae* non ignorantibus, quo artificio magnus *Archimedes* romanas naues comburere potuit, nec a tot saeculis immobilem Vestam quomodo stantem terram concutere potuisset.'

[1] *Works* (Napier, 1859) IX. 43, 44.

And, to speak the truth, this was a matter of congratulation for seventeenth-century Cambridge. For while we are not content that it should now be considered as exclusively 'the mathematical university,' or that the tripos in the last century should be called 'the mathematical tripos,' it appears that about 1635 it was not mathematical at all.

Wallis, who was at Emmanuel at that time, says[1] that mathematics were 'scarce looked upon as *Academical* studies, but rather *Mechanical*...And among more than Two hundred Students (at that time) in our College, I do not know of any Two (perhaps not any) who had more of *Mathematicks* than I, (if so much) which was then but little; And but very few, in that whole University. For the Study of *Mathematicks* was at that time more cultivated in *London* than in the universities.' Wallis adds that he first learnt logic, and proceeded to ethics, physics and metaphysics, consulting the schoolmen on such points.

But Aristotle and the Schoolmen were to be displaced within a very few years by the influence of Bacon and the discoveries of astronomy and physical science, and gradually in the Cambridge schools questions in moral and natural philosophy took the place of Aristotelian problems, and this (as Peacock observed[2]) without the slightest warrant on the part of the Statutes, or any formal alteration of them. During the latter half of the century when Barrow wrote, Descartes was in the ascendant, until just before its close, as we shall see, Newton was beginning to gain some footing in the academical disputations.

And when Newton was established the schools first clave to the *Principia* and by degrees (but not for another half century) revelled in fluxions. Afterwards when the Senate-house examination was getting the better of the Schools, the latter became almost exclusively 'philosophical' (i.e. addicted to the moral and mental science of the day) until they perished in the present century; while the mathematics migrated in a body to the Senate-house and have flourished there ever since[3].

---

[1] Hearne's *Longtoft*, I. pp. cxlvii.—cxlix.

[2] Peacock *On the Statutes*, 69.

[3] An interesting picture of the Cambridge schools, of Lax the moderator (mentioned p. 38), and the Senate-house, is given in the letters of W. Gooch (Caius), 1791, in an Appendix.

It will have been remarked that to get a degree in Arts at Cambridge in the last century a young man must have *some* knowledge of mathematics (indeed in the latter part of that period as much as or more than he could well acquire[1]), a trifle of colloquial Latin and of formal logic, as well as a little metaphysics;—-Newton,—*at least a part* of the *Principia,*—seems to have been always expected.

In later times (1818) it was considered a great concession on the part of the moderators to allow an aspirant to mathematical honours—indeed the only honours then attainable—to 'keep' in the Eleventh Book of Euclid instead of in Newton.

English mathematicians of the eighteenth century worshipped the genius of Newton, and few Cambridge men would have dreamt of such audacity as to attempt to advance upon his discoveries. And who shall blame them? But so it was that no progress was made. For example, with regard even to the mechanical part of his work in hydrodynamics, no advance was made in England upon the *speculations* of Newton until the time of Thomas Young[2] (M.D. Göttingen 1795, Camb. 1808). This remarkable man, who was destined to shake the Newtonian Emission Theory of Light, wrote *On Sound and Light* for the Royal Society while he was an undergraduate at Emmanuel, aged 26, in 1799.

Dr W. Heberden of St John's, writing of the examinations which he remembered about 1730, says that Locke, Clarke, and the most important parts of the four branches of natural philosophy were studied; while 'Newton, Euclid and Algebra were only known to those who chose to attend the lectures of Prof. Saunderson, for the college lecturers were silent on them. The works

[1] 'You may do anything with young men by encouragement, by prizes, honours, and distinctions: see what is done at Cambridge. But there the stimulus is too strong; two or three heads are cracked by it every year... some of them go mad; others are reduced to such a state of debility, both of mind and body, that they are unfit for anything during the rest of their lives. I always counselled the admixture of the study of natural philosophy, of classics and literature, and that university honours should be accorded to all. One thing I always set my face against; and that is, exercises in English composition.' Paley's *conversation in 1797 with* H. Best, *Personal and Lit. Memorials*, p. 171.

[2] Whewell, *Hist. Induct. Sciences,* Vol. II. Bk. vi. Ch. iv. § 2.

however of Dr Smith[1] and Dr Rutherford[2] naturally introduced a greater attention to the subjects of which they treated in the two great colleges:' which spread thence and soon became subjects in the public examination[3].

Dr Whewell (disposing of Professor Playfair's misrepresentations of Cambridge as if she were slow in recognising her hero[4]) shews that Newton probably taught the substance of the *Principia* in lectures at Cambridge before it was published in 1687, one or two of which had been heard in the publick Schools by Whiston [B.A. 1689], who became his deputy in 1699, and his successor in 1703; in which capacities he delivered lectures explanatory of Newton, which were published in 1707, 1710, *in usum juventutis Academicae.* Whewell writes,

'About 1694 the celebrated Samuel Clarke [of Norwich], then an undergraduate, defended in the schools a question taken from the philosophy of Newton: a step which must have had the approbation of the moderator who presided at the disputations: and his translation of Rohault with references to the Principia was first published in 1697; and not in 1718 as Professor Playfair has strangely supposed.' Rohault was indeed an expositor of the Cartesian philosophy[5], and Whiston calls this a good edition of ' a *Philosophical Romance:*' but the Newtonian Philosophy which had already crept into the notes was soon about to usurp the text, and to subjugate the editor. For he

---

[1] ROBERT SMITH, B.A. 1711, a cousin of Cotes, whom he succeeded as Plumian professor of astronomy and experimental philosophy 1716 — 60, succeeded Bentley as Master of Trinity 1742—68. He increased the endowment of the Plumian professorship, and founded the Smith's prizes 1768. He wrote a *System of Opticks* 1728, and *Harmonicks,* or the Philosophy of Musical Sounds, 1760.

[2] THOMAS RUTHERFORD, B.A. 1729, was one of the candidates for the mastership of St John's 1765. He was Regius professor of Divinity 1756—71. He wrote *Ordo Institutionum Physicarum* (dedicated to Dr Newcome) 1743, Nature and Obligations of Virtue, 1744,

System of Natural Philosophy (lectures on mechanicks, opticks, hydrostaticks, astronomy) 1748, Institutes of Natural Law (St John's College Grotius lectures) 1754—6, &c., &c.

[3] *Strictures upon the Discipline of* Cambridge, 1792, pp. 42, 43.

[4] Whewell (1821) *On the Statements of Prof.* Playfair *respecting the Univ. of* Cambridge (*Museum Criticum,* II. 514—519.) Monk thinks that Bentley learnt the secret of Newton's discoveries from his professorial lectures before 1680. *Life of Bentley,* I. 8.

[5] I have mentioned elsewhere that *even the Tripos Verses* attack the Cartesian system as early as 1694. This is a most significant fact.

republished the book in 1702 'with more copious additions from the principles of Newton, which could hardly "escape the no-tice" of any body who saw the book, since they are mentioned in the title page,' says Dr Whewell[1].

We next find Dr Clarke translating Newton's *Opticks* into elegant Latin, a performance which so much pleased the author that he gave the translator 100*l.* for each of his five children[2]. This was in 1706.

Long before this, indeed in the year when Clarke took his first degree (1694), Richard Laughton became tutor[3] of Clare Hall, Whiston's college. His lectures 'had probably been on Newtonian principles for the whole or the greater part of his tutorship; but it is certain that for some years [before 1710] he had been diligently inculcating those doctrines, and that the credit and popularity of his college had risen very high[4] in con-sequence of his reputation.'

The study of the new philosophy, and with it mathematicks generally, had gained some ground at our university when Sir W. Browne went there in 1707. It was about that time[5] that Laughton published 'a sheet of questions for the use of the Soph Schools,' on the mathematical *Newtonian* philosophy. It was in this year that ' the celebrated [Nic.] Saunderson [LL.D.] having acquired an extraordinary portion of mathematical knowledge, came to Cambridge [Chr. Coll.] with the intention of fixing himself in the university by means of it.' And though the subject was already occupied by Whiston, the blind geome-ter[6] was encouraged with the permission of the professor himself

[1] In a paper read before the Camb. Philosophical Society in 1851, and printed as 'Appendix G' to his *Philos. of Discovery*, Dr Whewell has shewn how the Cartesian Theory of Vortices was gradually (though very tardily) supplanted by the Newtonian system at Paris, when in 1741 a Cartesian Essay was rewarded with a prize along with three Newtonian.

[2] Whiston's *Histor. Memoirs of Clarke*, p. 13.

[3] 'The lectures of persons in that capacity Prof. Playfair considers as the only effective part of the University

system; and *according to him* these instructions were very late in receiv-ing the impression of Newtonianism.' *Whewell*, Mus. Crit. II. 517.

[4] Thoresby's *Diary* (8 July, 1714).

[5] Sir W. Browne's *Speech*, 1772. Nichols' *Lit. Anecd.* III. 322. Cp. Monk's *Bentley*, I. 288, II. 30 *n.*

[6] His blindness came on when he was one year old. A portrait of Saun-derson with his eyelids closed, in bands and cape, handling a skeleton-globe, was painted by Vanderbanck, engraved by G. Vander Gutch. Saun-derson's *Elements of Algebra* were

to give a course of lectures on 'the Principia, Optics, and Arithmetica Universalis of Newton;' Public exercises, or *acts* as they are called, *founded on every part of the* Newtonian *system*, are spoken of by Saunderson's biographers as very common in 1707. By this time those studies were extensively diffused in the university, and copies of the *Principia* were in such request that in 1710 one which was originally published at *ten shillings* was considered cheap at *two guineas*. In 1709 and the following year Ri. Laughton was enabled to stimulate the progress of the science in an official capacity in the university as he had done in Clare Hall. He was elected proctor: and instead of deputing another person to moderate, according to the usual custom, he chose to preside in the schools in person, and to discharge the office of moderator himself. Among his college pupils[1] were Francis Barnard, preb. of Norwich, and Martin Folkes, the celebrated president of the Royal Society in 1741. Another tutor of Clare, Ro. Green, in his *Principles of Natural Philosophy* (Camb. 1712), opposed the Newtonian philosophy[2].

Meanwhile Saunderson was teaching 'numerous classes of scholars in private Lectures annually[3]' with great success; and when Whiston was removed from the chair of Barrow and Newton in 1710, he succeeded to the Lucasian professorship. And the testimony of the next generation was that, although mathematics had become more generally understood since his

issued posthumously in 1740 (2 vols. 4to.) and of its 'Select Parts' many editions were published.

[1] Nichols' *Lit. Anecd.* III. 328, II. 578.

[2] Green's *Principles of Philosophy of Expansive and Contractive Forces*, Camb. 1727, was reviewed soon afterwards on the continent in *Acta Eruditorum*, 1729, No. VI. pp. 241 *sqq.* His *Encyclopædia*, or scheme of study for undergraduates, 1707, will be found reprinted in an Appendix to this present compilation.

'Dr Green maintained there is neither a Vacuum, in the sense of the moderns (Newton, Raphson, Keil, &c.) nor a Plenum in the sense of Descartes —he held some peculiar notions on

gravity—he maintained also, and offers proof of the possibility of squaring the circle. He examined also various other doctrines that are comprehended in Sir Isaac Newton's Philosophy as that of Sound, Light, and Colour, the Rainbow, Fluids, &c. He thought that the new systems tended to undermine the authority of Revelation, in which he appears to have been a sincere and zealous believer.' Dyer, *Privil.* II. ii. 200. Like H. Lee, Green opposed Locke's theory of the Mind. Saunderson said he was accounted mad. See De Morgan, *Budget of Paradoxes*, 80, 81.

[3] Dyer *Priv. Cant.* I. 539 *n.*

premature death in 1739 (aged 56), yet Saunderson was 'justly famous not only for the display he made of the several methods of Reasoning, for the improvement of the mind ; and the application of Mathematics to natural Philosophy,' but by the ' reverential regard for Truth as the great Law of the God of truth[1], with which he endeavoured to inspire his Scholars, and that peculiar felicity in teaching, whereby he made his subject familiar to their minds.' It may be remarked that Cotes, Newton's friend and disciple, and Bentley, who made Newton's philosophy known to the readers of general literature[2], resided in Cambridge in the first years of Saunderson's professorship, the one as Plumian Professor till 1716, the other (who survived both his colleagues) as Master of Trinity. Saunderson's *Elements of Algebra* and *Treatise on Fluxions* were published posthumously. Smith recommended Ri. Watson[3], then a sizar of Trinity, to read the latter work in 1757 soon after its publication.

Saunderson's successor was J. Colson of Sidney and Emmanuel who was brought to Cambridge by Dr Smith after being master of Rochester school and vicar of Chalk. He edited *Newton's Fluxions* 1736, and decyphered *Saunderson's Palpable Arithmetic*, prefixing it to the posthumous 'Algebra' 1740. Other works of his are mentioned in Cooper's *Biographical Dictionary*.

The next Lucasian professor was E. Waring, a senior wrangler, of Magdalene. He was appointed in 1760 at the age of twenty-five, before he got his fellowship. He wrote *Miscellanea Analytica de Aequationibus Algebraicis et Curvarum Proprietatibus, Meditationes Algebraicae, Meditationes Analyticae*, &c. The first chapter of his *Miscellanea Analytica* he circulated to defend the honour of the University, which had chosen so young a man to sit in the seat of Barrow, Newton, and Saunderson. Dr Powell of St John's attacked this production in some *Observations,* with which Waring grappled 'in a very able reply, for which he was indebted to Mr J. Wilson[4], then an under-

[1] Ri. Davies, M.D., *Epistle to Dr Hales* (*Bath*, 1759,) *p.* 14. Dyer, however, says that Saunderson was ' no friend to Divine revelation.' But he adds that ' he desired to receive the communion before he died.' *Privil. Camb.* II. ii. (= Suppl. Hist.) pp. 142-3.

[2] *Whewell,* l.c. *p.* 518.

[3] Watson's *Anecd.* I. 14. Dyer, *Privil.* II. i. 206.

[4] Wilson (of the *Theorem*), sen. wrangler 1761, was Paley's private tutor. A. De Morgan *Budget of Paradoxes*, 132, 133.

graduate of Peter House, afterwards a Judge of the Common Pleas.' Powell had the last word[1]. In 1765 G. Wollaston, of Sidney, joined with two Peterhouse men, J. Jebb and Ro. Thorp, in editing *Excerpta quaedam e* Newtoni *Principiis Philosophiae Naturalis*, cum notis variorum, 4to. This became a standard work at Cambridge. Isaac Milner, of Queens' (senior wrangler, 1744), succeeded Waring, 1798—1820. He had been previously professor of Natural Philosophy. He took little part in mathematical instruction, except so far as the examinations went. Long before this, Newton's name was familiar in the mouths of the most ignorant persons in the kingdom, such as Doiley in Mrs Cowley's *Who 's the Dupe?* (Act ii. sc. 2, 1779), who exclaims 'Newton! oh ay—I have heard of Sir Isaac—everybody has heard of Sir Isaac—great man—master of the mint!'

At Oxford the *Principia* was not so well received[2]. David Gregory, *secundus*, (editor of Euclid, &c., Savilian Professor), brought something of this philosophy from Edinburgh[3]; but the old Oxonians were somewhat jealous of his reputation.

In one place Hearne admits that Newton was 'a very great mathematician:' but in another he states that Sir Isaac Newton does not understand a bit of classical learning, only studies chronology for relaxation, and is beholden to others for the Latin of his books. Moreover that he took his *Principia* 'from hints given him by the late Dr Hook (many of whose papers cannot now be found), as well as from others that he received from Sir Christopher Wren, both of which were equally as great men as Sir Isaac[4],'—and had the advantage of being educated respectively at Christ Church, and Wadham College, *Oxon.* However J. Carswell or Caswell (Wadh. and Hart Hall), their Savilian professor of Astronomy (1709—13), did not give a very favourable character to Ro. Hooke; for while he considered him a good mechanician, he thought him inclined to overrate his own discoveries[5],

[1] Nichols' *Lit. Anecd.* II. 717.
[2] The anti-Newtonian J. Hutchinson's *Mosis Principia* appeared in two parts 1724—7. He was followed by J. Parkhurst (Clare) in articles *Jehova Eloheim*, &c., in his Hebrew lexicon, and by G. Horne and Jones of Nayland.

[3] Sir W. Browne (Pet. and Queens') published a translation of Gregory's *Catoptricks* and *Dioptricks.*
[4] *Reliquiae Hearnianae* ed. 2, II. 216 (*anno* 1724), 245, 277, 309, 310.
[5] Uffenbach, *Reisen* III. 182, which passage gives evidence of this Oxford

Jo. Spence of New College also gives currency to the ridiculous popular Anecdote (p. 175) that Newton could not make up a common account for himself even when he was master of the Mint.   If Cambridge desired to retort upon her sister she might with the advantage of truth on her side proclaim, that the learned and generous founder of the lectureships of geometry and astronomy at Oxford, the warden of Merton and provost of Eton, Sir Henry Savile, publicly confessed that a course of lectures on the definitions, postulates, axioms and first eight propositions of Euclid was a task which almost overwhelmed him[1].   Dr Whewell, however, takes a more liberal view of his words, and attributes them to the absorbing process of the commentatorial spirit working in a critic long and earnestly employed on one author.

Bp G. Horne at the age of 19 wrote a Satire on Newton, 'The Theology and Philosophy in Cicero's *Somnium Scipionis* explained.' Lond. 1751.   Two years later when fellow of *Magdalen* he wrote the more mature 'Fair, candid, and impartial State of the Case between Newton and Hutchinson.'

At the close of the eighteenth century, Dr Abram Robertson of Christ Church, Savilian professor of Geometry, and Dr Thomas Hornsby of Corpus, Savilian professor of Astronomy[2], were among those Oxford professors of whom Adam Smith had asserted in 1776 that 'the greater part...have for these many years given up altogether even the pretence of teaching.'   *Tempora mutantur.*

Algebra[3] lectures were begun at Cambridge on Lady Sadleir's foundation at the following nine colleges,—Emmanuel, King's, St John's, Sidney, Trinity, Jesus, Queens', Peterhouse, and

professor's interest in astronomical and practical mechanics.

[1] 'Exolvi per Dei gratiam, Domini auditores, promissum; liberavi fidem meam; explicavi pro meo modulo, definitiones, petitiones, communes sententias, et octo priores propositiones Elementorum Euclidis. Hic, annis fessus, cyclos artemque repono.' *Praelectiones.* See *Whewell*, Hist. Induct. Sciences, *Bk.* iv. *ch.* ii.

[2] Misprinted '*Anatomy*' in my *Univ. Society*, p. 87.

[3] Dyer (*Privil.* ii. ii. 205—209) gives an account of certain Cambridge algebraists—among them baron Francis Maseres (fellow of Clare), author of *A Dissertation on the Negative Sign in Algebra*, 1758,—and W. Frend (Jes.), author of *Principles of Algebra*, 1796-9. Both of these persons set themselves against Saunderson, Maclaurin and the rest of the world; for they rejected negative quantities 1, −1, no less than $\sqrt{-1}$; and, like Ro. Simson, 'made war of extermination on all that distinguishes algebra from arithmetic,' (*De Morgan.*)

Pembroke Hall. The foundress was widow of W. Croune, M.D. of Emmanuel, and died Sept. 30, 1706[1]. In the present century the remaining colleges were endowed with lectureships from the same foundation[2]. They were commuted for a professorship about 1860.

Dr J. Green, bp of Lincoln, says in the *Academic*, 1750, (p. 23), that 'Mathematicks and Natural Philosophy are so generally and so exactly understood, that more than twenty in every year of the Candidates for a Batchelor of Arts Degree, are able to demonstrate the principal Propositions in the *Principia*; and most other Books of the first Character on those subjects. Nay, several of this Number, they tell you, are no Strangers to the *higher-Geometry* and the more difficult Parts of the Mathematicks: and others, who are not of this Number, are yet well acquainted with the Experiments and *Appearances* in natural Science. In Morality, Metaphysicks, and Natural Religion, the Authors whose *Notions* are the most Accurate and Intelligible are generally read and well understood by many before they are admitted to this Degree.

'Logic they allow to be at present rather more neglected than it deserves; as Men run but too commonly into opposite Extremes; but the Error, they say, begins to be perceived and will probably be of no long Duration.' Dr Green is here mentioning the current opinion of the studies at Cambridge in 1750; not controverting its truth, but its significance.

For practical instances of their knowledge, as brought to the trial of examination, we have a tradition of Turner, tutor of Pembroke Hall in Pitt's time, that he thus advised an undergraduate, 'By all means do not neglect your *duodecimals*. I was Senior Wrangler in 1767 by knowing my duodecimals[3].'

---

[1] The lecturer's stipend at all but Emmanuel was at first £20, and in course of time was doubled.

[2] *Camb. Calendar*, 1802, p. 33. Cooper's *Annals*, IV. 77.

[3] Of T. Robinson of Trinity (seventh wrangler in 1772) it is recorded that he was 'well acquainted with natural philosophy, though but little with analytics,' and that for one of his disputations as an opponent in the schools 'he invented an argument against the doctrine of prime and ultimate ratios as taught by one of our ablest mathematicians; which (says his biographer, E. T. Vaughan, 1816, p. 29), I am assured has never yet been satisfactorily answered.' Robinson 'gained great credit from his mathematical disputations in the schools, the year previous to his first degree,' (*ibid.* p. 28), yet rather from his reasoning powers than from any great proficiency in Algebra and Fluxions....

In 1776 Wakefield, the second wrangler, retired from competition for the Smith's prizes because he ' was but a humble proficient in the *higher* parts of *Algebra* and *Fluxions*[1].' Then ten years later there is the astonishment of the expectant wranglers at being required to extract roots to three places of *decimals*[2]. And later we have a current story of an old fellow cautioning an aspiring student to make sure of his quadratic equations, because a *hard quadratic equation* made his fortune. This is no doubt a modern reproduction of the duodecimal story, but it was suited to the times (perhaps about 1815). However, the books read by candidates tell at once a more trustworthy and a more favourable tale.

About 1756 Ri. Watson of Trinity read L'Hôpital's Conic Sections. H. Gunning of Christ's (1784-8), who was fifth wrangler, does not give us much information on this point. He says merely that he read Euclid, Algebra, Newton and Paley. Maclaurin was their text-book in Algebra, supplemented by MSS. examples. Parkinson, his tutor at Christ's, lent him a manuscript on Mechanics (centres of oscillation, gyration, and percussion). On the eve of examination he crammed six forms out of Waring's *Meditationes Algebraicae*, with a view to the ' Evening Problems.' George Pryme of Trinity, B.A. 1803, is equally reticent, merely mentioning that ' one of the books then read for a degree was that of Roger Cotes, a great mathematician, who died at the early age of 33, of whom Isaac Newton said, "had Cotes lived longer we should have known something".' Dr Whewell considers the Cambridge mathematical course of that time to have included Newton's *Principia*, the works of Cotes, Attwood, Vince and Wood : ' by no means a bad system of mathematical education.' As early as 1774 a syndicate was appointed to prevent men reading too high—' in quaecunque recondita, quaecunque sublimia, impetu quodam fervido ruentibus.' And a grace of March 20, 1779, informed them that they would get no credit for advanced subjects unless they satisfied the examiners in Euclid and elementary Natural Philosophy. About 1780, when the examination began to be conducted on paper to a greater

Locke's Essay and Butler's Analogy, which he had studied attentively, were also of service to him in the examina-tion. (*p.* 30.)

[1] *Memoirs* (1804), I. 111.

[2] Gunning, *Reminisc.* I, ch. iii,

extent, much dependence was placed upon *Syllabuses*, traditional treatises called in later times 'college manuscripts'; and men attempted to foretell pieces of book-work likely to be set. At the close of the century the works of Wood and Vince established something of a standard and system of study, and about 1808 the French analytical method was introduced.

The tenth wrangler of 1796 mentions in his diary (1793-5) reading 'Trigonometry...Ratios and Variable Quantities... copied a syllabus of Mechanics (belonging to a friend)...Astronomy, Euclid XI (the college lecture subject)...Spherical Trigonometry....Vince's Conic Sections....Plane Trigonometry.... Fluxional Problems....Cotes, Newton Opticks....Hydrostatics.' His brother, W. Wordsworth (B.A. 1791), had learnt Euclid, books I—IV, VI, and simple and quadratic equations, at Hawkshead school. He had therefore (as he afterwards lamented) a full twelvemonth's start of the freshmen in his year[1].

At that period a complaint was made[2] against the mathematical method then in fashion.

'A short method of acquiring many truths is affected... it is deemed a terrible waste of time in training a youth for the examination of the Senate [House] to attempt to hamper him with the sound method of the antient geometricians. Algebraic calculations are generally effected, and attempted to be applied to every question, with the assistance of a little Geometry and Fluxional principles, which can be proposed in pure or mixed mathematics....It is evident that no person can understand the *Principia* without the analysis I allude to. But I object to the excess of analytical expressions, which are little more than operose combinations of letters by the common signs of composition which convey no permanent or useful ideas. As an illustration of what I mean to inforce, let me relate a fact which happened not many years ago, and will have a greater force than any thing which I can offer further on the subject.

'A bachelor of arts was some years ago a candidate for a fellowship; who had kept an exercise upon the 3rd section of the 1st Book of the *Principia*, and in the schools had occasion

---

1 *Memoirs of* W. Wordsworth, I. 14.   *By a* Member of the Senate. 1788.
2 *Considerations on the Oaths*, &c.   p. 18.

to talk a good deal about the motion of a body in a parabola, and
to shew some symptoms of knowledge of the fluxional calculus.
I believe too he was a wrangler. He was asked by one of the
senior Fellows to find the area of a given rectilinear triangle;
and to the astonishment of the poor old man, who thought himself absolutely mocked by the answer, replied that *he could do
it by fluxions*[1].'

The boys' schools about 1750, did little or nothing in the
way of mathematical preparation. 'Mr Ayscough...writing in
1797 says[2], Whatever may be the present usage [in grammar-
schools], it is within recollection that *fifty* years ago there were
sent from *capital* schools to the universities youths of good
abilities, and not by any means wanting in *grammar* and
classical learning, yet so little versed in common figures as to
be obliged to have recourse to a *master of a day school* in the
town for instruction *in the four fundamental rules of arithmetic*.'
But in 1792 Ingram complained[3] that the example of Cambridge had induced 'several of the schools in the kingdom' to
study the mathematics to the neglect of the classics, 'an evil of
some magnitude.'

About 1815-18, John M. F. Wright of Trinity (who but for
untoward circumstances might have taken a very high place)
gives a formidable list of books which he had read. When he
came to Cambridge he had read only *Ludlam's Elements* and
Walkinghame's Tutor's Assistant. In his Freshman's year he
added to this foundation Wood's Algebra with Ludlam or
Bridge; Woodhouse's Plane Trigonometry; and learnt to
write Newton's Binomial Theorem.

In his *second year* he applied his attention to old examination papers and 'College MSS.' and the problems in Bridge's
Mechanics. For Statics and Dynamics he read Wood, Parkinson, and Gregory. Then (after turning his mind to Paley's
Evidences and Moral Philosophy, Locke on the Human Understanding, and Dugald Stewart), he took up Parts II, III, IV. of
Wood's Algebra and Spherical Trigonometry, Garnier's Algebra
and Analyse Algébrique, Lacroix's Algebra, Cresswell's Spherics.
For problems and deductions he had recourse to Leybourne's

---

[1] *ibid.* p. 19.

[2] Hone's *Year Book*, col. 991.

[3] *Necessity of Introducing Divinity*,
&c., by *R. A. Ingram*, p. 101.

Mathematical Repository and Dodson's Repository. He compiled for himself a 'College MS.' of book-work, &c.; and read Conic Sections, Popular and Plane Astronomy in Bonnycastle, Laplace's Système du Monde, Newton's Principia, Sections I, II, III.

In his *last year* he read the Jesuits' Newton, (the college lecture subject); Monge's Géometrie Analytique, Lagrange's Mécanique Celeste; Vince, Dealtry, Lacroix, Fluxions; Françoeur's Mécanique and Mathématiques Pures; Poisson, Garnier,Gergonne's Annales Mathématiques, Journal Polytechnique, Leybourne's Mathematical Repository, Old papers, The 'small Lacroix' and his three large 4tos; Bossut's Hydrostatique and Hydrodynamique. He attends the following lectures:—Farish on machinery, Clarke on mineralogy, and the Plumian Professor (S. Vince, Cai.) who explained experimentally Mechanics, Hydrostatics, Optics, Astronomy, Magnetism, Electricity, Galvanism, &c.

Dr Parr, writing at the close of the last century, says with regard to the mathematical professors and teachers at Cambridge, that 'Dr [Ed.] Waring [Magd. Lucas. Prof.] and Mr [Sam.] Vince [F.R.S., Caius, Plumian Prof. 1796] in their writings have done honour to the science, not only of their University, but of their age. The profound researches of Dr Waring, I suppose, were not adapted to any form of commucation by lectures. But Mr Vince has, by private instruction, been very useful both to those who were novitiates [*sic*], and to those who were proficients in mathematics. Dr [S.] Halifax[1] (Jes., Arabic and Civil Law), Dr [T.] Rutherford[2] (S. John's, Divinity), and Dr [Ri.] Watson[3] (Trin., Chemistry and Divinity),

[1] Bp. *Hallifax* published Analysis of the Civil Law. 8vo. Camb. 1774. (Also Ogden's Sermons and an analysis of Butler's Analogy.)
[2] Dr *Rutherford* was the author of
1. Ordo Institutionum Physicarum. 4to. Camb, 1743.
2. On the Nature and Obligations of Virtue. 4to. Camb. 1744.
3. System of Natural Philosophy, being a Course of Lectures in Mechanics, Optics, Hydrostatics, Astronomy, read in St John's Coll. 2 vols. 4to. 1748. Camb. 31 plates.
4. Institutes of Natural Law. 2 vols. 1754—6.
[3] Bp. *Watson* printed Institutiones Metallurgicae. 1768. Theological Tracts, 6 vols. 1785. Chemical Essays, 5 vols. 1781, 1782, 1786.
(Also an Apology for Christianity, 1776. Apology for the Bible, 1796. Christian Whig's Letters, 1772.)

very abundantly conveyed the information which belonged to their departments sometimes in the disputes of the schools, and sometimes by the publication of their writings.'

Is. Milner of Queens', who sat in Newton's seat as Lucasian Professor, succeeding Waring in 1798, did not lecture, but took part in the Senate-house examinations, and got students to come and consult him.

In addition to such assistance as the professors thus afforded, there were at the several colleges the Sadlerian lectureships already mentioned (p. 72), supplementing the efforts of individual tutors. The University also provided a lecturer in Mathematics[1] in the person of the senior Barnaby lecturer with a stipend of £4 a year from the Vice-chancellor, the other Barnaby lecturers in Philosophy, Logic, and Rhetoric (or, previous to the Statutes of Edw. VI., in Terence), receiving only £3. 4s. from the bursar of Jesus College.

The *text-books* recommended by an anti-Newtonian at the commencement of the century will be found in the proper sections of Ro. Green's Ἐγκυκλοπαιδεία, printed among the Appendices of this volume.

The books (mathematical, physical, mechanical and hydro-statical) which were thought serviceable for the schools about 1730 I have digested in the following list from Waterland and Johnson. Similar lists of *Optical and Astronomical* works, and of *Ethical and Metaphysical* will be found below, at the close of two other chapters.

BOOKS

in use at *Cambridge* about the year 1730,

for *Arithmetic, Algebra, Geometry,*

Physics, Mechanics, and *Hydrostatics.*

Acta Eruditorum (Lipsiae) 1686, 1690, '91, '94, '95.
Acta Philosophica.

Bacon, F. (Trin.), Historia de Ventis. Lug. Bat., 1638; Lond. 1672.
———— Sylva Sylvarum, 1627, ed. 9, 1670.

---

[1] In 1534-6 the mathematical lectureship was commuted for lectures in Greek or Hebrew. A writer in the early part of the last century (*Caius Coll. MSS.* 604) considered the stipend as '£4 entirely flung away.'

Bartholin, Casp. nepos (Copenhagen) Physicks. Lond. 1703.
Bentley, Ri. (Joh. & Trin.) Boyle Lectures. Lond. 1693.
Bernoulli, Jac. (Basle, Heidelb.) de Gravitate Aetheris. Amst. 1683.
Boerhaave, Herm. (Leyden) Chymistry (Shaw) 4to. Lond. 1626.
Boyle, Ro. (*Oxon.*) History of Cold. Lond. 1665, 1685.
———— Physico-Mechan. Experim. *Oxon.* 1660. Contin^d, 1669; Lond. 1682.
———— Principles of Nat. Bodies. Lond. 1674.
———— Sceptical Chymist. *Oxon.* 1661, 1680.
———— Works (abridged by Shaw) 3 vols. 4to. 1725.
Bradley, Ri. (Camb.) on Gardening. Lond. 1626.
Browne, Peter (*T. C. D.*) Procedure of the Understanding. Lond. 1728.
Burgundiae Scholae Philosophia. 2 vols. 4to. Nürnb. 1682, Paris 1684, '7.
Burnet, T. (Clare & Chr.) to Keill in Appendix to his own Theory. Lond. 1698.
———— Theory of the Earth. Lond. 1681—9.

Cartesius, Réné (La Flèche) Principia. Amst. 1644, &c.
Castellus, Bened. (Montp.) de motu aquae. ital. Rom. 1628. english, Lond. 1661.
Caswell, J. (*Wadh.*) Trigonometry. Lond. fol. 1685.
Chambers, Ephr. Dictionary (sub vocibus *Air, Barometer, Circulation of Sap, Deluge, Dissolution, Diving Bell, Elasticity, Electricity, Fire, Fluid, Fossil, Gravity, Matter, Perpetual Motion, Pump, Sound, Syphon, Tarantula, Thunder, Vegetation*) fol. 1728.
Cheyne, G. (Edinb.) Philos. Princip. Lond. 1715.
Clarke, S. (Caius) Letters to Dodwell. Lond. 1706.
———— Letters between him and Leibnitz. Lond. 1717.
Clericus, Jean (Geneva) Physica. Cantab. 1700, 1705.

De Chales (Challes), Cl. Fr. Milliet (Turin) Cursus Mathematicus, fol. 4 vols. Lyons 1690.
————————— Euclid. *Oxon.* 1685, 1704, &c.
De la Hire, Philip. (Paris) Conic Sections. Paris, 1655, 1685.
De Lanis, Fr. Tert. (S. J.) Magist. Nat. & Art. Brescia 1684, 1692.
De la Pryme, Abr. (Joh.) in Philos. Transactions.
De l'Hôpital, Marquis, G. F. A. (Paris) Conics. London, 4to. 1723.
Derham, W. (*Trin.*) Letters. (Ray's.) Lond. 1718.
Desaguliers, J. Theo. (*Ch. Ch.*) transl. of Marriotte's Hydrostatics. 1738.
Descartes, see Cartesius.
De Witt, J. Conics. Amst. 1659.

Euclid, cura D. Gregory. fol. *Oxon.* 1703. Gr. and Lat.

Friend (or Freind), J. (*Ch. Ch.*) Praelect. Chem. *Oxon.* 1704, 1709, et alibi.

Gassendi, Pierre (Aix & Paris) Philos. Lond. 1658.
Gordon, Patrick (? T. C. D.) Account of Trade Winds. ? Geography Anatomized 1693, 1716.
's Gravesande, W. Ja. (Leyden) Philos. Newton. Lond. 1720.
———— Physic. Elem. Math. Lug. Bat. 1720.
Green, Ro. (Clare) Principles of Nat. Philosophy. (Solid Geom.) Camb. 1712, ibid. 1727.
———— Princ. Philos. of Expansive and Contractive Forces.

Hales, Steph. (C. C. C.) Vegetable Staticks. Lond. 1727.

Hammond's Algebra.

Harriott, T. (*S. Mary Hall*) Artis Analyticae Praxis. Lond. 1631.

Harris, J. (S. John's) Lexicon Technicum (sub vocibus *Deluge, Hydrostaticks, Perpetual Motion, Spring, Thunder, Vegetation*) 1708.

Hawksbee, F. (F. R. S.) Phys. Mechan. Experiments. Lond. 1709, 1719.

Helmont, J. Bapt. van (Louvain) Opera.

Hooke, R. (*Ch. Ch.*) Micrographia (Elzevir 1648). Lond. 1665, 1671.

——— Posthumous Works. Lond. 1705.

Huet, P. D. (Caen) Censura Phil. Cartes, 1689, Paris 1694.

Huyghens, Chr. (Lugd.) Opera Posthuma. Lug. Bat. 1703.

Jones, W. (F.R.S.) Abridgment of Philos. Transact.

——— Analysis per Quantitatum Series, Fluxiones ac Differentias. 4to. Lond. 1711.

——— Synopsis Palmariorum Matheseos. Lond. 1706.

Keill, Jo. (*Balliol*) Epist. de Legibus Attractionis. *Oxon.* 1715 ; 4to. Lug. Bat. 1725.

——— Examination of Burnet's Theory of the Earth. *Oxon.* 1698.

——— Introd. ad Phys. Lect. (1701, 1705, 1726). *Oxon.* 1715.

Kersey, J. Algebra. Lond. 1673—4, 1725.

Law, Edm. (Joh., Chr., Pet.) Translation of King's Origin of Evil. 1732.

Le Clerc, see Clericus.

Le Grand, Ant. (*Douay & Oxon.*) de Carentia Sensus in Brutis. Lond. 1675.

——— Instit. Philos. 1694.

Leibnitz, Godf. W. (Leipzig) and Clarke's Controversial Papers (1717).

Lister, Mart. (Joh. & *Oxon.*) Account of Trade-winds. (? 1683.)

Locke, J. (*Ch. Ch.*) Essay on the Human Understanding. Lond. 1690, &c.

Lowthorp, J. Abridgment of Philos. Transact. Lond. 1716.

Lucretius de Rerum Natura I. (Creech *Oxon.* 1695. Maittaire 1713.)

Maclaurin, Colin (Glasg. & Aberd.) Geometra Organica, sive Descriptio Curvarum, Universalis. Lond. 1720. 4to. (Algebra 1742).

Malebranche, Nic. (Sorbonne) Search after Truth. Lond. 1720.

Marriotte, Edm., see Desaguliers.

Michelotti Pet. Ant. de Separ. Fluidorum. 4to. Venice 1721.

Milnes, Ja. (? M.D. Camb., M.A. *Oxon.*) Conic Sections. *Oxon.* 1702, 1723.

Miscellanea Curiosa (Halley, Molyneux, Wallis, Woodward, &c.). Franc. and Leips. 1670—97.

Musschenbroeck, Pet. van (Leyden) de Cohaerentia Corporum.

——— Elem. Physico.-Math. Lugd. Bat. 1729.

——— Phys. Experim. de Magnete.

Newton, Is. (Trin.) Algebra.

——— Arithmetica Num. and Specios. Probl.

——— Optice. Lond. 1704.

——— Principia Mathem. (1687) ed. 2, Camb. 1713. ed. 3, 1726.

Newtonianae Philosophiae Institut. 12mo.

Nieuwentyt, Bern. Religious Philosopher (a translation, J. Chamberlayne, *Trin.*—Lond. 1718—19, 1730).

Ode, Jac. Phil. Nat. Principia. Traject. ad Rhen. 1727.
Oughtred, W. (King's). Clavis Mathem. Lond. 1631. *Oxon.* 1652, &c.; Transl. Halley, 1694.
Ozanam, Jacques. Cursus Mathem. Paris 1693, 1712.

Pardie. Geom. 1701.
Pell, J. (Trin.). Idea of Mathematics. 1650.
Pemberton, H. (Leyden). View of Newton. Lond. 1728.
Philosophical Conversations.
———— Transactions.
Polenus, J. (Padua) de Motu Aquae. 4to. Patav. 1717.

Quincy, J. Dispensatory. Lond. 1718; ed. 7, 1730.

Ray, J. (Cath., Trin.). Physico-Theol. Discourses. Lond. 1692, 1693, 1717, 1721.
Reflections on Learning (by T. Baker, Joh.) 1699, 1700, &c.
Rohault, Jacques. Physica (S. Clarke); ed. 4, 1718.

[Saunderson, Nic. (Chr.). Algebra (posthumous), 4to. Camb. 1740.]
Simpson, T. Algebra. Lond. 1737, 1746.
Simson, Ro. (Glasg.). Conics. 4to. Edin. 1735.
Stillingfleet, E. (Joh.). Origines Sacrae. Lond. 4to. 1662, fol. 1709.
Sturmius, J. Chr. (Altdorf). Auctarium.
———— Colleg. Experiment. siue Curios. 1672. 4to. Nürnb. 1675—85.

Tacquet, Andr. S. J. (Antwerp). Euclid (W. Whiston); ed. 3, Cantab. 1722.
Torricellius, Evang. De Motu projectil.

Varenius, Bern. Geographia (Newton) Camb. 1681; (Jurin) Camb. 1712, 1714.

Wallis, J. (Emman., Qu.; *Savil. Prof.*). Logic. *Oxon.* 1687, 1729.
———— Op. Mathemat. fol. 1699.
Ward, Seth (Sid. & *Trin.*) Idea Trigonom. In usum juvent. 4to. *Oxon.* 1654.
Watts, Isaac. Logic. Lond. 1725.
Wedelius, G. Wolfg. Theoria Saporum. Jen. 1703.
Wells, E. (? *Ch. Ch.*) Arithmetick, 1713. Lond. 1726.
———— Geography. *Oxon.* 1701; ed. 4, 1726.
———— Trigonometry. Lond. 1714.
Whiston, W. (Clare). Praelect. Phys. Mathem. Cant. 1710.
———— Theory of the Earth. Camb. 1737.
Wilkins, J. (*New Inn, Magd. H., Wadh.*). Mathem. Magick. Lond. 1648, 1691.
Wingate, Edm. Arithmetick. Lond. 1630, 1726.
Wolf, Christian., in Elementis Math. Mechanica. Genev. 1732.
Woodward, J. (Lambeth). Theory of the Earth. Lond. 1695, 1723.
Worster, Ben. Princip. Nat. Philos. Lond. 1722, 1730.

CHAPTER VIII.

THE TRIVIAL ARTS.

(*Grammar, Logic, Rhetoric.*)

Ignoramus. Sunt magni idiotæ, et clerici nihilorum, isti Universitantes: miror quomodo spendisti tuum tempus inter eos.

Musaeus. Ut plurimum versatus sum in *Logica.*—RUGGLE.

Lingua Tropus Ratio: Numerus Tonus Angulus Astra.—*Memoria Technica.*

THE first three words of the memorial line prefixed to this chapter were intended to denote the *triuium* of three elementary sciences which were to occupy the quadriennium of undergraduateship preparing the student for the 'mathematical' *quadriuium* in which he was to employ the succeeding triennium of bachelorhood before he could be qualified to rule as a Master in the arts-schools.

The same information is more clearly conveyed in the hexameter of the following couplet, which is traced to the first half of the xvth century.

Gram. loquitur, *Dia.* vera docet, *Rhet.* verba colorat:

Mus. canit, *Ar.* numerat, $\overline{Geo}$ ponderat, *As.* colit astra.

Neither of our universities has been able to undertake to teach the complete course of the Seven Liberal Arts in the limited period for which the majority of their students reside; and since the public and private schools have done their part of preparation it has been less necessary.

Cambridge selected *Mathematics* (covering three of the four quadrivial subjects), *Rhetoric* and *Logic,* two of the trivials, and *Philosophy* which may mean very little, or else (with *Theology*) may be, the employment of the Master qualifying himself for full teaching powers as Doctor.

The four *Barnaby* Lecturers (see above, p. 78) were appointed to read on these four select subjects.

They were so called because the nominees were annually 'pricked' for election on the eve, and appointed on the feast of S. Barnabas (June 10th, 11th)[1]. They were the '*ordinary*'[2] readers appointed by the University to give instruction to students living in the hostels or lodging-houses in Cambridge.

As time advanced and the age of matriculation at Cambridge became later, as boys' schools took the place originally occupied by the universities, it was taken for granted that undergraduates were already advanced in their *trivials*, so that 'Grammar' became *in possessiuo subauditum* of a freshman. *Grammar* meant originally the latin language acquired by means of Terence, Priscian, Boëthius, and Donatus. In the fifteenth century larger readings from Terence, Virgil, or Ovid, with some instruction in latin-verse composition, were added[3]. Queen Elizabeth's statute 50, § 21, allowed grammar to the choristers in Trinity and King's alone. A statute of King Edward VI. had confined the privilege to Jesus College. King Henry VIII's statutes for St John's Coll. (*cap.* 16) provided that grammar should be left for schools to teach, and prohibited it as a study in the university: *tum quia magnum studiis suis* (sc. τοῦ docentis) *impedimentum erit, tum quia maiora docenda in collegiis sunt, grammatica in ludis litterariis docenda est.* Three years before this, *i.e.* in 1542, the last degree in grammar at Cambridge had been taken. The curious proceedings for incepting in the obsolete degree in that faculty, the principal *exercise* being the 'purveying' and corporal punishment with 'palmer' and rod of 'a shrewde Boy' who received 'a Grote for his Labour,' have been frequently transcribed from bedell Stokys' account, written, I suppose, about 1558, when he was Registrary, in case that degree should be revived.

While our own university undertook to initiate her undergraduates in the advanced lore of the scientific *quadriuium*, Oxford seems not in past generations to have ventured with her younger sons beyond the *trivials* of philology. An Oxford

[1] Gunning's *Ceremonies*, pp. 109—113.
[2] They are so called in a decree of the Heads, 26 *May*, 1684.
[3] Mullinger, *Hist. Univ. Camb.* 22, 341, 349—50.

statute of 1588, which was not long observed, enjoined an examination for the B.A. degree *in grammaticalibus et logicalibus,* while according to the Laudian code of 1636 (which was *nominally* in force at *Oxford* until the end of the last century) the student in the first year was to attend lectures in *grammar.* The lecturer was to expound its rules from Priscian [6th century], Linacre [fellow of *All Souls* 1484], or some other approved writer, or to explain critically some passage of a greek or roman author. The student was also to attend lectures on *rhetoric,* founded on the works of Aristotle, Cicero, Hermogenes, or Quintilian. The Ethics, Politics, and Economics of *Aristotle,* and *logic,* were to be the subjects of the second year. *Logic, moral philosophy, geometry,* and the *greek* language, under the professor of greek, was the employment of the third and fourth years[1].

Oxford has always been faithful to logic[2] (*Dialectice*). For this her constancy Coleridge commended her[3], adding that it is 'a great mistake to suppose geometry any substitute for it[4].' But at Cambridge more direct attention used to be given to that art than is paid at the present time. Still the gymnastic training of the reasoning faculties for which logic is mainly valuable, is secured among us by the requirement of the geometrical system of Euclid. 'All geometrical reasoning' (says Dr Whewell[5]) 'may be resolved into a series of syllogisms,

[1] Oxford *Univ. Commission* Report (1852), *p.* 56.

[2] Among the effects of Chr. Tilyard, B.A. Oxon., who died in 1598, were 'Aristoteles's lodgicke' and 'Saunderson's lodgike,' i. e. *Institutiones logicae,* 1589, by *John* Sanderson (a Lancashire Roman Catholic, who studied at Douay and taught at Rheims and Cambray), and *not* Ro. Sanderson's *Compendium,* as I impertinently supposed, *Univ. Society,* p. 455.

[3] *Table Talk,* 4 Jan. 1823.

[4] So Harris says, *Hermes* (Pref. pp. xiv, xv. ed. 3, 1771), 'When Mathematics...are used not to exemplify *Logic,* but to supply its place; no wonder if *Logic* pass into contempt,

and if *Mathematics,* instead of furthering science, become in fact an obstacle. For when men knowing nothing of that Reasoning which is *universal* come to attach themselves for years *to a single species* wholly involved *in Lines and Numbers only,* they grow insensibly to believe these last as inseparable from all Reasoning, as the poor *Indians* thought every horseman to be inseparable from his horse.

'And thus we see the use, nay the necessity, of enlarging our literary views, lest even *knowledge itself* should obstruct its own growth, and perform in some measure the part of ignorance and barbarity.'

[5] *Of a Liberal Education,* p. 42.

and in its proper form consists of a chain of enthymems, or implied syllogisms; and in like manner, all other sound reasoning on all subjects consists of a like chain of enthymems.'

King James I. licensed W. lord Maynard, co. Wicklow, to appoint in the university of Cambridge a logic lectureship (tenable with a Johnian fellowship), July 20, 1620, with a stipend of £50; but it died a natural death in 1640[1]. About that period[2] boys brought with them to college some knowledge of some book of logic such as Seton's or Peter Ramus (the devotee of Logic though the rebel against Aristotle), supplemented in their first term by lectures on Keckerman or Molineus. Milton found fault with this system of commencing the nurture of students in arts with such hard fare as logic and metaphysics. At St John's in 1737-8 there were 'two logick-tables...join'd[3]:' while at Trinity in 1755 there were lectures and weekly examinations in Duncan's logic, &c.[4] In 1710 Bonwicke read *Burgersdicii institut. logic.*, and all the *fasciculus præceptorum logicorum Oxoniensis*[5]. John Jebb bears witness that the former book had been prescribed at Cambridge in the memory of their forefathers; but *then* (1775) the barbarous sounds of Darii and Felapton no longer grated on their ears[6].

.As in old times the mere study of the Sentences of Peter

[1] Cooper's *Annals* III. 135, 136.

Our Univ. Statutes of 1570 provided (*cap.* 4) that the professor of logic should teach the arguments of Aristotle or the Topica of Cicero.

[2] Mayor's *M. Robinson* 16 *n.*, 98.

Ramus when proceeding M.A. at Navarre astonished his examiners by choosing for his thesis that 'what Aristotle has said is all wrong' *Quaecunque ab* Aristotle *dicta essent commenticia esse.* Whewell, *Philos. of Discovery*, 99.

[3] Baker-Mayor, *p.* 1035, *l.* 32.

[4] *Bp.* Watson's *Anecdotes* I. *p.* 12, ed. 1818.

[5] Dean Aldrich published his popular *Artis Logicae Compendium* in 1692. It adopted an order independent of the *Organon.* Dr Tatham (rector of Linc.)

asserted that it was all derived from Sanderson. *Letter to* [Cyril Jackson] *dean of Ch. Ch.* 1807, *p.* 11. Cp. Sir W. Hamilton's *Discussions* 123, 148, 149, 168, 718 *n.*

[6] *Jebb's Works*, II. 357.

A curious instance of the estimation of logic as compared with skill in argument is to be found in the note to the names of the first wranglers on the tripos of 1786: Ds Bell, *Trin.*, Otter, *Jes.*, Hutchinson, *Trin.*, Lambe, *Joh.*; *Cum inter* Dm. Otter, Dm. Hutchinson, *et* Dm. Lambe, *nullum prorsus discrimen in rebus* Mathematicis *extitisse concedatur, secundum hunc ordinem disponuntur, hac sola de Causa, quia* Ds. Otter *in* dialecticis *magis est uersatus,* et Ds. Hutchinson *in* Scholis Sophistarum *melius* disputauit.

Lombard and the Summa of Aquinas must have given some
insight into the method of dialectics; so again during the
century, dating from about 1730, when the Cambridge disputations became more important and serious, some acquaintance
with logic was indispensable. Still it was confined to a narrow
groove; and we read of a professorial moderator (Kipling)
being puzzled more than once by a *disjunctive* syllogism[1].

In 1802 there were college lectures for freshmen in *Locke
and logic.*—How the author of the Essay on the Human
Understanding would have fretted, had his life been prolonged
a century, to find his work in such hateful company!

In 1772 the freshmen's lectures at Jesus Coll., Camb.[2], were
in Algebra and Logic.

Amhurst in his Terrae Filius of March 28, 1721, tells of an
Oxford logician who said that the best book which was ever
written, except the Bible, was *Smiglecius!* The Aristotelian
logic was most in vogue at that university, and the method of
the schools was kept in constant practice not only by the public
quodlibetical disputations, but by *daily* private 'acts' in the
colleges. A Brazenose scholar[3] wrote in 1742—'We are here
quite taken up with logic, which is indeed a very dry study.'
In 1767 dean W. Markham (abp. of York, and a writer of
Carmina Quadragesimalia) and the canons of Ch. Ch. formed an
important plan for reviving the School logic in their college.
But in the present century it had become useless to compel the
study of logic at Oxford, and the students hailed with joy the
proposal to leave the study to the option of candidates for
honours. On the other hand, (Abp.) Ri. Whately of Oriel, who
was made principal of S. Alban Hall in 1825, was convinced
that it ought to be a subject for honours. He published his
Logic in 1826, and this gave a considerable impetus to the
pursuit at a most important juncture[4].

[1] Gunning *Reminisc.* II. ii. *cp.* ch. x.
(A disjunctive proposition consists of
two or more categoricals so stated as
to imply that some one of them at
least is true, and generally that but
one can be true; as, 'It is *either* day
or night.' By denying all but one,
you infer the truth of the remainder;
or when it is implied that only one
can be true, by affirming one you deny
the rest.)

[2] Gilbert Wakefield's *Memoirs* (1804),
I. 82.

[3] *Oxf. Undergrad. Journ.* [Ri. Robinson *Qu.*] 1867, *p.* 166.

[4] Har. Martineau's *Biog. Sketches.*

How indispensable some knowledge of logic was in the schools at Cambridge, even when the disputations were on their last legs[1], may be seen by any one who examines '*A Guide to Syllogism* by C. Wesley, B.D. (of Chr. Coll.) 1832.'

Let us now pass to rhetoric, a study which in its modern sense Locke detested no less than logic.

Rhetoric in ancient days[2] was equivalent to the study of Quintilian, Hermogenes, and the speeches of Cicero, artistically considered. Statutably this was the study of the first year of the undergraduate's *quadriennium* (before he entered upon *logic*, the study of the two years of his Sophistry). There were Rhetoric Lecturers[3] at Cambridge in the last century, but I do not remember any evidence of their lecturing in the subject from which they took their title. In earlier times (1540) indeed we find John Jewel elected from Merton to a fellowship at Corpus, and there appointed reader in humanity and rhetoric[4]. He held those offices for seven years, and wrote a dialogue in which he comprehended the sum of the Art of Rhetoric. Again, a little later, we read of the Public Orator in Cambridge, George Herbert, of sweet memory, delivering public rhetoric lectures which D'Ewes attended in 1620. A century later Steele lamented (*Spectator*, Sept. 15, 1712) that at Oxford and Cambridge the nurseries of learning had grown 'dumb in the study of eloquence.' After that period the duty of the rhetoric lecturer seems to have been confined to looking over and correcting themes; but this was commonly neglected[5]. At St John's, in 1775,

---

[1] In the preceding generation *Duncan's* logic had been 'the best system... or at least that most favourably received at Cambridge...little more than an Abridgement of Locke's Essays.' (Dyer, *Hist. Camb.* I. 197, 198.)

[2] *Stat. Acad.* Cantab. 1570, *cap.* 4.

[3] In ancient times students of rhetoric, the composers of latin poems at Oxford, were honoured as *laureati* and their verses published on S. Mary's gates. Among the last were Ro. Whittington 1513, and J. Ball and T. Thomson 1514. Skelton was laureated

in 1493, and being vicar of Trumpington, was employed by the sister university to write latin letters (Cooper's *Annals* I. 251) as Caius Auberinus an Italian had been engaged in 1491 (*ibid.* 240). Erasmus produced his tract *de Conscribendis Epistolis* for us about 1512. Warton says that the 'poet laureate' was merely a graduate in rhetoric employed by the king.

[4] Wordsw. *Eccl. Biog.* III. 334.

[5] Dr G. Croft of Univ. Coll. Oxon., Bampton Lecturer 1786, an experienced schoolmaster, observes in his

attention was called by the master and seniors to this defect[1], and it was ordered that every student (except sophs in the term before they went into the senate-house) should give in four themes at least to the rhetoric-lecturer every term, yearly prizes being offered for their encouragement; and in 1782 they ordered that noblemen and fellow-commoners should not escape either these exercises or other lectures.

Practically, however, this study was not neglected. Cicero and Demosthenes, as well as Thucydides and Aristotle, were studied. The *thesis* which opened every Respondency in the Schools or in College Chapels[2], gave an opening for exercise therein, and the same purpose was yet better served by the College *Declamations*[3]. Lord Byron ridiculed these exercises in the present century[4]; but they had been much used in earlier times, and doubtless were of service to young men who were comparatively speaking under slight terror from

---

Plan of Education, 1784, p. 21, that 'the practice of modern time presupposes both [Rhetorick as well as Grammar] to have been taught in Schools.'

[1] Baker-Mayor, *Hist. of St John's* II. 1083, 1087. So, 30 July 1806, H. Kirke White (ed. Southey I. 253) writes to his brother Neville that the *Rhetoric Lecturer* of St John's, after a college examination, sent him one of his latin essays to copy for inspection, a compliment not paid to any of his competitors.

[2] *Hist. of* St John's, *Baker-Mayor*, 1036.

[3] Besides the 'theses,' *declamations* were statutably required as an exercise for a degree in arts, but the latter were never enforced seriously, except in 1748, when J. Ross was taxor and W. Ridlington proctor. The chief result was Chr. Anstey's expulsion. Cooper's *Annals*, IV. 261.

Symonds D'Ewes declaimed in S. John's chapel and in his tutor's 'lodgings' in 1619.

[4] But lo! no common orator can hope
The envied silver cup within his scope.
Not that our heads much eloquence require,
Th' Athenian's glowing style or Tully's fire.
A manner clear or warm is useless since
We do not try by speaking to convince.
Be other orators of pleasing proud:
We speak to please ourselves, not move the crowd:
Our gravity prefers the muttering tone,
A proper mixture of the squeak and groan:
No borrow'd grace of action must be seen,
The slightest motion would displease the Dean;
Whilst every staring graduate would prate
Against what he could never imitate.
Hours of Idleness. (1806.)

examinations. Thus at Oxford, at the close of the 17th century, we read of regular declamations at Magdalen[1]. In 1749, English Essays were read in the ante-chapel after divine service. And the Statutes of Hertford College, 1747, provided that undergraduates should make a Declamation (or else a Theme or Translation) every week, in english during their second and third year, and in latin during their fourth[2]. Bp. Ri. Watson, in 1756, set himself this same task for his own private exercise when a sizar at Trinity[3]. Two years later, the master and fellows of Peterhouse voted a yearly prize of three guineas' worth of books for the best declaimer in the judgment of the master, deans and tutors. Dr Hooper's Oration prizes, bequeathed in 1763, encouraged the same exercise at Trinity, but latin declamations were recited there by sophs in the chapel after Saturday evening prayers to large audiences at least as early as 1749[4]. The latin declamations in S. John's College Chapel have been discontinued within the last twenty years. Barnaby (or Ordinary) Lecturers in Logic, Rhetoric and Philosophy were appointed on Sir Ro. Rede's foundation, in addition to the University Mathematical Lectureship with the same title from early in the sixteenth century until quite lately. The Rede lecturers were put on a new footing in 1858.

[1] Johnson's *Life of the Poet* T. Yalden. Pointer, Oxon.

[2] About the same time there was a scheme afloat at Cambridge in Pembroke Hall for employing one tutor to teach pronunciation, and another to look over themes. This is mentioned in *Free Thoughts upon Univ. Education*, 1751, p. 34. Jebb, writing in 1772, says that 'elocution ...is utterly neglected.' *Works*, II. 272.

[3] Watson's *Anecdotes*, I. 20.

[4] Cumberland's *Memoirs*, p. 73. Some reminiscences of Trinity declamation in 1793 are given in my *Univ. Life in the 18th Cent.* pp. 588, 589. In the University Library (Z. 23. 10) is a copy of *A General Theorem for a* [Trinity] *Coll. Declamation.* By [C. V. le Grice], *with copious notes by Gronovius...* Cambridge: printed by Francis Hodson, 1796 (pp. 1—13). Another copy in Trinity Library [X. 14. 10], apparently reproduced privately in 1835.

CHAPTER IX.

HUMANITY.

Homo sum: humani nil a me alienum puto.
TERENCE, *Hauton Timorumenos*, I. i. 25.

THERE is, or there was, a common opinion which assigned to Oxford exclusively the study of Classics, and to Cambridge the sole pursuit of Mathematics.

The truth amounts to this, that since the Revolution and until the first quarter of the present century was waning, a degree could hardly be obtained at Cambridge without some application to geometry at the least, while at Oxford mathematical knowledge or skill won no academical distinction until our own time.

On the other hand, to speak of Cambridge as even by comparison the *non-classical* university, represents a gross misconception[1].

If the Great Rebellion had put a period to the colloquial use of the latin language in college halls and walks[2], we find it restored as the medium for college lectures, examinations and declamations, and for the public disputations, without

[1] Classical study was no doubt languishing for a time in the old age of Bentley, when Gray lamented to his friend West in 1736 that such pursuits were 'fallen into great contempt' at Cambridge. But not with Gray.

[2] Symonds D'Ewes talked latin in his walks in 1619. There was indeed an attempt on the part of the Commonwealth Committee (12 July, 1649) to enforce the colloquial use of greek and latin in the Universities. Cooper's *Annals*, III. 429. It was ordered at Queens' that nothing but latin should be spoken at dinner and supper except on scarlet-days, two days at Christmas, and Commemoration of Benefactors (26 Oct. 1676). In 1680 (Sept. 13) the exceptions were to be 'Sundays and Holydays.' About a century later the tables were turned and the utterance of three consecutive words of latin at dinner was made punishable with a fine or 'sconce'!

which no degree could under ordinary circumstances be acquired[1]. Until quite recently, no student of Trinity was accepted as candidate for a foundation-scholarship until he had written a latin epistle to the master, nor was any admitted without some knowledge of greek. Until 1 Oct. 1869 all academical graces were expressed[2] in the former language, of which we still have traces in the words *supplicat, placet, bene discessit, licet migrare*, &c., as the Cambridge undergraduate vocabulary contains *optime, exeat, redit, aegrotat*, and in past times had *dormiat, descendas;* as the Oxonian keeps *testamur.* But in the more serious process of study we not only find Cambridge students exercising themselves in writing and speaking and even thinking in latin by way of preparation for their 'acts,' but we know that not merely commentaries on classical authors but good mathematical treatises were accessible only in a scholarly guise. Indeed it was in the last century far more difficult for a student to become a wrangler without some fluency in reading and speaking latin, than it is now to gain a very high degree in mathematics without acquaintance with french, or in natural science without access to german treatises.

Indeed we may say with truth that the mathematical university has excelled in accurate scholarship; and her best mathematicians have been her best scholars[3]. If the names

[1] Mr Wace made a latin speech at the end of his proctorate in Oct. 1874. Dr Cookson made a Vice-Chancellor's speech in english the last time he held that office. Professor Selwyn remarked audibly, '*Placet materies, non placet lingua.*' He also wrote a latin epigram on the innovation. Adam Smith first lectured in english at Glasgow. Edinburgh had latin examinations in 1827.

[2] At least by the registrary. There was an order for latin in Nov. 1856.

[3] 'From the year 1752 to 1812 both inclusive, 122 gold medals have been presented to the best classical scholars among those whose names appeared in the first Tripos [i.e. Wranglers and Senior Optimes]. In this period there have been 860 Wranglers and 834 Senior Optimes.

The Wranglers have obtained:
    44 1st medals.
    36 2nd medals.
The Senior Optimes:
    14 1st medals.
    25 2nd medals.
The Proctor's Honours ·
    3 1st medals.
Thus, the Wranglers have obtained eighty, and the Senior Optimes thirty-nine medals in all. The Wranglers therefore have obtained *twice* as many medals as the Senior Optimes, and *three* times as many *first* medals.' *Classical Journal,* VI. 413 (modified).

of Newton and Barrow live, so also do those of Bentley and Porson. And we may consider it significant that Bentley was virtually third wrangler in 1680, and was instrumental in the edition of Newton's *Principia*, which was prepared by Cotes in 1709-17$\frac{12}{13}$, while Porson though only third senior optime in 1782 (being, as we may conjecture, pitted against skilful mathematicians in the Schools on account of his prestige as a scholar), was discovered in his fatal illness with an algebraical problem[1], as well as some greek and latin notes, written in his pocket-book. It was thought that he was intending to prepare an edition of the *Arithmetica* of Diophantus.

One good effect of the habit of encouraging colloquial latin we may observe in the intercourse of our learned men with continental scholars. With Bentley himself the language was so thoroughly established as the medium of literary commerce, that he wrote latin letters not only to P. Burman, Kuster, Hemsterhuys, and Graevius, his foreign correspondents, but even occasionally to Ri. Mead, F.R.S., to J. Mill, Edmund hall, and to E. Bernard, at Exeter Coll. *Oxon.* Among John Augustus Ernesti's correspondence (ed. Tittmann, 55-62) 1812,

A. S. writing from Chesterfield to the *Monthly Magazine* in 1797 (p. 186) gives a similar calculation. 'There have been in forty-one years, from 1755 to 1796 inclusive, eighty-two medallists. Of these, fifty-one were Wranglers;—thirty-one were Senior Optimes; consequently the proportion in favour of the Wranglers is so great that we may lay it down as a positive fact that the mathematical studies of Cambridge are not unfavourable to classical literature. I have not the least doubt that I could prove the superiority of Cambridge to its sister Oxford in these latter studies.'

[1] This problem—

$$xy + zu = 444,$$
$$xz + yu = 180,$$
$$xu + yz = 156,$$
$$xyzu = 5184,$$

kept the correspondents of the *Classical Journal* in calculation for some time in 1812. 'W. S.' gave a solution (with one value for each letter) in three lines: 'T. E.' followed with another filling as many pages: while 'Philo', with happier moderation, did the task in seven lines. *Ibid.* II. 722, 736; v. 201, 222, 411; Pryme (*Recollections*, p. 151), speaking of Porson and Dobree's fondness for algebra, refers the reader to Appendix to the *Reminiscences of* Charles Butler, *Esq.*, Vol. I. Note 3.

The following equation has been ascribed to Porson: τίς ὁ ἀριθμὸς οὗ τεμνομένου εἰς δύο ἄνισα μέρη, ἡ τοῦ μείζονος μέρους δύναμις μετὰ τοῦ ἐλάττονος μεταλαμβανομένη, ἴση ἔσται τῇ τοῦ ἐλάττονος δυνάμει μετὰ τοῦ μείζονος μεταλαμβανομένῃ; $x + y = 1$. (*Facetiae Cantab.* p. 144.)

is a series of four letters from Sam. Musgrave, commenced apparently without personal introduction in the spring of 1757[1].

As a specimen both of the friendly feeling of foreign scholars towards Englishmen, and of the esteem in which our native scholarship was then held on the continent[2], we may refer to the writings of David Ruhnken and his learned admirer and biographer Daniel Wyttenbach.

In 1777, Wyttenbach, a native of Bern, who had been invited to Leyden eight years before by Valcknaer and Ruhnken, persuaded the latter to assist him in starting a philological review at Leyden. This, under the title of *Bibliotheca Critica*, turned out to be a valuable enterprise. It was written mainly by younger men[3], such as the originator himself[4], and Henry Albert Schulten III. (whom Oxford honoured with the degree of M.A.) and Laurence van Santen (pupil of P. Burman II. who left Amsterdam about that time), but they had the advantage of Ruhnken's judgment, and occasionally of an article by himself[5], such as that on Tyrwhitt's Orphica de Lapidibus, Περὶ Λίθων, 1781, which was also mentioned in one of the short notices. The review went through twelve numbers (1777—1807), eight of which appeared before Ruhnken's death, in 1798. In these, a considerable proportion is devoted to english publications which meet in general with considerable commendation (excepting, A New System or an Analysis of Ancient Mythology, by *Jacob Bryant* (King's), vol. I. ed. 2, 1775,

[1] So, towards the end of the 18th century, all Burgess' foreign correspondents wrote to him in latin, except Villoison, whose communications were in french.

[2] Brunck, writing to Tyrwhitt, 28 April 1786, goes so far as to speak of England as 'le pays de l'Europe où la littérature Grecque est la plus florissante.' Luard, in *Camb. Essays*, 1857, p. 125.

[3] Wyttenbachii *Vita Ruhnkenii* (1799), p. 170 = Wytt. *Opusc.* (1821), I. 687, 688.

[4] 'Bibliothecam Criticam scribere instituenti (1777), primum dissuasor

mihi, deinde suasor fuit consilii: cujus postea neutrum poenituit.' *Vita Dav.* Ruhnkenii *auctore* Dan. Wyttenbachio (*Lug. Bat. et Amstelod.*) 1799, p. 170 = *Wytt. Opusc.* 1821, I. 684.

[5] 'Illa quam dixi Bibliotheca Amstelodami editur a discipulis meis. Quorum judicium interdum rego judicio meo, rarissime tamen censuras a me conscriptas interponens, nisi forte liber aliquis, qualis Tuus est, sua me elegantia ad talem scriptionem invitavit.' *Ruhnken* to *T. Tyrwhitt*, *Lug. Bat.* 9 Januar. 1783, with two copies of his Homeric Hymns, cum Epistolis Criticis, one for Toup.

Theocritus, by *T. Edwards* (Master of S. John's, Coventry, fellow of Clare) Cantab. 1779, and Apollonius Rhodius, by *T. Shaw*, fellow of Magd. Coll. *Oxon.* Clarendon Press, 1777[1]). The books thus noticed are V. T. Hebraicum Ben. Kennicott (*Wadham*, M.A. *Exon.* 1750) Clarend. Press, 1776, Lennep's translation of Bentley's Dissertation on Phalaris 1777, Aristotle de Poetica, T. Winstanley, Coll. Hertf. *Oxon.* 1780; Jonathan Toup's Longinus, *Oxon.* 1778, is fairly dealt with, although the editor (B.A. Exon. *Oxon.* M.A. Pemb. Camb. 1756) had treated the critic somewhat ungenerously[2]. About 1756, Ruhnken had struck up an acquaintance[3] at Paris with Samuel Musgrave then studying medicine, and T. Tyrwhitt who is described by Wyttenbach as *bene dives*. Musgrave's Euripides, Clarendon Press, 1778, is fully noticed, and in due course his correspondence with Schweighäuser, and his death in 1782[4].

Tyrwhitt's[5] *Babrius* 1776, and conjectures on *Strabo* 1783, as well as the *De Lapidibus,* are highly spoken of. Even two pseudo-Horatian odes which appeared in the *Gentleman's Magazine* Jan. 1778 do not escape the Dutchman's eyes. Again, the fact that the Leipsic press had thought it worth while to reproduce Joshua Barnes' text of *Euripides* is duly noted, as well as the appearance of the *Decretum Lacedaemoniorum contra Timotheum Milesium,* Oxon. 1777. The edition of five greek plays selected by J. Burton (C. C. C. *Oxon.*) and previously published by him as a Cambridge book under the title of Πενταλογία, was re-issued by T. Burgess then only an *undergraduate* of Corpus, *Oxon.* Clarendon Press 1779, and the republication under the editorship of the last named scholar

---

[1] There is a tradition that this editor looked eagerly in subsequent publications for some acknowledgment of his work, and at last discovered one brief recognition of one conjecture in the words '*putidè* Shavius.' The *Bibliotheca Critica* was not much more complimentary; nor indeed was Brunck. A happy *mot* of Shaw's is recorded in Best's *Memorials,* § XVII.

[2] Vita Ruhnken. p. 172 = Wyttenbachii *Opusc.* I. 686.

[3] Ibid. p. 71 = *Opusc.* I. 586, 587.

Among Ruhnken's *Correspondence,* is a familiar letter to ' Optimo amicissimoque viro *Sam. Musgrave* ' 9 Jul. 1780, and another 'Viro praestantissimo *Thomae Tyrwhitt,*' 9 Januar. 1783 (Ed. *Brunsw.* 1828, II. 718—722).

[4] *Biblioth. Crit.* II. i. 120, ii. 117.

[5] Ex iis qui nunc Critici in Britannia numerantur, dubito an quisquam ullo sit genere laudis Thomae Tyrwhitto anteponendus. *Bibl. Crit.* II. viii. 85.

(then B.A.) of the *Miscellanea Critica* of Ri. Dawes (Emm.) Oxon.
1781, are spoken of with approbation[1]. Of Burgess' remarks
it is said 'habent in juvenili redundantia magnam commenda-
tionem ingenii, eruditionis, et elegantiae ut minime dubitemus
eum......aliquando in praecipuis harum Litterarum doctoribus
numeratum iri.' Three years later the young author paid
Leyden a visit and began an intimacy with the professors[2].

Ruhnken himself, though according to his biographer *cibo
potuque, si quis alius, modicus* (in which case his portrait and
the popular rhyme attributed to Porson[3] belie him), was a man
of friendly disposition. When writing to Tyrwhitt in 1783 he
sent one copy of Homeric Hymns for Toup, who had not acknowledged his assistance in 1778 even by giving him a presentation copy of his Longinus. Among others whom he helped
are enumerated[4] S. Musgrave, M.D., and T. Burgess (C. C. C.
Oxon.), T. Morell (King's), J. Ross (St John's), R. Porson (Trin.),
and T. Edwards (Clare). Comparing our great english critic
with his own master Hemsterhuys 'ut Hemsterhusium ratione,
Bentleium ingenio, alterum alteri, praestare, et utrumque utraque facultate omnibus sui aevi Criticis longe antecellere cen-
sebat; ita primas partes ingenio, ingeniique Bentleio tribuebat:
eique (adds his pupil) sua ipse natura in omni Critices munere
similior erat[5].'

Among Wyttenbach's own correspondence after Ruhnken's
death in 1798, are twelve letters to Englishmen: W. Cleaver,
Bp. of Chester (B. N. C.), G. Williams, M.D., Corpus Christi, J.

[1] Ibid. II. vii. 114. Dawes' *Misc.
Crit.* had appeared previously in his
life-time in 1745, and was again re-
edited by Kidd in 1817, '27. The preparation for its publication in 1778—81,
won for Burgess the acquaintance of
Tyrwhitt, who became a kind friend
to him. Harford's *Burgess*, p. 21.
He received congratulations also from
Everard Scheidius, and from G. L.
Spalden of Berlin, whom he lionized
at Oxford in 1786, p. 113. Dawes'
literary character is discussed by
Monk, in his *Life of Bentley*, II.
367—371.

[2] (1784) 'Mox gratissimus advenit
hospes Thomas Burgessius Britannus:
cujus excellentem Literarum scientiam
rara quaedam ornabat animi probitas
morumque modestia; unde amicitia
cum praesente nobis conciliata, deinde cum absente epistolis officiisque
viguit.' Vita Ruhnkenii 189 = Wyttenbachii *Opusc.* I. 701.
[3] Ibid. 176 = *Opusc.* Wytt. I. 689;
Facetiae Cantab. 48.
[4] Ibid. 232 = *Opusc.* I. 743.
[5] Ibid. 222 = *Opusc.* Wyttenb. I. 733;
Altonae, 1831.

Randolph, Bp. of Oxford, and T. Gaisford (Ch. Ch.), J. C. Banks, and J. Brown about his own Plutarch[1], which was being printed by the Clarendon Press, though the war made communication difficult. He acknowledges presents from Walter Whiter of Clare, and from R. Porson, and sends his *Life of Ruhnken*, and other books to him, and to Burgess. Of Markland and Toup he wrote 'illum ratione, hunc ingenio Criticam factitare[2].'

On the whole it is most instructive to observe the lively interest taken in Holland both in English Philology and philologers contrasted with some jealousy of the French Academy[3]. And it is not unreasonable to attribute continental ignorance of our recent insular productions to the discontinuance of latin annotations and prefaces. That Wyttenbach should say to Banks in 1801, after the appearance of Porson's *Hecuba*, *Phoenissae* and *Medea*, 'Miror tantum ab eo in Euripide post summorum virorum curas, novi praestitum esse; et, si quid aliud, Literarum causa opto ut egregio viro vita et otium suppetat ad totum Euripidem perpurgandum,' is not so remarkable: but it *is* a significant fact that he had what he considered tardy news of the first (anonymous) edition of Porson's Aeschylus, and it is still more remarkable that the *Bibliotheca Critica*[4] should have heard of its fame and should contain the announcement 'Ceterum cognovimus novam item Aeschyli editionem institui Cantabrigiae a Rich. Porsono, V. Cl., de cujus acumine et doctrina bene nos sperare jubent egregia quaedam specimina privatim nobis cognita, necdum in vulgus edita,' so early as 1783, *twelve years before its first appearance* and while Porson was only a middle-bachelor.

Cambridge itself has seldom been long without a classical or literary magazine.

In Bentley's time the *Bibliotheca Literaria* was started by Sam. Jebb of Peterhouse (B.A. 1712) and Joseph Wasse[5] of

[1] Ruhnken (*Epist.* LXIII. 2 *Nov.* 1794, ed. *Altonae*, 1834) commended the simplicity of the dedication of his Plutarch:

'Academiae Oxoniensi
D. D.
Daniel Wyttenbach.'

[2] Vita Ruhnk. 218 = *Opusc.* Wyttenb. I. 729.

[3] Ibid. 71 = *Opusc.* I. 587. He speaks, however, with respect of Villoison, Larcher and Sainte Croix.

[4] II. viii. 140.

[5] When ridiculing Bentley, the great

Queens' (B.A. 1694, B.D. 1707) of whom Whiston reports that Bentley said, 'When I am dead, Wasse will be the most learned man in England.' He died however, in 1728, fourteen years before Bentley, at the age of sixty-six, leaving behind him an edition of Sallust, 1707, and of Thucydides (with Duker) 1732, and ten numbers of the *Bibliotheca Literaria* published in 1722-4, when his prolix account of Justinian pressed it to death. Other contributors were Dr C. Ashton of Jesus, Dr W. Wotton and S. Barker[1].

In 1731, John Jortin (Jes.) started the *Miscellaneae Observationes*[2] in sixpenny numbers, but the publication was transplanted to Holland after languishing eighteen months in England, and in its new soil it flourished perennially till 1739, and then blossomed at irregular periods till 1751, under the care of D'Orville and Burman.

In June, 1750, the *Student*, which had been started as a University Magazine at *Oxford* by Rawlinson, Johnson, Warton, Colman and Bonnel Thornton, incorporated the name of Cambridge on its title-page. Though addicted to trivialities it admitted some philosophical papers and a note or two on classical subjects[3].

Aristarchus, then on the brink of the grave, Pope did not refrain from flinging a stone at the memory of Wasse and at other verbal critics :

'How parts relate to parts, or they to whole,
The body's harmony, the beaming soul,
Are things which Kuster, Burman, Wasse shall see,
When Man's whole frame is obvious to a *Flea*.'
Dunciad, iv. 235—8 (1742).

[1] Nichols' *Lit. Anecd.* i. 242, 248, 258, 259, 262, 263 n., 706, 707.

[2] The signatures of Dr Taylor, Wasse, Thirlby, Masson, Barker, and other contributors are elucidated in Nichols' *Lit. Anecd.* ii. 559 n.

[3] In 1810 (Valpy's) *Classical Journal* began its eleven years' career. Among the contributors were P. P. Dobree, Trin., and 'E. H. Barker O. T. N.' [of Thetford Norfolk] Trin. (no degree), and G. Burges (Trin., B.A. 1807). It fell foul of its younger rival '*Museum Criticum*, or, Cambridge Classical Research,' 1814 and 1826 (Nos. i.—viii.) edited by (Bp.) C. J. Blomfield (Trin.), which reckoned E. V. Blomfield (Cai. and Emman.), J. H. Monk and W. Whewell (Trin.) among its supporters.
T. Kidd's editions of *Porson's Tracts* 1815, and *Dawes' Miscellanea Critica* 1817, '27, which last had already appeared at Camb. in 1745 and Oxon. 1781, contain 18th cent. work.
Philological Museum,1832—3, by J.C. Hare, Connop Thirlwall, Whewell, H. Malden, H. Alford, and John Wordsworth, of Trinity, to which W. Wordsworth, Landor, Fynes Clinton, Corne-

1792, Musei Oxoniensis Fasciculus I. Edited by T. Burgess of Corpus, *Oxon.* 1797, Musei Oxoniensis Fasc. II.

As a pleasing symptom of the good understanding established at the beginning of the century between English and foreign scholars, we may observe the transactions at the second-centenary festival of the university of Frankfort on the Oder[1]. In answer to an invitation from that society Drs Andrew Snape of King's, Henry Penrice of Trin. Hall, and Henry Plumtre of Queens', were delegated by the Senate to attend as representatives from Cambridge of the faculties of divinity, law, and physic. With them were associated W. Grigg of Jesus (afterwards of Clare) who was detained by an accident[2], J. Wyvil (Trin.), and Ludolph Kuster (*Neócorus*) the editor of Suidas, who went out thither *en route* for his greek professorship at Berlin, with Bentley's patronage and the scarlet (or, as he spells it, *charlad*) robes of a Cambridge LL.D.

Kuster's two attempts at writing english which are preserved among Bentley's correspondence (May and June 1706) can by no means be adduced in argument against the use of latin as a medium for the correspondence of learned men of different nations. The Cambridge deputation was singled out for especial honour among the representatives of numerous literary bodies by the King of Prussia and by Dr Strymesius the Rector Magnificus of Frankfort.

It appears from the sumptuous memorial-volume[3] which was printed at Frankfort that an invitation was sent to both our universities, but while congratulatory verses were contributed by Cambridge and Oxford alike, the latter university did not answer the invitation by sending a deputation; but her authorities were content with commemorating the occasion at

wall Lewis, and Sir Edmund Head contributed.

Journal of Classical and Sacred Philology, i—xii., 1854—60.

Oxford *and Cambridge Essays*, 1855, &c.

Journal of Philology commenced in 1868.

[1] Nichols' *Lit. Anecd.* IV. 236, IX.

823. Monk's *Bentley* I. 191. *Bentley's Corresp.* (Wordsw.) pp. 233—240. Cooper's *Annals*, IV. 75.

[2] In England.—See Reneu's letter (21 Mar. 170⅘) in an appendix to the present compilation.

[3] *Secularia Sacra Academiae Regiae Viadr.* 1706. foliQ. [Camb. Univ. Libr. 62=Nn, i. 35.]

home in their own theatre in five sets of latin verses and three
latin prose addresses, beside the oration of W. Wyatt of Ch. Ch.
(and S. Mary Hall) the public orator. One of the addresses
was the production of T. Burnet of New Coll., the bishop's son.
There appear also to have been three pieces of music performed,
one of them with the Sapphic ode. On the same day John
Ernest Grabe (who received a pension from the english crown,
and was engaged in editing the Septuagint ms. of the royal
library) was created D.D., while his namesake and the learned
Ezekiel Spanheim received the degree of D.C.L. as members of
the council or embassy of the King of Prussia[1].

In later times our communications with foreign universities
have not been many. S. John's indeed voted £10 to the Hungarian university of Debreczin in 1756; and the senate voted
£300 to the distressed professors of Wittenberg in 1814; and
the other day we sent a selection of our Pitt Press books to the
university of Leyden on the occasion of their tercentenary
festival (Febr. 1875). What our printers have done for some
foreign scholars will be mentioned in an Appendix.

We have no doubt lost much of the facility in latin which

[1] Academiae *Francofurtanae ad Viadrum* Encaenia secularia *Oxonii* in
Theatro *Sheldoniano* Apr. 26. Anno
Fundat. 201, annoque Dom. 1706 cele-
brata. Oxonii e Theatro Sheldoniano
An. Dom. 1706. *folio*. pp. A—L. [Bodl.
Bliss 653. Reproduced in the Frankfort *Secularia Sacra*.] One of the
speakers, Ri. Stephens, M.A., of All
Souls, after an address to ' *Anna Incly-
tissima Britannorum Regina*, Tuque
Frederice vere *Auguste Maxime Borus-
sorum Rex*,' who had inaugurated the
new Augustan age, and after a compliment to the recipients of the honorary
degrees (*qui hodie purpurati apud nos
incedunt*) remarks that our German
cousins had their *Beckmanns* [John
Christopher, historian and geographer,
Frankfort-professor of history, greek,
and divinity] and *Strimesii* [the rector]
'qui cum *Jano* nostro' [*cp*. Univ.
Life, *pp*. 32, 468, 605, 606] 'Ponti-

ficiorum detegent fraudes, cum *Ed-
vardo Wynnoque* Socinianos debella-
bunt.' [Jonathan Edwards of Ch. Ch.
and Jesus *Oxon.*, author of *a Preserva-
tive against Socinianism*.] ' Quali vero
oratione charissime *Sturmi* aut quibus
verbis te excipiam! qui Artis Mathe-
maticae summus magister, cum *Gregorio* [David, Savilian prof. astron.]
Hallaeove [Edmund, *Queen's*, Savilian
prof. geom.] nostro possis contendere:
patre tuo *Johanne* [J. Chr. Sturm of
Altdorf, died in 1703] tantum minor
ipsique sola aetate postponendus.' He
then prays that the eminent James
Jurin (of Trin. Coll. Camb. and Guy's,
died President of Coll. Physicians 1750),
may use his art to preserve them in
good health, '*Jurenio* enim non minor
in *Germania* quam in *Anglia Hoyo
Radcliviove* nostro tribuenda laus.'
He finishes up with a compliment to
Wyatt the orator of his university.

was possessed by university men in former generations. It is quite possible that even particular and critical accuracy in composition has tended to produce this reaction. Longer passages for latin composition were set, dissertations and annotations were seldom to be had in any other language, and greek authors were to be approached by the tiro through the medium of a latin version. There were but few English books of any kind to distract the student; and as for modern continental languages, he abhorred them. Indeed, had it not been for latin, it is doubtful whether English scholars would have had any intercourse with foreigners; for Bentley[1] could not understand dutch without Sike's help, and Porson[2] was 'sadly to seek' in german. But such notes as Ruhnken's in *Timaei Lexicon* would furnish the student with elegant latin modes of expression while he was studying Plato, the use of Aynsworth's[3] or Entinck's dictionaries would accustom his eye to serviceable phrases, while even his early reminiscences of *Propria quae maribus* and *Quae genus* (not to mention Erasmus) would provide him with such a vocabulary as is not now always to be found, a part of which facility was sometimes acquired half a century ago by the sedulous reading of Parr's preface to Bellendenus *De Statu*[4].

Dr Parr himself, when remarking on Gilbert Wakefield's literary character in a free and friendly strain, laid the blame of the incorrectness of the then respected critic's easy latin style, to his lack of a public-school education[5]. Similarly he traced the faulty latin of archbishop Potter[6], John Taylor, and Toup,

---

[1] *Bentley's* Corresp. *p.* 252, *l.* 31.

[2] *Life by* Watson, *p.* 416 *appendix*.

[3] Hearne mentions Aynsworth as a great connoisseur in English coins and as a non-juror, but suspected him of Calvinism. His dictionary 'in the manner of Littleton's' was finished (though not published) Aug. 1734. He kept a private school in London when at the age of 70. *Reliqu. Hearn.* II. 157, III. 13, 151. There are specimens of his calligraphy in various styles among Strype's correspondence (1707—8) in the MS. Collection in the Camb.

Univ. Lib. Adds. VI. 321, 330. *Littleton's* dictionary continued to be printed, 4to.; 5th and 6th editions, 1723, 1735.

[4] *Reminisc. of* G. Pryme, p. 136.

[5] Wakefield's *Memoirs*, II. 449. *Appendix G.* Gilbert Wakefield's credit as a scholar and a critic has been recently exploded by Munro's *Lucretius* (Introd.). Porson had already done something of the kind.

[6] Abp. John Potter, who commented on Plutarch and Lycophron, and Antiquities, went to Univ. Coll. *Oxon.*

&c., to the fact that their education had been confined to private schools, the critic being himself Harrovian by birth, by education, and by early employment as an assistant master[1].

Much of the accuracy of scholarship acquired by english students may be attributed to the care and attention which was paid to composition and especially to verse composition. The poets were much read—Juvenal, for example, at Westminster and, under Kinsman, the predecessor of Valpy and Donaldson, at Bury[2]—and large portions of their works were committed to memory, according to the good old Wykehamical practice of *'standing-up,'* at which George Williams (afterwards an Oxford professor) won his early laurels by reciting the Iliad[3].

It is interesting to observe how many university prizemen were educated at the public schools. A large number issued from Winchester in the mastership of Joseph Warton (1766— 95), who, if he was not a thorough master of a 'stiff greek chorus[4],' yet contrived to instil into his pupils something of that taste for classical poetry which was conspicuous in his father and brother. One day (about 1778) he brought in triumph into school to *pulpiteers*[5] an edition of a classical volume edited by an old Wykehamist undergraduate (possibly T. Burgess' edition of Burton's *Pentalogia*), and asked the senior praefect

from Wakefield School. It is fair to add that *Bentley* went to S. John's Camb. *from the same seminary.* Also, that Taylor was at Shrewsbury.

[1] Among Parr's own pupils was John Tweddell (of Trin., B.A. 1790), who had been previously under Dr Mat. Raine (afterwards Master of the Charterhouse) at Hackforth. Tweddell, who died at Athens aged 30, was a thorough *prizeman.* He published his *Prolusiones Academicae* in 1792-3, but collections more important and more mature were lost after his death. See Gunning *Reminisc.* i. ch. vii. ii. chh. i, iii.

[2] *Memoirs of* R. Cumberland, 32.

[3] M. E. C. Walcott's *W. of Wykeham,* p. 444. For anecdotes of Etonian repetitions see *Etoniana Ancient and*

Modern, p. 200.

[4] *W. of Wykeham* 360. Also Harford's *life of T. Burgess.*

[5] *i.e.* the assembly of 'Sixth Book' (the highest form) and 'Senior Part' of the Fifth who 'in Cloister Time' (after Pentecost) went 'up to books' together; boys in the Sixth being 'set on' in turn to translate some such author as Theocritus for the benefit of the others, among whom the lazy or dilatory would trust to this as sufficient preparation for their own innings which was to follow,—giving credit to their own memories or to the rapid use of 'smugglers' or little pencils sharpened at each end,—a questionable practice, for which I believe the equivalent 't' other-school notion' is *paving;* in America, *illuminating.*

W. Lisle Bowles 'When will you do a like work ?' If the boy
Bowles had been gifted with the spirit of vaticination as he was
with that of poetry, he might have answered, 'Within ten years'
time.'

The Wykehamical 'pulpiteers,' which I have described in a
note for the benefit of the uninitiated, seem to have had some
equivalent at Westminster·and at Bury, where Kinsman introduced the Westmonasterial system.   Cumberland speaks of
having been called on frequently to ascend the *rostrum* and to
recite and translate Juvenal for the benefit of the other boys.
He says that they practised (at Bury, 1743) 'challenging for
places' in construing and repetition[1].   Their other exercise was
composition.   The master[2] had introduced even an imitation of
the Westminster[3] Play of Terence, and when at one time he
stopped the custom, the boys acted Cato on their own account,
for which performance Cumberland had to learn the 10th Satire
of Juvenal as an 'imposition.'

At Westminster itself among the ushers (*hostiarios*) were
scholars of considerable taste and talent.

Samuel the elder brother of John and Charles Wesley.   He
was M.A. Ch. Ch. 1718.   In 1732 he left Westminster for
the mastership of Blundels at Tiverton.

Vincent Bourne, who went from Westminster to Trinity,
B.A. 1717; M.A. 1721.   He was a considerable writer of

---

[1] The more solemn *Challenges* of
Westminster School, in which boys
ask each other questions, have a parallel in the '*Fights*' at Twyford,
Hants.

[2] *Memoir of* R. Cumberland, *pp.*
23, 30—32.

[3] The electors at Westminster were
at the beginning of the century Atterbury, dean of Westminster, Smalridge,
dean of Ch. Ch., and Bentley, master
of Trin., 'and "as iron sharpeneth
iron" so these three by their wit and
learning and liberal conversation, whet-
ted and sharpened one another.' *Life
of* I. Newton (*Chalmers*) II. 11.

H. Fynes Clinton had read at South-

well before he went to Westminster in
1795, the whole of Horace and Virgil
except the Georgics, Caesar de Bello
Gallico, Sallust and Cicero's Catilin-
arian Orations.   In Greek S. John's
Gospel, Xen. Cyropaedia I.—IV., Homer
Iliad I.—V., Goldsmith's Rome, Lang-
horne's Plutarch.   *At Westminster* he
added nothing to his Latin stock, but
in Greek finished the Iliad, the Odyssey, Sophocles 4 plays, Euripides 2,
Lysias Or. Funebr., Thucydides and
Plato, Mitford's Greece: also English
poetry and Johnson's Lives, and Bell's
British Theatre.   With such preparation he went to Ch. Ch.

tripos-verses, which he published in a volume of *Carmina Comitialia* Cantabrigiensia, in 1721. His first production of that character (see note[1]) seems to have been composed on the extraordinary occasion of the Public Act in 1714, when Roger Long (afterwards master of Pembroke and professor of astronomy) gave the Musick-speech as prevaricator, and W. Law, who had been suspended for his tripos-speech two years before, produced a set of hexameters on the theme ' Materia non potest cogitare ' *Popham* I. 77—80). Law did not refrain from mentioning two living persons; he contrasted the quiescent humour of *D' Urfey*, and the peaceful triumph of Ormond, with the more fiery temperament of Milton and of *Marlborough* who returned from his voluntary exile that year.

But Vincent Bourne's muse was not content to slumber after he had taken his degree. She gave him the art of expressing in the elegiac distich which Catullus and others had borrowed from the greek, ideas more varied than Martial's, with a versatility and command of language less perfect than Ovid's, but in an englishman more remarkable. His *Poematia*

---

[1] Existentia Entium incorporeorum colligi potest Lumine Naturae. *In Magnis Comitiis*, The *Act*, 1714.

Deus est cognoscibilis Lumine Naturae. Com. Prior. 1715—16.

Mutua Benevolentia primaria lex Naturae est. Com. Prior. 1716—17 (in elegiacs, translated by Cowper).

Mundus non fuit ab aeterno. Com. Poster. 1715—16.

Lockius non rectè statuit de Particula Anglicana *But*. Com. Prior. 1717—18.

Planetae sunt habitabiles. Com. Poster. 1718—19.

Fluxus et Refluxus Maris pendent ab Actionibus Solis et Lunae. Com. Prior. 1719—20.

Camera Obscura. Com. Poster. 1720.

Laterna Megalographica. Com. Prior. 1720—21.

Sonus propagatur per Aërem. Com. Poster. 1721.

[Rationes Boni et Mali sunt aeternae et immutabiles. Com. Prior. 1706-7. (This, though included in Grant's edition of his poems, can hardly have been written by V. B.)]

V. B. printed in his volume of *Carmina Comitialia Cantabrigiensia* (Lond. 1721) eight other sets of tripos verses, as well as two poems ascribed generally to Jortin, but as they are all dated we can be sure that some of them were not his own composition: e. gr. ' Scorbutus et Chlorosis oriuntur a Torpore Spirituum Animalium.' In Vesp. Comit. 1698, when Bourne was two years old! He *may* have written the following,

Ordo Mundi probat Deum (' Quisquam ne in Terris,' &c.—another set on the same theme printed in his collection but dated 'In comitiis Prioribus 170⅗,' begins ' Cum Chaos.') In Com. Poster. 1717.

Systema Copernicarum. In Com. Prior. 1721—22.

Latine partim scripta partim reddita were printed at West-minster[1] in 1734, and the call for other editions and even its interpolation have attested the popularity of the collection. Bourne's pupil, the poet Cowper, translated one-and-twenty of his pieces, and Charles Lamb englished nine. It is some praise to have written the original for 'Little inmate full of mirth,' and for 'Her lessons were his true *Principia*'—but Dr Beattie went so far as to assert of the '*partim reddita*' (from Gay, Addison, A. Pope, W. Pope, Prior, &c.) that 'it is no compliment to say that in sweetness of numbers and elegant expressions they are equal to the originals, and scarcely inferior to anything in Ovid or Tibullus[2]'—a generous testimony from the countryman of Buchanan.

Bourne, though a worse disciplinarian than Dr Burton, must have supplied, not indeed by his teaching but by his composition, something of that style in versifying which played so prominent a part in the liberal education of the day. Many of his poems are cast in that elegant mould[3] from which the Christ Church *carmina comitialia* or Lent verses were and had been turned out; they were short latin epigrams composed on a motto, such exercises as under the name of *vulguses* Win-chester boys had to produce at the rate of three a week, and Westminster provided for the entertainment of liberal visitors.

This species of exercise was afterwards introduced at Rugby by Dr Arnold from Winchester, at which school the advanced scholars were called upon to produce epigrams *impromptu*, the

---

[1] Sam. Wesley translated his *Me-lissa*.

[2] Quoted in Mr Thompson Cooper's *Dict. Biog.*, where the date of V. B.'s first edition is misprinted '1724.'

[3] 'Lent Verses' were peculiar to Christ Church. Ro. Surtees wrote them as late as 1798. Six copies of six to twenty elegiac lines on his own subject were expected from each competitor, and the censor chose some of the best to be read publicly.

One volume of *Carmina Comitialia* was edited by C. Este 1723, the second by A. Parsons 1747—8. See my *Univ. Society*, pp. 310—314. Longer poems in heroic verse like the Winchester 'verse tasks,' were produced at Cambridge for tripos-verses, and at Eton for 'play'; a large number have been printed in *Musae Etonenses*. Many 'select' sets of verses produced (1638—1761) at Oxford, Cambridge and Winchester were printed in two vols. by E. Popham of Oriel in 1774, 1779. Accessions and the deaths of royal or academical personages afforded frequent opportunities for the composition of *gratulationes, luctus, epitaphia,* &c. XLVIII sets in Caius Coll. mss. 1750—90.

subject being announced when they were actually come 'up to books,' or in their 'fardel' or class in the presence of the 'posers' at the election. These were called *varyings*, either because they were originally metaphrases[1] (or transpositions) of classical verses into a metre different from that in which the author had written them, or because the *improvisatore* was expected (like our Cambridge 'varier' or 'prevaricator') to give a novel turn to the theme, or to vary the theses from affirmative to negative. Dr Whewell in his essay prefixed to *Napier's* Barrow, *vol.* IX, p. xix, says, 'A remnant of the like practice exists at Westminster School. There, on the day of election of scholars to Oxford and Cambridge by the "three Deans" (Ch. Ch., West[r]., and Mast. of Trin.), while the three dignitaries are at dinner in the college hall, they give out or are supposed to give out, subjects for epigrams; and not only are a swarm of epigrams produced by the scholars immediately after dinner; but the subject is *varied* from positive to negative, and modified in other ways.' Cp. Duport's *Praevaricatio* in the Appendix.

Thus when Dr Warton announced *Decus et tutamen* as a theme, a boy who was much twitted for a wig which he wore held it up when it came to his turn and said,

Haec coma quam cernis uarios mihi suppetit usus,
tutamen capiti nocte, dieque decus[2].

In quantity and metre as in other things accuracy is gained gradually, both by individuals and by the general community[3]. Not only did Paley[4] say *profŭgus* in his Cambridge *Contio* for a doctor's degree after his installation as subdean of Lincoln in

[1] There are some specimens of *metaphrases* in the Chapter Library, Westminster. Abp. Markham's (*Ch. Ch. and Westminster*) paraphrase of Simonides' Danae to Perseus in Latin hendecasyllables (Warton's *Adventurer* No. 89), would, I suppose, come under that denomination. Cp. *Zouch*, lxv. by *Wrangham* who (privately) printed Markham's xxvi *Carmina Quadragesimalia*. 1820. (In Trin. Coll. Lib.)

[2] A specimen of verses by a junior boy at Eton written in the Christmas holidays 1696 at Wotton, for his uncle John Evelyn, is preserved in Bentley's *Corresp.* p. 137.

[3] Barrow when 'Humanity Lecturer' at Trinity [1659] announced in facetious terms that the undergraduates, if they made false quantities in their themes, must not be surprised if they were punished in the buttery-book (*in promptuario*) by fines for syllables unduly lengthened and short commons for long syllables made short. *Works* (Napier) IX. 135.

[4] *Facetiae Cantab.* 126, 127.

1795, not only did Ri. Watson 'come up' in doubt as to the penultimate syllable of *fortuito* and *Areopagus*, but Sumner said μακαρίτης in the Senate House. J. Wilson of Peterhouse was *censured* in the Divinity schools by the Bp. of Peterborough and Dr T. Symonds (Trin.) for not saying *abolīta;* and Jacob Bryant of King's had, in 1802, to go back to Eton to learn that μεσίτης was incorrect[1]. T. Wilson, senior fellow of Trinity, was always known by the unfortunate word *parabōla*[2] which he let slip in the schools in 1747, and even in Vincent Bourne's *Eques Academicus* we find *refert* (in the sense of *interest*) put carelessly to close a pentameter. According to Reginald Bligh, Dr Plumptre of Queens' made several false quantities in his vice-chancellor's speech in 1777, which were thus strung together (as Kipling's grammatical blunders were by Porson)

Rogĕrus immēmor Robērtum denōtat hebētem[3].

The pronunciation of greek and latin has more than once taken the attention of our University.

Erasmus having improved the very small pittance of greek which he had picked up at Oxford, visited Cambridge in 1506. In 1511 he paid a second visit, and resided for two or three years in Queens', being appointed lady Margaret's professor in Divinity, and reading lectures in the greek grammars of Chrysolorus and Theodorus to a small class of poor men. Not long after his departure Ri. Croke of King's began his lectures, and in 1519 was formally commissioned by the University to continue them, and in 1522 was elected primary public orator. Several of his successors in that office—Redman, Smith, Cheke, and Ascham, were prominent in the establishment of greek learning and orthoëpy.

Thomas Smith of Queens' was greek reader in 1533, public orator in 1538, and primary regius professor in civil law in 1540. About 1535 he and his friends resolved to improve the current method of pronunciation, which allowed but two sounds

---

[1] Watson's *Autobiog. Recoll.* I. 7—9.

[2] Gunning *Reminisc.* II. ch. iv.

[3] Bligh's *Defence against the President and Fellows of Queens'*, 1780, p. 32, and his *Letters*, 1781, p. 5. This refers to Robert Plumptre, D.D., prof.

of Casuistry 1769—88, and president of Queens'. Russell Plumptre, M.D., of Queens', regius professor of physic 1741—93, was an elegant scholar. *Quarterly Rev.* XVII. 236.

to all the vowels and diphthongs of the greek language, long and short alike.

He began by accustoming his hearers to the novel sounds by introducing one now and then in his lectures on Aristotle's *Politics* as it were *lapsu linguae*, and sometimes pretending to correct himself. At the same time he proceeded with less caution in his readings of the Odyssey with a private class.

In Christmas-week the *Plutus* was acted with that pronunciation, and it became prevalent among the rising Grecians of Cambridge.

In course of time Smith paid a visit to France and held disputations with continental scholars[1] on this subject.

In the meantime Stephen Gardiner, Bp. of Winchester and master of Trinity Hall, had become for the first time chancellor of the university. In May of the year of Smith's return to Cambridge (1542) Gardiner sent to the V.-C. a public decree to enforce a return to the vulgar pronunciation[2]. Smith having had an amicable conversation with the bishop at Hampton Court ventured to write to him (from Cambridge 12 Aug. 1542) urging their reasons for dissenting from his judgement and desiring him to retract his decree on the ground that those who had approached him were not the learned men of Cambridge, but those who knew no greek;—that the passage of Theon on which he relied was corrupt[3], that Dio. Halicarn., Plato (Cratyl.), Ar. Nubes, Terentianus, Priscian and Suidas were on the side of the *etists* (as they came to be called);—that it was scarcely fair to blame them for not consulting him seven years before when he was not Chancellor and was away in France or Italy;—that they had not been precipitate but had begun with quite sufficient caution to satisfy all reasonable requirements; that when Radcliffe got up in the pulpit in the schools to oppose Cheke's pronunciation the 'boys' hooted him down.

[1] He did not meet with much favour. However in 1551 Roger Ascham (*Works*, 355) heard Theodoric Lange read greek in his lecture at Louvain according to Smith's pronunciation. He does not add whether that was the cause for which his class 'knocked him out' by making a din. Ascham's Scholemaster, *Mayor*, p. 221.

[2] Cooper's *Annals*, I. 401—403.

[3] The same emendation (αὐλὴ τρὶς πεσοῦσα for αὐλητρὶς παῖς οὖσα) was put forward by Cheke in his correspondence with Gardiner (ed. 1555). pp. 294—300, cf. 186, 334, and supported from Quintilian.

Some years later Smith printed his remonstrance at Paris[1], but meanwhile the Chancellor had waged war against his party, though with little success. Just one year after his original decree (which he pretended to have made 'by consent of the hol universite') Gardiner wrote to the Vice-Chancellor to assure him that he would not be 'deluded and contempned.' However exactly two years later he mentioned (in his correspondence relative to the offensive play *Pammachius*) that his late order was disregarded with impunity[2]. The following year (1546) Gardiner was superseded, but when he was restored to the chancellorship in Q. Mary's reign (1553) he found the new pronunciation still holding or gaining ground. Accordingly in October of the next year he sent injunctions[3] to use summary measures with the innovators. At this time Cheke was reading greek on the continent, having lately been set free from the Tower, whither his office of secretary of state to the lady Jane had brought him. Smith also and Poynet had had their vicissitudes and were retired from Cambridge. Nicholas Carr[4] (Pemb. and Trin.) had been Cheke's substitute and was now his successor, and gave no offence to the Chancellor on theological grounds. It appears however that these and some other orders of the same date were the cause of several leaving the university and of the persecution and deprivation of others especially in S. John's.

In reply to one of Gardiner's captious criticisms, Smith[5] had said that he and his friends had not ventured to reform the pronunciation of *latin*. It appears however that his disciples were equal to the occasion: for John Caius (fellow of Gonville, 1533, Greek professor at Padua 1541, master of his own college 155⅝—73) in his treatise against the etists charges them with

---

[1] De recta et emendata Linguae Graecae Pronuntiatione, *Thomae Smithi* Angli, tunc in Academia *Cantabrigiensi* publici prælectoris, ad *Vintoniensem Episcopum* Epistola. ('Cantab. 12 Aug. 1542') *Lutetiae*, ex officina *Roberti Stephani* Typographi Regij. 1568. Cum Privilegio Regis. (96 pages.)

[2] Cooper's *Annals* (15 May 1543) I. 406, *ibid* (12 May, 1545), 426.

[3] *ibid.* II. 92.

[4] He was buried in St Giles' Church. His monument, restored by Trinity Coll., is now in the south chapel of the new church.

[5] *De recta Pronuntiatione*, fol. 45 b. Smith wrote also (*Paris* 1568) a dialogue on the phonetic writing of english.

pronouncing the latin *i* like the english[1], with dividing vowels as *pulchrai* for 'pulcrae,' with using such forms as *olli, queis,* and as the Scotch or northerners, saying *saibai, taibai, vaita, aita,* for 'sibi, tibi, vita, ita[2].'

The new pronunciation he urged was peculiar to England— nay peculiar to *one place* in the island 'in quo per ea tempora oratores noui imperabant.' The pretence of a gain in perspicuity was frivolous, for scholars had wit enough to judge from the context, &c.; and as for antiquity Apollo himself made no distinction between λοιμὸς and λιμός. The Greeks themselves used nothing like this newfangled fashion; for the Patriarch who was in London in K. Edward's reign could not understand[3] Cheke's greek, and Cheke[4] could not understand the

[1] Evelyn having been present at the election of Westminster scholars to Trin. and Ch. Ch. (*Diary*, 13 May, 1661), observed 'their odd pronouncing of Latine, so that out of England none were able to understand or endure it.' Milton in the introduction to his *Accedence* (1669) says 'few will be persuaded to pronounce Latin otherwise than their own English.'

[2] *J. Caius* de pronunciatione Graecae et Latinae Linguae. *Londini* in aedibus *Johannis Daij.* an. Dom. 1574. (pp. 23.) Dr Sam. Jebb republished this and other treatises by Caius in 1729.

[3] In 1660 in his inaugural lecture as Greek Professor Barrow spoke of this unique and, as he considered, most antique method of greek pronunciation as greatly redounding to Cheke's credit. *Works* (Napier) ix. 140.

[4] Cheke himself had a correspondence with Gardiner which was printed at Basle in 1555 from the originals which, when on his way to Italy, after K. Edward's death, he lent to 'Coelius Secundus Curio' who dedicated the collection to Ant. Cook. It is entitled '*Joannis Cheki* Angli *De Pronuntiatione Graecae* potissimum linguae disputationes cum Stephano Vuintoniensi

Episcopo, septem contrariis epistolis comprehensae, magna quadam & elegantia & eruditione refertae. Cum gratia & priuilegio Imperiali. *Basileae*, per *Nicol. Episcopium* iuniorem 1555.' (Epistola nuncupatoria, pp. i—ix.) Gardiner to Cheke (1—17). Gardiner's Edict (18—21) Datum Londini 18 Calend. Junias, anno Domini 1542.—Cheke's first answer (22—162) 'I have made no changes in *latin* old or new.' Not long ago people used to say 'Timothéum, Philemónem, Sátanam, Jácobum, Maríam Magdálenem, Sálomem Jácobi.' Smith began when he was reading Aristotle. Ponet, Pickering, Ascham, Tong and Bill have adopted it. Radcliff 'qui nunquam diu cum bonis consentiebat' is our only opponent.—*Gardiner to Cheke,* July 10 (163—217), complains of Cheke's prolixity and arrogance.— *Cheke* to *Gardiner* (218—325) emends Theon and protests against the Chancellor's treatment of the scholars of his university.—*Gardiner to Cheke,* 4 Sept. (326—338) complains of his correcting him.—*Cheke to Gardiner* (339 —345) supplicates for liberty to retain the old pronunciation of Greek.— *Gardiner to Cheke* 2nd Oct. (345—349) refuses to relax his edict for uniformity.

Patriarch. Oxford could tell us well enough how the Greeks themselves speak, for Wolsey had imported a native Matthaeus Calphurnius to teach the language.

We learn from Caius that moderns wanted them to pronounce—'satis rusticè,' he fairly said,—φοῖβος, *toutois, cai, lobois, mousais, basilews, epeiros, tuptomai, chreia, chresimos, apophugen, husteron, kibdes, cuclops, korakeion, lewcon, hippewein, wyos, pais,* instead of the time-honoured *phoebus, toutis, cha, louis, musaes, vasileus, epirus, typtomae, chria, chrisimos, apophygen, ysteron, cibdis, cyclops, coracion, leucon, yppewin, yios, paes.* We may add to this Smith's testimony that for κενταύροις Gardiner would have said *Chentafris.*

It is curious to turn from these fierce contests in the infancy of greek scholarship in England to a protest against the substitution of accent for quantity which was prevalent in the early part of the eighteenth century[1].

Thomas Bentley, nephew of the great Aristarchus, was struck with the want of greek text books for the use of schools, where nothing of that language was read but extracts from Homer and Hesiod—so that when afterwards Demosthenes or Sophocles was put into their hands the youths could make nothing of them; and their verses were dull and archaic.

To remedy these defects he edited in 1741 Callimachus, Theognis, a century of epigrams from the Anthology, and the prose *Protrepticus* of Galen of Pergamos, with latin versions of all and notes to the first. The preface (pp. iii.—xviii.) is devoted to an expostulation against the depraved method of pronouncing greek at that time prevalent. We learn that no distinction was made between τίθημι and τίθεμαι, δίδωμι and δίδομαι, or ἀνάθημα and ἀνάθεμα; and that it was usual to make false quantities for the sake of accent not merely in proper names, as Δημοσθένης, Θουκυδίδης, Θηραμένης, Παρύσᾰτις, *Philotĭmus,* and *Musăgētes,* but in ἰᾱτρός, κίνδῡνος, ἀκρῑβής, ἄκρᾱτος, εὑρῑνος, εὑρῑζος, &c., &c. Thomas Bentley however

[1] In 1712 J. Hudson had edited G. Martinis *de Graecarum Litterarum Pronuntiatione* (with the *Atticista* of Moeris) at *Oxford,* and in 1717 Ja. Richardson of Blackheath had edited a treatise by R. Francklin, called '*Orthotonia* seu *de Linguae Graecae Tonis* Tractatulus.' Lond. 12mo. with additions. It had gone through four editions 1630—73.

shews that his own knowledge of quantity was not equal to what is within reach of each modern *tiro*; for when he asserts that there is absolutely no example of *gratuĭtus*, or *fortuĭtus*, it is probable that he was ignorant of the seeming exceptions which are treated as trisyllabic. It seems also strange now-a-days to appeal to Homer as the authority for the scansion of ἰατρός.

However the question of Accent or Quantity was not destined to slumber long.

In 1754, Henry Gally, of Corpus Christi College, Cambridge (B.A. 1717), published 'A Dissertation against pronouncing the Greek Language according to Accents [a quotation from Dio. Halicarn.]. *London*, Printed for *A. Millar* in the *Strand*, 1754.' pp. i—viii, 1—149[1].

The next year Dr Gally published a 'second edition, corrected. Price 2s.'

Dr Roger Long (B.A. 1700), master of Pembroke Hall, 1733, and Lowndean professor of Astronomy, 1750, replied with a pamphlet 'On Greek Accents,' 1755.

But Dr Gally found a younger and more formidable antagonist in John Foster, sometime fellow of King's (B.A. 1753; D.D. 1766), then under-master, and afterwards for a short period head-master of Eton, who took up the cudgels on the side of Vossius and the accents in an elaborate treatise, entitled 'An Essay on the different nature of Accent and Quantity, &c., &c., 1762.' I have not seen the first edition, but in our University Library[2] there is a copy of the 'second edition, corrected and much enlarged, containing some additions from the Papers of Dr Taylor and Mr Markland. With a Reply to Dr G's second Dissertation in Answer to the Essay. By *John Foster*, M.A., Late Fellow of King's College Cambridge. *Eton*, Printed by *J. Pote*, 1763.' pp. i—xxxi, 1—448.

[1] Camb. *Univ. Library*, Aa. 17. 20.

[2] xvii (=18) 6. 21. A third edition. *Lond.* 1820. Mr W. G. Clark in a paper *On English Pronunciation of Greek*, read before the Camb. Philosophical Soc. and printed in the *Journal of Philology* No. 2. pp. 98—108, in 1868, commends *Foster's* learning and judgment. When Mr H. A. J. Munro made known the results of his researches into ancient latin pronunciation about 1870, prof. Lightfoot and some others showed some interest in the sounds of the greek vowels, diphthongs, and double letters.

The former edition had called forth from Dr Gally 'A
Second Dissertation[1], &c. In Answer to Mr *Foster's* Essay *On
the different Nature of* Accent *and* Quantity. "Accentuum graecorum omnis hodie ratio praepostera est atque peruersa."
Bentl. Ep. ad Mill. 82. London, Printed for *A. Millar* in the
Strand, 1763, price 2*s.*' pp. i—xxiv, 1—95. He accuses Foster
of discourtesy, of misrepresenting Cheke, and of practically
confounding the meaning of the term *accent,* which he started
with defining.   Gally's own position was, that greek cannot
be pronounced according to our acute accent without violating
quantity.   The reply appended to Foster's 2nd ed.[2] is 'A
Review of some passages in the present Essay in a reply to
Dr G's Second Dissertation.   By the Author of the Essay.
Eton. 1763.' pp. 1—49.

W. Primatt, M.A. (Sid.) 1725, published '*Accentus Rediuiui.*
With an answer to Mekerchus, Is. Vossius, &c.   Camb. 1764.'
And S. Horsley, LL.B. (Trin. Hall) 1758, issued an anonymous
treatise 'On the Prosodies of the Greek and Latin Languages.
Lond. 1796.'

It has long been the pride of our schools and universities
that the practice of verse composition has created more skilful
metrical (and consequently, grammatical) critics (headed by
Bentley the discoverer of the *digamma*[3] and of *synaphea,* and
Porson who laid down the law of the *final cretic* and of the limits
of the tragic senarius in general) than are known even in
Germany.   Porson, as it is well known, thought little of verse
composition, except with some such purpose, and it is told
with what facility he was able to shew the errors in the first
edition (1789) of Godfrey Hermann's *de Metris,* which the
Cambridge scholar tacitly refuted in the Supplement to the
Preface of his second edition of the *Hecuba*[4].   The reiterated
'*Quis praeter Hermannum...?*' in the long note on *Medea* 675,

[1] Camb. *Univ. Library,* Aa. 17. 20.
[2] *Ibidem,* XVII. (=18) 6. 21.
[3] *i. e.* Bentley (about 1713) discovered
the importance of the *digamma* in relation to homeric metre. Its *name*
was known at Camb. as early as Cheke's
time, from the old grammarians.

[4] Hermann sent Porson a copy in
1796 on Heyne's suggestion. The
early writings of that scholar, then at
Leipsic, especially the first edition of
his *De Metris,* were very faulty. See
Mr Luard in *Cambridge Essays,* 1857,
pp. 161, 162.

(which commences with a sly reference to Wakefield's impudent suggestion at the end of his *Diatribe*, that Porson should make his notes more discursive) is perhaps Porson's most heartless attack upon the critical character of any contemporary. Among Hermann's *dicta* was the unfortunate 'nihil interesse quâ in sede trimetri anapaestus occurrat.' To this Porson rejoined, not by critical argument alone, but by an english translation of an Etonian's adaptation of an ancient epigram, as follows :

Νήιδες ἐστὲ μέτρων, ὦ Τεύτονες, οὐχ ὁ μὲν, ὅς δ' οὔ·
Πάντες πλὴν "ΕΡΜΑΝΝΟΣ· ὁ δ' "Ερμαννος †σφόδρα Τεύτων. [†μάλα]
The Germans in Greek
Are sadly to seek ;
Not five in fivescore
But ninety five more :
All, save only Herman,
And *Herman's a German. [* Or "he is a"]

He also treated the critic (who must have held some heresy about tribrachs) to a couple of *senarii* on his own prescription[1], all traces of their iambic kindred being effaced by the course of licentiousness to which they had been abandoned :

Ὁ μετρικὸς ὁ σόφος ἄτοπα γέγραφε περὶ μέτρων.
Ὁ μετρικὸς ἄμετρος, ὁ σόφος ἄσοφος ἐγένετο.

It is however fair to Hermann's memory to record that in 1796 he wrote (*De Metris*, p. 150), 'A trisyllabis pedibus tragici Graeci maxime abstinuerunt, quamquam etiam in pari sede, sed admodum raro anapaestus invenitur.' However, Porson would have said, 'in primo tantum pede, nisi sit nomen proprium quod alias ex iambico omnino excludendum esset.'

I do not suppose that the average scholar's familiarity with greek accentuation in the last century differed materially from what it is at present. One man, however, who passed for a critic (Gilbert Wakefield), had the boldness to publish a Bion and Moschus in 1795 without accents[2] (*Lond.* 12mo.), and with a flimsy apology for this slovenliness or want of scholarship which disfigured his selections from the tragedians in 1794, and his other books. Porson, in the opening note to his *Medea*, sets the matter in its true light, referring to the author of the *Diatribe Extemporalis in* Euripidis Hecubam *Londini nuper*

[1] *Classical Journal*, v. 298. Luard's Porson's *Corresp.* 87. Porson himself would hardly have written πλὴν

"Ερμαννος.
[2] Some better men, as Marsh and Tyrwhitt, did the like.

publicatam (1797), as he does in other notes, without mentioning his name.

It is interesting to observe how Porson chose the part of instructor of the academic youth[1] (indeed this characteristic of his writings not merely atones for, but fully justifies his delivering no lectures), and as such we may recognize him specially as the founder of that succession which in our time has borne fruit in the Shrewsbury greek iambics. In earlier days such greek verses as were written were either hexameters, more or less patched together from homeric hemistichs, or elegiacs of no style in particular.

After giving his due to Ri. Dawes[2], who in his old age picked up the niceties of greek criticism while master of Newcastle school, 1738-44, and produced the eleven ' *Canons* ' which bear his name, we must look upon the annotated editions of Euripides' plays by Ri. Porson (1797-1801), as commencing the improved method of scholarship[3] which flourished under the auspices of Monk, Dobree, Blomfield, and Dr Kennedy.

[1] 'Poteram et labori parcere et quieti meae fortasse consulere totam omittendo. Video enim a nonnullis, optimis quidem illis, sed nec satis eruditis et paullo iracundioribus uiris, omnem accentuum rationem despicatu haberi. Verum ii sunt opinor aetate iam prouectiores quam ut a me uel quicquam praui dedoceantur, uel recti quicquam addiscant. Vos autem, ADOLESCENTES, quos solos tutelae meae duxi, uos nunc alloquor. Aliquoties hoc argumentum tetigi ut ad Orest. 631 [al. 626] et alias ; iterum, ut opus erit tacturus. Si quis igitur VESTRUM ad accuratam Graecarum litterarum scientiam aspirat, is probabilem sibi accentuum notitiam quam maturrime comparet, in propositoque perstet, scurrarum dicacitate et stultorum irrisione immotus. *Nam risu inepto res ineptior nulla est.* Unum tantummodo in praesentia monebo. Quicunque huius doctrinae expers, codices MSS. conferendi laborem susceperit, is magnam partem fructuum eorum, qui ex labore suo in

Remp. litterariam redundare et poterant et debebant, disperdiderit. Qui hanc doctrinam nescit, dum ignorantiam suam candide fatetur, inscitiae tantum reus ; qui uero nescire non contentus ignorantiae suae contemptum praetexit, maioris culpae affinis est.'

It is also interesting to reflect that Bentley's Dissertation on Phalaris was evoked by one of those juvenile editions whereby Dean Aldrich (in imitation of his predecessor Fell) encouraged precocious critics, and which he made a new-year's-gift to the junior students of Christ Church. *Hearne-Bliss*, I. 83, Monk's *Bentley*, I. 64.

[2] Dawes' 7th canon, denying the use of οὐ μή with the 1st aor. conjunctive, though approved by Cobet, has been discredited by Mr Ri. Shilleto.

[3] A specimen of Porson's examination papers is printed in Kidd's *Tracts*, 392. Monk carried on the tradition of setting long passages for translation. *Herc. Furens*, 637—679 (Beck), is the specimen of Porson's.

The older type of versification found its encouragement also in the contest for the Browne medals, which was instituted in 1775. A selection of the successful compositions for that and for the Latin ode (which until the present century was always composed on the same theme with the Greek) was published by Valpy in 1810, under the title of *Musae Cantabrigienses*. For earlier specimens of Cambridge greek lyrics and hexameters we may refer to some copies by Michael Lort, B.A., Trin. 1746, Greek professor, 1759, and by T. Zouch, B.A., Trin. 1761, printed in Wrangham's *Zouch*, I. 375, 382, 387, as well as to the earlier collections of congratulatory verses, &c. in various languages, presented from time to time by the universities to royal personages.

It is not easy to collect such a list of books as will give a fair notion of the average course of reading at the university at any particular time. Many classical books arranged in the chronology of their publication will be found registered in an appendix to this volume.

Barrow had publickly declared[1], with satisfaction, that under Duport's professorship young students at Cambridge read Plato and Aristotle and the greek poets, philosophers, historians and scholiasts. A century later, Gray complained that Plato was very little known, and the same was, I suppose, true of Aristotle *à fortiori*.

---

[1] Orat. in Comitiis [1654]. *Works*, ed. Napier, IX. 36.

Cp. Dyer *Privil.* II, ii. 224, 'When Aristotle was the highest name in our Schools, Plato's appears to have been but little known; and at, and after, the Reformation, though he had many admirers, he was not generally received: nor am I aware that his writings are now (1824) taken much for lecture-books in the colleges. But as there have been published by Cambridge critics editions of his most admired Moral and Theological pieces (one of which is a favourite school-book), and lately have appeared in a splendid edition of Mr Gray's works,

published by Mr Mathias, some Remarks on Plato's Writings, with other original pieces, from Mr Gray's MSS. in Pembroke Hall Library; and as Mr Thomas Taylor has also I perceive just advertized The Theologies of Plato and Proclus in English; with these associations in my mind, I have ventured to say thus much of the Theology of Plato.'

Select Platonic dialogues, de rebus divinis, were edited by North, *Camb.* 8vo. with Latin version 1683. Forster edited five dialogues of Plato (*Oxon.*) 1745. Wilkinson's Ethica Aristot. *Oxon.* 1716. Taswell's Physica Aristot. (Bowyer), 1718.

Xenophon's *Anabasis* and *Cyropaedia* were a good deal read[1]. Samuel Pegge (Joh.) was preparing an edition of each about 1728, but he was forestalled by Hutchinson, whose publications (*Oxon.* 1727, 1735) became standard text-books. Porson added some notes to his Anabasis when Nicholson ('Maps') re-issued it in 1785.

Cicero *de Officiis* was another book commonly read. John Jebb delivered lectures thereon in Trinity Hall as Dr Ridlington's deputy in 1766. Portions of *Demosthenes* were pretty frequently edited—by Foulkes and Freind, 1715, Brook, 1721, Mounteney, 1747, J. Taylor (Joh.), 1748, &c. T. Johnson brought out *Sophocles* in 1705, 1708 and 1746, and Thomas Francklin (Greek professor, 1750—59, and member of the Westminster Club) published a translation. Ro. Potter (Emm.) did so for the entire Poetae Scenici 1777—88. *Euripides*[2] was set forth by Piers, 1703, J. King (King's), 1726, S. Musgrave, (the whole) 1756, 1778, Jer. Markland (Pet.), 1763, 1771, and Egerton, 1786. But for *Aeschylus* Stanley's edition, *Lond.* 1663, continued in use. However Askew projected an edition, and Needham had one ready for press, and Porson's was in progress. J. Burton's *Pentalogia* and Wakefield's selection have been already mentioned.

It is worthy of remark, that previous to the establishment of the Classical Tripos in 1822—4, the university proposed no examination in *Greek* to candidates for honours. At the same time an examination in the *Iliad* I—VI. and the *Aeneid* I—VI. was instituted for the *polloi*, who were not candidates for honours. At the same time a *previous examination* was established for all persons in their second year, the subjects being one Greek and one Latin classic, *e.g.* for 1826, *Herodotus* I. and

---

[1] Wells edited *Xen.* (*Oxon.*) 1703.

[2] Joshua Barnes (Emman.), the Greek professor, had edited *Euripides* in 1694 folio. His *Homer* 1711 (2 vols. 4to.) was an improvement on previous editions, and continued without a rival for nearly a century, although it was severely handled by Bentley, who observed that he believed Barnes had as much Greek and understood it about as well as an Athenian blacksmith. Cumberland's *Memoirs*, p. 28; *Bentley's Corresp.* 1. 411. Hearne was a great friend of his, and called him 'the best Grecian (especially for poetical Greek) in the world,' *Reliquiae*, I. 263, and accused Clarke of stealing his Homer from Barnes' edition (*Ibid.* III. 133).

Virgil, *Georgic* IV, as well as S. Matthew's Gospel and Paley's *Evidences of Christianity*.

There was just the one statutable ceremony by which the university required each candidate for the degree of Master of Arts to be examined in Greek by a bedel, or in the case of a member of King's College, or of a mandate degree, to read Greek to a bedel, but these forms were obsolete[1] before 1828.

Greek was of course required of candidates for university scholarships. Thus, in 1725, Snape, the provost of King's, gave Battie and the other candidates for the Craven a *viva voce* examination in Sophocles and Lucian[2]. At the beginning of the present century the usual requirements were some passages from Demosthenes, Sophocles (or Euripides), Tacitus (or other Latin prose author), and a Latin poet, to be translated into English prose. A piece of English prose to be turned into Latin, and *sometimes* into Greek. Questions in History, Geography and Chronology, and composition in Latin prose and verse, and sometimes Greek verse[3].

In a codicil to her will, dated 1739, lady Eliz. Hastings defined the examination for certain scholars at Queen's Coll. *Oxon.* in the following terms. At 8 *a.m.* to begin to translate eight or ten lines of an oration of Cicero into English, and as much Demosthenes into Latin; also two or three verses of the Vulgate into Greek. In the afternoon to write from eight to twelve lines of Latin on a question of practical divinity taken from the Church Catechism, and two distichs on a classical sentence.

When they had gone into residence at Oxford, the scholars elected were to spend four years on the arts and sciences, and a fifth in studying Divinity, Church History, and the Apostolic Fathers in the original: to study the Scripture, and to write exegetical notes daily for one hour. Before their fourth year to write a translation of part of S. Chrysostom *de Sacerdotio,*

[1] *Ceremonies,* Wall-Gunning, pp. 168, 171, 207.

[2] Nichols, *Lit. Anecd.* IV. 601.— Porson gained the Craven in 1781. A translation of an epitaph (14 lines) into Greek iambics (17) which he per- formed in that examination in less than an hour (with the help of Morell's *Thesaurus,* according to Dr T. Young) is preserved. Watson's *Porson,* p. 32.

[3] *Camb. Univ. Calendar,* 1803.

and when[1] B.A., to shew the provost notes of theological reading prescribed by the tutor.

The colleges, however, supplemented the requirements of the university in this respect. Not to mention the scholarship and fellowship elections at Trinity, among the subjects required of all the students in S. John's, from 1765 downwards, was, in one of their years at least, a play of Sophocles, a speech of Demosthenes or the like. A glance at the schemes of study, printed among the Appendices to this volume, will shew what was done at the smaller colleges in the first half of the century, while the following extract from the Cambridge *University Calendar* for 1802 (p. xiii), may be fairly supposed to represent the work of the close of the 18th century[2].

'Under the *third* head of Academical Studies come the *Belles Lettres* or *Classics*, which in most colleges are cultivated with great diligence and success; each term having some part of the best Classics appropriated to the lecture-room. An Oration of *Demosthenes, Lysias, Isocrates*, a *Greek Play, Longinus, Cicero, Quintilian*, select portions of *Herodotus, Tacitus, Thucydides*, &c., &c., afford exercises for the Pupils, and ample room for the Tutor to display his taste on the best writings of antiquity, and to compare them with parallel works in the modern languages. Compositions, Latin or English, are weekly delivered by the Pupils, either in writing, or *viva voce*, in their respective chapels.'

Ro. Surtees, at Christ Church 1796—1800, read all Herodotus, Thucydides and Livy, Plays of Aeschylus and Aristophanes, Xenophon's Anabasis and Hellenica, Demosthenes' public orations, Aristotle's Rhetoric, Pindar's Olympics, Diodorus Siculus, Polybius, Juvenal and Persius. He distinguished

[1] Poulson's *Hist. of Beverley*, i. 461, 5 n.

[2] A little earlier, in 1775, Jebb speaks of classical lectures in college for each sizar and pensioner only 'during the first year of residence,—which it is well known the said pensioner and sizar pay little regard to, as there is no general opportunity offered them by the university of distinguishing themselves in this branch of useful literature.' *Works*, iii. 275. Jebb generously states the exceptional case at S. John's under his late opponent Powell, who examined noblemen and fellow-commoners (as well as other students) in Greek and Roman Literature (*Ibid.* 276, 277).

himself in the terminal *collections*, an examination then conducted by the dean, tutors, and censors of the college. (*Memoir* by G. Taylor, p. 7.)

A chronological list of university classical books will be found in an Appendix to this volume. We will conclude this portion of our observation by noting what books were used by a man at Trinity in the early part of the present century (1815—16)[1].

Porson's *Hecuba*, Hermann and Seale *on Metres*, Scapulae *lexicon*, Dawes *Misc. Critica*, Bentley on *Phalaris*, Hoogeveen's *Particularum Doctrina*, Bos *Ellipses*, Preface to Franklin's *Sophocles*, Cumberland's *Observer*, Brumoy's *Greek* Theatre, Tyrwhitt's *Aristotle*, Horace *ad Pisones*, Gillies' *Hist. of Greece* (borrowing Mitford's more expensive book, and the *Travels of Anacharsis*), D'Anville's *Atlas*, Butler's *Aeschylus*, Drakenborch's *Livy*, Hooke's *Hist. of Rome*, *Polybius*, and Larcher's *Herodotus*.

In his second year,—Duker's *Thucydides*, Watts' *Scriptores Historici*, Campbell *on the Gospels*, Beausobre and Valpy on *New Testament*, Soame Jenyns' *Internal Evidences*, Jenkins' *Reasonableness of Christianity* and Butler's *Analogy*. He attended the Norrisian professor's 'dull and disorderly' readings of Pearson *on the Creed*.

With the third term of the second year mathematics began to demand the student's undivided attention.

---

[1] [J. M. F. Wright's] *Alma Mater*, I. 120, 163, 184, 195, 206, 219, 222.

CHAPTER X.

MORALITY. METAPHYSICS. CASUISTRY.

THE first number of *Mind* in 1876 contained a paper by the Rector of Lincoln College, Oxford, on the study of Philosophy in his University. In the next number Mr Henry Sidgwick followed with a sketch of the treatment which that important study has met with at Cambridge in the last two or three generations. The upshot is (so far as concerns our present inquiry) that at neither of our English universities was any serious interest taken in mental science or metaphysics at the commencement of the nineteenth century.

If we glance at the state of England at the close of the *seventeenth* century, this is very surprising; European thought seemed fully set upon such pursuits, and in our own country the minds of people below the higher ranks were affected by philosophical talk in a way unparalleled even at the present time.

The causes of such a change must be left for others to assign. What effect may have been produced by engrossing wars and commercial interests, by the revival of theological discussions and the increased importance of political questions; or again by the decay of coffee-houses, and the tax on pamphlets, or the revulsion produced by the fate of philosophical Paris, the reign of Decorum, and the growth of delicacy and apprehensiveness of un-orthodoxy—how far these or other powers may have conduced to psychological and ethical apathy, I must leave for others to determine. Suffice it to say, that the universities, if no better in this respect, were no worse than the nation at large. At the time when the university as a body was casting away the last pretence of examining in 'philosophy,' and even Locke and Paley had been discredited[1], about 1835, there was a band of Coleridgians among the younger fellows of Trinity.

This leads me to the remark that in gauging the philosophical reading of the University we must distinguish between works read by individual scholars more or less widely, and books which were actually or virtually acknowledged text-books received by the tutors, examiners, &c., representing a college or university.

Of the latter class the short catalogue subjoined to this chapter will give a fair notion for the former half of the century. The names of Plato, Hobbes, Descartes, Newton, Locke, Clarke[2], Spinoza, Leibnitz, Butler, Berkeley, Grotius, Puffendorf, Milton, W. Law, Ray, Cudworth, H. More, Hutcheson, King, Shaftesbury, Wollaston, Pearson, Hooker, Jeremy Taylor, and Sanderson will not escape us.

If we go through the names of other writers of the day we shall find that they were very few. Toland had been answered

---

[1] Sc. by Sedgwick's *Sermon*, 1832, printed in 1833, 1850. However, even as early as 1775, Jebb (*Works*, III. 271) speaks 'of ethics meeting with very slender encouragement, and the incomparable Locke being now almost as little honoured at the public time of trial as real science is said to be at the sister university.'

[2] Dr Sam. Clarke of Norwich (1675—1729), editor of Homer, afterwards a friend of Newton, was educated at Caius, where he obtained a fellowship (B.A. 1694). He combined his Boyle lectures (1704—5) under the title of *A Discourse concerning the Being and Attributes of God, the Obligations of Natural Religion, and the Truth and Certainty of the Christian Revelation.* He maintained the independent and necessary character of moral distinctions perceived by reason, and he declared Moral Right to be another aspect of Divine Command. Clarke's writings made some stir in the country. It was (I suppose) his tenets, and such as the great latitudinarian Cudworth had taught in the previous century (died at Christ Coll. Lodge, 1688, having been also Master of Clare, Hebrew prof., and fellow of Emmanuel), that Fielding ridicules in the philosopher Square (*Tom Jones*) with his 'Fitness of Things' and 'Eternal and Immutable Verities.' One of Clarke's other books, the *Scripture Doctrine of the Trinity*, was condemned by the lower house of Convocation. His draft of the Church Service mangled to suit unitarianism was adopted as the basis of Theophilus Lindsey's '*Book of Common Prayer Reformed for the use of the Chapel in* Essex Street.'

and was no longer a novelty. Anthony Collins (King's) and Matthew Tindal (*Linc. Exon. All Souls*) the deists and opponents of Clarke, and Bernard Mandeville (to say the least) an extravagant writer, could hardly be looked for in an academical list. Hume did not publish his first book till 1738, David Hartley (Jes.) in 1749, dying in 1757. Voltaire, Rousseau, Condillac, Montesquieu, and C. A. Helvetius had not broken silence. If Jonathan Edwards, of New Jersey, had already brought out his treatise on the Will it had not crossed the Atlantic, nor had (Kant's forerunner) J. C. von Wolff's heresies, which had caused his temporary ejection from Halle (1723—41), troubled our island.

Again, if we take our observations of Cambridge at the end of the century, we find Locke, Butler (*Analogy*), Clarke (*On the Attributes*), Law (*Theory of Religion*), and Berkeley still in favour, while Paley[1], Hartley, Rutherford, Gisborne, Burlamaqui are added to the list: Balguy and Hey having had a short popularity as moral theologians. Locke (with logic) was the freshmen's subject; the other books were kept for the second and third year. The efficiency of the lectures varied of course in different colleges. At S. John's, Dr Newcome, the master, who died in 1765, established a prize for the commencing B.A., who having gained mathematical honours should distinguish

[1] 'Fawcett,' who is classed with 'Locke and Paley' in the *Sizar A Rhapsody*, 1799, p. 89, is I suppose the Norrisian professor of Theology. R. H. C. writing in the *Monthly Magazine*, 1797, p. 266, says, 'It is a notorious fact, that in most colleges the classical and moral lectures are hurried over in the most slovenly manner, and without the least regard to the improvement of the students.'—A. S. rejoins (p. 360), 'It was not so in my time; or, perhaps, I may not have paid sufficient attention to what was doing in other colleges. In the college at which I was educated, we had lectures two evenings in the week in the Greek Testament, and once in a Greek or Latin author; and in the mornings, our lectures were alternately in the classics, and Locke or Moral Philosophy. These lectures were so far from being hurried over in a slovenly manner, that he must have been a very stupid fellow indeed who would absent himself from the latter, given by one of the first characters in the university, now a dignitary of the church. Many of his principles in morality I held in the greatest detestation, though I was formerly pleased with his liberality and his familiar mode of instruction.' Watson was assistant tutor at Trinity, 1761, but the reference is most probably to Paley, who lectured at Christ's 1768—76, to freshmen on Locke, Clarke and Butler; to sophs on moral philos. I cannot identify either A. S. or R. H. C. among the graduati.

himself by knowledge of Moral Philosophy. It was gained by J. Carr (5th wrangler) in 1767[1]. At Christ's Paley delivered about 1770 those lectures which he published with little alteration in 1785, under the title of *Moral and Political Philosophy*[2]. At Trinity the lectures delivered by the tutor, Thomas Jones (a scholar of Shrewsbury and S. John's, author of a *Sermon on Duelling* 1792), were much appreciated by the junior sophs, some of whom (about 1799, 1800) asked leave to attend them a second time. His bust is in S. John's ante-chapel.

Towards the end of the last century, Hartley was considered a great light among philosophical minds at Cambridge. He was a contemporary of Hume and a fellow-follower of Locke. His system (which was based on physiology) gathered up the floating materialism current at Cambridge, and was for a time adopted by Coleridge while he was at the University, as well as by Priestley and other Necessitarians and Unitarians[3].

The Oxonians seem to have discovered a short way with metaphysicians, both simple and practical in the extreme, and comparable with Prideaux's projected *Drone-Hall* :—

'The Emoluments of the Professorship in Morality' (says *Philalethes*, replying to Vicesimus Knox in behalf of his university, 6th Feb. 1790) 'are divided between the Proctors of each year: The very nature of their office must lead them to a most satisfactory discharge of the real duties of a Professor in Moral Philosophy.'

In few things perhaps is fashion more noticeable in her changes than in the matter of philosophical and metaphysical opinions.

---

[1] *Baker-Mayor*, 1030, *l.* 23 ; 1073.

[2] Cp. 'The tutors of Cambridge no doubt neutralize, by their judicious remarks, when they read it to their pupils, all that is pernicious in its principles.' [Best's] *Personal and Literary Memorials*, p. 166 (where the story of the king refusing 'Pigeon Paley' a bishopric is told). G. Pryme, *Recoll.* p. 38.

[3] Prof. Shairp's '*Study*' on *Coleridge*. (Coleridge was at that time, like David Hartley, associated with arians, and a member of the same college,—Jesus.) David Hartley, junior, his son and biographer, the inventor and M.P., was fellow of Merton. His devotion to natural history is exemplified (Best's *Personal and Lit. Memorials*, p. 223) by the horror he showed on having treated his friends to game before he knew it had been a specimen sent for his investigation—'*We have eaten a nondescript.*'

Even in the conservative schools of Oxford in the last century there were some symptoms of vacillation. In 1721 it was not infrequent for 'the tutors in their lectures upon many points of philosophy to tell their *pupils* that in the schools they must hold such a side of the argument; *but* that the other side is demonstrably the right side.'

Nicholas Amherst, who made this assertion in the xxIst number of his *Terrae-Filius* (a work by no means implicitly to be trusted), reiterated it in the preface to his edition of 1726, adding that the change was creeping from the colleges even into the schools, and that '*Locke, Clarke* and *Sir Isaac Newton* begin to find countenance...and that *Aristotle* seems to totter on his antient throne.'

He proved however to be not so very easy to dethrone. Throughout that century, at the ceremony for taking the degree of B.A. at Oxford, 'the student, when formally asked the heads of the predicables, formally replied, *Aristoteles pro me respondebit,* being touched on the head with a big copy of the Stagirite, and rising *baculo magis quam lauru dignus*[1].'

At Oxford, Aristotle has been in high favour from the fabulous times when the Queen's Scholar found him the readiest weapon against even that 'bristle-backt foe[2],' the wild boar, on that memorable occasion when

> 'instead of avoiding the mouth of the beast,
> He ramm'd in a volume, and cried *Graecum est!*'

In more historical times it was enjoined that nothing in the schools should be defended against Aristotle. This was prescribed by the Injunctions of Sir Chr. Hatton in 1589; whose predecessor, the Earl of Leicester, five years earlier had ordained that 'six solemn lectures be read in Aristotle.' Even at the time of the Great Rebellion it was observed in Parliament by Colonel Briscoe (Debate *Dec.* 12, 1656, *ap.* Burton's *Diary*), that '*est Aristotelis*' was in the University an unanswerable argument 'like *ipse dixit* with Pythagoras's own scholars.'

---

[1] [Ri. Robinson] *Oxf. Undergraduates' Journal*, 1867, p. 166.
[2] The Oxford Sausage, 1764,—Compare also the picture in *Oxford and Camb. Nuts to Crack*, 1834, p. 90.

Cambridge too required her sons to answer a question in 'Aristotle's Priorums,' but how far she elicited from them any understanding or love for his metaphysics or moral science is perhaps hardly doubtful. Even in our own times we have heard of the greek of Aristotle being well known in a certain manner, and diligently observed, while to give a second thought to the author's philosophy or its relation to the thoughts of ancient or modern times would have been considered to be extravagance on the part of the classical scholar.

Still, in the eighteenth century, although not 'so devote to Aristotle's Ethicks[1]' as her sister, Cambridge did not utterly neglect mental and moral science. Her Christ College Platonists (Ralph Cudworth[2], and Henry More) of the previous century had accepted with certain important reservations the Cartesian as opposed to the Aristotelian Philosophy which was upset in the second quarter of that century, and carried with it the ancient statutable subjects for disputations. The writings of Descartes are thought by Professor Playfair[3] to have kept their ground at Cambridge as late almost as 1720, more than thirty years after the publication of Newton's discoveries. But Dr Clarke, as we shall see, introduced first Descartes into the academic course, and subsequently Newton soon after taking his degree (B.A. Cai. 1694), and very shortly after those discoveries had been published (*Principia*, 1687). We find Ri. Laughton of Clare also encouraging the study of Newton, when tutor and moderator, ten or twelve years at least before the date assigned by Playfair to the introduction of that system.

---

[1] *Taming of the Shrew*, I. sc. 1.

[2] Cudworth lived just long enough to hear of Newton's discoveries, and died too soon to read Locke's Essay. Mullinger's *Cambridge in the* xviith *Century*, pp. 159—164.

[3] See [Whewell's] strictures on this statement in *Mus. Crit.* II. 515. Whewell was of opinion that no one at Cambridge had ever seriously entertained the cartesian theory of *vortices*. Des Cartes' general hypothesis, that all natural phenomena may be ac- counted for by matter and motion, was refuted by Barrow in a latin speech in 1652. See *Whewell to De Morgan* (*Todhunter*, II. 414), *Philos. of Discovery*, p. 179, and *Hist. Induct. Sciences*, Vol. II. Bk. vii. ch. iv. § 2. However, in one passage (*Works*, III. 280) Jebb seems to imply that *he* thought 'the vortices of Des Cartes' had been familiar and dominant at Cambridge. How far H. More the platonist was a cartesian is discussed by Dyer, *Priv.* II. fasc. ii. p. 219.

As early as 169⅘ Descartes' name as a philosopher had begun to be brought into disrepute in the tripos verses, and in 172¾ and subsequent years the Newtonian philosophy is upheld. 'Bobus' Smith, however, as lately as 1790, chose *Cartesii Principia* for the subject of one of his humorous copies.

But we may find a disturbing force even earlier than Newton, that is, in Bacon.

'Bacon's new philosophy,' says Dyer (*Hist. Camb.* I. 194), 'aspired to derange the old metaphysics and logic, and with them the old natural philosophy, the subtleties of the former being the foundation of the latter. It, however, left a space open for a more liberal philosophy, founded in the operations of nature and uniform experience. As far as logic and metaphysics went, that place was filled up by Locke's *Essay on the Human Understanding*, his inquiry being, in fact, a guide to *general* metaphysical reasoning, a philosophical analysis of the principles of logic (as some part is of grammar), and founded on the principles of Bacon, as the more sure method of philosophizing.'

Locke's Essay appeared in 1689, two years only after the publication of Newton's discoveries. It is certain that the author had been removed from his studentship at Christ Church[1] by King James' command, and had returned from abroad in William's fleet. His book was not treated with much favour by his own university.

At a meeting of the Heads of Houses at Oxford (which was pledged[2] to follow 'Aristotle and the entire peripatetic doctrine') so late as 1703, it was proposed to censure and discourage the reading of it[3]. John Wynne indeed (afterward bishop of Bath and Wells), a great tutor in *Jesus* College, abridged Locke's Essay, which he read to his pupils, and persuaded other tutors to do the like. Among these was Mr Milles[4], vice-principal of

---

[1] Curious letters between the E. of Sunderland and bp. Fell in Nov. 1684, relating to Locke's studentship and non-residence on the plea of health, were printed in 1750 in the 6th no. of the *Student*. He is said to have 'belonged to the late Earl of *Shaftesbury*.'

Fox Bourne states it fairly.

[2] *Stqt. Acad. Oxon.* VI. 2.

[3] Masters' *Life of* T. Baker, p. 118.

[4] *Thomas* Milles, M.A. 1695, was *vice*-principal; *John* Mills, or Mill, the Greek Testament critic, was *principal* 1685—1707.

Edmund-hall (bp. of Waterford), but Tom Hearne, when an undergraduate there (1697—1700), ' always declined' his lecture[1]. He tells us[2] that in January, 17$\frac{16}{16}$, Dr Charlett, of University College, commended Locke as fair in arguing, and as displaying wide knowledge in coffee-house conversation. At that same college, however, half a century later, when Sir W. Jones, the Oriental scholar, was an undergraduate (1765), the only logic in fashion was the logic of the Schools. When one of the fellows of Univ. College was reading Locke with his pupils, he carefully passed over every passage wherein that great metaphysician derides the old system[3].

Charles Kidman of Benet College (B.D. 1694) was one of the first to introduce the reading of Locke's Essay at Cambridge[4], where it took root and flourished until about the year 1830. Indeed, the Essay may be said while cast out from Oxford, not only to have flourished at Cambridge, but to have borne fruit. Not only did it become in itself a text-book, of which an analysis or 'Syllabus' was printed at Camb., 12mo. 1796 (pp. 38), and again in the form of a Catechism in 1824 (pp. 252), and other years; but it may be said to have produced such popular books as Duncan's *Logic*[5], and Paley's *Moral Philosophy*[6].

H. Lee, a fellow of Emmanuel (a philosopher of the same school as the anti-Newtonian, Ro. Green of Clare), did indeed, in 1703, publish '*Anti-Scepticism,* or Notes upon each Chapter of Locke's *Essay,* in four Books :' but this did not prevent 'the ablest metaphysicians' in our University from being proud to come forward as 'its critics and commentators. Hartley' (continues Dyer) 'was a disciple of Locke's school : his doctrines of the Mechanism of the Human Mind, and of the Association of Ideas, are but an enlargement of Locke's, or rather a deduction from it. His Doctrine of Vibrations is considered more his

[1] *Reliqu. Hearn.* III. 162, 163.
[2] *Ibid.* II. 28. Hearne also with his own hand inscribed a very honourable commendation of Locke in that author's presentation copies of his works to the Bodleian in 1704. (Macray's *Annals,* 124.)

[3] Ld. Teignmouth's *Life of Sir W. Jones,* 1815, p. 39.
[4] Disney's *Life of Sykes,* p. 3.
[5] Dyer, *Hist. Camb.* I. 198.
[6] A. Sedgwick's *Discourse* (original ed.), p. 49.

own; and though Hartley's *Observations* [*on Man, his Frame, his Duty, and his Expectations*, 2 vols. 8vo. 1749, by David Hartley, sometime fellow of Jesus Coll. Camb.] has not been made a Lecture-book in our colleges, it has been much read in the University. Dr Law, late Bishop of Carlisle, Master of Peterhouse, published in 1777 a fine edition of Locke's Works, together with a Life and Preface; and the Moral Philosophy of Dr Paley is fruit of the same tree, though damaged in the gathering[1].'

The Proctors' book contains, among additions to the statutes, a grace passed 14th Mar. 1855, on the recommendation of the syndicate, to the effect that candidates for mathematical honours should not be required to attend the 'poll' examination of Paley's *Moral Philosophy*, the New Testament, and Ecclesiastical History to which they had been insecurely bound by a loosely-worded grace on the recommendation of the Theological Syndics' Report 11 May, 1842.

The following essays on Moral, Political, or Social Philosophy deserve to be mentioned:—

On the Slavery and Commerce of the Human Species, Lond. 1783, and *On the Impolicy of the African Slave Trade*, 1787, by T. Clarkson (1st junior optime, 1783, Joh., where Wilberforce had taken his degree in 1781), who having gained the Middle Bachelors' Members' Prize, on the slave trade in 1785, wrote subsequently several other tracts on the same subject and on Quakerism.—Also, *Observations on the Nature of Civil Liberty*, &c. Lond. 1776. Three prize *Dissertations* (50 guineas each offered anonymously) viz: *On Gaming*, Camb. 1783., *On Duelling*, Camb. 1784., *On Suicide*, Camb. 1785. The three reprinted 1812, all by Ri. Hey, Magd. and Sid., 3rd wrangler and senior medallist, 1768; esquire bedell, 1772; LL.D., 1779. *Duelling* had been the subject for the Seatonian poem in 1774; no prize having been adjudged it was repeated for 1775, when C. P. Layard (Joh.) and S. Hayes (Trin.) were successful. The duel between two Pembroke-hall men (Applethwaite shooting Rycroft) in 1791, occasioned the sermon by T. Jones, mentioned on p. 123. See Aikin's *Athenaeum* XIII. (1808) 262, 539.

---

[1] Dyer, *Hist. Camb.* I. 195, 196.

List of Books
on Moral Philosophy and Metaphysics
recommended or
in use at Cambridge
in 1730.

Adams, J. (King's) On Self Murder. Lond. 1700.

Atterbury, Fr. (*Ch. Ch.*) Concio ad Clerum. Lond. 1709.

———— at Mr T. Bennet's Funeral, 1706.

Mr B. [=J. Balguy (Joh.)] Foundation of Moral Goodness. 1728.

Barbeyrac, Jean (*Lausanne & Groningen*) Puffendorf, with Prefatory Dissert. 1724.

Baronius, Vincent (O. S. B.) Ethica Christiana. Paris, 1666.

Bates, W. (Emm. and King's) On the Existence of God. Lond. 1676.

Bayle, Pet. (*Roterdam*) Dict. (s. vv. *Manicheans, Marcionites, Paulicians,* &c.),1695.

Bentley, Ri. (Jo. and Trin.) Boyle Lectures. Lond. 1693.

Berkeley, G. (*T.C.D.*) Dialogues. Lond. 1713.

———— Treatise on the Principles of Human Knowledge. Dublin, 1710.

Browne, Pet. (*T.C.D.*) Procedure of the Understanding. Lond. 1728.

Buddeus, J. F. (*Halle & Jena*) De Origine Mali.

Burnet, Gil. (*Aberd.*) F.R.S. De Statu Mortuorum. Lond. 1720, 1727.

———— On the xxxix. Articles. Lond. 1699, 1720.

Butler, Jos. (*Oriel*) Three Sermons with Preface. 1726.

A. C. [=Ant. Collins (King's)] On Liberty and Necessity, 1715. (*See* Gretton and Jackson).

Cartesii, Ren. (*La Fleche*) Meditationes 1630, 1641.

———— de Methodo. (1637) Camb. 1702.

———— Principia. Amst. 1644, &c.

Chambers (Ephr.) Dictionary (s. vv. *Abstract, General*) 1728.

Cheyne, G. (*Edinb.*) Philos. Princip. Lond. 1715.

Chubb, T. Reflections on Moral and Positive Duties.

———— Collection of Tracts, 4to. Lond. 1730.

Clarke, J. of Hull (Pet.) Foundation of Morality. York. n. d.

————, J. dean of Sarum (Cai.) Boyle Lectures on Origin of Evil. Lond. 1720, 21.

Clarke, S. (Cai.) On the Catechism. Lond. 1729.

———— Corresp. with a Gentleman at Cambridge.

———— ———— with Dodwell. Lond. 1706.

———— ———— Leibnitz. Lond. 1717.

———— On the Being and Attributes of God. Lond. 1706.

———— Evidences of Nat. and Revealed Religion.

Le Clerc, J. (*Geneva*) Logica. 1704. Lond. 1692.

———— Pneumatologia. Amst. 1692.

Colliber, S. Essay on Nat. and Revealed Religion.

———— Impartial Enquiry into the Being and Attributes of God. Lond. 1735.

Collier, Arthur (*New Coll.*)   Clavis Universalis.   Lond. 1713.

'Country Clergyman's Letters to a Deist.'

Cudworth, Ra. (Emm. Clare, Chr.)   Eternal and Immutable Morality.   Lond. 1731.

—— Intellectual System.   Lond. 1678.

Cumberland, Ri. (Magd.) de Legibus Naturae.   Lond. 1672.

Dawes, Sir W. Abp. (*Joh.; Cath.*)   Sermons.   Lond. 1707 &c.

Derham, W. (*Trin.*)   Astro-Theologia.   Lond. 1714, 1726.

—— Physico-Theologia.   Lond. 1713, 1727.

Episcopius, Simon (*Amsterd.*)   Instit. Theol.   Amst. 1665—71.

———— de Libero Arbitrio.

———— Respons. ad Quaestiones.

Fabricius, J. A. (*Hamb.*) de Veritate Rel. Christianae.   Hamb. 1725.

Fancourt, Sam.   On Divine Prescience.   Lond. 1729.

Felton, H. (*Edm. H.*)   On the Resurrection, 1725.

Fiddes, Ri. (*Univ.*) Body of Divinity, Vol. ii.   Preface on Morality.   Lond. 1720.

—— On Hell Torments.

—— Theol. Speculat.   Lond. 1718—20.

Filmer, Sir Ro. (Trin.)   Patriarchia.   Lond. 1680.

Fordyce, Dav. (*Marischal*)   Ethics.   (Lond. 1754.)

Gastrell, Fr. (*Ch. Ch.*)   Boyle Lectures.   Lond. 1703.

' Gloucestershire,' Gentleman of.   On Clarke's Attributes.

'sGravesande, W. J. (*Leyden*)   Elem. Phys.   Lug. Bat. 1720.

Green, Ro. (Clare)   Princip. Philos.   Camb. 1712.

Gretton, Phil. (Trin.)   Answer to A. C.   Lond. 1730.

—— Review of the Argument *à priori.*   1732.

Grew, Nehem. (Pemb.) Cosmologia Sacra.   Lond. 1701, 1710.

Grotius, Hugo (*Leyden*)   De Jure Belli et Pacis.   Paris 1625, Excerpta Camb. 1703.

—— Mare Liberum.   Lug. Bat. 1609, &c.

—— De Veritate Rel. Christ.   Lug. Bat. 1627.   Lond. 1711.

Gurdon, Brampton (Cai.)   Boyle Lectures.   Lond. 1721.

Hale, Sir M. (*Magd. Hall*) Primitive Origination of Mankind.   Lond. 1677.

Hoadley, Ben. (*Cath.*) Answer to Atterbury.   1706, 1710.

—— Measure of Submission.   Lond. 1706.

Hobbes, T. (*Magd. Hall*) de Cive.   Paris 1642.

—— Human Liberty.   Lond. 1654.   (Tripos § 3.   Lond. 1684.)

—— Leviathan, 1651, 1680.

'Homily against Rebellion.'   1568.

Hooker, Ri. (*C. C. C.*) Eccl. Polity. i.   Lond. 1593, 1723.

Huet, Pet. Dan. (*Caen*) Censura Philos. Cartes. 1689, Helmst. 1690.

—— Quaestiones Alnetanae.   Caen 1690.

Hutcheson, Fr. (*Glasgow*) Ideas of Beauty, &c.   Lond. 1725.

———— Illustr. of Moral Sense.   Lond. 1728.

———— The Passions.   Lond. 1728.

Jackson, J. (Jes.)   Defense of Human Liberty against Cato's Letters.   [T. Gordon and J. Trenchard.]

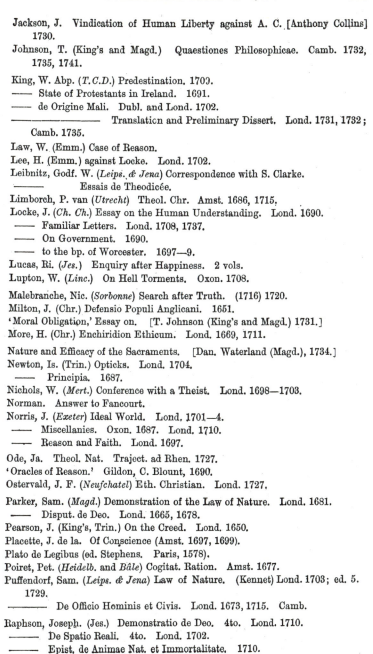

Jackson, J. Vindication of Human Liberty against A. C. [Anthony Collins] 1730.

Johnson, T. (King's and Magd.) Quaestiones Philosophicae. Camb. 1732, 1735, 1741.

King, W. Abp. (*T.C.D.*) Predestination. 1709.
—— State of Protestants in Ireland. 1691.
—— de Origine Mali. Dubl. and Lond. 1702.
———————— Translation and Preliminary Dissert. Lond. 1731, 1732; Camb. 1735.

Law, W. (Emm.) Case of Reason.

Lee, H. (Emm.) against Locke. Lond. 1702.

Leibnitz, Godf. W. (*Leips. & Jena*) Correspondence with S. Clarke.
—— Essais de Theodicée.

Limborch, P. van (*Utrecht*) Theol. Chr. Amst. 1686, 1715.

Locke, J. (*Ch. Ch.*) Essay on the Human Understanding. Lond. 1690.
—— Familiar Letters. Lond. 1708, 1737.
—— On Government. 1690.
—— to the bp. of Worcester. 1697—9.

Lucas, Ri. (*Jes.*) Enquiry after Happiness. 2 vols.

Lupton, W. (*Linc.*) On Hell Torments. Oxon. 1708.

Malebranche, Nic. (*Sorbonne*) Search after Truth. (1716) 1720.

Milton, J. (Chr.) Defensio Populi Anglicani. 1651.

'Moral Obligation,' Essay on. [T. Johnson (King's and Magd.) 1731.]

More, H. (Chr.) Enchiridion Ethicum. Lond. 1669, 1711.

Nature and Efficacy of the Sacraments. [Dan. Waterland (Magd.), 1734.]

Newton, Is. (Trin.) Opticks. Lond. 1704.
—— Principia. 1687.

Nichols, W. (*Mert.*) Conference with a Theist. Lond. 1698—1703.

Norman. Answer to Fancourt.

Norris, J. (*Exeter*) Ideal World. Lond. 1701—4.
—— Miscellanies. Oxon. 1687. Lond. 1710.
—— Reason and Faith. Lond. 1697.

Ode, Ja. Theol. Nat. Traject. ad Rhen. 1727.

'Oracles of Reason.' Gildon, C. Blount, 1690.

Ostervald, J. F. (*Neufchatel*) Eth. Christian. Lond. 1727.

Parker, Sam. (*Magd.*) Demonstration of the Law of Nature. Lond. 1681.
—— Disput. de Deo. Lond. 1665, 1678.

Pearson, J. (King's, Trin.) On the Creed. Lond. 1650.

Placette, J. de la. Of Conscience (Amst. 1697, 1699).

Plato de Legibus (ed. Stephens. Paris, 1578).

Poiret, Pet. (*Heidelb.* and *Bâle*) Cogitat. Ration. Amst. 1677.

Puffendorf, Sam. (*Leips. & Jena*) Law of Nature. (Kennet) Lond. 1703; ed. 5. 1729.
———————— De Officio Hominis et Civis. Lond. 1673, 1715. Camb.

Raphson, Joseph. (Jes.) Demonstratio de Deo. 4to. Lond. 1710.
—— De Spatio Reali. 4to. Lond. 1702.
—— Epist. de Animae Nat. et Immortalitate. 1710.

Ray, J. (Trin.) F.R.S. On Creation. Lond. 1691...1722.
— Physico-Theol. Discourses. Lond. 1692...1717.
'Republick of Letters,' Present State of the. *July* 1728.
Rohault, Ja. (*Paris*) Physica fr. Paris 1671; lat. Lond. 1682; engl. J. and S. Clarke 1710, 1718.
Rust, G. (Camb.) On Truth. Lond. 1682.
Rymer (?) Revealed Religion.

Sacheverell's Trial, 1710.
Salmasius, Cl. (*Heidelb.*) Defensio Regia. Amst. 1650.
Sanderson, Ro. (*Linc.*) De Obligatione Conscientiae. Lond. 1661.
————   —— —— Juramenti. Lond. 1722.
Scot, J. (*Oxon.*) Christian Life. Lond. 1681—6. Ed. 9. 1729.
Selden, J. (*Hart Hall*) Mare Clausum. Lond. 1630.
Shaftesbury, Ant. Ashley Cooper. Inquiry concerning Virtue (Characteristics II.) 1711—23.
Sharp, J. (Chr.) Abp. Sermons. Lond. 1729—35.
Sharrock, Ro. (*New Coll.*) De Finibus Virtutis Chr. Oxon. 1673.
Sherlock, W. (Pet.) On a Future State. Lond. 1705.
————— On Future Judgment. Lond. 1692, 1715.
Sidney, Algernon. On Government. Lond. 1698, 1704.
Smith, J. (Qu.) Select Discourses. 1660.
Spinoza, Benet. (*Amsterdam*) Opera Posthuma. 1677.
Stillingfleet, Ed. (Joh.) Irenicum. Lond. 1659.
————— Origines Sacrae. Lond. 1662.
Strutt, S. On Locke's chapter of *Power*.
Swinden, Tobias. (Jes.) Treatise of Hell. Appendix. Lond. 1714, 1727.

Taylor, Jer. (Cai.) Ductor Dubitantium. Lond. 1660.
Templer, J. (Trin.) against Hobbes. Lond. 1673.
Tillotson, J. (Clare) Sermons. Lond. 1707—12.

Ward, Seth (Sid., *Trin.*) Immortality of the Soul. Oxon. 1652.
Watts, Isaac. Logic. Lond. 1725.
Webster, W. (Cai.) Answers prefixed to [L. Maimbourg's] Hist. of Arianism. 1728.
Whitby, Dan. (*Trin.*) Ethics. Compend. in usum juvent. Oxon. 1684, 1713.
————— Appendix to 2 Thess. 1703.
Wilkins, J. (*New Inn, Magd. H., Wadh.* and *Trin.*) Nat. Religion. Lond. 1675.
Wollaston, W. (Sid.) Religion of Nature Delineated. 1724.

Of the Cambridge professors of CASUISTRY in the last century, two (Colbatch and Walker, 1707, 1744) were in different ways eminent for their connexion with Bentley, two (Dr Edmund Law[1], 1764, and Geo. Borlase, 1788) as members of

[1] Bp. Watson (*Autobiog.* i. 13.) calls Dr Law 'one of the best metaphysicians of his time.'

Peterhouse had some interest among the electors. They were, however, all men of some note in their day; but the last of them at least did not lecture; indeed, I believe Dr Whewell was the first to do so. Ro. Plumptre, master of Queens', who succeeded Dr Law in 1769, was the author of a pamphlet called *Hints respecting some of the Univ. Officers*, 1782. Casuistry seems to have been an extinct science with us in the last century[1]; and in the present this professorship took for a time the title of Moral Theology[2]. In the 17th century the Stuarts had encouraged this important subjective enquiry. It was a study after James I.'s own heart. Ro. Sanderson (Linc. Coll. Oxon.), chaplain to King Charles I. and, after the Restoration, bishop of Lincoln, was one of the most scientific expositors of this science. His *Ten Lectures*, delivered in 1647 and printed in 1660 (Praelectiones, 1661), were a most important contribution to the art. In 1678 were published *Nine Cases of Conscience*, which he had given out in two parts in 1666, 1668. A *Latin* version was printed at Cambridge in 1688. Some short tracts on Cases of Conscience were appended to an edition of his Life by Walton in 1685[3]. Among the divines who gave practical application to these principles were two men of very different dispositions,—*Jeremy Taylor* of Caius (and All Souls, Oxon.), author of *Ductor Dubitantium*, or the Rule of Conscience in all her General Measures, ed. 1, 1660, ed. 2, 1671;—and *Ri. Baxter*, who in his *Christian Directory*, published in 1673, propounds and answers many *centuriae* of subtle and practical doubts and cases of conscience with the nicety of S. Thomas Aquinas.

Bp. Joseph Hall (Emman.) of Norwich is referred to by Taylor (preface to *Ductor Dubitantium*). Hall wrote *Resolutions*

[1] A cause to which Jer. Taylor attributed the scarcity of English authorities was 'the careless and needless neglect of receiving private Confessions.' Preface to *Ductor Dubitantium* (or, as Whewell would have called it, 'Medulla Dubitationum'). Among authors he refers to W. Perkins (Chr.), who published *Aureae Casuum Conscientiae Decisiones*, Tribus Libris, &c. Basle, 12mo. 1609, translated from 'A Case of Conscience,' *Lond.* 1592, *Camb.* 1595, &c. and 'The whole treatise of Cases of Conscience,' *Lond.* 4to. 1611.

[2] Whewell and Grote abandoned the popular Paleian system, and revived the Butlerian principle of the *Moral Sense.*

[3] Sanderson's *Artis Logicae Compendium* had been printed for him at his own University in 1618.

and Decisions of divers practical Cases of Conscience, fol. Lond. 1649.

Tho. Barlow (*Queen's* Coll., Bodley's Librarian), the second bp. of Lincoln of that sirname, took up his predecessor Sanderson's work, by considering sundry *Cases of Conscience,* which were published posthumously in 1692.

H. Ferne, *S. Mary Hall* Oxon. and Trin. Coll. Camb., bp. of Chester, published in Dec. 1642 (Cambridge, E. Freeman and T. Dunster) *The Resolving of Conscience upon this Question* Whether...Subjects may take Arms and resist? *and* Whether that case be now? 4to. pp. 51. Also *Conscience Satisfied that there is no warrant for the Arms now taken up by Subjects.* Oxon. 1643, 4to.

J. Norman wrote *Cases of Conscience,* Lond. 1673, of which I know nothing.

Watt, so far as I am aware, does not record a single *eighteenth* century book of English casuistry; and indeed casuistry would be of small use without *canonists,* of whom even the commencement of that century could claim but the small list given in a note on p. 138, and perhaps Humphry Hody (*Wadh.,* Gk. Prof., and Archd.), and the Cambridge non-jurors, J. Johnson (Bene't), and Lawr. Howel (Jes.), and, perhaps one of the greatest, John Ayliffe, ejected fellow of *New College,* (author of 'the Antient and Present State of the University of Oxford,' 2 vols. 1714), who published his *Parergon Juris Canonici Anglicani,* 1726; also 'The Law of Pawns,' 1732, and 'A new Pandect of the Roman Civil Law,' (with a bibliographical list) fol. 1734.

CHAPTER XI.

LAW.

A Serjeant of the Lawe ware and wise,
That often hadde y been at the Parvis [1].

Chaucer's *Prologue*.

IN old times the faculty of Law undertook to teach the *jus utrumque*, and to give separate degrees in Canon and Civil Law [2].

The old English CANON LAW consisted of the body of legatine and provincial canons, promulgated and adopted in this country, as well as the Roman *corpus* of Decretals, Clementines and Extravagants collected in the twelfth and three following centuries. The *decretum* of Gratian of course included Mercator's forged additions to Isidore, on which so much of the pretensions of the See of Rome is founded.

Though there were separate degrees in Canon and Civil law, there was yet a close connexion between the two, so that (as Mr Mullinger shews) when Occam attacked one he aimed a blow at the other. They were connected also in the university course, *i.e.* a candidate for the doctor's degree was not allowed to enter on Canon law until he had heard lectures in Civil for

---

[1] *Parvis* (paradisus), a lean-to building, such as was used by the lawyers at S. Paul's, and by the scholars at S. Mary's church, Oxon. for the afternoon exercise of 'sitting in generals' or little-go (*in paruiso*) *iuramenti gratiâ*.

[2] In *Bedell* Stokys' *Book* (*ap.* Peacock *On the Statutes*) are given the proceedings at the '*Vepers in Canon and Civell*, and the *Commensment in Canon and Civyll*' as they were conducted about 1555.

three years[1]. It is interesting to observe from the information gathered in Mr J. B. Mullinger's early History of Cambridge (1873), how the study of law was from the first little encouraged in the universities; and, as respect for learning and culture increased, the law of the period met with disinterested *dis*couragement. And, on the other hand, when Pope John XXII. had ordered the Constitutions and Decretals to be read in the schools at Cambridge in 1317, that study had tended to exterminate others of greater estimation[2]. In the fourteenth and fifteenth centuries the statutes of several halls and colleges permitted a limited number of inmates to study Canon law with special permission, and a still smaller number to read Civil law.

Although a stop had been put to the ancient study by K. Henry VIII.'s royal prohibition, yet 'afterwards' (says Fuller) 'Scholars applyed themselves to the *reformed Canon-Law*...... to enable themselves for Chancellours, Officials, &c. in several Dioceses: yet so that *Canon-Law* did never after *stand by it self* (as subsisting a distinct Faculty wherein any commenced) but was annexed to Civil-Law, and the Degree denominated from the later. And although *Civilians* keep *Canon-Law* in *Commendam* with their own Profession, yet both twisted together are scarce strong enough (especially [1655] in our sad dayes) to draw unto them a liberal Livelihood[3].'

It is only surprising that the study did not expire altogether, considering the sudden failure of the *Reformatio Legum Ecclesiasticarum* (1551—3), on the death of K. Edward VI. English Canon Law had been limited, and, so to speak, embodied in the Statute law two years before Henry forbade its study. 25 Hen. VIII. *cap.* 19. § 7 gives express sanction to the then received canons, constitutions, &c. which are not contrary to the general laws of the realm. Even received *foreign* Canon

---

[1] They interpenetrated even in the university ceremonies. At the 'Vespers in Canon and Civil' (on the day before commencement) the proctor was to say 'to the yongest Doctour in *Cyvill* iff the Scolys be kepte in *Canon*, Domine Doctor, querratis Rationem Diversitatis. And iff the Scolys be in *Cyvyll*, the yongest Doctour in *Canon* shall aske Rationem Diversitatis.' *Bedell* Stokys' *Book* (1555) ap. *Peacock's* Statutes Univ. *Camb.* p. *l.*

[2] Dyer, *Priv. Cant.* I. 14, 534.

[3] Fuller, *Hist. Camb.* § VI. end.

Law was included under these terms according to *cap.* 21. § 1. Coke's opinion, as given in Gibson's Codex, p. xxix, was that 'when the Convocation makes Canons concerning matters which properly appertain to them, and the Sovereign has confirmed them, they are binding on the whole realm.' Lord Hardwicke, however, laid down that the post-reformation constitutions of the church, after royal confirmation, bind the *spiritual* body, as between members of that body, but not the laity[1], at any rate not so as to subject them to pecuniary penalties.

Lord Hardwicke, moreover, (when he was known as Mr Attorney-General Yorke) had laid down[2] that the law by which the university itself was governed internally was a compound of Civil and Canon Law, and that our universities (like that of Paris) had been, by various grants from the crown, freed from the courts of Common Law, the University courts being practically subject to the *jus utrumque*[3]. Such considerations may have in some measure modified the effects of that sweeping royal edict of the sturdy Tudor monarch to the partial results of which we have referred, and which is thus recorded:—

K. Henry VIII. 'stung (as Fuller says) with the dilatorie pleas of the *Canonists* at *Rome* in point of his marriage, did in revenge destroy their whole Hive throughout the Vniversities.' Accordingly, in his Injunctions of 1534-5, he ordered that thenceforward no degree nor even *lectures* should be given in Canon Law[4].

In Q. Mary's reign three persons graduated in that faculty[5]. It was admitted indeed that the Canon Law was supposed to be included in Civil Law : and a few enthusiasts, like Hearne, may have dreamt of a good time coming, when it should again

---

[1] This implies (I suppose) that the laity are not held to be so bound in *foro exteriore;—in foro conscientiae* every churchman is bound.

[2] [Hurd's] *Opinion of an Eminent Lawyer*, 1751. On the other hand Dr Chapman, in his *Inquiry into the Right of Appeal* (see my *Univ. Life*, 74, 630), had maintained that the university was subject to Civil only and not to Canon Law at all.

[3] Dyer, *Hist. Camb.* i. 75, 76. *Priv. Camb.* i. 443—5.

[4] Fuller, *ut supra.* He had something of a precedent in the prohibition of *Civil* law laid upon the university of Paris by Honorius III. in 1220, and not finally removed till 1679.

[5] Peacock *On the Statutes*, Appendix, p. *l.* note.

be recognized by a special degree. He even knew an M.A. of Balliol (C. Browne, 1716), who had intended to proceed to the Bachelor and Doctor of Canon Law; only he died[1]. Dr Gardiner, the Vice-chancellor of that time, told him that they could not indeed hinder him, but that it would be very troublesome.

A few university canonists are mentioned in the note[2].

Thomas Wood (New Coll.) LL.D. (1703) and Barrister at Law, author of the *Institute of the Laws of England* [1720; ed. 10, 1772], published anonymously in 1708 *Some Thoughts concerning the Study of the Laws of England, Particularly in the Two Universities*, in a Letter to the Head of a College in *Oxford*[3].

He says 'the *Canon* Law is......read and practised within the Universities. And even Divines think themselves under a necessity to read the *Institutes* drawn up by *Lancellot* [Antwerp, 1566], or *Corvinus*, and to consult the *Decrees* and the *Decretals* with the *chief* Canonists for settling of Cases of Conscience, and to inform themselves in Church History. *This* method also is so far commendable: and if Divines would inspect the Registers of our Ecclesiastical Courts and *Clark* [Praxis Fr. Clark in Foro Ecclesiastico, 1666], as to the general Practice, they might be sufficiently qualified for the Offices in those Courts; the Profits of which honourable Posts are often

---

[1] *Reliqu. Hearn.* Bliss III. 165.

[2] *David Wilkins*, received the degree of D. D. at Cambridge, 1717. *anno aetatis suae* 32. He edited *Leges Saxonicae* (1721), and *Concilia* A.D. 446—A.D. 1717. (4 Vols. 1737.)

Bp. Edm. Gibson, M.A.1694, Queen's Coll. *Oxon.—Codex Juris Ecclesiae Anglicanae.* Lond. 1713, Oxon. 1761.

Richard Grey, M.A. 1718-19, Lincoln Coll. *Oxon.* wrote (beside *Memoria Technica*) *A System of Ecclesiastical Law* (abridged from Gibson's Codex), 1730, for which the University conferred on him the degree of D.D.

Richard Burn, D.C.L. 1762, Queen's Coll. *Oxon.—Ecclesiastical Law*, 1760-65. For others see p. 134.

[3] Ed. 2, 1727. Bodl. *Godwin Pamph.* 22. Wood published also in 1712 (Bowyer's press, v. ed. 4. 1730) *A new Institute of the Imperial or Civil Law, with Notes; shewing in some principal cases,...how the Canon Law, the Laws of England, and the Laws and Customs of other Nations, differ from it. In Four Books.* 8vo. In 1756 an oration on the same subject was delivered in Trinity Hall chapel by [Sir] James Marriott, a fellow of the society, shortly before he took his doctor's degree. It was afterwards published under the title *De Historia et Ingenio Juris Civilis et Canonici, cum Comparatione Legum* Angliae.

of necessity given to the Laity over the Clergy......As to the common Business, *Lynwood*[1] [Constit. Provincial, 1557], *Degg* [Parson's Counsellor, 1676], *Godolphin* [Repertorium Canonicum, 1678], *Watson*[2] [Complete Incumbent, 1701], &c. are the Oracles which our best Canonists will vouchsafe to consult upon all occasions ; and every Student may quickly learn the skill of turning to an Index as well as the most celebrated Practisers.' (N.B. '*Degg*' = Sir Simon Degge.) But at this time it was practically only the *Civil* Law which was taught by the University professors.

CIVIL LAW was encouraged by archbishop Theobald and taught at Oxford as early as 1149, when Vicarius lectured on the Pandects. He was silenced by K. Stephen, and many of the text-books were destroyed by private persons. These books had been *pauperibus praesertim destinati:*—whence Oxford law-students were known as *pauperistae*[3]. So closely was the study of civil law entwined with that of the canonist, that the blow struck at the one by K. Henry VIII. was almost fatal to the other. In the first year of K. James (1603) there were rumours at Oxford that the very existence of the faculty of (Civil) Law was threatened[4], but, a demonstration being made in convocation by Dr Leonard Hutten (deputy Vice-chancellor), and Dr H. Marten of New College, letters were sent to the Chancellor and to the earl of Devonshire, and the danger was averted[5].

This study had been restored at Cambridge in 1654-5 on

---

[1] Lindewood was Chaplain to Abp. Chichely, Dean of Arches, and afterwards bp. of St David's in 1444. His *Constitutions* was one of the few books popular in the 15th century (Wordsworth, *Eccl. Biog.* [Tindall] II. 129) and by use it became practically the authoritative digest and Corpus Juris Canonici for England.

[2] The author is supposed to have been not Watson, but *Place* of York.

[3] Mullinger, *Hist. Univ. Camb.* (1873) p. 38. Malden's *Essay on the Origin of Univ.* p. 73.

[4] 'Before the end of the reign of Henry the VIII. a sufficient number of [*civilians*] could not be found for the public service, more particularly in foreign embassies and negotiations. It arose from a strong feeling of this deficiency that the Protector Somerset proposed to combine Clare Hall with Trinity Hall and the Hostel of St Nicholas in one great college for the study of the civil law: but the accomplishment of this project was defeated by the death of the young king.' Peacock, *Statutes*, App. A. *l.* note. Our first M.P.s, 160¾, were D.C.L.s.

[5] A. Wood's *Annals*, II. 281.

the petition of the university addressed to parliament and supported by the civilians of Doctors' Commons. Sir Matt. Hale, while he preferred the national system, used to lament the neglect of Civil Law as a *study*, so highly did he value the Digests or Pandects of Justinian as setting forth the grounds and reasons of the science[1]. The University degree continued to be required in the advocates of Doctors' Commons.

The Regius Professor of Civil Law at Cambridge was practically a Trinity Hall lecturer. Thomas Ayloffe was the first appointed in that century (1702). He was succeeded in 1714 by *Francis Dickins*, a friend of the famous T. Baker, the St John's *socius eiectus*. Of Dickins Zachary Grey says, 'No Professor (I may venture to say) from the Foundation ever made a greater Figure in the Chair, and few I believe have equalled him. His Command in the purest Latin Tongue, placed him upon a Level in that Respect, with two of our most celebrated Professors of Divinity, Dr Beaumont and Dr James, the one Master of Peterhouse, and the other of Queens' College; and was not supposed to fall greatly short of them in knowledge of the Questions and Management of the Disputations. And his Determinations upon some of the Questions that came before him were so excellent that they were much attended to and admired; and an eminent Divine has been heard to declare more than once, there were some Passages in St Paul's Epistles, he could not comprehend till he heard them explained by him in the most satisfactory manner from the Roman Laws[2].'

The requirements of the Cambridge statutes for a degree in laws were by no means small; but so utterly were they disregarded (perhaps for that very reason, as being hopelessly impracticable), that it was necessary in 1768 to *enact* that none should be admitted B.C.L. who could not produce a certificate to the effect that he had attended lectures for *three terms*. The statute required *five years*[3].

Nevertheless a harry-soph's gown[4] and a law degree con-

[1] Cooper's *Annals*, III. 463. Wordsworth, *Eccl. Biog.* IV. 540.

[2] Masters' *Life of* T. Baker, p. 110.

[3] *Camb. Calendar*, 1802, *pp.* 19, 20.

[4] 'The practice of studying civil law without reference to professional

tinued to be the refuge of the lazy and the dullard (as at a later period 'the botany poll' became); but the more respectable lawyers, on the other hand, were wont to contend for honours in the (philosophico-mathematical) tripos, thereby securing some amount of culture before devoting themselves to their professional studies.

Andrew Pemberton of Peterhouse, the university commissary in 1779, was sixteenth wrangler in 1751.

Francis Maseres of Clare, attorney-general of Quebec, and cursitor-baron of the exchequer, was 4th wrangler and primary senior chancellor's medallist 1752, and enjoyed some reputation as an algebraist.

Samuel Hallifax of Jesus and Trin. Hall[1] was 3rd wrangler and senior medallist in 1754. In 1770 he was law professor. He wrote an *Analysis of the Roman Civil Law*, which appears to have been employed as a text-book for lectures by Dr Joseph Jowett[2] (LL.B. Trin. Hall, 1775), his successor in 1781. It

views, and too often with a view of escaping the more severe studies which are required for the degree of bachelor of arts, has not tended to augment the estimation in which the faculty is held, notwithstanding the very laudable efforts which have been made by the present professor of civil law to maintain its credit and character.' [J. W. Geldart, LL.D. Cath. and Trin. Hall, was not succeeded by Sir H. S. Maine until 1847.] Peacock *On the Statutes* (1841), App. A. *p.* li. *n.* A *Quarterly Reviewer* says (1827, p. 262), 'The professor of civil law at Cambridge, where there is a college expressly endowed for this study, obliges all law-students to attend his lectures and examinations; and has of late years published the names of those who distinguish themselves classed in the order of merit. But as the university at large have little information and feel little interest concerning these proceedings, in which he is sole arbiter, his honours, like foreign titles, lose the greater part of their dignity the mo-

ment they pass the confines of the small territory where they have been conferred.'

[1] I have seen a printed notice of professorial lectures on the Civil Law to commence in Trin. Hall on Monday, 12 Nov. 1787, at 10 A.M.

[2] Dr Jowett, who was tutor of Trin. Hall, was a man of small stature. About 1790, he enclosed a little corner from the public way to plant as a garden, whereupon some one (Porson, it is said) wrote—

A little garden little Jowett made
And fenced it with a little palisade;
A little taste had little Dr Jowett,
This little garden doth a little show it.

Or in Latin,

Exiguum hunc hortum fecit Jowettulus iste
Exiguus, uallo et muniit exiguo:
Exiguo hoc horto forsan Jowettulus iste
Exiguus mentem prodidit exiguam.

The professor having afterward laid

contained the heads of Hallifax's own course of Law lectures, and was printed several times at Cambridge (1774, 1779, 1795). I believe it was the only thing printed by a regius professor of Civil Law at either university in the last century! Hallifax was also professor of arabic (1768), and bishop of Gloster and St Asaph (1781, 1789).

John Wilson of Peterhouse, of the Common Pleas, was senior wrangler in 1761.

Jeremiah Pemberton of Pembroke, the commissary in 1784, was 2nd wrangler and senior medallist in 1762.

Ri. Pepper Arden (lord Alvanley), of the Common Pleas, of Trinity, 12th wrangler in 1766.

Edward Law (lord Ellenborough) of Peterhouse, was 3rd wrangler and senior medallist in 1771.

Edward Christian of S. John's, first Downing Professor, was 3rd wrangler in 1779.

Not one of these took a degree in law except professor Hallifax, and that not until ten years after his degree in arts.

T. Wood, in the tract (1708) to which reference has been made already, asks, 'Why should not the COMMON LAW of England be studied at the universities; being "of infinitely more use amongst us even than the Civil and Canon Laws", and of more value (as he says) than the ordinary studies of those societies?' 'Because of this Ignorance you may often hear our Lawyers say, they had rather have any other Clients than Clergymen or Scholars; for they ask so many odd Questions, and will have a Reason for everything in their own way: whereas a good Reason in the *Schools* is not always a good Reason in a *Court*.' He shews the practical utility of a knowledge of Common Law for Country Gentlemen, University Residents, and the Clergy[1], whose predecessors used to study the

out his estate in gravel, the following postscript was added:—

Because this garden made a little talk,
He changed it to a little gravel walk.

The *false* reputation of having written the epigram, coupled with his notorious whiggery, cost (archd.) Fr. Wrangham a fellowship at Trin. Hall,

and a lawsuit. *Facetiae Cantab.* p. 200. G. Pryme's *Recoll.* 246. Gunning II. i.

[1] About 1658 Matthew Robinson, having left his fellowship at St John's Camb. for a country cure, was already 'by reading the councils well acquainted with the canon law.' Mayor's *Robinson*, p. 53.

Canon Law, while they do not now know anything of the
Common Law which has superseded it. He enumerates several
acts with which the Clergy ought to be acquainted: and,
after lamenting the want of a 'complete *System* of our Laws'
(p. 43), T. Wood commends among the 'methods then in existence, *Finch's Discourse of Law* as 'the most methodical Book
extant that ever was wrote by one of our Profession; it almost
follows the method of *Justinian's Institutes.*' Time however
required its revision and augmentation with reference to Coke
upon Littleton. *Wentworth* on the Office of an Executor
(rather than *Swinburn*[1] or *Godolphin*), and *Hale's* Pleas of the
Crown, should be read with books II. and III. of [Sir H.] *Finch's*
Discourse (a translation of *Nomotechnia* ou description del com-
mun Leys d'Angleterre, 1613). Pp. 44—54 contain accounts
of some supplementary works, 'abridgements' and books of reference recommended.

He concludes by observing that the Chancellor's Court at
Oxford 'might be so regulated as to conduce very much to
improve this Study' of Common Law: for the exclusive attach-
ment to the *Civil* Law is productive of great inconvenience and
disorder; while the use of *Common* Law is required in certain
cases by the letter of the University Statutes, &c.

Fifty years after this the celebrated William Blackstone
(*Pemb.*, fellow of *All Souls* and *Queen's*, afterwards, 1761—6,
principal of *New Inn Hall*, where Alberic Gentilis, who came
to be law professor at *Oxford*, in the 16th cent. had resided) was made first Vinerian professor of the Common Law of
England (1758), and delivered excellent lectures.

He virtually answered the question, which Wood had asked
fifty, and Sir J. Fortescue three hundred years before.

Blackstone shewed in his inaugural lecture or *Discourse* on
the Study of Law (4to. *Oxon.* 1758, pp. 40), that not only was

[1] H. Swinburne *on Testaments*, Ridley's *View of the Civil and Eccles.
Law* (1634), *Dialogues betweene a
D.D. and a Student in the lawes*
(1569), Bacon's *Elements of the Common Laws* (1630), Cowell's *Instit. juris
Anglic.* (Cantabr. 1609), Grotius *De
Jure B. et Pacis*, &c. were read by
Matt. Robinson in the middle of the
17th century. He had also some acquaintance with Canon Law. (*Mayor's*
Robinson, *p.* 53.) J. Godolphin's book
was called the *Orphan's Legacy.*

Common law unpopular at the universities because it was expressed in other languages beside latin (as Sir J. Fortescue had
remarked, *de Laudibus Legum Angliae,* printed about 1490),
but because the clergy had been jealous for their own law, and
had withdrawn from the rising *forum saeculare* in accordance
with a canon of 1217. Thereupon the municipal lawyers finding themselves excluded from the universities[1], had founded
their own colleges in the Inns of Court: and the universities
knowing Civil law to be founded on reason had not thought it
worth while to compete with the professional society in teaching
the Common law, which was not very valuable as an instrument
of culture.

Sir W. Blackstone had published his *Essay on Collateral
Consanguinity* (with reference to *All Souls*) in 1750 when he
took his doctor's degree, and soon afterwards his *Analysis of the
Laws.* The *Commentaries* first appeared at *Oxon.* in 4 vols.
1765—8. His successor in the professorship, Sir Robert Chambers (*Linc.* and *Univ.*), B.C.L., was, like him and *James* Blackstone (prof. in 1793), at once Vinerian Prof. and principal of
New Inn Hall. Chambers had been an Indian judge, and in
1791 was chief justice.

The next professor, Richard Woodeson (1777—93), D.C.L.
fellow of *Magd.*[2], published *Elements of Jurisprudence,* 1789 ;
and a *Systematical View of the Laws of England,* as treated in
a course of Vinerian Lectures read at Oxford. 3 vols. 1792—3,
re-edited in 1834. Dr G. Croft (in a *Letter to a Young Gentleman,* Wolverhampton, 1784) bears witness that 'no diligence
has been spared' in these lectures.

In the last century two medical and *six* Common-Law fel-

[1] In the last century and the commencement of the present, it was not
uncommon for gentlemen intending
for the law to leave the University
without taking a degree. This was
the case for example with *W. Boscawen*
(Chalmers' *Dict. Biog.*), who was a
gentleman-commoner of Exeter Coll.
about 1770, then studied at the Middle
Temple, and learnt the practice of
special pleading under Mr (afterwards

judge) Buller. However, in 1827 a
Quarterly Reviewer said (Pp. 236—7)
that a very considerable proportion
of English barristers were graduates,
though of attorneys not one in a
thousand, in spite of the privilege of
short service in an office granted to
graduates by 1 *and* 2 Geo. IV. *c.* 48.

[2] He is mentioned in Best's *Memorials,* § XVII.

lowships were founded at Oxford: at Cambridge only one of the former, and *none* in law[1].

Cambridge was more backward in getting an accredited teacher of Common Law.

Edward Christian of S. John's (3rd wrangler 1779) and Gray's Inn, had given lectures for three years[2], when, in May 1788, W. Annesley, M.P., master of Downing, gave him a professorship of Common Law. Half a year later, the university confirmed his title as 'Professor of the Laws of England' until such time as Downing College should be founded. The professor was one of the counsel in the long-contested suit between the university of Cambridge and the heirs of the founder, sir Jacob Downing. Christian became Downing Professor in 1800, but delivered his course of two dozen lectures in rooms in S. John's. His *Syllabus* was printed, Lond. 1797. Gunning says that his edition of Blackstone (the 12th), Lond. 1796, 'was very creditable to him[3].' His charges to the grand jury, as chief justice of the Isle of Ely were very queer; and he died in 1823 in the full vigour of his incapacity.'

At this period there was no proper lecture-room for the Professors of Civil and Common Law[4], and indeed the need of them was hardly felt, so lax were the requirements for the degree, while, in respect of the other studies of the university, law students were more 'wary and wise' than even Chaucer's lawyer, for they never made their appearance *in parvisiis* at all!

It was not till 1851 that *bona fide* examinations took the place of the old farcical 'disputations' for the degree of B.C.L. (Bachelor of Civil Law) at Oxford[5], yet some forty years earlier Professor J. W. Geldart had set himself to remove the stain upon his faculty at Cambridge[6], where it had for at least a

[1] F. W. Newman (Huber's) *English Universities*, Vol. II.

[2] I have seen a printed notice to the effect that Prof. Christian would commence one of his courses on the Laws of England on Monday 13 Mar. 1786 in S. John's Coll. at 11 A.M.

[3] Gunning *Reminisc.* I. vi.

[4] Ingram's *Necessity of Introducing Divinity*, 1792. *p.* 108 *n.* Camb.

Univ. Calendar, 1802. p. 33. Cooper's *Annals,* IV. 432.

[5] Cox's *Recollections*, p. 360.

[6] Malden's *Essay on the Origin of Universities*, p. 130. It is within the memory of man that a Law Professor in the Cambridge Schools was forced to say to a hopeless candidate, '*Descendas:*' the man replied, in latin equal to the occasion, '*Non descendebo.*' Another

century been considered the royal road to a degree for those
who took fright at the approaching art examination.

The Civil-Law Examination was commenced in 1816. It
appears however from the following quotation that in earlier
days also this degree had been fairly guarded.

·John Taylor, the critic, of S. John's, Cambridge, writes in
1755 to Andrew Coltee Ducarel, D.C.L., *S. John's, Oxon.*, one of
the first fellows of the Society of Antiquaries established in
that year, an interesting letter relative to the migration of a
friend from Oxford. He says that 'King's is esteemed the
cheapest' college, but he thinks they make up by high charges
in some particulars. Taylor adds 'there is a checque held upon
those that vibrate between Arts and Law,' in the shape of a
fine. Also he believed 'the common exercise must be kept
under the Law Professor: for though the University will give
him an *ad eundem* degree, they will not be so good-humoured
or indulgent as to suffer his *exercises* at Oxford to proceed *ad
eundem* also.' (Nichols' *Lit. Anecd.* IV. 666.)

One of the points of Ld. Chancellor Macclesfield's scheme
for University Reform was the provision of a Professor of the
'*Law of Nature and Nations.*' But although this plan[1] was
committed to writing in 1718, and printed by Gutch as a
curiosity in 1781, it was not till 1869 that a Professor of
International Law was appointed at Cambridge in virtue of
a bequest from Dr Whewell. At Christ Church there were
lectures on Puffendorf in 1738 (*West* to *Gray*, Dec. 2). His
de Officio Hominis et Civis juxta Legem Naturalem was also a
morning-lecture subject at Trin. Coll. Cant. in 1755. A System
extracted from Grotius *de Jure* was printed *at Cambridge in*
1703. And Rutherforth's *Institutes* 1754-6, were his Grotius
lectures at S. John's.

professor out of sheer pity asked one
person under examination from whom
he could get no answer to more strictly technical questions:—'If you go
down Chancery-Lane, what is the first
court you come to on the right?' But
the only answer he could elicit was,

'*The Old-Bailey.*' This unsuccessful
'harry-soph' shewed his wit when it
was too late by declaring that the professor had plucked him for not answering a question which was not in
any of the books.

[1] *University Life*, pp. 568, 579.

CHAPTER XII.

HISTORY AND MODERN LANGUAGES, WITS, POETS, ANTIQUARIES AND SAXONISTS.

Nerissa. What say you then to *Fauconbridge* the yong Baron of *Engʔand?*
Portia. You know I say nothing to him, for hee vnderstands not me, nor
I him; he hath neither *Latine, French* nor *Italian,* and you will come into the
court & sweare that I haue a poore pennie-worth in the *English.*

The Merchant of Venice, Act i.

IN very early times universities seem to have taken great interest in such geography and history as was known. As; according to a well known legend, Herodotus read his history at a panathenaic festival when young Thucydides was by, so we read that Giraldus de Barri (Cambrensis) recited his Topographia Hiberniae in the convention of the university of Oxford at the close of the 12th century, and Rolandius his chronicle in the presence of the professors and scholars of Padua.

Before the twelfth century the study of History meant reading the work of Paulus Orosius, a book founded on his master Augustine's *De civitate Dei*[1].

In later times a taste sprang up for rhyming chronicles, and *mirabilia mundi;* then for moral tales and anecdote, flowers of histories, illustrative of the Virtues and Vices, and (with the exception of the interesting and romantic character of their incidents) bearing scarcely higher claims to the title than the History of the Fairchild Family, or the story of Sandford and Merton. Such were the *Gesta romanorum* and the *Speculum historiarum,* printed in 1483. The era of the invention of printing brought forward the works of the chroniclers, which continued to be popular in the case of Holingshed and Foxe's

---

[1] In 1703, Cellarii *Notitia Orbis Antiqui* (also 1783), and *Historia Universalis* were printed at Camb. In 1712, 14, Varenii *Geographia* (ed. Ja. Jurin) was published there, Newton having edited it in 1681.

Actes and Monuments long after the Elizabethan times; as was the more modern Baker's Chronicle to the memory of recent generations.

Fulke Greville, Ld. Brooke, designing to found a professorship of History and Politics (*Civilis Scientiae*) at Cambridge, offered the post to G. I. Vossius (*epist.* 89, 90) 13 Sept. 1624. Eventually Is. Dorislaw, also of Leyden, was appointed, but offence was taken at the supposed political tendency of his first course of lectures on Tacitus. (*Ward* to *Usher*, 16 May, 1628.)

Oxford boasted a Reader of Histories or Professor of Ancient History from the foundation of W. Camden in 1622. Among those who held this office were (1773) W. Scott, Lord Stowell, (brother of Ld. Eldon; he was also Queen's Advocate, and then Judge of the High Court of Admiralty) of *Univ.*; and Tom Warton of *Trin.* the younger, who succeeded him in 1785, the same year that he was made poet laureat. Though there were then no such professors at Cambridge, we find Ambrose Bonwicke the younger reading the 'Jesuit Bussières' *flosculi historiarum delibati*, at St John's, in 1710. A century earlier Florus, Gellius, and Macrobius had been read, and in the 18th something was done at Bentley's suggestion (*Monk* I. 337) towards an account of modern geographical discoveries in an appendix by James Jurin, fellow of Trinity, to his edition of Bernhard Varenius in 1712.

In the last century, soon after Lord Macclesfield had been scheming for their benefit, Geo. I. founded for each university a professorship of *Modern History and Modern Languages* in 1724, to lecture, with a stipend of 400 *li.*, out of which they were, says Hearne (May, 1724[1]), to appoint two deputies, each to instruct twenty scholars[2] to be nominated by the crown, each of whom is to learn two languages, but yet not to deviate from the university course. Hearne himself thought that it showed the

---

[1] *Reliqu. Hearn.* II. 200. See also the end of the Report of the 1st Univ. Commission.

[2] According to the rules revised at Cambridge in 1772, not more than six-and-twenty pupils, nominated in certain proportion by the Heads of the different colleges. When W. Smyth of Peterhouse succeeded Symonds in 1807, he refused to restrict the number of his pupils.

depths to which learning had fallen in 1734, that 'nothing is now hardly read but Burnett's romance or libel, call'd by him *The History of his own Times.* 'Tis read by men, women, and children [1].'

Samuel Harris, of Peterhouse, was appointed first Modern Professor at Cambridge, October, 1724. K. George II. confirmed the letters patent for the professorships, and continued Harris in that office at Cambridge by a licence dated April 3, 1728[2]. His *Oratio inauguralis* is dated 1725.

The *Oxford* professors were :

D. Gregory, Ch. Ch. (appointed Oct. 27, 1724).

W. Holmes (pres^t. of St John's) 1736.

Jos. Spence, New Coll., 1743.—J. Vivian, Balliol, 1768.—T. Nowell, Oriel, 1771—1801.

In 1727 Dr Rawlinson, writing from Rome, expressed his approval of the new professorships[3] as likely to supply tutors for young noblemen and gentlemen in the place of 'impudent and ignorant French Hugonots and Scotch pedlers.' Hearne adds : 'To our shame at present be it spoken, both tutors and pupils come and go very little skilled in the languages : and that little they know of the learned languages is useless, as the pronunciation, especially in Italy, is widely different from ours, in a manner unintelligible to us and them, as the doctor, he says, found by experience[4].'

---

[1] *Ibid.* III. 125, 129.

[2] Cooper's *Annals*, IV. 185, 196.

[3] I am indebted to F. Madan Esq. of B. N. C. for a reference to the *Gloucester Journal* for April 19, 1725, containing a "List of the Gentlemen upon the New Establishment for the study of Modern Languages and History, in the University of Oxford," containing the following names :

Mr [Dan.] Burton, A.M. Stud. Ch. Ch.

,, [J.] Burnaby, A.M. Oriel.

,, [J.] Douglass, A.B. Balliol.

,, [Benj.] Pearson, A.B. Queen's.

,, [T.] Velly, A.B. Queen's.

,, [Walt.] Francks, A.B. Merton.

,, [H.] Bland, Gent. Com. Corpus.

,, — Reynolds, Fellow of New Coll.

,, [J.] Totty, Scho. Worc.

Mr [Gil.] West, Com^r. Stud. Ch. Ch.

,, [G.] Wyndham, Scho. Wadham.

,, [Sam.] Holcombe, Com^r. Trin.

,, [J.] Merrick, Scho. St John's.

,, [J.] Whistler, Com^r. Magd. Hall.

,, [W.] Saunders, Com^r. Wadham.

[4] *Reliqu. Hearn.* II. 311.

In the summer of 1728, J. Jebb of Christ's while waiting for a fellowship was hoping to be put on the new list of the Kings 'modern Scholars.' He trusted that his taking Holy Order would not disqualify him; for 'most on ye last List were of y^t Profession.' Before his ordination to the curacy at Sandy he had entertained the idea that a place on the Modern List might lead to a secretaryship in England or Ireland or to some envoy or nobleman, as

Shallet Turner of Peterhouse succeeded Harris at Cambridge in 1735, and in 1762 was followed by Lawrence Brockett of Trinity. We learn indeed from [Green's] *Academic* (pp. 22, 25), that about the year 1750 young men were imbibing a taste for modern languages, and that among those who were proficient therein were numbered many who were also skilful in the ancient tongues[1].

The poet Gray (then of Pembroke) succeeded Brockett in 1768 : but it is surprising to find that even at his death in 1771 there had not been a lecture delivered since the foundation of the professorship in 1724. Ill-health was the poet's own excuse, and it is stated that he liberally rewarded the teachers of French and Italian in the university. The terms of his patent allowed him to find a deputy in *one* of the two branches of his duty. At Oxford also in 1790 the professor employed an assistant in each language ;...each of them receives an annual stipend from the Professor, and...they attend their Pupils at their own Apartments in the Colleges[2].

It is to the credit of St John's college that at last was found a successor to Gray who did deliver lectures in History[3].

John Symonds (1771—1807) proposed a set of rules which were accepted by the heads in 1772, the Cambridge professorship being in general more unfettered than the corresponding one at Oxford. *Inter alia* Symonds arranged that the fees of Noblemen, Fellow-Commoners, and their attendant Private-tutors, should be devoted to remunerating the Language-Masters and buying books, maps, &c. He collected near 1000 volumes, each whereof was stamped *Scholae Historicae Cantabrigiensis Liber.* His course was to lecture (1) on *Rules* for the

---

[1] In another pamphlet belonging to the same controversy as the *Academic* it is asserted that if the professor of History would reside at Cambridge with his proper assistants a numerous audience would regularly attend his it had done for those in the last list; for such of the set as were taken any notice of. He understood French already, and something of Italian. (I am indebted to the Rev. H. G. Jebb for these particulars.)

lectures or classes. *Free Thoughts upon University Education; Occasioned by the present Debates at Cambridge...By a sincere well-wisher,* &c, 1751, p. 14. (Trin. Coll. Lib. x. 14. 14.)

[2] Philalethes' *Reply to* Knox, p. 9.

[3] I have seen printed notices of the Professor's Lectures to commence 'Monday, 13 Nov. 1775,' 'Tu. 18 April, 1780,' and 'Tu. 22 Nov. 1786.' Also a copy of Rules dated 1771.

Study of History, enumeration of *points* for subsequent discussion, and of *text-books*. (2) Causes of the Fall of Rome. (3) State of Commerce, Literature, Civil Government, Feudal System. (4) Christianity, centuries I—XV. These topics occupied a good many lectures, wherein the history of England, France, Spain, Germany, and Italy, was discussed, with allusions occasionally to the Eastern Empire, the Greek and Saracen, and, in later times, to Turkey. He made a great point of reprobating 'Intolerance in Religion and in Civil Government, whatever form that Government might bear. The matter and number of the lectures have been altered almost every year, the Professor sometimes omitting two or three entirely, which had been given before, in order to introduce new circumstances, which either study or reflection for the last *ten* years had *unhappily* afforded[1].'

He was succeeded in 1807 by W. Smyth, tutor of Peterhouse. He was a whig but did not obtrude his political sentiments upon his hearers. Though an admirable lecturer he would permit no notes to be taken[2], but in 1840 he published altogether five volumes of lectures on *Modern History* and on the *French Revolution*, which are still read. He sometimes explained points in political economy[3]. His lectures were eloquent, thoughtful and popular. But when the Previous Examination was established, a great part of his audience became too busy to continue their attendance[4].

The nearest approach to Polit. Economy lectures in the last century were Paley's (at Christ's), which formed the ground of his *Principles of Moral and Political Philosophy*[5], published in 1785. Ro. Acklom Ingram of Queens', senior wrangler in 1784, and afterwards tutor of his college, did indeed attempt to

[1] *Camb. Univ. Calendar* 1802, *pp.* 27—29. J. Jebb a thorough-going whig prepared 'some political or constitutional lectures' in the latter half of 1773 (Life by *Disney*, p. 50.), but I do not know that he ever delivered them. Possibly he was deterred by the fate of his Greek Testament class.

[2] *Facetiae Cantab.* 1836, p. 158.

[3] *Prof.* Pryme's *Recoll.* p. 120.

[4] Whewell, *Principles of Engl. Univ. Education*, p. 71.

[5] C. V. Le Grice of Trin. edited an *Analysis* of Paley's *Moral and Political Philosophy*, Camb. 1795. Smithson Tennant professor of chemistry who was killed in 1815 had projected a work on political economy (Dyer, *Privil. Camb.* II. ii. 99).

institute lectures on political economy[1], and went so far even
as to print 'a Syllabus or Abstract of a System of Political
Philosophy' in 1799, in the preface to which he advocated the
establishment of public lectures on the subject, 'but not meeting with suitable encouragement he declined persevering in his
plan[2].' Mr G. Pryme of Trinity delivered his first lecture in
March, 1816, and twelve years later received the title of Professor of Political Economy.

Adam Smith's '*Nature and Causes of the* Wealth of Nations'
was published in 1776. The author had left Balliol without
a degree, having been surprised when reading Hume's new
Treatise of Human Nature, by the college authorities, in 1741.
The remarks which he makes in book v. § 1, would not tend
to make it a work to be favourably received in Oxford. I do
not know that it was *commonly* read in Cambridge in the last
century[3], but Pryme[4] (the future professor) came across it at
the age of fourteen, in 1795, when his private tutor read it
with his older pupils, B. C. Raworth and A. C. Verelst, before
they went up to Trinity Hall and Clare; and Pitt, who took
his first degree (M.A.) in the year of its publication, shewed
himself so familiar with it (1780), that there is great probability
in his biographer's supposition[5] that he read it with Pretyman
(Bp. Tomline) in his protracted residence in Pembroke Hall.

If Walpole and Gray had been less exclusive and more
popular, and if Gray had worked as professor of Modern Languages, french and italian literature[6] might have taken more
hold at Cambridge than was the case. But while men are
much occupied in the study of greek and latin, their classical
tastes are already provided with as piquant diet as any of the
moderns could produce. As at the present day, a few students

---

[1] Dyer, *Hist. Camb.* I. 220.

[2] *Camb. Univ. Calendar* for 1802,
p. 159 n.

[3] The fact that a '*Complete Analysis
or Abridgment of* Adam Smith's *Wealth
of Nations*' was edited by Jer. Joyce
at Cambridge in 1797, makes it probable however that it *was*.

[4] *Autobiog. Recoll.* 23.

[5] See Stanhope's *Life of* Pitt, I. 17.

[6] In 1710, J. Byrom a scholar of
Trinity enquired for Bentivoglio's His-
toria della Guerra dalla Fiandra &c.,
Tasso, Ariosto, Marino, Fulvio, G.
Testi, Petrarcha &c., Father Paolo's
Hist. Concil. Trident. And in Spanish
Don Quixote, Quevedo's Visions, &c.

learnt from authorized teachers on their own account. Mons. René La Butte taught french from about the year 1742 till his death in 1790. He had been one of Bowyer's printers, and was the sole compositor of Gardiner's tables of logarithms[1]. Dr Conyers Middleton had introduced him at Cambridge, where he printed, married, and taught french with great reputation. A contemporary of his was Agostino Isola, who had the honour of instructing at a considerable interval of time the poets Gray and Wordsworth[2] in the italian language. He could boast of Pitt also among his numerous pupils. He was a native of Milan, but was forced to fly from his home because a friend had taken up an English book which Isola had carelessly left about. Charles Isola of Emmanuel, esquire bedell, 1797-18, was his son, whose little orphan, Emma, won the heart of Charles and Mary Lamb in one of their visits to Cambridge, and was adopted by them, until in 1833 she became Mrs Moxon.

The encouragement of modern languages was thought an object beside the scope of the university by some in 1788, when the author of *Considerations on the Oaths* complained (p. 39) that in 1782 the Syndics of the Press had employed the £500 arising from the tax on sheet almanacs to 'a fac-simile of the Beza ms.' (Kipling's celebrated performance), and '*Italian Sonnets.*' £50 was assigned 'To Sig. Isola towards printing a new edition of Tasso's *Gerusalemme Liberata*[3].'

H. F. Cary, the translator of Dante (1806, 1813), when at *Ch. Ch.* (B.A. 1794) was instructed in italian by U. Oliviero. T. J. Mathias (Trin.) was a good italian scholar.

How John Delaport proposed to stimulate conversation in the french language at Emmanuel Coffee-House in 1763, I have already narrated in my *University Social Life*[4]; where I have also given a note on the encouragement which the french

[1] Hone's *Year Book* 683. Nichols' *Lit. Anecd.* ii. 459, 726. Labutte's French Grammar was published in 1764; and in 1790 with a prefatory analysis of the subject.
[2] *Memoirs of* W. Wordsworth, i. 14. W. Gooch also learnt of him. See his letter in an Appendix.

[3] Agostino Isola printed some Italian Selections, translated into English verse by some Gentlemen of the Univ. of Cambridge, 8vo. Lond. 1778, Camb. 1788. Also Ariosto's *Orlando Furioso*, Camb. 1789, Lond. 1790.
[4] pp. 143, 144, 208 *n.*

language received in our collegiate foundations of the *fourteenth* century. Mr Thompson Cooper mentions that Herbert Marsh (Joh.) knew more german than the rest of his countrymen.

Something was done both by the universities and by individual colleges in enabling students to carry their researches in botany, oriental studies or any *specialité*, beyond the seas.

William Worts' will (1709)[1] was to provide, in process of time, when the interest should be sufficient, after endowing certain other things, an exhibition of £100 *per annum* for each of two young Cambridge bachelors of arts, who should be sent abroad severally for two years, and should write a descriptive letter every month to be placed in the Library.

It seems that the period of absence was ultimately extended to three years, and the required letters reduced to two. A list of Worts' bachelors is given below[2].

This was not altogether a new invention, for Barrow had leave to travel upon similar conditions in 1656, when he was a fellow of Trinity. He wrote his letters in Latin verse. Vernon the botanist had (as will be seen) a travelling-fellowship from Peterhouse at the end of the seventeenth century: and Fynes

---

[1] Cooper's *Annals*, IV. 86.

[2] Worts' Travelling Bachelors, Cambridge.

1767 P. H. Maty, Trin. Son of a hollander, 11th wrang. Translated Reisbeck's Travels 1787. Index to Philos. Transact. Review 1782-6.

1768 J. North, Caius, 7th wrang.

1770 Nedham Dynoke, Joh. 4th sen. opt.

1771 T. Kerrich, Magd. 2nd sen. opt. University Librarian 1797. Preb. Lincoln.

1772 Fred. Browning, King's.

1775 Alleyne Fitz Herbert, Joh. (Ld. St Helen's), 2nd sen. opt. 1st medal.

1777 C. [Manners] Sutton, Emm. 15th wrang. Abp. Cantuar. 1804. 'Description of five British species of Orobanche,' Linn. Soc. 1797.

1778 Edm. Morris, Trin. 1st jun. opt.

1779 H. Jacob, King's.

1780 W. Meeke, Emm. (fellow of Downing).

1782 J. Browne, Trin. wooden-spoon.

1783 T. Hardy, Sid. 5th jun. opt.

1786 T. Ellis, Caius, 3rd sen. opt.

1788 E. Morris, Pet. 10th wrang.

1789 H. Nic. Astley, Chr.

1791 Joshua Stephenson, Joh.

1792 J. Ellis, King's.

1794 Alex. Richardson, Bene't. 4th sen. opt.

1795 J. Singleton Copley, Trin. (Ld. Lyndhurst) 2nd wrang. 2nd Smith's prize.

1795 G. Caldwell, Jes. 10th wrang. 1st medallist.

1797 Roger Kingdon, Joh. 8th sen. opt. Translated a German theological work.

1798 Clement Carlyon, Pemb. M.D. 1813.

Moryson was similarly assisted in 1589. Sir William Browne made it a condition (1774) that his Peterhouse 'physick-fellows' should *not* have leave to travel.

Dr Radcliffe founded with an endowment of £600 *per ann.* two travelling-fellowships at Oxford for masters of arts 'entered upon the physick-line.' These were tenable for ten years and entailed travelling beyond the seas for five years at least; but rooms were provided in University College for the travellers. A list is subjoined in the notes[1].

Among travellers whom the universities produced, Edmund Chishull, *Corpus,* Oxon. was chaplain to the factory at Smyrna, 1698-1702, B.D. 1705. His *Travels in Turkey* were edited posthumously by Dr Mead in 1747, the author having written an appendix on Smyrnaean medals for Mead's Harveian oration in 1724. He wrote also a dissertation on the *Sigean Inscription* (1721), containing a review of a somewhat hasty private criticism of Bentley's. His *Antiquitates Asiaticae* (1724) contained an inscription from the Bosporus, which Bentley emended with marvellous sagacity, as circumstances afterwards contributed to shew. See Monk's *Bentley,* II. 156-9, 411, 412. T. Shaw (*Queen's* and *Edm. Hall*) who visited Barbary and the Levant about 1730, and J. Marshall (Chr.),

---

[1] Radcliffe's TRAVELLING MASTERS, *Oxford.*

1715 Noel Broxholme, *Ch. Ch.*
1715 Robert Wyntle, *Mert.*
1725 C. Peters, *Ch. Ch.* 'Of a Person bitten by a mad Dog,' 1745.
—— James Stephens, *Corpus* (resigned).
1731 Nat. Hickman, *Queen's.*
1735 J. Kidby, *Balliol.*
1741 J. Monro, *S. Joh.*
1745 G. Dowdaswell, *Ch. Ch.* (in Carmina Quadragesimalia, II.).
1751 Robert Lynch, *Corpus.*
1755 David Hartley, *Mert.* (M.P. Kingston-on-Hull) 'Argument on the Fr. Revolution,' 1794.
1760 Sam. Musgrave, *Corpus,* F.R.S.

(Medical and Classical works, 1760—81).
1761 J. Turton, *Queen's.*
1770 J. Colwell, *Trin.*
1771 Francis Milman, *Exeter.* Bart. F.R.S. 'Instances of the true Scurvy,' 1772.
1780 James Robertson, *Balliol.* (? 'On the Variation of the Compass at Jamaica,' 1806.)
1781 J. Sibthorpe, *Linc.*
1790 E. Ash, *Ch. Ch.* M.D., F.R.C.P., F.R.S. 'The Speculator,' 1790.
1791 James Haworth, *B.N.C.*
1800 C. Ri. Vaughan, *Mert.* (and *All Souls*) 'Narrative of the Siege of Zaragoza,' 1809.

who observed the astounding height of the Himalayas before Colebrooke, we shall have occasion to notice in the next chapter. Richard Chandler (fellow of *Magd.*, p. 12), having edited *Marmora Oxoniensia* for the Clarendon Press in 1763, and *Roman Antiquities* for the Dilettanti Society in 1769, was sent out by the latter body to travel in Greece and Asia. He published *Inscriptiones Antiquae...in Asia M. et Graecia praesertim Athenis Collectae*, Oxon. 1774. *Travels in Asia Minor*, Oxon. 1775. *Travels in Greece*, Lond. 1776. *History of Ilium and the Chersonesus of Thrace*, Lond. 1802. E. Daniel Clarke (Jes.), who travelled in Tartary, Circassia, Greece, Turkey, &c., belongs properly to the present century, as Sir G. Wheler (*Linc.*) is the property of the seventeenth.

The classical studies of a university with the leisure attainable in academic life, tend to produce a crop of no great value, though somewhat curious in its nature.

At the beginning of the present century the specimens of *facetiae* were useless and even noisome, but about the middle of the eighteenth there was a coterie of humorists who have left some reputation behind them. Such were Kit Smart (Pemb.), Joseph Warton (*Oriel*), and his more witty brother Tom Warton (*Trin.*), George Colman the elder and Bonnel Thornton (*Ch. Ch.*), and other contemporaries of Johnson and Shenstone. It may be that their time would have been better spent, and their peculiar talent better employed if there had been more encouragement in their day for application to classical and continental literature. However it does not seem that Porson's humour was much refined by his scholarship.

The generation of Pope (R. C.), Swift (T. C. D.), Prior (Joh.), Addison (*Qu.* and *Magd.*), Steele (*Mert.*), immediately succeeding Dryden (Trin.), was rather more hopeful. It produced the more elegant school of Chr. Pitt (*New Coll.*), Vincent Bourne (Trin.), and Samuel Wesley the younger (*Ch. Ch.*): but there was also Tom Brown and Edmund Neale (*alias* Mun Smith) expelled from *Christ Church*. Nicholas Amherst was removed from *St John's*, in an age which was not over particular, and Chr. Anstey (King's) was reprimanded. We may add to this list the minor wits who contributed to the *Oxford*

Sausage (1764). Herbert Beaver (*Corpus*), Michael Woodhull (*Linc.*), J. Kidgell (*Hert.*), Isaac Hawkins Browne (Trin. Coll. Camb.), and two Benet-Hall men, J. Hoadly and J. Duncombe. Ralph Bathurst, whose epigram was included in the collection, belonged to the preceding century. Among the poets and more respectable versifiers[1] we may mention T. Gray (Pet. and Pemb.), S. T. Coleridge (Jes.), W. Wordsworth (Joh.), W. Brome (Joh.), Elijah Fenton (Jes. and Trin. Hall), W. Whitehead (Clare), W. Mason (Joh. and Pemb.), W. Somerville (*New Coll.*), Gilbert West and G. Lyttelton (*Ch. Ch.*), T. Tickell (*Queen's*), W. Collins (*Qu.* and *Magd*), Ri. Jago (*Univ.*), W. Shenstone, S. Johnson, Heywood, Ri. Graves, Southern and J. Hawkins (*Pemb.*); C. Lloyd (Caius), G. Dyer (Emm.), Ro. Southey (*Ball.*). Beside these a large number of men tried their hands at translation. T. Creech (*Wadh.*) hanged himself at Oxford in 1700, thus avoiding the limit of our century. W. Gifford graduated at *Exeter*, as also did W. Tasker; W. Holwell and R. Polwhele and George Ld. Lyttelton at *Christ Church*, S. Barnet at *University*, and Dr S. Langley at *Pembroke*. Cambridge produced W. Tremenheere of Pembroke Hall, W. Clubbe of Caius, J. Duncombe of Corpus, Fr. Fawkes and Gilbert Wakefield of Jesus, G. Ogle of Sidney and R. Potter of Emmanuel; while Capel Lofft resided some time at Peterhouse.

Beside these, some of the more eminent men devoted a part of their energies to translation—as Ambrose Philips, Fenton, Broome, and Garth: Addison, Colman, Tickell, C. Pitt, and Yalden.

Joseph Trapp (*Wadham*) the professor of poetry gave a specimen of his skill in this department.

Of his successors in the professorship, which was tenable for five years, Ro. Lowth (*New Coll.*) and John Randolph (*Ch. Ch.*) were bishops, the latter with Ben. Wheeler (*Magd.*) being regius professors of Divinity: Ro. Holmes (*New Coll.*) was canon of *Ch. Ch.* and dean of Winchester; the Thomas Wartons, father (*Magd.*) and son (*Trin.*), have some reputation: Jo. Spence (*New Coll.*) was a friend of Pope and has preserved anecdotes of

[1] Ri. Duke and G. Stepney (Trin.), T. Otway J. Philips and W. King (*Ch. Ch.*), with Prior and Addison, belong properly to the seventeenth century.

him and of other contemporaries; he also published *Polymetis* (1747), a sort of eighteenth century 'Friends in Council' on art: J. Whitfield was student of *Ch. Ch.*, W. Hawkins fellow of *Pembroke*, and Ja. Hurdis[1] D.D., of *Magdalen*. All (with the exception I believe of Wheeler) were authors, most of them theologians, and almost all published their poetry praelections. Cambridge has never enjoyed the luxury of a professorship in this art.

The art and criticism of painting has been utterly neglected by the universities until quite lately, and nothing has been produced of any interest, except in the way of caricatures by such draughtsmen as the Kingsmen T. Orde, B.A. 1770, and James Bearblock, B.A. 1789. Tyson also used to etch.

In the more serious department of antiquities (and history) Oxford has produced J. Urry and Browne Willis (*Ch. Ch.*), T. Tanner (*Qu.* and *All Souls*), A. Charlet and Humphrey Wanley (*Univ.*), White Kennett and T. Hearne (*Edm. Hall*), Ri. Rawlinson and Andrew C. Ducarel (*S. John's*), and Joseph Spence (*New Coll.*).

Cambridge reared Jeremy Collier and F. Blomefield (Cai.), J. Strype (Kath. and Jesus), T. Baker (S. John's), J. Le Neve (no degree), S. Knight, Morris Drake Morris[2] and F. Peck (Trin.), S. Pegge, senior (S. John's), W. Richardson[3] (Emman.), W. Cole (Clare and King's), Jacob Bryant (King's), Ri. Gough and Michael Tyson (Bene't), Sir S. Egerton Bridges (Queens').

We should mention also the learned William Bowyer of S. John's (the pupil of Mr Bonwicke) who took John Nichols into partnership. In the palmy days of the *Gentleman's Magazine*, while *Sylvanus Urban* was a Nichols, it kept up a connexion with the literary men of Cambridge, and it has left us much valuable information concerning them. John Upton (King's), and T. Tyrwhitt (*Qu., Mert.*), as students of english must not be forgotten.

Some notices of academical STUDIES IN SAXON are to be found in the same authorities, Nichols' *Anecdotes* and the *Letters from the Bodleian*, vol. II. (1813).

---

[1] Praised by H. F. Cary, *Mem.* I. 52.
[2] Cooper's *Annals* IV. 162, 163.
[3] Richardson made collections for

Athenae Cantab. His edition of Godwin *De Praesulibus* was printed at Camb. 1743.

To these references I will add the following summary gathered from the studious bookseller, J. Petheram's *Historical Sketch of* Anglo-Saxon *Literature in England.* 1840. (chapters III—VI.)

At the Reformation the attention of English Churchmen turned naturally to the records of the Saxon Church. Abp. Parker, beside collecting and completing by facsimile the mss. which are now in the University Library and at his own college, Corpus Christi, employed J. Day, the celebrated printer, to cut the first saxon type in brass in 1566. About seventy years later W. L'Isle received the *imprimatur* from the Cambridge licenser for printing a *Saxon English Psalter.* A few years after this (1640) Sir H. Spelman (Trin.) designed by will to found a saxon lectureship at Cambridge, but it came not then into existence. He had already given an allowance to Abraham Wheelocke (Trin. and Clare) the arabic professor (see p. 163), who published Chronologia *Anglo-Saxonica,* with W. Lambard's *Leges Saxonicae,* Camb. 1644. The disturbance of property at the time of the civil war delayed the foundation of the professorship, but Spelman's grandson Roger carried it into effect after Wheelocke's death.

Fr. Junius the younger (Leyden), uncle of Is. Vossius, studied at Oxford and procured the cutting of Saxon type there in 1654. We must be content with naming James Usher, abp. of Armagh, who resided at Oxford and left his library to Trin. Coll. Dublin, W. Laud (*S. Joh.*), abp. of Canterbury, likewise a munificent collector of mss., J. Selden (*Hart Hall*), Sir Symonds D'Ewes (Joh.) and Meric Casaubon (*Ch. Ch.*).

The Cambridge type used by Wheelocke being too large, his successor W. Somner of Canterbury had his dictionary printed (1659) at the Oxford press, which was afterwards enriched by the type which lord Parker had given to Bowyer's press for miss Elstob's *Rudiments of the English-Saxon Tongue,* 1715.

At the end of the seventeenth century Oxford boasted several advancers of saxon studies. G. Hickes (*Joh., Magd. C., Magd. H.,* and *Linc.*), Edm. Gibson and Chr. Rawlinson (*Queen's*) and Humphry Wanley (*Univ.*). The greek professor E. Thwaites, of whom Hickes had a high opinion, had as many as fifteen saxon students (including T. Benson and Jos. Todhunter) at his own college, *Queen's.*

Several books in this department were printed at the close of the seventeenth century, but we will confine our list to the period which is more properly the subject of the present compilation.

1701. Vocabularium Gul. Somner, cura T. Benson (*Qu.*).

1705. Thesaurus Ling. Vet. Septentrional. G. Hickes (*Joh., Magd. C., Magd. H., Linc.*) with Catalogue of MSS., &c. Hum. Wanley (*Univ.*).

1708. Compendium or Latin epitome of Hickes' *Thesaurus*, by W. Wotton (Joh.), notes by G. Hickes (*Jo. &c.*), E. Thwaites (*Qu.*), and a transcript by Miss E. Elstob.

1708. Notae in Anglo Saxonum Nummos. E. Thwaites (*Qu.*).

1711. Grammatica Anglo Saxonica. (*Id.*)

1713. Versions of the Lord's Prayer, J. Chamberlayne (Trin.).

1719. Saxon Homilies, Gul. Elstob. (Cath. *Qu.* and *Univ.*) et Soror.

„ History of Kent. J. Harris, D.D. (Joh.).

1719—21, 1726. Complete Linguist. (Orator) J. Henley (Joh.).

1720. Textus Roffensis. T. Hearne (*Edm. H.*).

„ Canons Ecclesiastical. J. Johnson (Magd., and C. C. C. C.).

1721. Leges Saxonicae[1]. Dav. Wilkins (D.D. Camb.).

1722. Asseri Annales.

„ Bedae Hist. Eccl. J. Smith, D.D. (? Joh.) Camb.

1723. Hemingii Chartularium Vigorn. T. Hearne (*Edm. H.*).

1735. Conspectus Thesauri Hickesiani, a Gul. Wotton. Translated by Maurice Shelton.

1737. Concilia, a D. Wilkins (D.D. Camb.), enlarged from the edition of 1717.

1743. Fr. Junii Etymol. Anglīc. ed. E. Lye (*Hart H.*) *Oxon.*

1745, '53. Enquiry into Anglo-Saxon Government. S. Squire (Joh.).|

1751. Caedmon (projected edition). E. Lye (*Hart H.*).

1755. History of the Language prefixed to the Dict. S. Johnson (*Pemb.*).

1772. Asseri de r. gestis Alfredi, recensuit Fr. Wise (*Trin.*).

„ Anglo-Saxon and Gothic Dictionary, E. Lye (*Hart H.*) posthumously edited by O. Manning (Queens').

„ Leges Saxonicae. O. Manning (Qu.).

1774. History of English Poetry, Vol. I. T. Warton (*Trin.*) *Oxon.*

1778. Letter to J. Dunning by J. Horne [Tooke] (Joh.).

---

[1] This work had been commenced by W. Elstob (Cath. H. Camb.; *Qu.* and *Univ. Oxon.*), nephew of Dr Hickes, who had died in 1714. He translated the Saxon homily of Lupus and edited that on the Birthday of S. Gregory, 1709, &c. His sister Eliz. Elstob (whose portrait is in the initial G of that homily) was at least as good a scholar as her brother, and continued to work, in great poverty and without much encouragement, after his death. Their type being destroyed in the fire at Bowyer's (1712-13), Ld. Ch. Justice Parker gave them new type for her Saxon Grammar, from drawings made by Humphrey Wanley, at Ro. Nelson's request.

1786. Diversions of Purley. J. Horne [Tooke] (Joh.).
1787. Historical Account of the Textus Roffensis, with memoirs of the Elstobs and J. Johnson. S. Pegge (Joh.).
1798. Saxon and English (not Latin) illustrative of each other, exemplified in the errors of Hickes, Wilkins, Gibson, and other scholars. S. Henshall (B. N. C.).
1799—1805. History of the Anglo-Saxons. Sharon Turner.

The middle of the century appears to have had some restraining power for Saxon studies. Not only was there Lye's abortive edition of Caedmon, but Squire's Saxon Dictionary withered away[1]. And, yet more important, Ri. Rawlinson's (Joh.) purpose to establish a Saxon Professorship at Oxford was frustrated for a longer time than Spelman's had been at Cambridge in the preceding century.

It was not until the year 1795 that C. Mayo, fellow of S. John's, was appointed first Rawlinsonian professor. He was succeeded in 1800 by T. Hardcastle fellow of Merton.

[1] However Lye did publish in 1750 'Sacrorum Evangeliorum versio Gothica,' in 4to. Oxon. and his Junii Etymologicon, fol. Oxon. 1743, contains an anglo-saxon grammar.

CHAPTER XIII.

ORIENTAL STUDIES.

Arabicae linguae professor cras ibit in desertum.

Edm. Castell (1669).

AT this point some information relative to the study of the arch-science Divinity might have been expected to follow our account of Humanity and Morality.

This, however, has been postponed for another occasion, if it shall ever arise, when it is proposed to put together some collections on the kindred topic of *Religious Life at the English Universities* in the Eighteenth Century.

Nevertheless we here subjoin a few notes upon the study not of arabic only but of hebrew, as that may be considered simply as a branch of philology, though its literature is theological.

Some *additional information*, kindly communicated by Mr Bensly, will be found *in the concluding chapter* of this volume.

In the seventeenth century our English schools and universities were by no means behindhand in the study of hebrew. It was well done that the drudgery of learning the alphabet and grammar should be got over while the memory was young: and some traces of that system still linger at King's College Camb., and, if not now at Westminster, at the other London schools, and at King Edward VIth's school, Bury St Edmunds[1].

---

[1] Dr J. Covell, master of Christ's 1688—1723, was educated at Bury. He had a chaplaincy in Constantinople (1670—77.) and brought home some valuable eastern MSS. His pupil John Marshall (B.A. Chr. 1663-4, M.A. com.

There were even among the juniors at Cambridge in 1654, many (as Barrow quaintly said) who could have understood Adam when he gave names to all things[1]. He added that cabalistic studies were then pursued, and concluded by deploring the death of Abraham Wheelocke (Clare), the first arabic professor on Sir T. Adams' foundation[2], 1632-53. Wheelocke was also professor of saxon, and died while engaged upon the Polyglot Bible. His place was not filled up until a few years after the Restoration. His successor, Edmund Castell, who had been pensioner of Emmanuel and afterwards fellow-commoner of St John's, finding his lectures neglected the third year of his occupation of the chair, posted up on the Schools' gate the humorous notice which stands at the head of this chapter.

Simon Ockley of Queens' was author of an 'Introductio ad Linguas Orientales,' 8vo. *Camb.* 1706. 'Account of Barbary,' a version of Esdras II., and of an arabic life of Hai Ebn Yokdhan, and other works. He lived in very narrow circumstances; so much so that among Ellis' *Letters of Eminent Men*[3] is one addressed by him in 1717 to the E. of Oxford from the Castle prison, Cambridge, whence he wrote also the introduction to the second volume of his *History of the Saracens.* His 'Oratio Inauguralis habita Cantabrigiae in Scholis publicis. Kal. Febr. Anno 1711,' was published in 4to. in 1712 (Camb.). The first Lord Almoner's reader, 1724-9, was David Wilkins,

regiis 1705) spent many years in India and acquired unusual knowledge of the Puranas, Vedas and the rites of the Brahmins (Uffenbach *Reisen* III. 29). Prof. Cowell, in a paper read before the Camb. Philological Soc. (17 April, 1872) expressed his regret that Marshall did not publish his diaries *Harl. MSS.* 4250—4256) in 1680, as they were in advance of anything that was known in Europe till the present century. Is. Milles brought a knowledge of Hebrew to S. John's cir. 1657. *Life* (1721) p. 14.

[1] T. Comber of Trinity, who was master (1631, ejected 1645) was 'dexterous in Hebrew, Arabick, Coptick, Samaritane, Syriack, Chaldee, Per-

sian, Greek, Latine, French, Spanish and Italian, and well versed in the Greek and Latine Fathers, Schoolmen, Councels and modern writers.' Lloyd (*Memoirs*, 1668). He also relates (p. 619) of Ri. Crashaw the poet that '*Hebrew, Greek, Latine, Spanish, French, Italian,* were as familiar to him as *English*.' Brian Walton himself, though incorporated at *Oxford*, was Cambridge-bred (Magd. & Pet.).

[2] Cooper's *Annals* III. 247—9. The Lord Almoner's readership was not instituted till 1724.

[3] pp. 353, 354. Among Ockley's pupils about 1705 was J. Jackson (Jes.), theologian and biblical scholar.

(who appears, according to *Saxii Onomasticon* VI. 278, to have corresponded with the versatile orientalist Mathurin Veyssière Lacroze of Nantes, St Maur, Bâle and Berlin) editor of the 'Concilia' (D.D. 1717), who issued 'Novum Testamentum Copticum,' and was succeeded by Leonard Chappelow (S. John's, B.A. 1712), who had then been Adams professor for nine years. Chappelow published an edition of J. Spencer[1] 'de Legibus Hebraeorum,' 'Elementa Linguae Arabicae,' a commentary on Job and translations of Abu Ismael's 'Traveller,' and 'Six Assemblies; or, Ingenious Conversations of Learned men among *Arabians,' Camb.* 1767, from Schultens' edition of arabic idioms, proverbs, &c., with special reference to the elucidation of Holy Scripture[2].

He died in 1779, and was buried in S. Andrew the Great, Cambridge. John Jebb was a candidate for his place, but was beaten by the more popular Samuel Hallifax (B.A. Jesus; M.A. Trin. Hall), who held the readership and professorship as sinecures for two years, until he became professor of Civil Law[3]. Dr W. Craven followed him, but gave up the professorship when he became master of S. John's in 1795. His successor, Joseph Dacre Carlyle (of Christ's and Queens', B.A. 1779), had studied arabic with the assistance of David Zamio of Bagdad. In 1799 he went to Constantinople with Col. Elgin, visited the Troad, &c., and died in England, 1804. He published in arabic and latin (1792), 'Maured Allatafet Jemaleddini Filii Togri-Bardii, seu rerum aegyptiacarum annales ab A. C. 971 usque ad 1453,' and 'Specimens of Arabic Poetry,' 1796.

Among the Cambridge verses on the occasion of Q. Anne's accession in 1702 are *hebrew* poems by S. Townsend (M.A. Jesus 1701), Pet. Allix (B.A. Qu. 1702; M.A. Jesus 1706) and

---

[1] Master of Benet, 1667—93.

[2] Bp. Law, hypo-bibliothecarius in 1773, tried to get H. A. Schultens to make a catalogue of our Oriental MSS. *Baker-Mayor*, p. 714, l. 35. This portion of the catalogue was the worst done in the hasty list completed in 1752. The profr. added descriptions of Oriental MSS. where not noted. Among these is the entry 'Thin. *perhaps* Turkish.' Humphrey Wanley writing to Dr Charlett in 1699 noticed here one book described as '*liber valde peregrina lingua et characteribus plane ignotis exaratus,*' and recognized in it a late Arabic tract. Ellis' *Letters* (C. S.), p. 286.

[3] Disney's *Jebb*, 10, 20, 22.

Arthur Ashley Sykes (M.A. Corpus 1708.) Also one each in *arabic, persian,* and *turkish* by C. Wright, late fellow of Trinity. Some of these persian characters had to be supplied by substitute from the arabic fount. Wright's MS. aethiopic grammar is in Camb. Univ. Library.

Bentley boasted that between 1699 and 1708 oriental learning began again to be cultivated, first at Trinity under his own rule, and then by infection in the whole university. (*Corresp.* 449). His own reputation as a hebraist has been established by Mr John Wordsworth (*ibid.* 790), in the face of Middleton's disparagement of his proficiency in such studies. In a letter written in 1735 (*ibid.* 711) he wrote to an Oxonian about a *persic* ms. of the Gospels which had been sent from Ispahan to the university, and offered some acute remarks about its date.

In 1703 H. Sike (LL.D. 1705) succeeded Talbot as regius professor of hebrew. By his German connexion he was well known on the continent. Uffenbach much regretted[1] that he was not in residence at the time of his visit to Cambridge, and when he was in London he came across a young student of Breslau who was going to study eastern languages under our professor. When he put an end to his own life in his rooms in Trinity in 1712[2], his death caused much regret among foreign scholars as well as in England. In 1706 he paid a visit to Oxford and inspected the arabic and other oriental mss—corresponding[3] with Kuster at Amsterdam and Bentley at Cambridge. He edited the Evangelium Infantiae. (arab.)[4]

A Catalogue[5] of the oriental MSS., and other curiosities given by G. Lewis, archd. of Meath in 1726, was printed at the time in a small pamphlet. The seals on the books and the plates on the book-case bear his name and the date 1707.

Among our orientalists several distinguished themselves in the senate-house.

J. Parkhurst (Clare) was 6th wrangler in 174⅜.

---

1 *Reisen,* III. 84, II. 455.
2 Monk's *Bentley,* I. 328, 329. Luard's *Rud's Diary,* p. 8.
3 Bentley *Corresp.* 244.
4 Traject. ad Rhenum, 1697.

5 This catalogue was re-printed, with the omission of 'chop-sticks. Iterum chop-sticks' and the like, in the *Classical Journal,* No. xxxvi. and in Dyer's *Privileges,* I. 581 *foll.*

C. Torriano (Trin.) first junior optime in the same year, was hebrew professor 1753—7.

W. Disney (Trin.) hebrew professor 1757—71, was senior wrangler in 1753.

W. Craven (S. Joh.) arabic professor 1770—95, and Ld. Almoner's reader, was 4th in the same year.

S. Hallifax (Jes.) arabic prof. 1768—70, and Ld. Almoner's reader, was 3rd in 1754.

J. Jebb (Pet.) candidate for the arabic professorship was 2nd, and *Ro. Tyrwhitt* (Jes.) 13th in 1757.

W. Collier (Trin.) hebrew professor 1771—90, was 5th in 1762.

J. Porter (Trin.) hebrew professor 1790—95, was 5th in 1773.

J. Dacre Carlyle (Queens') arabic professor 1795—1804, was 10th in 1779.

H. Lloyd (Trin.) hebrew professor[1] 1795—1831, was 10th in 1785.

J. Palmer (Joh.) arabic professor 1804—9, was senior wrangler in 1792.

The hebrew professors do not appear to have produced much. A good deal of the instruction imparted at Cambridge in that language[2] in the middle of the century was given by Israel Lyons[3], a Polish silversmith (father of the botanist), whereas in 1741 the stipend (£2), due to the hebrew lecturer at Peterhouse, was devoted to increase the dean's salary[4]; eight years later it was agreed to allow £5 to Lyons 'for teaching such scholars the hebrew tongue as shall be appointed by the master and deans.' About 1764 John Jebb learnt from him[5], and

---

[1] I have seen a notice bearing the date '1 Feb. 1799' to the effect that the hebrew Professor (Lloyd) would give instruction gratis on Tuesdays and Thursdays, and oftener if desired.

[2] The Statutes required every M.A. qualifying for the degree of B.D. to attend the hebrew lecture *daily for seven years.*

[3] John Byrom learnt from him as early as 1733 when making one of his sojournings in Cambridge.

[4] By a college order, 28 Nov. 1659 the hebrew lecturer's place was conferred on Mr Skelton, the deputy junior dean, for his encouragement. The lectureship was allowed to lie fallow at least as early as 1700.

[5] Disney's *Jebb*, I. 10.

at the same time he was employed as teacher in S. John's College[1]. He died about 1770.

Knowing what sentiments Gilbert Wakefield expressed concerning greek accents, we are not so much surprised to read in his autobiography the following disagreeable remark: 'The chief motive for the recommendation of *points* in those who understand them, is, I fear, too often pride.' He confesses[2] that in 1775 he could not master *Lyons'* Hebrew Grammar[3], and threw it aside for *Masclef's*, which discards the points.

We may fairly say that Oxford did more than Cambridge for these studies. In the previous century we read of Ri. Kilbye (one of the translators of the Bible) as a hebrew professor well read in Rabbinical lore, licensing Jacob Barnet, a young jew (who subsequently made off when he had undertaken to be baptized), to give elementary lessons to students[4]. Archbishop Laud had been most munificent in presenting mss. to the University[5], and in his code of statutes he made knowledge of hebrew a condition for the degree of M.A. That it was fairly studied in the middle of the next century is regarded as notorious by a writer in the *Student* in Feb. 17$\frac{50}{51}$, who is advocating the revival of arabic[6]. In the second volume (pp. 377—380) is a paper on the hebrew root *achal*, a specimen of a supplement to the *Originals*. Another correspondent contributes a paper (II. 306—309) on *reading hebrew without points;*—all this in the midst of the facetiae of Smart and Warton.

Laud procured in 1620 the annexation of a canonry at *Ch. Ch.* to the hebrew professorship: he also endowed a chair of arabic, which was supplemented more than a century later by the lord Almoner's readership.

Speaking of the time of the Bartholomew Act of Uniformity (1662), Burnet says 'the young clergy that came from the universities did good service. Learning was then high at Oxford; *chiefly the study of the oriental tongues,* which was much raised by the Polyglot bible, then lately set forth. They read the

---

[1] *Baker-Mayor*, p. 1040. 1. 24.

[2] *Memoirs* (1804), I. 100, 101, 388.

[3] *The Scholar's Instructor* or Hebrew Grammar by I. Lyons, *Camb.* ed. 1. 1735, 1738, ed. 3. 1757.

[4] Mark Pattison's *Is. Casaubon*, 413. (a. 1610.)

[5] Hook's *Laud*, pp. 169, 173, 310.

[6] *The Student, or Oxford Miscellany*, I. 41—46.

fathers much there. Mathematics and the new philosophy were in great esteem. And the meetings that Wilkins had begun at Oxford were now held in London too in so public a manner that the king himself encouraged them much and had many experiments made before him[1].'

Edward Pococke of *Corpus* then held both professorships, but he died in 1691 ; and ere the century[2] opened Thomas Hyde of (King's, Camb. and) *Queen's*, was his successor both for hebrew and for arabic. In 1700 he had published his great work ' Historia Religionis veterum Persarum.' He wrote also on chinese weights and measures, on eastern games, and edited the Gospels and Acts in the malay language.

Thomas Hunt of *Hart Hall* (Prof. Laud. *Arab.* 1738. Reg. *Hebr.* 1747-74) printed latin orations 'De Antiquitate Elegantia, Utilitate Linguae Arabicae' and 'De usu Dialectorum Orientalium.' Kennicott published his posthumous 'Observations on the Book of Proverbs.'

Benjamin Blayney, B.A. *Worc.*, fellow of *Hart Hall*, was professor of hebrew 1787—1802. He published translations of Jeremiah and Zechariah, and in 1769 edited the Oxford Bible, like Mr Scrivener revising the marginal references.

Thomas Shaw[3], F.R.S. (who was professor of Greek 1747—51), fellow of *Queen's*, having resided at Algiers as chaplain to the english factory, and having visited eastern countries, published in 1738 his 'Travels in Barbary and the Levant,' containing observations and illustrations of the sacred and classical writings as well as other valuable information. Another edition in 1757 included his rejoinders to Pococke's strictures. He succeeded Felton as principal of *S. Edmund Hall*, and figures in the 'Oxford Sausage' as the '*Gaby*' of Herbert Beaver's the 'Cushion Plot,' and as a 'convert' in politics.

George Horne was admitted at *Univ. coll.* in his sixteenth

---

[1] Burnet, I. 332 = (folio) I. 192. *Oxon.* 1823.

[2] There is in Letters from the Bodleian (1813), II. 49—52 a letter from *Arthur Bedford (B. N. C.* author of Scripture Chronology 1730, &c.) to Dr Charlett *Univ.* (11 Dec. 1799.) recommending that the newly proposed professorship should undertake to teach *Chaldee* as well as *Syriack*, the alternate months throughout the year.

[3] Like his namesake (p. 94) he seems to have been a butt for the Oxford wits on account of the latin version of his name. *Biog. Universelle.*

year, and became fellow and president of *Magd. coll.* and Bp. of
Norwich. He was a follower of Hutchinson the learned hebraist, opponent of the Newtonian system, which Horne attacked
in the ironical 'Theology and Philosophy in Cicero's *Somnium
Scipionis* explained,' 1751. Soon afterwards he entered into a
dispute with Kennicott, but ultimately they became fast friends.
In 1776 appeared his 'Commentary on the Psalms' (2 vols. 4to).

Benjamin Kennicott entered at *Wadham,* but he won his
fees[1] for B.A. and a fellowship at *Exeter* by his Dissertation 'On
the Tree of Life' and 'On the Oblations of Cain and Abel' in
1747. Subsequently he was keeper of the *Radcliffe library,*
preb. of Westminster and (by exchange) canon of *Ch. Ch.* He
undertook the enormous work of examining the hebrew mss. of
the Bible, and finally brought out the hebrew Bible with Pro-
legomena and various readings in two vols. folio 1776 and 1780.
But while the work was in progress he had brought out specimens of his researches from time to time :—' The State of the
printed hebrew Text of the Old Testament considered.' *Oxon.*
2 vols. 1753—9. 'Annual Accounts of a Collation of Hebrew
MSS.' 1761—9, collected 1770. 'Dissertatio Generalis in V. T.
Hebr.' *Oxon.* 1780. Beside his còntroversy with Horne he had
a 'Correspondence with an Abbé' (Rome), 1771—3, and a
'Letter to J. D. Michaelis' on his strictures on the edition, 1777,
and pamphlets were interchanged between him and our T.
Rutherford (Joh.) on the Samaritan Pentateuch. 1761-2.

Robert Lowth was elected to *New College* from Winchester
in 1730. As professor of poetry he signalized himself by taking
up the subject of hebrew compositions[2]. His Prælectiones
'De Sacra Poesi Hebraeorum' came out in 1753, in which
certain passages relating to the book of Job were violently
attacked by Warburton in an appendix to the last vol. of his
second edition of the 'Divine Legation of Moses.' Lowth published a trenchant letter to the bishop in 1765. He became
bishop of S. David's, Oxon. and London.

Sir W. Jones, F.R.S., removed from Harrow to *Univ. coll.*
where he obtained a fellowship. When an undergraduate he

---

[1] Cp. the obsolete Camb. expression 'to *save one's groats.*'

[2] Lowth speaks in his Crewian oration as if the oriental professorships
were generally regarded almost as
sinecures at that time (1751).

was permitted to study arabic instead of attending the college
lecture, and he was appointed tutor to lord Althorp (E. Spencer).
About 1766 he began his Commentaries on Asiatic Poetry, after
the example of Lowth's hebrew praelections. He was employed to translate the K. of Denmark's eastern ms. life of the
Nadir Shah. He was appointed judge in the court of Bengal,
and at Calcutta instituted a Royal Society of Oriental Literature and Science, and applied himself to the study of Sanskrit.
He died suddenly in 1794 (aged 48): a monument by Flaxman
was put up in his college chapel.

Joseph White, D.D. (*Wadh.*), arabic professor 1774—1814,
published the Syriac N. T. Vers. Philoxen. from the Ridley mss.,
several miscellaneous works, and his lecture *de Utilitate Ling.
Arab. in* Studiis Theologicis... Oxon. *in Schola Linguarum*
1775. Also *Institutes of Timour or Tamerlane* from the Mogul
through Dr Hunter's Persian ms. by W. Davy. Oxon. 1780.
And Abollatiphi *Hist. Aegypt. Compendium.* Oxon. 1800.
Beside later productions. He gave persian lessons to Cary
(1794).

The first volume of the Oxford catalogue of Oriental MSS.
(hebrew, chaldee, syriac, aethiopic, arabic, persian, turkish and
coptic) was begun in 1766 by John Uri (a hungarian, pupil of
Schultens of Leyden), and issued in 1787[1]. The first part of
the second volume by Dr Nicoll came out in 1821, and the
conclusion by Dr Pusey in 1835. Uri's part is said to be
incorrect, and rendered less valuable by the discovery of many
forgeries palmed upon almost all orientalists except Pococke.

---

[1] *Notes and Queries*, S. IV. ix. 379,
380. Macray's *Annals of the Bodleian*,
pp. 199, 233. There was also *Notitia
Librorum Hebraeorum, Graec. et Lat.
Saec.* xv., *et Aldin. in Bodl.* published
at *Oxford*, 1795. We may also mention the following books proceeding
from the Clarendon press.
1716 Testamentum Novum Aegypti-
um, vulgo Copticum ex MSS. Bodl.
D. Wilkins.
1767 T.Hyde,SyntagmaDissertationum
(Arabic, Hebrew and Chinese trea-

tises) 2 vol. 4to. Plates, &c. Greg.
Sharpe, LL.D.
1775 Lexicon Aegyptiaco-Lat. a M. V.
Lacroze, ex cura C. Scholtz notas
et indices adj. C. G. Woide. 4to.
1778 Scholtz Gramm. Aegypt. cura
C. G. Woide, 4to.
   „   Testamenti Novi Versio Syriaca
Philoxeniana. J. White. 4to.
   „   Albucasis de Chirurgia. Arab. et
Lat. J Channing (*Ch. Ch.*) 4to.
1790 Pentateuchus Hebraeo-Samarit.
charactere hebraeo,B.Blayney,8vo.

CHAPTER XIV.

PHYSICK.

'How! you understand surgery,' answers the doctor, 'and not read *Galen* and *Hippocrates* ?' 'Sir,' cries the other 'I believe there are many surgeons who have never read these authors.' 'I believe so too,' says the doctor, ' more shame for them ; but thanks to my education, I have them by heart, and very seldom go without them both in my pocket.' ' They are pretty large books,' said the gentleman.

H. Fielding's *Adventures of Joseph Andrews*. i. xiv.

THE English universities, while aiming at educating professional men, never pretended in old time to give the final practical training which is required for every profession. Even in the education of the clergy, to which they gave their special attention, they attempted to educate them in scientific Theology rather than to impart even the elements of the pastoral profession.

So it was that young men intending to practise medicine or surgery, though they might receive the grounds of a valuable education, and some theoretical instruction, in one of the universities, were obliged to look elsewhere for practical knowledge to qualify them for their profession.

A *Quarterly Reviewer* stated in 1827 (p. 235) that of all the physicians then practising in England (three hundred licentiates of the College of Physicians and numerous unlicensed country practitioners) about one hundred had been educated at Oxford or Cambridge ; while of the six thousand members of the

College of Surgeons not six had graduated at either of our universities.

Let us see what were the relations in which the former of these learned colleges stood with our own in earlier times.

In 1701 (18 Nov.), it was ruled by Sir J. Holt that a university graduate in physic might not practise in London, or within seven miles of it, unless he had a licence from the College of Physicians[1]. 29 Nov. 1715, the Senate agreed to support our M.D.s' claims against such prohibition[2], and a similar course was adopted at Oxford. However, in $17\frac{16}{17}$ the universities were again defeated in the person of Dr West by the College of Physicians in the Court of King's Bench[3].

More friendly overtures were made between the two learned bodies in $17\frac{21}{22}$, the College offering to appoint their fellows entirely from the list of University Doctors[4], and the University of Cambridge undertaking, through the Public Orator (March 1), to make her degrees in medicine strictly conformable with the statutable qualifications. In 1750, on the demand of our Universities, the College agreed to exclude graduates of foreign universities[5]; and in 1753 it was decided in the case of Dr Isaac Schomberg of Trinity that an academic M.D. cannot claim to be enrolled F.R.C.P. as a matter of right[6].

There were but three Regii Professors of Physic at Cambridge in the last century[7] (Chr. Green, Cai. 1700: Russell Plumptre, Qu. 1741: ·Sir Isaac Pennington 1793—1817), which speaks well for their professional treatment of themselves, but I do not know that they ever lectured. Indeed most of our men

[1] Cooper's *Annals*, iv. 47, 48.

[2] Van Mildert's *life of* Waterland p. 16.

[3] Cooper's *Annals*, iv. 142, 145.

[4] *Ibid.* p. 168. This was enforced in the King's Bench in Easter term, 1797. Gunning's *Reminisc.* ii. ch. iii.

[5] Cooper's *Annals*, iv. 281. King Charles II. had made a similar order in favour of the universities' monopoly Feb. 12, $167\frac{4}{5}$. *Ibid.* iii. 566.

[6] Nichols' *Lit. Anecd.* iii. 27 *n*.

[7] In the preceding century professor F. Glisson (Caius), 1636-7, had made early observations on the nervous system which have since been universally adopted. (Whewell, *Hist. Induct. Sciences* iii. 427, 428.) William Harvey who discovered the circulation of the blood (1615-28) had been educated at Caius (and Padua), and was elected Warden of *Merton* in 1645. Glisson said that Wallis (Emman. 1635; fellow of Queens') was the first of his 'sons' who defended the then new doctrine of the Blood (Hearne's *Langtoft*, i. cl.).

learned in medicine found a field for their powers away from the University. However, it appears that when Is. Pennington held another professorship (that of *Chemistry*) in 1773—93, he found a deputy who gave satisfactory lectures in *that* subject,—J. Milner of Queens'[1]; while some years earlier we find a Botany Professor, Ri. Bradley, delivering and printing (at Bowyer's press 1730)[2] 'a Course of Lectures upon the Materia Medica... in the Physick Schools at Cambridge upon the Collections of Dr Addenbroke and Signor Vigani' deposited in Catharine Hall and Queens' College.

Among the colleges at least one (Peterhouse) had in past times a laudable custom of urging her fellows to determine themselves in the line of some faculty—going on 'the Law line,' or that of Physick, or of Divinity. Two physicians celebrated for their good-nature and other social and moral qualities were residents (though not fellows) in that society for some time. Sir Sam. Garth (B.A. 1679, M.D. 1691, Harveian Oration, 1697, *The Dispensary*, 1699), and Sir W. Browne (B.A. 1710, M.D. 1721), founder of the classical medals, and translator and editor of *Gregory's Elements of Catoptricks and Dioptricks*. By his will he gave the college two " κατ' ἐξοχὴν *Non-travelling*" *Physic Fellowships*[3]. Among resident practitioners was Ro. Glynn (Clobery) fellow of King's (B.A. 1741, M.D. 1752, Seatonian Prizeman 'The Day of Judgment,' 1757) who was physician to the poet Gray. Though he was a doctor of repute his favourite panacea was 'emplasma vesicatorium amplum et acre.' He was conspicuous for his gold-headed cane, scarlet cloak and three-cornered hat. In rainy weather he wore pattens, which is possibly the reason why until 1872 there hung at the gate of his college a notice forbidding their use. His funeral in 1800 was the last performed by torchlight in Cambridge. Like the author of the *Dispensary* he shewed much professional kindness to the poor. In [Mathias'] *Pursuits of Literature* Glynn is celebrated as '*dilectus Iapis*' and ἰατρικώτατος, φιλόδωρος καὶ ἀδωρο-δόκητος, φιλόπτωχος, γενναῖος, νέων διορθωτής, ὅσιος, δίκαιος,

[1] Gunning's *Reminisc.* Vol. i. chap. viii.
[2] Nichols' *Lit. Anecd.* i. 445, 446.
[3] *Ibid.* ix. 442.
[4] Gunning, *Reminisc.* Vol. ii. ch. iv. *Autobiog. of* G. Pryme, 46.

εὐσεβής, εἰς ἄκρον τῆς παιδείας ἐληλακώς. (1796). His portrait hangs in the libraries of Magdalene and Caius.

The following notices, preserved by Dr Webb, prove that Dr Glynn used to do some work as a teacher:

'On the 14th of March, 1750—1
Will begin
A *Course* of *Lectures*
on
The Medical Institutes.
İ. On the Animal Oeconomy.
II. On the Operations of Medicines.
III. On the History of Diseases.
By R. GLYNN.

Gentlemen who propose to attend these Lectures are desired to call upon Mr *Glynn* at King's College.'

And another to the following effect:
On Monday, March 2nd, 1752. Medical Lectures on the Structure and Use of the Principal Organs of the Human Body, will begin at 3 p.m. Anatomy Schools. 1st Course 2 Guineas; 2nd, 1 Guinea.

In Dr Webb's collections, vol. I. (Univ. Library), is preserved a copy of a printed ballad, 'Unfortunate old Clobery' (with a latin jingling version), to the tune of 'A Captain bold of Halifax,' relating to Dr Glynn and the 'Chest' fund at King's. (1780.) 8vo. pp. 16.

We will now pass on to our enumeration of scientific men.

Stephen Hales was preëlected fellow of Corpus, or Benet Hall, in April, 1702, and admitted Feb. 1703; B.D. 1711; F.R.S. 1718. '*Statical Experiments* on the Sap in Vegetables, and an attempt to Analyse the Air,' 1727 (being vol. I. of his *Statical Essays*). '*Hydraulick and Hydrostatical Experiments on the Blood and Blood-vessels*: also the Nature of certain Concretions,' 1733, forming vol. II. In 1733 he took the degree of D.D. at *Oxford* by diploma—why he took degrees in divinity instead of medicine I cannot say; '*Admonition* to Drinkers of *Spirituous Liquors*,' ed. 2. 1734; '*Experiments* of Sea-Water, Corn, Flesh, &c.; containing many useful Instructions for Voya-

gers,' 1739, in which year he was Copley Medallist of the Royal
Society; 'Observations on Mrs *Stephens's Medicines*,' 1740 ;
'On *Ventilation*,' 1743 ; 'On *Tar-Water*,' 1745 ; On '*Earthquakes*,' 1750. '*Crounean Lecture*, &c., *Job* x. 11, 12.' Hales
was foreign member of the Parisian Academy, Proctor in Convocation, Clerk of the Closet to the princess Augusta and
prince George (afterwards K. Geo. III.). Like Dr Burton, he
was a trustee for the new colony of Georgia, which Wesley
visited in 1735. (*Masters'* Hist. of C. C. C. C. 302 *sqq.*) He
planned his Statical experiments in his 'private Elaboratory in
Bennet College[1].'

About 1648—9, Dr Wilkins and Wallis had removed to
Oxford, and continued such philosophical discussions as they
had held for about four years in London,—in the rooms of
Wilkins in *Wadham* College. There, with Boyle, W. Petty,
Seth Ward, and other doctors of physic and divinity, they had
formed the nucleus of the Royal Society, and established the
Oxford Philosophical Society, which lasted till 1690. Most of
the founders of the Royal Society had removed to London after
about ten years' sojourn in Oxford. They were incorporated at
the Restoration, and had the honour of receiving and printing
the MS. of the *Principia*. In 1669, Evelyn applied to H. lord
Howard to effect an exchange of Arundel MSS. and scientific
books between the university of Oxford and the Society. An
unfortunate jealousy against the Royal Society appears to have
arisen at Oxford, so that Thomas Sprat of *Wadham*, in his
history of the R. S. (1667), found it necessary to argue that
Experiments are not dangerous to the universities. Still, two
years later, South, the university orator, took occasion to inveigh
against it at the opening of the Sheldonian Theatre, as Wallis
informed Boyle. Again, at the very close of that century
(1700), Dr W. King of *Ch. Ch.* satirized the Royal Society, or
at least Sir Hans Sloane their president, in two dialogues
intituled *The Transactioneer.* Sloane was created M.D. at
Oxford in the following year.

John Freind, one of the most eminent physicians of the
century, was M.A. *Ch. Ch.* 1701, having been joint editor with

---

[1] Ri. Davies, *General State of Education*, 1759, p. 44.

Foulkes of one of dean Aldrich's 'new year's gifts' (*De Corona*, 1696). The lectures which he delivered before the university in 1704 as Reader in Chemistry were published in 1709.

In 1671, Dr John Eachard, afterwards master of Catharine Hall, in '*Some Observations* upon the Answer to an *Enquiry into the Grounds and Occasion of the Contempt of the Clergy*,' gives an amusing sketch of the pert young academical sciolists of the day. 'And in the first place comes rattling home from the *Vniversities* the young pert *Soph* with his *Atoms* and *Globuli*; and as full of defiance of all *Countrey Parsons*, let them be never so learned and prudent, and as confident and magisterial, as if he had been *Prolocutor* at the first *Council* of *Nice*. And he wonders very much that they will pretend to be *Gownmen*, whereas he cannot see so much as *Cartes's Principles*, nor *Gassendus's Syntagma*, lying upon the Table; and that they are all so sottish and stupid as not to sell all their *Libraries* and send presently away for a whole *Wagon full of new Philosophy. I'll tell you, Sir*, says one of these small *whiflers*, perhaps to a grave, sober, and judicious *Divine*, the *Vniversity is strangely altered since you were there, we are grown strangely inquisitive and ingenious. I pray, Sir, how went the business of motion in your days? we hold it all now to be violent*,' and so on. The whippersnapper's criticism on the sermon is exquisitely sketched. Then follows a slash at the younger members of Gresham College (where the Royal Society twice found shelter), who ask 'to what purpose is it to *preach* to *people*, and go about to *save* them, without a *Telescope*, and a *glass* for *Fleas?*' Pp. 142—7.

Uffenbach visited the chemical laboratory at Oxford in 1710. The room had been fitted up for the original Royal Society in its early Oxonian days. He found the stoves in fair condition, but everything else in dirt and disorder. Dr Ri. Frewin (*Ch. Ch.*, where his portrait is hung), afterwards Camden Professor of Ancient History, did not seem to care about it, and White the demonstrator was a good-for-nothing man.

John Addenbrooke was B.A., S. Catharine's, in 1701, M.D. 1712. He is thought to have practised in Cambridge, which he endowed with £4000 to build the hospital, which was further assisted by the bequest of £7000 from J. Bowtell the bookseller.

Samuel and John Jebb of Peterhouse we have occasion to mention elsewhere. They took their first degree respectively in 1712 and 1757. The same society produced, beside Sir W. Browne (B.A. 1710), another fellow of the college of physicians, J. Clerke, B.A. 1738.

W. Battie, the Craven scholar, B.A. King's, 1726, was Lumleian lecturer, physician of S. Luke's hospital, and a mad-doctor of some repute. He published a *Treatise on Madness*, 1758, and *Aphorismi de Cognoscendis et Curandis Morbis*, 1762.

The William Heberdens, father and son, were B.A.s of S. John's in 1728 and 1788. The former lectured for ten years on the Materia Medica[1], having Sir G. Baker, Dr Gisborne, and Dr Glynn among his pupils. He presented his collection of specimens for illustration to the college; and he relinquished his fellowship in favour of a poorer man. His essay on *Mithridatium and Theriaca* (1745) is a specimen of his university lectures. His *Commentarii de Morborum Historia et Curatione* appeared posthumously in 1802[2].

George Shaw[3] of Magd. Hall, *Oxon.*, M.A. 1772; M.B., F.R.S., having been his father's curate for some time, chose to abandon the performance of clerical duties for the study of medicine, in which his heart lay. After attending lectures at the University of Edinburgh he returned to Oxford, where he graduated M.D. (1787) in order to qualify for the privileges of the College of Physicians. If he had not been ordained he would have been elected botanical professor. He was one of the vice-presidents of the newly established Linnaean Society, and lectured on Zoology at the Leverian Museum. He was also keeper of the Natural History department in the British Museum. (Born 1751, died 1813[4].)

I have already had occasion to refer to the 'Epistle to the Reverend Dr Hales[5],' by Ri. Davies, M.D., late fellow of Queens',

---

[1] A programme of the elder Dr Heberden's Course of Lectures is printed at the end of this chapter.

[2] Dr Munk's *Roll of R.C.P.* II. 142.

[3] Brother of *Putide Shavius.* See p. 94 n.

[4] H. Best in his *Personal and Lite-* *rary Memorials* pp. 224, 225, gives examples of his trick of quaint phraseology. Shaw wrote the scientific descriptions of the *Naturalist's Miscellany.*

[5] Stephen Hales, M.D., F.R.S., and D.D. *Oxon.* by diploma.

on 'the *General State of Education* in the Universities, with a particular view to the Philosophic and Medical Education, being Introductory to Essays on the Blood'—1759.

Dr Davies proposed to abolish 'close' fellowships and scholarships (*p.* 23), and the restrictions of tests and holy orders to Masterships and Fellowships (*pp.* 19, 30), to raise the number of professorships and public lectureships to *at least fifty* in each university, without limitation of tenure or requisition of celibacy, their stipends depending in part on the attendance of their pupils (*pp.* 33, 34), to sequestrate some existing fellowships for this purpose (*p.* 32), to make them generally terminable ten years after the first degree (*p.* 31), to encourage Colleges to devote themselves to some particular science or line of study (*p.* 35). (This was already in some measure the case with Caius and Trin. Hall.) He goes on to urge the need of *instruments* as well as books for carrying on experimental knowledge in mechanics, optics, practical Astronomy, &c., for *books* will not supersede Nature, since they are conservative rather than acquisitive : being useful rather to record past inventions than to forward fresh discoveries (*p.* 39). 'The Arts subservient to Medicine have no appointments to encourage Teachers in them. Anatomy, Botany, Chemistry, and Pharmacy, have been but occasionally taught [1759]; when some person of superior Talents has sprung up and has honoured the University by his first display of them there, before his passage into the world' (*p.* 40).

The author thought however that no place was so well fitted for the early training of Physicians (to be supplemented 'by due attendance at some public Hospital, which ought to be the finishing school of the clinical Physician') as the English Universities, on account of their discipline :—if only the Professors' lectures had not become a farce[1] ; those posi-

---

[1] The statutes were evidently intended for the education of medical students entering the University at a very early age. When in the 18th cent. men came up later from school or perhaps from some elementary practice in the profession or its trade, it was found impossible to keep them waiting for the whole statutable period required for M.D. (*eleven years*), so it was given up as impracticable. When T. Young, M.D., F.R.S., Egyptologer and discoverer of the principles of interferences in the Undulatory Theory

tions being looked upon as Dignities rather than Offices (*p.* 3). Love of Truth had given place to love of Disputation (*p.* 12), and the result of this neglect might be seen in the Patent Quackeries and Universal Remedies displayed in every newspaper (*p.* 4).

Among Dr Webb's (Clare) Collections, now in the Univ. Library, are two editions of a scheme of Dr Heberden's lectures, about 1741. One edition compresses them into 26 lectures.

' The Order of
A Course of *Lectures*
on the
Materia Medica.

I. (in two parts). Introductory, giving a general account of the Rise and Progress of the Materia Medica.

Of FOSSILS.

2. Of Waters.
3. Of Mineral Waters.
4. Of Earths, Sulphurs, Fossil Oyls, Bitumens and Ambar.
5. Of Sea-Salt, Alum, Nitre, Borax and Vitriol; of the Ores of Metals.
6. Of Quicksilver, and of Semimetals.
7. Of the perfect Metals.
8. Of Stones.

Of VEGETABLES.

9. Of the Aromatic Herbs, Leaves, Flowers, Seeds, Barks and Woods.
10. Of the Aromatic Roots : of the Acrid Herbs, Fruits, Seeds and Roots.
11. Of the Astringent Flowers, Fruits, Seeds, Barks, Woods, and Roots.
12. Of the Peruvian Bark.

(*Memoir* by Peacock ch. v.) was at Emmanuel in 1799, after studying at Edinburgh and Göttingen, there were no medical lectures at Cambridge except Prof. Harwood's, and they were addressed to a miscellaneous audience.

13. Of the Emollient Fruits, Seeds and Roots.

14. A general account of the use of Purging Medicines: [Of the Purging Inspissate Juices].

15. Of the Purging Herbs, Leaves, Flowers, Fruits, Seeds, Barks, Woods and Roots.

16. A general account of the use of Emetics: of the Emetic Herbs, Seeds, Barks and Roots : of Diuretics.

17. Of Narcotics and Opium.

18. Of Vulneraries, &c.

19. Of Gums ; [And a general account of Resins.]

20. Of Balsams, Turpentines and Resins.

Of Animals.

21. Of Insects, Fishes and Birds.

22. Of the Serpent-kind, Quadrupeds and Man.

Of Chemicals.

23. Explication of some Terms used in Chemistry.

24. Of the simple and compound Waters, Essential and Fixed Salts, Soaps, Caustic Stones, Expressed and Essential Oyls ; of the Preparations of Turpentine.

25. Of Spirit of Wine, Spirituous Waters ; of Vegetables, Vinegar, Tartar and its Preparations, Tinctures and Chemical Resins.

26. Of Ammoniac Salt, Spirit of Ammoniac Salt and Hart's Horn, *Spiritus Volatilis Oleosus*, Animal Oyl and Phosphorus.

27. Of Spirits of Sea-Salt, Nitre and Vitriol; of the Preparations of [Ambar], Sulphur, Steel, Lead, Tin, Silver and Copper.

28. Of the Mercurial and Antimonial Preparations.

29. General Rules for Prescribing.

30.⎫
31.⎭ Of the Antidotes [proper] to all the known Poisons.

[In this Course a Specimen of each Particular will be shewn, and every Thing is intended to be mentioned that is useful or curious regarding its Natural History, Introduction into the Materia Medica, Adulterations, Preparations, Virtues, Dose and the Cautions necessary to be observed in its use.

These Lectures will begin on *Monday, April the 4th*, at 2 o'Clock in the Afternoon, in the Anatomy Schools; and will be read every Day,

By W. HEBERDEN, M.D.]

The First Course is Two Guineas; *the Second*, One Guinea; *ever after*, Gratis.

[*Those Gentlemen, who intend to go, are desir'd to send in their Names*].'

In 1770 T. Okes published (8vo. *Camb.*) extracts from Hippocrates, with a new latin translation, notes, and emendations, incorporated in two latin dissertations delivered in the Schools.

Of the Sedleian professors of Natural Philosophy at *Oxford*, Thomas Hornsby (1782-1810) was the most eminent. He was fellow of *Corpus*, D.D. and Savilian Professor, 1763-1810, publishing several astronomical tracts in 1763 and the ensuing decade.

He was a good lecturer, and his natural philosophy classes were well attended although they entailed fees. Even his occasional fits of dizziness would not disturb the sequence of his remarks or explanations, though they might interrupt it. After his servant had placed him in his chair, and administered restoratives, he would resume his prism or air-pump as though nothing had happened[1].

J. Channing (*Ch. Ch.*) published *Albucasis de Chirurgia* (arabic and latin) at the Clarendon Press in 1778.

---

[1] H. Best's *Personal and Literary Memorials*, 219—221.

CHAPTER XV.

ANATOMY.

" Quando enim, obsecro, a conditâ Academiâ in tot canum, piscium[1], volu-
crumque neces ac lanienas sanguinolenta curiositas saeviit, quo vobis partium
constitutio et usus in animalibus innotesceret? O innocentissimam crudelitatem
et feritatem facile excusandam ! "

I. Barrow, In Comitiis. [1654.]

DISSECTION appears to have been no modern innovation at
Cambridge, for queen Elizabeth granted two bodies for
anatomical purposes to the medical students of Gonville and
Caius[2]. By a grace of Nov. 27, 1646, the three dissections
required by the University Statutes (capp. 15, 17) as a qualification for M.D., and the two required from students aspiring
to M.B., were revived, this exercise having fallen into disuse.
Five years later 'vividissections of dogs and such-like creatures'
were popular[3].

James Keill (younger brother of John Keill the Newtonian,
see in the index), 1673—1719, having studied medicine at
Edinburgh and Leyden, read anatomical lectures at Oxford,
and also at Cambridge, where he also took the degree of M.D.
in 1705.

In 1723 Parliament considered and rejected a clause facilitating the acquisition of the corpses of felons of Cambs. and
Hunts. for dissection by the Cambridge faculty.

---

[1] The first systematic ichthyologist
was Francis Willughby of Trin. Coll.
Cant., who studied for some time at
the Bodleian and afterwards travelled
all over the continent with Ray who
edited and then translated his *Ornitho-
logia* 1676-8, and. edited his *Ichthyo-
graphia* 1686, and other posthumous
works.

[2] *Historical MSS. Commission* Report, II. p. 118.

[3] Dr C. Ashton's MS. Collectanea on
the Statutes (Brit. Mus.) referring to
the V. Chancellor's Book p. 91. Statut.
cap. 32. Cp. Dyer *Privil.* I. 243.
Mayor's *Matt. Robinson,* p. 31.

In the spring of 1732, when John Morgan[1] of Trinity (B.A. 1721) was professor of Anatomy, a body was dug up in a village near Cambridge, and carried to Emmanuel College. A riot arose, and a warrant was issued to search the College, but in vain. The offence became common at this time, and in the same year (May 9, 1732) it was forbidden by grace of the Senate, Dr Mathias Mawson of Corpus being Vice-Chancellor[2].

The preparations for a private dissection in college-rooms at Cambridge are described in the satirical romance of *Pompey the Little* (II. xi.) in 1750, by F. Coventry, then an undergraduate of Magdalene. About fifteen years later (Bishop) Watson, when professor of Chemistry, procured a corpse from London and dissected it in his laboratory, with the help of E. Waring (Magd.), and W. Preston (Trin.), afterwards an Irish bishop. The remains were not properly buried, and their discovery would have led to the stoning of the operators had they been known[3].

The professorship of anatomy was founded by the University in 1707. The fifth professor (1753—85) C. Collignon[4], Trin. M.B. 1749, printed a *Compendium Anatomico-Medicum*, 1756, of the lectures which he used to deliver yearly in March. At the close of the century his successor, Busick Harwood of Christ Coll. and Emmanuel (M.B. 1785, M.D. 1790, Anat. Prof. 1785—1814, Med. Prof. Downing, 1801) used to give his lectures[5] opposite Queens' college at 1 p.m. at the latter end

[1] Cooper's *Annals*, IV. 181. John Byrom attended some of Morgan's earliest lectures (which met with good encouragement) when he was making a stay in Cambridge in Jan. 1728, and again in 1730 he met the elder (Henry) Coventry of Magdalen on his way to see the professor conduct a dissection on a human subject.

[2] Masters' Hist. of C. C. C. C. p. 196.

[3] Watson's *Anecd.* I. 237.

[4] In 1764 and 1771, '95, '96, Collignon published 'An Enquiry into the Structure of the Human Body.' *Camb.* 8vo. And in 1769 'Medical and Moral Tracts.' John Jebb attended his lec-

tures in 1776. Collignon's father came from Hesse Cassell and ministered to the dutch congregation in Austin Friars. The professor was educated under Kinsman at Bury, and was admitted pensioner of Trin. 1743. He was appointed deputy regius professor of Physic for Plumtre in 1779, and Downing professor of Medicine or rather professor in Downing College, 1783—5, as well as professor of Anatomy. I have seen a printed notice stating that Collignon would commence an anatomical course 16 Feb. 1779 at 3 p.m.

[5] I have seen notices of B. Har-

of the Lent Term. (In the early years of his professorship he used to dine at 2, and take his friends to his lecture afterwards at 4 *p.m.*) His course included '*Comparative Anatomy* and *Physiology;* in which the structure and œconomy of *Quadrupeds, Birds, Fishes*' [which, according to Gunning, occasionally re-appeared at his hospitable dinner table] 'and *Amphibia* are investigated[1]; the several organs which constitute the Animals of the different classes compared with each other, and with those of the Human Body; the most striking analogies pointed out, and remarkable varieties accounted for, from the Natural History of the Animals belonging to each class. *Pathological* remarks on the diseases to which man and other Animals are liable are introduced, with observations on the nature and effects of the Medicines usually employed for their removal. The *Anatomia* Medico-Forensis, together with the effects of various poisons, and also of suspended animation, and the recovery of drowned persons, occupy a share of these Lectures. At the commencement of the course, the Blood of various Animals is compared with that of the Human Species: the doctrine of *Transfusion* is investigated[2]: its probable advantages and defects enquired into, and the practice illustrated by an actual experiment[3].' So few medical students were there at Cambridge, that these lectures were designedly popular and unprofessional. He was assisted by a Demonstrator named Orange. Harwood wrote descriptions and histories of about twenty specimens which are enumerated in the *Catalogue of the Anatomical Museum* in the University of *Cambridge*, arranged according to the system of Bichât, 1820. (pp. i.—viii. 1—71.) The university purchased also for the use of the anatomy school the anatomical models which had been executed in wax for Sir Busick Harwood at Florence and Bologna.

wood's lectures for 1792, '94, '96: the time there stated is 4.15 p.m., in the Anatomy School opposite Queens'.

[1] In 1775, Thomas Martyn the Botanical professor published at Cambridge '*Elements of Natural History*' Vol. I. Part 1. 8vo. pp. 80, containing *Mammalia*, 289 species.

[2] Busick Harwood printed a *Synop-*

sis *of a Course of Lectures on the Philosophy of Natural History*. 4to. Camb. 1812. The *Scots Magazine*, Vol. LIII. p. 27, contains a curious description of a visibly effectual *transfusion of blood* from a sheep into a dog at one of his lectures. (1791.)

[3] *Camb. Univ. Calendar* 1802, pp. 26, 27.

In 1710 Uffenbach went to see the anatomy school at Oxford, and agreed with Borrichius that it was not to be compared with the anatomical theatre at Leyden. It was in charge of the celebrated Tom Hearne, who did not know the cast of a foot from the natural limb. Uffenbach also attended a lecture given by Dr Lavater, who being only lately appointed had no corpse provided for dissection, but gave a lecture (in English) on osteology.

Before 1738 Dr Nicholls had deserted the anatomy school at Oxford, and about that year Nathan Alcock, M.D. of Leyden, began lectures on his own account. He taught physic also, as the old W. Woodford (*New Coll.*) the regius professor (1730—59) made a sinecure of his office. The university was shamed into appointing a chemistry reader, T. Hughes, M.D., *Trin.*, and summoning Dr Laurence from London to lecture in anatomy. Alcock was allowed a room by his own college (*Jesus*). This was crowded, while the authorized readers addressed the walls of the empty museum, which at last they resigned to their rival. Alcock received his degree of M.A. after some opposition, and proceeded M.B. in 1744.

In the *Student, or* Oxford *and* Cambridge *Monthly Miscellany* (1750—1) are printed several papers relating to anatomical studies—viz.; *Twelve Experiments* on dogs and pigeons, by Mr F. G. Zinn (II. 12—19) forming part of a thesis read before professor Haller of Göttingen, in Oct. 1749. Alb. von Haller was F.R.S., and had declined the Oxford professorship of botany in 1747, as well as the invitation of Holland, Russia, and Prussia. A paper of his, *de nova tunica, oculi fetus claudente pupillam observatio*, was also printed in the Student (I. 261—4), and called forth a communication 'On the *Membrana Pupillaris*[1]' (p. 340) by 'R. B. *Philomed.*'

About this time (Dr M.) Lee's Ch. Ch. Readerships in Anatomy were founded, and rather later (1776) the anatomical theatre was commenced at Oxford. The Tomlin's lectureship held by the professor of medicine was founded in 1623, the

---

[1] Francis Sandys (M.D. 1739) is mentioned in Simmons' *life of* Dr W. Hunter pp. 14, 15 *n.* as discoverer of the *Membrana pupillaris.* He taught anatomy at Cambridge and made collections of anatomical preparations which passed at one time into Dr Hunter's possession.

Aldrichian professorship dates only from 1803.   J. Parsons (*Ch. Ch.*) was nominated Lee's reader in 1766, the year when he took his M.A., and three years before he was M.B. Under his direction the anatomical theatre was built; he provided excellent preparations, and read two courses of lectures in anatomy every year.   In 1780 Parsons was elected first clinical professor of the Radcliffe infirmary.

CHAPTER XVI.

CHEMISTRY.

"If he haue leasure to be idle (that is to study) he ha's a smatch at Alcumy, and is sicke of the Philosophers stone, a disease vncurable but by an abundant Phlebotomy of the purse."

J. Earle's *Micro-cosmographie.* [1628.]

JAMES KEILL, whom we have mentioned as an anatomist, translated Lemery's Course of Chemistry in 1698, thereby introducing English chemists to the current theory of the relations of acids and alkalis[1]. But ten years before that time, J. J. Beecher of Mentz had died, and G. E. Stahl was following out his observations, which had already borne fruit[2] in his *Zymotechnia Fundamentalis,* with an 'experimentum novum' sulphur verum arte producendi' (1697), which resulted in the enuntiation of the theory of *phlogiston,* the terminology of which was retained or adapted even by our Cavendish and Priestley in England in the latter half of the succeeding century, when they had passed to more positive observations and discoveries of the composition of water, and oxygen gas.

Long before a chair of Chemistry was endowed at Cambridge[3], we have Barrow's testimony[4] to the ardour with which

[1] Whewell, *Hist. Induct. Sciences,* III. 110.

[2] Whewell, *Hist. Induct. Sciences,* III. pp. 116—123.

[3] Uffenbach's visit to the Oxford chemical laboratory has been mentioned above (p. 176). Anthony Wood had gone through a course of chemistry in 1663 'under the noted chimist and rosicrucian, Peter Sthael of Strasburgh in Royal Prussia,' whom Ro. Boyle had brought to Oxford. Wallis, Wren, Bathurst and bp. Turner were his pupils. Also Locke, who was very troublesome at lecture and 'scorn'd'

to take notes. Wood paid £3 for the course. In Sept. 1683 the Oxford 'elabatory was quite finished' and R. Plot, J. Massey and some other scholars 'went a course of chemistry' and held friday afternoon conversations. In these meetings they were joined by Wallis, Bathurst, Aldrich, prof. Bernard, &c. (A. Wood's *Diary*). J. Friend's *Praelectiones Chymicae in quibus omnes fere operationes Chym. ad vera principia et ipsius naturae leges rediguntur* were published 8vo. Oxon. 1704.

[4] *Works* (Napier, 1859) IX. 46.

the study was pursued. In a speech delivered *in Comitiis* about the year 1654 he said : ' Equidem noui quorum animos ad haec studia igni chymico feruentius desiderium inflammauit: alios qui se Lullii, Villanouae et quae eiusdem farinae Philosophorum extant monumenta, immo et ipsius Paracelsi obscurissima scripta se capere et comprehendere non dubitarent; ne memorem alios egregios uiros, quorum magnanima audacia de Chrysopoeo Lapide nobilem siue fabulam siue historiam generosi fide amplecti non pertimesceret.'

Towards the close of the seventeenth century chemistry had been successfully taught at Cambridge for twenty years by a Veronese, John Francis Vigani. In the winter of 1692 Abraham De la Pryme went to his course, but ' by reason of the abstruceness of the art...got little or no good thereby.' He describes the 'Signior' as 'a very learned chemist, and a great traveller, but a drunken fellow[1].' 10 Feb. 1702—3, Vigani's services were acknowledged in the University by investing him with the title of Professor of Chemistry.

Bentley soon afterwards fitted up a chemical laboratory for him in the 'lumber hole,' eastward of Trinity bowling-green.

His two nearest successors, J. Waller, 1713, and J. Mickleborough, were Corpus men. Then followed J. Hadley of Queens' in 1756, the Plan of whose lectures was printed, Camb. 1758.

Two sets of lectures by professor Mickleborough with list of persons attending his courses in several years between 1726 and 1741 are preserved among the Caius College MSS. (619 = 342 *red*)[2]. In 1728 as many as three and twenty attended

---

[1] Diary of Abr. De la Pryme, p. 25 (*Surtees Soc.* No. 54). Monk's *Bentley*, I. 204. Cooper's *Annals*, IV. 53. Bentley's *Corresp.* Wordsw. 448. Rather more than a year later De la Pryme seems to have advanced in the study. He records in his diary ' 1694. *Febr.* 14. This day I received twelve little retorts and three receivers from London, to try and invent experiments, and all the things that I shall do I intend to put down in a proper book, and in imitation of the most learned

Democritus, to give them the title of χειρόκμητα, as he did his, which being interpreted implys the *Experiments of my own Personal Trying.* The retorts cost me 4*d.* a piece at London, and the receivers 6*d.*, and I pay'd for their carriage from thence hither 1*s.* 6*d.*'

[2] Another MS. at Caius [No. 460, a small 4to.; pp. 215, a few blank] contains *A Course of Chymistry in Four Books* by J. Yardley, Trin., M.A. 1704, a student in medicine in Vigani's time. *Bk.* I. contains some general

(the fee being one guinea), including Theodore Colladon, Genevensis, and a Cambridge apothecary. Only fourteen came to his fourth course in 1735[1], the list commencing with 'Charles Mason, A.M., Coll. Trin. Soc., Woodward Prof.; Sheppard Frere, Coll. Trin. Soc. Commens.[2],' &c., &c. The lectures embraced an encomium on Dr Friend, the first who applied the Newtonian philosophy to Chemistry. Calcinations. Distillation of Hartshorn. Analysis of Plants distilled in the Great Alembic. Distillation of Vitriol. Tinctures of Myrrh, Aloes, Saffron, Laudanum, Steel, and Antimony, and many by Digestion. Acids and Alkalis. Experiments of Phosphorus. A short course on the Four Elements.

In 1764, Ri. Watson of Trinity (afterwards bp. of Llandaff) was appointed, and his stipend augmented by the Government, with which he was in favour. Dr Watson 'knew nothing at all of Chemistry, had never read a syllable on the subject, nor seen a single experiment in it, at the time this honour was conferred' upon him: yet he had had the effrontery to signify his intention of reading chemical lectures in the University, to 'an eminent physician in London' who 'had expressed a wish to succeed Dr Hadley.' However he took to the subject, sent immediately after his election to Paris for an operator, and busied himself in his laboratory, so that in fourteen months he began to lecture to a very full audience. He delivered other courses in Nov. of the years 1766—8, and published volumes of Chemical Lectures in 1781, '82, and '86. In 1768 he printed *Institutiones Metallurgicae*, designed a series of chemical propositions in Rutherforth's system, and sent a paper on the *Solutions of Salts* to the Royal Society. In 1771 (when he printed an 'Essay on the Subjects of Chemistry, and their

---

Praecognita, Rules for Distillations, Cohobations, Sublimations, Extracts, Tinctures, Chymical Principles, Salts, Colours, Alkali Austera, Crystallization, Fermentation. *Bk.* II. Of Metals and Minerals. *Bk.* III. of Vegetables. *Bk.* IV. of Animals. Lutes and Fires. Calcination. Extraction. Coagulation. *Index.*

[1] In this year J. Rowning's (Magd.)

Natural Philosophy in four parts Camb. 8vo. commenced its appearance, being completed in 1744.

[2] I suppose this was the Mr Frere who accompanied John Byrom (Chetham Soc. 1855, p. 531) to Dr Long's astronomical lectures 29 Nov. 1733. He was educated at Bury and Trin. Coll. Camb., took no degree, bought Roydon Hall, Norf.

general division,' and a 'Plan of Lectures') a paper of his was noticed in the Journal Encyclopédique[1].

Dr Watson was enabled to conduct electrical experiments on so large a scale as to excite the admiration of professor Musschenbroek of Utrecht and Leyden. About 1747 he observed almost simultaneously with Franklin[2] 'positive and negative' (or as the former called them, 'more rare and more dense') electricity, and that when an electric body was excited, the electricity was not created, but collected. Watson published 'Institutionum chemicarum in praelectionibus academicis explicatarum pars metallurgica,' Camb. 1768, and 'Plan of a Course of Chemical Lectures,' Camb. 1771.

Isaac Pennington of St John's (finding a sufficient deputy in J. Milner[3]) succeeded Dr Watson in 1773; and when he was advanced to the Regius Professorship of Physic in 1793, his place was filled by W. Farish of Magdalene. He, finding that Chemistry was already being taught by Wollaston, the Jacksonian Professor, struck out quite a new line. 'The application of Chemistry to the Arts and Manufactures[4] of *Britain* presented a new and useful field of instruction, which, however, could not be cultivated with effect, without exhibiting whatever else was necessary to the full illustration of the subject. After having taken an *actual* survey of almost everything curious in the manufactures of the Kingdom, the Professor contrived a mode of exhibiting the operations and processes that are in use in nearly all of them. Having provided himself with a number of *Brass Wheels* of all forms, and sizes, such, that any

[1] *Anecdotes of* Ri. Watson (ed. 2) I. 45, 46, 53, 54, 64. Perhaps the most characteristic story of Bp. Watson's impudence is that told in J. S. Watson's *Porson* (pp. 79, 80,) where it is related that the professor having been recently primed with a quotation from Gregory, an author he had previously never seen, protested in a moderatorial speech '*Haec ex* Gregorio *illo* Nazianzeno, *quem semper in deliciis habui*' (an expression borrowed, by the way, from Erasmus). Porson alludes slyly to this audacity in his *Letters to* Tra-

vis, 223, 272. Watson's device of distilling wood in close vessels was said to have saved the government £100,000 a year for gunpowder (c. 1787).

[2] Whewell, *Hist. Induct. Sciences,* III. 12, 15, 22 (1837).

[3] Milner printed the 'Plan' of his chemical lectures, Camb. 1784.

[4] About 1750 Dr Charles Mason, one of the senior fellows of Trinity (B.A. 1722), a good mathematician, used to be much interested in practical mechanics, working at his lathe, &c. Cumberland's *Memoirs*, p. 106.

two of them can work with each other, the *Cogs* being all equal; and also with a variety of *Axles, Bars, Screws, Clamps,* &c., he constructs at pleasure, with the addition of the peculiar parts, *working Models* of almost every kind of *Machine.* These he puts in motion by a *Water Wheel,* or a *Steam Engine,* in such a way, as to make them in general do the actual work of the real Machine on a small scale; and he explains at the same time the chemical and philosophical principles, on which the various processes of the Arts exhibited, depend.

'In the course of his lectures he explains the theory and practice of *Mining* and of *Smelting* metallic Ores—of bringing them to nature—of converting, purifying, compounding, and separating the Metals, and the numerous and various Manufactures which depend upon them, as well as the Arts which are more remotely connected with them, such as *Etching* and *Engraving.* He exhibits the method of obtaining *Coal* and other *Minerals,* the processes by which *Sulphur, Alum, common Salt, Acids, Alcalies, Nitre,* and other *saline* substances are obtained, and in which they are used; the mechanical process in the formation of *Gunpowder,* as well as its theory and effects. He shews the arts of procuring and working *Animal* and *Vegetable* substances; the great staple manufactures of the country, in *Wool, Cotton, Linen, Silk;* together with the various chemical arts of *Bleaching,* of *Preparing* Cloth, of *Printing* it, of using *adjective* and *substantive* colours, and *Mordants* or *Intermediates* in Dying. He explains in general the nature of Machinery: the moving powers, such as *Water-wheels, Windmills,* and particularly the *agency* of Steam, which is the *great* cause of the modern improvement and extension of manufactures. He treats likewise on subjects which relate to the carrying on, or facilitating, the commerce of the country, such as *Inland Navigation,* the construction of *Bridges, Aqueducts, Locks, Inclined Planes,* and other contrivances, by which *Vessels* are raised or lowered from one Level to another; of *Ships, Docks, Harbours,* and *Naval Architecture.* On the whole, it is the great design of these Lectures to excite the attention of persons already acquainted with the principles of Mathematics, Philosophy, and Chemistry, to *Real Practice;* and by drawing their minds to the consideration of the most useful inventions of ingenious men, in all parts of the kingdom, to enlarge their sphere of amusement and instruction and to promote the improvement and progress of the Arts.

'These Lectures are given in the Schools in the Botanical Garden, alternately with those of the *Jacksonian* Professor, in the *Lent* and *Midsummer* Terms[1].'

In the vestibule of one of the most remarkable of European Laboratories, that of the chemical faculty in Bonn university, it is with some feeling of national pride that the Englishman will recognize among the select medallions of eminent chemists, &c., those of his own countrymen, Cavendish, Watt, and Davy.

The Hon. Henry Cavendish was matriculated Dec. 1749, he was admitted fellow-commoner of Peterhouse, being contemporary in residence with the E. of Euston (afterwards Duke of Grafton), Gray, and Jeremiah Markland. He left Cambridge just before the time when he should have taken his degree. As the 'three Articles' were then, and for about twenty years afterwards, required as a test for the degree of B.A., he may have been thereby deterred. Cavendish inherited some interest in science from his father, who was a meteorologist, and he himself has been ranked 'the third in order of time of the four great English pneumatic chemists of the 18th century: the other three being Hales, Black, and Priestley[2].' Sir H. Davy characterized him as "fearful of the voice of fame;" but now he is credited with being the real discoverer of the *Composition of Water*, to which Watt and Lavoisier have had their claims set up and demolished[3]. There is now a characteristic likeness of him in one of the windows of Peterhouse hall, from a cartoon by Mr Madox Brown, in his grey suit (once violet), and knocker-tailed periwig, standing with one hand

---

[1] *Univ. Calendar*, 1802, pp. 24, 25. Another sketch of Farish's lectures is given in *Facetiae Cantab.* 1836, p. 154; and another in the *Edinburgh Review* of the first number of the *Cambridge Philosophical Transactions* in 1821. In the reviewer's light sketch professors Clarke and Sedgwick are also noticed. I have seen a printed notice of the commencement of Farish's lectures for 1794.

[2] *Life of the Hon. H. Cavendish by* G. Wilson, M.D. (Cavendish Society's publications, 1851) p. 24.

[3] *Sir H. Ellis, Letters of Eminent Literary Men*, p. 427 (Camden Society).

behind his back, and his stockings hanging loose and un-gartered, like the boy Napoleon Bonaparte's[1].

Isaac Milner of Queens' was the first Jacksonian professor of Natural and Experimental Philosophy appointed in Cambridge (1783). According to the will of the founder, he and his successor, Fr. J. Hyde Wollaston, of Trinity Hall[2] (1792) paid great attention to the exhibition of 'facts' in Natural History, &c., at least three hundred experiments being exhibited annually[3]. But Milner's experiments in Optics, though entertaining, were 'very little more than exhibitions of the Magic Lanthorn on a gigantic scale[4].' When Vince broke through the bad example of preceding Plumian professors, by *lecturing* in Experimental Philosophy (1796), Wollaston devoted himself to Chemistry alone. Twelve students might receive nominations to attend these lectures *gratis*, four being reserved for Trinity.

William Hyde Wollaston[5], who studied medicine at Caius (M.B. 1788, M.D. and F.R.S. 1793), had a wider reputation than his namesake, as the discoverer of the goniometer for crystals, and was barely anticipated by Dalton in the rule of multiple proportions, a stepping-stone on the way of the atomic theory. With Smithson Tennant the Cambridge professor he detected the new metals palladium, rhodium, iridium and osmium in platinum ore, before Davy's discovery of potassium.

Tennant's other discoveries relate to the analysis of carbonic acid, the magnesian variety of limestone, the inflammable nature of the diamond, the chemical examination of emery, the nitrous solution of gold, and a mode of double distillation. Tennant was Copley medallist of the Royal Society 1804[6]. A notice of

[1] Wilson's *Cavendish*, pp. 167, 168.
[2] Afterwards Master of Sidney (1807).
[3] *Univ. Calendar*, 1802, p. 32.
[4] Gunning's *Reminisc.* I. viii.
[5] Whewell, *Hist. Induct. Sciences*, III. pp. 150, 151, 160, 181, 207 (1837). See also Munk's *Roll of R. C. P.* II. 381—3.
  Dr Webb preserved a printed paper

(dated 6 Dec. 1796) to the effect that 'in consequence of the election of Mr *Vince* to the Plumian Professorship, Mr *Wollaston* will discontinue his Lectures in Experimental Philosophy and intends to read *Chemistry* annually.' His apparatus was handed over to Vince, partly to use and partly to dispose of.
[6] Dyer, *Privil. Camb.* II. ii. 99.

his death is given in the next chapter, p. 199 *n.* Wright's account is not so accurate.

The Plan of Wollaston's chemical course was printed at Cambridge in 1794.

Later in the present century (1823) James Cumming of Trinity, the Cambridge professor of chemistry, determined the thermo-electric order of most of the metals within a few months of the discovery of thermo-electricity by Seebeck of Berlin[1]. Cumming's syllabus appeared in 1834 (Camb.)

In days when the Universities could not set before themselves the task of giving a good education to more than one or two classes of professional men, and when the ancient road branching at one point into its *triuium,* and again parting in a *quadriuium,* had become overgrown and impracticable for the heavier traffick of the Sciences, it was perhaps inevitable (though humiliating) that our ancient bodies should be content practically to abandon the work of pioneering students in the natural Sciences. 'What Science there was in England was in an attitude of hostility,' says the Rector of Lincoln College, speaking of Oxford at the time of *I. Casaubon's* visit about 1613[2]. 'Neither Selden nor Bacon were ever fellows of a college.' This is the more to be regretted when we think of Bacon's almost pathetic dedications to the universities, whereof one is now engraved upon the pedestal of his monument in Trinity ante-chapel.

In the seventeenth century the universities manifested some jealousy of the Royal Society[3], which (after some London meetings) was first established in Oxford in 164⅔. Even beyond the middle of the eighteenth century it beneficially centralised the best powers of the country on the Natural Sciences in their widest sense. Dr South, the University Orator, at the Encaenia in Oxford in 1669, took occasion to inveigh against it in his satirical vein, denouncing its members 'as underminers of the University; which was very foolish and untrue, as well as un-

[1] Dyer, *Privil. Camb.* III. 90.
[2] *p.* 417.
[3] Evelyn's *Diary* (July 9, 1669) *Univ. Society,* p. 287. *Reliqu. Hearn.* (anno 1731) Bliss III. 71. *ed.* 1. Huber's

Engl. Univ. (F. W. Newman) II. i. 82. Hobbes' sneer at the Royal Society is quoted by Dr Whewell, *Hist. Moral. Phil.* p. 53. Mayor's *Matt. Robinson* 104 *et passim.*

reasonable. In 1700 the tory W. King of Ch. Ch., LL.D., ridiculed the Royal Society and its president Sir Hans Sloane in the *Transactioneer*[1]. And Hearne (*Diary*, April 13, 1731) remarks that it 'sinks every day in it's credit both at home and abroad, occasioned in some measure by it's new statutes for election of foreigners and natives by posting up·their names in the public room ten weeks together. 'Tis observable (what I have been told by one of the fellows thereof) that this Society is now as much tinged with party principles as any publick body, and Whigg and Tory are terms better known than the naturalist, mathematician, or antiquary.'

[1] Johnson's *Life of* W. King. Sir Hans Sloane was president in 1727. He was secretary in 1693, whereupon he revived the publication of their *Transactions* which were commenced 6 Mar. 164$\frac{3}{4}$.

CHAPTER XVII.

GEOLOGY AND MINERALOGY.

" Terrible apprehensions and answerable unto their names, are raised of
Fayrie stones, and *Elves* spurs, found commonly with us in Stone, Chalk and
Marl-pits."

T. Browne, *Vulgar Errors*, ii. 5.

ALTHOUGH some of the chief men who were interested in
mineralogy and geology in the last century got their degrees
elsewhere , we find that both at Oxford and at Cambridge the
study of stones was not a novelty.   Two keepers of the Ashmolean, Ro. Plott (*Magd. H.*) and E. Llwyd (*Jes.*) established the
credit of *Oxford* in the 17th century.   The latter edited a
catalogue of english fossils in the Ashmolean Museum, under
the title of *Lithophylacii Britannici Iconographia*[2] (8vo. Lond.
1699; ed. 2. *Oxon.* 1760).   Llwyd's book has been useful ever
since, especially for the figures.

'A Lapidary or the history of Pretious Stones by T. Nichols
sometimes of Jesus-Colledge in Cambridge,' printed by T. Buck,
4to. Camb. 1652, was founded chiefly upon the *Gemmarum
Historia* of Anselm Boetius de Boot.   The classification of
stones by sizes tells of diligence and system at Cambridge, if
the science was but infantile.

The study of GEOLOGY may be said to have been begun at
Cambridge by the bequest of J. Woodward, M.D.[3] (dated 1 Oct.
1727) of his original collection of English Fossils (begun in
1695 with wonderful system and sagacity) in two cabinets with
their catalogues to that University, and at the same time the
foundation of the Geological Professorship or Lectureship

---

[1] e.g. Woodward from Lambeth,
his antagonist Sir J. Hill from Scotland, and in more recent times 'father'
W. Smith from Dublin.

[2] Whewell, *Hist. Induct. Sciences*,

iii. 495, 496.   Hearne's *Diary* (1706).
Bliss i. 107.

[3] 'Woodward; a man ridiculed by
Pope who was his contemporary, but
who was far in advance of his age in

with a view to opposing the theory of Dr Camerarius that
fossils were not of organic origin[1]. Dr Conyers Middleton of
Trinity (Bentley's 'fiddling Conyers',) was the first to fill it,
being elected in 1731. Upon Dr Woodward's death his collection of *Foreign* Fossils also was secured for £1,000 (*Reliq.
Hearn.* III. 18.)

The professor was bound to attend at the Museum and to
give oral instruction ' to all such curious and intelligent persons
as shall desire a view of them'[2]—he was expected also to deliver four lectures a year in latin or english, and to publish one
at least of them.

About 1732 was printed by Bowyer *Oratio* de novo Physio-
logiae explicandae munere ex celeberrimi *Woodwardi* Testamento instituto, habita *Cantabrigiae in Scholis Publicis* a Conyers Middleton[3] S. T. P., Acad. Cant. Protobibliothecario et
Lectori ibidem Woodwardiano.

Middleton's successor was Charles Mason of Trinity, known
as a practical engineer of a queer character. His ' Oratio Woodwardiana' appeared in 4to. Camb. 1734.

J. Mitchell of Queens' followed him (1762—4). Shortly
before he was made professor he had enunciated with novel dis-
tinctness the stratified structure of the earth's crust. (Philos.
Trans. 1760). His papers shewed that he had himself investigated the strata which occur between Cambridge and York[4].
His 'Essay on the Cause and Phenomena of Earthquakes'
(1760) is philosophical and in advance of his contemporaries.
His successor, Professor Sam. Ogden (Joh.) 1764, was a
remarkable preacher. T. Green (Trin.) 1778 spent some pains
in arranging the collections and books. J. Hailstone (Trin.)
1788 was a botanist and antiquary as well as a geologist. He
seems, from a comparison of the Calendars of 1802 and the fol-

---

perceiving the importance of collections
of organic and other fossils.' *Whewell.*
(Todhunter, I. 379.) His earlier works
were translated into french; *Amst.*
1735, &c.

[1] Woodward, like Ray and Whiston,
considered Geology in illustration of
the Mosaic record.

[2] *Facetiae Cantab.* pp. 151, 152.

[3] Middleton held the professorship
1731—4. The office of Protobibliothe-
carius was created specially for him in
spite of Bentley, Dec. 15, 1721. In
1845 it was consolidated with the Li-
brarianship. His scheme for the library is extant.

[4] Whewell, *Hist. Induct. Sciences,*
III. 501.

lowing years, to have been pretty constantly employed in giving descriptions to all comers for four hours twice a week, though he did not lecture. He made a collection distinct from Woodward's[1]. When Mr Hailstone died in 1818 there came forward a man who had studied geology for some time, G. Corn. Gorham of Queens' (B.A. 1809), known in theological controversy, and biographer of the botanists Martyn.

The successful candidate was Adam Sedgwick, who with boldness equal to Watson's, but with more striking success, undertook to get up his subject *after his election.* He lectured both in his auditorium and in the open air with characteristic energy.

Now, the Woodwardian, with the additions of the splendid Fletcher, Leckenby, and Walton collections, its fine series of fossil reptiles, and numerous other additions, many of them the result of Professor Sedgwick's work and liberality, is a museum of which the university may well be proud; while the most ancient foundation of Peterhouse has a choice practical selection of specimens on a smaller scale, gathered and arranged with loving care by the late Master, whose love of science and forethought have left a mark on the Woodwardian Museum also.

While Mr Hailstone was alive there arose an ardent disciple of the kindred science of MINERALOGY, Edward Daniel Clarke of Jesus, the famous traveller and discoverer of the Eleusinian ' Ceres' or Caryatid. He gave lectures in mineralogy, Feb. 17, 1807, which were enthusiastically received. The end of the following year he was made first *professor* of mineralogy at Cambridge. Hailstone was favourable to his lectures, which were delivered in the Botanic room by invitation from Tho. Martyn, who was become superannuated.

Clarke's lecture-room was thus described from recollection—

'We will wile away a few minutes over the beautiful specimens which are so delicately arranged upon the table, and the surrounding cases, from the primitive formation of granite to the costly stones and precious metals; the [gas] blow-pipes[2] too, [his own invention], whose intense heat in fusing metal has

<hr>

[1] Hailstone published '*Outlines of the Geology of* Cambridgeshire' 1816.

[2] Cf. Gunning's *Reminisc.* Vol. II.

chap. vii. and Whewell's *Writings and Letters* (Todhunter) I. 378.

so much assisted the science; the picture of the grotto of Anti-
paros, with its beautiful stalactites and crystal floor; the ingenious section of the strata of this island; the green god of the
New Zealanders; and a vast collection of curious and precious
things.... His earnest manner of recommending his darling
pursuit shows that his heart and soul are wrapt in it. To a
full audience he mentions the names of some ambitious travellers among his pupils who have brought him specimens from
Scandinavia, Switzerland, and the Pyrenees[1].' He was called
'*Stone* Clarke' as distinguishable from two other professors,
Bone Clark (anat.) and *Tone* Clarke [Whitfield,—(music)].

J. Holme of Peterhouse framed the syllabus for his lectures,
and assisted the professor to accuracy in details[2].

Many may like to have preserved the following *jeu d'esprit*
on Dr E. D. Clarke, attributed to professor Smyth of Peterhouse. It exists in various forms, and has been communicated
to me by Mr J. Willis Clark of Trinity.

> I sing of a Tutor renowned
> Who went roving and raving for knowledge,
> And gather'd it all the world round,
> And brought it in boxes to College.
> And because Mathematics[3] was clear,—
> Too clear for our Metaphysicians[3]—
> Introduced Dr *Gall* as I hear
> To enlighten his Academicians.
>
> Tol de rol, &c.
>
> His pupils flocked eagerly round
> When they heard there was nothing to bore 'em,
> But guess their surprize when they found
> A lot of old skulls placed before 'em.
> Astonished confused[4] and perplext,
> They stared at their Lecturer able,

[1] *Facetiae Cantab.* p. 153.

[2] Gunning *l. cit.* In [Wright's] *Alma
Mater* II. 31 Clarke's grief at his friend
Tennant's death is commemorated.
When Farish became Jacksonian Professor, S. Tennant succeeded him in
the chair of Chemistry (1813). He
was devoted to that science even as an
undergraduate (1786), and but for his
untimely end (which was owing, not to
drowning as Wright supposed, but to
the fall of a draw-bridge near Boulogne
in 1815) he would have left a lasting
name behind him. 'He was known
throughout Europe by several important discoveries, among others that
the diamond is the purest form of
carbon, which he explained in the *Philosophical Transactions*.' (G. Pryme's
Recoll. p. 115. Gunning's *Reminisc.*
II. ii.)

[3] *al.* 'Metaphysics.......Mathemati-
cians.'

[4] *al.* 'plagued.'

And the Freshmen expected that next
Old Nick would pop up through the table.

'Come round me, Sophs[1], Freshmen and all,'
Cried the Doctor, and sprang from his chair:
'You shall hear of the wonderful *Gall*,
And of skulls and[2] their mysteries rare.
Of Thought, how it comes and it goes,
And of Life in the marrow descending;
And I'll tell you what nobody knows,
And you'll see me begin at the ending.

'First there's life that must fashion and warm,
And when figure and form have begun
The skull is the seat of the charm,
'Tis there you must look for the fun.
And you've only to peep in the brain
Just to see how it bumps and it bends,
And when the whole matter is plain,
Why—'tis plain the whole mystery ends.

'Observe now this skull I pick out,
'Tis[3] hard; see how slowly it moulders;
And hence I conclude without doubt
'Twas on some Fellow Commoner's shoulders.
And *this*, by[4] the lines in the face,
Belonged to some fam'd Rhetorician.
And *this* by this little soft place,
Was the head of a Metaphysician.'

Then he talked in a *capital* strain
Of the Lion the Bear and the Fox,
Of Parrots with musical brain,
And of men with mechanical blocks,
That the Organ of Courage was clear
To the test of an Investigation,
And he talked till his Pupils looked queer
Of an Organ of Assassination.

Next he shewed how the Organ of Thought
Was developed, as easy as may be,
How Man to perfection was brought
By tinkering the nob of the Baby.
The Doctor grew more and more able
And his eloquence clearer and clearer,
Till he knocked round the skulls on the table
And knocked up the skull of each hearer.

---

[1] *al.* 'ye merry men all.'
[2] *al.* 'and of brains and of hair.'
[3] *al.* 'How hard! See, how little it moulders.'

[4] *al.* ...'by the marks in this place
Was the head of a Mathematician
And this, by the lines in the face.'

But[1] alas ! while the Doctor was prosing
Of Brains[2] and their wonderful parts,
  In entered a German[3] imposing
To sell him a lump of Red Quartz.
  Red Quartz ! There was no standing that,
And besides he had with him a gander
  Which he swore had grown jolly and fat
At the Tomb of the Great *Alexander.*

And *Flaxman* was now at the door,
To talk of the *Ceres*[4] divine;
  And *Bircham*[5] to settle the *Corps;*
And *Caldwell* to sell him bad wine.
  In the Court were five Lions from Town,
And a message came hot from the Master
  So that round about up-stairs and down
The plot thicken'd faster and faster.

Oh me ! cried poor *Clarke* in a stew,
And to lecture no longer was able,
  Off, whizz ! like a rocket he flew,
Overturning the skulls and the table.
  And he cried in a *whiff* as he went
That now nothing more was expedient,
  That in short they all knew what he meant
And that now he must be their Obedient.

So huzza for all Tutors and Lectures
And our able promoters of knowledge,
  And the rest of our learned protectors,
Not forgetting the Cooks of the College.
  And long may a Tutor be found
To explain Dr *Gall's* lucubrations,
  And his humbugging System profound
Of prancing and proud botherations.

After 1813, when he was translated to the Jacksonian professorship, Farish prefixed (in the *University Calendar* of 1814)
to his syllabus about mining, &c. (see above p. 191)—'the
natural history of minerals.' Hailstone and Clarke were already engaged for that subject.

[1] *al.* 'Thus far had the Doctor pro-
    ceeded.'
[2] *al.* ' sculls.'
[3] *al.*   'and pleaded
He'd brought him a lump of fine Quartz.'
Fine quartz ! '
[4] *the Ceres.* See p. 198.
[5] In 1803 Capt. S. Bircham of the

30th foot drilled the Cambridge Volun-
teers. Prof. Clarke was on the Committee and his college (Jesus) supplied
the largest contingent to the *corps*
after Trinity and S. John's. Ld.
Palmerston was one of his comrades.
Cp. Otter's *Clarke* II. 210. Cooper's
Annals IV. 478, 9. Gunning II. vii.

CHAPTER XVIII.

BOTANY.

Bernardus ualles, colles Benedictus amabat,
Franciscus uillas, magnas Ignatius urbes.

IF the fathers of the monastic orders had their tastes in scenery and situation, their degenerate posterity at Oxford and Cambridge in the seventeenth and eighteenth centuries took great pleasure in gardens. Paradise and Christ Church Walks, Merton and Magdalene Gardens, St John's Grove, New College and Wadham Gardens, Trinity Mount—beguiled the solitude of Earle, Addison, and Whitefield; while '*Kinges colledge backesides*[1],' the Groves of Peterhouse, Queens', and Trinity Hall, the Wilderness of St John's, the Gardens of Christ's, Emmanuel and Sidney, as well as the walks of Trinity, offered their attractions to Barrow-and Simeon. The avenue of the last-named royal foundation, with Coton Church in the distance, suggested to the sportive fancy of Porson a type of a clerical fellowship which he declined — 'a long dreary walk with a church at the end of it.' Many, perchance, would question the great critic's estimate both of the 'Coton grind' and of the Trinity-fellowship and country-Parsonage—

'Sheltered, but not to social duties lost,
Secluded, but not buried[2].'

However, gardens are not only suited for academic discussion and meditation, recreation and pleasant converse; but as they were in the days of Evelyn and Sir T. Browne, they

---

[1] See Speed's map of Cambridge, 1610.
[2] W. Wordsworth's *Excursion*, Book v.

may be made studies in themselves[1]. Lord Bacon wrote as
follows in 1605, 'We see likewise that some places instituted for
physic [*medicinae* (1623)] have annexed the commodity of
gardens for simples of all sorts, and do likewise command the
use of dead bodies for anatomies[2].'

The study of botany made one very great and important
step in the course of the last century. But if we say that
Charles von Linné, or Linnæus, of Sweden published his most
remarkable works about the middle of the century, and that
his system was introduced into our Universities about ten years
later, and that there were one or two families of enthusiasts
who kept the claims of their subject before our learned public,
we have said nearly all. If we may say that Newton belonged
to the seventeenth century, and left few behind to continue
his work, we might more fairly surrender Ray (d. 170$\frac{4}{5}$) to
that period, and assert that his work outstript our investigations for the next century in their claim to be recognized as
scientific. J. Ray was a student of Catharine hall, whence
he migrated to Trinity and became fellow of that royal foundation (1649)—but was afterwards deprived (though in holy
orders) for refusing to protest against the Solemn League and
Covenant. He subsequently conformed.

After his time English botanists seem to have contented
themselves with collecting plants, especially curiosities, and
in publishing catalogues. In such occupations and in herbarizing
expeditions considerable energy was expended. Even as early
as 1654 Ray's contemporary Barrow[3] asserted that Cambridge
freshmen could name and distinguish all plants that were to
be found in the fields and gardens of the neighbourhood.

When Uffenbach visited Oxford in 1710 he went (Sept. 19),
to the *hortus medicus* with Dr Büttner. They had an introduction to professor Jacob Bobart[4], an ill-favoured man, rather

---

[1] The colleges were intended apparently to be self supporting. To this
day Queens' has its own kitchen garden. Mr J. W. Clark has drawn my
attention to the *reditus orti* in the
old *computus* rolls, whence it appears
that in 1472 (e. gr.) Peterhouse made
what was then a handsome sum from

'*auelanis*' (nuts) and '*focalibus.*'
[2] *Advancement of Learning*, II. 'To
the King.'
[3] *Works* (Napier) ix. 46.
[4] The younger Jacob Bobart, who
like his father was keeper of the Oxford physick-garden (1683—1719.),
manufactured a winged dragon out

a gardener than a botanist. However he was devoted to his occupation, and published the work of his more scientific predecessor Rob. Morison[1]. The plants seemed to Uffenbach pretty numerous, but not to be compared with the treasures of Leyden and Amsterdam. Some specimens intended for the former place had found their way to Oxford, having been captured by a French privateer; afterwards when they were recognized Bobart kindly restored them to professor Hermann of Leyden. Büttner did not see a dozen plants which he considered rare.

Morison died in London Nov. 10, 1683, and the second professor Edwin Sandys of Wadham was not appointed by the University till 1720, if we may rely on an old Oxford Calendar. Jacob Bobart the younger (above-mentioned) succeeded Morison at least in the work of the place. His father Jacob, who died in $16\frac{79}{80}$, had also published (1648) a catalogue of the plants at Oxford, more than twenty years before the first professor was appointed. The botanical gardens seem to have descended from father to son in quite a patriarchal style. Beside the Linnæi at Upsal, and the Martyns at Cambridge, there were at Oxford the Bobarts, and Humphrey and John Sibthorp, father and son (1747, and 1784—96). These last were preceded by John James Dillenius of Darmstadt, who had followed Sherard to England in 1721, of whose foundation he was first professor in 1728. He had undertaken an edition of Ray's *Synopsis Stirpium Britannicarum.* He entered at

of a rat's skin which deluded several naturalists and was deposited in the museum. (Grey's *Hudibras* I. 125 *n.*) Cp. *Terrae-Filius* XXVI.

[1] However Cuvier and Whewell do not speak very highly of his system of classification. 'The most distinct part of it, that dependent on the fruit, was probably borrowed from Caesalpinus.' (Whewell *Hist. Ind. Sciences* III. 296.) Morison was an Aberdeen man wounded near Dee bridge in the Royal cause.—He retired to France where Charles II. found him, and after his Restoration made him superintendent

of the Royal Gardens, and 'first director of the Botanical Garden at Oxford.' He wrote 'Remarks on the Mistakes of the two Bauhins (1669), and 'Plantarum Historia universalis Oxoniensis' (the original volume) fol. Clarendon Press, 1680.

Morison was the Duke of Ormond's candidate for the Sedleian professorship. Ralph Bathurst wrote to the duke (their Chancellor) 16 Nov. 1675, to explain that botany was not enough for a professor of Natural Philosophy, and that they elected Dr Millington. (Warton's *Bathurst*, I. 138.)

St John's, and in 1735 received the degree of M.D. He died
in 1747, having publisht *Hortus Elthamensis*, and a *History
of Mosses.*

We have a quaint account of the dutch appearance of the
Oxford Physick Garden in 1707, from the pen of Thomas
Tickell (*Queen's*), in his poem of ' Oxford.'

> 'How sweet the landskip! where in living trees
> Here frowns a vegetable Hercules[1]!
> There fam'd Achilles learns to live again,
> And looks yet angry in the mimic scene;
> Here artful birds, which blooming arbours show,
> Seem to fly higher while they upward grow,
> From the same leaves both arms and warriors rise;
> And every bough a different charm supplies.
> So when our world the great Creator made'——&c. &c.

The '*Pocket Companion for* Oxford' 1761 (pp. 22—24),
dilates upon the architectural glories of the Physick Garden
adorned by the Earl of Danby, 1632. 'The Garden is divided
into four Quarters, with a broad Walk down the Middle, a
cross Walk, and one all round. Near the Entrance, one on the
R. and the other on the L. H., are two elegant and useful
Greenhouses, built by the University for *Exotics;* of which
there is as considerable a Collection, as can be met with any
where. One of the large Aloes was blown in 1750, and grew
to the Height of 21 Feet. In the Quarters within the Yew
Hedges, is the greatest Variety imaginable of such Plants
as require no artificial Heat to nourish them, all ranged in
their proper Classes, and numbered. At the lower end of the
middle Walk, near the Iron Gates, are two magnificent Yew-
Trees, cut in the Form of Pedestals (but of Enormous Size)
with a Flower-Pot on the Top, and a Plant as it were
growing out of it....Eastward of the Garden, without the Walls
is an excellent Hot-House; where tender Plants, such whose
native Soil lies beneath the Tropics, are raised and brought
to great Perfection; viz. the Anana or Pine-Apple, the Plan-
tain, the Coffee Shrub, the Caper Tree, the Cinnamon, the

---

[1] Mrs Alicia D'Anvers (*Academia:
or Humours of the Univ. of Oxford
in Burlesque Verse,* 1691, *p.* 16 *n.*)
speaks of ' A Tree cut into the shape
of a Giant the Face Alabaster' in the
Physick Garden, and another in the
shape of a crane.

Creeping Cereus, and many others. These Pine-Apples have nearly the same delicious Flavour as those in warmer Climates ; the Caper and the Coffee-Shrub also bear well.

' The Earl settled an annual Revenue for the Maintenance of the Garden, and furnished it with Plants and Herbs, for the Use of such Gentlemen of the University who study Botany, as a necessary Branch of Physic. This useful Foundation has been much improved by the late Dr *Sherard*, who brought from *Smyrna* a valuable Collection of Plants. He built a Library adjoining to the Garden, for Botanical Books, and furnished it with a curious Collection. One End of this Building hath, within a few Years been altered into a convenient Apartment for the Professor whose Salary is paid out of the Interest of 3000*l.* given by Dr *Sherard* for that Purpose. The Assistant to the Professor is paid by the University.' In 1764 Israel Lyons the younger, a native of Cambridge, lectured on botany at Oxford to a class of sixty or more, at the instance of [Sir] Joseph Banks who had learnt that science from him. He had some reputation as a mathematician.

The following botanical works were produced at Oxford :—

1648. Catalogus Horti Botanici Oxon. (by Jacob Bobart the elder.)
1658. Catalogus &c. priore duplo auctior. (by P. Stephan, W. Browne and Bobart.)
1672. Plantarum Umbelliferarum Distributio Nova. Ro. Morison.
1678. Plantarum Historia Universalis Oxoniensis, fol. Vol. I. (by R. Morison: posthumous.)
1690. Plantarum Hist. Universal. Oxon. Vol. II. (by Jacob Bobart the younger.)
1699. In Historiam Plantarum Adnotationes Nominum singularum plantarum linguâ Arabicâ, Persicâ, Turcicâ, by T. Hyde D.D. Queen's, oriental professor and keeper of the Bodleian.
1713. Vertumnus. An Epistle to Mr Jacob Bobart, Botany Professor of the univ. of Oxford and keeper of the Physick-Garden. (frontisp.) 12mo. pp. 1—33.
1732. Hortus Elthamensis. J. J. Sherard Dillenius[1].
1740. Historia Muscorum. J. J. Sherard Dillenius.
1794. Flora Oxoniensis exhibens Plantas in Agro Oxon. Auctore Jo. Sibthorp, M.D., F.R.S.

[1] Professor Dillenius of *S. John's* whom Sherard brought from Giessen and appointed his first professor was created M.D. in 1735. He scattered foreign and indigenous seeds in the country round Oxford. Dr Alcock used to find the plants when he went botanizing about 1740. *Memoirs of* Nathan Alcock (1780) p. 24.

1808. Flora Graeca & Florae Graecae Prodromus, vol. I. 8vo. J. Sibthorp
(the characters by Sir J. E. Smith.)

In the middle of the seventeenth century, Matthew Robinson, of St John's, was an ardent botanist at Cambridge, and
pursued the study after he left the university[1].

Adam Buddle, whose botanical collection Uffenbach saw in
the British Museum in 1710 (*Reisen* III. 202) took his degree at
Catharine Hall in 1681.

Among the records of permission for non-residence, which
were granted at Peterhouse from time to time, is the licence
of 'W. Vernon on the approval of the Visitor to be absent for
three or four years to improve his Botanick Studies in the
West Indies,' with the proviso that he shall certify yearly
that he is alive and unmarried. (Dated 23 Dec. 1697.) Vernon
collected plants in Maryland, as Hans Sloane did in Jamaica,
and John Banister in Virginia[2].

Of the minor botanists of Cambridge in the last century
we may notice Benjamin Stillingfleet the younger, whom Gray
described as a cheerful, honest and good-hearted man. His
grandfather was the bishop of Worcester, whose ex-chaplain
Bentley invited this young man to Trinity and then used
his influence to prevent his election to a fellowship, observing
that 'it was a pity that a gentleman of Mr Stillingfleet's parts
should be buried within the walls of a College.' The colour
of his stockings has been immortalized in our language as the
sobriquet for learned ladies such as delighted in his company.
He made in 1755, and published in 1761, the *Calendar of
Flora*, in Swedish and English, *Miscellaneous Tracts* by members of Upsal University, translated from the latin 1759, &c.,
and other works. He was one of the first (in 1757) to bring
the system of Linnæus into notice in England[3].

At the end of the century James Lambert, a senior fellow
of Trinity and regius professor of greek, was much addicted
to this study[4]. The *Quarterly Reviewer* said in 1827 (p. 263),
that the study of botany was then 'just awakened out of a
thirty years' slumber.'

[1] Mayor's *M. Robinson* pp. 31, 106.
[2] Whewell, *Hist. Induct. Sciences*, III. p. 291, ed. 1837.
[3] Boswell's *Johnson*, sub anno 1781. Nichols' *Lit. Anecd.* II. 336.
[4] Gunning's *Reminisc.* II. ch. iv.

The following books relating to Cambridge and Cambridgeshire botany have been printed :—

1660. Catalogus Plantarum circa Cantabrigiam nascentium I. Raius. 8vo.
1663. Ray's first Appendix ad Catalogum &c. 8vo. and 12mo.
1667. Edmundi Castelli Oratio. (Scripture botany elucidated from oriental writers [1].)
1685. Ray's second Appendix.
1716—27. Five Decads of a Historia Plantarum Succulentarum...quae in Horto sicco coli non possunt. (R. Bradley.) 4to.
1727. Methodus Plantarum circa Cantabrigiam nascentium (J. Martyn) 8vo. and 12mo.
1734. Bradley's Hist. Plant. Succulent. (reprinted posthumously).
1741. The Georgicks of Virgil with a Translation and Notes (partly botanical) by J. Martyn.
1749. The Bucolicks (ditto).
1754. On the Sex of Holly, by J. Martyn (*Philos. Transact.*)
1763. Plantae et Herbationes Cantabrigienses. T. Martyn.
——— A Short Account of Dr Walker's Donation to the Botanick Garden. T. Martyn.
——— Fasciculus Plantarum circa Cantabrigiam nascentium quae *post Raium* observatae fuere. Israel Lyons jun. (Bowyer).
1764. Heads of Botany Lectures (privately printed). T. Martyn.
1771. Catalogus Horti Botanici Cantabrigiensis. T. Martyn.
1772. Catalogus &c. *editio secunda.* (With Lectures and a Plan of the Gardens prefixed.)
1775. The Elements of Natural History. T. Martyn. *Camb.* 8vo.
1782. Heads of Lectures on Botany, Natural History and Fossils. T. Martyn.
1785. Rousseau's Letters on Elements of Botany. To a young Lady. T. Martyn.
1788. Thirty-Eight Plates to illustrate Linnæus' System of Vegetables and Rousseau's Letters. T. Martyn.
1786—93. Three parts of *Flora Cantabrigiensis* by R. Relhan (collected in 1802 and 1820.)
1787. *Heads of a Course of* Botanical *Lectures* delivered at Cambridge by R. Relhan.
1792—4. Flora Rustica. T. Martyn.
1793. The Language of Botany. A dictionary with critical Remarks. T. Martyn.
1794. *Horti Botanici* Cantab. *Catalogus* [2].
——— *Account of the Botanic Garden* at Cambridge [3].
1802, 1820. Relhani *Flora Cantabrigiensis,* see above.
1804, 1807. *Hortus Cantabrigiensis ;* or a Catalogue of Plants Indigenous and Exotic, by *James Donn,* Curator.
1807. T. Martyn's edition of P. Miller's *Gardener's and Botanist's Dictionary.* (A list of Fen-plants by W. Marshall, Esq. of Ely is given in G. Pryme's *Recollections,* pp. 147, 405.)

[1] A copy in Queens' Coll. Library, M. 14. 36.

[2] Queens' Coll. Library, Hh. 3. 31.

[3] *ibid.* P. 5. (11).

1829. A Catalogue of British Plants arranged according to the Natural
System, with the Synonyms of De Candolle, Smith and Lindley.
By Prof. J. S. Henslow. Camb. 8vo. pp. 40.

It appears that about 1588 John Gerard the herbalist
tried to move lord Burleigh to establish a botanical garden
in Cambridge, and to recommend him as 'Herbarist[1],' but
his project came to nothing, and the letter which he composed never had the Chancellor's signature. A similar attempt
to establish a physic garden at Cambridge was made a century
later (1695), which also met with no success[2].

Ri. Davies M.D. of Queens', writing to Dr Hales in 1759,
on the *General State of Education*, &c., says ' *Oxford* indeed
has long enjoyed a Botanic Garden, which since the time of
Mr *Sherard's* donations has been properly supported. There
has also been lately erected there a magnificent pile of
Building by the donation of a celebrated Physician of the
last age. But it has not proved a real enlargement of the
School of Science.'—The Library founded by John Radcliffe,
M.D., *Linc.* 1682, was originally entirely the Physical Library.
It was opened April 13, 1749.

The ground for the garden at Cambridge was actually
measured and the plan drawn in 1696, but through some
unknown impediment the scheme failed[3]. But the hopes of a
later generation were raised when the title of Professor of
Botany was conferred on Ri. Bradley[4], F.R.S., by a grace dated
Nov. 10, 1724. He was author of a large number of miscellaneous works on botany and agriculture. He died in 1732,
Nov. 5, while measures were being taken to deprive him on
account of his irregularities. It is said that he was chosen professor ' by means of a pretended verbal recommendation from
Dr Sherard to Dr Bentley, and pompous assurances that he
would procure the University a public Botanical Garden by his
own private purse and personal interest... with the mere view

[1] Cooper's *Annals*, II. 458, 459.
[2] Baker MS. xlii. 138 *b*, ap. Cooper's
Annals, IV. 30.
[3] Cole MS. XXXIII. 26, *Athenae* III.
312.

[4] Bradley's most important research
related to exotic succulent plants.
See preceding page, s. a. 1734, and
Nichols' *Lit. Anecd.* I. 446 *n*.

(it should seem) of obtaining the Botanical Chair[1].' How thoroughly Bentley was alive to the importance of this as of other branches of science may be seen from his correspondence (*Wordsw.* pp. 620—625) with the Rev. John Lawrence on *Silphium* and *Laserpitium.*

Bradley publicly repeated his promise in his lectures in 1729, but nothing was done. And as he usually neglected to read lectures the university made no difficulty to permit another person to do it. Mr John Martyn, F.R.S., who in his early days as a counting-house clerk had herbarised in St George's Fields, was 'recommended by Dr Sherard and Sir Hans Sloane as a proper person to execute the office. Accordingly in the next year (1727) in the Anatomy Schools he gave the first course that ever had been read there in that Science, with a view to restore this study on the spot which should seem most adapted to its growth, as having nourished the most eminent of all our english Naturalists, the excellent Mr Ray.' It appears, however, that Bradley was shamed into reading a course of Lectures on the *Materia Medica* in 1729, which he published in 1730.

John Martyn entered at Emmanuel in 1730. In the following year he had several conferences with Dr Mawson, the V. C., and Phil. Miller of the Chelsea garden[2] about the projected physick garden at Cambridge, but the ground (Brownell's) designed for it, was secured for some other purpose. In 1733 on Bradley's death J. Martyn was elected professor, H. Goddard of St John's and T. Parne of Trin. retiring.

He continued to lecture only till 1735, when other employment engaged his time. However, he did not lose his interest in the subject, but soon afterwards opened a correspondence with Linnaeus: and in 1741 he sent forth his botanical edition of Virgil's Georgicks dedicated to Mead, the astronomical portion being submitted to Halley. In 1749 his translation and notes of the Bucolicks followed.

He had a valuable botanical library (200 vols.) which with

[1] Gorham's *Memoirs of the* Martyns pp. 31, 32...113. Cooper's *Annals*, IV. 185.

[2] The interview between Miller and

Bentley, which the latter terminated abruptly with the celebrated '*Walker, my hat*,' is narrated by Monk (*Life* II. 406, 407).

his *Hortus Siccus* of foreign plants he bequeathed to the University on his resignation. The lack of a garden was still felt: indeed we are told that W. Heberden's course of experiments on *Medicinal* plants of Cambridgeshire, about 1748, was spoilt for want of one[1]. But it was left for Martyn's son to supply it. In 1761 Thomas Martyn (5th senior optime, Emman. 1756), tutor of Sidney, succeeded his father Joh. Martyn of Emmanuel (who survived exactly six years) as professor of Botany. In the following year Dr Ri. Walker, Bentley's Vice Master, endowed the new garden, where many plants had already been put in, and a greenhouse partially erected. He appointed T. Martin (*sic*) as first reader, and C. Miller first curator[2]. T. Martyn introduced the Linnaean system[3] into his first lecture in 1763, contemporaneously with professor Hope in Edinburgh.

Young Martyn's publications have been enumerated above, so far as they relate to Cambridge. In May 1766 he had but few pupils, and those inattentive. His curator C. Miller went to the East Indies in 1770, and the professor gratuitously supplied his place, receiving (till 1793) nothing but lecture-fees. Soon after he married the sister of the master of his college and took the incumbency of Triplow, but continued to lecture, though his subject was not at all popular: indeed in 1782 (if not in other years) he was forced to include natural history and geology in his course in order to secure an audience. Miller (who was son of the Chelsea curator) had worked satisfactorily for eight or nine years before his resignation. A good account of Sumatra was pirated from his papers for Philos. Transact. LXVIII. 160[4].

In May, 1784, a syndicate was appointed to build a lecture-room for the Botanical and Jacksonian Professors[5]. The Calendar of 1802 states that T. Martyn lectured in this room[6]

[1] Gorham's *Martyns* 117.

[2] *ibid.* 32, 33.

[3] Linnaeus when visiting England in 1736 had been coldly received by Hans Sloane, and Dillenius the Oxford professor refused to accept the sexual system. Thomas Martyn was a Rayian about 1750, but about 1751—3 the *Philosophia Botanica* and the *Species Plantarum* effectually drew him over to Linnaeus.

[4] Gorham's *Martyns* 111, 114 *n.*

[5] Cooper's *Annals* IV. 412.

[6] Mr Gorham however says that he delivered his last lectures in 1796. He died in 1825, and was succeeded

during the first half of the Midsummer term at 4 p.m.,
explaining the elements of Botany, and elucidating Linnaeus'
system. The doctrine of the Sexes in Plants, being the foundation of that system, was proved. The Theory of Vegetation
and other matters relative to the Physiology of Plants were
detailed; and finally, the more curious and useful species were
selected and exhibited. When he got old, Thomas Martyn lent
his lecture-room to E. D. Clarke, the professor of mineralogy.

A controversy between Sir J. E. Smith, M.D. (President of
the Linnaean Society[1]), and professor J. H. Monk (1818, 1819),
on the Cambridge Botanical Professorship, is bound up in a
volume of pamphlets[2] in the library of Trinity College, Cambridge. It arose from the successful opposition of the tutors of
most of the colleges[3], refusing to allow their pupils to attend the
lectures of one who was a member neither of the University
nor of the Church of England; Thomas Martyn having nominated Sir James as his substitute.

by J. S. Henslow the mineralogist.
Perhaps Ri. Relhan of Trin. was
Martyn's deputy at this time.

[1] He purchased the herbarium and
collections of Linnaeus.

[2] x. 14. 10. Cp. Cooper's *Annals,*

IV. 520, 521. Gorham's *Martyns*
242—9.

[3] Queens', Clare Hall, Benet Coll.,
Magdalene and Downing were not
represented.

CHAPTER XIX.

THE DEGREE OF MASTER OF ARTS.

'Non stabit pro forma.'

Specimen of Early Latin.

THAT candidates for the degree of B. A. had some instruction in Philosophy (probably as much as they *ever* had) we have already seen. But since the Reformation there does not seem to have been any great effort made to incite bachelors to spend their three years in the statutable pursuit of the University *quadriuium* of Music Arithmetic, Geometry and Astronomy. Still in 1787 the University still required of candidates for a Mastership in Arts three years continuance as B.A., and (in that capacity)

> Three Respondencies against M.A. Opponents.
>
> Two . . . . , B.A. . .
>
> One Declamation [1].

Hence we gather that even M.A.s were called upon to dispute [2]. (See *Statut. Acad.* cap. L.)

Accordingly the colleges [3] bade their bachelors to exercise themselves in Acts within their walls. It was in order to remunerate M.A. Fellows who acted as moderators in these college disputations, that college fees for M.A. degrees were levied originally from B.A.s. But, as I have observed, when

---

[1] *Considerations on the Oaths*...by a Member of the Senate. *Camb.* 1788. p. 43. Appendix I.

[2] But these 'acts' were *huddled* through all at one time, after the style of 'Hodiissime, Omnes Magistri estote' (Corbet's *Ballad.* 1615), for an *ad eundem* degree in the presence of an M.A. and a B.A., between the ceremonies of Admission and Subscription to the xxxvith Canon;— and for an ordinary M.A. 'performed privately' before his 'supplicat' was offered. *Ceremonies* Wall-Gunning *pp.* 167, 168 (1828).

[3] The Statutes of University College *Oxon.* ordered that a *moderator of the bachelors* should be appointed to pre-

undergraduates began to be admitted at a manlier age, there was a tendency at Cambridge to anticipate the course of study, and to require from undergraduates that mathematical knowledge which according to the statutes belonged rather to graduates. Shall we say that Oxford went further[1], and expected her undergraduates to be qualified as bachelors in the arch-science of Divinity?

It is not surprising that a man of Gray's calibre should rebel against the thraldom of mathematical and metaphysical lectures (1736); but towards the close of the 18th century, there was a growing vehemence in the protest against that state of affairs which continued until the foundation of the Classical Tripos in this century.

I have read two pamphlets of the year 1788, in which this complaint is set forth—that at Cambridge *mathematics* was made the only standard of merit and 'the only Introduction to a Fellowship[2].' 'Mathematics[3], with a little Logic, Metaphysics, and Moral Law, constitute the sum of the course of lectures: for Divinity, History, and Classical Knowledge scarce enter into the plan; Civil and Common Law never: so that unless a student have a taste for mathematical studies, he may as well not attend the public lectures.' And the like testimony was borne by R. Acklom Ingram of Queens' in 1792[4].

But if at Cambridge mathematics were dominant, this was not so at Oxford: while on the other hand she could not boast any more than her sister that she was free from the abuse of *huddling*[5], though she did not perhaps recognize the name. If I mistake not, the Cambridge Schools had the dust swept from them and the daylight let into them many years before the Oxford examination was made efficient.

It has been stated, that real examinations may have taken

---

side over the disputations of the bachelors. Dr Stanley informed the Commissioners in 1852 that the office was still retained in name.

[1] Cp. [Southey's] *Espriella* ii. 79.

[2] *Remarks on the Enormous Expence in Education*, 1788, *p.* 13.

[3] *Considerations on the Oaths*, 1788, *p.* 16.

[4] *The Necessity of Introducing Divinity into the regular Course*, &c. by R. A. Ingram. *Colchester* &c. 1792. *p.* 122.

[5] Dr Knox (ap. Gradus ad Cantab. s. v. *Huddling*) says that at Oxford 'droll questions are put on any subject; and the puzzled candidate furnishes diversion by his awkward em-

place in Oxford up to the thirteenth century, but they had completely fallen into disuse at all events after the end of that century[1]. Two years after the statutes of 1636[2] a supplementary statute introduced at Oxford a principle which had been recognized at Cambridge a century before : viz. that of a real examination for the degree in arts; the degree having depended virtually upon a plurality of votes, although nominally upon the old scholastic exercises, which for a long time past were become a practical nullity[1]. And it would not now have been prudent politically to encourage the freedom of disputations. So pass examinations were established.

It seems a startling statement, but so far as I am aware there was *no such thing at Oxford as an honour examination for degrees* until the nineteenth century[3].

The same wave of interest in university examination which distressed Powell and Jebb at Cambridge about 1770, seems to have stirred a ripple on the tranquil waters of Isis. In 1773 was printed *Considerations on the Public Exercises for the First and Second Degrees in the University of Oxford.* This pamphlet was circulated in Cambridge, and was considered by Jebb as 'an ingenious performance[4].' The writer mentions that the question had been mooted at 'an occasional meeting of several respectable Members of the University,' and had been subsequently commended by the V. C. to the serious consideration of the Heads of Houses and the Proctors. He proposes to make the examinations really public by having fixed days for their performance, a change which would also induce men to commence their residence at one time of year: that there should be two regular Examiners or Censors holding office perhaps for three years. The first week in Lent Term should be an exami-

barrassment. I have known' (he adds) 'the question on the occasion to consist of an enquiry into the pedigree of a race-horse.'

[1] *English Univ.* V. A. Huber (F. W. Newman, 1843) ii. pt. 1, p. 59.

[2] The statutes of Laud required as a qualification for M.A. three years study after the degree of B.A. As-

tronomy, Metaphysics, Natural Philosophy, Ancient History and Hebrew, as well as the continuation of the study of Geometry and Greek which were to occupy the latter part of the undergraduate course.

[3] See Bp. Mant's *Life* (Trin. Coll. *Oxon.* 1797; fellow of Oriel) p. 62.

[4] Jebb's *Works* ii. 304.

nation-week for all who were candidates for a bachelor's degree the ensuing year, and another week or four days in Act (Trinity) Term for candidates for their second degree. The examinations to be held in presence of Congregation in the Theatre or the Nat. Philos. Schools, to be conducted generally by the Examiners, any member of Congregation having a right to take some part in examining (as under the then existing régime at both Universities). It would have been a formidable ordeal if conducted in latin in the Theatre, each examinee appearing in one rostrum and answering the two examiners who were to sit in the other rostrum. Private examination would the more grow into disrepute if it were reserved for those who had been 'plucked' in the public scrutiny. The author approved on the whole the matter prescribed by the statutes for examination. He wished however to make *mathematics* a more important subject than it was then made at Oxford. He proposed therefore six books of Euclid, the nature and use of Numbers, particularly vulgar and decimal Fractions, and the Elements of Algebra, reserving (as we shall see) higher subjects for the second degree. In addition to the other recognized subjects (grammar, rhetoric, logic, ethics, greek classics, and speaking latin) he proposed to examine in the historical part of the New Testament, and in the XXXIX Articles. And to arrange the names of the successful candidates *in three classes*—the 1st and 2nd only being published:—thus virtually making the modern distinction between '*pass* and *class.*'

So much for the author's *proposal* (in 1773) for a new examination for B.A. at Oxford. Let us pass to the state of things which then was, and which continued to be till the beginning of the present century. The Oxford statutes required from candidates for the degree of B.A.—

I. *disputationes in parviso* ['generals' and 'juraments']¹, a

---

¹ Wood records that this exercise, having been in early times the pride of Oxford, fell into desuetude but was revived in 1601, and in 1606 each candidate for B.A. was required to swear that he had ' answered' in *Parvisiis* or generals, or at least had been once prior opponent. At that time the proctors appointed certain M.A.s as *Supervisors.* (Wood II. 271, 291, 726 —8.) About 1645 acts and exercises were discontinued, and all undergraduates under sixty years of age were on military duty. (*ibid.* II. 475.)

disputation on three questions in grammar or logic from 1 to 3 p.m. Each Student was to hear others perform in his 2nd, 3rd, and 4th years. This was systematically neglected. In his 3rd year he was to be created a *senior soph* after performing these disputations twice himself (this was called *generals*); after which he was to keep one such disputation (*juraments*) every term. The questions were trite and uninteresting, and when a student was once Senior Soph he merely went into the schools every term and proposed one syllogism *juramenti gratia*, and was said to be 'doing juraments.' One great defect in the working of this statute was the frequent absence of proctors and regent 'masters of the schools,' so that as a general rule there was no one to watch the proceedings.

II. *answering under bachelor.* The student disputed upon three questions in grammar, rhetoric, ethics, politics, or (more often) in logic, a B.A. taking the office of *moderator.* This was performed twice in the Lent of his third or fourth year for an hour and a half. The proctors and masters visited the schools in Lent more often than in *parviso*, but still they did not always watch the entire time. (*p.* 56.)

III. *Examination* in grammar, rhetoric, logic, ethics, geometry, greek classics, fluency in the latin tongue. The proper examiners were three regent masters, but as the custom of the regents taking this duty by rotation had long since become obsolete, the candidate usually *chose his own three examiners*, and then got their *liceat* from the proctor. This examination was quite *private*. This was the main point which the author of the 'Considerations' wished to reform. He proposed to add to the statutable exercises, one latin and one english *declamation* to be delivered publicly in the Theatre in Act Term.

The writer of another Oxford pamphlet of that period[1] remarked that at Cambridge 'they are generally supposed to expect more than we [Oxonians] do from a Candidate for the First Degree, in proportion as they expect less from a Candidate for the Second.' Doubtless the statutable exercises (viz. three respondencies to an M.A., two respondencies to a B.A., and one declamation) for a Cambridge M.A. were trifling[2], and generally

[1] *Considerations on the Residence usually required for Degrees,* &c.—   Oxford 1772—*p.* 19.
[2] *Stat. Acad.* Cantab. 1570, *cap.* 7.

stultified by 'huddling' or by the forfeiture of caution-money, and indeed of no account except so far as some of the Colleges kept their bachelors employed by 'acts' and 'declamations.' We may gather from these *Considerations on the Exercises* (1773) that if the *statutable* requirements for an Oxford M.A. were not inconsiderable, they were in the last century by no means so creditably observed as were the Cambridge exercises for the *first* degree.

Our university indeed seems never to have pressed the revival of the exercises of those who, being bachelors, were proceeding to their *next* degree in Arts. For a long while— even almost till 1840—'the incepting masters of arts crowded (*huddled*) to the schools, sometimes on a day preceding, sometimes within a few minutes of the presentation of their *supplicats*, to keep, *juramenti gratiâ*, the statutable exercises[1].' It was allowed that the repetition of *two lines* of Virgil's first Eclogue or the same quantity of Aen. I. would do for a *declamation;* and as for the three disputations or 'acts' which the statute (cap. 7) required, they might be summarily despatched in one compendious form[2]—the 'respondent' asserting

'Recte statuit Newtonus—Recte statuit Woodius—Recte statuit Paleius.' The 'opponent' was allowed to attack these all-embracing positions with a scarcely less positive

'Si non recte statuerunt Newtonus, Woodius, Paleius, cadunt quaestiones.

Sed non recte statuerunt Newtonus, Woodius, Paleius.

Ergo cadunt quaestiones.'

Between such combatants it would have been sheer presumption for a moderator to interpose. It remained only for the opponent to become respondent (and *vice versa*), and to go through the same nonsense—and *there* were *six acts* and *two declamations* finished, and two *supplicats* earned, in less than two minutes ! It needed only that the first and second disputants should have said the *same* couplet of Virgil for their

---

[1] Peacock *on the Statutes*, 1841, p. 86.

[2] Porson's juvenile theme—
    'Nec bene fecit Brutus occiso Caesare, nec male fecit, sed interfecit'—

while it emulated these modern Cantabs in brevity, had the advantage of them in wit. (See *Facetiae Cantab.* p. 199.)

declamations to reduce the formula to its lowest and simplest terms, and to absolute barrenness. It seems strange that the 'bold interpretation' of the Heads in 1608 (25 May), which virtually excepted the clause '*iustum trium annorum spatium*' (cap. 7) from the apparently plain prohibition '*nec plures proponant terminos in quibus studuerint in academia*' &c. (cap. 21), should not have been imitated by abrogating the remainder of *cap.* 7 of the University Statute, rather than that the farce of 'huddling' should continue in the 18th and part of the 19th centuries to rival the promenade '*ad oppositum*' whereby the commencers of the 16th century almost to our own time have mounted to the degree of doctor (or M.A.). Yet we might be inclined to regret that the university had the heart to improve away that quaint old step worn by so many worthy feet, now that the doctorate is dignified by an ascent of more becoming altitude.

The *Oxford* requirements for M.A. were

I. *determination.* A solemn exercise opening with prayers and *contio* in St Mary's on Ash Wednesday. Then the dean of each college walks in procession to the Schools, at the head of his determining bachelors, and there holds a disputation for the tedious period of *four hours.* He reads a copy of verses, proposes arguments upon three questions to every determiner of his house: which questions are to be defended against him by a determined or senior bachelor, who responds for the determiner and is therefore called his *Aristotle.* ['Aristoteles pro me respondebit.'] In the course of Lent the determiner is required to hold two disputations, each on three questions in grammar, rhetoric, ethics, politics, or (more often) logic; in which he is always to maintain the doctrine of Aristotle and the Peripatetics. Though the questions themselves and the arguments were not good for much, the exercises of Ash Wednesday itself were respectable, the V. C. being usually present as well as the deans and a fairly large audience of determiners, &c.; but the other days in *quadragesima* were comparatively neglected and made to do double duty as 'answering under bachelor' for the degree of B.A., and as 'determinations' for M.A. This exercise was often held in the afternoon,—an inconvenient time.

II. *disputationes apud Augustinenses* [1]—to be performed from 1 to 3 p.m. for the degree of M.A. by a determined Bachelor. He might be called upon to repeat the exercise in the subsequent years of his *triennium.* No one was present except the candidate and the moderating master of the Schools. It was an exercise which might well be discontinued.

III. *disputationes quodlibeticae*—responding to a certain regent master on three questions, and to any other disputant on any question whatsoever. This had become the merest farce, and might (it was urged) be dropped with advantage.

IV. *sex solennes lectiones*—three original dissertations in Natural, and three in Moral philosophy, to be delivered in the Schools between 1 and 2 p.m. These were intended to stimulate original invention and research, but had so degenerated that they were held *pro forma* in an empty school, and had long since obtained the title of *Wall Lectures* [2], being then 'scarce known by any other name. An attempt has lately been made in one of our Colleges to restore it to its ancient dignity and utility, by obliging every Bachelor to read his solemn lectures publicly in the College Hall: a regulation which does honour to the Society [3].' The author proposed to have these lectures read publicly in the Theatre, and to give honours of some sort for excellency therein.

V. *binae declamationes*—to be delivered (at 2 p.m.) without book before the proctor on a thesis assigned or approved by him. This was intended as an exercise in polite learning and elegant composition. In old times one candidate affirmed the thesis, a second denied, and a third arbitrated 'in the way of *ambigitur.*' It was suggested that this system should be re-

---

[1] When dean Fell was V.C. in 1646, 1647, he revived for a time the strict discipline and the interest of this exercise, vulgarly known as *doing Austins.* It took its name from the custom of scholars at Oxford disputing with the *Augustinian* monks, who had a reputation for exercises of this kind. The proctor appointed a B.A. as his '*collector* in Austins' who had authority to match the disputants together at his discretion. (See my

Univ. Life pp. 315, 317.)

[2] See above, p. 10.

[3] This was a provision of the *Rules and Statutes of* Hertford College (*Hart Hall*) as early as 1747. See my *Univ. Life* p. 576. At *Christ Church* towards the end of the century a man (apparently an undergraduate) was chosen to read an essay each week in hall. While H. F. Cary was in residence (*Memoir* i. 66) Canning was frequently thus distinguished.

vived, the declamations held publicly in the Theatre in Act
Term, and one of the two made in the english language.

VI. *examination*—as for B.A., only the subjects are geometry, natural philosophy, astronomy, metaphysics, and history
(including geography and chronology), greek classics, and hebrew, and latin conversation yet more perfect. The writer of
the pamphlet proposed to regulate the examination, as has been
stated on p. 216, and to add to the fixed subjects Euclid xi, xii,
some system of Conic Sections, Trigonometry, Logarithms, and
Algebra applied to Geometry. Also the Epistles in the New
Testament, the XXXIX Articles, and the book of Genesis in
hebrew.

This scheme seems to have produced no immediate effect at
Oxford in 1773. Accordingly we find Mr G. V. Cox, the Oxford
esquire bedel, recollecting the sad decay at Oxford[1], when
Cambridge examinations for B.A. were in a comparatively
healthy condition. At Oxford 'it seems (1868) the trial is
strict when one takes a Master's or Bachelor's, but slack when
you come to the Doctor's Degrees, and *vice versa* at Cambridge.'
But at Oxford in 1797 there were traditional schemes, skeletons, or '*strings*' of questions, examples of syllogisms, used by
the Examiners or Masters of the Schools, as well as by the
examinees[2],—sometimes wound up by a latin epigram. 'It is
well known to be the custom for the *candidates* either to present
their examiners with *a piece of gold,* or to give them a handsome entertainment.'

Cox quotes a contemporary english epigram (*pp.* 36, 37),
supposed to be spoken by a well *satisfied* examiner. In 1799
(he continues) the examination for the B.A. degree, under the
old system, 'had dwindled into a formal repetition of threadbare
"Questions and Answers" (in Divinity, Logic, Grammar, "et in
omni scibili"), which had been transmitted in manuscript from
man to man, and were unblushingly admitted, if not adopted,

[1] Cox's *Collections and Recollections of* Oxford, *pp.* 34, 35.
[2] In the *Gent. Mag.* vol. L. pp. 277, 278, an example is given of an 'argument' in Generals at Oxford. These were to be had ready made and were called 'strings.' 'Schemes' are defined as 'collections of all questions which will be probably asked in the sciences.'

even by the "Masters of the Schools."' These were Regent-Masters of the year, whose duty it was by virtue of their Regency to go through this ceremony, for a mere ceremony it had become. The more scrupulous, joining in the increasing cry for a new Examination-Statute, hung back from the farce; but each year was sure to produce a few Masters who did not object even to dine with the *examined* after the fatigues of the morning! Well might such a state of things expire with the expiring century!

'The "New Examination-Statute" was already on the anvil, and was being worked into shape; Dean Cyril Jackson [Ch. Ch., 1783—1809], Dr [John] Eveleigh [provost of Oriel, 1781—1814], and Dr [John] Parsons [Mr of Ball., 1798—1819], were labouring hard for the revival of scholarship and the credit of our Alma Mater' [Oxon.][1]. The new Public Examinations Statute came into action rather feebly indeed at first in 1802; but the claimants for honour degrees were, in the years from 1802 to 1806, only two, four, three, one, three respectively.

Professor F. W. Newman bears witness to the efforts of Eveleigh and Jackson in the interest of Oxford examinations. He bestows also deserved praise upon Dr Eveleigh's successor, the provost of Oriel, Dr Coplestone (bishop of Llandaff)[2].

He says, translating Huber's *English Universities*, 'In proof of the degeneracy of the University Studies in the last century[3], I need only refer to Kuettner's *Beiträge zur Kenntniss von England*. Kuettner's account refers more immediately to the second half of the 18th century; but if any alteration had by then taken place, it was for the better: so that the earlier

---

[1] *Gent. Mag.* XLIX. pp. 35, 37, 45.

[2] *Huber* and *F.W.Newman*, English Universities, 1843, vol. II. part ii. pp. 513, 514; 501.

[3] 'Mr John Scott [Lord Eldon] took his Bachelor's Degree in Hilary Term, on the 20th February, 1770. "An Examination for a Degree at Oxford," he used to say, " was a farce in my time. I was examined in Hebrew and in History." "What is the Hebrew for the place of a skull?" I replied "Golgotha." "Who founded University College?" I stated (though, by the way, the point is sometimes doubted) "that King Alfred founded it." "Very well, Sir," said the Examiner, "you are competent for your Degree."' Horace Twiss' *life of Ld. Eldon*, I. 57, quoted in the Oxford *Univ. Commission Report*, p. 59. Mr G. V. Cox (*Recollections*, p. 34 *n.*) loyally regards the anecdote told against his university as a mere '*post prandium* joke.'

period *à fortiori* deserves the severest censure justly applicable to the later.' After quoting Amhurst's example of an Oxford *disputatio quodlibetica*, 'a short *string* of syllogisms, upon a common question, *An datur actio in distans*,' as it was disputed about 1718[1];—Huber adds, 'Such jokes as these are among the less ordinary effusions of talent. Generally the whole party—Moderator, Opponent, and Respondent—passed the prescribed half-hour in reading or talking[2]........

'Doubtless the young men who carried off the various University and College prizes from the year 1801 to the end of the war, were morally superior to the mass; yet of these but few can have become permanent residents in Oxford, as so few Fellowships were as yet thrown open to any sort of fair competition. The first College which in this respect became celebrated was Oriel.'

The same movement, at the beginning of this century, which improved the B.A. examinations in Oxford, revived also for a time the qualification for the M.A. degree. We happen to have a minute account of their working in the life of Daniel Wilson (bp. of Calcutta), who was born in 1778. It will be as well to sketch his studies up to that time[3].

'He continued during the six months of his student life [as private pupil of Josiah Pratt, in 1798] to rise at 5 o'clock and retire at 10 o'clock. One hour's exercise in the day sufficed him. At breakfast the *Spectator* and Johnson's *Lives of the Poets* were read through. Hebrew, Greek, Latin, and elementary parts of mathematics occupied the morning. The after part of the day was assigned to divinity, logic, history, natural philo-

[1] *Terrae Filius*, 1721, No. xxi. The Respondent chooses to maintain the negative, and simply says *negatur minor, negatur antecedens*, &c. after each syllogism. The opponent takes as his example the power of the fear of the Vice Chancellor upon a student who has committed a breach of the statute by wearing a hat (*galerus*). The Moderator ends with a ridiculous *distinctio* about the *bedels* and the imagination of the offender.

[2] However lax the *University* may

have been, we must not omit to notice that *individual Societies* were more particular. In 1720 we find *John Wesley* acquiring skill in logic at *Christ Church*, and improving it in 1726—8, when as 'Moderator of the Classes' in *Lincoln Coll. Oxon.* he presided at disputations *six times a week*. (*Life by* Southey, Coleridge *and* C. C. Southey, 1846. pp. 27, 37, 39.)

[3] Bateman's *Life of* D. Wilson. 1860. pp. 49—67.

sophy, geography, and general literature. The books read were, The Holy Scriptures in *Hebrew* and *Greek*, Hooker's *Eccl. Polity*, Doddridge's *Lectures*, Fuller's *Calvinism and Socinianism*, Rowning's *Natural Philosophy*, Drallois' *Epitome of Logic*, Chisseldon's *Anatomy*, Adam's *Geography*, *Anacharsis' Travels*, Wilcock's *Rome*, Bisset's *Life of Burke*, Blair's *Lectures*, and Payne's *Epitome of History*.

'Seventy or eighty years have witnessed great changes and improvements in our universities. All testimony goes to shew that towards the end of the last century religion had little life there, and learning little encouragement[1]. The Classes and the Tripos which now gauge a man's ability and assign him his proper place were then unknown. At *Oxford* ... the examination was a mere form. *A man chose not only his own books, but his own examiners.* It was consequently the very general custom to choose the easiest books and the most indulgent examiners. There was no audience. The three Masters of Arts, who were the examiners, and the undergraduates to be examined, were alone present; and it was not unusual to proceed to the Schools from a pleasant breakfast, or to adjourn after a successful termination of the day's labours to a good dinner!

" Quid solidus angulus ? "

Such was the question of an examiner in the schools : and receiving no answer from the respondent, he answered himself by grasping the corner of the desk at which he stood, and saying,

"Hic solidus angulus."

'Such is a specimen of the traditionary stories of the day; and it might be capped by many of the same kind.......

'Before the last century had closed many changes had begun, and many abuses were corrected. The authorities of the university appointed examiners, and publicity was given to the examination. Though there was not as yet any fair and impartial criterion of ability, such as the Classes have since presented, yet the opinion of the Examiner was publickly ex-

---

[1] It will, I think, have appeared from the foregoing pages that this remark does *Cambridge* scant justice.

pressed, and sent through the university the gradually widening circle of commendation or disgrace.

'It was in November, 1798, that Daniel Wilson entered into residence at Oxford ... in St Edmund's Hall. It was but a small society, and perhaps at that time better known for its piety[1] than its learning. Still he says that he found the men reading what required from him five hours' preparation daily.

'During the short vacation in March, 1799 ... he was giving more time to Hebrew and Greek. He makes also a successful application [to his father] for permission to have a private tutor, in order to work at Thucydides. "I am perfectly well," he says, "in health, not as yet experiencing any inconvenience from my studies. Very few days pass when I do not walk for about an hour."

'In 1799 he leaves Oxford for the Long Vacation, July 1st, and returns October 17th, to set to work at Herodotus, and Livy, the Hebrew Bible, Hutton's *Mathematics*, and Rollin's *Ancient History*. He now also began to talk Latin familiarly with his friends, Bull and Cawood. Tradition says that he translated and re-translated the whole of Cicero's Epistles. In the vacation he had devoted his mornings, from 9 o'clock till 2;—the first hour in Hebrew, the second in Greek, and the third in Latin; reading French and then English after dinner if time allowed.' He had fortunately acquired regular habits by being in business in his early youth.

He was examined for his B.A. degree early in June, 1801; and for that of M.A. about the same time in the following year.

It appears that in May, 1800, an examination statute provided that there should be a strict public examination for the degree of M.A. at Oxford as well as for that of B.A. This regulation induced men to forego their second degree, or to seek it at Cambridge, so that the decree fell into neglect and desuetude.

'But Daniel Wilson came under its operation whilst it was in vigorous action, and we are thus enabled from his second

[1] It was famous for the expulsion of six '*pious students*' in 1768, (a transaction more proper to the records of *University Religion in the* 18*th Cent.*). Few of the larger societies could have found so many to expel.

examination to supply what was lacking in the details of the first.

'He writes to his friend Cawood and makes very light of it. "You seem," he says, "to make a great deal more of the examination I have just passed than it deserves. I can scarcely help smiling at what you say, and at the anxiety you feel. I only gave three days for direct preparation, and you need not give one. But since *omne ignotum pro magnifico*, I will tell you what really took place." He then goes on to say that he was examined with his friend Wheeler and a Christ Church man. The books he took up in *Greek* were Thucydides and Herodotus. But in *Latin* he made no selection; he took up all: *omnes optimae aetatis auctores—omnes aureos auctores*—are the expressions he employs. His friend Wheeler followed his example in the Latin, and took up Sophocles and Longinus in the Greek. In *Hebrew* Daniel Wilson stood alone.

'A book was first put into his hand called *the Gentleman's Religion,* and he turned a page of it into Latin. The Greek Testament followed. He read part of St Mark xiii, and answered questions about the Temple erected in the time of Vespasian and the prophecies concerning it in the Old and New Testament. Livy was then opened and a page translated. This led to many historical questions. Up to this time, he confesses, he was not without apprehensions, not knowing where the examination might lead him: but now all fears subsided. Latin being finished, Hebrew came on. He took up the whole Hebrew Bible: but the examiner (wisely perhaps for himself) confined his examination to the first Psalm, and some grammatical questions which were readily answered. His friend having passed a similar ordeal, they were now bid to sit down whilst others were called on, approbation being expressed with what they had done.

'Whilst sitting apart the junior examiner, as if casually, asked whether Wilson had read *Physics,* and then put certain questions such as "Whether the angle of refraction was equal to the angle of incidence?" "Whether a ray of light passing from a thin into a denser medium would be deflected from the perpendicular?" &c.; all of which were of course answered. *Mathematics, Logic* and *Metaphysics* were passed by; one of the

THE DEGREE OF MASTER OF ARTS.

sciences only being required by the statute. When he was again formally called up, the third Book of *Thucydides* was selected, and he was put on at one of the speeches. Neither this nor the *historical questions* connected with it, gave him any difficulty. *Xenophon* followed instead of Herodotus (which was his book) : but he took things as he found them ; and the passage selected was (he says) neither obscure nor difficult.

'Thus ended the examination : and the Senior Examiner confirmed his former sentence by saying in a loud voice that Wheeler and Wilson had done themselves the greatest credit, and obtained the highest honour. The Christ Church man gained his *testamur*, but nothing more ; and *six* men were rejected. There were about one hundred auditors.'

This new examination for the Oxford M.A. degree seems soon to have degenerated, and existed barely for half-a-dozen years. Mr G. V. Cox in his *Recollections* (p. 57) speaks of it as 'fast becoming an "examination made easy," for it never, I believe, ended in *plucking*, and seldom attracted an audience.' This testimony of an accurate observer shews how fast and utter was its decline, for Mr Cox was admitted to New College *only two years* after Wilson saw *six* men rejected and *a hundred* persons present. The M.A. examination was discontinued towards the end of 1807[1].

'A *Gentleman* in the *City*,' writing 'to his Friend in *Oxford*[2],' Nov. 25, 1700, says ' I am glad to hear from you that the study of the *Mathematicks* is Promoted and Encouraged among the *youth* of your *University*[3].' He concludes however (*p.* 33) that mathematics must be 'more generally study'd at our *Universities* than hitherto they have been.' Still it is below the dignity of those Bodies, that their students should be 'taught the practice of any rule without the true and solid reason and demonstration of the same.' So that the common *Compendiums* are to be reprobated[3].

---

[1] See also Abp. *Whately's* Evidence (p. 25), Oxford *Univ. Commission* 1852. ' In *fact* it was *not* public, all the Undergraduates and Bachelors making it a point of delicacy never to attend, because several of those examined were men of middle age, and many clergymen.'

[2] ed. 2. 1721. Bodl. *Godwin Pamphlets*, 22.

[3] *ibid.* p. 35.

It is amusing to compare with the foregoing pages an account of the Oxford examinations when they had come to be empty forms, as they are indignantly described by Vicesimus Knox in his seventy-seventh Essay (*ed.* 1782). He had taken his M.A. degree at *S. John's,* Oxon. in 1753.

'The youth whose heart pants for the honour of a Bachelor of Arts degree must wait patiently till near four years have revolved. But this time is not to be spent idly. No; he is obliged during this period once to oppose, and once to respond in disputations held in the public schools—a formidable sound, and a dreadful idea; but on closer attention the fear will vanish and contempt supply its place.

'This opposing and responding is termed in the cant of the place *doing generals.* Two boys or men as they call themselves agree to *do generals* together. The first step in this mighty work is to procure arguments. These are always handed down from generation to generation on long slips of paper, and consist of foolish syllogisms on foolish subjects of the formation or the signification of which the respondent and opponent seldom know more than an infant in swaddling cloths[1]. The next step

---

[1] 'These commodious sets of syllogisms are called *strings,* and descend from undergraduate to undergraduate in a regular succession ; so that when any candidate for a degree is to exercise his talent in argumentation he has nothing else to do but to enquire among his friends for a string upon such or such a question, and to get it by heart, or read it over in his *cap*... I have in my custody a book of *strings* upon most or all of the questions discuss'd in a certain college very famous for their ratiocinative faculty; on the first leaf of which are these words,

Ex dono Richardi P——e primae Classi Benefactoris munificentissimi.

...I will present the reader with a short *string* of syllogisms upon a common question as it was disputed about three years ago; Dr B[aro]n being then vicech[ancello]r (1715—18.)...it was really a *new* one (which...is a very

great rarity), and was, I believe, made by the disputant himself.

Intrent Opponens Respondens *et* Moderator.

Opponens. Propono tibi, domine, hanc quaestionem, (viz.)
—An datur actio in distans.
Respondens. Non datur actio in distans.
Opp. Datur actio in distans ; ergo falleris.
Résp. Negatur antecedens.
Opp. Probo antecedentem ;
Si datur fluxus virium *Agentis* cum distat *Agens,* tum datur actio in distans.
Sed datur fluxus virium agentis cum distat agens.
Ergo datur actio in distans.
Resp. Negatur minor.
Opp. Probo minorem ;
Vice-Cancellarius est agens ;

is to go for a *liceat* to one of the petty officers called the Regent-Master of the Schools, who subscribes his name to the questions and receives sixpence as his fee. When the important day arrives the two doughty disputants[1] go into a large dusty room, full of dirt and cobwebs, with walls and wainscot decorated with the names of former disputants, who to divert the tedious hours cut out their names with their penknives or wrote verses with a pencil. Here they sit in mean desks opposite to each other from one o'clock till three. Not once in a hundred times does any officer enter; and if he does he hears one syllogism or two, and then makes a bow and departs, as he came and remained, in solemn silence. The disputants then return to the amusement of cutting the desks, carving their names or reading Sterne's *Sentimental Journey* or some other edifying novel.

Sed datur fluxus virium Vice-Cancellarii cum distat Vice-Cancellarius.

Ergo datur fluxus virium agentis cum distat agens.

Resp. Negatur minor.

Opp. Probo minorem;

Si Disputans Parvisiis vel aliquis Galero indutus timet et patitur, dato spatio inter Vice-Cancellarium et Disputantem vel Galero indutum, tum datur fluxus virium Vice-Cancellarii, cum distat Vice-Cancellarius.

Sed Disputans Parvisiis vel aliquis Galero indutus timet et patitur dato spatio inter Vice-Cancellarium et Disputantem vel Galero indutum:

Ergo datur fluxus virium Vice-Cancellarii cum distat Vice-Cancellarius.

Resp. Negatur tum minor, tum sequela.

Opp. Constat minor ex perfectissima Academiae disciplina et experientia; et valet sequela quoniam *incutere timorem alicui* est *agere* in aliquem.

Moderator. Distinguendum est ad tuam probationem.

Terror non procedit a fluxu sive ex effluvio Vice-Cancellarii; sed Bedelli forsitan (viz. *Whist[leru]s* et *M—ck Muss[endi]nus*) baculis suis incutiunt terrorem.

Et dico secundo quod imaginatio Disputantis sibi incutiat terrorem; quippe nihil est *materialiter* terrificum vel in *Baronio* vel in *Whistlero*, vel (utcunque obeso) in *Mussendino*; sit quamvis *formaliter.*'

(Terrae Filius, xx, xxi.)

[1] Knox says nothing of any *moderator* who according to Amhurst's account (1721, March 24.) is always present and 'struts about between the two *wordy* champions during the time of action, to see that they do not wander from the question in debate, and when he perceives them deviating from it to cut them short, and put them into the right road again; for which purpose he is provided with a great quantity of *subtle* terms and phrases of art such as *quoad hoc*, and *quoad illud, formaliter* and *materialiter, praedicamentaliter* and *transcendentaliter, actualiter* and *potentialiter, directè* and *per se, reductivè* and *per accidens, entitativè* and *quidditativè, &c.* all which I would explain to my *english* reader with all my heart, *if I could.*'

When this exercise is duly performed by both parties they have a right to the title and insignia of *Sophs*; but not before they have been formally *created* by one of the regent masters, before whom they kneel while he lays a volume of Aristotle's works on their heads and puts on a hood a piece of black crape hanging from their necks and down to their heels; which crape it is expressly ordained by a statute in this case made and provided shall be plain and unadorned either with wool or with fur.

'And this work done a great progress is made towards the wished-for honour of a bachelor's degree. There remain only one or two trifling forms and another disputation almost exactly similar to *doing generals,* but called *answering under bachelor* previous to the awful examination.

'Every candidate is obliged to be examined in the whole circle of the sciences by three masters of arts *of his own choice*[1]. The examination is to be held in one of the public schools, and to continue from nine o'clock till eleven[2]. The masters take a most solemn oath that they will examine properly and impartially. Dreadful as all this appears there is always found to be more of appearance in it than reality; for the greatest dunce usually gets his *testimonium* signed with as much ease and credit as the finest genius. The manner of proceeding is as follows: the poor young man to be examined in the sciences often knows no more of them than his bedmaker, and the masters who examine are sometimes equally unacquainted with such mysteries. But *schemes* as they are called, or little books containing forty or fifty questions on each science are handed down from age to age from one to another[3]. The candidate to be examined em-

[1] 'It is a notorious truth that most candidates get leave of the *proctor* by paying his man a crown (which is called his *perquisite*) to choose their own *examiners*, who never fail to be their old *cronies* and *toping* companions.......It is also well-known to be a custom for the *candidates* either to present their *examiners* with a *piece of gold*, or to give them an handsome *entertainment.*' Terrae-Filius, No. XLII. (8 *June*, 1721).

[2] 'and again from *one* in the after-

noon, if the *examiner* thinks fit, as long as he pleases.' *Ibid.*

[3] 'As I told my reader, that for *disputations* they have ready-made *strings* of syllogisms; so for examination they have the *skeletons* of all the arts and sciences in which they are to be examined, containing all the questions in each of them which are usually asked upon this occasion and the *common answers* that are given to them; which in a week or a fortnight they may get at their tongue's end....Many a *school-*

ploys three or four days in learning these by heart, and the examiners having done the same before him when they were examined, know what questions to ask, and so all goes on smoothly. When the candidate has displayed his universal knowledge of the sciences he is to display his skill in philology. One of the masters therefore desires him to construe a passage in some Greek or Latin classic, which he does with no interruption just as he pleases and as well as he can. The statutes next require that he should translate familiar English phrases into Latin. And now is the time when the masters shew their wit and jocularity. Droll questions are put on any subject and the puzzled candidate furnishes diversion by his awkward embarrassment. I have known the question on this occasion to consist of an enquiry into the pedigree of a race-horse. And it is a common question after asking what is the *summum bonum* of various sects of philosophers, to ask what is the *summum bonum* or chief good among Oxonians, to which the answer is such as Mimnermus would give[1]. This familiarity however only takes place when the examiners are pot-companions of the candidate, which indeed is usually the case; for it is reckoned good management to get acquainted with two or three jolly young masters of arts, and supply them well with port previously to the examination. If the vice-chancellor and proctors happen to enter the school, a very uncommon event, then a little solemnity is put on very much to the confusion of the masters as well as of the boy who is sitting in the little box opposite to them. As neither the officer nor any one else usually enters the room (for it is reckoned very *ungenteel*) the examiners and the candidates often converse on the last drinking-bout or on horses, or read the newspaper or a novel, or divert themselves as well as they can in any manner till the clock strikes eleven, when all parties descend and the *testimonium* is signed by the masters. With this *testimonium* in his possession the candidate is sure of success. The day in

boy has done more than this for his breaking up task !' *Terrae-Filius*, XLII.

[1] τίς δὲ βίος, τί δὲ τερπνὸν ἄτερ χρυσῆς Ἀφροδίτης ;

τεθναίην ὅτε μοι μηκέτι ταῦτα μέλοι κρυπταδίη φιλότης καὶ μείλιχα δῶρα καὶ εὐνή—

Mimnermus, Fr. 1.

which the honour is to be conferred arrives; he appears in the Convocation house, he takes an abundance of oaths, pays a sum of money in fees, and after kneeling down before the vice-chancellor and whispering a lie, rises up a Bachelor of arts.

'And now if he aspires at higher honours (and what emulous spirit can sit down without aspiring at them?) new labours and new difficulties are to be encountered during the space of three years. He must *determine*[1] in Lent, he must do *quodlibets*, he must *do austins*, he must declaim twice, he must read six solemn lectures, and he must be again examined in the sciences, before he can be promoted to the degree of Master of Arts.

'None but the initiated can know what *determining, doing quodlibets*, and *doing austins* mean. I have not room to enter into a minute description of such contemptible *minutiae*. Let it be sufficient to say that these exercises consist of disputations, and the disputations of syllogisms, procured and uttered nearly in the same places, time and manner as we have already seen them in *doing generals*. There is however a great deal of trouble in little formalities, such as procuring six-penny liceats, sticking up the names on the walls, sitting in large empty rooms by yourself or with some poor wight as ill employed as yourself, without having anything to say or do, wearing hoods and a little piece of lambskin with the wool on it, and a variety of other particulars too tedious and too trifling to enumerate.

'The declamations would be an useful exercise if it were not always performed in a careless and evasive manner. The lectures are always called *Wall* Lectures, because the lecturer has no other audience but the walls. Indeed he usually steals a sheet or two of Latin out of some old book, no matter on what subject, though it ought to be on natural philosophy. These he keeps in his pocket in order to take them out and

---

[1] Amhurst mentions (*Terrae-Filius*, XLII) some abuses connected with the quadragesimal *determinations :* the unstatuteable fees and treats of the *collectors* (the two determiners who arranged the classes for the proctors) and their partiality in assigning *gracious days* (half-time days) to those who paid them handsomely, while they *posted* or *dogged* the poor men (*i. e.* assigned to them the opening or closing day of the period) and never gave them *commodious schools* in the scheme. In the preface to his edition of 1726, he says that he hears that since 1721 'the *collectors* have been lately curb'd in their *exorbitances*.' p. xviii.

read them if a proctor should come in ; but otherwise he solaces himself with a book, not from the Bodleian but the circulating library.

'The examination is performed exactly in the same manner as before described; and, though represented as very formidable, is such a one as a boy from a good school just entered might go through as well as after a seven years' residence. Few however reside; for the majority are what are called *term-trotters*, that is, persons who only keep the terms for form-sake, or spend six or eight weeks in a year in the university to qualify them for degrees according to the letter of the statutes.

'After all these important exercises and trials, and after again taking oaths by wholesale, and paying the fees, the academic is honoured with a Master's degree, and issues out into the world with this undeniable passport to carry him through it with credit.

'Exercises of a nature equally silly and obsolete are performed in a similar manner for the other degrees[1].'

That it was most unfair to speak of 'our English universities' as though Cambridge in 1782 were in the same condition as Oxford with respect to the process for degrees, is manifest, and is scarcely excusable on the plea of ignorance.

With regard to Oxford, in an improved condition, a Rugby boy destined to be an eminent professor of that university wrote the following sagacious remarks comparing it with Cambridge in May, 1843.

'I have been led from attentive observation lately to look upon the two rival systems of Oxford and Cambridge as being neither of them perfect in themselves, from their being each confined to one part of education. Cambridge, I should say, from its verbal criticism and philological research, as well as its mathematical studies, imparts a system of education valuable not so much for itself as for the excellent discipline which prepares the mind to pass from the investigation of abstract intellectual truth to the contemplation of moral subjects. Oxford, on the contrary, seeks without any such medium to arrive at

---

[1] V. Knox, *Essays Moral and Literary* I. 332—6. (1782) 'On Some Parts of the Discipline in our English Universities.'

the higher ground at once, without passing through the lower, leading the mind before it has been sufficiently disciplined to investigate the highest and most sacred subjects at once. Cambridge men too often view the intellectual exercise as sufficient in itself, instead of as a preparation for higher things; Oxford men without any such preparation, which they affect to despise, proceed to speculate on great moral questions before they have first practised themselves with lower and less dangerous studies. And this, I look upon it, is the cause of the theological novelties at Oxford—men apply to the most sacred things powers which ought first to have been disciplined by purely intellectual exercises. The one, if I may so express myself, raise a scaffolding and too often rest contented with that; the other endeavour to build the house either with no scaffolding at all, or at least a very slight one—and a most unsubstantial structure it generally proves. The fault of Cambridge, you see, is not the fault of system, but its abuse; in Oxford the plan seems to me radically wrong, and consequently, if followed out to the full, cannot do much good. Cambridge appears to have seen that the province of a university is not to give a complete education, but to furnish the mind with rules, drawn from lower subjects, to be applied in after life to higher; Oxford wishes to give a complete education, and by attempting too much, does the whole very imperfectly[1].'

[1] *The Miscellaneous Writings of* J. Conington *M.A.* i. xvii, xviii.

CHAPTER XX.

MUSICK.

" Mvs canit, Ar numerat, Geo ponderat, As colit astra."

We will now pass to the consideration of those studies which in mediæval times were named the Quadrivium[1], and considered as the most advanced treasures attainable by the seeker after Arts, though 'smally regarded' by the universities in the Elizabethan era.

Music, the art intended by mediæval scholars, was something very different from the sweet tones which cheer many modern mathematicians; and even from the knowledge of harmonics, nodal lines, strings, and thorough bass, which has a charm for the intellects of some of them. The *musice* which a bachelor in ancient times had to study in order to qualify himself as Regent Master was little more than an acquaintance with *metre*. It was however necessary that all clerks should be at least '*bene can.*', i. e. able to *sing* well[2]: accordingly, in the 16th century, the determiners were 'examined in *Songe* and wrightynge[3]' on the 5th thursday in xl^ma. Bishop Cosin, in his zeal for divine service, took care in like manner that the scholars of his foundation should have instruction *in phonasco*. The rule still existed in some of the old institutions—as at

---

[1] W. Harrison's *Description*, Holinshed's Chronicle (1577) 73 *b*. Cooper's *Annals*, II. 351. The Cambridge University .statutes of 1570 prescribed (*cap.* IV.) that the *professor of mathematics*, if he were teaching *cosmography*, should expound Mela, Pliny, Strabo or Plato; if arithmetic, Cuth-

bert Tunstall (*Ball. Oxon.* and King's Hall Camb.), *de arte supputandi* (1522, commended in De Morgan's list), or Jerome Cardan of Pavia; &c. if *geometry*, Euclid; if *astronomy*, Ptolemy.

[2] Harrington *Nugae Antiquae*, II. 158.
[3] *Bedell* Stokys' *Book.*

Winchester College in the present century, where the 'children' before admission being asked if they could sing, answered, as a matter of course, somewhat indirectly, by *saying* a stanza of 'All people that on earth do dwell.'

Degrees in Music seem at all times to have been rather uncommon in England, and lectures from the professor in that faculty still more rare. Of the so-called 'Musick Lectures' at Oxford in the 17th century, an account will be found in my *Univ. Life*, p. 308. It will there be seen that voices and violins were employed. An act in musick at Cambridge in 1620 is described, *ibid.*, p. 280; but Bedel Buck (1665) speaks of a Music Act as not always forthcoming *in Die Comitiorum*[1]. So in his account of the Oxford Commencement (1714), Dr Ayliffe says, '*if there be any Person* taking a Musick Degree, he is to perform a Song of 'Six or Eight Parts on *Vocal* and *Instrumental* Musick, and then he shall have his Creation from the *Savilian* Professors, &c.' In Walmisley's time (1836—56), these exercises at Cambridge were usually performed in Trinity Chapel[2]. Dr Ro. Smith, the master of Trinity, who printed a book on Harmonics (1749, &c.) had a correct ear. He would not use a harpsichord until, by a contrivance of his own, he had divided the semitones into their proper flats and sharps. Bishop Spencer Madan (Trin. 3rd wrangler 1749—50) had a great passion for music, and sang well[3]. Dr Smith instructed and patronized Joah Bates (fellow of King's, Craven scholar, 1760), who was director of the original Handel Festival in Westminster Abbey, and the Pantheon, and founder of the 'Ancient' concerts in Tottenham Street[4].

---

[1] At Cambridge there is a grace '*Cum in Academia nullus sit in Musica Doctor*, Placeat Vobis, ut A.B. Senior Procurator, istiusmodi Doctoris munus pro hac vice suppleat.' (Wall-Gunning *Cerem.* 1828. *p.* 124. In a statute of 1608 it was ordered that the *comitia* or great Commencement should be closed with a musick act, *cum hymno ab huiusce facultatis inceptore.* A letter in Amhurst's *Terrae-Filius*, no. x, dated '*Wadham-college*, Jan. 22. 1720—21,' says that there had not been seen in the schools 'the face of any lecturer in any faculty, *except* in *poetry* and *musick*, for three years past; that all lectures besides were entirely neglected.'

[2] MS. note in the Registry, by Romilly. 'Father' (Bernard) Smith was a member of Bentley's London Club and built the chapel organ which was completed by Chr. Schrider his son-in-law. Monk's *Bentley*, I. 205.

[3] Cumberland's *Memoirs*, 109, 105.

[4] Gunning's *Reminisc.* I. *ch.* ii.

Among the deans of *Christ Church*, H. Aldrich was fond of music, and composed anthems and certain well-known catches. Cyril Jackson, on the other hand, publicly manifested his ignorance and his contempt for the art[1].

Dyer relates how the music professor, J. Randall (King's), attended Gray regularly for three months in 1768 to set music to the poet's ode for the Installation of the D. of Grafton; he complied with the author's taste in adapting the music to the Italian style; but when he came to the chorus, Gray exclaimed, 'I have now done:—make as much noise as you please[2].'

For some account of the increased taste for music and '*fiddling*' at both universities in the middle of the last century, and Tom Hearne's contempt for 'one *Handel* a foreigner' in 1733, I may again be permitted to refer to my *University Life*, pp. 199—204. J. Byrom ordered Corelli's *Sonatas* when he was a scholar of Trinity in 1710.

For the following list, I am indebted to the Compilers of a Collection of Anthems for the Cathedral Church of Lincoln 1875[3].

Graduate Anthem Writers.

J. Alcock, organist of Lichfield and Tamworth Mus. B. (*Magd.*) 1755.

H. Aldrich, dean of *Christ Church*, died 1710.

S. Arnold (Chapel Royal), director of the R. A. of music 1789, Mus. D. (*Magd.*).

T. Attwood, pupil of Mozart at Vienna, organist of S. Paul's 1795.

J. Christmas Beckwith, organist of Norwich, Mus. D. (? *Magd. Hall.*)

W. Boyce, Chapel Royal, Mus. D. Camb. 1749.

J. (Whitfield) Clarke, Mus. D. Dublin, organist of S. John's and Trinity and professor of Music at Cambridge.

W. Croft, organist of Chapel Royal and Westminster Mus. D. (*Christ Church*) 1713.

W. Crotch, Mus. D. (*S. Mary Hall*), professor of music at *Oxford*, 1797.

Maurice Greene, organist of S. Paul's and Chapel Royal, Mus. D. and professor at Cambridge 1730.

Manchester Register, i. 58 (Chetham Soc.) Cooper's *Dict. Biog.*

[1] H. Best's *Memorials*, no. xxii,

[2] *Privil.* Camb. ii. pt. iii. (=*Supplement to Hist.* Camb.) p. 36. A friend of Southey's (*Ball.* Coll. 1794) had a *harpsichord* in his rooms. Such instruments were still in use at Oxford as late as 1805. W. Battie had a *spinnet* at King's about 1724.

[3] The collection of 570 anthems contains 15 by Boyce, 14 by Greene, 10 by Croft, 9 by Attwood, 8 each by W. Hayes and Nares, 7 each by Crotch and Kent, 4 each by Aldrich, Whitfield-Clarke and Weldon, 2 each by Beckwith and King, one each by Arnold and P. Hayes; none, so far as I observe, by Alcock, Norris or Stephen.

W. Hayes[1], organist of *Christ Church* and *Magdalen*, Mus. B. (Magd.) 1735, professor at Oxford.

Philip Hayes (son), organist of *Magdalen*, Mus. B. (*Magd.*) 1763, professor at Oxford.

Ja. Kent, organist of Trinity College Cambridge and of Winchester.

C. King, choir of S. Paul's, Mus. B. (*Merton*) 1707.

Ja. Nares, organist of York and Chapel Royal, Mus. D. Cambridge 1757.

T. Norris, organist of *Christ Church* and *S. John's*, Mus. B. Oxon.

J. Stephens, organist of Salisbury, Mus. D. Cambridge 1763.

J. Weldon, pupil of Purcell, organist of *New College* about 1705.

King's College Anthems were published in 8vo. Camb. 1706.

The following lines, of which a ms. copy is preserved among Dr *Webb's Collections* in the University Library, may be thought worthy of notice for the reference which they have to Joah Bates, 'Jemmy Twitcher,' Beverly, &c.[2]

'*Mr* Jennar's *Song.   Sung at Lord* Sandwich's[3].

> Ye Friends of sound Harmony, Mirth and good Chear;
> Who would sing out the old and sing in the New Year.
> You that Fiddle for pleasure, for Fame, or for Bread;
> Come and list at Lord *Sandwich's* Kettle Drum Head.
>   derry down down derry down.

[1] The music professors Hayes, father and son, had been preceded in that professorship (1682, 1718,) at Oxford by two Richards Goodson likewise father and son, organists of *Christ Church*.

[2] The Persons mentioned are as follows,—

Felice Giardini, violinist, born at Turin 1716, died at Moscow, 1796.

Joah Bates, fellow of King's, B.A. 1764. Secretary to Ld. Sandwich.

C. Jenner, Pemb., B.A. 1757.

Ld. Sandwich, Trin. LL.D. 1769.

? T. Champness, Trin. B.A. 1762.

Wade Gascoigne, Trin. LL.D. 1757.

? C. Norris, fellow of Trin. B.A. 1766.

J. Beverly, Chr., 1767.

Busy.

Desborough.

Ant. Shepherd, B. A. Joh. 1743. M.A. Chr. 1747. (Plumian Prof. 1760.)

Rokeby.

? J. Ward (Dudley), LL.D. 1769.

[3] The following anecdote (about 1770), quoted in the *Quarterly Review* (1813. IX. 391, 392) of the 2nd ed. of Meadley's *Life of Paley*, has some interest in this connexion.

' "When the hall of Christ's College, which had been promised through the interest of Dr Shepherd, was fitting up for a benefit concert for Ximenes, a Spanish musician, warmly patronised by Lord Sandwich, Mr Paley and Mr Law peremptorily insisted that the promise should be recalled unless satisfactory assurance was given that a lady then living with his lordship, and who had been openly distributing tickets, should not be permitted to attend. At first the senior tutor, who was in habits of intimacy with Lord Sandwich," (a very reputable connexion for a divine and an instructor of youth) " objected to the idea of excluding any lady from a public concert: but afterwards when they urged that standing in a public situation as instructors of youth it was their duty to discountenance every sort of immo-

For now from the Cares of the Helme he descends;
And blowing his Whistle, he summons his Friends;
And nothing he leaves them to wish or desire,
Except for Giardini a little less Fire.

*   *   *   *   *   *

Now the Masters all mount in a terrible Row,
And tun'd is each Fiddle, and Rosin'd each Bow,
And Giardini when got in his †Tantrums and† Fits
Frights the poor Dilettanti quite out of his wits.

At the Harpsichord now Joah Bates takes his place;
Tho he casts a Sheep's Eye on his dear Double Bass,
To the Heart Strings it grieves him to quit it so soon,
For tho he mayn't play it, he'll put it in tune.

But when he begins to sprawl over a Chorus
And lays the whole matter so clearly before us:
No Hearer so stupid but soon understands,
He's full Son to *Briareus*, and Heir to his Hands.

Charles Jenner sits trembling close to his right side,
And soon as a hard Solo passage he spied,
He swore that alone he could do it all right,
Tho' he makes the same Blunder but every night.

Sam Champness comes lagging, but well propt with Ale
He will roar you as sweet as a young Nightingale;

*   *   *   *   *   *

While Gascoigne who plays on the Hoarse Tenor Fiddle
And for ever is coming in wrong in the middle;
With more Wit than Musick is cracking his Jests,
Which he thinks better Fun than dry counting of Rests.

John Beverly[1] long had been Fidling the Bass,
But his Fingers so long seldom hit the right place;
So the great double Bass to take up he did beg,
Where he measures the Stops by the length of his Leg.

Giardini for Absentees now looks about,
If Desborough's call'd to a worse crying out;
Or if any loose Straglers, the practise would balk,
If Rokeby or Ward take a Ride or a Walk.

---

rality, and threatened to appeal to the Society in case of his refusal, the assurance was given and the *arrangement* suffered to proceed." Be it remembered, that of these two cham- pions of morality and decorum, the older [W. Paley] was then no more than twenty-eight.'

[1] The notorious Esquire Bedell (1770), to whom Gunning devotes part

Lord Sandwich mean time ever active and steady
  Eyes the Drums with impatience, and cries an't you ready?
Knows who are alert, and who always ask pardon;
  And who are the Men must be fetch'd from the Garden.

When the Band is all marshall'd from front to the rear,
  And Miss Ray[1], and Norris, and Busy appear;
When impatience to start shines in ev'ry man's Face,
  Steals in Dr Shepherd a tuning his Bass.

But now hush'd is each noise, and on each raptur'd ear
  Break such sounds as the angels stand list'ning to hear;
Handel rouses, and hearing his own Thunder roar,
  Looks downward from Heaven, and calls out encore.

Dr Webb's collection in the University Library contains, beside the foregoing song (vol. I.), a '*programma*' (W. Richardson, Coll. Pet., V.C.) forbidding persons *in statu pupillari* from attending a public concert, 30 June, 1770 :—Also the programme of a Concert held in the hall of Trinity College on Friday, 26 June, 1772, at 6 p.m.:—Another (three pages 4to) of a concert in the same place 30 June, 1775.

of the 5th chapter of the first vol. of his *Reminiscences*. Beverly got an honorary degree from the proctors in 1767, and a good deal of money from the heads of colleges, &c. in various years.

[1] Miss *Raey*, òr Wray, mother of Basil Montagu, Q.C. (Chr.) 6th wrangler, 1790. She was shot (1779) when coming from Covent-Garden theatre by an unhappy admirer. She was doubtless the person whom Paley and J. Law obliged Dr Shepherd to exclude from the concert in their college hall.

CHAPTER XXI.

ASTRONOMY.

Sir Roderick (*examining* Immerito, *a candidate for preferment*). Sirrah, boy, write him down a good astronomer.
Page (*aside, writes*) ' As colit astra.'

The Return from Parnassus (1602), i. 3.

THOUGH of old time the subjects of *Arithmetic* and *Geometry* were reserved for *Bachelors* in Arts to study, we have already said all that we have to say thereanent on the topic of the Mathematical Tripos.

Concerning *Astronomy* we have still a few remarks to make.

The Cambridge professors seem as a rule to have done their duty by this science. First and foremost we have Newton, who by exact scientific reasoning proved the guess of Descartes[1] in his general hypothesis of matter and motion to be true, but in a different sense for the material universe.

Isaac Newton of Trinity was Lucasian Professor 1669—1702, and had his private observatory in the college[2].

---

[1] In illustration of the question in dispute between Whewell and Playfair on the hold which Cartesianism had at Cambridge I omitted (p. 125) Eachard's (Master of Cath. Hall) humorous description of the 'young pert *Soph*' criticizing the country parson's Easter Sermon. 'What a good Text was here spoyled to divide it into this and that, and I know not what, when it would have gone so easily into *corpus* and *inane;* or into the three *Cartesian* elements. Besides, like an old dull Philosopher, he quite forgat to suppose the motion of the *vortexes* upon which the grand business of the *Hypothesis* of the Resurrection alto-

gether depends.' *Some Observations* upon the Answer to an *Enquiry into the Grounds and Occasion of the Contempt of the Clergy* 1671, p. 144. Cp. above p. 176.

[2] Humphrey Wanley was staying in Cambridge in *Sept.* 1699. He wrote thus to Dr Charlett of *Univ. Coll. Oxon.* 'Here was a great preparation for observing the Eclipse, a room darkened, telescopes fixed and everything put in order on purpose, and happy that man that could be admitted; but after some hours waiting for black Wednesday *parturiunt montes,* the gentlemen having dined with Duke Humfrey came out very gravely

His deputy and successor W. Whiston, of Clare, took interest in this pursuit. He records[1] how Sam. Clarke and his father Alderman Clarke, of Norwich, about 1707 or 1708, 'happened to be viewing Saturn's Ring at *Norwich*, with a Telescope of 15 or 16 ft. long; when without any prior Thought or Expectation of such a thing, as Mr *Clarke* assured me, they both distinctly saw a fixed star between the Ring and the Body of that Planet: which is sure evidence that the Ring is properly distinct from the Planet, and at some distance from it: which, tho' believ'd, could hardly be demonstrated before.'

When Whiston was deprived of his professorship and catechetical lectureship Oct. 30, 1710, he retired to London, and gave astronomical lectures, which were attended by Addison and Sir R. Steele. But just before this he published his *Praelectiones Physico-Mathematicae*, and three years earlier (1707) he had been especially energetic, editing Newton's nine years' professional lectures on Algebra under the title of *Arithmetica Universalis*, as well as *Praelectiones Astronomicae*[2] of his own. In the month of May of that year he and Roger Cotes the young Plumian professor began a course of experiments, from which each of them composed a dozen lectures in hydrostatics and pneumatics.

Roger Cotes, of Trinity 1706—16, just mentioned, is numbered among our professors of Experimental Philosophy[3]. He

into the warm sun cursing their tables, &c., and were as well laughed at as the Sons of Art in London, who hired the monument for the same purpose.' *Letters from the Bodleian*, I. 97.

[1] Whiston's *Memoir of* S. Clarke (1730), p. 14.

[2] *Praelectiones Astronomicae*, Cantabrigiae *in Scholis publicis habitae*, *Quibus accedunt* Tabulae *plurimae* Astronomicae Flamstedianae *correctae*, Hallianae, Cassianae, *et* Streetianae. *In Usum Juventutis Academicae*. Pretium 5s. 6d. 1707.

Praelectiones Physico-Mathematicae, Cantabrigiae *in Scholis publicis habitae*. Quibus *Philosophia Illustrissimi*

Newtoni *Mathematica explicatius traditur ; et facilius demonstratur.* Cometographia etiam Halleiana *Commentariolo illustratur. In Usum Juventutis Academicae. Typis Academicis* 8vo. *Pretium* 4s. 6d. An english ed. *Lond.* 1716.

Whiston lectured also on the Ancient *Eclipses* of the Sun and Moon for about a year before he was banished 1709—10. *Memoirs of the Life of* W. Whiston (1749), I. pp. 135, 173, 181. His *New Theory of the Earth* (1695) continued to be read at Cambridge.

[3] Cotes was elected unanimously the year after he had taken his first degree ! Bentley calls him 'Post mag-

is very widely celebrated for his 'property of the circle,' and on the continent Gauss has done honour to his interpolation method for the value of integrals. Mr J. W. L. Glaisher informs me that a method which is even now just beginning to find its way into Cambridge teaching, the treatment of optics by the methods of modern geometry, of which Gauss is the modern founder, is really due, so far as its principles are concerned, to Cotes.

Cotes by his College observatory and experiments 'involved himself in a debt[1] which his modesty permitted to prey upon his health; and which put an end to that valuable life at the age of thirty-four. A Person renowned for his great skill in classic literature [Bentley] then presided in the College; a spectator of *Cotes's* distress: Into which he had been plunged upon expectations or promises that the expenses should be born (*sic*) by that opulent College. But the only regard paid him was by the Epitaph composed in classic elegance; which is inscribed on his monument in Trinity College Chapel. After death every Virtue is sure to meet its reward[2].' Monk's life of Bentley (i. 202, 401) *by no means bears out this imputation.*

In 1714 the Plumian and Lucasian Professors were con-

num illum Newtonum Societatis hujus spes altera et decus gemellum ; cui ad summam doctrinae laudem Omnes morum virtutumque dotes In cumulum accesserunt ; Eo magis spectabiles amabilesque, Quod in formoso corpore Gratiores venirent.' (*Epitaph.*) Vincent Bourne also wrote epitaphic lines in his memory. Three years before Cotes' death Brook Taylor (LL.B. St John's) had discovered (simultaneously with John Bernoulli and James Hermann of Basle) the *centre of oscillation* of bodies in motion rigidly connected by a lever. Taylor published in his *Method of Increments,* 1715, a problem in vibrating strings. He was the discoverer of the *theorem* which bears his name. He contributed to the Philos. Transactions, 1712—23. He died in 1731, but his *Contemplatio*

Philosophica was not printed till sixty years later. (Whewell *Hist. Induct. Sciences*, Vol. II. Bk. vi. Ch. VI. § 10; Bk. viii. ch. II.)

[1] There was a college observatory in the 2nd court of S. John's (1765), of which Isaac Pennington (then a Soph) had charge in 1766 with a stipend of £15 per annum. He was required to deliver observations to the master and seniors. In 1764 a pair of 16 in. diam. globes were ordered, price not exceeding 10 guineas ; but it was two years before they were procured. *Baker-Mayor*, 1071—1073.

[2] Ri. Davies' *General State of Education in the Universities* with a particular View to the Philosophic and Medical Education : to Dr Hales. Bath. 1759. Sold by M. Cooper, London. (*Bodl. Gough Camb.* 66), p. 43.

stituted *ex officio* of the Commission for discovering the longitude at sea. (Cooper's *Annals*, IV. 120).

Antony Shepherd (M.A. Chr., B.A. Joh.) printed in 1776 'A description of the experiments intended to illustrate a course of lectures on the principles of natural philosophy, read in the observatory at Trin. coll. Cambridge,' as Plumian professor[1].

At the close of the century another of the successors of Cotes as Plumian Professor, Sam. Vince of Caius (1796—1822), used to lecture *inter alia* upon Astronomy; giving experiments and explanations of instruments[2]. He printed a 'Plan' of his course, Camb. 1797. It may have been on account of Vince's sufficiency that the special Professor of Astronomy of the later (Lowndesian) foundation, W. Lax of Trinity (1795—1836), gave 'no lectures[3]' at the end of the last century. It certainly was on account of Vince's lectures that Wollaston the Jacksonian professor lectured in chemistry only instead of alternating with experimental Philosophy, and in his turn Farish took to Mechanics.

The first who had held the office of Lowndes' professor of Astronomy, was Dr Roger Long of Pembroke (1750—71), the friend of Gray. His famous 'Zodiack,' constructed with the help of Jonathan Munns, the tin-plate worker, has been noticed in *Univ. Life*, p. 662. It has only recently been discarded by the society to which he bequeathed it. Until Vince was appointed Plumian Professor, F. J. H. Wollaston of Trin. Hall, professor of Natural and Experimental Philosophy (1792—18), gave alternate courses on Astronomy with Chemistry, but in 1795 he abandoned the former. An account of the work of their successors at the commencement of the present century may be found in [Wright's] *Alma Mater*, ii. 34 (relating to 1818), and *Facetiae Cantab.* 1836, *p.* 159.

In 1792 Mr Ingram complained[4] that our University had need of a good *Observatory*, and a convenient room for the pro-

---

[1] The covenant of Trin. Coll. with the Plumian Trustees, Feb. 9, 1705, is given in *Cooper's Annals*, IV. 69 *n.* The Observatory over the King's Gate is mentioned.

[2] *Camb. Univ. Calendar*, 1802, pp. 23, 24.

[3] *Ibid.* p. 30.

[4] *The Necessity of Introducing Divinity*, &c. p. 108 *n.*

fessors in Divinity and the professors of Civil Law and Common
Law to read their lectures in.

In 1768 there had been a project for building a Music Room
and Amphitheatre for professional lectures, started by Walter
Titley's donation, but it fell through.

There were small Observatories in our principal Colleges—
over the 'great' or ' King's ' gate of Trinity, and in St John's [1].
The former was erected by subscription of Bentley and his
friends (Jan. 170$\frac{5}{6}$) and stored with the best astronomical instruments which science could at that period produce,—partly at
the expense of the library fund. Beneath this Cotes, and after
him his cousin Ro. Smith, Bentley's successor, resided as Plumian
Professor. Sir I. Newton, and after him Vice-master Walker,
occupied the rooms to the north of the gate, and W. Whiston
those to the south [2].

The following list may interest Oxonian Astronomers and
Geometricians :—

A *Catalogue of* Instruments *Made and Sold by* John Prujean *near* New-
College *in* Oxford. *With* Notes *of the* Use *of them*[3].

Holland's Universal Quadrant,
His Arithmetick Quadrant, serving to take Heights by inspection.

Oughtred's Quadrant,	His Double Horizontal Dial.
Gunter's Quadrant,	His Analemma,
His Nocturnal.	Collins's Quadrant.

Mr *Halton's* Universal Quadrant for all Latitudes with Mr Haley's notes.

Orontia's Sinical Universal quadrant.	*Napier's* Rods.
Mr *Caswel's* Nocturnal.	Mr *Haley's* Nocturnal.
Mr *Tomson's* Pantametron.	Mr *Pound's* Cylinder-Dial.
Mr *Edward's* Astrolobe. [*sic.*]	Mr *Hooper's* Dialing Scales.
Scales for Fortification.	Scales for Surveying, Dialing, &c.

And most other Mathematical Instruments.

John Keill (1671—1721), born at Edinburgh, studied under
David Gregory at the university there, and following him to
Oxford, entered at Balliol, and exhibited experiments illus-
trative of the Newtonian philosophy by means of an apparatus
of his own invention : he also examined Burnet and Whiston's
Theories of the Earth. In 1700 he lectured on natural phi-

[1] Baker-Mayor 1041, 1073.
[2] Monk's *Bentley*, I. 202, Bentley's
Corresp. pp. 448, 449, 786. Walker
preserved Newton's rooms as far as
possible *in statu quo*, adding Bentley's
famed hat to his relics.

[3] Advt. at the end of *Globe Notes
by* R. Holland, Oxford, *Printed for*
Henry Clements, 1701.—*Bodl.* Godwin
Pamph. 1238. Another list will be
found among W. Gooch's remains in
the Appendix to this volume.

losophy as deputy for the Sedleian Professor, Sir T. Millington. In the following year he published *Introductio ad veram Physicam.* Having been elected F. R. S., he took the part of Newton against Leibnitz in the Fluxional Controversy (1708). After paying a visit to America (1709) as treasurer to the exiled Palatines, he returned to Oxford, and was made Savilian Professor[1] of Astronomy the same year. He again took up the cudgels for Newton against the Cartesians, in a Paper before the Royal Soc., *On the Rarity of Matter,* &c. In 1711 he became Decypherer to the Queen; and in 1713 took the degree of M.D. Two years later he edited Euclid; and in 1718 he read an '*Introduction to the true Astronomy, or* Astronomical Lectures *in the* Astronomical School of *the Univ. of* Oxford,' which was published in 1721, the year of his death. He is said to have been the first who introduced the love of the Newtonian Philosophy at Oxford by his lectures in 1704, laying down very simple propositions which he proved by experiments and from those he deduced others more complex, which he still confirmed by experiments; till he had instructed his auditors in the laws of motion, the principles of hydrostatics and optics, and some of the chief propositions of Sir I. Newton concerning light and colours.

This account of John Keill's positive method is given by his successor *Desaguliers* in the Preface to his *Course of Experimental Philosophy.*

John Theophilus Desaguliers (1683—1749) was born at Rochelle, brought to England after the Revocation of the Edict of Nantes, and sent to Christ Church. B.A. Ordained Deacon 1710. The same year, having removed to Hart Hall, he read lectures on Experimental Philosophy, as successor in that readership to John Keill, who was visiting New England. Having married and taken his M.A. degree in 1712, he commenced lectures in London in 1713; was made F. R. S. under Newton's presidency in 1714. Published *Fires improved,* and quarrelled with Edmund Curll for advertising it too much.

---

[1] Keill's master, David Gregory of Balliol, had held this professorship (1691—1709). The chair had been filled in earlier times by Seth Ward and Chr. Wren. Jo. Caswell (or Carswell) who succeeded Gregory left a very favourable impression on Uffenbach, who conversed with him on telescopes in 1710. *Reisen,* III. 180.

Lectured before K. Geo. I. in 1717. B.C.L. and D.C.L., 1718. With Dr Stephen Hales he invented and exhibited an engine for sea-soundings in 1728. His electrical experiments and papers in the Philos. Transactions, &c. are enumerated in Kippis' *Biog. Brit.*

James Bradley of Balliol, who succeeded Keill as Savilian Professor of Astronomy in 1741, made constant obervations, and discovered and settled the *aberration of the fixed stars* (1727) from the progressive motion of light combined with the earth's annual motion, and the *nutation of its axis* (1737). He succeeded Halley as astronomer royal. Two of the Savilian professors of *Geometry* also held that post—Edm. Halley of Qu. himself, and his successor in the professorship (1742), Nat. Bliss of Pembroke. Halley, while at Oxford, had published observations on a spot in the sun, by which its motion on its axis was established, in 1676—two years before he was admitted M.A., and just before his important visit to St Helena.

On the evening of June 3rd, 1769, the tower of New College was used by Mr Lucas a fellow, and Mr Clare of St John's, to observe the transit of Venus; the Savilian Professor Hornsby was in the Schools' Tower; and Mr Nitikin (a Russian) and Mr Williamson of St Alban Hall, in the Infirmary[1]. Cyril Jackson, then A.B. and Student of Ch. Ch., and several others, were stationed in other places, not particularly fitted for the purpose[2]. This shows how much a proper observatory was then needed at Oxford. The foundations for such an one (the Radcliffe) were laid soon afterwards, in June 1772.

In Sept., 1750, a Cambridge man wrote to the Student or Oxford Monthly Miscellany (I. 339) commending the study of astronomy to future country gentlemen, and to all university men. He says, 'I fancy they will find it no inelegant transition from a chapter in *Smigletius* to a lecture in *Keil.*' He concludes by proposing to commence astronomical communications to the *Student,* and refers to an account of the early history of the science by G. Costard[3], fellow of Wadham, in his *Two Letters to* Martin Folkes, Esq., 1746.

---

[1] Mackenzie E. C. Walcott, *W. of Wykeham and his Colleges,* pp. 335, 336, [Green's] *Oxford during the Last Century* (Slatter and Rose), p. 22.

[2] *ibid.* p. 29.

[3] Vicar of Twickenham; author of *Observations illustrating the Bk. of Job,* 1747. *Hist. of Astronomy,* 1767, &c.

A list of Books in use at Cambridge
about the year 1730
for Optics and Astronomy.

Acta Eruditorum Lipsiae. anno 1683.

Bentley, Ri. (Trin.) Boyle Lectures, Serm. viii. Lond. 1693.

Boyle, Ro. (*Oxon.*) Works, abridged by Shaw. 1725.

Bullialdus, Ismael (Boulliau) De Lineis Spiralibus, Paris, 1657.

Burgundiae Philosophia. (Cf. p. 79 supra.)

Burnet, T. (Clare and Chr.) Theory of the Earth. Lond. 1681—9.

Cartesius, Renat. (La Fleche) Dioptricks.

——— Meteor.

——— Principia. Amst. 1644.

Chambers, Ephr. Dict. (sub vocibus *Halo, Light, Moon, Parhelion, Rainbow.*) 1728.

Clarke, S. (Caius) Demonstration of Sir I. Newton's Philos.

Clericus, J. (Geneva) Physica. Cantab. 1700, 1705.

De Chales, C. F. M. (*Soc. Jesu,* Turin) Cursus Mathem. Lyons, 1690.

Derham, W. (Trin.) Astro-Theol. Lond. 1714, 1726.

Domekins, G. Peter. Phil. Newton. Lond. 1730.

Fabri, Honorat. (Rome) ii. de Homine. Paris, 1666.

Flamsteed, J. (Jes.) 1672—1713.

Gassendi, P. (Aix and Paris) Astron. 1702.

's Gravesande, W. J. (Leyden) Physico-Math. Lug. Bat. 1720.

Gregory, Dav. (Edinb., *Oxon*) Astron. folio *Oxon.* 1702. engl. Lond. 1715.

——— Catoptricae et Dioptricae Sphericae Elementa. Oxon. 1695. (Lond. 1705, 1715, 1735.)

Harris, J. (S. John's) Astron. Dial. (ed. 3. 1795.)

Hooke, R. (Ch. Ch.) Posthumous Works. 1705.

Huyghens, Christian. Discursus de Causis Gravitat. Lug. Bat. 1724—8.

——— Opusc. Posthuma. Lug. Bat. 1703.

——— Planetary Worlds, or Cosmotheoros. Hagae. 1698. Lond. 1699.

Johnson, T. (King's, Magd.) Quaestiones (Opticae pp. 27, 28).

——————————————————— (Astronomicae pp. 32, 33) Camb. 1732 ; ed. 3. 1741.

Keill, John (*Balliol*) Examination of Theorists on the Earth. Oxon. 1698.

—— Introd. ad Astron. Oxon. 1715.

Lowthorp, J. (Joh.) Abridgment of Philos. Transactions, 3 vols. 4to. Lond. 1716.

Malebranche, Nic. (Sorbonne) Search after Truth. (1674), Transl. T. Taylor. Lond. 1720.

Miscellanea Curiosa (Halley, Molyneux, &c.)

Molyneux, W. (F. R. S.) Dioptricks. 4to. Lond. 1692.

——— in Misc. Curiosa, ii. 263.

Musschenbroeck, P. van. (Leyden) Elem. Physico-Math.

Newton, Is. (Trin.) Lectiones Opticae. Opticks, 4to. Lond. 1704.

——— Optice. lat. ed. S. Clarke. Lond. 1706, 1728.

——— Principia Math. Lond. 1687. Camb. 1713.

Ode, Ja. Phil. Nat. Principia. Traject. ad Rhen. 1727.

Pemberton, H. (Leyden, Gresham Coll., F.R.S.) View of Newton. Lond. 1728.
Philosophical Conversations.
——————— Transactions.
Riccioli, Giov. Bapt. (Parma) Almagestum Novum. Bologna 1651—69.
Rizzett, Giov. de Luminis affectionibus, or the present State of the Republick
of Letters.
(Rizzett, Giov.) a Confutation of.
Rohault, Jac. Physica. ed. 4. (by S. Clarke) 1718.
Rowning, J. (Magd.) Opticks.
Smith, R. (Trin.) Opticks, Camb. 1728, 1738.
Tacquet, Andr. (Soc. Jesu, Antwerp) Catoptricks (1669).
Wallis, J. (Emm. Qu. Savil.) Opera Mathemat. Oxon. 1687—99.
Whiston, W. (Clare) Praelectiones Astronom., Camb. 1707.
———————————————————— Physico-Mathem., Camb. 1710.
——————— New Theory of the Earth. Lond. 1696, 1725.
Worster, Ben. Princip. Philos. Lond. 1730.

It may be well to supplement this index, and that on pp.
78—81, with a chronological list of

Some Mathematical Books printed since 1730.

1731. Euclid *Oxon.*
L. Trevigar, Conic Sections (in usum juvent. Acad.) Camb.
1734. Is. Barrow's (Trin.) Mathematical Lectures (Bowyer).
Inquiry into the Ideas of Space. Treatises by J. Clarke, E. Law, &c.
1737. W. Whiston (Clare) New Theory of the Earth. Camb.
1738. Ro. Smith (Trin.) Complete System of Opticks (ed. 1. 1728). Camb.
Roger Cotes (Trin.) Hydrostatical and Pneumatical Lectures (Bowyer).
1739. R. Dunthorne (Dr Long's servant, Pemb.) Astronomy of the Moon.
Camb.
——————— Tables of the Moon's Motion. Camb.
1740. Nic. Sanderson (Chr.) Elements of Algebra.
1741. ——————————————— 2 vols. 4to. with Memoir.
1742. Roger Long (Pemb.) Astronomy, 4to. vol. I. Camb.
Colin Maclaurin (Glasg. Aberd.) Complete System of Fluxions. Lond.
1744. R. Smith (Trin.) Harmonics. Camb.
P. Parsons (Sid.) Astronomic Doubts. Camb.
1747. J. Keill (*Ball.*) Euclidis Elementa. ed. 4. *Oxon.*
Ralph Heathcote (Jes.) Historia Astronomiæ. Camb.
1748. Colin Maclaurin (Glasg. Aberd.) Account of Newton's Discoveries. Lond.
——————— Algebra, in 3 parts. Lond.
——————— Geometra......Descriptio Curvarum (ed. 2. with Life.)
Lond.
H. Owen (*Jesus*) Harmonia Trigonometrica.
T. Rutherforth (S. Joh.) System of Nat. Philosophy. Camb.
1749. R. Smith (Trin.) Harmonics. Camb.
Edm. Halley (*Queen's*) Tabulae Astronomicae. 4to. Lond.
1752. ——————————— Astronomical Tables, 4to. Lond.

1756. James Ferguson, Astronomy on Newton's principles. Lond. (also 1757, 1764, 1772, 1778.)
1758. Menelai Sphaerica. E. Halley, J. Costard. *Oxon.*
1759. R. Smith (Trin.) Harmonics ed. 2. Camb.
Isr. Lyons junior. Treatise on Fluxions.
1760. W. S. Powell (S. Joh.) Observations on Waring's Miscellanea Analytica.
James Ferguson, Lectures on Mechanics, Hydrostatics, Pneumatics and Optics. Lond.
1762. E. Waring (Magd.) Miscellanea Analytica de Æquationibus algebraicis et curvarum Proprietatibus. 4to. Camb.
W. Jones, Essay on Nat. Philosophy. *Oxon.*
1765. Excerpta quaedam e Newt. Principiis. J. Jebb et R. Thorpe (Pet.) G. Wollaston (Sid.) 4to. Camb.
1767. Syntagma Dissertationum. (partly scientific). Hyde. *Oxon.*
1768. James Ferguson, Easy Introduction to Astronomy.
1769. Astronomical Observations at Camb. 1767, 68. W. Ludlam (S. Joh.) Lond.
1770. E. Waring (Magd.) Meditationes Algebraicae. 4to. Camb.
James Ferguson, Introduction to Electricity. Lond.
1771. W. Ludlam (S. Joh.) Hadley's Quadrant, with Supplement. Lond.
1772. E. Waring (Magd.) Proprietates Algebraicarum Curvarum. 4to. Camb.
W. Ludlam (S. Joh.) On the Power of the Wedge. Lond.
1774. The Academick Dream (a poem against the excessive study of Mathematics) 4to. Camb.
1776. E. Waring. Meditationes Analyticae. 4to. Camb.
1778. T. Kipling (S. Joh.) Elementary part of Smith's Optics.
1780. W. Ludlam (S. Joh.) on Newton's Second Law of Motion. Lond.
J. Bonnycastle, Scholar's Guide to Arithmetick. 12mo. Lond.
1781. S. Vince, Conic Sections. Camb.
1782. E. Waring, Meditationes Algebraicae (ed. 3.)
1783. J. Bonnycastle, Introduction to Algebra. 12mo. Lond.
1784. G. Atwood (Trin.) Rectilinear Motion. Camb.
————— Analysis of Lectures on Nat. Philosophy.
Roger Long's (Pemb.) Astronomy, 2 vols. Camb. (see 1742—64.)
1785. E. Waring (Magd.) Meditationes Analyticae. ed. 2. 4to. Camb.
T. Parkinson (Chr.) System of Mechanics and Hydrostatics, 2 vols. 4to. Camb.
W. Ludlam (S. Joh.) Rudiments of Mathematics. Lond.
1786. J. Bonnycastle. Introduction to Astronomy in a Series of Letters. Lond.
1787. W. Ludlam (S. Joh.) Rudiments of Mathematics. Camb.
1789. F. Wollaston (Sid.) General Astronomical Catalogue. Lond.
J. Bonnycastle. Elements of Geometry. Lond.
1790. S. Vince (Cai., Sid.) on Practical Astronomy. Camb. and Lond.
1792. Archimedes cum Eutocii Ascalon. commentariis. J. Torelli. *Oxon.*
1793. S. Vince (Cai., Sid.) Plan of Lectures on Nat. Philosophy. Lond.
F. Wollaston (Sid.) Universal Meridian Dial. 4to.
1794. T. Newton (Jes.) Short Treatise on Conic Sections. Camb.
E. Waring (Magd.) On the Principles of Human Knowledge (Suppressed).

1794—1852. S. John's Coll. Algebraical Equation and Problem Papers. W. Rotherham (Camb. 1852.)

1795. James Wood (S. Joh.) Algebra, vol. I. Camb.

S. Vince (Cai., Sid.) Fluxions. Camb. (=vol. II. of Wood's series).

1796. T. Manning (Cai.) Arithmetic and Algebra, I. Lond.

James Wood (S. Joh.) Mechanics. Camb. (=III. i.)

S. Vince (Cai. and Sid.) Hydrostatics (=Wood's Series III. ii.)

1797. S. Vince (Cai., Sid.) Astronomy vol. I. 4to. Camb.

1798. T. Manning (Cai.) Algebra, vol. II. Lond.

Astronomical Observations (Greenwich 1750—62) J. Bradley (*Ball.*) and N. Bliss, *Oxon.*

James Wood (S. Joh.) Elements of Optics. Camb. (=IV. i.)

1799. S. Vince (Cai., Sid.) Principles of Astronomy (complete=Wood's Series, IV. ii.)

1800. S. Vince (Cai., Sid.) Plane Spherical Trigonometry. Logarithms. Camb.

——— Principles of Hydrostatics. Camb.

———————— of Fluxions. Camb.

J. Stephens (? S. Joh.) Method of Ascertaining the Latitude of the northern hemisphere. 4to. Camb.

F. Wollaston (Sid.) Fasciculus Astronomicus. 4to. Lond.

CHAPTER XXII.

CONCLUSION.

Reliquum est Σπάρταν ἔλαχες, ταύταν κόσμει.

M. T. C. *ad Atticum*, IV. 6.

WHILE we thoroughly accept the position that, if Cambridge is our mother, Oxford is our aunt[1]; and while we admit the vigour of the latter in the seventeenth and nineteenth centuries, we shall hardly be considered unfairly prejudiced if we declare our opinion that there were more certain signs of vitality and usefulness in our north-easterly university in the eighteenth century, at least in the latter half of it.

Matters at Cambridge are apt to be at a level (not always of necessity a dead level), shewing something of the natural characteristics of the country and the town in which her lot is cast. Their beauty is retiring, and the point from which they may be seen is sometimes far to seek. The elegancies and the virtues of Oxford are more prominent, more obvious, even to those who do not look for them.

We may draw a parallel similarly for the intellectual character as it is trained by the traditional method of each university. Oxford shews her sons how they may make the most of each point of excellence and turn the smallest details to advantage. Cambridge may be colder and duller, but her purpose is to aim immediately at nothing higher than preparing the ground with care and laying the foundation conscientiously.

The one aims at producing all, and is in danger of losing the whole : the other is content with one thing at a time;—*that* at least is gained, though often nothing is built upon it.

Again, let us carry the contrast of the sister universities

---

[1] Lakes' *Ballad* in answer to Ri. Corbet on K. James I's visits to the universities in 1614, 1615. Cp. Fuller's *Hist. of* Camb., preface, 1655.

into comparison with the genius of the two centuries preceding our own; Oxford beauty and Cambridge plainness, the Athenian and the Spartan, may be thought to correspond with similar characteristics,—the one of the seventeenth, the latter of the eighteenth century.

To take for example one particular where the comparison favours Oxford; a particular where Oxford had a right to pre-eminence, on the ancient and noble theory that to aim at *all* science is to aim at Theology: we may observe that theological controversy, the study of the sacred languages by raw students, and even reverent care for ceremonial details, was a growth of the seventeenth rather than of the eighteenth century, and seemed more at home at Oxford than at Cambridge. A similar backwardness (we should hardly call it a deficiency) was, I believe, noticeable in our university with regard to physical science.

In mathematics (if not in metaphysics) Cambridge could turn the tables on her sister, at least in the latter half of the seventeenth century. But these were the foundations on which all subsequent study, in Theology and the other sciences, was to be built.

To these subjects she clung, the like foundation she continued to lay, under the guidance of more skilled master-builders, and with greater energy, during the eighteenth century.

In that period a new species of Theology, of a character exclusively protestant and alarmingly negative, the product of the Revolution, was taking the place of the anglican Divinity of Laud or of Cranmer.

It was not a great step from Hoadly to Clarke, and so to Theophilus Lindsey to Gilbert Wakefield and William Frend. Those were men of Cambridge education, though no doubt their university was not well satisfied with the superstructure which they raised upon her grounding. How far she produced any better theologians we may perhaps consider hereafter: suffice it to say that when she next produced a decided 'school' of notability, it was not a school of able and learned theologians, but a band of earnest men whose strength lay not in science but in subjective religion. As for Oxford, if the theological bent of eighteenth century character was not agreeable to her traditions, she was content to slumber; at least she raised no powerful opposition to the floods which for a season were overwhelming the field of Divinity with a dull and level surface of dead water.

But now let us look to the work of *preliminary* training which rightly or wrongly Cambridge did pretend to do exclusively.

We may take for example the year 1793 (when Kipling, Is. Milner and others called Frend to account for his pamphlet, and refused the use of the Cambridge University press to a fasciculus of Wakefield's *Silva Critica*), a time which was allowed to be in the dark ages of the Universities.

At Cambridge were circulated the following notices, of which I have printed copies before me; and I know not how many similar evidences of vitality may have perished in the dust-heap.

Of the three instructors thus advertising their courses of lectures, one, namely Vince, was not a professor in 1793. He was promoted three years later and continued to lecture and publish as Plumian professor.

'*Cambridge*, Oct. 10. 1793.

On Monday, Nov. 18, at *four* o'Clock in the Afternoon,
The Rev. *S. Vince*, A.M., F.R.S.,

Proposes to begin his *Philosophical Course* of Public Lectures in the *Principles* of the *Four Branches of Natural Philosophy*, With the Application to a great Variety of *Problems*, and on the *Principia* of Sr. I. Newton, with the most useful *deductions*.

To be continued every Monday, Wednesday and Friday.

That Part of the Course which contains the Lectures on the *Principia*, will for the Conveniency of those who shall then have commenced Sophs, be given at the End of the present and Beginning of the next Term.

And on Tuesday, Nov. 19, at the same Hour, he proposes to begin his *Mathematical Course* of Public Lectures on the Principles of *Arithmetic, Algebra, Fluxions, Trigonometry, plain* and *spherical, Logarithms, Ratios*, &c., &c.

To be continued every Tuesday, Thursday and Saturday. Each Course to be attended a second Time gratis.

Terms of attendance are 5 Guineas for each Course. They who purpose to attend are requested to send in their Names[1].'

The next notice tells that the Jacksonian Professor (F. J. H. Wollaston) will begin to lecture on the same subjects to candidates for the degree of B.A., and in the ensuing January will instruct questionists.

Another (preserved accidentally like the others) signifies that the Professor of Anatomy (Busick Harwood) will lecture on Human Anatomy and Physiology. This shows that some attempt at least was made to supply professional education.

Such is a specimen of the *pabulum* which was provided in the University. If in the next place we peep into the private diary[2] of a scholar of Trinity written that same month of November, 1793, we find him reading 'Ratios and Variable Quantities,' transcribing a Syllabus of Mechanics, attending certain lectures and declamations, beside other literary reading and conversation. The diary breaks off in the middle of the month and is resumed in the following spring, when the writer appears to be studying Euripides *Hippolytus*, Sophocles *Oed. Coloneus*, Lowth *de Sacra Poësi*, Grecian History, Locke, Astronomy, and attending Mr Tavel's college lectures on Euclid Bk. XI, and Spherical Trigonometry, and professor Wollaston's public lectures aforementioned.

But, not to confine our investigations to one college, we find that at S. John's there were the annual examinations which had been established nearly a quarter of a century before :

[1] A similar notice dated *'Trinity Hall*, Nov. 2, 1793,' informs students that the Rev. F. Wrangham, with the Assistance of Basil Montagu, M.A. Chr. will deliver (at 4 p.m.) a Course of Lectures upon—

'*Mathematics* and *Natural Philosophy*. The Mathematical Part will include *Algebra, Fluxions*, &c. The Philosophical Part the *Four Branches, Newton's Principia*, &c., Illustrated by a Variety of Problems.

Terms of Attendance 5 Guineas each

Part: or 8 Guineas the whole course.'

This was I suppose a private venture of Wrangham and Montagu. The former lost his election three days after this date. Shortly after this the friends formed an elaborate plan of taking pupils at Cobham (Gunning's *Reminisc.* II. 1). On seeing their latter prospectus Sir James Mackintosh remarked 'A boy thus educated will be a walking encyclopædia.'

[2] Printed in my *Univ. Life*, 589—591.

These were conducted *viva voce* except in the mathematical subjects, in which we have evidence that *printed* papers were set as early as 1793.

The following S. John's examination paper for 1794 (or a year or two earlier[1]) has been preserved by Mr W. Rotherham.

'S. JOHN'S COLLEGE. CAMBRIDGE.

(cir. 1794.)

1. $20 + \dfrac{7x^2}{3x} - 6 = \dfrac{352 - 12x}{10}$.

2. $4x - \dfrac{15 - x}{2} = \dfrac{30y}{12}$

$15x - 8y = 35 - \dfrac{2x + 5y}{5}$

3. $x^2y^4 - 7xy^2 - 945 = 763$

$xy - y = 12$

4. A shepherd had two flocks of sheep, the smaller of which consisted entirely of ewes, each of which brought him 2 lambs. Upon counting them he found that the number of lambs was equal to the difference between the two flocks, and that if all his sheep had been ewes and had brought him 3 lambs apiece, his stock would have been 432. Required the number in each flock.

5. A countryman, being employed by a poulterer to drive a flock of geese and turkeys to London, in order to distinguish his own from any he might meet on the road, pulled 3 feathers out of the tails of the turkeys and 1 out of those of the geese, and upon counting them found that the number of turkey feathers exceeded twice those of the geese by 15. Having bought 10 geese and sold 15 turkeys by the way, he was surprised to find as he drove them into the poulterer's yard, that the number of geese exceeded the number of turkeys in the proportion of 7 : 3. Required the number of each.

6. Two persons, A and B, comparing their daily wages, found that the square of A's wages exceeded the square of B's by 5; and that if to the square of the sum of the fourth powers of their wages, there was added 4 times the rectangle contained by the square of the product of their wages and the square of the difference of the squares of their wages, augmented by 12 times the 4th power of the product of their wages, the aggregate amount would be 1428£ 1s. Required the wages of each.'

If our scholars in the eighteenth century did not pretend to the studiousness of some in earlier days,—such as Henry Hammond who spent thirteen hours in study when he was in

[1] *'Algebraical Equation and Problem Papers proposed in the examinations of* St John's College Cambridge, *from the year* 1794 to 1852.' pp. 1, 2. See the preface, p. ii.

residence in *Magdalen* College Oxon[1], or even of Robert Sanderson (eighteen years his senior), who was content with eleven
hours while at *Lincoln* College[2] (M.A. 1608);—we find that a
wrangler of the year 1796 read (at least while a questionist) on
an average nearly ten hours *per diem;* once or twice, as much as
twelve hours and a half. About ten years earlier, Gunning
having remarked that some people supposed Vickers of Queens'
would run Brinkley (of Caius) hard for the senior wranglership
as he read twelve or fourteen hours daily, Parkinson, the tutor
of Christ's observed, "If he means to beat him, he had better
devote six hours to reading, and six hours to reflecting on what-
he has read[3]." Probably the books then required in the tripos
were more exhausting than those studied in the seventeenth
century. However, we find that in the early part of the
eighteenth century Waterland expected students to study in
the vacations as hard as they did in term-time, while Sir W.
Hamilton complains that in the latter part (called somewhat
strangely 'the Augustan Age of Cambridge[4],') the mathematical examination entailed too severe a strain upon the brains of
the examined[5]: and this was before the French analytical
studies had become popular[6], and even before Waring's works
were published. Paley indeed, as quoted above, p. 66, did in his
later years make some such statement as to the severity of the
preparation, but he did so not altogether as blaming the system
or its requirements, and I should venture to think that he over-
stated the havoc made among weak brains. He himself was
quoted[7] as an instance of exceptional immunity from the dele-
trious effects of being senior wrangler, which may remind us of
the Cambridge 'Don's' tale of the no less disastrous effects
attributed to a contest of later times, when one old university
man represented himself as the only survivor of a certain crew
who had rowed a hard race against Oxford not very many years

[1] Fell's *Hammond*, ed. 2. (1662), p. 8.
[2] [Bliss] *Oxoniana*, iv. 84.
[3] Gunning's *Reminisc.* i. ch. i.
[4] *Quarterly Review*, Oct. 1817. xviii.
235.
[5] *Edinburgh Review*.
[6] Playfair had stigmatized the neglect of analysis in England in his review of La Place. *Edinb. Rev.* vol. xi.
Jan. 1808.
[7] *Quarterly Review*, July 1818. ix.
390.

before.   His hearer was inclined to think that there must be
some truth in this charge of destructiveness against boating, for
he had been told in confidence *a similar tale* by *five* of his
friend's seven colleagues.   Of one thing there could be no doubt,
that the coxswain was no more.

We may be inclined to think in the other case that the
brains *reported* to have been cracked would have given way
without the tripos coming in contact with them.

In addition to the evidence which we have just now brought
forward, our Appendices on the Trinity fellowship and scholarship elections, and the S. John's 'May' examinations, will supply
some information (supplementary to what has been already
printed at the beginning of this compilation) about the measure
of study pursued at Cambridge in the last century, especially in
individual colleges.

Even now we have no regular admission examination previous to matriculation except at Trinity and Trinity-hall; we
learn[1] that there were such examinations at Cambridge about
1787, but they were not universal nor efficient: such a system
is indeed established generally in Oxford, but the Quarterly
Reviewer hailed it as a comparatively recent innovation at some
colleges (*e. g.* Oriel and Balliol) in 1827 (p. 259.)   The same
writer speaks also of terminal examinations, the Oxford 'collections[2],' in the colleges of both universities.

---

[1] *Considerations on the Oaths required by the Univ. of* Cambridge, &c.,
&c. *by* a Member of the Senate, 1788.
p. 9.   *Abraham de la Pryme* thus describes his admission a century earlier
in May, 1690.

'I was admitted member of St John's
College the day following.   First I was
examined by my Tutor, then by the
Senior Dean, then by the Junior Dean,
and then by the Master [Dr Gower];
who all made me but construe a verse
or two apiece in the Greek Testament,
except the Master, who asked me both
in that and in Plautus and Horace
too.   Then I went to the Registerer
to be registered member of the College,

and so the whole work was done.   We
go to Lecturs every other day in
Logics, and what we hear one day we
give an account of the next.   Besides,
we go to his [our tutor's] chambers
every night and hears the Sophs and
Junior Sophs dispute, and then some
one is called out to conster a chapt in
the New Testament which after it is
ended then we go to prayers, and then
to our respective chambers.'   *Surtees
Soc.* (1870) liv. p. 19.

[2] *Collections.*   An examination at
the end of term on the subjects of
college lectures, &c.   Cp. the Wykehamical term 'gatherings.'

The system of tuition underwent some modifications.

I suppose it was within fifty years of the establishment of our Elizabethan academical constitution (1570—1620) that the college tutors[1] supplanted the university teachers and professors, and undertook their work[2]: so much so that enrolment under a tutor as sponsor was required. However, it was not until 1630 that each student was obliged to be under a tutor of his own college (the Laudian system). As 'pupil-mongers' the college-tutors took classes more or less formal;—in fact something between our modern college-lectures and private tuition. When the age of admission became later, and students and tutors no longer 'chummed' together in the same rooms, the parental relationship in which the tutor stood to his pupil was lost (it had died out probably before the accession of George II.), and only one or two tutors (such as Paley and J. Law at Christ's) made any attempt to revive it[3]. In days when non-residence[4] of fellows was unusual, and the senior tutor's lectures became obsolete, and when the importation of fresh mathematical lore made the contest of the tripos dependent on less obvious

[1] The earliest tutor's accounts which I know are those of several pupils of Whitgift (1570—76) when he was *Master* of Trinity. See *British Mag.* xxxii. 361, 508, 650. from MSS. in Lambeth library.

[2] That is, the formal lectures which are universal in our larger colleges. In colleges where there are but two or three men engaged upon one subject, or a few men so slow or so backward as not to be able to profit by the inter-collegiate or other lectures, the tutors find it desirable to adopt something very like the older system in addition to the now more ordinary formal lectures for those who can use them.

[3] The tutorship at Christ's was held about the middle of the century by Dr Ant. *Shepherd* (B.A. 1743, Plumian Prof. 1760-96. Cp. p. 238). After the eminent *W. Paley* (senior wrangler, 1763) and *J. Law* (2nd wrangler and senior medalist, 1766; Bp. of Elphin)

had undertaken respectively the moral philosophy and divinity, and the mathematical and natural philosophy lectures for some time, they demanded to be taken into partnership. Paley continued his work till 1776, but Law went out of residence in 1774, and was succeeded by *T. Parkinson* (senior wrangler, 1769; archdeacon of Leicester) the writer of a treatise on mechanics (4to. Camb. 1785) who was H. Gunning's tutor. The lectures in classics, logic and moral philosophy, Grotius, &c., were taken by *J. B. Searle*, the writer on metres, who was 2nd medallist and 7th wrangler in 1774.

[4] Leave of non-residence was granted in the 17th century only under very exceptional circumstances. See particulars concerning Ro. Mason of S. John's (1624-7), Mayor's Baker, 491 *l.* 11, 494 *l.* 30. It would be interesting to know when the present relaxation of the rule of residence began.

methods of preparation, the private tutor rose into corresponding importance. In 1782 and 1795 we find newly-admitted bachelors of arts taking one or two pupils even before they were elected fellows, from which body alone the regular college-tutors were taken. Watson himself[1] took pupils when he was only a junior soph in 1756.

Professor G. Pryme says[2] that in 1800 he and many others found the regular college-lectures in term-time sufficient instruction without private 'coaching.' He was sixth wrangler in 1803.

Bp. Watson, who prided himself on his liberality, puts forth a general charge of unfairness in examining against 'the *Johnians*,' instancing the result of his own tripos (1759) as a case in point. W. Abbot the moderator had, he affirms, placed Millington Massey[3], of his own college, and one of his private pupils, as senior wrangler, 'in direct opposition to the general sense of the examiners in the Senate-House,' who declared in Watson's favour. I doubt whether the professor was correct in styling Abbot 'the leading moderator[4].' However, he says that the case was notorious, and that old Dr Smith, the Master of Trinity, sent for him, and told him 'not to be discouraged, for that when the *Johnians* had the disposal of the honours, the second wrangler was always looked upon as the first.' I am afraid we must admit that a Trinity moderator (Lax in 1791) was similarly charged by a Caius man.

Our Cambridge examination system, with its accurate and absolute arrangement of honour-men in the class-list, a system devised or adopted by the sagacious masters of continental

---

[1] *Anecdotes*, p. 16.—J. Evelyn had at *Balliol* in 1637 a private tutor who had not then been elected fellow.

[2] *Reminisc.* p. 48.

[3] Millington Massey was of Manchester School. He was afterwards chaplain to visct. Weymouth, rect. of Corsley-Wilts (*Camb. Chron.* 21 *May*, 1768) and died 26 Dec. 1807 (Hoare's *Modern Wilts*, III. (1) 18.)

[4] The tripos for the year 1759. Lynford Caryl, D.D. *Jes.* V.C.

J. Willey, M.A. *Chr.* } Proctors.
T. Metcalf, M.A. *Joh.* }

Adam Wall, M.A. *Ch.* } Mod[rs].
W. Abbot, M.A. *Joh.* }

D[r]. W. Stevenson, *Joh.* } V.C. and
S. Berdmore, *Jos.* } proctors'
Nic. Browne, *Chr.* } Honorary
J. Hawes, *Jes.* (medallist) } 'optimes.'
M. Massey, *Joh.* (senior wrangler).
Ri. Watson, *Trin.*
P. Forster, *Jes.*
&c., &c.

education[1], is of necesssity liable to suspicion of unfairness, but it is gratifying to know that such a charge has been very rarely brought against its decisions. Watson was of opinion that a plan which he introduced in 1763, whereby the preliminary 'classes' (pp. 45—53) under examination were composed no longer of all the men of one college, but of groups of men whose proficiency had been ascertained to be approximately equal, tended to do away with an element of inequality[2].

Such instances of partiality as that to which he referred were particularly attacked by a grace of 21 June, 1777, which prohibited any examiner from having as private pupil any one who was within a year of his tripos. However there seems to have been occasion soon afterwards (when the Smith's prizeman T. Catten, or Catton, afterwards tutor of S. John's, who was expected to be senior wrangler, was put below two others) for a more stringent law (25 Jan. 1781), incapacitating from his degree any student[3] who should read with any private tutor as a senior soph or questionist, indeed within two years of his degree-time; but no security was demanded[4]. By graces of 9 April 1807, 3 July 1815, and 19 May 1824, the prescribed period was reduced from two years to a year and a half, then to one year, and finally to *six months;* and so I suppose it still stands in the ordinance-book.

[1] The university of Louvain (founded in 1425) which presents a singular instance of our English *collegiate* system among foreign universities, and which was said to have been recently under the influence of the Jesuits, for whose church Leopold William laid the first stone in 1650, possessed a complete *tripos system* at least as early as 1627 (Vernulaeus, ii. 6. *ap.* Sir W. Hamilton's *Discussions*, Appendix, III. B). *There* they strictly prescribed even the quota to be furnished by each college to the first and second class. It is curious to observe that Jebb's curious statement that the Cambridge senior optimes were limited to the number twelve in each year, (see above, p. 49,) *was strictly true of the Louvain second class.*

[2] *Anecdotes of* Ri.Watson (1818),I.29.

[3] Dr Webb's collection contains a printed copy of a grace to abolish private tutors for any except *pensionarii maiores* (fellow-commoners) and noblemen; and, in favour of the 'coaches'—*Queries addressed to Every Impartial Member of the Senate,* 24 Jan. 1781 (4to pp. 3). Also *The Triumph of* Dulness, *a Poem : occasioned by a late grace...*1781. (4to. pp. 15.)

[4] Whewell, *University Education* (1837), p. 75. *Of a Liberal Education* (1845), §§ 269—275,

The office of college-tutor[1] being often monopolized by a senior fellow (for few juniors can have had the spirit which enabled Paley to insist on being taken into partnership), and residence being the rule, there was some temptation for newly-elected fellows to indulge in idleness after the severe tax which the tripos is said to have laid upon them, and then to take one or two private pupils, instead of pursuing their own studies, as the constitution of the university required.

I have said that the establishment of *tutors* on the part of the *colleges* tended to make the *professorships* on the part of the *university* superfluous so far as lecturing went.

At the end of the last century, I believe not more than one in three of the Oxford Professors gave lectures; several of them are not reported to have written or studied in their chairs. Some particulars on these points I have given in another place[2].

At the same period nearly one half of the Cambridge professors gave lectures; of the rest, Porson, Watson, Hailstone, Lax, and (perhaps) Milner[3], were doing useful work. One interesting particular has been pointed out, *i.e.* that out of the thirty-three professorships now enumerated in our Cambridge Calendars no less than twelve[4] (or fourteen) owe their origin to the

---

[1] The TUTORIAL FEES *per quarter* appear to have varied thus

in the years	1570-76	1721-67	1767-1802	1802	1877.
	s. d.	*£ s. d.*	*£ s. d.*	*£ s. d.*	*£ s. d.*
Nobleman	13 . 4	6 . 0 . 0	8 . 0 . 0	7 . 10 . 0	10 . 0 . 0
Pensioner {? major	10 . 0	3 . 0 . 0	4 . 0 . 0	3 . 15 . 0	7 . 10 . 0
{? minor	6 . 8	1 . 10 . 0	2 . 0 . 0	1 . 17 . 6	4 . 10 . 0
Sizar	? ?	15 . 0	{ . 15 . 0 { aft. 1*l.*	18 . 9	1 . 10 . 0

The statistics for the period 1697-1721, *I have not been yet able to discover.*

[2] *University Social Life in the* xviii[th] *Cent.* 83—87.

[3] Frend and Reginald Bligh severally charged Milner in print with inefficiency; but either of them had a personal grudge against him.

[4] Chemistry,1702. Plumian Astron. and Exper. Philos., 1704. Anatomy, 1707. Royal, Modern History, 1724. Ld. Almoner's Arabic, 1724. Botany, 1724. Woodwardian, Geology, 1727. Lowndean, Astronomy and Geometry, 1749. Norrisian, Divinity, 1777. Jacksonian, Natural and Experimental Philosophy, 1783. Downing, Laws, (1788) 1800. Downing, Medicine, 1800. To these may be added Sadlerian, Mathematics, 1710, and Hulsean Divinity (Christian Advocate), 1789, both re-modelled in 1860. Whitehall Preacher, 1724.—The Battie Scholarships were founded in 1746, Seatonian Prize, 1749. Chancellors' Medals, 1751. Members' Prizes, 1752. Worts' Tra-

eighteenth century, while Oxford was endowed with only seven[1] in *that* period, as compared with eight founded *in the seventeenth century* when Cambridge gained only four. Perhaps the donations to the Bodleian in the last century made up this inequality to Oxford, though we must not forget the royal present of books to the whiggish university. However, Cambridge did not owe her professorships to her politics: at least she received no more from the Crown than did her tory sister. Indeed lord Macclesfield proposed by his scheme in 1718 (see *Univ. Life*, pp. 568, 569) to bribe students from disaffection in both universities by government favours. How far this scheme of the lord chancellor's was carried into effect I cannot say. Perhaps his representations may have suggested the establishment of the Modern History and Languages professorships in 1724[2].

To what extent the Universities were affected by the privileges or the disabilities which characterized the age, it is no easy task to estimate.

Of the territorial assignment of endowments in the way of county fellowships, &c., we shall have occasion to speak elsewhere[3]. The paucity of lay-fellowships, so far as it was a disadvantage to the university and the church, produced such results indirectly rather than immediately. This matter will fall more naturally under the head of religious life. However,

velling Bachelorships, 1766, Smith's Prizes, 1768. Sir W. Browne's Medals, and Scholarship, and Hulsean Prize, 1774. Norrisian Prize, 1780. Mr Potts enumerates about seventy benefactors to the *colleges*, some of whom founded more than one exhibition, prize, &c., in the last century.

[1] At *Oxford*:—Birkhead, Poetry, 1708. Royal, Modern History, 1724. Rawlinson, Anglo-Saxon and Lee's Anatomy, cir. 1750. Vinerian Laws, 1755. Litchfield, Clinical, 1772. Lord Almoner's Arabic, 1775. We might add, the modifications in the Oxford Botany Professorship in 1728 and 1793. Radcliffe's Travelling Fellows, 1715. Whitehall Preacher, 1724. Chancel-

lor's Prizes, 1768. Bampton Lecturer, 1780.

[2] It is interesting to find that two of his suggestions (1718) anticipated the principles of modern changes (1860) in the most ancient foundation of Peterhouse :—the limited tenures of fellowships (10 years for laymen, and 20 for clerical fellows, compulsory according to his scheme, which, however, provided strict rules against non-residence) and the life-long tenure for the tutors after 15 years' service. The rotation of college offices, which is now practically a rule, was also one of his devices.

[3] Appendix V.

it must be confessed that Cambridge and Trinity college came near to lose Porson, ostensibly at least through scarcity of lay-endowment[1].

The condition of celibacy, which is even now with a few exceptions required in fellows, found some assailants in 1765—6, 1783, and 1793—8[2]; but it is not unlikely that its abolition at such a period would have had disastrous effects: at least, to judge from Gunning's picture of society in Cambridge, many of the dons would, in all probability, have fallen an easy prey to undesirable matrimonial connexions to an extent hardly to be anticipated in the present day. The abiding part of the society in each college being clergymen, it was to be expected that the education there should be either theological, or at least not such as should train students and their teachers for any profession rather than for Theology. To this perhaps we may attribute the smallness of the effect produced by the Universities upon the professions of Law and Physic, and upon the studies of those professions. (See above, Chapters XI. and XIV.)

It was observed (p. 173) there were 'physick-fellows' in one of the colleges. We may add that at S. John's college, Cambridge, there were two law and two medical fellowships, not indeed yet quite extinct. In 1627, K. Charles issued a mandate to the college to exempt from the necessity of proceeding to holy orders John Thompson, M.A., who had applied himself to the study of civil law[3], and was employed in the King's service, being M.P. for Cambridge; and in 1635 two fellowships were assigned to law by royal letters[4]. K. Charles II. likewise continued his fellowship for an M.D., Henry Paman, while he travelled in 1662[5].

---

[1] H. F. Cary of *Ch. Ch.*, the translator of Dante, tried unsuccessfully for a lay-fellowship at Oriel in 1794. *Memoir* by his son, I. 53, 61.

[2] *University Life*, 353—7. To the bibliography of this subject there given we may add the title of the following pamphlet, of which there is a copy in Peterhouse library [E. 10. 23 (8)], '*A Fragment on Matrimony:* Supposed to have fallen out of the pocket of a learned Fellow of —— College; and found near the Senate House. March 21, 1798.' pp. 8. In it 'Toleration of Marriage,' the pamphlet by C. Farish (Qu.), brother of the professor, is ridiculed.

[3] The act of Hen. VIII. allowed Ecclesiastical jurisdiction to D.C.L.s in spite of marriage.

[4] Mayor's Baker, 293 *n.*; 493, l. 30.

[5] *Ibid.* 542, l. 40.

We read occasionally in earlier time of Cambridge doctors of Civil Law[1], but our university still keeps up a nominal recognition of Canon Law by dubbing all and every one of her legal graduates bachelor, or doctor, of *Laws* (LL.B., LL.D.). Oxford, however, has not kept up even this semblance, for she knows only the degree in Civil Law (D. C. L.); nevertheless when one of her doctors of Civil Law becomes an Ecclesiastical Judge he adopts almost always (as Dr W. G. F. Phillimore informs me) in legal documents the Cambridge style of doctors of *Laws*.

Chichele's foundation for canonists at *All Souls* has, under the University Commissioners, been applied to fellowships for proficiency in Law and Modern History.

But we are warned not to wander in either direction beyond the limits of the eighteenth century. Suffice it therefore to say that we hope if Mr Mullinger continues his early history of the University, he will give us some account of the influence which the clergy and the universities have exercised upon the practice and the study of laws. Sir Robert Phillimore has already given a brief historical outline (which might be perused with much profit at the present time when the question of the history of ecclesiastical and lay courts is so important) in the *Preface* to the 1st volume of his *Commentaries upon International Law* (1854) pp. xix.—xxxvi[2].

---

[1] e.g. the primary representatives in parliament of the university, at the beginning of the reign of James I. Cooper's *Annals*, II. 3.

[2] The list of authorities there given and the pages referred to in the text suggest several of the following names of some judges, advocates, writers on international or ecclesiastical law, &c., who though educated at one or other of our universities, have not been commemorated either in chapter XI, or on p. 134 among the canonists, &c.

Sir G. Hay. *Joh.* (B.C.L. 1737).

Dr J. Bettesworth, *Ch. Ch.* (B.C.L. 1744).

Dr G. Harris *Oriel* (B.C.L. 1745) translated Justinian's Institutes.

Sir Ja. Eyre, Commoner of Winton and *Merton* (M.A. 1759).

Jer. Bentham, *Queen's* (B.A. 1764, aged 16), attended Sir W. Blackstone's lectures.

Sir Soulden Lawrence, Joh., 'legista,' or Law fellow, B.A. 1771, son of the eminent Oxford anatomical reader.

H. Addington, Vist. Sidmouth, (Commoner of Winton and *B.N.C.*, univ. prize essay. 1779).

Sir Joh. Littledale, Joh. (B.A. 1787).

Sir Alex. Croke, *Oriel* (B.C.L. 1787).

Sir N. C. Tindal, Trin. (B.A. 1799).

Sir Lanc. Shadwell, Joh. (B.A. 1800).

Some among these (like others mentioned in *ch.* XI.) took high places in the Cambridge tripos and were fellows of their Colleges, as may be seen from

When professor Mayor's "Cambridge *in the Reign of Queen Anne*' is in the hands of the public the name of John Marshall of Christ College will, I presume, be better known among indian scholars. Although he was in advance of his age[1] we must be content for the present to relegate him to the seventeenth century, when he travelled, until he is formally introduced in the company of Uffenbach with proper dignity by the professor himself.

The discoverer and editor of the Missing Fragment of the latin translation of the ivth book of Ezra has kindly sent me a memorandum of the following testimony of Ewald in praise of our Cambridge professor, Ockley's version[2] of the Arabic translation of that book barely mentioned above.

'Es freut anerkennen zu können, dass Ockley, welcher den fachkennern auch als übersetzer der Wagidäischen geschichte der eroberung Syriens bekannt ist, hier eine im ganzen nicht blos lesbare sondern auch zuverlässige übersetzung gegeben hat. Zwar irrt er einige mahl ziemlich stark: für seine zeit aber, muss man sagen, war er nach diesem zeugnisse ein ausgezeichneter kenner des arabischen. Auch merkt man leicht, dass er hier überall mit liebe arbeitete.'

It appears that the recovered fragment had been seen in a Complutensian MS. by John Palmer (Joh.), who held the Adams professorship of Arabic (1804—19), and afterwards augmented its endowment by his bequest. His journal has been recently brought to light, and its contents have been described in the *Journal of Philology*.

Mr Bensly, to whose unsparing kindness I am indebted for the following information also, has shewn me that there is much interesting matter to be collected relative to Cambridge and

the Univ. Calendar, which will also testify to the early honours of many of our judges at the commencement of the 19ᵗʰ century. A complete list of our 18ᵗʰ century university jurists would probably contain many eminent names here omitted.

Among those who did not stay at Oxford long enough to take a degree (see above, p. 144 *n.*) might be mentioned — W. Murray Ld. Mansfield (born 1705) of *Ch. Ch.*, J. Freeman Mitford Ld. Redesdale (born 1748) of *New Coll.*, and Ro. Plumer Ward (born 1765) of *Ch. Ch.*

[1] See above pp. 156, 162, 163 *n.*

[2] 'Printed in the Appendix to vol. iv. of Whiston's *Primitive Christianity Reviv'd.* Lond. 1711.

Oxford oriental studies in the period preceding that with which we are specially concerned. The following remarks, however, relate more closely to the 18th century[1].

Dr Humphrey Prideaux asserted[2] that he had the offer of the hebrew professorship vacated by Pococke, and ultimately filled, as we have seen (p. 168), by Dr Hyde, but that he refused it because he 'nauseated' at once the study of hebrew and residence in *Christ Church*, which would have been his abode, as it had been in the days when he published the *Marmora Oxoniensia*.

Mention ought to have been made above of Jean Gagnier, a parisian orientalist who renounced his orders on account of the obligation to celibacy, and declared himself a protestant. 'His principal works' (says Mr Thompson Cooper) 'are an edition of Joseph Ben Gorion's History of the Jews,' with a Latin translation [4to *Oxon.* 1706]; an edition of Abulfeda's "Life of Mohammed," in Arabic and Latin [fol. *Oxon.* 1723]; and Vindiciae Kircherianae, seu defensio Concordantiarum Graecarum Conradi Kircheri, adv. Abr. Trommii animadversiones." [1718.]' Gagnier received the degree of M.A. at Cambridge *per litteras regias* in 1703, and afterwards settled at *Oxford*[3]. He died 2 March, 1740. The work done by the oriental professors as university officers was not great: they may have been discouraged, as Castell was in the previous century, by some decline in the interest shewn by students in their special study, till (as we have seen) they lost the habit of lecturing, and satisfied their consciences, or the requirements of the age, by contributing their copy of verses to the collection of *luctus et gratulationes*[4] and the like, on those public occasions which were found for them indeed with toler-

---

[1] W. Bedwell made vast collections for an arabic lexicon, which are now among the MSS. in the University Library. These materials Castell used for the arabic portion of his polyglott lexicon. See H. J. Todd's *Memorial of* Brian Walton, I. 106. Pattison's Is. Casaubon, *p.* 329.

For a notice of the arabic taylor, H. Wild, who came from Norwich to Oxford, see Macray's *Annals of the* Bodleian, pp. 141, 142.

[2] Letters to Ellis, *Camd. Soc.* (1873),

p. 150.

[3] Among the *Graduati Oxonienses* is 'Gagnier (John) *Wadh.* B.A. Oct. 24, 1740.—M.A. July 2, 1743;' who was, I suppose, son of the above-mentioned orientalist.

[4] One of these collections, that on Q. Anne's accession in 1702, has been already noticed pp. 164, 165; and a list of such collections of verses, none of them of course exclusively oriental, may be found in my *University Life*, pp. 609—10. Mr Bensly has kindly

able regularity. At least one of them went so far as to give up for a time even the pretence of residence, and to take pupils in Edinburgh[1].

taken the trouble to note the names of oriental versifiers in several more of these sets at different periods. He does not speak very highly of the composition.

anno. 1697. A hebrew poem, auctore T. Bennet A.M. coll. Joh. Soc.

1700.	hebrew	P. Allix, coll. Regin. alumno.
	hebrew) arabic)	Simon Ockley, A.B. Coll. Regin.
	hebrew	Greg. Clarke, Aul. Cath. alumno.
1715.	hebrew) (greek and) .... latin))	Phil. Bouquet, S.T. et ling. S. Prof.
	hebrew....................	Jo. Wake, Coll. Jes. alumno.
1751.	arabic	Leon. Chappelow.
	hebrew	Th. Harrison, A.M., Coll. Trin. Soc., Ling. S. P.
	hebrew	Fleetwood Churchill, Aulae Clar. alumno.
	hebrew	Rob. Hankinson, Coll. Chr. Soc.
	arabic	Ri. Forester, A.M., Aul. Pemb.
	hebrew	R. Sutton, Trin. Coll.
	hebrew	Th. Evans, A.B., Coll. Jes.
1760.	arabic....................	L. Chappelow, Ling Arab. P.
	hebrew	Guil. Disney, Ling. Hebr. P.
	hebrew	S. Hallifax, Aul. Trin. Soc.
	hebrew	Ja. Sheeles, A.B., Coll. SS. Trin.
1761.	arabic....................	L. Chappelow.
	hebrew	Guil. Disney, Ling. Hebr. Prof. Reg.
	hebrew	H. Flitcroft, C. C. C. Soc. Comm.
	arabic....................	Jo. Wilson, Coll. Trin. alumno.
1762.	arabic....................	L. Chappelow, Ling. Arab. Prof.
	hebrew	Guil. Disney, Ling. Hebr. P. Reg.
	hebrew	J. Cowper, A.M., C.C.C.
	hebrew	H. Flitcroft, A.M., C.C.C.
	hebrew	Ja. Eaton, Coll. Div. Pet. alumno.
	arabic....................	J. Wilson, A.B., Coll. Trin.
1763.	arabic....................	L. Chapellow, Ling. Ar. Prof.
	hebrew	Guil. Disney, Ling. Hebr. Prof.
	arabic....................	S. Hallifax, Aul. Trin. Soc.
	hebrew	T. Bennett, Coll. Trin.

[1] His advertisement (on the fly-leaf of *The British Indian Monitor*, vol. I. 1806) is thus expressed,

'Education.

The Rev. Henry Lloyd, D.D. formerly a Fellow of Trinity College, and now Regius Hebrew Professor, at Cambridge, continues to receive into his house a limited Number of Pupils, who may require a complete Private Education, or to be prepared, either for an English Public School or Uni-

It will be seen that this statement, with which this concluding chapter must now be brought to an end, touches upon a blot in Cambridge history.

Before he began to search the records themselves, the writer, trusting to vague report, expected to find those records disfigured with very many blots of this kind.

He rejoices to say that he now believes that the annals of Cambridge study in the eighteenth century (like some ancient manuscript more spoken of than read) on closer inspection shew more fair pages and reveal more honest work than he at least had hoped to find.

As for the sister university: it is difficult even at Sparta not to praise the Athenians. But modern Oxford needs no praise from the writer; while he has already said how dim he thinks her glory had become a century ago. It may be that those who have a deeper knowledge of Oxford history and records will find grounds for modifying his belief in the unfavourable accounts of Oxford which have been quoted in this book. Some of them no doubt were penned by enemies of Athens. Possibly the writer himself, if he could have accepted the invitations of hospitality which were not wanting, would have found some records of late eighteenth century activity at Oxford which escaped him when he last had leisure to search her treasure-houses.

As to his own work, he would be well pleased if, of the subjects so imperfectly and unskilfully treated in the several chapters of the present book, each one were properly handled in a monograph by one who had given his attention to that special

versity, the East India College at Hertford, or the Seminaries in Edinburgh. With a view to facilitate the progress of Oriental Literature in his native City, and render himself essentially useful to those of his young countrymen who may have, or expect appointments to India, Dr Borthwick Gilchrist, formerly Professor in the College of Fort William, &c. &c., has offered his occasional Assistance, in this Branch of Instruction.

No. 1. South Side, George Street. Edinburgh.'

Dr Henry Lloyd fellow of Trinity, 10th wrangler in 1785, was Ling. Heb. Prof. Reg. 1795—1831. He proposed to translate Eichhorn's *Introduction to the Old Testament*. See Classical Journal, III. 243. *Life of* Geddes, pp. 545, 546 (*Geddes* to *Eichhorn*). Sir W. Hamilton's *Discussions* (ed. 1. 1852) p. 508.

branch of science or literature. Each monograph then might shew what advances have been made since the commencement of the nineteenth century, and we should see how in the places where a century ago were blots and blanks (as in the instance of Cambridge oriental studies cited above), the vellum is clear, the letters now painfully and severely traced are beginning to follow one another, and by the blessing of the Divine Illuminator whose is 'the silver and the gold,' the glory will at last crown the work of the faithful hearts and hands labouring in our Colleges and Universities.

And to Cambridge men this page would say

SPARTAM , NACTVS . ES

HANC . EXORNA.

APPENDICES.

APPENDIX I.

Relliquiae Comitiales

Duport 1631; *Shepheard
& Raleigh* 1615.

RELLIQUIAE COMITIALES.

Saec. XVII.

1. Duport's PRAEVARICATOR'S SPEECH. Camb 1631.
2—4. Notes of Shepheard's MUSICK-SPEECH, the TERRAE-FILIUS, and Raleigh's PHILOSOPHER'S SPEECH. *Oxon.* 1615.

WHEN I was hunting up the antiquities of the Cambridge *comitia*, and especially particulars relating to the B.A. disputant 'Mr *Tripos*' and the M.A. *Praevaricator* or Varier, which are printed in my *University Life*, pp. 207—307, I mentioned, on dean Peacock's authority, what he called 'a beautiful specimen' of a praevaricator's speech by Dr James Duport.

I felt no doubt that it was a well-known MS., but to my surprise on enquiry no tidings of its *habitat* could I find, until after a lapse of two years my eye was attracted by a record of it in the Donation-book in the library of Gonville and Caius. Through the kindness of the past and the present librarians, E. J. Gross, Esq. and the Rev. H. B. Swete, I am able to print the production; but in what sense the former dean of Ely called it a beautiful specimen the reader (if there be one sufficiently gentle and patient) will judge.

It is certainly curious as the somewhat juvenile production (as M.A. of the first year) of one who was, as I have elsewhere described him, 'Greek professor (1639—54), vice-master of Trinity (1655), prebendary of *Langford Ecclesia* in Lincoln Cathedral, archdeacon of Stow and dean of Peterborough. His earliest important publication was an *epitaphium* on the death of Bacon, and his last act at Trinity was to take part in the election of Newton to a scholarship in 1664; and almost his last deed was in 1679 to send Barrow a subscription of £200 for the building of Trinity library. While he was an undergraduate in 1622—6 he wrote several *carmina comitialia*, which we call usually "tripos verses."' He was also a royal chaplain, a popular tutor of Trinity, and, in 1668—79, master of Magdalene. His father, Dr John Duport, had been master of Jesus college (1590—1618), where James Duport was born in 1606.

The '*Musae* Subsecivae *seu Poetica* Stromata auctore J. D.' were printed in 1676. Many of them have a comitial character.

The entire composition may be compared with the speech of Darby of Jesus (thirty years later), which has been printed from the Hunter ms. (44.9) by the Surtees Society, *Hutton Correspondence*, preface x—xvi, and with the more juvenile *prolusio in feriis aestivis* (1628) in Milton's Prose Works.

Caius Coll. Library M.S. 627 (= 250, red.)

PRAEVARICATIO M^{RI} DUPORT *Trin. Coll. Socij. Anno Dom.* 1631.

Quaestio sic se habet.

Aurum potest produci per artem Chymicam.

Salve Dignissime Doctissimeque—Quem si vel nominare audeam suspensus sim: Salvete et vos Procuratores ambo. Tu imprimis Senior Procurator qui me creasti antequam esses Pater. Tu etiam qui ἐξ ἑτέρου sedes, simul et Magistri Regentes et non-Regentes et vos qui propter gravitatem videmini Patres, et vos qui propter levitatem estis: necnon et vos Viri Oxonienses, qui Bicipitis Parnassi culmen habitatis alterum, alterumque hoc jam praegnans spectatum venistis, et Jovis instar gravidum Minervâ caput. Parturit hodie mons noster, parturiet modò vester. Parturiunt montes en prodit ridiculus mus. Ergo quid mihi vobiscum? Ego non sum vester Praevaricator, quia non sum gigas (re) Terrae-Filius[1]. Heu habuistis virum Terrae-Filium Gigantem scilicet virum staturâ eminenti at secundus Praevaricator inter nos (si id nescitis) est sui Anni ffilius natu minimus. Corpulentus ille plura secum adduxit corpora, ego unum tantummodo, idque perexiguum[2]. Jamque ad vos descendo Fluctuans et inconstans Academicorum vulgus, quorum tantum vertices mihi apparent. Quidni ego vos dicam capita Academiae? Video equidem vestrûm omnia ora atque oculos in me esse conversos. Liceat mihi celsitudinem etiam vestram salutare, qui nos omnes despicitis qui tam attenti huc mihi adestis et veluti oculis ac auribus suspensi inter fumos ab ore meo pendentes. Liceat mihi vobis valedicere antequam scala nostrae orationis convertatur. Ego humillimus vester Praevaricator vobis aliquot gradibus superior jubeo vos malè audire. Foeminas utcunque heri in primo loco positas ego tamen posthabeo quippe cùm nihil ferè audiunt nec intelligunt tantum vident id manticae quod a tergo est. et certè opus est vestrâ patientiâ quae tam diu sedetis et nihil intelligitis.

Aures vestrae non sunt vobis usui, quaeso eas mihi accommodate: ego aurum ex illis extraham. Ab eis enim subjectum nostrae quaestionis viz.: Aurum dependet; ex iis igitur aurum potest produci. Quid plura? Corona undique Spectatissima, Spectatissimaeque, valere plurimum jubet Hodiernus Praevaricator qui quantus est totus totus est vester; sed non vacat diutius salutationibus immorari. Causidicus sum non Aulicus, nam pro Auro causam ago. Hesternus

---

[1] One of the jests of Tom Brown, the irregular *Ch. Ch.* wit (cir. 1680), was an argument in favour of the greater antiquity of Oxford as compared with Cambridge on the ground that Adam was *terrae filius* before he became a *praevaricator.*

[2] Barrow frequently alludes to the short stature of Duport his preceptor and predecessor in the greek professor's chair. *Works* (Napier), IX. 37, 141. The

following extract from Pepys' *Diary* (8 Feb. 1662—3) notices this personal peculiarity to which Duport himself so goodhumouredly alludes. 'I walked to White Hall to chappell where there preached little Dr Duport of Cambridge ...the most flat dead sermon both for matter and manner of delivery that ever I heard, and very long beyond his hour, which made it worse.'

Praevaricator ad compotationem vos invitavit, nec mirum cùm fuit Vinitor at cibum vobis non apposuit, quare non mirum si adhuc ipse esuriat, uti dixit, cum in Corpore Academico nondum sit completus Venter (i.) completus Magister Artis[1]. Vinum vobis non dedit, fortasse quia non venistis cum paratâ pecuniâ. Convivium vobis paravit, sed Academici vix solvendo esse solent. Ut igitur fidem cum illo servetis, aurum apporto quod pro symbolis detis, nam si desit vobis pecunia Aurum potest produci per Artem Chymicam. Bonum mehercule omen in ipso limine Quaestionis aurum reperio. Cum igitur aurum ultrò se tractandum offerat, quis nisi mentis inops oblatum respuit? Sic itaque aggredior. Pulcherrima Domina, amor et deliciae humani generis, splendor tui vultus perstringit oculorum meorum aciem. At quid est obsecro quod tam subitò palles? Laboras eo morbo qui dictur *Noli me tangere*, et recte mones, nam excellens sensibile corrumpit sensum[2]. Ego vero Auditores (fatebor enim) jamdiu Auri amore captus carmen hoc encomiasticum de eo scripsi, quod, si placet, recitabo.

Si quid est quod nos amamus,
Illud Aurum appellamus :
Aurea aetas aureum vellus
Et in vere Aurea Tellus.
Intonsus fflavus est Apollo
Quoniam aureum habet Pollo.
Nam ut Crinis est tonsura
Sic et Auri est cæsura.
Sed haec magis criminalis,
Licet utraque Capitalis[3].
Est et Regi Aureus stultus
Et nonnullis aureus vultus.
Si agit aureus fluit sermo
Ut Causidici in Termo.
En et Patri Aureus pileus[4]
Et ad dextram aureus filius.
Aureus Annulus est Doctori[5]
Χρυσοῦν στόμα Professori.
Habet Papa aureas Bullas
Quae nunc habent vires nullas.
Legendam auream Papistae
Qui obtrudunt sunt sophistae.

[1] Alluding to the introduction to Persius' Satires.

[2] Mr H. Jackson refers us to Aristotle,—τῶν αἰσθητῶν αἱ ὑπερβολαὶ φθείρουσι τὰ αἰσθητήρια. *De Anima* II. 12. παντὸς μὲν καὶ αἰσθητοῦ ὑπερβολὴ ἀναιρεῖ τὸ αἰσθητήριον. *Ibid.* III. 13.

[3] Cp. 'It is no English Treason to cut French Crownes, and to morrow the King himselfe will be a Clipper.' *The Life of Henry the Fifth*, Act iii.

[4] '*In Vesperiis Comitiorum...* The V. C., not being a Father is in his Scarlet Gown, his Cap being *garnished with gold Lace;* but if he be a Father, then he goeth in his Cope; and so do the other Fathers *with their Caps garnished.*' *Bedel* Buck's *Book*, (1665).

[5] The *Ring* among the *insignia doctoralia* is explained by Bentley in the speech printed before his Terence, as the emblem of liberty.

Nam verba haec sunt dividenda
Aurea est, sed non Legenda.
Quidam Asinus est Aureus
Qualem pinxit Apulejus.
Et si habeat metallum
Aureum dixero Caballum.
Demostheni, si causa fugit,
Aureus bos in lingua[1] mugit.
Aureus nitor est in stellis,
Aurei baculi sunt Bedellis.
Si qua divite fluit venâ
Illa Aurea est Camoena.
Aurea mala ex Hispaniâ
Missa capimus; ô Insania.
Ἐχθρῶν ἄδωρα δῶρα καλά,
Aurea suut, sed tamen mala.
Et si qua videtur Bella,
Illa Aurea est Puella.
Si quid est quod nos amamus
Illud Aureum appellamus.

At quid ego infelix procus versibus hisce amatorijs aurum emollire mihi conciliare satago? Nunquàm nunquàm recte illi persuadere potero ut mecum una sit et permaneat. Cùm igitur Academici aurum tam durum sit, ut nequeat flecti, ad vos accedo. Aequissimi Judices modo causae meae faveatis, hem vobis aurum. Si quid est apud me auri Judices, quod sentio quam sit exiguum, quaeso obtestorque vos, ut id potius Crumenae meae quam magnitudini vestrorum beneficiorum tribuendum putetis. *Aurum potest produci*, &c. Primus terminus quaestionis est satis conspicuus. Aurum tamen sumitur multis modis. Et primo aurum sumitur vel directè vel indirectè. 2° sumitur vel largè vel strictè: Aurum strictè vel praecisè sumitur a Fratre oppidano; Aurum largè sumitur a largâ conscientiâ. Nam ut forma extenditur ad extensionem materiae, ita aurum extenditur ad extensionem conscientiae; Sed qui sic extendit aurum ad extensionem Conscientiae, dignus est qui extendat collum ad extensionem Carnificis. 3° Aurum sumitur vel inclusivè vel exclusivè, exempli gratiâ respectu Crumenae Senioris **Fratris** aurum sumitur inclusivè, respectu meae, exclusivè. 4° Aurum sumitur vel spontaneè, vel invitè, spontaneè ab omnibus, invitè, a nemine. 5₀ Aurum sumitur vel pro voce ut ab Academicis, vel pro re ut ab oppidanis. Cum sumitur pro voce est vox ad placitum vel potius pro placito. 6° Aurum sumitur vel absolutè et sine respectu vel respectivè et conditionaliter. Aurum conditionaliter sumitur vel a priori vel a Posteriori. 7° Aurum sumitur vel aequaliter vel inaequaliter, Aurum aequaliter sumitur inter Procuratores. Aurum inaequaliter

[1] Cf. βοῦς ἐπὶ γλώσσῃ. Aesch. *Agam.* 36. Duport may have noticed on the same page (*Adagia* 520 b. 1617) in which Erasmus treats of *Bos in lingua* a reference to the tale of Plutarch and Gellius concerning Demosthenes' indisposition from ἀργυράγχη.

sumitur inter Fratres, et (quod mirum est) inter etiam socios. 8°
Aurum sumitur vel in Crœso, vel in Crasso, vel in Grosso. Aurum
in Crœso est aurum Fœneratoris, in Crasso Aurum diuitis, in Grosso
aurum notarii Causidicalis. 9° Aurum sumitur vel simpliciter, et
tunc est grave, vel non simpliciter, sive additamento aliquo, et tum
est leve. Aurum sumitur multis praeterea vijs et modis, quos ego
lubens ignoro :—et tantum de varia Acceptione Auri.
Sequitur ejus Definitio.
Aurum est intestina pestis lateus in venis et visceribus Terrae.
Vel quoniam nonnulli cùm Aurum tractent sibi videntur Caelum
digito tangere, Aurum potest definiri ut Caelum, Quod est corpus
solidum, rotundum, lucidum, et per orbem mobile. Sed quotuplex
est Aurum? Hem vos Socij, Bona Nova[1], hodie futura est Auri
divisio: Nam aurum sumptum in communi est dividendum, et
primum non incommode me futurum existimo, si distinguam de
Auro juxta tritum illud Hebraeorum proverbium[2] *in loculo, in poculo,
in oculo*. Aurum in loculo est corpus squalidum, rubiginosum, senile
et siccum, quod facile suis terminis continetur. Aurum in poculo
est aurum potabile, seu corpus humidum, quod difficulte suis terminis continetur. Vel aurum in poculo, seu poculum aureum est corpus
solidum, seu succi plenum ; Aurum in oculo est dives facies aut
vultus pretiosus. Et hoc Aurum Aristoteles libro millesimo Me-
teoromineralium, capite proximo post ultimum sic describit. Est
meteoron ignitum ex multitudine vaporum e ventriculo in cerebrum
ascendentium ortum, et ad mediam faciei regionem erectum, ibique
haerens mediocriter rutilans et scintillans. Idem in libro centesimo
physiognomonicometallicorum, capite immediate praecedente primum,
ait, quòd hoc Aurum facile producitur per artem potandi. 2° etiam
Aurum non distribuitur cuique secundum Intellectum, ut patet ex ejus
definitionibus iu Collegio factis. potest tamen ita dividi, ut Intellectus in Aurum in actu, in Aurum in habitu, in Aurum in potentiâ.
Aurum in actu fit recipiendo Imagines impressas in manum per vim
apprehensionum. Aurum in habitu est aurum melioris, vel cum quis
ex imaginibus prius receptis comparavit sibi habitum auri. Aurum
in potentiâ est Aurum Academicum, vel cum quis habet naturalem
propensitatem ad recipiendum Aurum, illud tamen actu non recipit
ob aliquod impedimentum, putà oppidanus quispiam qui profecto
habet naturalem inclinationem ad aurum meum recipiendum, cubicu-
lum meum advenit, fores clausas invenit, et sic discedit, ille jam
propter indispositionem medij, aurum a me actu non recipit habet
tamen illud in Potentiâ.

[1] '*Bona nova*'—one of the mysteri-
ous formulae uttered by one of the
bedells at the ancient ceremony of 'the
order of the questionists'—i. q. '*Good
news !*' See *Univ. Society*, p. 209.

[2] Here there are some hebrew letters
which are incorrectly written in the
MS. Dr Schiller-Szinessy has kindly
pointed out the Talmudic reference,
which is also quoted in Buxtorf *Lexicon*

Chaldaicum Talmudicum et Rabb. col.
1032 s. v. כיס—Apud Talmudicos
בשלשה דברים אדם ניכר בכיסו בכוסו
בכעסו *in tribus rebus homo cognoscitur,
In loculo suo, in poculo suo, et in ira
sua,* Erubhin fol. 65. col. 2. Duport
happily imitates the triple assonance
of the original b$_e$kiso, b$_e$koso, b$_e$ka'so
(purse, cup, temper), though *oculo* is
not a perfect representative of the last.

Hoc Aurum in ·potentiâ insignes habet virtutes et operationes
quas recensere possum sed festino. Aurum igitur 3º est vel probatum
vel non probatum. Aurum Medici probatum est ; Aurum Causidici
non est probatum, quia adhuc sub judice lis est. Porrò Aurum non
probatum multas habet species, quarum hae sunt praecipuae

> Quod sumitur pro voce dandâ
> Aut pro Lege abrogandâ
> Aut pro˙ causâ adjuvandâ
> Aut pro pœnâ declinandâ
> Aurum est sed non probatum.
> Quod corrumpit Judicem,
> Et quod ditat pellicem
> Quod crëat Pontificem
> Et ducit ad Carnificém,
> Aurum est sed non probatum.
> Quod Laicos facit Cardinales
> Clericosque temporales
> Quo honores sunt venales
> Etsi sint sacerdotales
> Aurum est sed non probatum.

Sed ut Auri natura clarius elucescat, sciendum est quòd Sol et
Terra multos genuerunt filios, inter quos metalla licèt nomine sunt
μετὰ ἄλλα revera tamen non sunt postponenda. Inter metalla Aurum
est Terrae filius primogenitus, malè fit[1] omni conversioni simplici,
nam ex quo Aurum habuit primogenituram, inde primogenitura
habuit Aurum, quod me miserum docuit experientia. At quod dixi,
num Aurum est Terrae filius ? statim erit praevaricator[2], et num
aliquando causam prodit ? videant Causidici, nos ignoramus, ut ut
Aurum est omnium metallorum facile princeps.

> Ergo Crates stulte fecit
> Aurum in mare qui projecit
> Rectè Croesus qui Solonem
> Admisit tanquam morionem
> Ob insanum dictum ejus,
> Aurum ferro esse pejus.
> Ego Aurum longe mallem
> Quàm tam sordidum metallum.
> Sapiens Midas vesci auro
> Mallet quàm praepingui tauro
> Mallet fame cruciari
> Quàm non Auro saturari.
> O quàm egregius Alchymista
> Quàm arte celebris in istâ
> Quàm ad unguem hanc callebat
> Aurum tactu quod cudebat
> O si Aures tetigisset

[1] ? sit.
[2] 'Terrae filius...praevaricator.' Cp. the jest cited on p. 274 n.

Illasque in Aurum convertisset
Aureus Asinus tunc fuisset
Et gloriari potuisset
Sicut audit Rex Gallorum
Midas Rex est Asinorum
Sic si mens me male fallis
Aurum Rex est in metallis.

Sed Aurum est bonum sui diffusivum praesertim inter nos Academicos, et angustis his mendicantium Fratrum rythmis includi
gravatur.

Qualitates in Auro praedominantes sunt splendor et gravitas, cùm
enim sit solis et Terrae filius ab utriusque naturâ participat, a sole
splendorem mutuatur a Terrâ gravitatem. Quidni ego hanc coro-
nam Auream dixero? Splendidissima siquidem est et gravissima
ffoeminarum conventus non est corona verè Aurea, sed fucata, nam
splendida est sed tamen levis. Subjectum Auri est duplex; subjectum capax et subjectum tenax. Subjectum capax, ut Procurator
Causidicus. Subjectum tenax ut avarus. De Avaritiâ haec obser-
ventur. 1⁰ Avaritia est virtus Cardinalis, et Avarus qui Aurum
colit est Papista qui abhinc Cruces[1] inde adorat Imagines. 2⁰ Avaritia
est omnium malorum materia prima, quia ejus appetitus numquam
satiatur. 3⁰ Avaritia Graecè non dicitur φιλοχρυσία sed φιλαργυρία.
quia eo tolerabilius est Aurum, quàm Argentum ; quo magis meretur
veniam qui vino inclinatur quàm qui cerevisiâ. Motus Auri, ut est
omnis corporis gravis, duplex est, vel naturalis a superiori ad inferio-
rem, et tendit ad perfectionem. Vel violentus[2] et contra naturam ab
inferiori ad superiorem, et tendit ad corruptionem, ut Academijs quibusdam transmarinis (non dico nostris) motus Auri a Discipulo
Collegij ad Magistrum. Sed videtur Aurum ut et Angeli moveri
in instanti, qui nullam invenit resistentiam ; Nam Auro omnia
cedunt. Sed respondeo revocando Aurum ad Lydium Lapidem Phy-
losophicum, quia successio motus non tantum provenit a resistentiâ
medij ; Nam quod Aurum non usque adeo in instanti movetur ad
manum Causidici, ratio est ob intercapedinem terminorum. Sed quis
locus Auri? O Aurum vbi es? De Auri loco seu vbi, sunt hi
Canones. Aurum meum nescio ubi est. Senior Frater plerumque
habet Aurum ad vnguem. Aulicus Phantastes plus habet Auri ad
calcem quam ad manum. Aurum Aulici non est in suo loco, quia
gravitat, nam a Crumenâ decidit ad calcaria. Inter Nobiles et
Generosos tàm Aulicos quàm Academicos, mos nuper obtinuit nec
cultrum in vaginâ gestare, nec Aurum in Crumenâ. Judex cùm suo
Auro est in loco Definitivè. Aurum signatum est in loco cùm titulo
Regis circumscriptivè. Aurum nunquam est in Crumenâ mea repletivè.

Quaeritur hic a Chymicis an Aurum possit nutrire hominem?
puto, quia primò admittit concoctionem. 2⁰ Quod possit in succum
et sanguinem converti illud potest nutrire. Aurum potest in succum

---

[1] *Cruces.* on the reverse of the coin.   Cudworth *Int. Syst.* **Praef. ad mit.**
So the coin itself.   See p. 284 *n.*   Aristot. *Eth. Nic.* I. v. 7.
[2] For *uiolentus* = non-natural   cf.

et sanguinem una converti gò[1] : 3° Aurum est nutritivum quia est somnificum, exempli gratia, exhibeat aliquis petitionem ad Senatum alicujus Vrbis aut Academiae, aurumque eis porrigat pro suppositorio, et statim annuent graviora capita. Praeterea Judex qui alioqui etiam dormire solet super Tribunal, sumat mediocrem quantitatem Auri et facilè connivebit. Vnus adhuc scrupulus de Auro restat. (viz.) Cur apud Homerum Apollinis sacerdos Χρύσης dicitur, vates Κάλχας? Quid aeri cum vate, quid auro cum Sacerdote? Ego certe dicere nolo, vos dicite Pontifices in sacris[2] quid facit Aurū? Profecto facit sacerdotem. Sed num Homerus hoc vidit? Sed ego nimis prodigus sum et vos de Auro meo plus satis accepistis et faeminarum aures jam antea Auro sunt oneratae. Post Aurum sequitur 'Potest' sive Potestas sequitur Aurum, immo Aurum quid non potest? *Potest* est duplex, aut potest hoc, aut potest nihil ; verbi gratiâ, si quis quaerat quid potest hominem ad sacerdotium promovere? dico Aurum potest hoc. At Virtus sine Auro potest nihil. Aurum potest, ex. gr. quid si Aequitas causae vincere nequit in Judicio? Aurum potest. Quid si Virtus nequit hominem ad honorem evehere? Aurum potest. Quid si Doctrina nequit Socium, aut Discipulum Collegij efficere? Aurum potest. Tantum potest Aurum, et tantum de 'potest.' Jam ad productionem producendus est sermo. *Aurum potest produci,* sed quaedam limitationes adhibendae sunt. Nam

Ex Avarorum loculis
Ex Praevaricatoris joculis
Et ex plenis poculis,
    Aurum produci non potest.
Ex mendaci saeculo
Ex meo subligaculo
Ex nostra cista communi
    Aurum produci non potest.

In caeteris casibus quaestio tenet
Aurum produci potest.

Ex generoso Patris filio
Ex quadrato Patris pileo
Ex oblongo Bedelli Bacillo
    Aurum potest produci.

Circa modum producendi Aurum quaeritur an Auri productio sit cum motu vel sine motu. Respondeo. Aurum non re-sidentium producitur per quietem sine motu, quia nullus motus est discontinuus. Aurum Judicis producitur per motum circularem. Aurum Causidici vel producitur per motum directum a termino ad terminum, vel per motum obliquum, seu indirectum et sine termino. Aurum Tabernarij producitur, vel per motum irregularem quorundam Planetarum errantium ab uno signo ad Aliud; vel per motum circularem, Capitis sub mitrâ. Cum autem sex sunt species motus, sc : Generatio et Corruptio, &c.[3] Auri productio fit per omnes has sex species. Aurum meretricium, seu Aurum Laidis, producitur per Generationem; sed hoc Aurum est spurium et adulterium. Aurum Magistratuum producitur per corruptionem. Aurum Foeneratoris producitur per augmentationem, sed hoc meâ non interest. Aurum Tonsoris producitur per incrementum capillorum, aut potius per excrementum. Aurum Mancipij producitur per diminutionem ferculi. Aurum etiam producitur per diminutionem et eclipsin. Praevaricator non producit sibi aurum per praevaricationem. Denique Aurum

---

[1] *gò :* =, Ergo ualet consequentia.
[2] Persius II. 68, 69 : where the read-

ing is *sancto.* (al. *sacro,* al. *sanctis*).
[3] Aristot. *Categ.* c. 14 *ad init.*

Tabellarij producitur per motum lationis. Oritur hic Controversia inter Chymicos, an Aurum potest produci a nihilo? puto, nam qui potest nihil in Aurum convertere, ille potest Aurum ex nihilo producere, sed aliquis potest nihil in Aurum convertere. Major patet, minor probatur. Qui Aurum suum jam in nihil convertit, ille potest nihil in Aurum convertere, sed aliquis Aurum suum jam in nihil convertit; et hoc liquido constat. Deindè Malum est nihil et Aurum est bonum, sed aliquis potest bonum ex malo producere, ut Causidicus ex malo consilio potest bonum Aurum producere, idque per conversionem, mutando scil: finitos in infinitos. Sed objiciat aliquis. Quomodo ex malis causis bonum effectum, vid: Aurum, potest produci? Respondeo, hoc fit per Artem Chymicam, aut enim est fallacia non causae pro causâ, Aut Cliens supponit quod non est supponendum.

Quanquàm verò Aurum potest fieri ex nihilo, tamen non potest produci in instanti. Si quis ad Sacerdotium citò pervenire nequit nè miremini: Aurum non potest produci in instanti. Si hoc Anno laboremus penuriâ Doctorum; ne miremini; Aurum non potest produci in Instanti. Dicet Adversarius Aurum hodiè producitur per Creationem, et Creatio est productio momentanea, et fit in instanti. sed haec ratio nullius est momenti. Nam etsi pater Creat, tamen ffilius aliquid praesupponit. Deinde Aurum non producitur in Instanti, quia gradatim et successivè acquiritur. Nam Pater acquirit Aurum per gradus, senior ffrater per successionem. Hactenus de Auri productione. Productionem Auri sequitur 'Per' sive unusquisque persequitur Auri productionem. *Aurum potest produci Per* 'Per' est duplex, per fas, per nefas. Aurum utroque modo producitur. Per iterum est triplex. Per se, per Alium, per Accidens. Vt in Academijs quibusdam exoticis, ignavum quoddam pecus, quod fucus dicitur, degunt in Collegijs; qui fructum et proventum societatum capiunt per se, concionantur, reliquisque exercitijs funguntur per alium, student per Accidens. Ignavi praelectores Academiae legunt nec per se, nec per alium, si quando legunt, legunt per Accidens. sed nimiùm fortassè de Per, seu patris Per nimium.

Aurum potest produci per, sed per quid? Non cuivis contingit adire Corinthum, nec cuivis est Aurum facere. Immò hoc Artis opus, non Virtutis. *Aurum potest produci per Artem.* Et primum hoc supponimus pro fundamento Aurum necessario esse habendum. Ergo aut per Artem, aut per Naturam, sed Aurum non est a Naturâ, quia quod est a Naturâ, non est in nostrâ potestate sed Aurum est in nostrâ potestate. Quod sumitur in electione est in nostrâ potestate, sed Aurum frequenter sumitur in Electione. gò[1]. Deinde nullus Habitus est a Naturâ, sed Aurum est habitus quia acquiritur longo studio et industria et est difficulter et aegre mobile a subjecto. Aurum saltèm acquiritur. Aurum est habitus in procuratore, quia augetur, et intenditur per additionem gradus ad gradum. Sed hic Cautione opus est, nam si actus intenditur a Magistro, iste Habitus Procuratoris diminuitur.

[1] i.e. *Ergo* the syllogism is proved.

Quid si dicamus Aurum non esse ipsum habitum sed dispositionem, hoc est gradum ad habitum, vel dispositionem ad gradum sine qua nemo aut habitum aut gradum sumat. Nam ut agens per naturam, non inducit ad formam in materiam, nisi dispositam, ita agens per Artem, Bedellus scil., non imponit habitum alicuj, nisi per aurum priùs rectè disposito et praeparato.

2⁰. Generalitèr sic arguo, quod producitur per apprehensionem simplicem, per compositionem et Divisionem, per propositionem, aut per discursum, producitur per operationem Intellectus, et ex Consequenti per Artem sed Aurum ita producitur gò[1] e.g. Aurum Pharmacopolae producitur per apprehensionem simplicium. Aurum quorundam Officiariorum Academiae producitur per Compositionem. Aurum Sociorum producitur per Divisionem. Vt voluntas sequitur dictamen intellectus, ita Seniores Collegij (ut par est) sequuntur dictamen Magistri. Intellectus proponit voluntati hunc vel illum eligendum, et per hanc propositionem Aurum saepe producitur: Denique Aurum Dunkerkorum[2] producitur per discursum, discurrendo ab uno cubiculo ad aliud.

3⁰. Aurum producitur vel per Artem, vel per Scientiam. Non per Scientiam, nam facilè producitur sine Scientiâ vt Medicus, si habet Praxin, potest producere Aurum sine Scientiâ. *Ergò* relinquitur quòd Aurum producitur per Artem. Proptereà vt Artes tractantur methodo Analyticâ, sic Aurum, et quandocunque ego nummum produco ex Crumenâ meâ—si forte quis Aureus[3] exit, quando haec rara avis est—si quis tamen Aureus exit, statim vtor methodo Analyticâ, resolvo Aurum in solidos, et solidos in denarios. Sed hoc est contra regulam Chymicorum, qui dicunt Aurum fieri ex argento vivo, non contra argentum ex Auro. Resp. Argumentum meum non est vivum, imò fere mortuum est, nam diu fuit consumptione. Jam Artes per quas Aurum producitur sunt vel manuales vel mentalés. Artes manuales sunt mechanicae, nam Aurum acquiritur παντι τροπῳ καὶ μεχανη (*sic*) praecipuè vero sunt duae furandi et ludendi in quibus Aurum producitur dexteritate quadam ex materiâ viscosâ, et vnctuosâ, contemperatâ cum Argento vivo, seu Mercurio, et hoc propriè est Aurum facere. Artes mentales sunt multae, ut adulandi, mentiendi, fallendi, pejerandi, simulandi, dissimulandi, aequivocandi, &c. In his Artibus Aurum producitur virtute lapidis Philosophici, per reservationem specierum in Intellectu, seu per verbum mentis, seu (ut loquitur Faber in libro περὶ χρυσοποιητικοῦ) per mentalem reservationem, seu per commutationem quandam Geometricae proportionjs, quâ verba damus pro Auro. Fidicines, et notarii Aurum producunt per Artes instrumentales; Aurum non producitur per Artes liberales, quia clientes hodiè non accipiunt Aurum, sed dant, et Patroni non dant Aurum sed accipiunt. Quales demum sunt ipsi Patroni, hi tamen sunt quos hodie pascunt homines. Gaudeo si quid tibi feci aut facio quod placeat, et id gratum fuisse

---

[1] *Ergo*, the syllogism is proved.
[2] *Dunkirk privateers.* See Nares.
[3] A parody on Persius i. 45, 46.

adversum te habeo gratiam, vt Socius in Collegio, dicerem vt Socia[1] in Comoediâ Simonj. Aurum itaque per multas Artes producitur, sed dotissimum per Artem Chymicam. Martialjs[2] in laudem hujus Artis nullibi sic cecinit.

Barbarus aurifluas sileat Pactolus arenas
Ostentet flavum Gens nec Ibera Tagum.
Nec Florae templo molles laudentur honores,
Dissimulet quaestum vrbs cornibus ipsa frequens.
Aëre nec vacuo totidem pendentia signa
Laudibus immodicjs avis[3] ad astra ferat.
Nec nimiùm jactet currus Hobsonus avitos
Vnde tot extraxit fulva talenta senex[4].
Nempè omnis Chymicae cedat labor Aurificinae ;
Vnum pro cunctis fama loquatur opus.

Lapis Phylosophicus est hujus Artis materia prima, et certè eas tantùm in potentiâ ; hunc tamen vt inveniant Alchymistae nullum non movent lapidem. Sed non ex quovis ligno fit Mercurius, nec ex quovis lapide fit Phylosophus, ut loquuntur Chymici. Vbi igitur reperitur ? Resp : effoditur ex Aureis montibus in Eutopiâ ; sed quia ejus figura nec longa, lata, nec profunda, nec quadrata nec rotunda, sed quadrangulo-circularis, aut quadratura circulo aequalis. Ex hoc lapide phylosophico Aurum producitur vel per Conversionem vel per Extractionem : per Conversionem sic sutor producit aurum per conversionem vestimentorum. Bedelli per Conversionem capuciorum. Per extractionem sic (ni fallor) Alchymista aliquis ex Patris pileo Aurum extraxit, heri enim fuit Aureus. Sic duo litigantes sunt duo lapides Phylosophici, ex quorum mutuo afflictu et collisione Causidicus Aurum extrahit per Artem Chymicam. Videntur autem hi lapides non esse phylosophyci quia non quiescunt in propriis locis, sed sursum feruntur ad Londinum contra naturam. Sed respondeo, ascendunt ne daretur vacuum in aulâ Westmonasteriensi. Johannes de lapide scripsit, sed nihil de Lapide philosophico. Et Chymici cum tot ubique videant lapides non possunt invenire philosophicum. Ego tot invenio Philosophos ut vix possim videre lapides prae lapidibus. Nam omnes sumus lapides et cum Paedagogis loquor ex poetâ. Genus durum sumus et documenta damus. Magistratus seu Priores viri sunt Magnetes. Sed magnetes nostri aurum attrahunt non ferrum. Quaedam ex ffaeminis sunt adamantes. Fidus Amicus

[1] *Sosia.* The quotation is from Terence *Andria*, I. 1. 14, 15 (=41, 42).
[2] This is however a parody of the opening of his *Spectacula.*
[3] Professor Mayor suggests that some proper name (as in Martial) is here intended — such as *Davis* or *Clauius.*

[4] Hobson had died on the 1st of January last past (1630—31), and had been buried by Fuller in S. Benet's chancel notwithstanding the plague. The rhymes under one of his portraits, no less than his benefactions to Cambridge, bear testimony to, his thrift.

Achates. Quid quot in hoc fluctuant pelago, tot capita veluti saxa video, et scopulos prominentes? Quaedam acutae sunt Charybdes, quaedam obtusae Syllae. Video et marmora (ni fallor) sudantia, et si fronte ulla fides, sunt inter vos lapides pretiosi, smaragdi et carbunculi. Sed quid video lapides in sublimi pendentes? Ni fallor, non sunt philosophici, ni forte ascendant ad bonum naturae communis, scil : ut prospiciant Vniversitati. Supponamus iam hosce lapides cadere (cadere enim possunt nisi aliquid supponeretur) contendo ego, quod etiam si daretur vacuum, motus eorum tamen esset in tempore, quia per aliquot horarum spatium moverentur. Praevaricator vester videtur esse lapis philosophicus, nam si vllus sit lapis Philosophicus, profecto ille lapillus est, imò lapillulus et fere nullus.

Vos etiam lapides qui in centro estis videmini Philosophici tàm quia estis in proprio loco naturali, tam quia id etiam sedulo cavetis a quo maxime abhorret philosophia (viz :) ne quis locus sit vacuus. Videmur inquam ego et vos lapides esse philosophici, sed non sumus, nam a vobis ne quid gry[1] quidem Auri extrahi potest, imò nec per Artem Chymicam. Vos graviora capita lapides vere philosophici cavete vobis, aderit mox Alchymista, qui si vos videat, probè contusos et contritos dabit, vt quintessentiam a vobis extrahat. Sed durum est haec dicere. Nam quid hoc est nisi lapides loqui? Satis ergo de lapide Philosophico. Videamus jam quaenam genera hominum optime hanc artem callent. Papa qui ex peccatis venialibus, seu potius venalibus aurum extrahit, optimus est Chymicus. Promus Collegialis, qui ex panum exustulis[2] aurum potest extrahere, et ex doliorum faecibus suum aurum expromere, novus homo est, sed vetus Chymicus. Ignis ille fatuus Causidicus bene lectus est in Arte Chymicâ, qui Aurum de crumenâ extrahit, et tamen causa non patet. Qui Aurum adulterinum cudit est malus Chymicus, quoniam est suae fortunae faber. Nam qui sic Aureas fingit cruces[3], ligneam habebit pro mercede, et qui obliquè lineam secat crumenae prope nodum alterutrum in via eclipticâ vt Aurum extrahat virtute Chymicâ, pendebit in lineâ rectâ cum nodo sub capite virtute carnificis. Qui coram mendico manum in crumena imponit, et nihil extrahit est malus Chymicus. Oppidani per miram quandam Artem Chymicam Aurum ex suis cornibus producunt. Nam bos Oppidanus non pacatur, nisi Aurum in ejus cornua fundatur. Vespasianus[4] et Virgilius   *   *   * fuerunt optimi Chymici.
Liceat mihi par ex Chymicorum epigrammate proponere.

[1] *οὐδὲ γρῦ.* Aristoph. *Plutus* 17.
[2] *exustulis* (sic) probably an error for *frustulis* or *crustulis.* Cp. Earle's character of 'An old Colledge Butler.' *Microcosmographie* (1628).
[3] 'Crosses' were coins marked something like the reverse of our florin (cp. *kreuzer*). So Shakespere
Fal. Will your Lordship lend mee a thousand pound, to furnish me forth?

Just. Not a peny, not a peny: you are too impatient to beare crosses.
The second Part of King Henry the Fourth. Act i. Sc. iii.
Clo. For my part, I had rather beare with you, then beare you : yet I should beare no crosse if I did beare you, for I think you have no money in your purse. *As you like it.* Act ii. Sc. iv.
[4] Sueton. *Vesp.* 23.

Χρύσον ἀνὴρ εὑρων ἔλιπε βρόχον, αὐτὰρ ὁ χρυσὸν
ὃν λίπεν οὐκ¹ εὑρων ἤψεν, ὃν εὑρε, βρόχον.

Quod sic transfero,

Reperiens Aurum,† relinquit laqueum ille aperto²
Aurum qui amisit se perimit laqueo.

Circa hanc Chymicam multi sunt scrupuli, 1° quando ille laqueum
suum in aurum mutauit. *Respon:* fuit conversio per Accidens.
2° Quando alter Aurum suum in laqueum mutavit. *Resp.* fuit
conversio simplex. 3° Quaeritur an js qui Aurum amisit, potuit
se suspendere propter negligentiam, hic est nodus difficultatis. *Resp.*
Tamen si laqueum stricte sumas, potuit; aliter non. Deinde in-
ventio fuit in tensione, sed applicatio laquei fuit in executione.
Vsus Artis Chymici probatur hjs experimentis.
Primò. Sumat aliquis grana meritorum, 10 uncias Absolu-
tionum, et sex pondera Indulgentiarum, vna cum fasciculo reliquia-
rum, vnguento, sale, et saliva benè contemperatis, haec omnia
ponantur in pileum Cardinalis, et simul concoquantur in Aquâ
lustrali super ignem purgatorij, qui exuffletur ab incendiarijs Jesuitis
spiritu seditionis, et sic ebulliant donec ad nihilum redigantur, et
extrahetur Aurum optimum per Artem Chymicam.
Secundo. Sumat Causidicus septem scrupulos Controversiae
12 grana ignorantiae, et sex uncias fraudis, et Mercurij, cum pari
quantitate plumbei cerebri, et perfrictae frontis et perfractae conscientiae, vna cum aliquot subpaenis, Demurris, et Returnis; hae
omnia in perâ vulgo dicta Buckramiâ bene vncta simul concoquantur super Ignem contentionis, ex spinis Quaestionum legaliun
compactum, et sic ebulliant a mense Michaelis ad Octavas Hylarij
et extrahetur Aurum optimum per Artem Chymicam.
Tertio. Sumat Calendariographus, seu trivialis Astrologus 10
pondera mendaciorum cum totidem scrupulis dubiorum, et duobus
fragmentis eclipsium, et aliquot sectionibus et minutis motus diurni,
tum frustum zodiaci amputetur falce saturnicâ, particulâ Aurei
circuli et aequatoris, haec omnia colligat zonâ virginis, simul concoquantur in sinistro cornu Arietis, super fascem Lunaris hominis
ascensum et sic ebulliant a solstitio hyemali ad aequinoctium vernum
et extrahatur Aurum optimum per Artem Chymicam. Aur m
inquam conflabitur ex ventis; idque cito, quia ex tempore, et
opportune, quia tempestate.
Quarto. Sumat Foenerator 20 libras Avaritiae cum totidem
minis extortionis, Aequali pondere oppressionis quae Argento vivo,
sulphure, et Plutone (mercurio dicerem) proportionaliter temperata
commolantur ad pûlverem, vna cum aliquâ portione novi haeredis,
haec omnia simul concoquantur in vetere Marsupio in lachrymis
viduae, sine igne, ut parcatur sumptui, et sic decoquantur a centum

---

¹ for οὐχ...ἤψεν &c. Let us hope
that the copyist and not the future
Greek professor was responsible for
the cacography and accentuation. The

epigram is in *Anthol. Pal.* ix. 44. Cf.
Auson. *Epigr.* 22.
² *linquit...reperto.*

ad decem, donec ffoeneratori aliquid inde ultra Principale ebulliat, haeres verò totum decoxerit. Vnum praeterea est observandum. Ingeminet ffoenerator hoc verbum hebraicum a Judaeis olim hujus Artis Magistris usurpatum הב הב (i) Da, Da. et tunc extraheretur Aurum optimum per Artem Chymicam. Quintò. Sumat Philosophus lapidem suum, et quadraturam circuli, cum duobus uncijs Ideae Platonicae, item aliquot scrupulos Quidditatum, cum nullo pondere Argumentorum, item duos asses μετεμψυχώσεως Pythagoricae, et 9 atomos Democriti Sphaerarum harmoniâ bene temperatos, Evellat praeterea 12 crines in suâ barbâ, eosque inter caetera ingredientia (velut coquus quidam) artificiose permisceat, haec omnia simul ponantur in vacuum et contundantur in infinitum, donec resolvantur in materiam primam, tunc Anaxagorae inpendat aquam, ex nigra nive genitam et in ea concoquantur super Ignem fatuum qui exuffletur folle Curiositatis et sic ebulliant vsque ad Annum Platonicum et extrahetur Aurum optimum per Artem Chymicam.

Ergo Philosophus facit aurum; sed num Aurum facit philosophum; dubito, dico tamen. Aurum in potentiâ aliquando facit Philosophum in actu.

Dico 2⁰: Aurum in habitu non facit Philosophum, quod sic probo. Aurum est Senior Frater inter metalla, vt jam dictum est, et vlterius etiam probari potest, quia aetas aurea fuit prima. Aurum inquam in habitu est senior frater, et Senior Frater nunquam facit philosophum, et ratio est quia haeres possideat Terram tenurâ Liberâ, Philosophus vero tenet in capite.

Nil obstat tamen quin Senior frater aliquando sit Alchymista, nam (ut inquit ille) in satyrâ quidam Prodigus haeres est optimus Chymicus, Terram qui vertit in Aurum. Quod si veritas Quaestionis adhuc in dubio est, statim probabitur experientiâ. Si quidem Philosophus Aurum solidum et grave producit per Artem suam (meum quantumvis leve ne respuatis) et fruatur ille per me licet auro suo, si modo aliquid per artem suam hodie possit producere, non equidem invidebo, miror magis[1]. Certè Praevaricator vester est imperitus Chymicus, et credibile est emendari tempora, cum per hanc praevaricandi artem Aurum non producitur, sat (mihi fuerit) si aurum in fronte vestrâ (id est) serenitatem produxero. Aurum meum Intentionale est non reale. Et hoc aurum aequaliter inter vos divido. Junior socius, si modo sit bonus socius, et si capax sit, erit aequalis seniori, aliter authoritate mihi commissâ suspendo illum ab omni Auro tàm suscepto quàm suscipiendo. Et huc usque Chymicus vester arti suae insudarit, et pro eâ, quâ est facultate nullâ, aurum nihil, imò nec solidum produxit, Vestrum solummodo calculum in lucro ponit; Vobis (vix) placuisse illi erit instar Auri, et Albus Favoris vestri lapillus pro lapide Philosophico. Dixi.

The other documents in the volume (ms. 627, Gonv. & Cai.) which contains (i.) 'Praevaricatio Mri Duport.' are

---

[1] Vergil. *Ecl.* i. 11.

(ii.) Oratio ad Augustissimum Potentissimum Serenissimum
Invictissimum Monarcham Carolum ab Oratore Pub-
lico Dre Critton[1], edita (pp. 1—3).

(iii.) Oratio habita 5° Nov. Anno 1617 in Collegio Trin. Au-
thore Edm. Stubbs, A.B. (pp. 1—7).

The following rough notes of a 'Musick Speech' at *Oxford* about
1615, and of the laboured jests of a 'Terrae-Filius' are likewise
preserved among the mss. of Gonville and Caius College.

Though the text is a mere memorandum, such documents are now
so uncommon, and these relate to a circumstance of such literary
interest, that I have determined to print them, leaving emendation
to the reader.

Caius Coll. ms. 73 (74). fol. 341.

MUSICA PRAELECTIO. Shepheard. Coll. Lincoln : Oxon.

Textus Ex libro Boetij *de Music* :

1° Commendatio Authoris Boetii.

2° In Verbis Spectatur Musices { 1. Modulatio
{ 2. Modus { Doricus
{ Ionicus.

3° Modus Doricus (*Jacobo* Regi gratissimus) est sedatum genus
musices et grave.

Cantio.

4° Modus Ionicus (qui modernis usitatior) musices genus malae,
foemininum lasciviolum. Eius exemplum quid aliud, quam Cantus ille
famosissimus de adventu Regis ad Oxon. factus a Cantebrigien-
sibus, cuius quidem modum potius Ironicum quam Ionicum dixero.
Nomen illius. Neque cantus est neque cantio, neque cantilena, neque
harmonia, sed anglice *a Ballad.* Cantebrigienses sunt balatrones.
Auscultemini vero paulisper, et modulamen hujus *Ballad* audibitis ;
audivistis fidicinem agit (fides gemit) modulatio praemittitur, inde
mox crescit *Ballad.* Vnum vobis praemoneo. Hunc ipsum Cantabrigiae *Ballad* (postquam Oxoniam venit) latinè loqui didicisse. Nam
Cantabrigienses nec Musices professorem habent qui possit illum fidi-
bus canere[2] nec illum ipsi possunt latinam linguam docere : Sed sic est.

Oxoniam advenit Rex
cum nobilium choro
Plenus huic occurrit grex
in oppidi foro
Rusticani Oppidani qui vocantur Aldermani
Convenerunt uti ferunt & Jacobo obtulerunt.

[Haec nobilissima illa cantio in qua Cantebrigienses stupidi ho-
munciones Academiam nostram florentissimam derident ludunt &...[3]]

---

[1] Ri. Creyghton, Trin., Public Orator, 1627—39, succeeding Herbert.

[2] It is true that the Cambridge
music professorship was not founded
till 1684; but that at *Oxford* even was
not in existence in 1615, nor indeed
till 1626. The term *professorem* therefore must be used loosely as equivalent to *doctorem*, as it is commonly
in the title 'S.T.P.' in the theological
faculty. At Cambridge there was the
provisional grace quoted above p. 236
note 1.

[3] *erased* 2dâ manu.

Sed si minus accuratus forsan factus fuisset sub sordidis Cantabrig. Ejus verbum] *tigellis*, ab ingeniis *paludinosis*[1]. fecerat nostro Guilielmo ut opinor qui in consilium vocato.——&c. in opprobrium Cantabrigiensium nulla habita personarum differentia distinctioneve, & totius Universitatis Cantebrigiae[2]. Haec Viri egregii Oxonienses volui silentio servasse. Sed postquam Sicelides musae paulo asperiora canebant esse mei duco et virorum omnium haec ita agitare &c. Nuper enim egregium quidem virum nostrum Caecilius non privato sermone sed publicis Comitiis inter suos Cantebrigienses vellicaret. Sed quid tu homo Caecili[3]? Oh. Novimus & qui te[4]. Apud Oxoniam studuisti aliquid literarum parasti, nunc instar prolis asininae in matrem recalcitras &c. nulla Caecilii eruditio. Homo stupidus stolidus triobularis Wakus[5]....disertus Universalis. Sed vos forsan studitani egregii virum ignoratis; Describam ergo illum vobis. Incipit. Sed malo [Ciceronis] verbis illum describere.

Ex 2da & 3[a] Ciceronis actione *in Verrem* loca tria desumpsit et tria folia plus minus impressionis *Orationum*, libello protenso in Caecilium, praelegit.

In Vesperiis Comitiorum
Julii 9.

Terrae Filius. Publicè professus Cantebrigienses fuisse indoctos &c. : nec philosophos, nec poetas. Scribere tamen carmina, quibus invideant Skeltonus & Eldertonus, &c.

Se velle Hopton, Greshamum, Dad. &c. precio conducere, ut Cantebrig. nomina annuis Kalendariis reponeret, &c.

Philosophus Respondens *Raleigh* In tertia quaestione, *An quisquam sibi stultus videatur*, neminem quidem nominavit; dixit vero ——Quos tandem homines video? Peregrinos. Oh navis Stultifera nostras appulit oras. Ubi omnis generis habentur stulti. & dein post descriptionem aliquorum stultorum. Dii boni (inquit) quot navi stultifera huc delati sunt! Unus & maximus omnium nebulo (quantum novi) non adest: in *Caecilia* (ut opinor) dormitantem reliquerunt.

---

[1] So (Bp.) Ri. Corbet ridiculed Cambridge under the name of *Lutetia* in his ballad at this period.

[2] A pun deliberately written *manu secundâ*.

[3] Mr Cecill of S. John's, Cambridge, moderated at the divinity disputation before K. James, 13 May, 1615, and fainted in the act. He wrote *Aemilia*, which had been acted in his coll. at the king's former visit in 1614—15.

[4] Vergil. *Ecl.* iii. 8.

[5] *Wakus.* Thomas Wake, Fellow of Gonville and Caius, acted the character of *Cola* monachus, frater,' and '*Pyropus*, vestiarius' in the original cast of Ruggle's *Ignoramus* before the king. Ruggle left him by will a ring of 40*s.* value. 'Anthony Sleep of Trinity, and Wake of Caius College, used to have many encounters at the tavern: but Wake never had the better at the wit unless he had it at the wine, and then he used to cry out, "O Tony, melior Vigilantia Somno."' Thoms' *Anecd. and Traditions*, p. 39, *ap.* Halliwell's *Cambridge Coffee-house Jests*, p. 59. The more famous Sir Is. Wake was at *Oxford* (Wood-Bliss ii. 539), fellow of Merton and public orator. Of him and Ant. Sleep K. James is reported to have said that in Cambridge one Sleep made him wake, and in Oxford one Wake made him sleep. (MS. Sloane, 384.)

APPENDIX II.

LETTERS FROM CAMBRIDGE,

1704-5—1791.

THANKS to Mr G. Williams' Catalogue and Index to the Additional mss. (sometime known as the Baumgartner Papers) in the Camb. Univ. Library, we can easily collect the threads which connected the life of WILLIAM RENEU with the famous JOHN STRYPE.

In Nov. 1696, his father, Peter Reneu, wrote from London asking Strype to take the boy Willy, aged 7 years, as his pupil at his parsonage of Low Leyton in Essex (where Strype lived sixty-six years, though never inducted). Terms, £20 and presents offered, £30 accepted, (MS. Add⁴· Camb., tom. I. part ii. no. 165).

The boy was kindly treated by his tutor (I. ii. 166), to whom, when he was sent back after holidays (11 Oct. 1698—8 Sept. 1699—23 May, 1700), in his tenth, eleventh, and twelfth years, being found very troublesome at home, requests were forwarded to the effect that Willy should be kept more strictly, whipt now and then, and taught dancing instead of playing with the foot-boy and children in the village (III. ii. 259, 260 : I. ii. 231).

The history of W. Reneu's Cambridge career must be told by the letters here printed from the originals of the Strype Correspondence in the 'Baumgartner' collection. I will add merely that he took his degrees at Jesus College, B.A. 1708, M.A. 1712, and that he continued his friendship with the Strypes, writing to the historian (28 Oct. 1712) to recommend him to take care of his health after an attack of fever (IV. i. 60), and to his supposed widow, offering assistance and counsel (2 April, 1720), when a false report of her husband's death had been published in the London newspapers (IV. iii. 337).

1.]   MS. ADDˢ· CAMB. I. ii. 263.

(Endorsed by Strype 'Will Reneu's Greek¹ Letter.')

These
To yᵉ reverend Mʳ John
Strype
Living att Low Leighton
In Essex.

Γουλιελμὸς ὁ τοῦ Ρενευίου διδάσκαλον
αὐτοῦ αἰδοιότατον ἀσπάζει.

Κᾂν, ὁμολογέομαι, χάριτας ἀξίας σοὶ μηδαμῶς ἀναδιδόναι δύναμαι,
ὀρέγομαι δὲ τὶ τῆς εὐχαριστίας 'μοῦ σημεῖον σοὶ ἀποδεικνῦναι, ὑπὲρ τῆς
σοῦ εὐμενείας μεγάλης. Σὺ γάρ, γινώσκω, εὐσεβείαν ἐις τὴν ἐμοῦ ψυχὴν
ἐγχεῖν ἐφρόντισας, καὶ τὸν νοῦν μού τοῖς γράμμασιν πλουτίζειν. Καὶ
χάριν ἔχω σοι, ὥστε, ὅταν παρὰ σοῦ δόμῳ μακρότερον οὐκ ἔμεινον, μὲ²
παρὰ διδασκάλῳ ὄντως εὐσεβεῖ καὶ σοφῷ ἀμνηστέω τὴν τῆς σοῦ ἀγαθῆς
γυναίκος εὐμενείαν, ἀλλὰ τῇ αὐτῇ εὐχαριστέω.
Ἀσπάζε παρ' ἐμοῦ, δέομαι, τὰς σοῦ θυγατήρας. Πᾶσα ἡ οἰκία ἡμῶν σε
ἀσπάζει.
χαίρε. Ἡμέρ. ιή. τῆς μηνος ποσειδεῶνος. αψδ...

[18ᵗʰ Jan. 170⅘.]

2.]   I. ii. 266.
To the Reverend Mʳ
John Stripp, at his
house in
Lowleyton.

London 24ᵗʰ September 1705.

Sir, The Inclosed I Receaved some days agoe from Mʳ Gregg seeing
you were soe kinde as to promise to goe with mee to see willy sedle
In the Vniversity pray lett me know what day will be fitt for you
suppose twas munday next, wee may bee there a Tueusday about
noone, and soe tarry all wensday or tell [i. e. till] Thursday night
or a fryday att noone you may be Sett at your house, by this meanes
youl have noe occation to trouble any body to preach for you.

I Intend to take a coach wholy for our self, soe wee can goe
& come as wee please my service to your lady and the two young
ladies I Rest,
                          Your humb. Servant
                              P. RENEU.
[P. S.] Sir
    Pray Returne mee the letter, If the above tyme is fitt for you
assoone as I have your answer I shall hyre the coach & a munday

---

¹ There are some earlier letters, in
latin, from W. R. (1702—3) in ms.
Adds. III. i. (Nos. 42, 43).
² It is possible that Billy intended

to write μή. In any case his greek,
faulty as it was, would have conveyed
the boy's meaning to Strype if not to
' Mm Strype and yᵉ Misses.'

(God willing) bee with you about 10 or 12 of the clock and soe goe only to Bishopps Stafford [Stortford], we shall have 4 horses to the Coach.

3.]   MS. Add⁵· III. i. 88.

(Endorsed by Strype   ' Wᵐ Renew's first Letter
                          to me from Jesus Coll. Camᵉ.
                          ? Nov. (sic) 9. 1705.')
These
For y Reverᵈ Mʳ Strype
   Living att
      Lowleighton
In Essex.

                      Cambridge 8ᵇᵉʳ 9 1705.
Honoured Sʳ

This is to let you know yᵗ your freind Mʳ Salter is dead, he died on Sunday about 4 of yᵉ Clock in yᵉ Afternoon, when he is to be buried I can't tell, but they say he can't keep long, for his legs were mortifyed 2 or three days before he dyed.

I like the Colledge very well and I find my Commons with yᵉ addition of an half penny worth of Cheese or butter full enough for yᵉ most part.   The Lads are very civil and kind to me, and now and then they ask me to come to their Chambers and I do the same to yᵐ again :   But among themselves they are up to the ears in division abou high Church and Low Church Whig and Tory.   But for my part I strive to leave yᵐ when I find they are going to yᵗ sport.

Mʳ Trencher my Chamber fellow is a very good natured young gentleman and very civil to me, & I dont doubt but he and I shall agree very well together.   For yᵉ present I read nothing but a Chapter of yᵉ Epistle to yᵉ Romans every morning in greek to Mʳ Grig : But I shall do something else in a little while.   I hope you got home safe on Saturday.   I understand I am to make some petty speeches and disputations in yᵉ Hall next term, I wish they were well over, but I believe I am more afraid than I shall be hurt when I come to it.   Pray my humble service to Mm Strype and yᵉ Misses, I hope Mʳˢ Stryp has got rid of her intermitting Feavour. I am
                       Honᵈ Sʳ Your most obliged freind
                               and humble Servant
                                   W. RENEU

If I can do you any
Service here at yᵉ University
I shall be very glad to do it.
I did not write you in Latin
because I was afraid yᵉ post
would be gone before I could
finish yᵗ and some other
Letters I had to write.

4.]   MS. Add^{s.} II. i. 89.

  Endorsed by Strype   'Billy Renew in Latin
                             from Cambridge
                             Nov. 18...Recepi Nov. 21.'

G : Reneu viro Reverendissimo sapientissimo
[do*] ornatissimo D^{no.} Johanni Stryp S. P. D.

Vir Colendissime

    Multum me pudet, ut mihi literas anglicas tibi danti tu dares
Latinas sed ex benignitate tuâ spero te negligentiam meam exusa-
turum esse ; Et hanc et omnes dum tecum manserim, culpas com-
missas optimè enim scio te et jam meum bonum optare et semper
optasse consuluisseq ; Sed ut tu maximè sic ego meijpsius bonum et
felicitatem non curavi nec consului, deerat, deerat, inquam, ex mea,
nunquam ex tua parte, ad maximum meum dolorem nunc temporis
Luctumq.

    Ago tibi gratias etiam quam maximas quam plurimasque pro
bonis tuis sapientibusq consilijs sperans me ea observaturum esse et
secundum illa actiones meas Regulare.

    Tutor meus (vir benignus doctusq) Lecturas mihi ex Burgodiscio
de institutione Logices et ex graeco Testamento indies ad Horam
octavam praelegit.   Commendat autem mihi ut Legam Terentium
et quosdam alios authores Classicos.   Et die Lunae, die Mercurij, et
die Veneris ad tertiam horam Lecturas mihi et Contubernali meo
Legit mathematicas.

    Praeceptori meo colendissimo doctissimoq die Mercurij proximo
Literas dabo Latinas (Deo volente) si ante id tempus illum videris,
saluta illum fratremq Danielem meo nomine precor.   D^{nus} Grigg et
Trenchard se tibi commendant officiosissimè.   Vale.   [A*] E. Collegio
Jesu Cantab : 14 Cal : Mensis Dec. 1705[1].

* erasures.

[1] Strype's own letters to his mother
when he was a freshman at Jesus are
so curious that it may be worth while
to reprint them here from the originals instead of the common inaccurate
copies.
    Endorsed '1662.   One of my first
Letters to my Mother from Jesus Coll.
Cambr.'
    Good Mother,
    Yours of the 24th instant I gladly
received expecting indeed one a Week
before, but I understand both by
Waterson and yrselfe of y^r indisposed-
nesse then to write.   The reason y^o
receive this no sooner is, because I
had a mind (hearing of this honest
woman's setting out so suddenly for
London from hence and her business'
laying so neer to Petticoate lane,) that

shee should deliver it into y^r hands, y^t
so y^o may better & more fully heare of
me, and know how it fareth wth me.
She is my Laundresse make her wel-
come, and tell her how y^o would have
my linnin washed, as y^o were saying
in y^r letter.   I am very glad to hear
y^t y^o & my Brother Johnsō do agree so
well, y^t I believe y^o account an un-
usuall courtesie y^t he should have you
out to the cake-house.   however pray
Mo, be carefull of y^rselfe and do not
over walk yrselfe for y^t is wont to bring
y^o upō a sick bedd.   I heare also my
Bro Sayer is often y^r visitor : truly
I am glad of it, I hope y^r children may
be comforts to y^o now y^o are growing
old.   Remember me back again most
kindly to my Bro Sayer.   Concerning
y^e taking up of my things, tis true

[For Mrs Strype, on the same sheet]

Hon^d M$^m_{:}$

I am glad that you are got pretty well again of your fever which you had when I was with you last.   And I am much obliged to you

I gave one shilling to much in y^e 100, but why I gave so much, I thought indeed I had given y^o an account in y^t same letter: but it seems I have not. The only reason is, because they were a schollers goods: it is com̄on to make y^m pay one shill more than the Townes people. Dr Pearson himselfe payed so, and severall other ladds in this Coll. and my Tutor told me they would exact so much of one being a schollar and I found it so. Do not wonder so much at our com̄ons: they are more y^n many colledges have. Trinity it selfe (where Herring and Davies are), wch is ye famousest Coll. in ye University, have but 3 halfpence. We have roast meat, dinner and supper throughout ye whole weeke; and such meate as y^o know I do not use to care for; and y^t is Veal: but now I have learnt to eat it. Sometimes nevery^e-lesse, we have boyled meat, wth pottage; and beef and mutton, wch I am glad of: except Frydays and Saturdays, and sometimes Wednesdays; wch days we have Fish at dinner, and tansy or puddings for supper. Our parts y^n are slender enough. But there is y^s remedie; wee may retire into ye butteries, and there take a halfpenny loafe and butter or cheese; or else to the Kitchin and take there what wee will y^t ye Cook hath. But for my part I am sure I never visited the Kitchin y^t, since I have been here, and ye butteries but seldom after meals; unlesse for a Cize [or Size, or Sice] y^t is for a Farthingworth of small-beer: so that lesse than a Penny in Beer doth serve me a whole Day. Nevertheless sometimes we have exceedings: then we have 2 or 3 Dishes (but y^s is very rare): otherwise never but one: so y^t a cake and a cheese would (as they have been) be very welcome to me: and a neat's tongue, or some such thing; if it would not require too much mony. If y^o do intend to send me any thing, do not send it yet, until y^o may hear further of me: for I have many things to send for wch may all I hope be put into y^t box y^o have at home: but w^t they are, I shall give y^o an account hereafter, w^n I would have y^m sent:

And y^t is w^n I have got me a chamber; for as yet I am in a chamber y^t doth not at all please me. I have thoughts of one, wch is a very handsome one, and one pair of stairs high, and y^t looketh into the Master's garden. The price is but 20 shill. per annum, 10 whereof a knight's son, and lately admitted into y^s Coll. doth pay: though he doth not come till about Midsummer, so y^t I shall have but 10 shill to pay a yeare besides my income which may be about 40s. or there abouts. Mother I kindly thank y^o for y^r Orange pills y^o sent me. If y^o are not to straight of mony send me some such thing by the Wom̄a, and a pound or two of almonds and raisons. But first ask her if she will carry y^m; or if they will not be too much trouble to her. I do much approve of y^r agreeing with ye carrier quarterly; he was indeed telling me of it, y^t y^o had agreed wth him for it: and I think he means both y^{rs} and mine. Make your bargaines sure wth him. I understand by y^r Letter y^t y^o are very inquisitive to know how things stand wth me here. I believe y^o may be well enough satisfied by ye woman. My breakings out are now all gone, indeed I was affraid at my first coming it would have proved ye Itch: but I am fairly rid of it. But I fear I shall get it, let me do what I can: for there are many here y^t have it cruelly. Some of y^m take strong purges y^t would kill a horse, weeks together for it, to get it away, & yet are hardly ridd of it. At my first coming I laid alone: but since, my Tutour desired me to let a very clear lad lay wth me and an Alderman's son of Colchester, wch I could not deny, being newly come: he hath laid wth me now for almost a fortnight, and will do till he can provide himselfe a Chamber. I have been wth all my acquaintance who have entreated me very courteously: especially Jonathan Houghton. I went to his Chamber ye Friday night I first came, and there he made me stay and supp wth him, and would have had me laid wth him that night, and was extraordinary kind to mee. Since we

for your kind offer of sending me a Cake, which you may be sure when ever it comes will be very wellcome for though we have pretty good Commons yet we have not such a vast deall but we can make shift with a bit of Cake after y^m. Pray my humble service to M^r [sic] Susanna and Mrs Hester Stryp.

I remain
Hon^d. M^m

Yours at command

W. RENEU.

[On the third page, for J. Strype.]

I have sent you as you were pleased to order me ye inscriptions of ye monument of Mr Rustat and Boldero, wch are accurately and exactly written. Mr Rustat's monument is written all in great Letters and is as follows.

Tobias Rustat yeoman of ye Robes
   To King Charles the Second

Whom he served wth all duty and faithfulness
In his Adversity as well as prosperity
The greatest part of the Estate he gathered
By God's blessing, ye Kings favour, and his own industry
He disposed in his Life time in works of Charity

have been together pretty often. He excused himselfe y^t he did not come to see me before he went, & that he did not write to me since he had been come. Hee hath now, or is about obtaining £10 more from the Coll. Wee go twise a day to Chappell; in the morning about 7, and in the evening about 5. After we are come from Chappell in ye morning wch is towards 8, we go to ye Butteries for our breakfast, wch vsually is 5 farthings; an halfpenny loafe and butter, & a cize of beer. But sometimes I go to an honest house neere ye Coll, and have a pint of milk boyled for my breakfast. Truly I was much troubled to hear y^t my Letter to Ireland is not yet gone. I wish if Mrs Jones is not yet gone, that it might be sent some other way. Indeed I wish I could see my Cosen James Bonnell here within 3 or 4 years, for I believe our University is lesse strict to observe Lads that do not in every point conforme, y^n their's at Dublin, though our's be bad enough. Pray remember me to my Uncle, and all my friends there, w^n y^o write. Remember me to my cozen James Knox, I am glad y^t he is recovered fr̄o his dangerous sickness, w^tsoever it is; for I cannot make any thing of it as y^o have written it. And then, for want of Paper, I end, desiring heartily to be remembered to all my friends, excuse to my Bro^r an sister, y^t they have not heard from me yet, next week I hope to write to y^m both. Excuse my length, I thought I would answer your Letter to ye full. I remain y^r dutifull Son,

J. Strijp.

These
   For his honoured
      Mother Mrs Hester
Strijp. Widdow, dwelling
      in petticoate lane, right
         over against ye 5 Ink-Hornes
            Without Bishopsgate,
   In
         London.

[Baumgartner Papers, 7. *Strype Corresp.* IV. i, 8.]

And found y⁰ more he Bestowed
Upon Churches, Hospitalls, universities and Colleges
The more he had at the years end.
Neither was he unmindfull of his kindred and Relations
In making yᵐ provisions out of what remained.
He dyed a Bachelour y⁰ 15ᵗʰ of March
In y⁰ year of our Lord 1697 aged 87 years.

Mʳ Boldero's Monuments inscription in little letters

> Terra quam premis, Lector, sacra est
> Memoriae Edmundi Boldero
> S. T. P.
> Viri (saeviente Bello civili) de Ecclesia
> Anglicanâ optime meriti, utriq Carolo
> Devotissimi, & hujus Collegij Custodis
> Dignissimi, qui obijt 5ᵗᵒ die Julij, Anno Christi 1679
> Ætat. suae 72ᵈᵒ.
> Desine plura inquirere, et te talem praestes.
> Quod superest deest sed resurgam.

5.]   MS. Addˢ· III. Part ii. letter 266.

Endorsed 'Will Reneu's Letter
to me March 1705
before his¹ going to
Frankford.
Recepi Mar. 23.
1705-6.'

These

For ye Reverⁿᵈ Mʳ John Strype
at his house in Lowleyton
In Essex

Vir ornatissime

Tempore fere bimestri intermisso cujus spatium, antea tibi re-
sponderem, mihi concessisti, jam iterum ad te Literas do.
Eadem adhuc utitur Methodo Tutor meus optimus, qua olim, &
omnimodis seipsum verum & fidelem amicum mihi & toti nostrae
familiae ostendit & quantum ad me attinet, puto, nullam majorem
felicitatem mihi evenire potuisse quàm Cantabrigiam venienti illum
fore Tutorem; quandocunq mecum ambulet vel sedeat (ut non rarò)
non de nugis & rebus inanibus (ut solent plurimi) Loquitur, sed

¹ A slight inaccuracy. At least in
this letter Reneu speaks of going as
far as Harwich. His tutor Mr Grigg
went farther and fared worse, for he
had a fall which detained him at
Brunswick (Cooper's *Annals* IV. 75 n.)
while the rest of the deputation from
Cambridge attended the Jubilee of
Frankfort-on-Oder University. See
above p. 98.

tantum de rebus optimis & utilissimis & de ijs, quae summa mihi commoda afferant.

Scribis mirari admodum in Επιγραφη RVSTATI nullam adferri Rationem corpus ibi humandi. Ratio quidem haec est, Rustatus monumentum in Domo sua per octo annos habuit et ipse scriptionem fecit jussitq ne Verbum quidem ad eam Inscriptionem addi vel mutari post mortem ejus—Scribis etiam Lineam ultimã Inscriptionis Bolderianae intellectu difficilem esse, puto autem illam nill aliud velle nisi hoc; *Quod superest*, i.e. Reliqua pars mei, nempe anima, de qua nihil hic fertur *Deest*, i.e. non in hoc tumulo jacet *sed resurgam*, i.e. sed etsi separantur[1] nec simul esse possunt[1] in hoc tumulo anima et corpus Resurgam totus animã et corpore conjunctis.

Amicus tuus dominus Salterus £100 huic collegio Legavit.

Multum dolet Uxoris tuae Dominae Stryp aegritudo, praesertim cum jam Longo tempore male se habuit.

Tutor meus D^{nus} Grigg Contubernalisq Trenchard Francofurtum versus juxta Viadrum fluvium in Germania ituri sunt Ab Academia ad Jubile die vicesimo tertio mensis Apr: servandum, me Comite usque ad Harwich. Saluta totam familiam optimam tuam nomine meo, Tutoris and Contubernalis. Vale.

Mensis Martij die 21 1705-6

6.] MS. Add^a. III. ii. 279.

Endorsed 'From Wm Reneu
July 9 1706
Rec^d. July 11.'

For ye Reverend Mr John Strype | Minister |
at Low Leighton
In Essex.

Cambridge July 7th 1706

Hou^d, S^r

I received yours of ye 2^d of this month and am obliged to you for accepting so small a present in good part.

I humby thank you for your kind admonition viz: to write my Father a Letter of thanks for being at ye expence of my Journey &c But I have done it already.

I have also kept a Journall of my travails part of which I copied and sent my Father beleiving it would please him.

You make an Apology for continuing my Monitor still; I am not such a one as Horace gives a description off Who is

Monitoribus Asper

but instead of that I humbly thank you & own myself infinitely obliged to you for your care and kindness to me and you may be

---

[1] separantur *and* possint *are faintly suggested* secunda manu. The irregular way in which this letter is written in the original suggests that Reneu stopped pretty frequently to consult his Littleton.

sure there is nothing that greives me more than to think I can make
no Return for such repeated favours.

I am very glad to hear your Lady is in a way of Recovery from
a very dangerous fit of sickness by drinking Asses milk, pray God it
may perfect her cure.

I am glad to hear Daniel improves in Behaviour and Learning,
Pray my Love to him & service to M^r and Mrs Moreland when
you see them.

I have not heard whether I shall go to London or not as yet, for
my part I shall be very glad to see my old freinds but very content
also to stay if my Father had rather I should.   Pray my humble
service to your Lady and two Daughters and please to accept ye same
from

Your very much obliged and

July 9th M^{r}Grigg goes   humble servant
to London this week or   Wm RENEU
next and I dont know
but I may come along
wth him.

7.]   MS. Add^s III. ii. 285.

From W. Reneu to J. Strype
written   from   Putney Sept^{ber} 9th 1706.

[Received Strype's last letter when making a stay of three weeks
in London.   Sends transcripts of the monumental inscriptions in
Putney Church......]

'I believe, Mr Strype, you will be at a Loss for ye Coats of Arms
belonging to these monum^{ts}, which you know I cant Blazen, therefore I believe this must be your Remedy; to come hither, and
because the succussation of your Horse is so great, only to come to
london upon him, and come hither by water one day, and go away
ye next, tho we should be much gladder of your longer stay with us.
Pray present my humble service to Mrs Strype & your two Daughters
& please to accept ye same from

S^r) your most obliged humble servant
Wm RENEU

My Tutor is at the Bath and writes he shall not return till about a
fortnight hence, at which time, I shall accompany him to Cambridge.

8.]   Ibid. III. iii. 293.

For ye Rever^d Mr John Stryp
    Minister att his house
        In Lowleyton
            Essex.

Jes: Coll: January 2. 1706 [i.e. 1706-7.]

Hon^d S^r
    The great and noble work you are about, and ye lyttle news I

have had to send you of Cambridge hath been y⁰ Cause of my not
writing to you thus long. I'm sure, good S, you cant admitt y⁰
thoughts of my having forgotten a person, whom I have y⁰ greatest
reason to, & I dare say, always shall remember with all y⁰ Reverence
& Respect imaginable. But I 'm thoroughly persuaded you 'll
beleive me therfore will not detain you any longer on that Subject.

Cambridge at present is pretty quiet but about a quarter of a
year ago, there was a little stir about one Tudway Mr of Musick
who having been accused by one Plumtree Dr of Physick of some
scandalous and Toriacall Reflections on y⁰ Queen, was degraded &
expelled y⁰ University by y⁰ Vice Chancellor & y⁰ Heads. Most of
y⁰ Tory or rather Iacobite party blame their proceedings very much
as too rigorous upon him but y⁰ Whigs say just y⁰ contrary, but in
fine y⁰ thing is done & irrevocable.

I believe since I wrote to you last I have taken other Books to
read, being now at length climbed up to y⁰ degree of Junior Sophista.
At which time we begin to study Physicks & naturall Philosophy.
I go to lectures to Mr Grigg (whom I love entirely & and who strives
in all things to ρmote my welfare & Learning I'me sure) every morning In Clark's physicks, to Mr Townsend in y⁰ afternoon in Rohault's
Physicks; and I am not a little taken with y⁰ study of naturall Philosophy. The Books I read by my self are Tull: Tusculan Questions
& Homer. besides english Books. We have no Books coming out
at present as I hear off. Be pleased to present my very humble
service to Mᵐ Stryp & y⁰ young Ladies. If you have any service to
command me here at Cambridge I am and always shall be

Reverend S) your most ready, faithfull and obedient

humble servant & freinde

I wish you all an happy new
year.

9.]   MS. Add III. i. 140.

Endorsed 'Wᵐ Renew Frō Jesus Coll.'

These
For y⁰ Revᵈ Mʳ John Strype
  Minister of Low leyton
  In Essex
per London

                      .... ay y⁰ 6ᵗʰ 1707.

Honᵈ S

       I received a letter from you about 6 weeks agoe, and have
deferred y⁰ answering of it till now, least by my too frequent letters
I should interrupt you in perfecting yᵗ noble & Learned work you
are about to present y⁰ publick with. This reason I am persuaded
will keep you from imputing my long silence from disesteem or for-
getfulness of you.

I humbly thank you for telling me yᵉ right use I should make of Philosophy which was to admire the great Creator of all things whose Power goodness and wisdom so eminently shone in them; I shall make this use of it, and shall also take care not to let it swallow up all my time; for I am sensible I shall receive abundance more advantage from yᵉ study of yᵉ Languages than from yᵉ study of that; but I should not so wholly neglect it, as when I come up in yᵉ Hall or Schools not to be able to say one word. I have bought Patrick's Grotius which I think very well answers your Caracter of it. Mʳ Newcome and I hold very good acquaintance, we give one another a visit every now and then; he is a very studious and sober Lad: Another of my School-fellows is admitted of Emanuell fellow-Commoner, he was 3 forms below me at school (but fellow-commoners are seldom extraordinary scholars). There is another yᵗ was form-fellow wᵗʰ me, admitted pensioner of Katharine Hall, he is an extraordinary ingenious Lad, and Mʳ Moreland expects hee'll be a great Honour to his School. — My year is so very large yᵗ though I have been half a year Junior Soph I have not gotten a Scholarship, nor can't expect one these 6 months. Its Largeness has brought another inconvenience upon me, viz. that I neither have nor shall keep much exercise in Colledge which would have helpt to wear off yᵗ faulty Bashfulness which I have. I don't know whether I may expect a fellowship, for there are several to be served before me, if they stay.

My Tutor went to London about a month agoe, and from thence to yᵉ Bath. I received a letter from him on Sunday night last, dated yᵉ 28ᵗʰ Apˡ. wherein he wrote, he intended to leave Bath in about 3 weeks. I'me very sorry for my Uncle's misfortune, which I may be sure is no small affliction to my poor mother and all our Family, I pray God support them under it; nothing I doe here shall be an additionall greif to them if I can help it.

Here is a sad accident has happened to 2 Lads[1], one of Sidney colledge and another of ours, who going to yᵉ Tavern got most sadly drunk, and about 11 of yᵉ Clock at night meeting a man (the poor man was going to the Chandlers for a little Tobacco, and coming out again) one of yᵐ stuck him into ye breast, and not being able to make his Knife enter there far enough because of a bone that hindered; he run behind him and stuck him into yᵉ Back between one of yᵉ small Ribs, upon wᶜʰ he run away to colledge, but yᵉ other lad, being so drunk yᵗ he could not run, was taken and carried to yᵉ Tolebooth ; yᵉ poor wounded man bled (its thought) one ⅓ part of yᵉ Blood in his body and was given over by yᵉ surgeon, but yᵉ Blood stooping he's thought to recover, wᶜʰ I pray God he may; for if he does not, yᵉ Lads will go nigh to be hanged; if he does recover, it will cost yᵐ £30 a piece, if not more, to make him amends to pay yᵉ surgeon. My humble service to Mrs Strype and the young Ladies, and accept this Long Letter from

Sʳ Your much obliged humble servant

W. RENEU.

[1] Remington (Sidney). Lister (Jesus).

The lad y^t did it, is said to be of Sidney colledge not of ours. He of our Colledge is not under Mr Townsend. I believe they will both [be] either expelled or Rusticated, though one did not stab him. All this happened on friday night last.

Since I wrote this letter I hear that they were both expelled privately yesterday in y^e Afternoon by y^e Caput.

10.]   MS. Add^{a.} III. iii. 300.

'Billy Reneu
in Greek & Latin'

These
For Mr John Stryp Living
At Low=Leighton
near y^e Stocks
Essex

[28 Dec. 1707.]

wth care

Γουλιελμὸς ὁ Ρενευίου τον διδασκαλον ἀιδοιότατον ἀσπάζει

Τὰς σοῦ ἐπιστολὰς τῆς ἡμέρας ἐικόστης καὶ δευτέρης τοῦ μηνὸς ποσειδεῶνος ἐιληφα. Οὐδὲ μοὶ ἡ χαρὰ ἐστὶν μικρὰ ὅτι ἀι μοῦ ἐπιστολαὶ σοὶ ἐυγνωμονες 'ἦσαν χάριν τε σοὶ ἔχω ὑπὲρ τῆς παρακλήισως σῆς δηλαδὴ, ὡς παιδείαν ἑλλενικὴν σπουδάζοιμι, καὶ ὡς μὲ ἀυτὴν σπουδάζειν παροξύνοις, εἶπας, ὅτι τῇ ἀυτῇ παιδείᾳ ὁι ἄριστοι φιλόσοφοι καὶ ὁι ἀρχαιότατοι τῆς ἐκκλησίας Πατέρες χεχρωμένοι 'ἦσαν, καὶ ὅτι ἀυτὴ μὲ ἀπο τῶν δημοδέων σχολαστικῶν ἀφορίζοι· καὶ ὑπὲρ πάσης τῆς ἄλλης παρακλήσιως σοῦ χάριν σοὶ ἔχω μεγάλην.

Mathematica omnes meas horas otiumque, quod alitèr scribendo collocarem consumant nec aliquod inter omnia mea studia illis difficilius est, sed, etsi nunc multi sudoris sunt, alacritèr illis Laborem impendo ; animo evolvens, quantas voluptates et commoda postea mihi praebebunt.

Pater Maïerq fratrem Danielem a Dom. Memmingi schola removerunt ; nam non omninò doctior factus est, quantum ad Literas Romanas, etsi quatuor annos apud Illū manserit. Et Dom. Morlandus, Patre cupiente in domum accepit. Ita ut jam Sodales sumus. Totas Literas Graeco Idiomate scripserim, sed putavi res non tam congruas esse illi stilo. Ideoque partim Latine scripsi. Saluta, precor, meo & totius familiae nomine Dominam tuam Dominulasq. Omnes nostrae Domus bene se habent ; idemq de tuâ opto. Vale. Londini mensis Decembris Die vicesimo octavo.

11.]   Ibid. III. part iii. n°. 338.

Endorsed ' Wm Reneu 1708
His Questions w^h he
kept his Act.'

For y^e Rever^d. Mr John Strype
at his house in
Low = Leighton
Essex.

by London

Hon^d. Sir

Since my Last you have not done me y^e favour to
let me hear from you: I hope I need not impute it to any thing,
but your having abundance of business on your hands which has
engrossed all your time and kept you from thinking of Cambridge.
We are very quiet here this vacation and have ye best opportunity
of studying that can be. I hope I shall make good use of it and
fit myself to take my Degree honourably at Christmas. In order
to it I have kept an act in ye Schools upon these Questions.

Philosophia naturalis non tendit in atheismu,
Materia non potest cogitare.
Materia est divisibilis in infinitum.

I was baited 2 or 3 hours by 3 opponents and then came down
without much disgrace. Next term I shall be opponent once or
twice perhaps and then I shall have kept all my exercise in y^e
Schools; till I come to be middle Bachelour. I remember you told
me 'twould not be ungratefull to you to hear how we performed
here, y^t you might see ye Difference between your time and mine,
otherwise I had not troubled you wth this impertinence.

I have a peice of very ill news to send you i.e. viz. y^t one
Whiston our Mathematicall Professor, a very learned (and as we
thought pious) man has written a Book concerning ye Trinity and
designs to print it, wherein he sides wth ye Arrians; he has showed
it to severall of his freinds, who tell him it is a damnable, heretical
Book and that, if he prints it, he'll Lose his Professorship, be
suspended ab officio et beneficio, but all won't doe, he saies, he
can't satisfy his Conscience, unless he informs ye world better as
he thinks than it is at present, concerning ye Trinity.

Mr Grigg gives his humble service to you. Be pleased to give
mine to Mrs Strype and ye young Ladies. And believe me to be as
I truly am,

Sir

Your respectfull freind & Servt.

Jes: Coll: Aug: 10th. 1708.

Wm RENEU.

12.]   MS. Add⁵· III. part ii. letter 146.

Endorsed by Strype
'1708 Jan.
Wᵐ Renew Bach of Art.
My Book of yᵉ Annals
Yᵉ Judgmᵗ thereof at Cambridge.'

For yᵉ Revᵈ. Mʳ John Strype
Minister of Low = Leyton
In Essex
                                        [25 Jan. 1708-9.]
by London

Honoured Sʳ)   Last fryday I got over all yᵉ Troublesome business attending my Degree and was capped by yᵉ Vice Chancellour;
news I fancy that won't be very ungrateful to you; who have alwaies
shown such a kind concern for my wellfare & happiness. Preparation
for my Degree has kept me hitherto from reading your learned History &c a book, all yᵉ most ingenious men confess yᵐ selves mightily
obligèd to you for; & willingly own it to be a work no one could undertake & perfect, but yʳ self, as you have certainly done to all their
satisfactions; I intend within a little while to set about it and
read it over, I don't doubt, wᵗʰ a great deal of Pleasure. But I
believe I shall first see you at your own house; for I intend to be
at London (if yᵉ Weather alters and mends yᵉ Roads) within ten
dayes. In yᵉ mean time I fancy, my Father would be glad you'd
dine wᵗʰ him one day, and you'd particularly oblige me, if you'd
tell him he must expect pretty large Bills, this Degree-time[1]. I
have this day sent him up a very large one, which I don't know
how hee'll like. But intend he shall have no more such; for now
I me[2] Bachelour, I know I can find severall ways to retreave my
Expences, and live for threescore pᵈˢ pʳ Ann: very handsomely,
and that he's willing to allow me.
    Please to present my humble service to Mʳˢ Strype and yᵉ Young
Ladies, & excuse yᵉ freedom taken wᵗʰ you (in pretending to employ
you) from

                            Your aff:ᵃᵗᵉ humble Servᵗ.

                            W. RENEU

Jes: coll: Jan: 25:
        1708-9.

[1] Not only because of fees, but for
treats to the 'fathers' disputants and
friends in college.
[2] I me = I'm. Similarly "I'll" was
sometimes spelt "I'le," but with the
apostrophe; *ex. gr.* in Nevile's *Poor
Scholer* (1662), ii. 4.

13.]   Ibid. III. ii. 159.

Endorsed 'Mr Wm Reneu Oct 4. 1709
Mr Wort's 3000£ how
disposed in Charity
to y^e University.
Reneu fair for a Southern
Fellowship at Jesus Coll.'

Dear & Honoured Sir,

Whether I writ to you, or you to me, last, I can't
tell ; however I'me sure if I did your good nature will easily excuse
a supernumerary Letter, & ye same, I hope, will forgive me, if I was
in your debt.

As for College matters (about w^{ch} (upon my account) you used
to be kindly inquisitive) there's little or no alteration in them : I
have not got a better Scholarship, nor is there any Southern fellowship dropt; so y^t I continue in statu quo : But I can tell you a
piece of news wch I dare say won't be disagreeable ; y^t now if a
Southern Fellowship should drop, I have no senior to oppose me ;
and I'me persuaded no Junior can turn me out, by reason of y^e
Master's good opinion of me (how well I deserve it I don't know)
& my acquaintance with near half the fellows, things neither of
y^m despicable : so y^t in all probability I shall be coelected ye next
vacancy. To promote this my kind Father, upon my Request sent
ye Master ½ a Chest of Florence and as much to Mr Grigg ; which
you may be sure won't be to my Disadvantage in y^t particular, if
it does me no signall piece of service. I thank you S^r for your
service sent by Mr Wyat, who would not be so kind as to call
upon me, tho he was but 2 doors off ; otherwise we had drunk
y^r Health together.   Mr Grigg desires to be remembred to you ;
he continues as true and substantiall a friend as ever, and watches
all opportunities of doing me service as far as he's able. I beleive
you have not heard of a noble Charity left us by Mr Wm Worts
deceased, formerly Master of Arts of Caius College in this university; and in his Will as well dispos'd of, in ye opinion of every
body as 'twas possible it should be, it was thus. This gentleman
left 3000 in ye Bank thus to be disposed of. When ye interest of
ye 3000 amount to 1500, y^t 1500 is to be laid out to build Galleries for ye Bachelours of Arts and undergraduates in St Maries
Church. This it will doe in 7 or 8 years. The 3000 still lying
in ye Bank till ye Interest of it amounts to 1500 more ; this 1500
is to be spent in making a Causeway from Emanuell College to
Hog Magog : and ye 3000 is to continue in ye Bank, till ye Interest
amounts to 800 more, wch 800 is to be out at use & will bring in

at common interest 40 p^r Annum for ye Repair of ye Causeway &
Galleries.   After this ye 3000 is to remain in Bank till it raises
4000 or 200 p^r Annum for ever which is to bear ye Charges of
two persons to be sent out by ye Vice Chancellour to travell into
foreign parts, who are obliged to send a Journall of their observations every month to him.   They are to be out 3 years and then
other two are chosen by Mr Vice Chancellour and they are to come
home.   When ye 3000 has yielded ye above-mentioned Interest 'tis
to be put into ye University Chest.   The Vice Chancellour &
master of Trinity for ye time being, and others ye most substantiall
heads of ye University are made Trustees.   Now I think no Charity
of y^t value could have been better disposed off.   For as to ye Building of Galleries in St Maries, y^t you know was as much wanted as
any thing could be; for besides ye undecency of seeing so many
Gentlemens sons *standing* in ye Isles; ye want of seats brought in
y^t ill Custom of talking & walking about ye Church all ye service,
so y^t there's is often such a noise, one can hardly hear ye minister,
let him have never so good a voice; but by this means this will
be regulated.   Then you know ye causeway to ye Hills is very
necessary, for by means of Coaches & Carts & ye Chalkiness of
ye Road in winter time 'tis hardly possible to get to them; and
they are ye Pleasantest places as well as wholesomest y^t we have
about us.   The other Parts of his Charity you can see the use of
as well as I can tell you, therefore I'll conclude; and I had need,
I fancy, for this long relation will tire you.   My humble service
to Mrs Strype & your Daughters.   I am

Your Respectfull freind & serv^t

W RENEU

Camb: oct 4 . 1709

Mr Barker Senior fellow and President of Magdalen College
died last night; he was almost about y^r standing, therefore I
acquaint you with it, and you may possibly know him.—Verbum
non amplius addam.

14.]   MS. Add^a. III. part iii. n°. 353.

To ye rev^d Mr John Strype
Minister of
Low Leyton
In   Essex.

Febr: 10th 1709—10.

Dear & honoured Sir,
                I should not have deferred answering y^r Last
kind Letter and thanking you for ye token you sent by Dr Newcombe
thus long, had not I been plagued almost ever since with greivous

sore eyes. I have been bloodied in ye Temple veins & in ye Arm, been purged almost a dozen times & been blistered and used all y remedies imaginable for this last Q^r of a year & have hardly diverted ye Humour so much, but y^t upon ye least Cold it threatens me with a return. I have left off all ye exercises as shooting hunting coarsing football &c which can possibly endanger my catching cold; so y^t I hope I may have an opportunity of fixing to hard Study now; which I have left off so long, y^t I am perfectly tired of non-studying; having drained my whole Storehouse of amuzements. To draw ye Rheum & humours from my Eyes I am advised to smoak very much which I dare not let my Father know, he's so averse to it y^t I beleive he had as live see me dead or at least blind (and to be so, is death to a Student) as with a pipe in my mouth : I have smoaked, so y^t I can receive no prejudice any other way, than by his anger, but I'll take care to conceal it from him, if possible, whenever I take a pipe. I would have writ to you when D^s Newcome[1] went home, but my eyes were bad & I had some business on my hands which prevented me : He took his degree very honourably, and I believe will have an *optimè* ; you have not forgot how those are disposed of[2]. I see you are again employed at ye Printers for a good while ; I shall see you either there or at your own house very shortly I hope, for I intend to make my freinds a visit ye latter end of this or ye beginning of next month. I won't detain you any longer from y^r Arch B^p. Parker for fear ye Publick should suffer by my means. I am

Dr Sir Your respectfull freind
& Servant W. RENEU.

My humble service to
Mrs Strype & y^r Daughters.

15.] Ibid. III. iii. 372.

Endorsed by Strype ' May 1710
Mr Reneu of Jesus
His Exercises [as Middle B.A.] To make
ye Speech May 29.'

H^d S^r.
    I waited upon y^r freind Mr Baker as soon as I could conveniently, and delivered him ye Papers you sent by me; ye half guinea he desired me to return you (wch I have sent to my B^r John for you) and to tell you, one of y^r Books will be a much more acceptable present to ye young Painter. I have been so pestered with exercise in College and in ye Schools ever since I came down y^t I have hardly had time to write to any one otherwise you might have

---

[1] H. Newcome, Emman. B.A. 1709. M.A. 1713.
[2] An early instance of a reference to Cambridge *honours*. Reneu implies that these complimentary marks of distinction were conferred in Strype's time (B.A. 1665).

assured yourself of a Letter before this. I have very little time to spare at present for I am preparing a Thesis for the Bachelour Schools, being to come up ye Beginning of May & besides have a Speech for ye twenty ninth of May upon my hands for our Hall : I shall take w^t pains I can to make a good one, it may possibly do me some service against I set for a fellowship. Little Brown [1] is come to Coll : I shall take care to miss no opportunity of doing him Service, since you have recommended him to me—I hope Mrs Strype has got rid of ye Distemper she was afflicted wth w^n I saw you last. I wish you both all health and happiness, and am sincerely

Y^r Respectfull & aff^{ate} humb^e Servt.

W. RENEU

Pray my Service to all freinds but particularly D^s Newcome.

Apr. 25th 1710.

16.]   III. iii. 384.

Endorsed by Strype   'June   1710
Mr William Reneu from Cambr.
Thanks for my directions in
delivering his Speech May 29
To recomend him to ye Bp. Ely.'

Hon^d Sir,

I should be very much to blame if I did not take the first opportunity of writing to you to thanke you for your last kind Letter, wherein you showed so many proofs of ye Sincerity of your affection to me in y^r good wishes & advice : I take it very kindly I'll assure you, that you'd trouble y^r self to write me word what method you thought properest for me to take in my speech for ye 29th of last month ; it was finished before ye Receipt of y^r kind instructions, but I had ye satisfaction to see ye method I had taken in making it did not differ very much from y^t you prescribed. I found a great deal of benefit by ye latter part of y^r advice about pronunciation and moderate action, and laid aside in great measure y^t fearfulness I am so unfortunately prone to, by being forewarned of it by you. I thank you for y^r kind representation of me to my Father & Mother I hope they'll have no reason to complain of me for any thing I do here. My Father is a little hard upon me in making me find my self Cloaths and all sorts of conveniences & necessaries out of the 50^{lb} p^r An: he allowes me and ye scholarship I have wch is about 10^{lb} more ; I wish he don't hinder me of ye fellowship, I expect by forcing me to live so close in College for fellows expect to be treated now & then by youngsters that expect to be members of their Society. I'll try all wayes I can to save money but fear my Father must allow me ten pounds pr An. more. Please to order y^r Bookseller to deliver ye book I subscribed for, to my Father ; I have no time to look it

[1] T. Browne, Jes., B.A. 1713.

over yet, being engaged in studies preparatory to an examination, if a fellowship should chance to drop quickly. If ye Bp of Ely knows my Name, it may be of Service to me, I should be obliged to you if you'd let him know, I was under your care heretofore. I have had a little feaver for these five or 6 dayes, but I thank God its gone of, and I hope to set to Study very hard to morrow morning, and to continue it all summer. I have ye best opportunity y^t can be for there's hardly any one left in ye College because of y^e long vacation. I shall notwithstanding be ready & willing to spare you an hour as often as usuall to converse with you by letter. I hope Mrs Strype & y^e young Ladies are well, please to give my service to y^m Mr Grigg gives his to you. I sent to my B^r Reneu to pay you the $\frac{1}{2}$ Guinea I rec^d of you for y^e Painter, Mr Baker expects you'll send y^e Book to him y^t he may give it y^e Young Gentleman. I am

Your respectfull freind
& humb. Servt.
W. RENEU

Jun: 11th 1710.

17.]   Ibid. III. iii. 400

Endorsed 'Oct 1710
Mr Wm Reneu
To speak on his
behalf to y^e Bp of Ely.'

Jes: coll: oct^r 31: 1710.

Hon^d Sir,
       Though your not answering my last letter shows you are very busy and don't care to be disturbed, yet I can't forbear troubling you with this, to let you know you may do me a very signall piece of service without much inconvenience to yourself. The thing is this; y^t when you wait upon ye Bp. of Ely (w^m I think you visit pretty frequently when he's at London) you'd be so kind as to mention me as your freind and Scholar and one whom you would fain have fellow of Jes: coll: I think you told me you mentioned me heretofore to his Lordship; but I beg of you to take ye first opportunity to do it again; for if his Lordship be a little prejudiced in favour of me I shall certainly be fellow very shortly; for Mr Darby^1 ye person y^t was praeelected, has got preferment which incapacitates him for a fellowship, so that I am next oars now and may probably be elected in 6 months time: If it should happen so I'm sure 'twould be a very agreeable surprize to all my freinds, to my Father especially who would gladly be at less charge for my education. You see, Sir, how free I make with you, but

---

^{1} H. Darby, M.A. Jes. 1707.

I know you'll excuse it since I had no freind y^t was intimate with ye Bishop as yourself or I beleive so heartily desirous of my success in y^t point as your self.—Be pleased to give my humble service to Mrs Strype & your Daughters :   I am

Hon^d. Sir,

Your respectfull & affectionate
freind

Poor Mr Whiston   and Servant
being resolved not   W. Reneu
to recant is to be
expelled in 2 or 3 days.

18.]   MS. Add^s. III. iii. 402.

Endorsed 'Nov. 1710
            Mr Wm Reneu from Cambr.
            About coming up for a
            Fellows^r & going w^th
            me to ye Bp of Ely.'

Dear and honoured Sir,

            The news of a Gentleman's (Southern[1] fellow of our College) being so ill y^t his Life is despair'd of, has made Mr Allix[2] (another fellow) resolve to hasten to London to make w^t interest he can for a Brother of his my Junr: My Tutor advises me to be as quick in my motions as allix ; I intend therefore (if ye Letters y^t come in tomorrow night bring word of his death) to be in London on munday night; in order to wait upon ye Bp. of Ely ye next day: if I could have ye happiness of your company thither it would be mightily for my interest I'm sure and I should be very extraordinarily obliged to you.   If you'll meet me at ten a clock on Tuesday morning; after we have drunk a dish of Chocolate, wee'll set out for Ely house, if you please: for there's nothing like striking while ye Iron is hot.   My humblest Services to y^r good Lady & Daughters, I am

Hon^d. Sir Y^r aff^ate. humble
Servant
W. Reneu

Jes: 18: 9^r: 1710

---

[1] *i.e. australis.* See below, Appendix V.
[2] *Peter Allix* (B.A. Queen's 1702) fellow of Jesus, D.D. 1717. His brother *William* was B.A. at Jesus 1709, but never got a fellowship.

19.]   Ibid. III. iii. 406.

Endorsed 'Nov. 1710
Mr Peter Reneu
To assist wth ye Bp
of Ely in pcuring
a Fellowp for Wm Reneu' [his son]

Sir)   London 20th Nouember 1710

Yesterday Receaued the Inclosed from my sonn from Cambridge
for you, hee aduises that Doctor Stanhopes curate is very Ill whoe
is a fellow of Jesus colledge att the Receit of said letter I went
to Docter bradford[1] & hee & I went to the bisshopp of Ely, &
desired him if said curate should dye to prefferre my sonn to the
said fellowshipp hee would not Ingage noe further than only this
that when a vacancy comes the colledge Recommends two & hee
gives to him that has the best capacity & Recommendation, wee
weare half ann houre with the bishopp only wee three I told him
that you had spoaken with him in behalf of my Sonn, 'tis vncertain
or vnknowne weather said curate bee dead or not if dead then my
sonn will bee here this night or will aduis how it goes with the
said curate by the post, you shall know p tomorrow what aduis
wee haue either by my sonn or by the post which I think is
necessary before you take any further trouble, seeing that Doctor
bradford & I haue already bein with the Bishopp my service to
mrs strippe & yr Daughters accept the same from)

                                        Your humb Servant
                                        P RENEU
Sir
my wife Giues you and made
strippt & yr Daughters her seruice.

20.]   Ibid. III. iii. 405.

Letters from (β) W. Reneu
and (α) his father Peter Reneu
'concerning a fellowsp of Jesus Coll
wch he obtained.'

(α)   London 20th november 1710
   Sir)
Tis now about six of the clock in the Evening. I wrote to
you this morning a Letter now this serves to acquaint you that my
sonn is come from cambridge & says the Gentleman that was a

───────────────
[1] S. Bradford of Bene't, D.D. 1705.   in succession, bp. of Carlisle and
afterwards Master of his College and   Rochester.

fellow of their colledge is dead, I have acquainted you what doctor
bradford & I had done yesterday with the Bishopp of Elÿ. J
Reffere you to what my said sonn writhes you—in this Letter
& Rest

Your humble seruant

P Reneu.

(β)
    Sir

      Hon.ᵈ Sir,
             The gentleman I wrote to you about died last
saturday morning : In my letter I desired you'd please to call upon
me on Tuesday morning, but my Father having been wᵗʰ yᵉ Bp of
Ely I believe you need not put your self to any inconvenience
of yᵗ sort : If you are acquainted with our Master you speaking
a good word for me to him, may be of use to me, but I believe
nothing else you can do will reward your pains ; However if you
come to town I shall not excuse you unless you let me see you.
I am very heartily tired with my Journey, therefore can't write
you any particulars of yᵉ Proceedings at Jesus Coll : since yᵉ death
of this Person but shall be glad to acquaint you with yᵐ tomorrow
or yᵉ next time you come to London over a dish of Thea or
Chocolate ; My humblest service yʳ Lady & daughters.   I am

Hᵈ Sir

Yʳ humb' Servant

Wᵐ Reneu

Lond : 9ʳ yᵉ 20 . 1710.

21.]   MS. Addˢ. III. iii. 409.

        Endorsed 'Dec 1710
            Mʳ W. Reneu. Upon his
            being Fellow of Jesus.
            The trouble yᵉ Bp of Ely
            put him to.
               The Master his Friend
               His Thanks to me.'
    Hon.ᵈ Sir,
            I have been in such a continual hurry of business upon
my coming into my fellowship, that I have hardly had time to
think of my freinds, much less to write to them.   My Father told
me upon his acquainting you with my success you expressed a
very great satisfaction, wᶜʰ I am much obliged to you for : I shall
always very gratefully resent yʳ kind Care of me and think my
self now more particularly obliged to repeat my thanks for all your
kindnesses.   Your visit to yᵉ Bp of Ely[1] had not yᵉ good effect

<hr />

[1] John Moore, 1707—14.

you & I expected for he gave me all ye trouble he possibly could, put off my business from day to day and at last sent me to Dr Clark in order to baulk me of ye fellowship; I have forgiven him, but I have resolved never to have any thing to do wth him if I can avoid it. All ye fellows blame and are vexed at him heartily and I beleive respect me the more for coming of so well, and I dou't doubt but I shall live very comfortably & happily among y^m. ye Master likewise takes more than ordinary notice of me & has promised to direct me in my Studies & is every way as kind as I can desire. My humble services to your good Lady & Daughters, I wish you all a happy new year & am

Your respectfull humb
Servant
W RENEU

31 Decr. 1710
Mr Grigg gives his humble
service to you.

22.] Ibid. III. part iii. n° 432.

Endorsed 'Aug. 1711
Mr Wm Reneu from Cambr
Congratulation.
His intent of taking Orders
A Living to be held wth his
Fellowship.'

To the rev^d Mr J^no Strype
Minister of Low=Leyton
in Essex
present
2 D . C.

Hon^d Sir,
  'Twas with y^e greatest reluctance I left London without taking my leave of you, but my Journey was so sudden that I could not pay my respects to half my freinds, so y^t I hope you wont take it ill.
  I most heartily congratulate you upon y^r institution into y^r new living, I'll assure you Sir it was one of ye most agreeable peices of news I met with all ye while I was in town; long may you live to enjoy it, blest with health and all ye comforts this world can afford. Mr Grigg gives his humble service to you and joins in ye same wish. I am now returned to College in much better health than I left it, and am in hopes nothing will prevent me of half a years hard study to prepare for holy orders, there's a small College Living will be void about y^t time, & I beleive 'twill fall to my share if I'm capable of it, and for y^t reason I shall put on a Cassock ye sooner the value of it is just 20 per an̄m, it is three

miles distant from cambridge and a place where there are no Criticks so y^t a young man need not be much concerned tho' his sermons are not extraordinary, and may emprove his preaching faculty there better than any where else where there's a more awfull assembly. You see, I take ye freedom to acquaint you with all my designs, as thinking I shall hardly prosper in y^m unless you approve of y^m. My humble service to y^r good lady and Daughters—I am

H^d Sr Your most respectfull humb.

Servant

Wm Reneu.

Aug: 3. 1711.

23.]   MS. Add^s. IV. (i.) 40.

A letter from W. Reneu to Strype dated March 12 1711—12, condoling with Strype on his own severe illness and the sudden death of his eldest daughter.

24.]   Ibid. IV. (i.) 60.

A letter from Reneu to Strype 'Dear and ever honoured freind & ffather,' dated Jes. Coll Cambridge Octr 28 : 1712. advising Strype to take better care of his health on recovering from fever.

'I have got two pieces of preferment since I saw you viz: Steward of ye College & Taxor of ye university. A College living likewise of 20 per Añn ^{lb} staies for me.'

The next seven letters have been kindly communicated to me by the Rev. H. Gladwin Jebb, rector of Chetwynd. They give a vivid picture of Cambridge undergraduate life in 1739—46.

25.]   Thomas Goodwin [B.A. 1740, afterwards fellow of Trinity.]

For
Mr Samuel Jebb
at Mr Jebb's
in Chesterfield
Derbyshire
by Caxton
Bag.   Oct^{br} ye 7th 1739

Dear Jebb.   I have made bold to trouble you wth a Letter wch considering the friendship subsisting between us & the

News I shall impart I judg'd wou'd not be wholly unacceptable to you.

Yesterday came on the Election for fellowships when there were seven Vacancies & nine Candidates : one of yᵉ persons yᵗ were thrown out was Leigh¹, yᵉ Other you don't know—We have had here since you left College a very malignant Distemper of wᶜʰ have died two of Sᵗ John's whose names I have forgot, & of our own College Sharp in whose place is succeeded Wakefield², & a great many others have been dangerously ill but are recover'd—my self having far from enjoyed my health all the Summer—

There is a current Report at our Table wᶜʰ I am far from crediting & hope is groundless yᵗ you intend no more for College, your Uncle having wrote to Mʳ Wilson³ to cut out your Name— Mʳ Leigh is just recovered of a fit of Sickness but I believe not yᵉ Common one, who sends his service to you wᶜʰ is all at present worth communicating

from your affectionate friend & Servᵗ

Trin Coll. Camb: T. GOODWIN.

26.]   To the same from John Hinckesman⁴ of Queens'.

Cambridge Queen's [*sic*] College May 15ᵗʰ
1740

Dear Sʳ

I would not have neglected so long to write to you if I had not been at a Loss for something to fill up a Letter with, for I do assure you we have had very little news ever since I came up. This is yᵉ only reason why I have deferr'd writing so long, it is not because you have not answer'd my Last Letter, for be assur'd I stand upon Punctilio's as little as any man can do, which are (as you very Justly say) very pernicious & tend to yᵉ total Devastation of all Friendship & Correspondence.

I believe I have hitherto forgot to inform you yᵗ yᵉ Gownsmen & Townsmen quarrell'd & had a pretty good Battle, tho' not very long which begun in this manner. 2 of King's College were walking upon yᵉ Regent Walk one Sunday in yᵉ Dusk of yᵉ Evening and happened to meet with some of yᵉ sink of yᵉ Town (*for as you know very well⁵* none of yᵉ Tradesmen wou'd be guilty of so base an Action, it being as much as their Credit is worth) who had yᵉ impudence to oppose them, upon this a Great number of

---

¹ Timothy Lee, Trin. B.A. 1736; D.D. 1752.
² G. Wakefield, Trin. B.A. 1740.
³ J. Wilson (Trin. B.A. 1717 ; D.D. 1749) wrote Aug. 28, 1739 to John Jebb [B.A. Joh. 1725, *Chr., afterwards dean of Cashell] at Mansfield, to say that he would not cut his nephew young Samuel Jebb's name out of the boards in spite of his father Joshua Jebb's letter, but should wait till he saw him.
⁴ B.A. 1742.
⁵ The paper is torn and the words in *italics* are conjectural.

Gownsmen, who were in yᵉ Theatre Coffee House, rush'd out and drove yᵉ Pitiful Scrubs all round yᵉ Town; who when they saw that yᵉ Togatæ had yᵉ better of yᵉ Battle, run into Houses for Weapons and more assistance, and acted yᵉ parts of Cowards so much yᵗ they even fought with Spits & Fire Shovels.

The Vice Chancellor interpos'd and put an End to yᵉ Battle.

Lee although he promis'd so fair that he would pay me yᵉ money that he owes you in a short time; has never so much as mention'd it since. he & I have broke of Acquaintance long since & I don't know why, unless it be because I woud not lend him money, when he wanted it. he also has been yᵉ cause of Hurst[1] doing so too.

I hope now in a Month or 6 Weeks time I shall be at my desir'd Haven, & enjoy your pleasant Company; which will afford me no small delight.

I am your sincere Friend & Humble Servant

J. Hinckesman.

P.S. Be pleas'd to give my Service to all your good Family; & to all Enquiring Friends. & should take it as a Favour if you wou'd give my Humble Service to Mʳ Burrow[2] & all yᵉ Family[3]...

27.] J. Hinckesman 'to Mʳ Samuel Jebb
       at Chesterfield in Derbyshire.
       Per Caxton Bag.'

Cambridge Queen's College
May 9. 1741.

Dear Sʳ

I receiv'd yours of 22 of last month; and am fully convinc'd that your not writing to me was wholly owing to your long hurry of Business; and that you are very excusable upon this account.—I was very much amused with yᵉ Sketch that you gave me of your London Journey, and shoud have been very glad if you cou'd have so contrived as to have come down by Cambridge; assuring your self that no one cou'd have met with a more welcome reception than you, my very worthy Friend.—but since it was not consistent with your Business to return this way home; I must still desire to enjoy your pleasant company, hoping that my longing desire in process of time will be in some measure gratified; Gratified did I say? how can I ever be satisfied with your engaging Company, your mellifluous Tongue good Nature, & all yᵉ aimiable Qualifications yᵗ adorn our Social Life.—which you are possessed of.—but 'tis time to proceed to Business.

I fancy you must with great reason think that I am very much to blame in not sending you your Life of Tully[4] before this time,

---

[1] Perhaps *Thomas Hurst*, a freshman at Trinity, Tim. Lee's and (lately) Sam. Jebb's college.

[2] Mr Burrow was Vicar of Chesterfield.

[3] Two or three words torn off.

[4] Middleton's; a new publication.

and that I do you a great deal of Injury in depriving you of both y͏ͤ Advantage & pleasure of this Admirable Composure; I confess I am to be blam'd about this affair, when I consider that I hinder you from perusing a Book worthy of Tully himself; but S͏ͬ, be pleas'd to pardon my neglect, assuring you that I have never had an opportunity of sending it to you; altho' M͏ͬ W. Burrow has been up twice since it was publish'd and is now up, he has never been so Civil as to let me know when he came up neither of these Times, nor has never sent to ask whether I had any thing to send into y͏ͤ Country; which I am much surpriz'd at.—The Books I have very safe, & have had them very neatly Bound by M͏ͬ Wilson's order.—Be pleas'd to give my Service to your Father and all y͏ͤ family, with a great many Thanks for my Bill.

We have no news or else shoud have been glad to have given you a hint.—I am, Sir, Y͏ͬͦ most sincerely

J. HINCKESMAN.

28.]   Thomas[1] [brother of John] Hinckesman

      To M͏ͬ Samuel Jebb
        At his Fathers house
By Caxton ⎰ In Chesterfield
  Bagg   ⎱ Derbyshire
               These.

Sir

    I hope These will find you, with the Rest of your family in good health and all our Friends in Chesterfield.—I intended to have wrote to you, before this time, But imagined you was scarce settled after youre Journey; and another Reason was, we have been sitting for Scholarships lately, and I have now the pleasure to acquaint you, that I am Elected Into that Number. There were thirteen of us satt it proved A general Election.—as To The Examination you know the Nature of it very well, and therefore shall say no more to that, But hope to talk that over with you in the Vacation, and then shall have an Opportunity of Thanking you for your kind assistance in Directing me to A College which in my Opinion Is preferable to all in the University.—My Bro͏ͭ is very well and Desires his Service To all your Family, but you in particular, and says he will answer for himself about not writing.

    As to what news we have stirring here I think there is not much lately; we have had A famous Consert In oure Halls perform'd by two singing women from London,—their Names were Chiara's very much liked by all that heard them, joined with several Instruments of Musick, which made it very agreeable. My Bro͏ͬ and I was at it, they performed three Nights in the University.—this is most of the News we have except a Fellow of Queens College is

¹ T. Hinckesman, Trin. A.B. 1745.

Dead of the Small Pox[1].—Mr Wilson is very well, and when I was at his Room and told him that you had taken a journey to London he said he hoped you would take Cambridge in your Return home, he shoud have been glad to see you here, and Desired his service to you.

By this time I have tired your patience,
Therefore in the Conclusion I am
Your very humble
in haste Servt, Thos, HINCKESMAN
Cambridge Trinity College
May the 6th 1742

PS) As to the night in which we are to have our Treats it is next Monday night, I Believe; we are to be swore in[2] to morrow.

I had the Two Bournes, Wood, & Heathcote[3], at my Room lately, and they were all very well.

29.]   John Hinckesman to Mr Samuel Jebb
at Chesterfield
in Derbyshire
p Caxton Bag.

Cambridge Queen's Coll: May 15.
1742.

Dear S.^r

I am very sorry to think that I have been ye Cause of so long & so profound a silence betwixt you and me; I cou'd not have thought that such a Trifle as this of writing first shou'd have prevail'd betwixt you and me; especially when I had so often in my former Letters acquainted you that I shoud always take ye opportunity of writing to you, when I had any thing that woud afford you pleasure in ye Perusal.

I own that I have committed a fault in not writing to you sooner, & that you have Just reason to give me the name of a very bad Correspondent, but S.^r if you will give yourself leave to consider how troublesome it is to a man to sit down to write a Letter when he has nothing of Novelty to entertain his Friend with; nothing that can afford ye least pleasure; I hope you will think me in some measure excusable, & put a better construction upon this Misdemeanour.—you may assure yourself if I cou'd have scrap'd together any tolerable Stock of Cambridge Occurrences to have furnish'd a Letter out withal I should not have been so long ye Delinquent.—but to proceed to Business.—

[1] Carew died 5 April, 1742. He was buried in the college chapel.
[2] Sc. *Jure discipulorum in fundat. Coll. Trin.*
[3] Laurence Bourne, Queens', B.A.

1744, fellow.
John Bourne, S. John's. B.A. 1745.
John Wood, S. John's, LL.B. 1747.
Ralph Heathcote, Jesus, B.A. 1744, D.D. 1760.

My Brother is now settled in College, & Likes College very well : he keeps in y⁰ first Court up one pair of Stairs in y⁰ Turret which is but one Stair Case from where you kept.— I fancy my Brother told you that he had had success, & about his proceedings in it. So that I need not dwell upon this.

We have had 3 very fine Consorts here, one of which was perform'd in your Hall ; which my Brother and I had the Curiosity to go and see, The vocal Musick perform'd by y⁰ Italians was really exquisitely fine, & sung with a great deal of Humour & Judgement ; y⁰ Instrumental Likewise was prodigiously entertaining : in short it was a continued Scene of Mirth & Gaiety.—they found such Great Encouragement that they wou'd very gladly have perform'd a fourth time if they cqu'd have got Leave from y⁰ Vice=Chancellor.—they stay'd here so long after their performance & was so much caressed by y⁰ Gownsmen, that y⁰ Proctor's intended to have visited them, if they had not Just gone of in nick of Time.

I am very sorry to hear that you are likely to be depriv'd of your Bosom Favourite B. B. you know whom I mean, but hope that you are a man of so much resolution, that you can bear up against these strong byasses, & not suffer yourself to be overturn'd by y⁰ wheel of Fortune.—I hear that 'twill certainly be a match betwixt her & Mʳ Watts, and likewise 'tis Just upon y⁰ Point.— I have wrote to my mother by this Post to desire your Father to draw a 14̶ Bill, which I shou'd be glad if you woud hasten him in ; Be pleas'd to pay my Compliments to him & all y⁰ Family.— I saw Mʳ Goodwin of your Coll: the other Day he has been in Coll: about a Fortnight. I am your

very Humble Servant
in haste)   J. HINCKESMAN.

Mʳ Wilson desires his Service to you.

30.] John Hinckesman
     To
          Mʳ Samuel Jebb
             at Chesterfield
By London   in Derbyshire.

Westcammel Novʳ 5ᵗʰ 1745.

Dear Friend Jebb
              I humbly beg your pardon for not writing to you before this time, but I hope, you will think me somewhat excusable when you know the true reason of it.

I have been pretty much taken up since I came here in making preparation for Priest Orders, which I took at Michaelmas, and the more so, because not only the Bishop but the Dean and Chapter examine the Candidates at Wells.

This made me take some pains in Qualifying myself for such an examination.

Perhaps it may not be disagreeable to give you a hint of the method they have here.

The Bishop upon one of the days examines all the young Gentlemen privately himself; and then y⁰ next day following the Dean & Chapter come to y⁰ Palace and they examine all the Candidates before the Bishop one by one.

A Little Digression may not be improper.

The Country hereabouts is very fertile and abounds with Wood, the chief of it is Elm ; you wou'd be a Little surpris'd to see what Quantities we have of it here, every Close is full of it.

We have very fine Prospects here, they are so extensive that in some parts you may (upon y⁰ hills especially) command 30 or 40 miles about ; which makes it very agreeable upon a fine clear day, to take a view.

You may imagine that the Prospect in some parts of the County must be a good deal obstructed by reason of y⁰ high & Lofty Elms.

I should be glad to employ my Pen longer did not the Solemnity of the day call upon me to commemorate the invaluable blessing, the miraculous Deliverance, and the wonderfull Discovery of the horrid & barbarous Conspiracy against our Prince, our Peace, and our Religion ; which was fully design'd by them to be put in actual execution.

Be pleas'd to pay my Compliments to your Father Mrs Jebb & all the Family.

Pray be so good as to pay my Best Respects to Mr Wall and tell him I received his Letter the other day. remember me to Mr Smith. I desire you will write soon. May every good & Loyal Subject most devoutly & thankfully acknowledge the happy deliverances of this day, and may we all unite in blessing & praising God for his peculiar mercies as upon this day shew'd to us, his Unworthy Creatures. May we all (duly affected with their malicious intentions as upon this day) unite in defending Our King & our Country against the violent Attempts, the daring insults, the bloody plots & contrivances that now hover over us. in great haste.

I am dear Jebb your very sincere Friend

JOHN HINCKESMAN.

31.]   Thomas Hinckesman
    To
        Mr Saml Jebb
            In Chesterfield
By Caxton ⎰ Derbyshire
    Bagg ⎱

Dear Sr
            The impertinence of this I am inclined to think yr good nature will excuse.

I have often thought of enquiring after your Welfare in this form but knowing your diligence in business was loathe to Intrude unseasonably, & shoud this Occasion any let or hindrance I shoud be sorry.

If a small portion of time coud be spared from a thing so commendable as Industry a little intelligence from Chesterfield woud be Acknowledged as a great Favour.

You may reasonably expect I shoud relate some News as we have the papers every day from London. The chief news we have is the daily Accounts of ye Rebels dispersing very much & that the Pretender has but a small number with him at present.

In looking over my Memorandm^s I found I was entrusted with your Subscription to Dr Parns[1] Sermons wch I am sorry I have not had it in my power to Execute as yet, the D^r has not published his sermons nor can I hear w^n they will be printed off. Upon Enquiry I was told the reason why he did not print them was because The D^r coud not get such paper as he liked. There is a good number of Subscribers that are thus disappointed.

> My Complim^{ts} wait upon Mr Jebb &c. & then give me leave to say I am y^r most Obed^t
>
> T. HINCKESMAN
> Cambridge Trin: Coll:
> March ye 4th 1745—6.

P S.
Please to give my
due respects to our
Family when you
have an opportunity

LETTERS and other remains of W. GOOCH, of Gonville and Caius College, extracted[2] from a MS. volume in the University Library, 1786—91.

WILLIAM GOOCH of Caius was the second wrangler and second Smith's prizeman in 1791, W. Lax, *Trin.* and T. Newton, *Joh.* being moderators, Peacock, *Trin.* senior wrangler, Cross, *Pemb.* third[3].

[1] Andrew Pern, Peterhouse, B.A. 1728, D.D. 1739.

[2] The publication of the remainder of the volume would I think be a pleasing task to any one who is interested in eighteenth century travels and voyages.

[3] W. Gray, *Pet.*
Ro. Hankinson, *Trin.* } aegrotats in the first class.
T. Wingfield, *Joh.*

T. Causton, *Joh.*
W. Heath Marsh, *Corpus.*
T. Bewicke, *Jes.*
Jos. Gill, *Joh.* } Proctor's honorary optimes.

In the University Calendar Gooch is described as 'Astronomer in a Voyage of Discovery, and murdered by the natives of Owyhee[1].'

The Cambridge University Library contains a volume[2] [Mm. 6. 48.] of his letters and correspondence of his friends from which the following are selected.

Alderman C. Nichols of Yarmouth, J.P., who had been his 'chum' at school, observes that W. Gooch had an advantage for his academical career in having been educated under Tilney at Harleston, which had sent up to Cambridge two senior wranglers, *S. Vince* (1775) and *T. Brinkley* (1788), who were both resident at Caius in his time, the one being Plumian Professor and the other a tutor.

The following account is interesting in itself.

Receiv'd	£.	s.	d.
Scholarship to Lady 87	4	9	6
Lady Middleton's Bounty[3]	20	0	0
Sr. Jn. Berney's Do.	5	5	0
Scholarship to Mich. 87	4	13	2
Total Income	34	7	8
Total expenses	28	9	1
Ballance due to Mr Gooch	5	18	7

[Endorsed
'Copy of my Bill
at College
to Xmas 1787.']

Mr Gooch's Account to Christmas 1787	£.	s.	d.
Commons	3	4	7
Cook	1	1	3
Butler	0	14	6
Bookseller	0	7	6
Draper	2	8	6
Grocer	1	18	10
Ironmonger	0	8	3
Taylor	0	19	0
Joyner	6	2	0
Bedmaker	0	7	6
Cobler	0	4	0
Coals	1	13	3
Cash	2	2	0
	21	11	2
Admission Fees	0	14	1
Do Mich. 86	0	10	6
Do Xtmas 86	0	7	9
Do Lady. 87	0	14	0
Do Midsr. 87	0	9	9
Sundrys	0	8	1
Fire Irons	0	6	6
Kittle	0	3	0
Mich. 87	0	14	9
Laundress	0	14	6
Feather Bed	1	15	0
	28	9	1

[1] The particular island was called *Woahoo*, near Hawaii.

[2] Purchased at Dawson Turner's sale, 1859.

[3] In this Vol. of MS. are preserved Letters of thanks to lady *Middleton* 10 Dec. 1786 (with a copy in Greek character for his own edification) and to *E. Mundy* Esqre, M.P. Derby, 5 Nov. 1790.

32.] W. Gooch to his Parents at Brockdish
Harleston, Norfolk.

Nov. 6. [17]90
Cambridge

H^d Parents

I'm surpris'd I didn't mention the Hare, I know I intended it,
& to have requested you to return my thanks to Mr Pitts for it, as
I saw it came from his by the Direction—I gave it to Brinkley—
I'm sorry Mother you should make yourself at all uneasy about a
Malady of which I was almost recover'd when I wrote last, & as
I didn't feel my Health affected I'm vex'd with myself for mentioning it. However it is now entirely gone off, & certainly was never
owing to any great exertion, as I don't practice any such violent
exercise as you seem to imagine—Peacock kept a very capital Act
indeed and had a very splendid Honor of which I can't remember
a Quarter, however among a great many other things, Lax told him
that " Abstruse and difficult as his Questions were, no Argument
(however well constructed) could be brought against any Part of
them, so as to baffle his inimitable Discerning & keen Penetration[1]
&c. &c. &c.—However the Truth was that he confuted all the
Arguments but *one* which was the 1st Opponent's 2nd Argument,—
Lax lent him his assistance too, yet still he didn't see it, which I
was much surpris'd at as it seem'd easier than the Majority of the
rest of the Arg^s—Peacock with the Opponents return'd from the
Schools to my Room to tea, when (agreeable to his usual ingenuous
Manner) he mention'd his being in the Mud about Wingfield's 2nd
argument, & requested Wingfield to read it to him again & *then* upon
a little consideration he gave a very ample answer to it.—I was
third opponent only and came off with " *optime quidem disputasti*[2]"
i.e. " you've disputed excellently indeed " (quite as much as is ever
given to a third opponency)—I've a first opponency for Novr 11th under
Newton against Wingfield & a second opponency for Novr 19th under
Lax against Gray of Peter-House. Peacock is Gray's first opponent
& Wingfield his third, so master Gray is likely to be pretty well
baited. His third Question (of all things in the world) is to defend
Berkley's immaterial System.

Mrs Hankinson & Miss Paget of Lynn are now at Cambridge,
I drank tea & supp'd with them on Thursday at Mr Smithson's (the
Cook's of St Johns Coll.) & yesterday I din'd drank tea and supp'd
there again with the same Party, and to day I'm going to meet
them at Dinner at Mr Hall's of Camb. Hankinson of Trin. (as you
may suppose) have been there too always when I have been there ;
as also Smithson of Emmanuel Coll. (son of this Mr Smithson).
Miss Smithson[3] is a very accomplished girl, & a great deal of

---

[1] See above, p. 38. Gunning mentions *Reminisc.* I. iii. that Lax offended
ex-moderators &c. by lengthening the
disputations and giving high-flown
compliments.

[2] See above, p. 38.

[3] When he left England W. Gooch
not only wrote to Miss Smithson,
whom he called ' Goody Two-Shoes,'
but provided that his parents in his

unaffected Modesty connected with as much Delicacy makes her very engaging.—She talks French, and plays well on the Harpsichord. Mrs H. will continue in Camb. but for a day or two longer or I should reckon this a considerable Breach upon my Time ;—However I never can settle well to any thing but my Exercises when I have any upon my Hands, and I'm sure I don't know what purpose 'twould answer to fagg *much* at my Opponencies, as I doubt whether I should keep *at all* the better or the worse they being upon subjects I've long been pretty well acquainted with.—Yet I'm resolv'd when I've kept my first Opponency next thursday *if possible* to think nothing of my 2nd (for friday se'nnight) till within a day or two of the time—One good thing is I can now have no more, so I've the luck to be free from the schools betimes, for the term doesn't end till the middle of Dec^r.—The only thing that remains to be determined about my having Beevor of Ben'et (Nephew of Sr Thomas, as I think I told you) is whether he comes to my Room an Hour in the day or I go to his : for I understand by Chapman of Ben'et that he expects me (contrary to all custom) to go to his, but he's mistaken : every Body would then expect the same or have reason to be affronted, and so I should be dancing about the Town every day after my pupils, (as a french or Music-Master does for 3 guineas a Quarter) you would certainly blame me to submit to this I don't doubt.—I mention'd it to Brinkley who is perfectly of my opinion.— I expect one pupil from St Johns already (which is a very likely college to afford me more)—I've written a Letter of Thanks to Mr Mundy & inclosed the Copy.—I know nothing more to say this time but that I am

Your ever dutiful Son

WILL^M GOOCH.

O,—I haven't look'd among my shirts yet—well, will you excuse that for a few days.—I haven't told you neither that Smithson of Emmanuel & I entertain'd the Ladies last night with fire-works.

Adieu.

33.] The following letter is a journal scribbled with tired fingers between the hours of examination early in 1791.

' *Monday* $\frac{1}{4}$ aft. 12.

We have been examin'd this Morning in pure Mathematics & I've hitherto kept just about even with Peacock which is much more than I expected. We are going at 1 o'clock to be examin'd till 3 in Philosophy.

' From 1 till 7 I did more than Peacock ; But who did most at Moderator's Rooms this Evening from 7 till 9, I don't know yet ;—

absence should keep her and her parents supplied with letters in regu- lar rotation, one on her 20th Birth-day, 1st Oct. 1792,

but I did above three times as much as the Senr Wrangler last year, yet I'm afraid not so much as Peacock.

Between One & three o'Clock I wrote up 9 sheets of Scribbling Paper so you may suppose I was pretty fully employ'd.

' *Tuesday Night.*

I've been shamefully us'd by Lax to-day ;—Tho' his anxiety for Peacock must (of course) be very great, I never suspected that his Partially (sic) w^d get the better of his Justice. I had entertain'd too high an opinion of him to suppose it.—he gave Peacock a long private Examination & then came to me (I hop'd) on the same subject, but 'twas only to *Bully* me as much as he could,—whatever I said (tho' right) he tried to convert into Nonsense by seeming to misunderstand me. However I don't entirely dispair of being first, tho' you see Lax seems .determin'd that I shall not.—I had no Idea (before I went into the Senate-House) of being able to contend at all with Peacock.

Wednesday evening.

Peacock & I are still in perfect Equilibrio & the Examiners themselves can give no guess yet who is likely to be first ;—a New Examiner (Wood of St. John's, who is reckon'd the first Mathematician in the University, for Waring doesn't reside) was call'd solely to examine Peacock & me only[1].—but by this new Plan nothing is yet determin'd.—So Wood is to examine us again to-morrow morning.

Thursday evening.

Peacock is declar'd first & I second,—Smith of this Coll. is either 8th or 9th & Lucas is either 10th or 11th.—Poor Quiz Carver is one of the οἱ πολλοι ;—I'm perfectly *satisfied* that the Senior Wranglership is Peacock's due, but *certainly* not so very indisputably as Lax pleases to represent it—I understand that *he* asserts 'twas 5 to 4 in Peacock's favor. Now Peacock & I have explain'd to each other how we went on, & can *prove indisputably* that it wasn't 20 to 19 in his favor ;—I *cannot* therefore be displeas'd for being plac'd second, tho' I'm provov'd (sic) with Lax for his false report (so much beneath the Character of a Gentleman.)—

N.B. it is my very *particular Request* that you dont mention Lax's behaviour to me to any one.

Friday Morning $\frac{1}{2}$ aft. 12.

Brinkley has now been to us (all this Coll. have been supping together & are not yet dispers'd—we're supping in Lucas' Rooms.—) to shew us the Tripus which is as beneath[2]—

---

[1] See above, p. 55.
[2] This is printed exactly as in the Camb. Univ. Calendars except that the names Walker, Trollope, Oakes, Foster, Young (bis) Rogers and Westerman are spelt by Gooch Walpul,

324   UNIVERSITY STUDIES.

[The following inscription, treasured doubtless by Gooch's friends, shews how this *college* then encouraged her sons to distinguish themselves in the *university* contests. Cf. pp. 30, 47, 48.]

In
Scholis Philosophicis
Optime inter suos Caienses respondenti
D. D.
Franciscus Schuldham M.D.
Collegii Gonv. & Caii Socius.
Premium meruit
Gulielmus Gooch
A.D. 1791.

34.]   [Caius Coll. 1791.]

Hon^d. Parents

I arriv'd at Ixworth at 10 o'clock yesterday morning, left Ixworth at 11, arriv'd at Kennett by 1, left Kennett at 2 and arriv'd at Camb. at a little more than a Quarter past 4.

I left the Mare (quite cool) at Prior's (Jesus Lane), and in my way to Caius call'd at Mr Smithson's to see his son (of Emm.) who is indispos'd with a swelling in his side, which they cannot yet bring to a head.—Professor Harwood attends him.—I stopt there but a Minute, on account of one of my Breeches knees being wetted with a misty Rain which lasted almost all the way from Kennett—so I came home and chang'd them and then went back to Smithson's to Tea agreeable to an Invitation they gave me when I first call'd.—After Tea Smithson Junr and I play'd at Cribbage, nor could I get away by fair means till after supper; so you may guess what havock a Man off a long journey made among the Dainties of a Cook's Table[1]. This morning Heming of St John's breakfasted with me and I read with him an hour, after which I wrote the inclosed letter to Barmby.— After Commons I arranged my Linen which came Last Night, and then spoke to Beevor of Ben'et about Reading[2], he propos'd beginning tomorrow, but I insisted on reading an hour with him this Evening, and so I did from 7 to 8. So tomorrow we are to begin to read regularly from 12 to 1;—I drank Tea this afternoon with Heming when we agreed to have the hour from $\frac{1}{2}$ aft. 10 till $\frac{1}{2}$ aft. 11.—I've likewise seen Gingel[3], who will begin tomorrow to read French with me (from 4 till 5 in the afternoon).—I went to Chapel to-night and sat in the Bachelors' Seat for the first time, immediately after Chapel I call'd on Mr Belward, deliver'd M^r M's Letter and bled him for a couple of guineas.—Hankinson went up to London (to meet his Father there) the Night before I came. Peacock doesn't return till Octr. no more does Hankinson.

Trollop, Oaks, Forster, Younge (bis) Roger and Waterman. Pelham has the 'M^r' before his name and 'Marsh Bene't' is inserted as 10th jun. opt. above Churton. (The names of the colleges of course are not given exactly according to the uniform style of our Calendar).

[1] See above, p. 321.
[2] See above, p. 322.
[3] Possibly Ginkell a son of the marquis of Athlone. The 5th son took his degree (A.M.) at Trin. in 1804.

I haven't call'd at Pleasance's yet to speak to Miss E. but intend doing it tomorrow Morning.—I'm now going to sup with Hepworth where I shall meet Chapman of this Coll. & Tylney. Chapman[1] has an Act on his Hands for next Friday.—He will be a very high Man next Year.

You'll be good as to forward the inclos'd letter to Yarmouth immediately.—Present my respects to all Friends, and believe me

your ever dutiful son

W. GOOCH.

[A month or two after he had taken his B.A. degree Gooch was contemplating and making arrangements for the political and scientific expedition from which he never returned.]

35.]   W. Gooch to his father
        Mr Gooch, Brockdish, Harleston, Norfolk

Hon^d Parents

I've nothing particular to write about, but being o' th' Mind to write something I'm set down to it (as you see) tho' I can't find a clean sheet of Paper to write upon[2]. Perhaps you'll like to know what Instruments[3] I'm to take abroad so I'll give you a copy of the Catalogue (they are most of them the same that went with Captn Cooke).

1. An Astronomical Clock.
2. A Journeyman Clock.
3. An Alarm Clock.
4. A Good Watch wth Second Hand.
5. An Achromatic Telescope of 46 in. Focus wth a divided Object Glass Micrometer.
6. A Reflecting Telescope.
7. A Verticle Circle with an Azimuth-circle, for taking altitudes and Azimuths.
8. A Transit Instrument of 4 Feet with a Level and upright wooden Posts.
9. A Marine Dipping needle.
10. A small Pocket compass.
11. A Set of Magnetic Bars to change the Poles of the dipping needle.
12. A Burton's Theodolite with stand.
13. A Hadley's Sextant by Dollond.
14. Another by Troughton.
15. Two large Thermometers.
16. Two Thermometers with wooden scales by Ramsden.
17. A portable Barometer by Burton.
18. A Bason to hold Quicksilver with Glass Roof.
19. Quicksilver in a Bottle.
20. A Night Telescope.
21. A Steel Gunter's Chain.
22. A Knight Azimuth Compass by Adams.
23. A Portable Tent Observatory.

besides Books[4].

[1] Cp. p. 34. Benedict Chapman was 6th wrangler in 1792, and afterwards tutor of Caius, and master (1839—52).

[2] The paper was covered with astronomical diagrams and a calculation of readings of a thermometer, observations &c. taken 1774, July 22nd Obs. mer. zen. Dist. ☾ L. L. 69°: 20′. 8″.

[3] Cp. another list on p. 245.

[4] The following books left behind him at Cambridge were sold by auction at the White Bear Inn on Saturday Nov. 23rd, 1793.

Homeri Odyssaea, 2 vol. Kent's Lucian. 18s.

Burton Trag. Select. Johnson's Sophocles. 9s.

Virgil Lug. Bat. 1666. Florus Var. 7s. 6d.

Allen's Demosthenes, 2 vols. Milne's

326 UNIVERSITY STUDIES.

I shall set off for Camb. on Monday Morning and be admitted in the Afternoon. I shall leave Greenw^h. on Sunday.—I have to talk to you in a Letter soon about you coming to see me at Camb. for I must pass the *major* part of the Time I have to be in England *there*, on account of its being necessary for me to read French and Spanish— I've been thinking that if the ship were she [to] be appointed *immediately* as it will take 3 months [to] Man and Victual her you could come to Camb. ab^t a month hence, & about a month after your return I could come to you and stay a month with you.—What say you? Don't hear a word tho' of M^r K's coming.—I should like to hear what you think of this Plan as soon as you can write.—(Direct to CAMB. tho.')

From y^r dear Boy

BILLY.

P.S. I want you to promise (Father) to let me give you a lecture every day regularly on Popular Astronomy, when I come home.— Nothing is more easy to comprehend, and I'm convinc'd you'll think it entertaining after the first two or three Lectures.—You will then know what I'm about when abroad, and will have a clear Idea (from the Lat^s. and Long^s. of the Places) how we reckon time, &c.(for in every diff. Longitude the time of noon is different) and a hundred other little things which you would like to know, you w^d. then be able to find out.

36.]   Mr Gooch by favor of the Revd Mr Etheridge.

Hon^d Parents

Mr Etheridge being in Cambridge I shall take an opportunity of conveying a Letter to you by him and inclose one of Vince's to his Brother.—You may probably have seen in the Papers that old Mr Salter is dead, so that there is a Caius living and therefore another fellowship vacant. Tis suppos'd that North[1] (the sen^r fellow) will refuse it and choose to remain a fellow all his Life, and that Belward will wait for the Mastership; if so, Buck the third in the seniority will take it—Tis one of the best (being about £600 per Ann.) I'm

Conic Sections, Cockman's Tully's Offices. 7s.
Tooly Cic. de Officiis. Rollin's Quintilian. 5s. 6d.
Cole's Dictionary, Locke on Human Underst. 8s.
Simpson's Geometry, Emerson's Mechanics. 5s. 6d.
Cotes' Lectures, Simpson's Fluctions. 11s.
Whiston's Euclid, Parkinson's Mechanics, Hellin's Mathematical Essays. 11s. 6d.
Mayer's Lunar Theory, 5 small Astron. tracts by Maskelyne. 3s.
Vince's Precession of Equinoxes, Excerpta a Newtono. 3s.
Encyclopaedia Britannica, 15 half vol. 6li. 5s.
Duty 6s. 3d. *Commission* 16s.
[1] J. North took the rectory of Ashdon, Essex. He died in 1818.

now reading Spanish agreeable to Dr Maskelyne's Wish with Mr Isola who is himself an Italian, but is reckon'd an excellent Spanish Master as well as an Italian Master;—(There isn't a Spaniard in Camb.)—I'm about to begin Don Quixote in the Original.—While on Ship Board I shall want some study for amusement and that I may have[1] a Variety, I'll take Latin, Greek, French, Spanish, and Italian Books, that I may be improving myself in the Classical way or getting a Knowledge of the most useful modern Languages according as I find myself o' th' mind.—I'm going to Greenwich again tomorrow fourtnight and expect to be appointed tomorrow three weeks, Mr E. is now about leaving Camb. so that I must conclude immediately.

Y^r dutiful Son, W. GOOCH.

. . . The names of the Board of Longitude

Kepple	J. Smith (Mast^r of Caius)
C. W. Cornwall	E. Waring (Magd. Coll.)
T. Frankland	A. Shepherd[2] (another who examin'd who ex-
Rodney	amin'd Peacock and me).
J. Young	J. Marriott
R. Harland	T. Orde
Howe	G. Rose
Jos. Banks	P. Stephens
N. Maskelyne	C. Middleton
T. Hornsby	J. Smith.

I believe my chief Business will be to assign the Bounds of the English territories in South America.

The Ships...the *Discovery* sloop of war, Capt. Vancouver, and the *Chatham*, Lieut. Broughton.

Gooch himself followed in the *Daedalus*, Capt. New; 6 guns and 6 swivels, 30 hands in all. Gooch's salary (he continues) is to be 400 a year, which may be nearly doubled by selling to the Chinese the furs which he will get from the natives in exchange for large sheath-knives, small axes, copper saucepans, kettles, &c., spike-nails, beads, &c. He has a present of 1 doz. bottles of preserved gooseberries, and will take a medicine chest.

In a letter from the Downs near Deal, 31 July 1791, he gives an Inventory of his outfit.

I. *Contents of the Upper Drawer in Bed Room.*

1. A Roof Machine.
2. Quicksilver.
3. Three coloured Wedges.
4. Two Thermometers.
5. A set of Magnetic Bars.
6. Two Bottles of Powder'd Bark.
7. A Map of the World.
8. A small Inkstand.
9. A Cribbage Board.
10. Peppermint Drops.
11. Two spare centers and Punches for Dipping Needle.
12. A gross of Cottons for Lamp.
13. Some small wax Candles.
14. Epsom Salts.
15. Calcin'd Magnesia.
16. Two large screw drivers.

---

[1] fagg at (*in an erasure*).

[2] Dr Shepherd (see *Index*) was now Plumian Prof.; he was F.R.S. and Master of Mechanics to the king. His portrait is in Univ. Lib. Cole, MS. 26, 120, 208.

17. A Paper of Ink Powder.
18. A Tortoise shell box with a few beads in it.
19. Hair Powder and Pomatum.
20. Two Ink Cakes.
21. A Box of Wafers.
22. Three steel writing Pens and one steel ruling Pen.
23. A Glass Pestle and Mortar.
24. An Artificial Horizon and Spirit Level.

II.   *Contents of Middle Drawer in Bed-room.*

1. 26½ quires of Paper.
2. Two Pounds of Tea.
3. Four fishing Leads.
4. Ten sticks of sealing wax.
5. Shade for Lamp.
6. Instructions, &c.
7. A case of Drawing Instruments.
8. A small Brush.
9. Elliott's*Medical Pocket-Book*with written instructions *per* Mr Rideout.
10. Ten Pieces of Sponge.
11. *Doctrine of Eclipses.*
12. *Astronomy of Comets.*
13. Sutton's *duodecimal Mensuration.*
14. Hellin's *Mathematical Essays.*
15. Maskelyne's Paper *on the Diff. Refrangibility of Light.*
16. Maskelyne's *Rules for Ref. & Par.*
17. Maskelyne's *Remarks on ye Equa. of Time.*
18. Dollond's *Improvement of Refracting Telescopes.*
19. Toaldi *de Methodo Longitudinum ex observato Lunae transitu per meridianum.*
20. Waring,   *Form of the Lunar Method.*
21. Maskelyne's *Folio Tables.*
22. Vince *on the Succession of the Equinoxes.*
23. Essay *on the most Commodious method of Marine Surveying.*
24. *An Account of the prismatic Micrometer.*
25. Mayer's *Theory of the Moon.*
26. A Parcel of Glass Beads.

III.   *Contents of the lower Drawer.*

63 Quire of Paper.

IIII.   *Contents of the Upper Shelf in the Closet.*

1. Schrivellis [sic] *Greek Lexicon.*
2. Homer's *Iliad,* 2 vol.
3. Sherlock *Sermons,* 4 vol.

4. Simpson's *Fluxions,* 2 vol.
5. Ainsworth's *Dictionary.*
6. Cotes' *Lectures.*
7. *Requisite Tables,* 3 copies.
8. *Old Requisite Tables.*
9. Robertson's *Navigation.*
10. Clerke's [sic] *Attributes.*
11. Hutton's *Mathematical Tables.*
12. Buchan's *Domestic Medicine.*
13. Delphino's *Spanish Grammar,* 12mo.
14. *History of Spanish America,* 12mo.
15. *Don Quixote* in Spanish, 3 vol. 4to.
16. *Don Quichotte* (French) 6 vol. 12mo.
17. *Telemaque,* 12mo.
18. Baretti's *Spanish Dict^y.* folio.
19. Medicine Chest.
20. Dressing Box.

V.   *Contents of the Second shelf in the Closet.*

1. Seven Vol^s. of *Longitudes,* 4to.
2. *Don Chiciotte* (Italian) 2 vols., 12mo.
3. *Eton Latin Grammar,* 12mo.
4. *Don Quixote* English 4 vol. 12mo.
5. *General Tables for the Moon's Distance from the Sun and 10 Stars.* Folio.
6. *Devil on Sticks,* 12mo.
7. Keill's *Astronomy.*
8. Bottarelli's *Dictionary* Eng. Fr. Ital. 3 vol. 16to.
9. Harwood's *Greek Testament,* 2 vol. 12mo.
10. The *Nautical Almanacks* for 1769, '73, '74, '91—96, 12mo.
11. *Telemachus,* 2 vol. 12mo.
12. De Moivre's *Miscel. Anal.* 4to.
13. Parkinson's *Mechanics,* 4to.
14. *Latitudes from Mer. Alts.* 4to.
15. Wyld's *Practical Surveyor.*
16. Gardiner's *Logarithms.*
17. Greek Grammar, 12mo.
18. *Graecae Sententiae,* 12mo.
19. Gardiner's *Practical Surveying,* 12mo.

VI.   *Contents of the third Shelf in the Closet.*

1. *Tables of Refraction and Parallax,* 4to.
2. Guthrie's *Geography,* 4to.
3. Taylor's *Tables,* 4to.
4. Mayer & Mason's *Tables,* 4to.
5. Vince's *Practical Astronomy,* 4to.
6. Mackenzie's *Maritime Surveying,* 4to.

7. Green's *Astronomical Observa-tions*, 4to.
8. Wales' *Astronomical Observations*, 4to.
9. Two blank Journals, Folio.
10. Bode's *Celestial Charts*, Folio.
11. Six Quire of Paper.
12. Chambaud's *French Grammar,* 12mo.
13. Bayly's *Astron. Observations*, 4to.
14. Taylor's *Logarithms*, 4to.
15. Two small Blank Books.
16. Martin's *Mariner's Guide.*
17. *Seaman's Daily Assistant*, 4to.
18. Nelson's *Practice of True Devotion*, 12mo.
19. *Requisite Tables*, 8vo.
20. *Court Register* for 1789, 12mo.
21. *Common Prayer Book*, 12mo.
22. Do. in Greek, 12mo.
23. *Diable Boiteux*, 2 vol. 24to.
24. *Nat. Sines Tang'. & Sec'.* 24to.
25. A Clothes Brush.
26. Gunter's Scale.
27. A Pocket Compass.

VII. Contents of the fourth shelf of the Closet.

1. Three Loaves of Sugar.
2. 14lb. Moist Sugar.
3. A Powder Flask.
4. Spirits of Wine.
5. Two Balls of Cord.
6. Two Brace of Pistols with moulds for Bullets.
7. A Mould for Musquet Bullets.
8. A Tea Pot.
9. A Gunter's Chain.

10. A Bagonet.
11. A Lanthorn.
N.B. More things to be put in.

VIII. Contents of the Shelf over the Drawers in the Bed Room.

1. Part of the *Preface* to Taylor's *Logarithms* with Log^a. of Numbers, 4to.
2. Guthrie's *Plates*, folio.
3. A Station Pointer.
4. A Circular Protractor.
5. A Variation Chart.
6. A Miniature Picture.

IX. Contents of the Shelf over the Table.

1. Two Hangers.
2. An Umbrella.
3. A Shark Line.
4. Two Cod Lines.
5. A Walking stick.

Other articles...stow'd away at Portsmouth.

A Slate, Slate Pencils, Table Cloth, Trunks, Books, Candlesticks, Red Ink, Razor Strap, Hand Brush, Fungus, Drawing Books, Cards, Stool, Extinguisher. A Box for Wash Ball or Soap, Beads, Screws, Spermaceti Oil, Snuffers and Snuf Dish, Wafers, Wire Shirt Buttons, Metal Buttons, Moulds, Cartharge Paper, Blankets (for Trade at Nootka), Decanters, Beakers and wine glasses, Cloak Bag, Iron and Brass Wire.

There remain in the volume, still un-published, so far as I am aware, a few other letters written before his departure, his letters and journals (from Rio Janeiro) on board the *Daedalus,* plan of S. Iago harbour (Port Praya), a few characteristic sketches and engravings sent home, letters from his father to the Smithsons, their dreams [1] after his death, his will, and a mass of correspondence from Greenwich about his pay, testimonials, &c. A letter from his father to Rev. Ri. Belward thanking the authorities of Caius College.

W^m. Gooch's last letter is dated '*Daedalus,* S.S. off *Karakakooa-Bay, Owhyhee*[2].' May 2nd 1792.' He leaves the letter in charge of 'Tàmehàmehà[3] (King of this Island) for him to deliver to any English ship which may touch and expect to be in England before the expiration of 1793.' He looks forward to seeing them 'toward Autumn, 1794.' On the 13th May 1792, he, with two of his comrades, was murdered by the natives on the neighbouring island of *Woahoo*[4], or *Oahoo*, where they had landed.

[1] 24 Jan., 4 Mar., 5th July, 1794.
[2] Hawaii.
[3] Kamehamaha.
[4] Cp. Cook's *Voyages* bk. III. chh. xi, xii. (Jan. & Feb. 1778.) bk. v. chh. v, vi. (27 Feb. 1779.)

APPENDIX III.

'ADVICE', &c. WATERLAND'S STUDENT'S GUIDE.
1706—40.

'ADVICE TO A YOUNG STUDENT. With a *Method* of Study for the Four First *Years*.' 1706—40.

This Scheme was drawn up by DANIEL WATERLAND for his pupils at Magdalene College Cambridge, about 1706, when he was dean and tutor. The latter office he continued to hold even after he was advanced to the Mastership in 1713. It was *printed* piratically, in the Republick of Letters for December, 1729.

I have a copy of the Authorized '*Second Edition*' (anonymous) 8vo. pp. 32. Printed for J. Crownfield, 1730.

Another edition came out in 1740, which is printed among Waterland's Works VI. 299—324 (Van Mildert); the lapse of time having required some change in the text books, &c., recommended.

[I have indicated some of the alterations suggested by the edition of 1740 by square brackets, and others in the foot-notes.]

The tract of which I give a summary was intended to serve as a *Student's Guide* to supplement tutorial advice and to encourage method in study.

I. *Directions for a Religious and Sober Life.* Waterland recommends constant attendance on the prayers in Chapel—*early hours*—(Van Mildert mentions, I. 11, that Waterland's own example in this respect was of a remarkable character. His contemporary, the father of dean Cyril Jackson, used often to tell how a light was seen in Waterland's window when most of the world were asleep. His intense application to his studies is thought to have shortened his life)—Reading the Bible—Books of Devotion e. gr. *The Whole Duty of Man*, [The New Whole Duty of Man], *Taylor's Golden Grove* [Nelson's Devotions], or *Prayers us'd by King William*, in 12mo., or in *Tillotson's* Sermons vol. XIV, to be used at least till 'a Facility of praying extempore' be gained.

To these he adds *Thomas à Kempis*, *Nelson's Festivals*, *Goodman's Winter Evening's Conference* and the *Gentleman Instructed*.

'Never go to any Tavern or Alehouse unless sent for by some Country Friend; and then stay not long there nor drink more than is convenient.'

'Covet not a large and general Acquaintance but be content with a very few Visitants, and let these be good...

'Come in always before the Gates are shut, Winter and Summer; and before Nine of the Clock constantly, when your Tutor expects you at Lectures in his Chamber.'

'For the sake of peace and order bear with some little Rudeness and some imperious Carriage [from your seniors in College] if any be so foolish as to use them towards you : Not but that you may have Redress upon any the least Grievance by complaining to your Tutor.'

'Avoid Idleness, otherwise called *Lounging*.'

II.   *A Method of Study.*

The generality of students are intended for Clergymen, and as such must take the Arts in their way.

PHILOSOPHY (including *mathematics, geography, astronomy, chronology* and other parts of *physics*; besides *logic, ethics* and *metaphysics*) CLASSICAL learning and DIVINITY, are the three heads.

Waterland refers students of LAW and PHYSIC to their tutors for special advice.

III.   *Directions for the Study of Philosophy.*

'Begin not with PHILOSOPHY till your Tutor reads lectures to you on it.'

For the first half year at least attempt nothing beyond the text-book of the lectures.

Devote mornings and evenings to Philosophy : afternoons[1] to classics, as requiring less coolness.

'After you have come to a competent Knowledge in Philosophy,' make a *commonplace* book of the Questions discussed in your authors with references, *pro* and *con*.

'Set a Mark in the *Margin* of your Book when you do not understand any Thing and consult other books which may help to explain it: Or, if you cannot thus master the Difficulty, apply to some Friend that can, or to your Tutor.'

IV.   *General Directions for the Study of Classicks.*

'Let your *Afternoons*[1], as much of them as can be spared from Afternoon Lectures, if you have any, be spent in reading Classick Authors, *Greek* and *Latin*.' In the order mentioned; one at a time if possible straight through not too fast.   Consult *Dictionaries, Lexicons, Notes,* Friends or Tutor.

---

[1] So the writer of *Hints to Freshmen at the University of Cambridge* ('Curvo dinoscere rectum, &c.) 4th ed. London printed for J. Mawman Ludgate-street; and J. Deighton. 1822.' evidently a rigid supporter of Mathematical studies says (*p.* 7.) 'It is a good custom to set aside a part of the afternoon for *literae humaniores.*'

Read *Terence, Tully* and *Virgil* over and over again as models. Be provided with some books of Greek (*Potter's*) and Roman *Antiquities* (*Kennet's*) which you may once read over and afterwards consult upon occasion.

You may add to them *Echard's* Roman History.

'Have a *Quarto* Paper Book for a COMMON PLACE [in Mr Locke's method] to refer any Thing curious to;' rather to keep up your attention and for present profit than for future use.

In COMPOSITION rather imitate and vary, than copy out.

'When you are to make an Oration (after you have considered well the Matter) read one of *Tully's* on a similar Subject. Consider the Argumentative Part by itself, which *Freigius's* Analytical Notes will assist you in... However the bare reading of [Cicero's] Compositions will make your thoughts more free and more just than otherwise.'

'You may be taught in an Hour or two's time, by your Tutor how to use the *Maps* or *Tables*' which you should have before you when reading History or even Oratory and Poetry.

V. *General Directions for Divinity.*

The study of Divinity should be commenced in the early years of residence. It is well for a young man to keep the main object of his education in view; and many are ordained soon after taking their degree. The ordinary studies are so useful grounding for a Divine that Waterland recommends the study of divinity for the first part of a student's residence to be confined to his 'spare hours on *Sundays* and *Holydays*;' and on each of them he advises him to read and make *Abridgments* of a couple of sermons (which will take about 3 hours apiece) in a quarto paper book, marking general and particular heads according to an example given. Later in their course they should devote their mornings only to philosophy, afternoons to classics, and evenings as well as Sundays and Holydays to Divinity, 'or however to the reading the best English writers such as *Temple, L'Estrange, Collier* [*Spectator* and other writings of *Addison*] and other masters of *Thought* and *Style*.'

In the 4th year 'endeavour to get a general view of the several controversies on foot from *Bennet's* Books; and some Knowledge of *Church History* from Mr *Echard* and *Du Pin's Compendious History of the Church* in 4 vols. 8vo.; and then if you have Time undertake *Pearson* on the *Creed*, and *Burnet on the Articles*.'

VI. *A course of Studies Philosophical, Classical and Divine, for the first four years.*

The following scheme of course is not intended to be rigidly adhered to in all cases. Waterland begins 'the Year with *January*, though few come so early to College: If you happen to come later, yet begin with the Books first set down.'

		PHILOSOPHICAL.	CLASSICAL.	RELIGIOUS.
1st year.	Jan. Feb.	Wells'[1] Arithm.	Terence.	Sharp's Sermons. Calamy's Sermons.
	March April	Euclid's Elem.	Xenophontis Cyri Institutio.	Spratt's Sermons. Blackhall's Sermons.
	May June	Euclid's Elem. Burgersdicius'[2] Logick.	Tully's Epistles. Phaedrus' Fables.	Hoadly's Sermons. South's Sermons.
	July Aug.	Euclid's Elements. Burgersdicius.	Lucian's Select Dialogues. Theophrastus.	South's Sermons.
	Sept. Oct.	Wells's Geography[3].	Justin. Cornelius Nepos.	Young's Sermons.
	Nov. Dec.	Wells's[4] Trigonometry. Newton's Trigon.	Dionysius's Geography.	Scot's Sermons & Discourses, 3 vols.
2nd year.	Jan. Feb.	Wells's[5] Astron. Locke.	[10] Causin deEloquentia. Vossius' Rhetorick.	Tillotson's Sermons, Vol. i. folio.
	March April	Locke's Hum. Und. [6] De la Hire Con. Sect.	Tully's Orat.	
	May June	[7] Whiston's Astron.	Isocrates. Demosthenes.	Tillotson's Sermons, Vol. ii. fol.
	July Aug.	Keil's Introduction.	Caesar's Comment. Sallust.	
	Sept. Oct.	Cheyne's Philosop. Principles.	Hesiod. Theocritus.	Tillotson's Sermons, Vol. iii. fol.
	Nov. Dec.	[8] Rohaulti Physica.	Ovid's Fasti. Virgil's Eclog.	
3rd year.	Jan. Feb.	Burnet's Theory with Keill's Remarks.	Homeri Iliads, edit. Clarke.	Norris' Practical Discourses, 1st & 2nd Parts.
	March April	Whiston's Theory with Keill's Remarks.	Virgil's Georgicks. ——— Aeneids.	Norris' Practical Discourses, 3rd & 4th parts.
	May June	Wells' Chronology. Beveridge's Chron.	Sophocles.	Claggett's Sermons 2 vols.
	July Aug.	[9] Whitby's Ethicks. Puffendorf's Law of Nat.	Horace.	Atterbury's (Lewis) Sermons, 2 vols.
	Sept. Oct.	Puffendorf. Grotius de Jure Belli.	[11] Euripides, Piers' edit.	Atterbury's (Francis) Sermons.
	Nov. Dec.	Puffendorf. Grotius.	Juvenal-Persius.	Stillingfleet's Sermons.

In a later edition are substituted
[1] Wingate's Arith.
[2] Wallis' Logick,
[3] Salmon's Geography.
[4] Keill's Trigonometrice.
[5] Harris' Astron. Dialogues.
Keill's Astron.
[6] Simpson's Con.

[7] Milnes' Sectt. Conicae.
[8] Bartholin's (as well as Rohault's) Physics.
[9] The Compendium of Ethics, with Hutcheson and Fordyce.
[10] Cambray on Eloquence.
[11] King's Euripides instead of Piers', or the select plays in 8vo.

		PHILOSOPHICAL.	CLASSICAL.	RELIGIOUS.
4th year.	Jan. Feb.	Baronius' Meta- physicks.	Thucydides.	Jenkins's Reasonable- ness of Christianity.
	March April	Newton's Opticks.	Thucydides.	Clarke's Lectures. Grotius de Verit. R.C.
	May June	Whiston's Praelect. Phys. Math.	Livy.	Bennet of Pop.[1] Abridg.L.C.Conf.of Qu.
	July Aug.	Gregory's Astronomy.	Livy.	Pearson on the Creed with King's Crit. Hist.
	Sept. Oct.		Diogenes Laertius.	West on the Resurrec- tion.
	Nov. Dec.		Cicero's Philosoph. works.	Burnet's Articles.

Waterland adds to the Table for each year remarks on the use, merits and defects of the books recommended. I have room only for a few of them.

The hardest Philosophical and Classical Books are reserved for the 4th year.

The Sermons are not arranged in any particular order. Waterland gives this character of them.

Sharp's, Calamy's and *Blackhall's* are the best models for an easy, natural and familiar way of writing. *Sprat* is fine, florid and elaborate in his style, artful in his method and not so open as the former, but harder to be imitated. *Hoadly* is very exact and judicious, and both his *style* and *sense* just, close and clear. The other three (South, Young, and Scot) are very sound, clear writers, only Scot is too swelling and pompous, and *South* is something too full of *wit* and *satire*, and does not always observe a decorum in his style. *Tillotson* may be corrected by *Lupton's* Oxford Sermon, *Whitby's* Appendix to II. Thess. and "The Religion of a Church of England Woman" p. 339, &c.

"*Norris* is a fine writer for style and thought, and commonly just, except in what relates to his World of Ideas, where he sometimes trifles."

If there is more time the following Sermons may be added— [those in *brackets* are not mentioned in the two first editions.]

Lucas'.	[Seed's 4 vols.]
Barrow's.	[Butler's.]
Brady's.	[Waterland's.]
Hickman's 2 Vols.	[Blair's 4 vols.]
Bragg's.	[Abernethy's.]
Beveridge's.	[Bishop Sherlock's.]
Tilly's.	[Balguy's 2 vols.]
Fiddes' 3 vols.	[Dodwell's 2 vols.]
[Fothergill's.]	

---

[1] i.e. T. Bennet's (Joh.) *Confutation of Popery, Abridgement of the* London Cases, and *Confutation of Quakerism.*

APPENDIX.

For the 4th year's Divinity see ch. v. at end [1].
If you have learnt Hebrew at school keep it up all the time you
are at Cambridge. Otherwise devote some months wholly to it after
your degree. After going through the four years' course if you intend
to take Holy Orders soon (after learning Hebrew if necessary) read
through *Grotius, Patrick,* or some good Commentator. You may
read *Josephus'* History and *Du Pin's* Canon of the Old Testament *pari
passu.* Then proceed to the New Testament with *Whitby,* looking
occasionally into *Grotius* or *Hammond.* Then, if you have time,
read the Church writers up to the 4th century at least, first seeing a
character of their works in *Dupin,* or *Cave,* or *Bull,* referring to
Bingham's Ecclesiastical Antiquities when necessary.

To qualify yourself for a Preacher, in addition to the above-
mentioned Sermons [2], study the following :

Bull's Latin works, Grabe's folio (1703).
Nelson's Life of Bull with his *English* works, 4 vols. 8vo.
Nelson's Feasts and Fasts.
Stanhope's Epistles and Gospels, 4 vols.
Kettlewell's Measures of Obedience.
  „   *On the Sacrament.*
  „   *Practical Believer.*
Scot's Christian Life.
Lucas' Enquiry after Happiness, 2 vols.
Hammond's Practical Catechism.
Fleetwood's Relative Duties.
Stillingfleet's Origines Sacrae.
Burnet's History of the Reformation.
F. Paul's History of the Council of Trent.
Clarendon's History.
Bennet's Common-Prayer.
  „   *Rights of Clergy.*
Cosin's Canon of Scripture.
Stillingfleet's Cases.
Norris' Humility and Prudence, 2 vols.
  „   *Reason & Faith.*
Ditton's Moral Evidence.
Wilkin's Natural Religion.

[1] See p. 332.
[2] Tom *Hearne* in a list which he
began to make for a young divine in
1711 agrees with Waterland in recom-
mending,
Chillingworth, Dodwell,
Hammond, Sanderson,
Pearson, The London Cases
  with Mr Bennet's
  Abridgment.
He adds:
Laud against Fisher, Jewell,
Hooker's Eccl. P. Reynolds
and the Cambridge Concordance.
(*Reliquiae Hearn.* Bliss, ed. 2. i. p. 232).

Prebendary W. *Gilpin* in his Dialogues published posthumously 1807,
recommends for ordinary candidates
for orders :

Pearson, Butler, Barrow, Sanderson,
Tillotson, Burnet on the Articles, as
well as Lardner, Mede, Newton on
the Prophecies, Law's Serious Call,
G. Herbert's 'Parson to the Church,'
Smiglecius ('a heavy dry logical
work') and Saurin's and Bourdelon's
Sermons (which were translated by
R. Robinson the Cambridge Baptist,
1770—1784).

Dean *Sherlock's* Works.
Potter's Church Government.
History of Montanism.
Ostervald's Cases of Corruption.
      „   *Nature of Uncleanness.*
[Sherlock, Bp. of London on Prophecy.]
[„   Trial of the Witnesses.]
[*Observations on the Conversion of St Paul.*]
[*Wollaston's Religion of Nature.*]
[*Conybeare's Defence of Revealed Religion.*]
[*Butler's Analogy.*]
[*Watts' Scripture History.*]
[Archdeacon *St George's Examination for Holy Orders.*]
[Stackhouse's *History of the Bible.*]
Nichol's Defensio Eccl. Anglicanae.
Wake's Catechism.
Clagget's Operation of the Spirit.
Chillingworth.
Cave's Primitive Christianity.

Wingate's Arithmetic is an introduction to Mathematics.
Euclid preferred to other geometrical books (see Whiston's Preface to Tacquet).
Pardie may be read afterwards and will prove entertaining.
Wallis' logic is read in lectures and is useful for definitions. Mathematics more useful than Logic towards "the conduct of the understanding." The Tutor's help is pre-supposed on the pupil's beginning *Keill's* Trigonometry.
Hammond's, Maclaurin's and *Simpson's Algebras* recommended.
Simpson's Conic Sections may be read by one who understands Euclid and is necessary for those who would understand Astronomy. *Keill* is more difficult, *Cheyne* easy to one who understands the two former. Add *Bentley's* Sermons and *Huygens'* Planetary Worlds. In *Rohault's* Physics read the Opticks—the foot-notes are the valuable part in the rest of the work. With this read Wells's ['*Desaguliers'* and *Rowning's*' (*later ed.*)] Mechanics, Statics, and Optics adding *Le Clerc's* [*Bartholin's*] Physicks, for heads. In addition to *Wells* and *Beveridge* use *Strauchius'* Chronology.
With *Grotius* and *Puffendorf* (the abridgment by the latter himself) may be used as well *Sanderson's* Prælectiones (for Casuistry) and *Placette* of Conscience.
Malbranche and *Norris'* Ideal World may be added to the metaphysical works.
The B.A. "if he design not presently for Orders[1]" may add to his stock of Philosophy

---

[1] Rob. *Masters* in his History of C. C. C. p. 207, ed. 1, 1753, speaks of the need of encouragement to Bachelors of Arts to stay and study in College so that they should have better preparation for the Christian ministry.

Varenius' [Salmon's—(later ed.)] Geography.
Newtoni Principia.
Ozanam's Cursus Mathem.
Sturmius's Works.
Hugens' Works.
Newtoni Algebra.
Milne's Conic Sect.

[*Saunderson's* Algebra.]
[*Smith's* Opticks.]
[*Musschenbroek's* Philosophia.]
Molineux's Dioptricks.
[*Baker* on the Microscope.]
[*Chambers'* Dictionary.]
[*Hale's* Statistics.]

As to the Classical books recommended[1], a Greek and a Latin Book should be read alternately.

Rapin's 2 vols. may be read with *Cambray, Vossius,* or other rhetoric.

Read *Bossu* Of Epic Poetry before *Homer* and *Virgil.*

The B. A. may continue his Classical Studies, if he has time, by reading any of the following :

Aristot. Rhetorica.
Epictetus.
M. Antoninus.
Herodotus.
Plutarch.
Homeri Odyss.
Aristophanes.
Plato de Rebus Div.
Callimachus.
Herodian.
Longinus.
Veteres Orator. Gr.
Plinii Epist. et Panegyr.
Seneca.

Lucretius.
Plautus.
Q. Curtius.
Suetonius.
Tacitus.
Aulus Gellius.
Lucanus.
Florus.
Martialis.
Catullus.
Manilius.
Ovidii Epist. et Metam.
Eutropius.

[1] John *Wesley's* Scheme of Study when B.A. at Lincoln Coll. in 1726 was,

S.   Divinity.
M. }
Tu.} Classics.
W.   Logic and Ethics.
Th. Hebrew and Arabic.

F.   Metaphysics and Natural Philosophy.
Sat. Oratory, Poetry and especially composition.

He seems moreover not to have neglected Mathematics. *Life* by Southey Coleridge and Southey, I. p. 37.

APPENDIX IV.

ΕΓΚΥΚΛΟΠΑΙΔΕΙΑ, OR A SCHEME OF STUDY.
RO. GREEN. 1707.

ROBERT GREEN (or Greene) fellow of Clare—B.A. 1699, M.A. 1703, D.D. (Com. Reg.) 1728—Author of *Principles of the Philosophy of Expansive and Contractive Forces*, Camb. 1727 (see above 69, 127).

Ἐγκυκλοπαιδεία, or A Method of Instructing Pupils, 1707 (pp. 8) 4to. [in *Gough Cambr.* 67 *Bodl. Lib.* endorsed '*Dr Green of Clare Hall's Course of Lectures.*' There is a copy at Cambridge in the Library of Queens' coll. P. 5. (10)].

'The first half year's Exercise from the *Commencement* to *Christmas*.

Every Week make
{ A Theme *Lat.* A Copy of Verses *Lat.* A Translation out of a *Greek* Orator into *Latin*, or out of a Roman into English.

The first half Year's Study to Christmas.

Every Day read
1. The Lesson in the *Greek* Testament Morning and Evening with the *Critici Sacri* or *Synopsis*.
2. A Sermon in Dr *Tillotson* or some other Piece of the best and most genuine *English*, *Sprat*, Sir *William Temple*, *Clarendon*, *Burnet's* Theory, &c.
3. Some Lines of *Homer*, *Virgil* or *Horace*, *Terence*, &c.
4. Let the rest of the Day be divided betwixt the *Roman* and *Greek* Orators or Historians.

Continue the same method of Reading as much as possible all the following years, to which add

FIRST YEAR.

From Christmas to the Commencement half a Year.

1st Lecture from 1 to 2 or 3—*Greek* Classick Learning .... { Homer, Pindar, Hesiod, Theocritus.

2nd Lecture from 8 to 9 or 10—Latin Classicks { Virgil, Horace, Juvenal, Persius.

From the Commencement to Christmas half a Year.

1st Lecture—Chronology and Geography { *Cluver* and Maps, *Varenius*, *Gordon*, Petavius, Helvicus, Strauchius, Beverege.

2nd Lecture—History, *Greek* and *Latin* { *Thucydides, Herodotus, Livy, Sallust, Paterculus.*

Exercise.

Translate out of the *Greek* or *Latin* Orators into *English* every Week which are therefore to be explained every Monday Morning from 10 to 11. The best *English* writers as before, are likewise for that reason to be studied in order to form from thence a good Stile upon the Model of the Ancients, as also Pleadings and Speeches made in Parliament, together with the choicest sermons and *English* Tracts on other subjects; besides accidental Exercises are to be perform'd suitable to the studies peculiar to this year, in Classicks, History, Chronology, &c.

Every Sunday and Holiday thro' the Year.

1st Lecture—Upon the Scriptures { 1st, To shew the Validity and Necessity of them. 2ndly, Explain half of the Gospels of St *Matthew*, St *Mark*, St *Luke*, St *John*, the Acts, *Grot., Hamm., Whitby, Critici Sacri, Synopsis.*

2nd Lecture { Upon the Heresies, Schisms, Blasphemous Tenets of the Ancient and Modern Times. } Their History, Their Confutation, From { Scripture, Reason. } { *Vincentius Lirinensis, Cave's Histor. Literar., Roger's* Articles, *Epiphanius, Philastrius.*

SECOND YEAR.

From Christmas to the Commencement.

1st. { Logick—*Burgersdicius, Lock.*
Ethicks and Law of Nature { *Puffendorf de Officio Hom.*
—— *De Jure Belli et Pacis.*
Cumberland, Tully's Offices.

2nd. Elements of Geometry { *Euclid, Sturmius,*
Pardies, Jones.

From the Commencement to Christmas.

1st. { Metaphysicks { *Le Clerk, Lock,*
Baronius, Malebranche,
Templer against *Hobbs.*
Corpuscular Philosophy { *Cartes, Rohault, Varenius,*
Le Clerk, Boyle.

2nd. { Arithmetick { *Wells, Tacquet,*
Jones.
Algebra { *Pell, Wallis, Harriot, Kersey,*
Newton, Cartes, Harris,
Oughtred's Clavis, Ward, Jones.

Exercise.

Declaim in *English* every Monday Morning betwixt 10 and 11, besides Disputations in *Latin,* solving Problems in Arithmetick and Geometry, and other Exercises proper to the Studies of this Year.

Every *Sunday* and Holiday thro' the Year.

1st. Explain the other half of the Gospels St *John* and the *Acts.*

2nd. { Explain the several Doctrines of our Religion and compare 'em with those of other Religions and shew { The Reasonableness of those we are to believe, The Excellency of those we are to practice. { *Limborch* Articles, *Usher's* System, *Hammond's* Catechism, Primitive Christianity, *Beveridge* on the Catechism, *Jenkins.*

THIRD YEAR.

From Christmas to the Commencement.

1st. Experimental Philosophy and Chymistry of Minerals, Plants and Animals. { *Philos. Transact. Leipsick Acts,* Boyle, *Lemmery, Collegium Curiosum.*

2nd. Anatomy and Philosophy.
- 1st. of Animals { *Keil, Gibson, Blankard, Drake, Cowper, Harvey, Borellus de motu Animalium.*
- 2nd. Plants and Vegetables { *Grew, Philos. Trans. Miscell. Curios.*
- 3rd. Minerals, their minute parts { *Hook's Micrograph, Lewenhoek.*

From the Commencement to Christmas.

1st. Opticks, Dioptricks, Catoptricks, Colours, Iris. { *Gregory, Rohault, Dechales, Barrow's Lectures,* Newton, Cartes, *Hugens, Kepler, Molyneux's Dioptricks.*

2nd. Conick Sections, and the Nature of Curves. { *De Witt, De la Hire, Sturmius,* Marquis de *l'Hopitall,* Newton, *Millnes, Wallis.*

Exercise.

Translate every Week a piece of *Demosthenes* into *Latin* to be explain'd every Monday Morning betwixt 10 and 11, besides other Exercises appropriated to the Studies of this Year.

Every Sunday and Holiday thro' the Year.

1st. Explain half of the Epistles and Revelations, those to the *Romans, Corinthians, Galatians, Ephesians, Philippians, Colossians.*

2nd.
- 1st. Give an Ecclesiastical History of the Primitive Discipline and Government and Constitution of the Church, and then of the present Churches and compare 'em. } *Beveridge's Apostolical Canons, English Canons.*
- 2nd. Of the Practice, Worship, Virtues, Sufferings, &c. of it and of the present. } *Cave's Prim. Christ. Lives of Apost. Basilius Magn. summa moralium.*

FOURTH YEAR.

From Christmas to the Commencement.

1st. Mechanical Philosophy, Staticks, Hydro- staticks, Flux and Reflux, Percussion, Gravitation, &c. } *Marriot, Keil, Hugens, Sturmius, Boyl, New- ton, Ditton, Wallis de motu, Borellus, Halley's Miscell. Curiosa.*

2nd. Fluxions, Infinite series, Arithmetick of Infinites. } *Wallis, Newton, Raphson, Hays, Ditton, Jones, Nieuwentius, Marquis de l'Ho'pitall.*

From the Commencement to Christmas.

1st. Astronomy { Spherical Hypothetical Practical Physical } *Gassendus, Mercator, Bullialdus, Horoccius, Flamstead, Newton, Gregory, Whiston's Praelectiones and Kepler.*

2nd. Logarithms and Trigonometry { *Sturmius, Briggs, Vlacq, Gelli- brand, Harris, Mercator, Jones, Newton, Caswell.*

Exercise.

Declaim in *Latin* every *Monday* from 10 to 11, besides other Exercises adapted to the Studies of the Year, as resolving of Pro- blems by Fluxions, &c.

Every Sunday and Holiday thro' the Year.

1st. Explain the other half of the Epistles and Revelations, those to the *Thessalonians, Titus, Philemon, Hebrews,* those of St *James,* St *Peter,* St *John,* St *Jude,* and the Revelations.

2nd. Give an Ecclesiastical History of the Councils and other Transactions in the Church. } *Du Pin, Baronius, Cave's Lives of the Fathers, Histor. Literar., Bisciola, Centuriat. Magdebur- genses.*

Conclude the Night Lecture with an Office out of Dr *Hicks's* Reform'd Devotions, and the Prayer for Christ's Holy Catholick Church. Instead of the Lessons in Dr *Hicks,* let every one in his turn read a Lesson out of the *Greek* Testament in the same place where they are prescrib'd.

Add to this Method on Thursdays

1st. Lecture on the *Greek* 2nd. Lecture on the *Latin* } Poets, { 1. *Theocritus, Hesiod, Homer, Pindar,* &c. 2. *Virgil, Horace, Juvenal, Per- sius,* &c.

So that the first half year may be either employ'd in Classicks, as is before prescrib'd, or devoted to other Studies.'

APPENDIX V.

EXAMINATIONS FOR FELLOWSHIPS AND SCHOLARSHIPS, &c. AT TRINITY COLLEGE, CAMBRIDGE.

ZOUCH'S HINTS. THE ANNUAL 'MAY' EXAMINATION FOR FRESH-
MEN AND JUNIOR SOPHS. OLD EXAMINATION PAPERS, &c., &c.

UNTIL the present century[1] Trinity was the only college in Cambridge where the fellowships were open without territorial appropriation.

All the other colleges[2] (with the exception of King's) filled up each vacancy by electing if possible some one whose name had been matriculated as belonging to the same COUNTY[3] as the outgoing fellow.

The counties were thus distributed for Peterhouse in 1630 (by a statute superseding *Warkworth* cap. xii.) into *north* (Boreales) and *south* (Australes) by a line drawn from Yarmouth to Machynlleth.

NORTHERN. Bedford, Cheshire, Cumberland, Derby, Durham, York, Hunts, Lancaster, Leicester, Lincoln, Norfolk, Northampton, Northumberland, Notts, Rutland, Salop, Stafford, Warwick, Westmoreland, Worcester,—Anglesea, Caernarvon, Denbigh, Flint, Merioneth, Montgomery.

SOUTHERN. Berks, Bucks, *Cambridge*, Kent, Cornwall, Devon, Dorset,. Essex, Gloster, Herts, Hereford, *Middlesex*, Monmouth, Oxon, Southampton, Surrey, Sussex, Suffolk, Somerset, Wilts,—Brecon, Caermarthen, Cardigan, Glamorgan, Pembroke, Radnor.

---

[1] However the system of 'close' fellowships and scholarships had been denounced as early as 1759 in the *Epistle of* Ri. Davies *M.D. to Dr* Hales (p. 23): and in 1788 the author of *Remarks on the Enormous Expence in the Education...at* Cambridge (p. 30) suggested the parliament should interfere.

[2] In one instance a royal dispensa-

tion was granted, in 1639, to S. John's, and in 1776 that society resolved (if the master thought it worth while) to petition the sovereign for the removal of the restriction of counties. Mayor's Baker pp. 523, 1072.

[3] Hooker appears (*Keble* I. 15.) to have been entered at Corpus, Oxon. as of two counties, Devon and Southampton.

There might be four fellows at one time from Middlesex or Cambridgeshire, but only one each from any of the others (the whole of Wales counting as one) except by royal dispensation.

If it happened that there was no candidate of the right county ready, the election would I suppose lie between the men of any northern (or southern) counties which had no representatives in the existing body of fellows.

In 1785, Henry Gunning did not enter at S. John's because Cambridgeshire was filled by the bishop of Ely's fellow, and a professor's son, already admitted, was prepared to step into his shoes. He went therefore as a sizar to Christ's, where the Cambridgeshire fellow was likely soon to vacate his berth. This state of things continued at S. John's till the end of the century, when Dr Wood was scandalized at their finding themselves precluded from electing Inman the senior wrangler of 1800.

In the middle of the seventeenth century 'a fellowship examination included versification, *vivâ voce* questions and other exercises,' but the election was liable to be influenced by the party spirit which then ran very high, as well as by personal interest[1].

When Bentley was made Master of Trinity in 1700, he found the custom of examining the candidates for fellowships (and scholarships) in the chapel *vivâ voce* before the master and seniors. In order to give an opportunity for the performance of written exercises and time to weigh and deliberate upon the merits of the men, Bentley soon after his appointment ordered that they should be examined by each of the electors at his own apartments[2].

We have in the memoirs of his grandson Ri. Cumberland a full account of the working of the scheme under his successor Dr Smith in 1752.

Although *on rare occasions*[3] even a junior bachelor had been invited to stand for election and had been successful, it was until that year contrary to rule that middle bachelors even should be eligible.

'It would hardly be excusable in me' [says Cumberland] 'to detail a process that takes place every year, but that in this instance the novelty of our case made it a matter of very great attention. When

Mayor's *Matt. Robinson*, 28 *n*, 36 *n*. At S. John's there is some evidence of laxity in fellowship elections about 1622, but in 1634 and 166¾ we find reference to examination. Mayor's Baker 488 l. 15; 504 l. 26; 543 l. 12. In Dr Worthington's *Diary* we find a brief account of a fellowship examination at Emmanuel in puritan times. *Nov.* 18, 1657, afternoon, Sir Jones (co. Lancaster), Sir Gibson (co. Suffolk), Sir Pulling (co. Hertford), sat in the parlour for a fellowship. They were examined by Mr Shelton the dean and Mr Jewell the lecturer, and they answered in an equality. Next day, after discussion among the master and fellows, who gave their votes by

juniority, S[r] Jones the northern was elected.

When Dr Gooch (bp. of Bristol) claimed the right of examining Mr Gibbs or any other candidate for a fellowship as master of Caius in 1737, the fellows rejected his declaration at a Chapel-Meeting, 5 Sept. *Caius MSS.* 602 (10).

[2] Monk's *Bentley*, i. 159, 160.

[3] Isaac Newton 1667, Ri. Bentley jun. 1723, Rogerson Cotter (M.P. for Charlesville) 1771, T. Robinson (of Leicester) 1772, Ri. Porson 1782. In the present century there were only a few instances, until 1830 when there were ten vacancies and the rule was abolished.

the day of examination came we went our rounds to the electing seniors; in some instances by one at a time, in others by parties of three or four; it was no trifling scrutiny we had to undergo, and here and there pretty severely exacted, particularly, as I well remember by Doctor Charles Mason[1], a man of curious knowledge in the philosophy of mechanics and a deep mathematician.... He gave us a good dose of dry mathematics, and then put an Aristophanes before us, which he opened at a venture and bade us give the sense of it. A very worthy candidate of my year declined having anything to do with it, yet Mason gave his vote for that gentleman, and against one, who took his leavings. Doctor Samuel Hooper gave us a liberal and well-chosen examination in the more familiar classics....

'The last, to whom in order of our visits we resorted to, was the master[2]; he called us to him one by one according to our standings, and of course it fell to me as junior candidate to wait till each had been examined in turn. When in obedience to his summons I attended upon him, he was sitting, not in the room where my grandfather [Bentley] had his library, but in a chamber up stairs, encompassed with large folding screens, and over a great fire, though the weather was then uncommonly warm : he began by requiring of me an account of the whole course and progress of my studies in the several branches of philosophy, so called in the general, and as I proceeded in my detail of what I had read, he sifted me with questions of such a sort as convinced me he was determined to take nothing upon trust ; when he had held me a considerable time under this examination, I expected he would have dismissed me, but on the contrary he proceeded in the like general terms to demand of me an account of what I had been reading before I had applied myself to academical studies, and when I had acquitted myself of this question as briefly as I could, and I hope as modestly as became me in presence of a man so learned, he bade me give him a summary account of the several great empires of the ancient world, the periods when they flourished, their extent when at the summit of their power, the causes of their declension and dates of their extinction. When summoned to give answer to so wide a question, I can only say it was well for me I had worked so hard upon my scheme of General History.... This process being over, he gave me a sheet of paper written through in Greek with his own hand, which he ordered me to turn either into Latin or English, and I was shewn into a room containing nothing but a table furnished with materials for writing, and one chair, and I was required to use dispatch. The passage was maliciously enough selected in point of construction and also of character, for he had scrawled it out in a puzzling kind of hand with abbreviations of his own devising : it related to the arrangement of an army for battle, and I believe might be taken

---

[1] C. Mason, B.A. 1722, D.D. 1749, Woodwardian Professor 1734. 'A true modern Diogenes' who exercised himself at his blacksmith's forge and

lathe, and in bell-ringing.
[2] Robert Smith, B.A. 1711, LL.D. 1723, D.D. 1739, Plumian Professor 1716, Master of Trinity 1742.

from Polybius, an author I had then never read. When I had given in my translation in Latin, I was remanded to the empty chamber with a subject for Latin prose and another for Latin verse, and again required to dispatch them in the manner of an impromptu. The chamber into which I was shut for the performance of these hasty productions was the very room[1], dismantled of the bed, in which I was born. The train of ideas it revived in my mind were not inappositely woven into the verses I gave in, and with this task my examination concluded....

'The next day the election was announced, and I was chosen together with Mr John Orde, now one of the masters in Chancery.... When I waited upon the electing seniors to return my thanks, of course I did not omit to pay my compliments to Dr Mason[2].'

When he had become superannuated Cumberland was invited by his Trinity friends to offer himself a candidate for the Lay-fellowship then vacant by the death of Mr Titley the Danish envoy. There were only two fellowships of this description. He was successful against a considerable number of competitors; but he soon afterwards vacated it by marriage[3].

When T. Robinson was a successful candidate in 1772, we find the examination for Trinity fellowships still conducted by the electors 'separately and privately. Mr [Stephen] Whisson [ex-tutor and bursar] did not examine by formal and set questions, but rather in the way of conversational inquiry: and his questions were much calculated to ascertain the degree of general knowledge which the student had obtained. "Can you tell me, sir, what were the discriminating tenets of the ancient philosophers?" and the like[4].' This system of examining was obviously liable to objections, and at last in 1786, ten of the junior fellows had occasion to remonstrate that some of the seniors had taken part in the election without examining the candidates. Their representation after some heart-burnings[5] was speedily effectual, and a new master, Dr Postlethwaite, about three years later, instituted the public fellowship-examinations, which have ever since prevailed at Trinity.

The scholarship election went through a similar change. Professor Pryme contrasts the formal sitting in hall, which had already become established in his own time (1800), with the irregular proceedings which his uncle Owen Dinsdale remembered (B.A. 1762) when Dr Smith was master, and when the seniors sent for one, and sometimes two or three students together, and examined them in some Greek or Latin book in their own rooms, and afterwards they

[1] The *Judges' Chamber* in Trinity Lodge.
[2] Memoirs of *Ri. Cumberland*, 4to. 1806, pp. 106—110.
[3] *Ibid.* 148.
[4] E. T. Vaughan's *Life of* T. Robinson, pp. 32, 33.
[5] Involving an appeal to the Royal Visitor (*coram* lord Thurlow). See Cooper's *Annals*, IV. 424, 425. Gunning's *Reminisc.*, vol. II. chap. IV. Monk's *Bentley*, II. 423, 424. The memorial of the junior fellows is recorded in the Gentleman's Magazine, LVI. 1138.

would say to each other, "So and so has done well, I think he will do for a scholar," or the contrary, as it might be[1].'

We may now turn to a still earlier record :—

John Byrom, almost before he was matriculated, was one of nineteen candidates who ' sat' (so the phrase was even in Bentley's time) for ten vacancies among the scholars in 1709. They carried their latin epistles to the master and seniors at the end of April. On May 7th he had been ' examined by Dr Stubbs the vice-master already, and he promises fair.' The following Monday and Tuesday were appointed for more regular examination, which was conducted by Bentley, Stubbs, and Smith (then one of the seniors). On Wednesday they ' made theme for Dr Bentley, and on Thursday the master and seniors met in the chapel for the election ; Dr Smith had the gout and was not there. They stayed consulting about an hour and a half, and then the master wrote the names of the elect, who (continues Byrom) shewed me mine in the list. Fifteen were chosen and four rejected, two of them pensioners, Mr Baker's pupils, the other two sizars, one Sophister, the other a Lancashire lad of our year.

' Friday noon we went to the master's lodge, where we were sworn in in great solemnity, the senior Westminster reading the oath in Latin, all of us kissing the Greek Testament. Then we kneeled down before the master, who took our hands in his and admitted us Scholars in the name of the Father, Son, &c. Then we went and wrote our names in the book and came away, and to-day gave in our epistle of thanks to the master. We took our places at the scholars' table last night. To-day the new scholars began to read the lessons in chapel and wait in the hall, which offices will come to me presently.' (*Chetham Soc.* 1854, pp. 5, 6.)

The following is a Scheme of Study preserved in Wrangham's *Zouch*[2]. It relates apparently to Trinity College about the middle of the century.

' Mr ZOUCH'S

Directions for Study.'

(Drawn up for Thomas Zouch, perhaps by his brother Henry, about 1756, in which year the latter was admitted a Pensioner of Trin. Coll. Camb., under the tuition of the Rev. Stephen Whisson ; and elected Scholar of that society in the ensuing year.)

' Read authors according to a method. Be particularly cautious to read them slowly, and if possible, never pass over a difficulty ; but stop till by your own endeavours, or the instruction of others, you have overcome it. Thus will you proceed in your studies with equal pleasure and improvement.

---

[1] *Autobiographic Recollections of G.* Pryme, p. 47.

[2] *The Works of the Rev.* Thomas Zouch, *D.D.*, *F.L.S.*, *rector of Scray*-ingham and prebendary of Durham, with a Memoir by the Rev. Francis Wrangham, pp. xxviii, xxix.

'Read a chapter in the Greek Testament every day. Let this rule be invariably observed.

'Spend very few evenings in company.

'Read with critical accuracy the following books in the course of the ensuing year, exclusive of all due attention to your Lectures: Demosthenes, and Select Orations of Cicero; Select Tragedies of Sophocles, and Euripides; Juvenal and Persius. Horace will be always in your hands.

'Be particularly accurate in all your compositions. *Litera scripta manet.* Propose to yourself subjects for Themes and Declamations. Your stile can only be formed by continual use.

'Occasionally read some of our best English Poets, whenever you find yourself fatigued with more severe studies.

'Always attend Lectures, whether classical or philosophical. If you omit them once or twice, you will be at a loss to proceed with your Lecturer.

'Endeavour to be clear in your knowledge, and answer the questions proposed to you with diffidence and timidity.

'Converse with yourself as much as possible, and learn to think. When you return from Lectures, examine yourself strictly, whether you understand them or not. Recall the subjects of them often to your mind, and familiarise them to yourself by frequent meditation.

'When you have heard a Sermon, Declamation, or other Academical Exercise, endeavour to recollect the heads, and copy them into a book appropriated to that use.'

The following are the earliest Trinity College examination-papers that I have seen.

Questions
at the Fellowship Examination
Trinity College Cambridge 1797.
(*Set by* W. Collier, 5*th wrangler* 1762,
regius professor of hebrew.)

Questions Historical.

1. What were the different forms of Government under which the Jews lived by various names? what were those names? what were the successions of the forms of Government, and at what periods did they appear?

2. What are the four ancient Monarchies? what is their date, succession, and by what means and events did Cyrus establish his empire?

3. Whence proceeded the colonies of the East into the West, or Greece? what were the names of the Colonists? where did they respectively settle, and when?

4. Why was the southern part of Italy called Magna Graecia? and whence in the middle, or more northern parts, did the Etruscans proceed?

5. Whence arose the war between Athens and Sparta?
6. What was the rise of the Punic wars? what was their final event? and what effect did that event produce on the Roman Republic?
7. How many were the families of the Caesars, and with whom did they begin and end?
8. By what Nation was the Roman Empire finally destroyed? and what were the principal causes which brought it to it's fall?

Questions Geographical.

1. What is meant by the River and the Sea in the Sacred writings?
2. What is the relative situation of Jerusalem and Samaria? and what the names of the mounts in them, on which the respective temples were built?
3. What are the sources and directions of the principal rivers? and the general directions of the chains of the mountains in Asia, Africa, Europe, and the two Americas?
4. Which are the principal Istmi on the face of the earth?
5. What are the Islands in the Aegean Sea renowned for the birth or habitation of illustrious writers?
6. What is the situation of the Fortunate Islands? what is their modern name? and what is there most distinguished in one of them?
7. What places in the earth appear to have been contiguous to Continents, and are now divided by some great convulsions of nature?
8. What are the principal volcanoes on the surface of the globe?

Questions Grammatical.

1. Is language most probably a gift of the Creator, or an effect of human institution?
2. Whence arises the diversity of languages, and in what manner was it most likely effected?
3. What was the most ancient form of characters to express ideas; and what improvements ensued?
4. What was the most ancient alphabet, the number of the first letters? and the additions afterwards made?
5. What is βουστροφηδον, and what instances [of it have been discovered?]
6. What is the digamma? why so called [? and what examples do you know of its] application in Latin from the Greek?

[*The paper contained five other questions which are torn in the copy¹.*]

¹ There is no nº 7. owing to a typographical error, the rest so far as I can conjecture ran as follows :
'8. What is the smallest number of the [................ acknowledged
by the] Grammarians?
9. What is Markland's doctrine of the [...........................
........] from the Latin?
10. What is the use of particles in

The May Examination.

The 'May' examination in lecture-subjects was introduced at Trinity under Dr Postlethwaite in 1790, that for the junior-sophs was in the main mathematical; until 1818 senior-sophs were not examined. Prof. Pryme gives the following instances of the minute questions set in 1800.

'Give the names of the four Roman Legions that were stationed in Britain when Agricola was governor.'

And two or three years later,—

'What was the year, month and day of the birth of Cicero?'

Until 1809 only about one-half of the names were classed, those in the first class receiving prize books which were presented between the courses of the Commemoration dinner, while the band in the gallery played *See the Conquering Hero comes* and *Rule Britannia* (the only tunes beside *God save the King* which they knew) alternately.

In 1809 professor Pryme with good effect increased the number of classes from four to eight, with a ninth *below the line;* and ever since 1813 that system has become established[1].

The following was an early college examination-paper.

FRESHMEN.

Trinity College Cambridge, 1799.

(Set by T. Young, M.A. 1797, 12th wrangler 1794, afterwards tutor.)

Demosthenes *De Corona.*

1. What was the origin and ground of the accusation? Date the accusation and trial by Olympiads, and by years before Christ. Give the outlines of the cause; state its merits; and mention the event of the trial.

2. Cicero says, "Hanc mulctam Aeschines a Ctesiphonte petiit quadriennio ante Philippi Macedonis mortem." Can this be right?

3. Give a sketch of the lives of Aeschines and Demosthenes; and compare their merits as statesmen and Orators.

4. Give some account of the causes and progress of Philip's success, from his coming to the throne of Macedon to his death.

5. What was the extent of Alexander's power and influence in Greece and Asia at the time of this oration?

6. What was the state of Thebes at the same time? And how, and by whom, was it brought into that state?

all lan[guages? and what are your own opinions] on the subject?

11. What is the best manner of rendering [.............. and what is the rule] for applying Hic et Ille?

12. What is the distinguishing ex-cellence [of the writings of Virgil, and which of the] imperfections of Lucretius did he avoid?

[1] Cp. Monk's *Bentley*, II. 424. Pryme's *Autobiog. Recoll.* pp. 52, 53, 90, 91.

7. Give the Geography and history of Cirrha, and the Cirrhaean plain.

8. What was the relative situation of the following places—Thermopylae, Delphi, Amphissa, Elatea, Thebes, Athens, Eleusis, Cheronea? And what the distances of Eleusis and Elatea from Thebes?

9. Demosthenes says, και μετα ταυτα ευθυς δυναμιν συλλεξας, και παρελθων ώς επι την Κιρραιαν, ερρωσθαι φρασας πολλα και Κιρραιοις και Λοκροις, την Ελατειαν καταλαμβανει. Does this imply that Philip entirely neglected the punishment of the Amphisseans?

10. Explain the following terms, from the Athenian antiquities : Αρχοντες. Αρχοντος. Μνησιφιλου. Συγκλητου εκκλησιας. Πρυτανεις. Συμμοριαι. Οι τριακοσιοι.

11. Describe the constitution of the Athenian democracy, as settled by Solon ; and state the proportion which those who enjoyed the benefits of it bore to the whole population of Attica.

12. Give an account of the origin, constitution, and political use of the Amphictyonic council.

13. Demosthenes says—Ουτε γαρ ην πρεσβεια προς ουδενα απεσταλμενη τοτε των Ελληνων. Aeschines, speaking of the same time, says—Πρεσβειας, ἁς ητε εκπεπομφοτες κατ᾽ εκεινον τον καιρον εις την Ελλαδα. How is this to be accounted for ?

14. What is the strongest reason for thinking that in the decree of the Byzantines, we ought to read Εν τα ἁλια, instead of Εντεαλια ; and κτασιν γᾶς και οικιᾶν, προεδριαν εν τοις αγωσι, ποθοδον ποτι ταν βωλαν και τον δαμον, πρατοις μετα τα ιερα, instead of κτασιν γᾶς, και οικειαν προεδριαν εν τοις αγωσι ποτι ταν δολον, ποτι ταν βωλων και τον δαμον, παρα τοις περι τα ιερα ?

15. Of what materials was the crown composed ?

APPENDIX VI.

ANNUAL COLLEGE EXAMINATIONS AT S. JOHN'S, CAMBRIDGE, 1765-75.

Dr William Samuel Powell, B.A. 1738, was elected master of S. John's College Cambridge in 1765. 'In the very first year of his mastership he applied himself to the establishment of those college examinations which before his time were unknown in our university, and which form so excellent a test of proficiency in the various subjects of lectures. The examination lists still preserved in S. John's, which were all drawn up with great care and consideration by Dr Powell himself, as long as he presided over the college [till 1775], bear strong testimony to the acute discrimination, the strict impartiality and the resolute industry with which he conducted and perfected this his favourite scheme.' By prizes and punishments he overcame the opposition which the young men at first presented.

'He allowed the students of no year to pass without examination in one of the Gospels, or the Acts of the Apostles; no talents or acquirements being permitted to compensate for the neglect of this.'

The entry in the S. John's coll. conclusion-book is as follows.

5th July, 1765. 'Agreed that the examiners annually chosen shall by themselves or their sufficient deputies examine the under-graduates, both fellow-commoners and others publickly in the hall twice a year, the time and subjects to be determined by the master.'

In 1772, John Jebb of Peterhouse, being concerned to think that so many young men spent the early part of their course (and fellow-commoners the whole of it) idly or vieiously in default of any intellectual interest, drew up a scheme to the following effect :—

That there should be an annual examination to engage every student every year (no exemption being made in favour of Kingsmen, noblemen or fellow-commoners[1]) to be conducted by six or seven

---

[1] At Cambridge in 1675 exercises were required of fellow-commoners in *some* of the colleges, but not in others. (Dyer *Privil. Camb.* I. 368.)

For the university, Ri. Watson (Trin.) when he was moderator had advocated the examination of noble-men and fellow-commoners, and the

examiners (chosen according to the proctorial cycle) before the division of the May term.   It should comprise the law of nature and of nations, chronology, set periods of history, select classics, metaphysics, *limited* portions of mathematics and natural philosophy, moral philosophy, and metaphysics.   In their last examination before the tripos all should shew a knowledge of the four Gospels in Greek, and of Grotius *de Veritate.*   Candidates for holy Orders to have special lectures *after* their first degree in arts.   About one third of the men might have honours, and prize-books should be given stamped with the university arms.   The examination to occupy three days; from 9 a.m. to 12, and from 3 to 6 p.m.   Any candidate when not actually under scrutiny of the examiners might be summoned to the library or to some part of the senate-house by any regent or non-regent for private examination.

Jebb's scheme met with much opposition from Farmer and other Emmanuel men, Whisson the librarian and prof. Hallifax, but especially from Dr Powell and other Johnians, who were jealous for their own college examination[1], which did much to recommend their society to the public.   Accordingly in 1774, Jebb modified it in certain technicalities, changing also the time from May to November, reducing the subjects to latin and greek classics, elements of geometry and algebra, and (if I rightly comprehend it) proposing not to examine the students of all years, but only to give one previous examination before the degree, except for noblemen and fellow-commoners who should have a second one in Locke, natural philosophy, and modern history[2].

Dr Powell died in 1775, but Jebb by renouncing his Orders in that year had not improved the prospects of his scheme.   In 1773 he had seen a syndicate appointed without opposition, but in 1774 his propositions having passed the caput were thrown out by one

---

institution of a general annual examination, in 1766 and earlier years. *Autobiog. Anecd.* I. 47.

Thomas Jones (see p. 123), who had been an undergraduate of S. John's but took his degree (1779, senior wrangler, being private tutor to the 2nd) from Trinity, where he became senior tutor, having a larger 'side' than any of his predecessors, was moderator in 1786, 7, and introduced a grace by which fellow-commoners were subjected to the same academical exercises as other undergraduates. *Memoir by* Herbert Marsh, Aikin's Athenaeum, 1808, XIII. 261, cf. ibid. 539.

[1] A writer in the P. S. to a Letter in the *Gentleman's Magazine*, April 14, 1774 (copied in Bodl. *Gough Cambr.* 67) speaks of 'Open Examinations in private Colleges at which all the Scholars must and all the Fellows may be present' as supplying the

desideratum at Cambridge. This, which was Dr W. S. Powell's *panacea*, was made the argument against Jebb's project for a yearly compulsory university examination.   See Mayor's *Hist. of St John's, pp.* 1066—1068.

'One Master in Cambridge' (continues the MS., referring to Dr Powell, Master of S. John's 1765—1775,) 'introduced such Examinations in his own College some years ago, soon after his Election to the Mastership there: the Master assigns the books and subject for the Examination a sufficient time beforehand, appoints proper Examiners in the several branches....The Master has allways [sic] made it a Rule to be Present himself at these College Examinations.'

[2] J. Jebb's *Works,* I. (= *Memoir*) 45—51, 59—82, 88—91, 110—118. II. 255—390. III. 268—282.   Cooper's *Annals,* IV. 367, 369, 371, 382.

vote in the non-regent house. But all his efforts, and his clever wife's, were of no avail; his own vote was declared forfeited by statute in Feb. 1776, and he retired from Cambridge.

In 1821 Dr Wordsworth's scheme for an examination in Classics and Theology was rejected in the non-regent house, but in May 1822 he and others procured[1] the establishment of the Classical tripos, and Homer and Virgil for the 'Poll,' and two months earlier the Grace for the Previous Examination was passed[2].

Account of Annual Examinations

in S. John's at the time of Jebb's movement

1773—5.

From a ms. paper in the Bodleian[3].

'Dec. 1773.

' The subjects for the Examination in June 1774 will be

For ⎧Plain and Physical Astronomy
the ⎨Butler's Analogy
Sophs. ⎩3^d 10th and 13th Satyres of Juvenal.

Junior ⎧Mechanics
Sophs ⎨1st vol. of Locke
　　⎩Cicero's 2nd Philippic.

　　　⎧Algebra
Freshmen ⎨Logic
　　　⎩Demosthenes περι στεφανου.

' For all years the last 14 Chapters of St Matthew.'

[Then commences on the same page an official report of the result of the examination, written in a fair clerkly hand; but dated ' *June* 1774' by the writer of the list of subjects.]

' *Of the third year*[4] Sheepshanks, Hall, Mr Burrell and Wright 2^dows [sic., for secundus] have the prizes. Phillips, Hart and Caulet are the next. These seven distinguished themselves as having studied Physical Astronomy and even also are superior to the rest in all the subjects. But Wilkinson was very near them in plain Astronomy and Butler: Tighe, Willis, and Bateman did well and Thornhill also in the Classic.'

[We have omitted to transcribe the report 'of the 2nd year' and

---

[1] Whewell, *Of a Liberal Education*, § 218; *Sermons* (1847) p, 381.

[2] Baker's *Hist. of S. John's*, Mayor, 1055, 1071.

[3] *Gough Camb.* 67. the contents of which volume relate mainly to Jebb's Examination Schemes.

[4] The Johnians who went out in the tripos of 1775 were as follows;—

Wranglers.		Sen. optt.	
*Coulthurst	2nd	Wilkinson	4th
*Sheepshanks	4th	Phillips	8th
Hart	8th		
*Heberden	9th	*Jun. opt.*	
Hall	10th	*Tighe	8th
		* fellows.	

'of those who were now examined for the first time,' but the following extracts may be profitable] 'Collins would have been thought before some of the others. But though it was verily ill health which prevented him from being examined at Christmas he could not be considered in the distribution of the prizes....Burton... should not have neglected the Greek Testament. Mr Townshend was thought to be the best in Cicero but he had not studied the other parts. Of those examined for the first time "No one appeared to deserve a prize for the ms." [? = Mathematicks[1]].

'Pyke obtained a prize and one of the best exhibitions by his constant attendance at Chapel. Cooke, Collins, Poston and Smith sen[r]., who were next to him in regularity, have also exhibitions on this account.

'The behaviour of the Fellow Commoners[2] in this point has been observed, as notice was given last year that it would be.

'Among them Lord Midleton and Lord Powis whilst they stayed here were exemplary. Mr Broderick also has deserved much praise, and some who have been but a short time have given reason to expect from them like behaviour.

'There is no other part of their conduct by which they can merit greater honour or shame.'

[Then in the original hand follow :—]

'*Subjects of the next examination* Dec. 1774.

'Hydrostatics and optics
2nd Vol. of Locke
Antigone of Sophocles
6 first books of Euclid
Hutchinsons Moral Philosophy
21 Book of Livy
Stanyans Grecian history except ye 1st Bk. of ye 1st vol.
Horace's Art of Poetry
For all the years S[t] Marks Gospel.'

[There is subsequently a short report of the examination in the above subjects.]

'*Of the Sophs* ...

'Mr Kinnersley would have received more praise, had it not been remembered how much better he appeared last year.

'Mr Townshend by his translation of Sophocles showed his abilities

---

[1] An algebraical problem attributed to Dr Powell commencing 'A silversmith received in payment for a certain weight of wrought plate' is inserted in Bland. See preface to W. Rotherham's S. John's Coll. Papers, 1794—1852 and p. 256 *supra*.

[2] At this period (says Jebb, *Works*, III. *l.c.*) 'the noblemen and fellow-commoners also sometimes receive instruction in the chamber of the public tutor, but are never called upon by the *university* to give any public proof of their proficiency in learning.' For the reform introduced in this matter ten years later see above p. 88, and compare pp. 14, 15.

to be of the firstrate, and then left everyone to lament that he had
not applied them to any other subject.

'Lord powis appeared very well in Sophocles.

Of the Second year.

'Seven excelled in every part, they were Portal, Mr Broderick,
Hughes jʳ, Mr Villiers, Mr Otley, Pigott, Smith senʳ.

The third year
is only distinguished into classes ...

'The subjects of the examination in June 1775 will be

| For the Sophs. | { | Plain and Physical Astronomy. Butler's Analogy. The two first books of Lucretius. |

| For the Junʳ Sophs. | { | Mechanics. The first volume of Locke. The Phoenissae of Euripides. |

| For the Freshmen. | { | Algebra. Logic. Mounteney's Demosthenes. |

For all the year's St Lukes Gospel[1]'.

I have selected the following specimen from half a dozen ms.
EXAMINATION PAPERS in Caius Coll. Library [731 *red*], probably of
the end of last century.

I cannot say with any certainty whether the said papers were
produced or used originally in the College of Vince and Gooch.
There is in the Gonville and Caius College Library a collection of
latin exercises, epitaphic verses &c. by Emmanuel men and others;
also notes of Chemistry lectures by a student of Trinity, as well as
the miscellaneous reliques of the Schools, of which specimens are given
below in our eighth Appendix.

[1] On the same page and in the same hand, but dated 1769 Decᵇʳ. 'It was hoped yᵗ yᵉ Instruction given last year to such of the present Sophs as then appeared very much unprepared wd. have been sufficient to have mad em more diligent. But as it seems to have had no Influence some further trial must be made to do em good. J—— for a total neglect of his studies & for an obstinate refusal to be examined is Suspended from taking a degree till yᵉ end of May term after the usual time & his grace will not then be allowd unless he comes to the 3 next examinations with the year below him & behaves himself better yⁿ he has yet done. W. C. A. and M. must be examin'd in private about Ladyday, that it may then be determind whether they can or cannot be allowd to proceed to their degree. I. must be examin'd hereafter with his own year & yᵉ same is thought proper for P—— tho he is not so deficient as the others here named.'

(1) To find the area of a Parabola generated by a line revolving about the focus.

(2) Suppose that within the Earth's Surface the force of Gravity varied inversely as the Cube of the distance, to find the absolute time in which a Body would descend thro' the Space S.

(3) To find the time of oscillation in an Epicycloid.

(4) To find the force by which the oscillations of a Pendulum would become *isochronal* in any Curve.

(5) To find the attraction to a Sphere, the attraction of each particle varying inv^y as Dist.

(6) Prove that Within a Spheroid the attraction varies in the same right line as the distance from the Center.

(7) To find the *Latitudinal* Aberration of a ray incident parallel to the axis of a Spherical Reflector.

(8) Find the effect of the Precession of the Equinoxis upon the right Ascension and Declination of a given star.

(9) Prove that the altitude is the Log. of the Rarity, the Modulus being the Height of an homogeneous Atmosphere.

APPENDIX VII.

ANTIQUITIES OF THE TRIPOS-LISTS AND CALENDARS.

PROCTORS' SENIOR OPTIMES. HONORARY AND AEGROTAT DE-
GREES, 1750—97. JUNIOR PROCTOR'S MEMORANDUM, 1752.
SOME NOTES ON THE OLD UNIVERSITY CALENDARS, 1796, &c.

HONORARY AND AEGROTAT DEGREES.

As the *proctors' optimes* (or degrees granted without examination,
by the prerogative of the vice-chancellor, proctors and moderators)
and *aegrotat* degrees are (with very few exceptions) omitted from the
lists as they are printed in the Cambridge University Calendar, it
may be as well to publish the following list of them extracted from
the records in the Registrary's office. The *dagger* represents a mys-
terious mark in the subscription-book. I have added the *asterisk* for
those who obtained fellowships, and the μ for medallists.

This column shews in what colleges
the *patronage* for the year was
vested.

1750-51. *Adam Wall, *Chr.*	
*C. Hedges, *Pet.*	}[1] V.C., *Pet.*; Proctors & Moderators, *Pemb.* & *Chr.*
*E. Delaval, *Pembr.*	
†*H. Pelham, *Corpus.*	
1753. Is. M. Rebow, *Trin.*	
W. Amos, *Jes.*	
*G. Robinson, *Trin.*	}{ *Jes.*; *Jes.*, and *Trin.*; *King's* and *Magd.*
W. Chafin, *Emm.*[2]	
1754. C. Hope, *Joh.*	
†μ*S. Hallifax, *Jes.*[3]	}{ *Jes.*; *Clare* and *Joh.*
*Fleetwood Churchill, *Clare.*	
†μ*H. Emsall[4], *Joh.*	

[1] These four names *are* printed in
the *Calendar* between the senior-wrangler's name and Cardale's (Pembr.). In
the Grace Book K., they sign their
names even before the senior-wrangler
Hewthwaite.

Adam Wall wrote *University Ceremonies*, 1798.

†*H. Pelham* was fellow of Peterhouse.
E. Delaval, see p. 15.

[2] *Chafin* (see pp. 29, 363) is put at
the head of the senior optimes; the
other three stand above the 2nd wrangler. Chafin's was practically an aegrotat degree.

[3] *Hallifax*, fellow also of Trin. H.,

1755.	μ*East Apthorpe[1], *Jes*..................	*Chr.; Qu.* and *Sid.*
1756.	Obad. Lane[2], *Emm*..................	*Pet.; Caius* and *Emm.*
1757.	Walter Rawlinson, *Trin.*	
	J. Rouse, *King's*	*King's; Cath.* and *King's.*
	Humfrey Primatt[3], *Clare*	(the ' conduct' nominated by *King's* as moderator, was rejected.
1758.	J. Hepworth, *Corpus*	
	*G. Leycester, *Trin.*	*Corpus; Pet.* and *Trin.*
	Ri. Harvey, *Corpus.*	
1759.	W. Stevenson, *Joh.*	
	*S. Berdmore, *Jes.*	*Jes.; Chr.* and *Joh.*
	*Nic. Brown, *Chr.*	
	μ*J. Hawes, *Jes.*	
1760.	*S. Reeve[4], *Caius*	*Caius; Corpus,* and *Pemb.*
	F. Dodsworth, *Chr.*	
1761.	E. Bourchier, *Chr.*	
	†*J. Wycherly[5], *Qu.*	*Magd.; Queens'* and *Clare.*
	J. Castell, ⎱ *Caius.*	
	R. Heaton, ⎰	
1762.	Jos. Locke, *Qu.*	
	T. Wagstaff, *Chr.*	*Queens'; King's* and *Magd.;*
	*J. Twells, *Emm.*	*Pet.* and *Magd.*
	*W. Strong, *Trin.*	
1763.	G. Scurfield, *Joh.*	
	Booth Hewitt, *Jes.*	*Clare; Jes.* and *Trin.;*
	*Hopkins Fox, *Trin.*	*Pet.* and *Trin.*
	Ro. Lewis, *Jes.*	
1764.	C. Pigott Pritchett, ⎱ *Joh.*	
	W. Colchester, ⎰	*Sid.; Pet.* and *Joh.*
	*Ri. Bell ⎱ *Clare*	
	*J. Freeman ⎰	
1765.	Matthias D'oyly, *Corpus*	
	*J. V. Brutton, *Sid.*	*Corpus; Chr.* and *Sid.;*
	J. Wright, *Chr.*	*Trin.* and *Sid.*
	Julius Hutchinson, *Sid.* (Bar[t].)	
1766.	T. Craster, *Joh.*	
	C. Foot, *Joh.* ? *Emm.*	*Joh.; Caius* and *Emm.;*
	Ro. Tilyard, *Caius*	*Caius* and *Sid.*
	†*Ri. Halke[6], *Corpus*	
1767.	W. Johnson, *Caius*	*Caius; Pet.* and *Trin.*
	J. Beverly[7], *Chr.*	
1768.	*Edm. Smith[8], *Magd.*	*Trin. Hall; Cath.* and *Trin.;*
	J. Lingard, *Cath.*	*Pet.* and *Trin.*
	J. Burrows, *Trin.*	
1769.	H. Byne, *Joh.*	
	*Bert. Russel, *Trin.*	*Trin.; Queens'* and *Joh.;*
	Ro. Outlaw, *Qu.*	*Pet.* and *Joh.*
	G. Metcalf, *Trin.*	

professor of arabic & of law, Bp. of Gloster and S. Asaph;—his name *is* printed in the Calendar, perhaps because he was a medallist. Yet cp. 1755, 1759.

[4] †*Elmsall* stands at the head of the senior optimes: he was fellow of Emmanuel.

[1] *E. Apthorp* advocated S. P. G. in print 1765; wrote *Discourses on Prophecy,* 2 vols. 1786, and Sermons.

[2] *Lane* comes after the 3rd wrangler.

[3] *H. Primatt* wrote *Mercy to Animals,* 1766.

[4] *Sam. Reeve* (suicide at Commencement, 1789, when senior proctor.)— His name follows the senior's, and *Dodworth's* comes after the 2nd wrangler's.

[5] †*J. Wycherley,* fellow of *Sid.*

[6] *Ri. Halke,* fellow of *Clare.*

[7] *J. Beverley,* the notorious esquire bedell 1770—1826.

[8] *Edm. Smith,* D.C.L. *Oxon.*

1770. *G. Watson[1], *Trin.*
    C. E. de Coetlogon, *Pembr.*
    J. Penneck[2], *Trin.*
         Emm.; Chr. and *Pet.; Trin.* and *Chr.*

1771. *J. Stanhawe Watts, *Caius.*
    Ri. Wish, *Trin.*
    G. Cuthbert, *Chr.*
         King's; Clare and *King's; Clare* and *Joh.*

1772. H. Williams, *Trin.*
    G. Bryant, *Corpus.*
    Nic. Lechmere Grimwood, *Joh.*
         Pemb.; Corpus and *Joh.; Trin.* and *Corpus.*

1773. G. Whitcher, *Pembr.*
    J. Pettiward,   } *Trin.*
    H. [Boulton] Crabb, }
    W. Avarne, *Emm.*
         King's; Magd. and *Joh.; Corpus* and *Joh.*

1774. *J. Mirehouse, *Clare.*
    *T. J. Mathias[3], *Trin.*
         Jesus; Pembr. and *Jes.; Joh.* and *Chr.*

1775. W. Hickin, *Magd.*
    W. Dickinson, *Trin.*
    Egerton Leigh, *Sid.*
    *E. Balme, *Magd.*
         Magd.; Queens' and *Sid.; Sid.* and *Joh.*

1776. G. Isted, *Trin.*
    *H. W. Majendie[4], *Chr.*
    Ri. Relhan[5], *Trin.*
    †*Nic. Simons[6], *Chr.*
         Emm.; Emm. and *King's; Emm.* and *Magd.*

1777. *W. Grigson, *Caius*
    S. Edmundson Hopkinson, *Clare*
    J. Forster, *Trin.*
    *ffoliott-Herbert Cornewall[7], *Joh.*
    Ja. Cullum, *Chr.*
    Jos. Lodington, *Sid.*
         Joh.; Trin. and *Caius.*

1778. *J. Prettyman[8] *Pembr.*
    *T. Crick, *Caius.*
    J. Raper,   } *Joh.*
    W. England[9], }
    J. Newell Puddicombe[10], *Pemb.*
         Queens'; Pet. and *Joh.; Jes.* and *Joh.*

1779. *T. Horncastle Marshall, *Clare*
    Hor. Hammond, *Corpus.*
    J. Beevor, *Chr.*
    Ri. Eaton,   } *Joh.*
    C. Curteis, }
         Corpus; Chr. and *Clare; Chr.* and *Jes.*

1780. ....
         Cath.; King's and *Corpus.*

1781. *Walt. Whiter, *Clare.* aegr.
    Bethell Robinson, *Chr.*
    J. Greame, *Trin.*
    ?E. Jacob, *Pembr.*
    J. Lomax, *Cath.*
         Chr.; Pemb. and *Trin.*

---

[1] *G. Watson*, D.D., master of Doncaster.

[2] *J. Penneck* migrated to Peterhouse.

[3] *T. J. Mathias*, author of *Pursuits of Literature*, 1794—7, &c. &c., edited *Gray's works*.

[4] *H. W. Majendie*, Bp. of Chester and Bangor.

[5] *Ri. Relhan*, F.R.S., F.L.S., wrote *Flora Cantabrigiensis*, 1785.

[6] †*Nic. Simons* was also fellow of *Clare.*

[7] *ff-H. Cornewall*, Bp. of Bristol, Hereford, and Worcester.

[8] *J. Pretyman*, archd. of Lincoln, brother of Bp. G. Pretyman-Tomline.

[9] *W. England*, D.D. author.

[10] *J. N. Puddicombe*, fellow of Dulwich Coll. author of *Albion Triumphant*, 1781, and a *Poem* to the opponents of the *Slave Trade*, 1788.

1782. J. Chestney, *Pet.* aegrot.
       F. W. Blomberg[1], *Joh.*
       Owen Jones, *Jes.*   }   *Jes.; Joh.* and *Jes.*
       T. Robinson[2], *Joh.*
       †*A. Owen[3], *Chr.*

1783. *Matt. Wilson, *Trin.* 'aegrot. in 1[ma] classe   } { Quaestionistarum cen-
       Walthall Gretton, *Trin.* aegrot. in 2[da] classe } { sebantur a Modera-
                                                 toribus.'

       Hugh Owen, } *Joh.*
       Ja. Salt,   }
       Johnson Towers, *Queens'*   }   *Jes.; Queens'* and *Magd.*
       *J. Haggitt, *Clare*
1784. T. Ewbank, *Cath.*   }   *Clare; Cath.* and *Pet.; Sid.*
       *Jos. Twigger, *Cath.*   }   and *Trin.*
1785. T. Harrison, *Trin.* aegrot. in 1[ma] classe.
       S. Heyrick [Hill] *Trin.* aegrot. in 3[ia] classe.
       Baptist J. Proby, *Trin.*
       Barry Robertson, *Joh.*   }   *Magd.; King's* and *Sid.;*
       G. Wollaston, *Clare*   }   *Queens'* and *Sid.*
       Roger [Freston] Howman, *Pembr.* }
1786. Ja. Losh, *Trin.* aegrot. in 2[da] classe.
       Ro. Bradstreet[4], *Joh.*
       Chr. Wilson, *Sid.*   }   *Pembr.; Trin.* and *Emm.;*
       T. Whitaker, *Emm.*   }   *Trin.* and *Magd.*
       Ja. Reeve, *Joh.*
1787. J. Longe, *Trin.*
       T. Wallace, *Corpus*   }   *Sid.; Chr.* and *Joh.;*
       J. Vachell, *Pembr.*   }   *Trin.* and *Joh.*
       *Wilfrid Clarke, *Pet.*
1788. J. Ashpinshaw[5], *Emm.*
       Lanc. Pepys Stephens, *Pembr.* }   *Emm.; Pembr.* and *Clare;*
       J. Hughes, *Qu.*   }   *Joh.* and *Trin. Hall.*
       J. Milnes, *Jes.*
       *J. Blunt, *Joh.* } aegrot. in 2[da] classe.
       T. Carter, *Trin.* }
1789. P. [W.] Jolliffe, *Joh.*
       C. Hayward, *Caius.*   }   *Pet.; Caius* and *Corpus; Trin.*
       J. Crawford, *Joh.*   }   and *Trin. Hall.*
       J. Bennett, *Clare*
       *W. Pugh, *Trin.* aegrot. in 1[ma] classe[6].
1790. J. Rideout, *Jes.*
       Nath. Stackhouse, } *Joh.*   }   *Jes.; King's* and *Qu.;*
       Alex. J. Scott[7], }   }   *Trin.* and *Qu.*
       Ro. Bransby Francis, *Corpus*
       *T. Butler, *Trin.*, aegrot. in 1[ma] classe.

---

[1] *F. W. Blomberg* was D.D.

[2] *T. Robinson*, author of *Sketches in Verse* 1796, religious treatises, &c.

[3] †*A. Owen* was fellow of *Emmanuel.*

[4] *Ro. Bradstreet*, author of *The Sabine Farm, a Poem*, 1810.

[5] *J. Ashpinshaw* was LL.D.

[6] 'I heard him keep his Act, in which he displayed extraordinary learning, but no great knowledge of the subjects under discussion; hence he considered that Hailstone had conferred on him a very appropriate honour when, after complimenting him on the composition of his Thesis he added, "*Erudite disputasti.*" Pugh's name did not appear on the Tripos, probably on account of ill health; but he was elected Fellow..., and it was understood he had passed a remarkably good examination. When he took his B.D. degree [? 1799] he read a very learned and eccentric Thesis, which was entirely written on the covers of letters.' *Reminisc.* ii. ch. ii. by H. Gunning, who gives other anecdotes of Pugh.

[7] *A. J. Scott* was D.D. per reg. litt. 1806.

1791.   *W. Gray, *Pet.* ⎫
       Ro. Hankinson, *Trin.* ⎬ aegrot. in 1ma classe.
       T. Wingfield, *Joh.* ⎭

       T. Causton, *Joh.*
       W. Heath Marsh[1], *Corpus* ⎫
       T. Bewicke, *Jes.*   ⎬ *Joh.; Trin.* and *Jes.*
       *Jos. Gill, *Joh.*   ⎭

1792.   W. Townley, *Trin.*
       H. J. Wollaston[2], *Sid.*   ⎫ *Trin.; Pet.* and *Joh.;*
       Ja. Drake, *Joh.*   ⎬ *Sid.* and *Joh.*
       Warre Squire Bradley, *Joh.* ⎭
       J. Taylor, *Trin.* aegrotat.

1793.   *J. Hepworth, *Caius,* aegrot. in 1ma classe.
1794.   Ri. Ashworth, *Emm.*   ⎫ aegrot. in 1ma classe.
       Legh Richmond[3], *Trin.* ⎭
1797.   Dewhurst Bilsborrow[4], *Trin.*   (*Caius; Clare* and *Emm.;*
                                                Pet. and *Joh.*)

       *W. Webb, *Clare,* aegrot. in 1ma quaestionistarum classe.

At this point the record of honorary and aegrotat degrees breaks off. Of the former the *University Calendar* of 1804 (p. 141) testifies that the custom of conferring them had of late years been abandoned. Of aegrotat degrees no record was kept subsequently until Mr Luard became registrary, and they are not printed in the Calendar with the exception of the name of R. Kalley Miller of Peterhouse (1867) who was first Smith's prizeman. They now appear however on the back of the tripos-verses as of old, though that custom was discontinued after 1797 for many years.

It will be observed that among the early medallists three members of Jesus College had been somewhat questionably qualified for competition by an honorary degree. The name of S. Hallifax (1754) is even printed in the Calendar as if he had been third wrangler, while East Apthorpe (1755) and J. Hawes (1759) are not so immortalized.

In the years 1757, '58, '61, '62, '64, 1766—8, 1770—72, '76 the names of the 'gratuitous honorati' stand immediately after the senior wrangler's. In a few years (1754, '59, '63, '65, '69) they are even put before him! In 1773—5 and 1777—82 they stand at the head of the senior optimes. In 1783 they are degraded to the head of the junior optimes, and after 1797 they disappear. It will be seen that a smaller proportion of the gratuitous honorati had gained fellowships latterly.

The first aegrotat degree was registered in 1778. Others, as will be seen, were granted in 1781, 1782, 1783 (the class, see p. 45, being recorded for the first time and the names placed above the senior optimes, while those of the 'proctors' optimes' were put down to head the junior optimes), 1785, 1786, 1788—94, 1797. From that date the record is not kept until we come to the tripos papers of the present century.

[1] W. H. Marsh translated the Satires of Juvenal into English Verse, 1804.
[2] H. J. *Wollaston,* King's Chaplain.
[3] *Legh Richmond* wrote *Supposed*

Abstinence of Anne Moore, 1813, *Sermons,* &c.
[4] *D. Bilsborrow* mentioned in Dr Wordsworth's *Diary,* ap. *Univ. Life,* 588, 589.

Many original lists of the old 'classes' have been preserved by the late Dr Webb of Clare Hall in the first of his large albums or, more strictly speaking, blue-books, which are now in the University library.

The following document is perhaps a unique Junior Proctor's paper (1752).

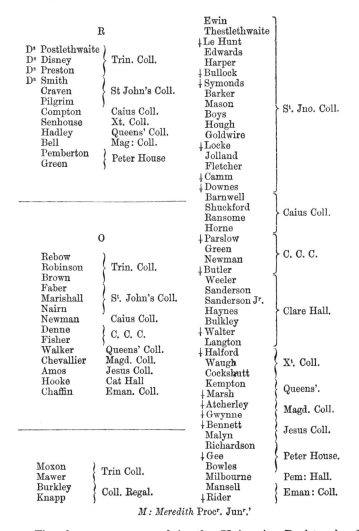

```
                    R                    Ewin            ⎫
                                         Thestlethwaite  ⎪
Dˢ Postlethwaite ⎫                       +Le Hunt        ⎪
Dˢ Disney        ⎬ Trin. Coll.           Edwards         ⎪
Dˢ Preston       ⎪                       Harper          ⎪
Dˢ Smith         ⎭                       +Bullock        ⎪
Craven           ⎫                       +Symonds        ⎪
Pilgrim          ⎬ St John's Coll.       Barker          ⎪
Compton          ⎭ Caius Coll.           Mason           ⎬ Sᵗ. Jno. Coll.
Senhouse           Xt. Coll.             Boys            ⎪
Hadley             Queens' Coll.         Hough           ⎪
Bell               Mag: Coll.            Goldwire        ⎪
Pemberton        ⎫                       +Locke          ⎪
Green            ⎬ Peter House           Jolland         ⎪
                                         Fletcher        ⎪
_____          +Camm           ⎪
                                         +Downes         ⎭
                                         Barnwell        ⎫
                                         Shuckford       ⎬ Caius Coll.
                                         Ransome         ⎪
                    O                    Horne           ⎭
                                         +Parslow        ⎫
Rebow            ⎫                       Green           ⎬ C. C. C.
Robinson         ⎬ Trin. Coll.           Newman          ⎪
Brown            ⎭                       +Butler         ⎭
Faber            ⎫                       Weeler          ⎫
Marishall        ⎬ Sᵗ. John's Coll.      Sanderson       ⎪
Nairn            ⎭                       Sanderson Jʳ.   ⎪
Newman             Caius Coll.           Haynes          ⎬ Clare Hall.
Denne            ⎫ C. C. C.              Bulkley         ⎪
Fisher           ⎭                       +Walter         ⎪
Walker             Queens' Coll.         Langton         ⎭
Chevallier         Magd. Coll.           +Halford        ⎫
Amos               Jesus Coll.           Waugh           ⎬ Xᵗ. Coll.
Hooke              Cat Hall              Cockshutt       ⎪
Chaffin            Eman. Coll.           Kempton         ⎭
                                         +Marsh          ⎫ Queens'.
_____          +Atcherley      ⎭
                                         +Gwynne         ⎫ Magd. Coll.
                                         +Bennett        ⎭
                                         Malyn           ⎫ Jesus Coll.
                                         Richardson      ⎭
Moxon            ⎫                       +Gee            ⎫ Peter House.
Mawer            ⎬ Trin Coll.            Bowles          ⎭
Burkley          ⎫                       Milbourne         Pem: Hall.
Knapp            ⎬ Coll. Regal.          Mansell         ⎫ Eman: Coll.
                                         +Rider          ⎭
```

M: Meredith Procʳ. Junʳ.'

The above was preserved in the University Registry by Mr Romilly, who says in a note 'I have no idea of the meaning of this.'

I think his attention must have been distracted by some of the frequent interruptions to which his office is subject, or he would speedily have conjectured that 'R' stands for *respondents*, 'O' for *opponents*. I suppose it was a memorandum taken from the reports supplied by college-tutors (see above p. 34) for the guidance of the moderators in pitting opponents against respondents for the acts.

All the names above the lower line in the left-hand column, twenty-six in number (*cf.* p. 48), after some shuffling in order, were dignified with a place on the first tripos, in *com. prior.*; all these respondents and four of the opponents being distinguished as the wranglers of the year.

'Chaffin...Eman. Coll.' is W. Chafin whose act has been described (pp. 29, 30), and whose name appeared among the *gratuitous honorati* of his year (1753) though not with the first trio of them, Rebow, Robinson and Amos.

The names beginning with *Moxon* (inclusive of those in the right-hand column) afterwards appeared in the poll.

†⫟† Those to which an inverted *obelisk* is prefixed are *erased in the original* ms. Their owners mounted up to be junior optimes (in *Comitiis posterioribus*), which Mr Romilly did not observe.

The following, without appearing on this Junior Proctor's Paper, were added to the list of the 'poll.' Were they bye-term men?

J. Longe	*Magd.*	J. Casborne	*Emman.*
J. Cradock	} *Cath.*	J. Hallam	} *Queens'*
E. Tyrwhitt		J. Foster	
	R. Sherman *Clare.*		

THE CAMBRIDGE UNIVERSITY CALENDAR.

Although a complete series of these Calendars is not very commonly to be found, there are such collections in the University library and at Peterhouse and Pembroke. Dr Edleston of Gainford also possesses a set.

The first issue (like a few of the subsequent ones) was the venture of a private member of the University. This was in

1796. Edited by G. Mackenzie, B. A., Trin., pp. 190. It commences with two pages on the Origin of the University.

1797. By J. Beverley (esquire bedell), pp. 248. Mr Romilly ascribes this also to Mackenzie.

1798. *No publication.*

1799. By B. C. Raworth, Trin. Hall, assisted by Ri. Sill and W. Webb of Clare, pp. 161 (purposely abridged).

1800. By a member of Trinity Hall [B. C. Raworth], pp. 120.

1801. B. C. Raworth, pp. 168. Dedicated to Archd. Gretton, Master of Magdalene, V. C.

1802 (Feb. 15). B. C. Raworth, price 5s., dedication to D. of Gloster, pp. i—lviii, 1—205, index, list of college servants (Butlers, Cooks, Porters, Chapel Clerks, Barbers, Jips, or Bed-Makers, favouring the derivation from γύψ[1], Master of the Union Coffee House), List of London Coaches. This Calendar is by far the most entertaining, by reason of the circumstantial Introduction founded upon Jebb's account 1773[2]. Such authorities have furnished much information for this present compilation.

In the 'Advertisement' prefixed to the Calendar for 1801 Raworth had made this queer reference to Is. Milner. Complaining that he 'should be obliged in some instances, to withhold *any* expression of gratitude'—he continues,

'A remark of this sort seemed necessary to account for the *laconicism* which characterises the statement at * Queen's college in particular. To obviate any charge of inattention the Editor feels himself bound thus publicly to declare, that application (he believes) was made not as hitherto, to the *communicative* Vice-President [F. Knipe, B.D.], but to the highest authority, the PRESIDENT; from whom (*considering his usual activity in University Affairs*), information was confidently expected. A reservedness on this occasion, might possibly proceed from *Indisposition*.'

'* A Librarian's place of 10£ per annum and several Scholarships...are considered as amongst the number of Omissions. For the truth of these assertions the Editor has however *no* authority to state, and less inclination to make any comments. Such is the report!'

The Calendar for 1802 in its Advertisement says: '...Through the polite permission of the Rev. and Right Worshipful the Vice-Chancellor, the several names in the *Triposes* have been again compared with the Subscription Book in his possession; yet, notwithstanding this precaution, the *capricious* manner in which some living Characters have therein subscribed, with regard to the spelling of their names, renders in some few instances, accuracy an impossibility...

'*Four* well-known Publications have been freely consulted...

'Our Sister University having done us the honor to adopt our Examinations as her model, and to publish a List (though incomplete, the *Bachelors* being omitted) of her *Graduates;* it is hoped she will soon exhibit as fair, candid and impartial a statement of her *Colleges, Emoluments* and *Honors* as is this year presented of the University of Cambridge.

'*Trinity Hall*, February
        15th, 1802.'

The book was published in stiff paper boards, bluish grey, bordered by a running pattern of arrow-heads, with a salmon-coloured back, in the form shewn on our next page, only with a height (6⅜ inches) which our procrustean sheet has warped.

---

[1] Some of the earliest Calendars contain a note on the words *tripos* and *harrisoph*.

[2] Works II. 285—299. It appeared also in *Gent. Mag.* See above, pp. 33, 45.

An universally interesting and useful Publication.

THE
CAMBRIDGE
UNIVERSITY CALENDAR,
FOR THE YEAR
1802.

CONTAINING

a list of the several colleges,
and their
present respective members;
with all the

Fellowships, Scholarships, Exhibitions and Prizes,
Fees for Degrees, &c.

UNIVERSITY OFFICERS AND PROFESSORS,
For a CENTURY past;
copies of the TRIPOSES
and

The Moderators of each Year;
Medallists and Prizemen;
University Ceremonies;
Travelling Bachelors;
Senate-house examinations, &c., &c.

By BENJAMIN CLARKE RAWORTH, A.B.
TRINITY HALL.

CAMBRIDGE,

Printed and Sold by F. Hodson, Corner of Green-Street.
For Nicholson, *Cambridge;* Rivingtons, *St Paul's Church*
Yard; and Lunn, Soho Square *London:* and may be had,
on application, of all Booksellers in the *United Kingdom.*

Colleges. Prizes.
)(
Prize-Men.

CAMBRIDGE
UNIVERSITY
CALENDAR

Scholarships
)(
Exhibitions

Profs. Officers
)(
Triposes

Exercises
)(
Fees for Degrees

Senate-House
)(
Examinations,
&c.

1802.
Price 5s.

NICHOLSON'S

CIRCULATING LIBRARY,

Near the Senate-House, Cambridge,

Established Fifty Years.

Subscription 7s. 6d. per Quarter;

For which each SUBSCRIBER is allowed to have
FIFTEEN BOOKS at once.

A Quarter's advance to be paid at the time of Subscribing.

STATIONARY,

Of all Kinds, and of the best Quality, and on the
lowest Terms.

NEW PUBLICATIONS, and Books of every Description
procured on the Shortest Notice.

BOOKBINDING executed in a variety of plain or
elegant Fashions.

Cambridge: printed by F. Hodson.

1803. 'The Cambridge University Register...by John Beverley, M.A.—Cambridge : printed for and sold by the Editor and by J. Deighton, Cambridge :' also Rivingtons, Lunn, and Hatchard. Printed by R. Watts ; pp. i—viii, 1—206 ; no dedication ; date, May 24. Apology for late appearance. Problem papers by consent of the Moderators. Wall's *Ceremonies* makes it unnecessary to print so long an account of University customs as in 1802, except about the Schools and Senate House.

From 1802 onwards there is a pretty full account of the professors. With the year 1804 the name of the publishers (Deightons) takes the responsibility of the production, which is dedicated to Pitt and the E. of Euston ; printed at the Univ. Press, pp. 232. In 1801—25 the cut of *Alma Mater Cantabrigiae* and the motto 'Hinc Lucem et Pocula Sacra' appears on the title and boards. From 1826 to 1841 various views of the Senate-House take its place. In the earliest editions the Univ. arms are engraved on the last numbered page of the volume. Until the middle of this century there is nothing which can be fairly called a kalendar except a list of the chief terminal engagements, fairs, &c.

With the year 1811 advertisements of Deighton's mathematical publications are appended ; in 1816 their other books are enumerated and Life Insurance is advertised. In 1830 a catalogue of *Oxford University Press* books is given.

1806 contains summaries of the poll for representations of the University in parliament in 1780, 1784, 1790, 1806. Also of members of the University and of the Senate. (pp. 295.)

1807 refers to Pitt's gait, and to his statue. This Calendar contains a meteorological journal for the year 1806, registered in the University library at 2 p.m.

1812 records Pitt's installation.

The lists of stage coaches appear in 1802 and regularly precede the index from 1805—41. But in 1842 'the list of coaches is altogether omitted, as owing to the frequent changes in the time of their starting, consequent on the progress of the different railroads, &c., its insertion would not have given information that could have been depended upon.' There is an advertisement of the Post Office in Sidney Street.

1862. Political Economy lectures fully noticed.

APPENDIX VIII.

SPECIMENS OF ARGUMENTS, &c. OF THE QUESTIONISTS
in the Schools at *Cambridge*.

1772—1792.

From the MSS. in
Gonville and Caius College Library.

THE CAMBRIDGE SCHOOLS.

ARGUMENTS AND QUESTIONS, AND MODERATORS' NOTICES.
1772—1792.

WHEN a part of the foregoing Compilation was already in the press I learnt that there was a collection of 'Schools' Arguments,' &c. preserved in the library of Gonville and Caius College.

If this had been discovered a few weeks earlier, the Reader should have been spared the sight of the imitation which has been offered above (p. 39).

As through the kindness of the College officers it is now in my power to give the genuine article, an account of the aforesaid collection is appended in this place with specimens of its contents.

Bibl. Coll. Gonv. & Cai. MS.   (a thin 4to.)
Contains,

   I.   About two dozen papers of 'arguments' or sets of syllogisms (some sets filling two leaves) 1772-92.

   II.   Fourteen notices on small slips of paper bearing three questions (cp. p. 35), the 'respondent's' name and the date for which the 'act' is to come on. These do not bear the moderator's signature, being only copies to be served on one of three opponents by whose names they are usually 'backed.'

I. SPECIMENS OF ARGUMENTS[1], &c.

The words here printed in *italics* are written compendiously by *symbols, abbreviations,* or *initials only* in the original mss.

'*Quaestiones Sunt*

Rectè statuit Newtonus in octavâ Sectione Libri primi.
Methodus Fluxionum rectè se habet.
Male statuit Berkleius, Figuram istam quae Tactu et istam quae Oculo percipitur nullam inter se habere similitudinem.

[Probo] Contra *primam* [Quaestionem].

Si vi variantè ut A^{n-1}, $V^2 \propto P^n - A^n$, *cadit quaestio.*

Si posito indice n pari numero idem evadat valor V^2, sive P sit +, sive −, hoc est, sive corpus a finitâ distantiâ sive a distantiâ plusquam infinitâ, ut vocatur, descendat, *valent consequentia et argumentum.*

Probo aliter :—

Si corpus projectum ad *angulum* rectum velocitate acquisitâ cadendo ab infinitâ altitudine, vi $\propto \dfrac{1}{x^3}$, circulum describat, *cadit quaestio.*

Si in hoc casu nullum sit decrementum distantiae, *valet consequentia.*

Si *igitur* area curvilinea eique aequalis sector circularis descriptus evanescat, hoc est corpus nunquam recedat a puncto projectionis, *valent consequentia et argumentum.*

Probo aliter :—

Si in Spirali reciprocâ arcus $z \propto \dfrac{1}{x}$, ideoque $\dot{z} \propto \dfrac{\dot{x}}{x^2}$, *cadit quaestio.*

Si fluxio temporis $\dot{t}$ semper $\propto \dot{z} x^2$, in hoc casu igitur $\dot{t} \propto \dot{x}$, *valet consequentia.* ·

Si secundum Newtonum $\dot{t} \propto \dot{x} \times \dfrac{Q}{\sqrt{ABFD - z^2}}$, *valet consequentia.*

Si vero $\sqrt{ABFD - z^2}$ non sit constans Quantitas, *valent consequentia et argumentum.*

---

[1] Compare the specimen, &c. on p. 39. In the note 2 at the foot of that page I fear the word '*minor*' has been used incorrectly. Also it would be more correct to say that the proper meaning of *consequentia* being forgotten it was sometimes used loosely for *consequens*. In the latter days of the 'schools' there was considerable carelessness or ignorance of the terminology displayed. Professor Fowler has kindly furnished the following succinct explanation.

(antecedent) (consequent)
If A is B, C is D...Major Premis.
    A is B.   ....Minor Premis.
∴ C is D.   ....Conclusion.

The *connexion* between the Conclusion and Premises is called the *consequentia*, or in a Hypothetical Syllogism the term is also used of the connexion between the Antecedent and Consequent of the Major Premis.

Probo aliter :—

Si positò quòd corpus describit semicirculum ad centrum virium

$$xy = \frac{-a\,\dot{x}}{\sqrt{a^2 - x^2}}, \; cadit \; quaestio.$$

Si *igitur* fluxio temporis $t = \dfrac{-x^2\,\dot{x}}{2\sqrt{a^2 - x^2}}$, *valet consequentia.*

Si distinctâ hâc fluxione in duas partes fiat

$$= \frac{\dot{x}\sqrt{a^2 - x^2}}{2} - \frac{a^2\,\dot{x}}{2\sqrt{a^2 - x^2}},$$

valet consequentia.

Si divisâ etiam area *VCI* tempus repraesentante in duas partes, quorum altera est sector circularis, altera triangulum, fluxio sectoris sit *aequalis* parti ultimae hujus expositae fluxionis, fluxio autem trianguli non sit *aequalis* parti primae, *valent consequentia et argumentum.*

Probo aliter :—

Si aequatio ad Apsides sit hujusce formulae $x^{n+3} - ax^2 + b = 0$, *cadit quaestio.*

Si posito $n + 3$ numero impari negativo, et P maximâ distantiâ plusquam infinita, fiat haec aequatio hujusce formulae

$$x^m - cx^{m-2} + d = 0,$$

valet consequentia.

Si haec aequatio duas habeat possibiles radices affirmativas, *valent consequentia et argumentum* [1].

[Probo] Contra *Secundam* [Quaestionem].

Si crescente x uniformiter crescat x^2 accelerato motu, *cadit quaestio.*

Si totum incrementum x^2 *aequetur* incremento genito velocitate

---

[1] The Caius collection contains another paper of four arguments against *Newton* I. 8., *viz*, the 1st and 2nd of the above repeated and two others as follows:—

'Si Equatio Apsidum cum corpus projiciatur cum *Velocitate* per plusquam *Infinitam* Distantiam cadendo acquisitum (!) sit hujusce formulae

$$x^{n+3} + ax^2 - b = 0, \; cadit \; quaestio$$
$$[x^{n+3} + p^{n+1}x^2 - p^{n+1} + a^{n+1} \cdot q^2 = 0].$$

Si posito $n = -3$ haec Equatio fiat

$$x^2 - 1 + \frac{p^2}{a^2} \cdot q^2 = 0, \; valet \; consequentia.$$

Si ex hac Equatione semper sit Apsis, *valent consequentia et argumentum.*

Probo Aliter :

Si sumat Newtonus in *Corollario* tertio Propositionis quadragesimae primae in *spirali Elliptica, angulum* descriptum a *Corpore* in Trajectoriâ *proportionalem* esse seu in data *Ratione* ad Sectorem *Ellipticum* seu ad *angulum* correspondentem Circuli, posito quòd Secans hujusce posterioris *anguli* distantiae semper sit *aequalis, cadit quaestio.*

Si positâ hâc Ratione 2 : 1 distantia corporis a centro fiat infinita quando in Trajectoria perfecerit duos rectos, *valet consequentia.*

Si ad hunc *angulum* distantia fiat Curvae asymptotos, igiturque *Velocitas* finita ad infinitam Distantiam sit ad *Velocitatem* finitam ad finitam Distantiam in Ratione infinitè magnâ, *valent consequentia et argumentum.'*

primâ uniformi + incrementum[1] genitum acceleratione solâ, *valet consequentia.*

Si haec incrementa sint fluxiones, prima et secunda, ideoque per methodum fluxionum totum incrementum $x^2 = 2x\,\dot{x} + 2\,\dot{x}^2$ *valent consequentia et argumentum.*

Probo aliter :—

Si fluxio areae hyperbolicae inter 1 et 1 + x contentae, vel fluxio logarithmi 1 + x, sit aequalis $\dfrac{\dot{x}}{1 + x}$, *cadit quaestio.*

Si hâc in serie infinitâ extenso et sumptu fluenti, fiat fluens $x - \dfrac{x^2}{2} + \dfrac{x^3}{3} -$ et cetera, *valet consequentia.*

Si eodem modo inventa fluens $\dfrac{-\dot{x}}{1 - x}$ fiat $-x + \dfrac{x^2}{2} - \dfrac{x^3}{3} + ...,$ *valet consequentia.*

Si igitur sumpto x ex utraque parte 1, areae hyperbolicae inter ordinatas ad tria ista puncta ductas contentae, sint aequales : vel quod idem est Ratio 1 − x : 1 sit aequalis Rationi 1 : 1 + x, *valent consequentia et argumentum.*

[Probo] Contra *Tertiam* [Quaestionem].

Si in picturâ lineae inter se parallelae repraesententur lineis ad punctum quodvis convergentibus, *cadit quaestio.*

Si nota sit talium linearum proprieta, quòds utpote ex diversâ parte eas spectes, nunc prorsùm nunc retrorsùm videntur convergere, *valet consequentia.*

Si igitur hae lineae, mutato loco dissimiles figuras ad oculos, similem vero semper figuram ad tactum repraesentent, *valent consequentia et argumentum.*

Wollaston, Sid. Coll. Opponat primus.   *Wilson,* Trin. Coll. Respondeat.
     Octr. 30, 1782.   *Gambier,* Sid. Coll. Opp. 2.
I. Milner, Mod^r.   *Massey,* Coll. D. Joh. Opp. 3.'

The above are the arguments which F. J. H. Wollaston, who came out senior wrangler in 1783 (and was Jacksonian professor 1792-1813) brought against Matthew Wilson of Trinity (*aegrotat* in the first *class*) when he kept his act under Milner of Queens' the senior moderator. It will be observed that as first opponent he brought only five 'arguments' against the *first* 'question'; but two against the second, and one against the third to make up the usual eight. (See above pp. 37, 38).

Our next selection introduces Joseph Watson (also of Sidney) who was destined to be third wrangler in 1785 and fellow of his college, posing Sewell of Christ's who seems to have taken no degree. He was to be followed on the same side by Lax of Trinity (the senior wrangler, subsequently moderator) who when keeping one of his own

---

[1] The symbol + seems already to have become prepositional. However the genders and terminations in the MS. are hardly classical.

acts on another occasion, at an interval of a few weeks perhaps, met in Watson his own opponent.

'Quaestiones Sunt.

(1) Solis Parallaxis ope Veneris intra Solem conspiciendae a Methodo Halleii recte determinari potest.

(2) Recte statuit Newtonus in tertia sua Sectione libri primi.

(3) Diversis sensibus non ingrediuntur Ideae communes.

[Probo] *Contra primam* [Quaestionem].

Si asserat Halleius Venerem cum Soli sit proxima Londini visam, a centro Solis quatuor minutis primis distare, *cadit quaestio.*

Si in Schemate posuit semitam Veneris ad os Gangeticum quatuor etiam minutis primis distare, *valet consequentia.*

Si spectatoribus positis in diversis *parallelis* Latitudinis non eadem appareat distantia atque non licet eandem visibilem sumere distantiam in hisce duobus locis, *valent consequentia et argumentum.*

Aliter :

Si in Figurâ Halleianâ centrum Solis correspondeat cum loco Spectatoris in Tellure, *cadit quaestio.*

Si locus centri Solis a vero centro amoti ob motum Spectatoris fit curva linea, *valet consequentia.*

Si composito motu Veneris uniformi in rectâ lineâ cum motu Solari in curvâ lineâ fit Semita Veneris in disco Solis curva linea, *valet consequentia.*

Si Longitudo hujusce lineae non rectè determinari potest, *valent consequentia et argumentum.*

Aliter :

Si Spectatori ad os Gangeticum posito ob terrae motum motui Veneris contrarium contrahatur transitûs tempus integrum, *cadit quaestio.*

Si assumat Halleius contractionem hanc duodecim minutis primis temporis *aequalem,* et deinde huic Hypothesi insistendo eidem tempori aequalem probat, *valent consequentia et argumentum.*

Aliter :

Si posuit Halleius eandem visibilem semitam Veneris per Discum Solarem ad os Gangeticum et portum Nelsoni, et hanc semitam dividat in aequalia horaria spatia, *cadit quaestio.*

Si motus horarius Veneris acceleratur vel retardatur per motum totum Spectatoris in medio transitu, quò magis autem distat, minus acceleratur vel retardatur, *valet consequentia.*

Si *igitur* ob motum Veneris acceleratum ad os Gangeticum et retardatum ad portum Nelsoni hi motus non debent representari per idem spatium, *valent consequentia et argumentum.*

Aliter :

Si secundum constructionem Halleianam spectatori ad portum Nelsoni, posito tempore extensionis majore, major etiam fit transitûs duratio, *cadit quaestio.*

Si secundum eandem constructionem posito quòd Spectatori ad os Gangeticum tempus contractionis majus sit duodecim minutis primis, evadat tempus durationis majus etiam, *valet consequentia.*
Si hae duae conclusiones inter se pugnent, *valent consequentia et argumentum.*

[Probo] Contra Secundam [Quaestionem].

Si vis in Parabolâ ad Infinitam Distantiam sit infinitesimalis secundi ordinis, *cadit quaestio.*

Si Vis sit V^{ls} [or V^{ts}; ? *variabilis,* or *verticalis*] igiturque ad infinitam distantiam sit infinitesimalis quarti Ordinis, *valent consequentia et argumentum.*

Aliter :

Si *Velocitates* ad Extremitates axium minorum diversarum Elliṛsium quarum Latera recta aequantur sint inter se inversè ut Axes minores, *cadit quaestio.*
Si Locus Extremitatum omnium Axium minorum sit Parabola, *valet consequentia.*
Si *Velocitas* corporis revolventis in istâ Parabolâ sit ad *Velocitatem* ad mediam distantiam correspondentis Ellipseos ut $\sqrt{2}$: 1, *valet consequentia.*
Si *Velocitas* in *Parabola* sit inversè ut Ordinata, *valent consequentia et argumentum.*

[Probo] *Contra Tertiam* [Quaestionem]:

Aut Cadit tua Quaestio aut non possibile est hominem ab ineunte aetate caecum et jam adultum visum recipientem visu dignoscere posse id quod tangendo priùs solummodo dignoscebat. Sed poss. &c.
Si eadem Ratio quae priùs eum docebat dignoscere tangendo inter Cubum et Globum eum etiam docebit intuendo rectè dignoscere, *valent minor et argumentum.*

Feb. 20. 1784	Sewell X^{ts} Respond.
Watson 1st Opp^t.	Lax *Trin.* 2^d Opp.
	Riley S^t. *John's* 3^d Opp.'

We will add in conclusion a specimen from the days when the 'moral' question (cp. pp. 37, 40) was the most insisted on.
After *one* argument against Maclaurin cap. III. sectt. 1—8, 11—22 ; on pulleys, there follow those against the second question 'Recte statuit Paleius de Criminibus et Poenis'—there is no third question on the paper unless the sections from Maclaurin counted as two.

'*Probo aliter* [1] *contra secundam.*

Si, qui Facinus in se admittit, Poenas isti Facinori adjudicatas pendere debet[2], *cadit quaestio.*

---

[1] *aliter:* I suppose that the owner of this paper was not the *first* opponent.

[2] *debet,* as a matter of abstract justice visiting inherent guilt. *Paley's* view

Si, Criminis particeps aequè culpabilis est ac qui Crimen perpetrat, *valet consequentia.*

Si, verò secundum Paleium, qui primus Aedes alienas Furti Causa intrat majores hoc ipso Facto meruit Poenas, *valent consequentia et argumentum.*

Probo aliter :

Si, communi Bono potius quam Commodis privatis consulendum sit, *cadit quaestio.*

Si, vita alterĭus[1] est omnibus (*al.* Civitati) commune Bonum, *valet consequentia.*

Si, exinde sequitur quòd non debent malefacientes mortem unquam subire, *valent consequentia et argumentum.*

Probo aliter :

Si qui in Insidiis incidunt non debent aeque multari ac si quid Mali ultro fecissent, *cadit quaestio.*

Si, quò majore facilitate malefaciunt, eò gravioribus Suppliciis plectuntur Homines, *valet consequentia.*

Si, secundum Paleium, qui ea quae Furti sunt obnoxia surripiunt, Morti Jure damnantur, qui vero saepe pejora§ faciunt levius puniuntur, *valent consequentia et argumentum.*

§ Perjurum nimirùm numellâ[2] includunt quod Ignominium solum affert. Mortis verò supplicium non solum infert Ignominium (sic) sed etiam Vitae Privationem.'

II. NAMES OF THE DISPUTANTS.

* *The* asterisks *denote* fellows of colleges.

	RESPONDENT	OPPONENTS
1771. (Nov. 27)	C. Buckland, *Sid.*	{ (*desunt* { *nomina*)
1780. (Nov. 29)	E. Moises, *Qu.* last wrangler.	{*Mont. F. Ainsley, *Trin.*, 3rd wrangler. {*T. Catton, *Joh.*, 4th wrangler, tutor. {*A. Wood, *Magd.*, 6th sen. opt.
1782. (Oct. 30)	Mat. Wilson, *Trin.* aegrotat in 1st class.	{*F. J. H. Wollaston, *Sid.*, senior wrangler, { Jacksonian Prof. { J. E. Gambier, *Sid.* { Roger Massey, *Joh.*, last wrangler.
1784. (Feb. 20)	W. Sewell, *Chr.*	{*Jo. Watson, *Sid.*, 3rd wrangler. {*W. Lax, *Trin.*, senior ——, Lownd. Prof. {*Ri. Riley, *Joh.*, 5th ——

was that punishments are merely conventional securities for social or political convenience.

[1] There are, or there were until lately, preserved in a college at Oxford certain traditional theses for common use in the Divinity Schools, throughout which compositions the *quantities of all words were marked* and the Greek quotations spelt in western characters, for the convenience of any who should aspire to the B.D. degree with ' small latin and less greek.'

[2] *Numella*, the pillory, was the statuteable punishment for perjury, a more serious offence (it is urged) than some which were in those days visited with capital punishment.

,,	*W. Lax, *Trin.*	{*Jo. Watson, *Sid.*, 3ʳᵈ wrangler.
(??)	senior wrangler, &c.	{*Edm. Stanger, *Joh.*, 6ᵗʰ ——.
		{*J. Bourdieu, *Clare*, 7ᵗʰ ——.

1791.   *T. Allsopp, *Emm.*
(Nov. 15)   11ᵗʰ wrangler.
{?Jos. Hargrave, *Magd.*
{ W. Meyrick, *Joh.*
{ E. Cuthbert, *Jes.*, 10ᵗʰ senior opt.

,,   Ja. Stanley, *Pet.*
(Nov. 18)   ' wooden-spoon '.
{ R. G. Blick, *Pet.*
{ J. Pepper, *Jes.*
{ Jonath. Alderson, *Pemb.*

,,   F. C. Wilson, *Trin.*
(Nov. 28)   3ʳᵈ wrangler.
{*E. Maltby, *Pembr.*, 8ᵗʰ wrangler, Bp. Durham.
{*T. Jack, *Joh.*, 4ᵗʰ ——.
{*T. Allsopp, *Emm.*, 11ᵗʰ ——.

,,   *G. F. Tavel, *Trin.*
(Dec. 1)   2ⁿᵈ wrangler, tutor.
{ T. Chevallier, *Pemb.*, 14ᵗʰ senior opt.
{*Jo. Allen, *Trin.*, 7ᵗʰ wrangler, Bp. Ely.
{*E. Maltby, *Pembr.*, 8ᵗʰ ——, Bp. Durham.

,,   Ja. Legrew, *Joh.*
(Dec. 13)   last wrangler.
{*J. Cubitt, *Caius*, 8ᵗʰ senior opt.
{ T. Woodcock, *Sid.* (& *Cath.*), 15ᵗʰ wrangler.
{*T. Comings, *Trin.*, 5ᵗʰ wrangler.

,,   W. Turner, *Chr.*
(Dec. 14)   12ᵗʰ senior opt.
{ J. H. S. Cary, *Chr.*, 14ᵗʰ wrangler.
{ Adams,
{ Is. Nicholson, *Qu.*, 6ᵗʰ senior opt.

,,   ?W. Evans jun., *Chr.*
(Dec. 15)
{ J. Dickson (=Dixon), *Qu.*
{ C. Mules, *Cath.*
{ Ja. Allison, *Joh.*

1792.   *Godf. Sykes, *Sid.*
(Feb. 6.)   10ᵗʰ wrangler.
{ Paul Belcher, *Joh.*, 12ᵗʰ senior opt.
{ J. Peers, *Magd.*, 5ᵗʰ wrangler.
{ J. Hepworth, *Caius*, aegrotat in class 1.

,,   *W. Manning, *Caius.*
(Mar. 8)   9ᵗʰ wrangler.
This was apparently a provisional memorandum, from which the moderator selected *Deacon, Heming,* and *Belcher* as opponents.
{ ?. Deacon, ?.   } 1ˢᵗ.
{ *T. Dickes, *Jes.*, 11ᵗʰ wrangler.   }
{ *S. B. Hemming, *Joh.* & *Cai.*   }
{ *C. Isherwood, *Magd.*, 5ᵗʰ wrangler } 2ⁿᵈ.
{ H. Scott, *Pemb.*, 3ʳᵈ senior opt.   }
{ Paul Belcher, *Joh.*, 12ᵗʰ sen. opt. 3ʳᵈ.

,,   T. Fancourt, *Qu.*
(Mar. 19)   8ᵗʰ senior optim.
{*H. Atkinson, *Caius*, 6ᵗʰ senior opt.
{*J. G. Perigall, *Pet.*, 4ᵗʰ junior opt.
{ Mountain, *Corpus.* (?=S. J. M. *Caius.*)

,,   *J. Maul, *Chr.*
(Mar. 20)   16ᵗʰ wrangler, tutor.
{*T. Dickes, *Jes.*, 11ᵗʰ wrangler.
{*H. Hasted, *Chr.*, 6ᵗʰ ——.
{ W. W. Currey, *Qu.*

,,   T. Fox, *Cath.*
(Mar. 21)   last wrangler.
{ Paul Belcher, *Joh.*, 12ᵗʰ senior opt.
{*C. Isherwood, *Magd.*, 15ᵗʰ wrangler.
{*G. Grigby, *Caius*, 2ⁿᵈ senior opt.

(??)   *C. Heberden, *Joh.*
13ᵗʰ wrangler, senior medallist.
{ T. T. Fenwicke, *Joh.*, 4ᵗʰ wrangler.
{ J. Maule, *Chr.*, 16ᵗʰ ——, tutor.
{ C. H. Wollaston, *Sid.*, 14ᵗʰ ——.

The following is a list of the THESES or QUESTIONS mooted, in the Caius collection, so far as they can be easily ascertained. It will give a fair specimen of the subjects argued in the Cambridge arts or philosophy ' schools' in the last quarter of the eighteenth century.

From Newton's Principia, Book I, Sections i; ii and iii (1791); iii alone (1784, 1792); vii 1791 &c.; viii 1782, 1791 &c.; xii Propˢ. 1—5 1780; —— Propˢ. 39, 40; 66 and six foll. corollˢ.; 66 and seventeen corollˢ. 1780. Book II. Prop. 34 (n. d.).

From Cotes Prop. 1 &c.; Centripetal force; five trajectories 1791. Parabola of projection 1791.

Halley's determination of the Solar Parallax 1784.

Correction of the aberration of rays by Conic Sections.

The method of Fluxions.

Smith de focalibus distantibus.

Maclaurin cap. III. Sectt. 1—8, 11—22.

Morgan on Mechanical forces; on the Inclined Plane.

Hamilton on Vapour.

Berkeley on Sight and Touch 1782.

Montesquieu Laws I. 1. 1791.

From Locke Faith and Reason 1771; Can matter think? 1780; Signification of Words vol. II. chh. 1, 2.

Wollaston sec. 2.   On Happiness.

From Paley On Penalties; On Happiness 1791; On Promises 1792.

Free Press 1771.

Imprisonment for Debt.

Duelling.

Slave Trade.

Common Ideas do not enter by different Senses, 1784.

Composite Ideas have no absolute existence.

Immortality of the Soul may be inferred by the light of nature (two years).   But no more than that of other animals (once).

The Soul is Immaterial.

Omnia nostrâ de causâ facimus.

APPENDIX IX.

BRIEF ANNALS

OF THE

CAMBRIDGE UNIVERSITY PRESS.

A CHRONOLOGICAL LIST OF *CLASSICAL* AND OTHER *WORKS*
PRODUCED CHIEFLY AT THE UNIVERSITIES
OR BY MEN OF UNIVERSITY EDUCATION
IN THE 18TH CENTURY.

THE UNIVERSITY PRESS.

BEFORE coming to our chronological list (such as it is) of classical
and other books printed at the Universities and elsewhere, I will put
together a few notes relating to the UNIVERSITY PRESS which have
occurred in the course of my investigations, as any adequate account
of this institution is still a *desideratum,* and materials for such a
sketch are scattered, if not scanty.

Edmund Carter in his Hist. of Camb. p. 467 (1753), having
thrown out a hint that Caxton (whom he calls a native of Cambridgeshire) might have erected a press here, states that 'the first Book we
find an Account of, that was Printed here, is a Piece of *Rhetoric,*
by one *Gull. de Saona,* a Minorite; Printed at *Cambridge* 1478 ;
given by Archbp. *Parker* to *Bennet* College Library. It is in Folio,
the Pages not Numbered, and without Ketch Word, or Signatures.'

This statement has been shewn to be fallacious. Not only was
Caxton on his own testimony a man of Kent, but this Rhetorica
Nova though 'Compilatum ... in alma Universitate Cantabrigie,
Anno Domini 1478⁰,' was 'Impressum ... apud Villam Sancti
Albani, Anno Domini 1480 [1].'

While therefore we acknowledge that a printed book was produced at Mentz in 1457, at Westminster in 1477, at Paris in 1470,

[1] In 1480 (6. Nov.) it was forbidden
by statute for the keeper of the Camb.
Univ. Chest to accept book's printed or
written on paper as a caution or pledge.
(Cooper's *Annals,* I. 224.)

In 1510 Wynkyn de Worde printed in
London *Roberti Allyngton* Oxoniensis
Sophismata cum consequentiis: in usum
scholae Cantabrigiensis.

and at Oxford in 1478[1], Cambridge must fall back upon Carter's next paragraph.

'There was one *John Sibert*, a Printer at *Lyons*, in the year 1498; who Probably was the John Siberch that Settled here, and stiled himself the First in *England*[2] that printed both *Greek* and *Latin*.'

It does not appear that he printed any book here entirely in Greek character. He was a friend of Erasmus, who mentions him and his brother Nicholas in a letter written to Aldrich (afterwards Bp. of Carlisle) from Bâle 25 Dec. 1525. Croke who lectured in greek is said to have brought him over. Siberch printed at Cambridge in 1521 (with the royal arms)

Galen de Temperamentis, translated by Linacre.
Abp. *Baldwin de Sacramento altaris*. (Trin. Coll. Lib. G. 8. 15.)
Oratio ad Card. Wolseium per H. Bullock[3], *cum annotationibus marginalibus*.
　　Cantabrigiae, per Joannem Siberch. (4to. S. John's Coll. Lib. S. 3. (1).)
Erasmus de conscribendis epistolis. Cantabr. Mense Octobri.

Watt records three other books under Sibert's name in this same year, and one (Papyrii Gemini Eleatis Hermathena) in the next. Mr Cooper (*Annals* I. 304) says that he printed two books in 1522.

No books of Siberch appear after 1522. Seven or eight years later the proctors' accounts mention proceedings against one Sygar Nicholson of Gonville hall, stationer of Cambridge, for harbouring lutheran books; and faggots for burning them cost the university a groat[4]. About the same time, in the year 1529, the university petitioned Wolsey in the interest of sound doctrine, to procure the royal licence for three booksellers, men of reputation, gravity, and foreigners (under the provision 29 Ric. III. *c.* 9), who might value books properly and import foreign publications. In 1530 (4 May) the king summoned to London twelve commissioners from each university to consider the propriety of licensing certain theological works[5].

In 1534 (20 July) the King by letters patent licensed the university to elect from time to time three stationers and printers who were to reside and to print and sell books licensed by the Chancellor and his vicegerent or three doctors. Accordingly Nicholas Speryng, Garrot Godfrey and Segar Nycholson were appointed[6].

Nevertheless we find no record of any book printed after the days of Siberch 1522 till the year 1584[7]. At Oxford there was a still longer cessation (1519 to 1585). And at Cambridge it is said that the Stationers' Company on some complaint of privilege seized the university printing-press.

[1] Bowyer and Dyer pleaded for the correctness of the date MCCCCLXVIII. on Jerome's *Exposicio in Simbolum*, but S. W. Singer's tract has confirmed the opinion of Conyers Middleton.
[2] 'Jo. Siberch primus utriusque linguae in Anglia impressor.'
[3] The *Bovillus* of Erasmus, fellow of Queens' about 1506.
[4] Cooper's *Annals*, I. 329. *Athenae* I. 51.

[5] *Annals*, I. 342—3.
[6] *Ibid.* I. 368—9. Fuller (*Hist. Camb.* § 4) on the authority of Coke asserts that 'This University of Cambridge hath power to print within the same "omnes" and "omnimodos libros"; which the University of Oxford hath not.'
[7] Dyer, *Suppl. Hist. Camb. = Privil.* II. fascic. iii. *p.* 17.

When Ro. Wakefield migrated from Cambridge to Oxford and delivered hebrew lectures, his oration *de utilitate linguae arabicae et hebraicae* was printed, in 1524, not at either university but in London by Wynkyn de Worde, and even there a third was omitted for lack of hebrew type : what he had was cut on wood.

In 1577 (18 July) lord Burleigh wrote[1] to discourage our authorities who were proposing to employ Kingston (a London printer) under academical privileges to print psalters, prayerbooks, and other english books in spite of the royal patents of W. Seres, Ri. Jugge, J. Day, &c. He thought, however, that they might employ a man on schools' notices, &c. 3 May 1582 Thomas Thomas (Thomasius, called 'that Puritan Cambridge printer' by Penry, *Martin Marprelate* Ep. I.) was licensed sole printer at Cambridge. He was fellow of King's. While he was engaged on a book of Whitaker's and had other works announced, the press, &c. was seized by the Stationers' Company of London[2]. After some overtures for conference and arbitration in the summer of 1583, lord Burleigh inspected the charter and gave his protection to the university printer in March (? 1583-4). About the same period the university authorities made regulations respecting booksellers, bookbinders and stationers at Cambridge.

The following books printed at Cambridge by Thomas are in Trinity College library.

Yves Rouspeau and John De l'Espine. Two Treatises of the Lord his holie Supper. Translated from the French, small 8vo. 1584. [H. 2. 26.]
An Exposition upon certain chapters of Nehemiah. By Bp. Ja. Pilkington. 4to. 1585. [5. 16 a. 7.]
Harmony of the Confessions of Faith of Christian and Reformed Churches. 8vo. 1586. [D. 1 a. 14.]

There is a full notice of Thomas in Cooper's *Athenae Cantab.* II. 29, 543.

As Wolsey had anticipated that the introduction of printing would strike a blow at the peace of the church, so the fears which (*mutatis mutandis*) Abp. Whitgift entertained were verified in the printing of a book in the presbyterian interest by Walter Travers. It was seized while in progress at Legatt's press in 1584[3]. 11 Feb. 1585—6, the senate followed the example of Oxford in prohibiting the purchase of such books as were printed in London, &c., when an edition had already been brought out, or should be in contemplation at the university presses[4]. In 1586 Abp. Whitgift wrote to prohibit the publication at Cambridge of the *Harmony of Confessions* which had been stopped in London. Mr Cooper suggests[5] that he afterwards revised and passed it. At all events there is the copy already mentioned in Trinity Library. On May-day 1588 the V. C. and heads wrote to lord Burleigh to complain that the London Stationers had pirated the latin dictionary of which Thomas the

[1] Cooper's *Annals*, II. 357.
[2] *Ibid.* II. 393, *sq.* [3] *Ibid.* II. 400.
[4] *Ibid.* II. 415.
[5] *Ibid.* II. 425. Six weeks earlier

(p. 424) the Star-chamber had most narrowly restricted the number of presses and apprentices at each University to 'one at one tyme at the most.'

Cambridge printer himself was compiler, and other books, whereby he was 'almost utterly disabled[1].'

Thomas died soon afterwards, having injured his health by the assiduity with which he compiled his dictionary[2]. He was buried in Great S. Mary's Church, 9th Aug. 1588. He was succeeded at the university press by John Legatt or Legate, a London Stationer, who married Agatha, daughter of Chr. Barker, the royal printer.

Copies of Legatt's small Terence were seized in London by the Stationers' Company, who threatened again to reprint Thomas' dictionary in 1589—90. The university invoked the aid of lord Burleigh and of J. Aylmer, Bp. of London[3]. In 1591 Legate in his turn was accused by the Stationers of having violated Barker's privilege to print the Bible and N. T., and Day's by publishing the Psalms in metre[4]. Sir Ro. Cecil vindicated the university and her printer. At the close of the year (6 Dec. 1591), the Stationers passed a self-denying ordinance, granting to Cambridge the privilege of choosing foreign books from the Frankfort mart for reprinting[5]. In 1596 (22 Nov) the Ecclesiastical Commissioners charged the university printer with having infringed the right of the Queen's patentees by printing the Grammar and Accidence, but after diligent search no copies could be reported[6].

Among books printed at Cambridge before the close of the sixteenth century by the elder John Legatt (who was the first to use the device of the *Alma Mater Cantabrigia* and *Hinc Lucem et Pocula Sacra* round it) were the following. (Watt supplies a list four times as long; *Bibl. Brit.* II. 595 *y*-—596 *g*.)

Terentii Comoediae (nonpareil roman). 24to. 1589.
Ciceronis de Oratore (copies described as 18mo. Trin. Coll. 24to, Queens' Coll., 32° Cracherode ap. Dibdin.) 1589.
W. Perkins' Golden Chaine, transl. R. Hill. 12mo. 1592.
G. Sohn's A Briefe and Learned Treatise of the Antichrist. Transl. from the Lat. by N. G. 12mo. 1592.
Dr Cowell's Antisanderus. II. dialogos continens Venetiis habitos. 4to. 1593.
The Death of Usury; or the Disgrace of Usurers. 4to. 1594.
W. Whitaker's Pro Auctoritate S. Scripturae adv. T. Stapleton. 1594.
W. Perkins' Exposition of the Creed. 1595.
I. R. De Hypocritis vitandis. 4to. 1595.
R. Abrahami praecepta in monte Sinai data Judaeis negativa et affirmativa; Lat. Phil. Ferdinand. 4to. 1597.
W. Perkins' Exposition of the Creed. New edition. 8vo. 1597.
——————— A Reformed Catholike, 8vo. 1598.
——————— De Praedestinationis Modo et Ordine, &c. 18mo. 1598.
Job and Ecclesiastes paraphrased, &c. Theod. Beza. 12mo. 1600.

Although John Legate did not die until 1626 Cantrell Legge (called Legate by Dyer) succeeded him in 1607 or 1608. John

---

[1] *Ibid.* II. 456, 7.
[2] Thomas' dictionary went through five impressions in eight years (1580—88). To the 10th was added, beside Legate's improvement, a supplement by Philemon Holland with a new

English Latin dictionary.
[3] Cooper's *Annals*, II. 477, 478.
[4] *Ibid.* II. 491, 492.
[5] *Ibid.* II. 510, 511.
[6] *Ibid.* II. 559.

Legatt the younger having obtained a licence to print Thomas' dictionary went and settled in London.

In 1620—21 (29 Jan.) the university by G. Herbert confided their apprehensions from the Stationers, who were grasping at a monopoly for foreign books, to Abp. Abbott and Ld. Ch^r. Verulam [1]. In 1621 and the following year the university obtained redress by the king's grant for selling their cheap and correct edition of Lilly's grammar, but J. Bill, Bonham Norton, W. Barrett, Clement Knight and other London printers combined to refuse the book [2]; whereupon the university ordered all graduates to use no other edition than their own, and university authors to offer their copy in the first instance to the university press : copy-right, &c., to be enjoyed by the printer only while he remained in office and not to descend to his family.

A royal proclamation, 1 April 1625, in answer to the representation of the universities, forbad the importation of cheap and inferior reprints of latin books. This was repeated 1 May, 1636 [3].

About 1627 Thomas Buck of Catharine-hall and Roger Daniel entered into partnership as university printers. In 1628—9 they (with *John* Buck) were accused by the Stationers of having broken a decree of the Star Chamber, but the lord Chief Justices, after consultation with six other judges, advised the Privy Council (18 March) that no patent for sole printing restrained the privileges of the university press under the licence of the Chancellor or V. C. and doctors [4]. However in 1629 (16 April) the Privy Council limited the privilege of the university to a yearly impression of 3,000 *Lilly's Grammars*; and *Common Prayers with singing-psalms* in 4to. and medium folio, without restraint of number, only on condition that the *Bible* was bound with them [5].

In 1632 Buck used beautiful hebrew type for the quotations in Mede's *Clavis Apocalyptica.* In the same year he printed an 8vo. Greek Testament [6]. In 1635 Dr Beale, V. C., was blamed for licensing *Five Discourses* by Ro. Shelford of Peterhouse, on account of their anti-puritanical tendency [7].

In 1637 the Star Chamber defined the jurisdiction of university licences [8], and exempted from their cognizance 'Bookes of the

[1] *Ibid.* III. 138, 139.
[2] *Ibid.* III. 142—4.
[3] *Ibid.* III. 175, 176; 275.
[4] See the charter of 6 Feb. 1627—8, *ibid.* III. 199.
[5] *Ibid.* III. 213.
[6] In 1634 when ' the practice held in Cambridge for printing almanacks, &c.' was drawn up for the information of Oxford, the following particulars were added—All other school books so many as they can print with one press : and almanacks (such copies as are brought them) without restraint of number. There was then however a three years' covenant to print only 500 reams yearly, the Londoners to purchase all

that were not required in Cambridge itself. (Gutch, *Collectanea,* I. 284, quoted in Cooper's *Annals,* III. 266.) About 1636-7 the Stationers hired these monopolies for a term of three years.—Cooper's *Annals,* III. 285.
[7] Cooper's *Annals,* III. 268.
[8] Ayliffe in his *Antient and Present State* of Oxford, Part 3, Vol. II. p. 242, informs us that the University of Cambridge was more prudent and observant than his own in having the defect in the charter of 14 Hen. VIII. rectified so as to secure great privileges for the Press. King Charles I. in 1635, at the suggestion of Abp. Laud, enlarged the privileges of the Oxford printers.

Common Law, or matters of State¹.' Roger Daniel was summoned before the Commons and reprimanded in 1642 (Aug. and Sept.) for printing 'the Book set forth in the Defence of the Commission of Array².' A few months later he was arrested for printing *Resolves in Cases of Conscience* by Dr H. Fern, afterwards Bp. of Chester. The blame was shifted to the V. C. Dr Holdsworth, and Captain Cromwell was instructed to send the doctor up in safe custody at his own charges. In 1649 a parliamentary ordinance (29 ? 20 Sept.) recognized the universities (with London, York and Finsbury) as privileged printing places³, and this was more clearly asserted 7 Jan. 1652—3⁴.

It was in 1642 that Buck and Daniel printed a fine edition of Beza's Greek and latin Testament⁵. Ten years later Buck sent forth exquisite and correct editions of Gataker's *Antoninus* and the *Poetae Graeci Minores:* also Stephens' *Statius* a little earlier. In 1650 Buck had become sole printer, but he resigned in 1653 (though he survived till 1688) and was succeeded by John Field.

Field took a lease of the ground near Queens' College and built the house and printing-office, which was in use until the present century.

In 1662—3 there were unsatisfactory overtures between our printers and the London Stationers relative to the Order in Council of April 1629, in which lord chancellor Clarendon and Dr Sancroft (Emm.) &c. corresponded⁶.

Field printed a good variorum edition of Andronicus Rhodius in 1679, but his attention was mainly devoted to small Bibles and Prayer Books (of which he executed a greek edition). Twelve errata in the Cambridge 4to Bible (1663) are noted on a page in vol. XVIII. Letters and MSS. of the D. of Northumberland at Alnwick Castle. Ri. Atkyns' work on the Origin of Printing came out in 1664.

About 1669 ' it appears that there was a treaty pending between the London Printers and the University, which was broken off on the 7th of July, when the Heads agreed that John Hayes should have the printing for £100 a year⁷. Carter mentions Edward Hall as a printer about 1688: he says also that while Hayes was still printing in the house which Field had built, Cornelius Crownfield, a dutch soldier, was at work in 1696 in another building (which was known afterwards as 'the *Anatomy School* and *Elaboratory*') until Hayes' death in 1707, when he removed to what then became the only university printing-house. Jonathan Pindar seems to have had some status as a Cambridge printer; he lived a few months after the death of Crownfield, who was an excellent typographer.

Crownfield had printed Joshua Barnes' *Euripides* (1694) which was considered a very fine edition. Two years later Bentley worthily

¹ Cooper's *Annals*, III. 287, 288. This was more clearly expressed after the Restoration by a temporary act in 1662. *ibid.* 501.
² *Ibid.* III. 332.
³ *Ibid.* III. 336, 337.
⁴ *Ibid.* III. 429, 453.
⁵ As to the Saxon type about this period see above p. 159.
⁶ Cooper's *Annals*, III. 506, 507.
⁷ *Ibid.* III. 537.

directed his energy to renovating the university press[1]. Improvements were made in the buildings, presses and type obtained by a public subscription, aided by a loan of £1,000, secured by the Senate ; and Syndics of the Press were appointed by a Grace of 21 Jan. 1697—8[2], which is given below.

Crownfield appears to have been 'Inspector of the Press' both before and after the death of Hayes ; his stipend in that capacity was fixed 9 Nov. 1698 at 10s. a week to be paid monthly or quarterly.

Bentley, to whom a complimentary grace had given absolute discretion in this particular, procured from Holland 'those beautiful types[3] which appear in Talbot's *Horace*, Kuster's *Suidas*, Taylor's *Demosthenes*, &c.' (Monk I. 74.)

It appears[4] that Matthew Prior of S. John's (the poet) was engaged A. D. 1700 in a negotiation for procuring greek type for us from the Paris Press.

'" With the History of the Cambridge press," adds [T. Philipps] the Historian of Shrewsbury, " I am not acquainted. In the year 1700, that learned Body applied to the French Ministry for the use of the Greek Matrices, cut by order of Francis I. This application, owing to national vanity, proved unsuccessful. See extracts of French King's MSS. Vol. I. p. 101. But 'the University appear to have procured others of greater beauty, from that country. The type of Dr Taylor's Demosthenes is precisely the same which John Jullieron, printer of Lyons, employed in 1623 in Nicholas Asemanni's Edition of the Anecdota of Procopius for Andrew Brugiotti, Bookseller at Rome."' Nichols' *Lit. Anecd.* IV. 663, 4.

The following extract, which is taken from the preface to the Medea and Phoenissae of Euripides edited by W. Piers[5], Cantabr. *Typis Academicis*, 1703, and dated '*è Coll. Emman.* Cantabr. 3 *Novembr.* 1702,' testifies to the advance which was made at this time.

'Si *Typorum elegantiam* mireris, gratias meritò ingentes habeto *Illustrissimo Principi* Carolo *Duci* Somersetensium *munificentissimo nostrae Academiae Cancellario*, cui Cordi est *nostrum* imo *suum* denuò revixisse *Typographéum*[6].'

[1] Monk's *Bentley*, I. 73, 74, 153—6. Cooper's *Annals*, IV. 34.

[2] *Theta*, p. 428. There is another grace 2 Dec. 1749 (*Kappa*, p. 123). See also the year 1737.

[3] 'Already (1701) some handsome editions of Latin Classics had been printed with those types and dedicated to the use of the young Duke of Gloucester. *Terence* 1701 had been edited by Leng of Catharine Hall, afterwards Bishop of Norwich ; *Horace* [1699 4to ; and 1701 4to and 12mo] by Talbot, the Hebrew Professor ; *Catullus Tibullus* and *Propertius* by the Hon. Arthur Annesley, Representative for the University; and *Virgil* by J. Laughton of Trinity.' Monk's *Bentley*, I. 154. Watt *Bibl. Brit.* attributes the *Virgil* 'Henr. Lonthono'. These classics (including an edition of Talbot's *Horace*) came out in 4 vols. 4to 1701.

[4] *Manuscrits de la Bibliothèque du Roi*, Paris, 1787, I. xciii. *seq.*

[5] The editor wrote his name Peirs (A.B.) 1684, and Peirse (A.M., S.T.B.) 1688, 1695. He was fellow of Emman. and rector of N. Cadbury.

[6] There was printed twice at least at Oxford a 'Specimen of the Several Sorts of Letter given to the University'

Here the earliest extant minute-books of the Curators of the Cambridge Press supply some interesting information about this revival of typography which was promoted, as we have just seen, under the noble patronage of the Chancellor by the agency of Dr Bentley, who as yet had his residence in his 'librarian's lodgings' at St James', when he was employed to order types on behalf of the Senate.

Bentley was preaching the Commencement Sermon the Sunday after the Duke of Somerset wrote the following letter;—which, with the other extracts, Mr Clay has with the permission of the Syndics of the Press kindly copied from their Order Book[1].

PETTWORTH June the 29th 1696.

GENTLEMEN,

As I have ye honour to be a servant to you all, soe am I ever thinking of w^t may be most for y^r interest, and for ye support of that reputation, and great character wch ye University have soe worthily deserved in ye opinion of all good, and of all learned men: & in my poore thoughts, noe way more effectuall, than the recovering ye fame of y^r own printing those great, and excellent writinges, y^t are soe frequently published from ye Members of y^r own body; wch tho' very learned, sometimes have been much prejudiced by ye unskillfull handes of uncorrect printers. Therefore it is, y^t I doe at this time presume to lay before you all, a short, and imperfect Scheame (here enclosed) of some thoughtes of mine, by way of a foundation, for you to finishe, and to make more perfect; wch tho' never soe defective at present, yett they have mett with aprobation among some publick spirited men (much deserving the name of friends to us) who have freely contributed eight hundred pounds towards ye Carying on this good, and most beneficiall worke.

Now, Gentlemen, their is nothing wanting of my part, to endeavour the procuring the like sume againe from others, but y^r aprobation, and consent, to have a Presse once more erected at Cambridge: and when that shall bee resolved on, then to give a finishing hand (like great Masters as you are) to my unfinished thoughtes, that I may bee proude in having done some thing, y^t you think will bee for your service; wch I doe hope will bee a meanes to procure mee a general pardonn from you all, for laying this Matter before you, having noe other ambition, than to bee thought your most obedient and most faithfull humble servant,

SOMERSET.

---

of *Oxford*, by Bp. Fell, 4to 1695, 8vo 1706.

The Clarendon Printing-House was commenced 22 Feb. 17$\frac{11}{12}$. (Ayliffe's *Antient and Present State of* Oxford, Part II. Vol. I. pp. 476, 7.) On the Saxon type of this time see above p. 160 *n*.

[1] For the knowledge of the existence of these interesting records I am indebted to the observation of Mr C. J. Clay, M.A. University Printer.

Grace for appointment of Syndics

      Placeat vobis, ut D^{nus} Procancellarius, Singuli Collegiorum Praefecti, D^{ni} Professores, Mr Laughton Coll. Trin. Academiæ Architypographus, Dr Perkins Regin. Mr Talbot and Mr Lightfoot Trin. Mr Nurse Joh. Mr Beaumont Petr. Mr Moss CCC. Mr Banks Aul. Pemb. Mr Leng Aul. Cath. Mr Pierce Eman. Mr Wollaston Sidn. Mr Gael Regal. aut eorum quinque ad minus, quorum semper unus sit D^{nus} Procancellarius, sint Curatores Præli vestri Typographici.

                 lect. & concess. 21 Jan. 169$\frac{7}{8}$

[The names of T. Bennett, T. Sherwill, and Laughton of Clare were added by a Grace of Oct. 10].

Aug. 23rd 1698

    1 Agreed then at a meeting of y^e Curators of y^e University-Press, y^t Mr Jacob Tonson have leave to print an edition of Virgil, Horace, Terence, Catullus, Tibullus and Propertius in 4to with ye double Pica Letter: he paying to such persons as shall be appointed by ye said Curators 12^s p. Sheet for ye impression of 500 copies: 14^s for 750; and so in proportion for a greater Number[1]: and y^t Dr Mountague, Dr Covell, Mr Leng, Mr Laughton and Mr Talbot shall sign ye Articles of ye agreement above mentioned, on ye part of ye University.

    2 Agreed at ye same time, y^t Mr Edmund Jeffries have leave to print an Edition of Tully's works in 12mo with the Brevier Letter: he paying 1^l. 10^s. ye sheet for 1000 Copies.

    3 That Cornelius Crownfield have leave to send to Roterdam for 300^l weight of ye double Pica letter in order to ye Printing of Virgil, Horace, &c in ye manner above mentioned.

    Placeat vobis, ut Auditores Cistæ communis audiant etiam quotannis computum officinæ typographicæ

           lect. & concess. 10 Octob. 1698.

Octob. 17. 98.

    Present Dr James Vicechancellour, Dr Covell, Dr Blithe, Dr Roderick, Dr Smoult, Dr Perkins, Mr Barnet, Mr Laughton, Mr Leng, Mr Beaumont, Mr Pearse, Mr Wollaston, Mr Talbot, Mr Bennett.

    1 Agreed y^t all resolves made at any meeting of ye Curatours for the press be entered in ye Register for ye Press.

    2 That ye Major part of ye Curatours present at any Meeting shall determine who shall write ye resolves then made into ye said Register.

---

[1] A few weeks later (9 Nov.) it was ordered that the compositor should receive 4s. 6d. and the corrector 9d. per sheet. The press man 2s. 8d. per 'Rheam' for printing both sides of each sheet.

The next week they found they must allow 'a boy for attending ye workmen at ye press' 1s. 6d. a week.

An earlier and fuller statement on the cost of printing, drawn up by the Cambridge University printer in 1622, forms part of Mr Thompson Cooper's communication to the *Bookseller*, 24 Feb. 1860.

3 That all graces granted by yᵉ Senate relating to yᵉ Press be entered into yᵉ said Register.

4 That there shall be a general meeting of yᵉ Curatours upon yᵉ first Wednesday in every Month.

5 That yᵉ general monthly meeting shall determine, wᵗ persons shall be delegates for yᵉ said Month.

6 That the sᵈ delegates appointed by them shall meet weekly on Wednesdays at 2 of yᵉ clock in yᵉ afternoon.

7 That every Editour shall appoint his own inferiour Correctour to attend yᵉ press.

8 That no Editour shall have power to appoint any inferiour Correctour to attend yᵉ Press, but such as shall be approved by the delegates, & yᵗ yᵉ allowance for yᵉ Correctours labour be set by yᵉ delegates.

The delegates for this month are Mʳ Vice-Chancellour, Mʳ Peirse, Mʳ Leng, Mʳ Talbot, Mʳ Bennett. [Piers, Laughton, Banks and Bennett were ordered to attend the next month.]

Wednesday Octob. 26. 1698.

1 Ordered, yᵗ Mʳ Cornelius Crownfield do go to London to procure an Alphabet of Box flourish't Letters, and to retain Workmen for the Press, and to take care for yᵉ Carriage of Mʳ Tonson's Paper: and to hasten yᵉ return of yᵉ double Pica Letter from Holland.

2 Upon yᵉ proposall of Mʳ Talbot of Dˢ Penny[1] to be his correctour for yᵉ edition of Horace with yᵉ approbation of yᵉ delegates; agreed, yᵗ the said Dˢ Penny be spoken to to undertake yᵉ said office of Correctour.

Wedn. December yᵉ 7ᵗʰ 1698

Memᵈᵘᵐ That Dʳ James [the ex-V.C.] delivered in a number of papers & letters (which had been in his custody) relating to yᵉ press, which were put in a paper box to be kept in yᵉ drawer.

January yᵉ 4ᵗʰ 1698

At a meeting of Eight of yᵉ Curators—

Ordered that Mr Talbot have full power to treat about & procure a Rolling press fit for yᵉ service of yᵉ Printing house the charges thereof to be defrayed out of such money as he shall receive upon subscriptions to yᵉ press at London.

---

[1] At the next meeting, this young student of Queens' (afterwards prebendary of Norwich) was assigned [9d., or] ⅛ of the compositor's allowance for each sheet carefully corrected.

At the same time (2 Nov. 1698) Ro. Nicolson was appointed 'Messenger of the Press' to summon the Curators (not being Heads or Professors) to the general meetings.

Will this circumstance in any way account for the paradox started by Prof. A. De Morgan in *Notes and Queries* (3ʳᵈ S. vol. IV. p. 170,) that 'Maps' (John Nicholson, son-in-law of Ro. Watts) was porter of the university library all his life?

Agreed also that 4 pence p week for copy money be allowed to yᵉ workmen at yᵉ Press & half a crown p Quarter for cleaning yᵉ Press,

---

March 4 1698

1 Orderd, that a particular account of each Body of Letter, & of all Tooles & Moveables belonging to yᵉ New Printing House be taken in writing in yᵉ presence of the Delegates for yᵉ weekly meetings of this Month, and yᵗ it be entered into yᵉ Journal Book by yᵉ person appointed to keep that Book : and yᵗ yᵉ said account be sign'd by yᵉ Delegates, & Mr Crownfield yᵉ Printer.......

3 Order'd, That all Combinations, Verses, and other exercises upon Public Occasions be printed only at yᵉ University's New Printing House.

May 3ʳᵈ 1699

Ordered—that 400 lbs. weight of Paragon Greek Letter be sent for to the Widow Voskins in Holland.

At a general meeting of the Curators June 7ᵗʰ 1699

Order'd that Dʳ Green & Dʳ Oxenden or either of them do examine Dʳ Bentley's account in relation to our Press, and upon his delivery of the Vouchers relating to it, and all other things in his hands belonging to the University Press ; give him a full discharg ; and likewise take a discharg of him for the Summ of four hundred and thirty three pounds received by him of the University.

---

1 'At a General Meeting of the Curatʳˢ Septebʳ yᵉ 6ᵗʰ 1699 'twas then agreed yᵗ Mr Crownfield be order'd to buy twelve Gallons of Linseed Oyle and a rowl of Parchment.

2 Order'd yᵗ yᵉ Sashes be renew'd

3 Order'd yᵗ twenty shillings per annū be allow'd to Printers for their weigh-goes¹.'

'Feby 12ᵗʰ 170⁵⁄₆ Agreed then also yᵗ foreign booksellers be treated with for an exchange of an hundred Suidas's, for a number of bookes wᶜʰ shall be esteem'd of equal value, & yᵗ Catalogues of proper bookes wᵗʰ their respective prises, be procur'd from them to be approv'd of by yᵉ University.'

(At p. 31 of the Syndics' Minute Book is given a list of books to be sent over by Mr Wetstein in exchange for 100 copies of Suidas.)

'June 15ᵗʰ 1708 Agreement with Profr. Barnes to print the Odyssee & Iliad of Homer.

---

¹ The printers' *way-goose*, or jour- neymen's entertainment, allowed origi- nally for making new paper windows at Bartlemy-tide, has been duly com- memorated in Hone's *Every-day Book* I. 1133. Halliwell has '*Way-goose*. An entertainment given by an appren- tice to his fellow-workmen. *West*.'

'March 2nd 17$\frac{12}{13}$ Agreed y^t Mr Crownfield have leave to publish his proposals for y^t Reprinting Robt. Stephens's Thesaurus of y^e Lat: Tongue, Dr Kuster of Rotterdam Editor.

'March 31, 1725   Entered then Terence in 4to with Dr Bentley's notes for Mr Crownfield.'

Many of the publications of the press after this period will be found recorded in the following pages[1]. There are however no entries in the minute-book from April 24, 1725, to Jan. 15, 173$\frac{8}{9}$.

In 1735 Conyers Middleton wrote on the origin of printing.

In 1737 a syndicate was appointed with plenary powers for three years[2]. Within that period (viz. 12 Geo. II.) an Act of Parliament repealed the clause of the Copyright Act of 1710 (8 Ann. c. 21) whereby vice-chancellors had been empowered to set and reform the prices of books[3].

A grace of 27 May, 1752 (*Kappa* p. 184) provides that the major part of a *quorum* of the Press Syndics (five, including the V. C.) have power to transact business. (Gunning, *Cerem.* p. 406.)

When Crownfield died in 1742[4] his successor had already been found, viz. Joseph Bentham. He was appointed 'Inspector of the Press in the room of Mr Cornelius Crownfield' by an order of the Curators (28 March 1740[5]), on condition that, if the profits of the place should not arise to £60 *per annum*, the Univ. should make good the deficiency.

The following entries are taken from the Curators' minute-book.

'Memorandum—Jan. 26, 1741—2

Mony due to the University Decr 24, 1741 from the Journeymen in the Printing House being chiefly what was advanced to them in the time of the Frost last winter, and when there was a deficiency of work.'

'Decr. 15, 1742   Entered the ninth edition of Dr Bentley's Phileleutherus Lipsiensis, for Mr Thurlbourn.'

Feb. 19, 1749   Amongst other books is entered 'Mr Masters's List of ye Members of C.C.C.'

Joseph Bentham[6] was free of the Stationers' Company. Carter says (*Hist. Camb.* 1753, p. 470) of him : 'He is allowed by all Judges to be as great a Proficient in the Mystery as any in *England*; which the *Cambridge* Common Prayer Books and Bibles, lately Printed by him, will sufficiently evince.' Thus in his time the Curators agreed (11 Dec. 1740) to print small Bibles 9000 price 2s.

---

[1] Bentley's *Horace & Terence*, Davies' & Pearce's editions of works by *Cicero*, Taylor's *Demosthenes* and *Lysias* may be here mentioned.

[2] Monk's *Bentley*, I. 156 n.

[3] Cooper's *Annals*, IV. 241. *ibid.* 96.

[4] He was buried in the chancel of S. Botolph's.

[5] Carter says *Hist. Camb.* that Bentham was 'chose in 1739.'

[6] Nichols, *Lit. Anecd.* VIII. 451. Dyer, *Priv. Camb.* Vol. II. *fascic.* ii. p. 85 : *fascic.* iii. pp. 24, 25. He printed his brother James' history of Ely their native place in 1765. Their other brother was Dr E. Bentham, of *Ch. Ch., C. C. C.*, and *Oriel*, editor of *Orationes Funebres*, and some instructive works.

and 1000 on large paper at 2s. 6d. Half a year later, nonpareil Bibles 11000 small paper, 1000 large paper.

Dyer mentions S. Squire's Plutarchus *de Iside et Osiride*, which was printed in 1744 by Bentham. In 1743 a bill was filed against him by T. and Ro. Baskett the royal printers, for having brought out in 1741 an abridgment of certain Acts of Parliament. After protracted hearings it was decided in the Court of King's Bench (24 Nov. 1758) that the University is 'intrusted with a concurrent Authority to print Acts of Parliament and Abridgments' within the university, by letters patent of K. Hen. VIII. and K. Charles I.[1].

In 1775, in consequence of a decision in the Common Pleas[2], by which it was ruled that the Crown has no control over the printing of almanacks, the Company of Stationers ceased to pay the annual sum (above £500) for which they had hired the University's share of the monopoly (which Ld. North attempted to re-establish in 1779[3]). In the same year an Act of Parliament[4] secured for the universities the copyright of school-books, &c., bequeathed to them.

Bentham died 1 June 1778, after which John Archdeacon (a native of Ireland) conducted the typographical department for Cambridge.

In 1781 Gutch's *Collectanea Curiosa*, containing *inter alia* (I. 282 *seqq.*) several papers and documents on the subject, was published at Oxford. In that year (though Mr T. Carnan the litigious bookseller of S. Paul's Churchyard had twice overthrown the universities' privilege) a new almanack duty act[5] granted £500 *per annum* to each university, which sum was at Cambridge by the grace of 11 June, 1782, placed at the disposal of the Syndics of the Press for the publication of new works or editions of old works. The grace is printed in Gunning's *Ceremonies*, p. 407, and in *Ordinationes Academiae Cantabrigiensis*, *Cap.* IX. *Sect.* 2. v. 5 (1874, p. 153) as follows:

June 11, 1782.

'*Government Annuity.*

Cum ad graves librorum imprimendorum sumptus sublevandos omnigenaeque adeo eruditionis studium promovendum, annuo quingentarum librarum reditu Academiam nuper auxerit munificentia publica; ne aut nostra negligentia deflorescat tantus publice habitus literis honos, aut in alios usus transferatur quod doctrinae ampli-

---

[1] Cooper's *Annals*, IV. 301.

[2] *Ibid.* IV. 374; cp. 390, 391.

[3] Basil Montagu (*Enquiries*, &c. respecting the *Univ. Libr.* 1805, p. 4 n.) attributes to Bp. Law a pamphlet *Observations concerning Literary Property*. Cambridge, 1770.

[4] Stat 15 Geo. III. c. 53.

[5] Cooper's *Annals*, IV. 390 n., 401. Stat. 21 Geo. III. c. 56.
The paper duty act of the same year

(Stat. 21 Geo. III. c. 24) allowed a drawback to the Universities in respect of paper used in printing books in the latin, greek, oriental or northern languages. Cooper's *Annals*, IV. 402. In 1794 another act added 'Bibles, Testaments, Psalm-books, and Books of Common Prayer' to the list. *ibid.* IV. 451. Since the abolition of the paper duty this advantage has been lost to the University.

ficandae sacrum esse oporteat; placeat vobis ut Typographici Preli
Curatores in hac etiam parte Syndici vestri constituantur, atque ut
quingentae quotannis librae, si ipsis necessarium videatur, vel in
novas veterum scriptorum editiones apparandas, vel in recentiorum
opera divulganda insumendae iis hoc nomine e Communi Cista ero-
gentur ; ita tamen ut singulis annis ante finem mensis Junii quicquid
ab iis in hujusce negotii procuratione factum fuerit ad vos in scripto
referre teneantur.'

Dr Ro. Plumptre, Pre^t of Queens', in his *Hints concerning University Officers*, 1782, p. 10, suggested that the Vice-chancellor
should be exempted from his official presidency of the Press Syndicate. It appears from Porson's history that in 1783 a syndic of the
Press did not understand the distinction between *collating* and *collecting* mss. Watson's *Porson*, p. 39.

In 1783 the *University Statutes* were printed in 4to.

Dr Webb's Collection (Univ. Lib.) contains a copy of the grace of
1782 concerning the £500. Also a V. C.'s notice to the Syndics of
the Press in the autumn of that year. A grace-paper proposing to
appoint more competent syndics 23 Dec. 1784, on the ground that
the house purchased (in 1762) in Silver St. was damp, and injury
had been done to the contents. ·In the same collection among documents belonging to the year 1785 there are a few which relate to the
management of the press, viz.;

(*a*) A grace to regulate the Press Syndicate, appointing for
three years only.

(*b*) Remarks by the proposers (4to. pp. 3).

Of the existing Syndicate 3 were appointed in 1761.

3	,,	,,	,, 1765.
3	,,	,,	,, 1776.
7	,,	,,	,, 1782.

(A duplicate is filed *s. a.* 1790 probably by mistake).

(*c*) Dr R. Plumptre who had been V.C. in 1762, made answer
(7 Feb. 1785) in four 4to pages, that only £20 damage had been
reported in 1778, and no further mischief had occurred. He would
gladly be dismissed, but not with disgrace.

(*d*) In rejoinder the complainants assert that substantial repairs
had never been made in the Silver Street buildings. (4to. pp. 3.)

The last page (56) of *Considerations on the Oaths* (1787) displays
the following ' *Extract from the Account of the Syndics, laid on one
of the tables in the Senate House, June* 27, 1787.

	£	s.	d.
To Mr Relhan towards the expences of printing his Flora Cant.	50	0	0
To Sig. Isola towards printing a new edit. of Tasso's Gierusalemme Liberata . .	50	0	0
To Profess. Waring new edit. Med. . . .	52	10	0
Prof. Cook's ed. Arist. Poet.	25	8	11

	£	s.	d.
Mr Ludlam's Introd. to Algeb. and an Introd. to the first six books of Euclid .	24	5	11
Mr Ormerod's Rem. 14 Sect. of Dr Priestley's Disquisition	4	19	0

This is an account of the expenditure of the Government annuity commuted as we have seen from the almanack-duty and augmented in 1782.

To a grant made by the Syndics from this fund the publication of the present Compilation is due.

Some objections were made against the title of the University to enjoy this grant by the writer of *Considerations on the Oaths*, Lond., 1787, p. 39. He objected also to the way in which it had been spent; viz. upon the '*facsimile*' of the Beza manuscript,' and 'Italian sonnets.' Dr T. Kipling's performance as editor of the former of these productions was at the time severely criticised from various quarters, and Mr Scrivener on a closer examination (*in emendandis*) has seen cause to confirm that censure which in the first instance was probably provoked as much by the man and his preface as by the exercise of any powers of discernment in Kipling's contemporaries such as Porson then, and our modern critic more recently has brought to bear upon his work. But this is a topic for the study of Divinity, the Frend controversy, &c.

However, *so far as the press is concerned*, the 'facsimile' in 2 vols. folio in 1793, is a very fine piece of work in uncials.

Sig. Agostino Isola's *Tasso* (for which £50 was granted) was grudged also by the writer of *Strictures on the Discipline of the Univ. of* Cambridge, 1792, p. 47. Dyer also complained in 1824, *Privil. Camb.* Vol. II. *fascic.* iii. *p.* 36, that the fund (which he says was called *the Poor's fund*) was devoted to printing 5 vols. of Simeon's *Skeletons of Sermons*, 1796, and Joseph Milner's *History* and *Sermons*, while it had been refused to Gilbert Wakefield for the 4th and 5th numbers of his *Silva Critica*. But Dyer would have been shocked to hear from the later editor of *Lucretius* that Wakefield was a poor Scholar in more senses than one.

In the latter part of the eighteenth century W. Ludlam (Joh.) complained that the press was extremely defective in mathematical types[1], so that he was actually obliged to make many a brass rule himself. This (says Dyer) had been fully remedied before 1824 when he wrote.

For some time (e.g. in 1794) J. Burges' name was coupled with J. Archdeacon's, and when the former retired Burges succeeded to his post[2].

[1] Nichols' *Lit. Anecd.* VIII. 414. Dyer, *Privil. Camb.* Vol. II. fasc. iii. p. 25. Ludlam published at Cambridge, *Mathematical Essays* (Ultimate Ratios, Power of the Wedge, &c. &c.) 1770, 1787.

Rudiments of Mathematics for the use of Students in the Universities. 1785.

[2] Mr Archdeacon retired to Hemingford, Hunts., where he was buried as Joshua Barnes had been.

In 1800 the university undertook the publication of Hoogeveen's *Dictionarium Analogicum* in 4to[1].

The celebrated *english* Porson *greek*, or 'Great Porson Greek'
type was designed by its eponymous hero, (who like the late Mr
Shilleto was as fine a calligrapher as he was a scholar,) and cut under
his direction by Austin of London, with the assistance of Mr Watts,
then University Printer[2]. However it was not used until after
Porson's death. Monk's *Hippolytus* (1811), and the second edition
of C. J. Blomfield's *Prometheus* (1812), were the earliest works
on which it was employed.

In 1804 the secret of the method of manufacturing stereotype
plates was bought from Mr Wilson, of Duke St., Lincoln's Inn
Fields, and he was employed to teach the process, and two presses,
Earl Stanhope's invention, were purchased. 'At the same time
too' (says Dyer) 'it was agreed upon by the Syndics, that certain
premises which hitherto had served the purpose of a warehouse
should be converted into a printing-office, the old printing-office
being then in a ruinous condition; which appointment therefore
gives at the same time the date of the first designing of a new
printing-house by the University, and of their commencing the
stereotype printing;—for they agreed upon both at the same time[3]'—

In the same year (4 Mar. 1804) the privilege of the Universities
solely to publish Bibles, New Testaments, and Common Prayer
Books was upheld in the House of Lords against the Richardsons
and Tegg, who had sold in London such books printed by the King's
printer in Scotland[4].

In 1805 Basil Montagu (Chr.) published a pamphlet (pp. 1—21,
1—20) of *Enquiries* and *Observations* respecting *the univ. library*, and
its right to a copy of every book published[5].

It was resolved at a meeting at the Thatched-House Tavern at
which the Marquess Camden presided (18 June, 1824), to apply
part of the surplus fund contributed for the Statue of Pitt erected in
London, to the building a new University Press in Cambridge. On
1st July the Senate appointed a Syndicate to purchase the houses
in Trumpington Street, between Silver Street and Mill Lane. The
first stone of the Pitt Press (designed by E. Blore) was laid 18 Oct.
1831, and it was opened (also by the Marq. Camden) 28 April, 1833,
and the key was formally delivered to Dr Webb the vice-chancellor[6].

---

[1] Oxford had done as much for Wyttenbach's *Plutarch*, 1795, &c. and
afterwards published Caravella's *Index
Aristophanis*, Creutzer's *Plotinus*, and
several editions by Bekker and Din-
dorf.

[2] Dyer (*Privil.* II. iii. 33) speaks of
a '*brevier* Porson greek' used in London for Valpy's Stephani Thesaurus,
and a fount of 'great Porson greek'
cast for the Clarendon Press at *Oxford*.

[3] Dyer, *Privil. Camb.* II. iii. 30, 31.

[4] Cooper's *Annals*, IV. 480.

[5] A copy in Peterhouse library E. 10.
23 (12). B. Montagu shews that legis-
lation (1662—1775, and the case of
Beckford v. *Hood* 1798,) had not diminished the privileges of the three
libraries, but that not six per cent. of
the books published in London about
1803 (he gives a list) were in the
Cambridge University Library.

[6] Cooper's *Annals*, IV. 572, 573.

The following list of—

CAMBRIDGE UNIVERSITY PRINTERS

may perhaps provoke those who are able to correct and complete it.

[John Siberch 1521 and 1522]
Nic. Speryng ⎫
Garratt Godfrey ⎬ 1534
Segar Nicholson, *Gonv.* ⎭
Nic. Pilgrim ⎫ 1539
Richard Noke ⎭
Peter Shers 1546
John Kingston 1577
Thomas Thomas, *King's* 1582—8 ('1583' *B.*; '1584' *Carter*)
John Legate 1588—1607
[John Porter 1593]
Cantrel Legge 1607—27 ('1606' *B.*; '1608' *Dyer*)
Thomas Brooke, *Clare,* esquire bedell[1], cir. 1614
Leonard Green 1622
John Buck, *Cath.* esquire bedell, 1625
Thomas Buck, *Cath.* esquire bedell, 1627—53 ('1625' *B.*)
Roger Daniel 1627—50 ('1632' *B.*; cf. Cooper's *Annals* III. 213).
Francis Buck 1630
John Legate 1650 (*B.*) Carter calls T. Buck 'sole printer' at this time.
John Field 1653 ('1655' *B.*; '1654' *Carter* and *Dyer*)
John Hayes 1669—1707
Matthew Whinn, *Joh.* registrary, 1669
John Peck, *Joh.* esquire bedell, 1680
Hugh Martin, *Pemb.* esquire bedell, 1682
Dr James Jackson 1683
Jonathan Pindar 1686, died in 1743
[Edward Hall, cir. 1688]
Henry Jenkes 1693
Cornelius Crownfield 1696—1742, 'Inspector of the Press' 1698—
    1740 ('1706' *B.*; 'sole printer 1707' *Carter*)
Joseph Bentham, Inspector of the Press 1740—78 ('1739' *Carter*)
John Baskerville 1758
John Archdeacon 1766—1793
John Burgess 1793—1802 ('Burges' *Univ. Calend.*)
Richard Watts 1802—1809
John Smith 1809—1836
John William Parker 1836—1854
Charles John Clay[2], *Trin.* 1854.

For several of the earlier names in the above list I am indebted
to a paper on the Cambridge University Press in the *Bookseller* of
24th Feb. 1860, contributed as I understand by Mr Thompson
Cooper.   Where a date differed from what I had put down independently, I have added it with the letter *B.*   I have omitted 'John
Deighton 1802' as belonging more properly to the list of Agents.

[1] For the convenience of university
business, when the working manager
was not a matriculated person, it
seems to have been a common practice
in the 17th century, before a Press
Syndicate was in existence, to nomi-
nate a university officer as Inspector
of the Press.

[2] The University entered into partnership with Mr Clay and Mr G.
Seeley, under a Grace passed 3 July
1854, Mr Seeley acting as the London
Agent.   On Mr Seeley's retiring in 1856
a new partnership between the University and Mr Clay was effected by a
Grace of 12 Mar. 1856, which has been
confirmed by subsequent deeds of partnership.   Cf. Gunning's *Cerem.* 248.

A CHRONOLOGICAL LIST OF ENGLISH XVIIITH CENTURY EDITIONS OF ANCIENT CLASSICS, &c. &c.

THE following list has been compiled in the main from the annals of Bowyer's press, Nichols' *Lit. Anecd.* vols. I—III., Saxii *Onomasticon Literarium*, Dibdin's *Introduction to a Knowledge of Rare Classics*, &c., edd. 1802, 1827. *The Classical Collector's Vade-Mecum*, 1822, Watt's *Bibliotheca Britannica* 1824, Dr P. Bliss' *Sale Catalogue* 1858, and some MS. collections kindly lent by Professor J. E. B. Mayor.

A few patristic, literary and scientific books are included, as well as the titles of other educational books mentioned already in the body of this volume.

Names belonging to *Oxonian* (or *continental*) editions are printed in *italics*, since it is supposed that the list will give a tolerably fair impression of the proportion of classical works produced each year or series of years in the several English universities, or by men of university training or connexions.

It will be observed that if *Oxford* was behind-hand in developing her educational system *as a university*, she was none the less most productive of individual literary enterprise.

When no size is registered the book is inferred to be in octavo ; the compiler however does not feel perfect confidence in his authorities on this score, as accuracy is not very common in this particular, 8vos being often described as 4tos, and 4tos as folios. One is tempted to think that the collectors sometimes classed their books according to the sizes of the shelves which their *extra large paper* copies occupied unread and undisturbed.

1701 Catullus Tibullus et Propertius. 4to. Camb.
    Horace. Ja. Talbot (Trin.). 2 edds., 18mo. Camb.
    Orationes ex Poetis Latinis. *Oxon.*
    Phaedrus. T. Johnson (King's and Magd.). Eton.
    Puffendorf de Off. Hominis et Ciuis. Ed. 6. Camb.
    Roman History. W. Wotton (Joh.).
    Sallust. W. Ayerst (*Univ.*). *Oxon.*
    De Suida Diatribe. L. Kuster (Camb.). 4to. Camb.
    Terence. J. Leng (Cath.). 4to and 8vo. Camb.
    Virgil. J. Laughton (Trin). 4to. Camb.
    Virgil (Tonson). Camb.
    Cosmologia Sacra, Nehem. Grew (Pemb.). Lond.
    De Veteribus Cyclis. H. Dodwell (T. C. D. and *Oxon.*). 4to. *Oxon.*
    Geography. E. Wells (*Ch. Ch.*). *Oxon.*
    Introductio ad veram Physicam. J. Keill (*Ball.*).
    Vocabularium Gul. Sumner, cura T. Benson (*Qu.*).
1702 Catullus Tibullus et Propertius. A. Annesley, earl of Anglesea (Magd.).
    4to. Camb.

Epictetus, Cebes, &c. Gr. Lat. 18mo. *Oxon.*
Euclid, Tacquet. W. Whiston (Clare). Camb.
Irenaeus. J. E. Grabe (*Oxon.*). Fol. *Oxon.*
Lycophron, ed. 2. J. Potter (*Linc.*). Fol. *Oxon.*
Annales Thucyd. et Xenophon. H. Dodwell (T. C. D. and *Oxon.*). *Oxon.*
Virgil. 4to and 8vo. Camb.
Cartesius De Methodo. Camb.
Clarendon's History (1702—4). *Oxon.*
Conic Sections. Ja. Milnes (*Oxon.*). *Oxon.*
Astronomia, D. Gregory (Edinb. and *Oxon.*). Fol. *Oxon.*
1703 Novum Test. Graecum. J. Gregory (*Magd. H.*). Fol. *Oxon.*
Cyril Hierosol. T. Milles (3 indices T. Hearne). Fol. *Oxon.*
Appian. Translated by J. Dryden (Trin.).
Aschami et Sturmii Epistolae. *Oxon.*
Euclidis Opera. D. Gregory (Edinb. and *Ball.*). Fol. *Oxon.*
————— Tacquet. W. Whiston (Clare). Camb.
Euripidis Medea et Phoenissae. W. Piers (Emm.). Camb.
Eutropius and Messala Corvinus. T. Hearne (*Edm. H.*). *Oxon.*
Geographi Minores. J. Hudson (*Qu. Univ.* and *S. Mary H.*). Ed. 2.
Institutiones Juris ex Grotii De J. Belli ac Pacis excerptae. 12mo. Camb.
Justinus. T. Hearne (*Edm. H.*). *Oxon.*
Justin Martyr Apol. H. Hutchinson. *Oxon.*
Maximus Tyrius. J. Davies (Qu). Camb.
Plini Caec. Secundi Epist. et Panegyr. T. Hearne (*Edm. H*). *Oxon.*
Xenophontis et Ciceronis Oecon. E. Wells (*Ch. Ch.*). *Oxon.*
Xenophontis Opera. 5 vols. E. Wells (*Ch. Ch.*). *Oxon.*
Anti Scepticism (on Locke's Essay). H. Lee (Emm.).
Genders of Latin Nouns. Ri. Johnson (Joh.).
A Journey to Jerusalem. H. Maundrell (*Exon.*). *Oxon.*
Linguarum Septentrional. Thesaurus. G. Hickes (*Joh., Magd. C., Magd. H.,* and *Linc.*). *Oxon.*
1704 M. A. Antoninus. *Oxon.* (After the Camb. Gataker of 1652.)
Introductio Chronologica. W. Holder (Pemb. and *Oxon.*). Ed. 2. *Oxon.*
Ductor Historicus. Vol. 2. T. Hearne (*Edm. H.*). *Oxon.*
Dionys. Halicarn. J. Hudson (*Qu., Univ.* and *S. Mary H.*). 2 vols.
Dionysius Periegetes. E. Wells (*Ch. Ch.*). *Oxon.*
Geoponica. P. Needham (Joh.). Camb.
Herodian. Ed. 3. *Oxon.*
Homeri Ilias. *Oxon.*
Lucian. E. Leedes (Pet.). Camb.
Peculiar Use, &c., of certain Latin Words (for Exercises). W. Willymot (King's). Camb.
Foedera. T. Rymer (Sid.) [1704, &c., vols. 16, 17, after his death in 1714, by Ro. Sanderson (*Linc.*)].
Euclid, Cl. Fr. M. De Challes (Turin). *Oxon.* Ed. 2.
Optice. Is. Newton (Trin.). Lond.
Praelectiones Chymicae. J. Freind (*Ch. Ch.*). *Oxon.*
1705 De Bibliorum Textibus. H. Hody (*Wadh.*). Fol. *Oxon.*
Ductor Historicus. Vol. 1. ed. 2. T. Hearne (*Edm. H.*). Lond.
Anacreon. Joshua Barnes (Emm.). Camb.
Anacreon Christianus (psalms, &c.). Joshua Barnes (Emm.). 12mo. Camb.
Homeri Odyssea. *Oxon.*
Justinus. T. Hearne (*Edm. H.*). *Oxon.*
Linguarum Septentrion. Thesaurus. G. Hickes (*Linc.* &c.). *Oxon.*
Litania et Ordo Caenae Dom. *Oxon.*
H. Lukin de Religione. S. Priest (Queens'). *Oxon.*
Ovid Tristia (Delphini). Camb.
Reflexions on Ant. and Mod. Learning. W. Wotton (Joh.). Ed. 3, with a Defence.

Sophoclis (4 plays). T. Johnson (King's and Magd.). 2 vols. *Oxon.*
Suidas. L. Kuster (Camb.). 3 vols. fol. Camb.
Catoptricks, &c. D. Gregory (Edin. and *Oxon.*) engl. W. Browne (Pet.). Lond.
Physica. J. Le Clerc (Geneva). Camb. Ed. 2.
Posthumous Works of Ro. Hooke (*Ch. Ch.*). Lond.
1706 Lexicon in N. Test. Gr. lat. Dawson. Camb.
Academiae Francofort. ad Viadr. Encaenia. *Oxon.*
Antiquities of Greece. J. Potter (*Linc.*). 2 vols.
Apollonius Pergaeus de Sectione Rationis. E. Halley (*Qu.*). *Oxon.*
Athenagoras de Resurrect., &c. E. Dechair (*Linc.*). *Oxon.*
Caesar. J. Davies (Qu.). Camb.
Ciceronis Orationes (Delphini). Camb.
Ciceronis De Oratore. T. Cockman (*Univ.*). *Oxon.*
Graecae Linguae Dialecti. Mich. Maittaire (*Ch. Ch.*). Lond.
Terence, Andria, Adelphi and Hecyra. W. Willymott (King's).
Grotius Baptizat. Puer. Instit. et Eucharistia. *Oxon.*
On the Being and Attributes of God. S. Clarke (Caius). London.
Introductio ad Linguas Orientales. S. Ockley. (Qu.). Camb.
Pro Testimonio Fl. Josephi de Jesu Christo. C. Daubuz (Qu.). Lond.
Newton's Optics. Lat. S. Clarke (Caius).
King's College Anthems. Camb.
1707 Biblia Graeca. J. E. Grabe (*Oxon.*) 4 vols., 1707—20. *Oxon.*
Novum Test. Graecum. J. Mill (*Qu.* and *Edm. H.*). Fol. *Oxon.*
Epictetus et Theophrastus. H. Aldrich (*Ch. Ch.*). *Oxon.*
Encyclopaedia, a Scheme of Study. Ro. Green (Clare). 4to.
Horatius cum lectionibus variis. 12mo. Camb.
Minucius Felix. J. Davies (Qu.). Camb.
Sallust. Jos. Wasse (Qu.).
Theodosii Sphaerica. Gr. Lat. J. Hunt (? *Ball.*). *Oxon.*
Virgilius ex edit. Emmesiana. Camb.
Litterae a pastoribus et professoribus Genev. una cum respons. univ. Oxon. Fol. *Oxon.*
Praelectiones Astronomicae. W. Whiston (Clare).
Newtoni (Trin.) Arithmetica Universalis. W. Whiston (Clare).
1708 Cicero Disp. Tusc. J. Davies (Qu.). Camb.
Compendium of Hickes (*Joh.*, *Magd. C.*, *Magd. H.* and *Linc.*).
Corpus Statutorum Oxoniensium. 12mo. *Oxon.*
Ignatii Epistolae. A. M. Salvini. *Oxon.*
Livius. T. Hearne (*Edm. H.*). 6 vols. *Oxon.*
Nepos. Ed. 2. *Oxon.*
Some Thoughts on the Study of the Laws of England. T. Wood (*New C.*). *Oxon.*
Sophoclis Antigone et Trachiniae. T. Johnson (King's and Magd.). Camb.
Lexicon Technicum. J. Harris (Joh.).
1709 Novum Test. gr. engl. E. Wells (*Ch. Ch.*). *Oxon.*
Antonini Iter Britannicum. T. Gale (Trin.) [edidit Rog. Gale (Trin.) fil.]. 4to. Lond.
Cicero Quaest. Tusc. J. Davies (Qu.). Camb.
Dionysius Periegetes, gr. lat. E. Wells (*Ch. Ch.*). *Oxon.*
Ephrem Syrus. E. Thwaites (*Qu.*). *Oxon.*
Hierocles Philos. P. Needham (Joh.). Camb.
Ignatii Epistolae. J. Pearson (King's), and T. Smith (*Qu.*). 4to. *Oxon.*
Leland Script. Britt. A. Hall (*Qu.*). *Oxon.*
Menander et Philemon, Le Clerc. Ri. Bentley (Joh. and Trin.; *Wadh.*).
Oxford and Camb. Miscellany Poems. Lintot (Nichols' *Lit. Anecd.* ix. 164).
Spelman's Aelfred. T. Hearne (*Edm. H.*). *Oxon.*
Chemistry Lectures. J. Freind (*Ch. Ch.*).
1710 Apollonius Pergaeus. Edm. Halley (*Qu.*). Fol. *Oxon.*
Annot. in 2 priores Aristophanis Comoedias. Ri. Bentley (Joh., Trin. and *Wadh.*). Fol. Amst.

Synopsis Canonum Eccl. Latinae.   Laur. Howell (Jes.).
Dionysii Orbis Descript. comment. Eustathii.   *Oxon.*
Historical Account of the Heathen Gods and Heroes.   W. King (*Ch. Ch.*).
Longinus.   J. Hudson (*Qu.*, *Univ.* and *S. Mary H.*).   *Oxon.*
Lucian.   E. Leedes (Pet.).
Emendationes in Menand. et Philemon.   Philel. Lips. [Ri. Bentley] Traj.
    ad Rhen.
Sallust, &c.   Jos. Wasse (Qu.).   Camb.
Triglandii Paedia Juris.   *Oxon.*
Cosmologia Sacra.   Neh. Grew (Pemb.).   Ed. 2.   Lond.
Euclid, Tacquet.   W. Whiston (Clare).   Camb.
Praelectiones Physico-Mathematicae.   W. Whiston (Clare).   Camb.
1711 Antiquitates Rutupinae.   J. Battely (Trin. C. Camb.).   *Oxon.*
Herodotus, Vita Homeri.   4to.   Camb.
Homer.   Joshua Barnes (Emm.).   2 vols. 4to.   Camb.
Horace.   Ri. Bentley (Joh., Trin. and *Wadh.*).   2 vols. 4to.   Camb.
Juvenal Transl.   J. Dryden (Trin.).
Orationes ex Poetis Latinis.   *Oxon.*
Oratio in publicis Acad. Oxon. Scholis in laudem T. Bodleii.   Edm. Smith
    (*Ch. Ch.*).   Lond.   (Bowyer.)
Ovid's Metamorphoses, englished by Sir S. Garth (Pet.), &c.   Fol. Lond.
Plautus.   2 vols.   Lond.   (Tonson.)
Pomponius Mela.   J. Reynolds (King's).   4to.   Exeter.
Praelectiones Poeticae.   Jos. Trapp. (*Wadh.*).   *Oxon.*
Velleius Paterculus.   *Oxon.*
Symposium Luciani, Platonis, Xenophontis, Plutarchi.   C. Aldrich
    (*Ch. Ch.*).   *Oxon.*
Grammatica Anglo-Saxonica.   C. Thwaites (*Qu.*).
1712 Essay on 2 Arabic MSS., Bodl.   J. E. Grabe (*Oxon.*).
Chrysostom de Sacerdotio.   J. Hughes (Jes).   Camb.
Caesar.   S. Clarke (Caius).   Fol.   Lond.
Dionysius Periegetes.   J. Hudson (*Qu.*, &c.).   *Oxon.*
Minucius Felix.   J. Davies (Qu.).   Camb.
Moeris Atticista.   J. Hudson (*Qu.*, *Univ.* and *S. Mary H.*).   *Oxon.*
De Graecarum Litt. Pronunc.   G. Martin.   *Oxon.*
De Ordine Vocabulorum, &c.   J. Ward.   Lond.
Oratio Inauguralis.   Simon Ockley (Qu.).   4to.   Camb.
Theophrasti Characteres, variorum.   P. Needham (Joh.).   Camb.
Varenii Geographia.   Ja. Jurin (Trin.).   Camb.
Maps of Anc. and Mod. Geography.   E. Wells (*Ch. Ch.*).
A New Institute of Imperial or Civil Law.   T. Wood (*New C.*).   Bowyer,
    Lond.
Conic Sections.   Ja. Milnes (*Oxon.*).   *Oxon.*
Principles of Natural Philosophy.   Ro. Green (Clare).   Camb.
1713 Newtoni Principia.   Ed. 2.   Roger Cotes (Trin.).   Camb.
Horace.   Ed. 2.   R. Bentley (Joh., Trin. and *Wadh.*).   8vo.   Camb.; also Amst.
Horace.   T. Bentley (Trin).   12mo.
Emendation of Menander and Ep. ad Millium (reprint).   R. Bentley.
Dissert. on Ep. of Phalaris.   R. Bentley (Joh., Trin. and *Wadh.*).
Menander et Philemon, gr. lat.   J. Clerc.   Ed. R. Bentley.   Camb.
Codex Juris Eccles. Angl.   Edm. Gibson (*Qu.*).   Lond.
De Parma Equestri Woodward.   H. Dodwell (T. C. D. and *Oxon.*) and T.
    Hearne (*Edm. H.*).   *Oxon.*
Plato de Republica. varior.   Edm. Massey.   Camb.
Poetae Vett. Lat. · Mich. Maittaire (*Ch. Ch.*).   Lond.
Justinus.   Lucretius.   „   „   „
Paterculus.   Phaedrus.   „   „   „
Sallustius.   „   „   „
Compendium Ethices.   D. Whitby (*Trin.*).   *Oxon.*
Physico-Theologia.   W. Derham (*Trin.*).   Lond.
Principia Mathem.   Is. Newton (Trin.).   Ed. 2.   Camb.

1714 N. Test. Graecum. Superintended by Maittaire. Lond.
    Reasonableness and Certainty of the Christian Religion. R. Jenkin
      (Joh.). Ed. 4.
    Spicilegium SS. Patrum, &c. J. E. Grabe (*Oxon.*). *Oxon.*
    Astro-Theologia. W. Derham (*Trin.*). Lond.
    Cicero de Oratore. Ja. Proust. *Oxon.*
    Homer Iliad. Morel. *Oxon.*
    Theophrastus transl. Eustace Budgell (*Ch. Ch.*). Lond.
    Geographia Varenii. Ja. Jurin (Trin.). Camb.
    Short Introduction to Grammar. *Oxon.*
    Grammatica Latina. *Oxon.*
    Ductor Historicus. T. Hearne (*Edm. H.*). Complete. Lond.
    Trigonometry. E. Wells (*Ch. Ch.*). Lond.
1715 Greek Testament. 12mo. Bowyer. Lond.
    Acta Apost. Gr. Lat. litt. maiusc. cod. Laudian. Bodl. T. Hearne (*Edm.
      H.*). *Oxon.*
    Commentaries on S. Paul's Epp. E. Wells (*Ch. Ch.*). *Oxon.*
    A Help for Underst. H. Scriptures. E. Wells (*Ch. Ch.*) 7 vols. 4to. *Oxon.*
    Aristeas. Hist. LXX. Interpp. Grabe, transl. Lewis. 12mo. *Oxon.*
  ?Irenaeus. Jo. Pottanus. 2 vols. Fol. *Oxon.* [Watt. I. 535 *u.*]
    Clem. Alexandr. J. Potter (*Linc.*). *Oxon.*
    Vindication of Sibylline Oracles. W. Whiston (Clare).
    Liberty and Necessity. Ant. Collins (King's).
    Epist. de Legibus Attractionis. J. Keill (*Ball.*). *Oxon.*
    Introd. ad Phys. Lect. J. Keill (*Ball.*). *Oxon.*
    Demosthenes et Aeschines de Corona. P. Foulkes and J. Friend (*Ch. Ch.*).
      Ed. 2. *Oxon.*
    Cicero de Finibus. J. Davies (Qu.). Camb.
    —— de Oratore. Ja. Proust. *Oxon.*
    Doctrina Philosophorum ex Cicerone. *Oxon.*
    Epictetus. E. Ivie (*Ch. Ch.*). *Oxon.*
    Euripidis Medea and Phoeniss. Joshua Barnes (Emm). Lond.
    Herodoti Clio. Camb.
    Musaeus Hero and Leander. Engl. Verse. A. S. Calcott. *Oxon.*
    Catullus, Tibull. Propert. Mich. Maittaire (*Ch. Ch.*). 12mo. Lond.
    Virgil. *Id.*
    Florus. *Id.*
    Ovid. *Id.* 3 vols.
  ?Horace. *Id.*
    Nepos. *Id.*
    Dictionary of Classical Geography. L. [and S.] Eachard (Chr.).
    Σκελετος Cantabrigiensis. Ri. Parkeri. Ed. T. Hearne. *Oxon.*
    Puffendorf de Off. Camb.
    Euclidis Elem. J. Keill (*Ball.*). *Oxon.*
    Catoptricks, &c. D. Gregory (Edinb. and *Ball.*), engl. ed. 2. W. Browne
      (Pet.). Lond.
1716 N. T. Coptice. David Wilkins (Camb.). *Oxon.*
    Aristotelis Ethica. var. G. Wilkinson. *Oxon.*
    Cicero De Officiis, var. ? J. Cockman (*Univ.*). *Oxon.*
    —— De Senectute, engl. S. Hemming (*Qu.*). *Oxon.*
    —— De Oratore. Zach. Pearce (Trin.). Camb.
    —— De Claris Oratoribus. Ja. Proust. *Oxon.*
    Horatius. Mich. Maittaire (*Ch. Ch.*). 12mo. Lond.
    Caesar. *Id.*
    Q. Curtius. *Id.*
    Juvenal. *Id.*
    Martial. *Id.*
    Athenae Britt. History of *Oxford* and Cambridge Writers. Miles Davies.
      Lond.
    De dea Salute. G. Musgrave. *Oxon.*
    Hist. Plant. Succulent. (decas I.). R. Bradley (Camb.). 4to.

1717 Baskett's Imperial Bible (vellum). 2 vols. Folio. *Oxon.*
Aristotelis Ethica Nicom. W. Wilkinson (*Qu.*). *Oxon.*
Cicero De Officiis, &c. T. Tooly (*Joh.*). *Oxon.*
—— De Amicitia, &c. T. Tooly (*Joh.*). *Oxon.*
Dionysius Periegetes. J. Hudson (*Qu.*, *Univ.* and *S. Mary H.*). *Oxon.*
Ovid Metamorph. transl. S. Garth (Pet.). Fol. Lond.
Aristarchus Anti-Bentleianus. Ri. Johnson (Joh.).
Antient and Present Geography. E. Wells (*Ch. Ch.*).
Musae Anglicanae. *Oxon.*
Εἰκὼν Σωκρατική. S. Catherall. *Oxon.*
Treatise on Opticks. Is. Newton (Trin.). Bowyer. Lond.
1718 Aesop. J. Hudson (*Qu.*, *Univ.* and *S. Mary H.*). *Oxon.*
Aesop. 12mo. *Oxon.*
Cicero De Nat. Deor. J. Davies (Qu.). Camb.
—— De Finibus. J. Davies (Qu.). Camb.
—— De Finibus, Paradoxa. T. Bentley (Trin.). Camb.
—— Rhetorica. Ja. Proust. *Oxon.*
Horace Odes, engl. H. Coxwell. 4to. *Oxon.*
Longinus. J. Hudson (*Qu.*, *Univ.* and *S. Mary H.*). *Oxon.*
Phalaris. C. Boyle (*Ch. Ch.*).
Physica Aristotelica mod....in usum Juv. Acad. Taswell. Bowyer. Lond.
Miscellanea in Usum Juvent. Acad. J. Pointer (*Mert.*). *Oxon.*
Virgil Aen. engl. Jos. Trapp (*Wadh.*).
Remarks on Italy. Jos. Addison (*Magd.*). Lond.
Optica Newton., lat. S. Clark (Caius). Ed. 2. Bowyer. Lond.
Pharmacopoeia Bateana. T. Fuller, M.D. Cantab. Bowyer. Lond.
Clemens Romanus. H. Wotton (Joh.). Camb.
Lactantius. J. Davies (Qu.). Camb.
Ray's Correspondence. W. Derham (*Trin.*). Lond.
Physica Ja. Rohault. S. Clarke (Cai.). Ed. 4.
1719 Apostolical Fathers, &c. W. Wake (*Ch. Ch.*). Ed. 3. Bowyer. Lond.
Ignatius, &c.
Justin M. Dialogues. S. Jebb (Pet.). Bowyer. Lond.
Clavis Ling. Sanctae. Nic. Trott (*D. C. L.*). Fol. *Oxon.*
Dissert. ad J. Clericum Epist^{ris}. de Quinctiliano. Mich. Maittaire (*Ch. Ch.*).
4to. Lond.
De Asse. J. Ward (Gresham). Lond.
Hierocles. P. Needham (Joh.). Camb.
Lucan. M. Maittaire (*Ch. Ch.*). 12mo. Lond.
Pomponius Mela. J. Reynolds (? King's). 4to. Lond.
Saxon Homilies. W. Elstob (Cath. H., *Qu.* and *Univ.*), &c.
1720 Vet. Test. Vol. 3. ? G. Wigan (*Ch. Ch.*). Lond.
Bibliotheca Biblica. S. Parker (*B. N. C.*). 4to. *Oxon.*
Cambridge Concordance. Fol.
Origines Ecclesiasticae. Jos. Bingham (*Univ.*). Bowyer. Lond.
Theologia Speculativa, Body of Divinity. Ri. Fiddes (*Univ.*). Lond.
Valesii, Eusebii, &c. Hist. Eccl. W. Reading. 3 vols. Fol. Camb.
De P. Pilati epist. T. Woolston (Sid.). Lond.
Cebetis Tabula. T. Johnson (King's and Magd.). Eton, Lond.
Cicero De Senect. &c., engl. S. Parker (*B. N. C.*). *Oxon.*
Josephus. J. Hudson (*Qu.*, *Univ.* and *S. Mary H*). 2 vols. Fol. *Oxon.*
Textus Roffensis. T. Hearne (*Edm. H.*).
Chronological Tables. A. Blandy (*Pemb.*). *Oxon.*
Institute of the Laws of England. T. Wood (*New C.*).
Canons Ecclesiastical. J. Johnson (Magd. and Benet.).
1721 Proposals for Gk. Test. R. Bentley (Joh. and Trin.). 4to. Lond.
Anacreon. Josh. Barnes (Emm.). Ed. 2. Camb.
Batrachomyomachia gr. lat. M. Maittaire (*Ch. Ch.*). Lond.
Cicero De Divinat. et De Fato. J. Davies (Qu.). Camb.
Demosthenes Fals. Legat. H. Brooke (*B. N. C.* and *All S.*). *Oxon.*
Demosthenis Orationes LXII. *Oxon.*

Inscriptio Sigea. Edm. Chishull (*Corpus*). Lond.
Carmina Comitialia. V. Bourne (Trin.).
Introduction to True Astronomy. J. Keill (*Ball.*).
On the Usefulness of Mathematical Learning. Ed. 2. M. Strong (*Linc.*). Oxon.
Petra Scandali (Schism. Eccll. Orient. and Occident.). Arabic version. J. Gagnier. *Oxon.*
Leges Saxonicae. D. Wilkins. (Camb.)
1722 Inquiry into Authority of Complutensian N. T. Ri. Bentley (Joh. and Trin. and *Wadh.*). Lond.
Beda Hist. Eccl. J. Smith (Joh.). Bowyer. Lond. and Camb.
A Kempis Imit. Xti. and Three Tabernacles. W. Willymot (King's). Bowyer. Lond.
Bibliotheca Litteraria I. II. S. Jebb (Pet.), &c. (Camb.). Bowyer. Lond.
Justin M., Trypho. Styan Thirlby (Jes.). London.
Tertullian adv. Haeret. et Theophili Apol. J. Betty (*Exon.*). *Oxon.*
Theophilus ad Autol. engl. Jo. Betty (*Exon.*). *Oxon.*
Aelius Aristides. S. Jebb (Pet.). 2 vols. 4to. *Oxon.*
Oppian Halieutica. W. Diaper and J. Jones (*Ball.*). *Oxon.*
Plini Epp. et Panegyr. M. Maittaire (*Ch. Ch.*). Lond.
Vidae Poemata. T. Tristram (*Pemb.*). E. Owen (Joh.). *Oxon.*
Miscell. Graecor. Scriptt. Carmina, gr. lat. Mich. Maittaire (*Ch. Ch.*). 4to. Lond.
De Obligatione Juramenti. Ro. Sanderson (*Linc.*). Lond.
Euclid. Andr. Tacquet (Antw.), W. Whiston (Clare). Ed. 3. Camb.
1723 Aretaeus Cappadox (medical). J. Wigan (*Ch. Ch.*). Fol. *Oxon.*
Bibliotheca Litteraria III.—VI. S. Jebb (Pet.). Bowyer. Lond.
Cicero (Manutii). F. Hare (King's). Camb.
—— Disp. Tusc. J. Davies (Qu.). Ed. 2. Camb.
Epictetus. E. Ivie (*Ch. Ch.*). Ed. 2. *Oxon.*
Epistola Critica ad F. Hare (King's), Jer. Markland (Pet.). Camb.
Euripidis Medea et Phoeniss. W. Piers (Emm.). Ed. 2. Camb.
Terentius. J. Leng (Cath.). Camb.
Carmina Quadragesimalia. C. Este (*Ch. Ch.*). *Oxon.*
Vida de Arte Poetica. 12mo. *Oxon.*
Hemingii Chartularium Vigorn. T. Hearne (*Edm. H.*).
English Particles. W. Willymott (King's). Lond.
Conic Sections. Ja. Milnes (*Oxon.*). *Oxon.*
1724 Anthol. Graec. Delectus Westmonast. *Oxon.*
Antiquitates Asiaticae. E. Chishull (*Corpus*).
Bibliotheca Litteraria VII.—X. Bowyer. Lond.
Britannia Romana. J. Pointer (*Mert.*). *Oxon.*
Longinus. Zach. Pearce (Trin.). Lond. •
Terence. Fr. Hare (King's). 4to. Lond.
Religion of Nature Delineated. W. Wollaston (Sid.).
1725 Anacreon. Mich. Maittaire (*Ch. Ch.*). Lond.
Anthol. Poem. Gr. Minor. Westmon. *Oxon.*
Cicero Quaestt. Acad. J. Davies (Qu.). Camb.
[Horace. John Pine. 2 vols. Lond.]
Phileleutherus Lipsiensis on Collins' 'Freethinking.' Ri. Bentley (Joh. Trin. and *Wadh.*). Ed. Camb.
Theophrastus transl. H. Gally (Benet). Lond.
Vida Christiad. E. Owen (Joh.). *Oxon.*
Gradus ad Parnassum. Lond.
New Theory of the Earth. W. Whiston (Clare). Ed. 2. Lond.
1726 Ignatius. *Oxon.*
Sum and Substance of IV Evangelists. *Oxon.*
Liber Precum Eccl. Cathedr. Oxon. *Oxon.*
Petra Scandali. J. Gagnier. Ed. 2. *Oxon.*
Three Sermons and Preface. Jos. Butler (*Oriel*).
Euripidis Hec. Orest. Phoen. J. King (King's). 2 vols. Camb.

Isocratis, &c., Orationes Selectae.   Phil. Fletcher.   *Oxon.*
Demosth. et Aeschinis Oratt.   P. Foulkes and J. Freind (*Ch. Ch.*).
   Oxon.
Terence, Phaedrus and Publ. Syrus.   R. Bentley (Trin.).   4to.   Camb.
Sibylla Capitolina.   *Oxon.*
Poemata Card. Maffaei Barberini.   Jo. Brown (*Qu.*).   *Oxon.*
   Urban VIII.
Tasso's Aminta.   P. B. Du Bois (*S. Mary H.*).   *Oxon.*
   J. Faber.   *Oxon.*
Astro-Theologia.   W. Derham (*Trin.*).   Lond.
Terrae Filius.   N. Amhurst [*Joh.*].
Arithmetick.   E. Wells (*Ch. Ch.*).   Lond.
Geography.   E. Wells (*Ch. Ch.*).   *Oxon.*
Principia Mathem.   Is. Newton (Trin.).   Ed. 3.   Camb.
1727 Holy Bible.   2 vols. fol.   *Oxon.*
   ———— arranged for the Clementine Libr. by E. Warren (? *Bras.*).
   4to.   *Oxon.*
The Sacred Classics defended and illustrated.   Ant. Blackwall.   Lond.
Caesar.   J. Davies (Qu.).   Ed. 2.   4to.   Camb.
Cicero De Legibus.   J. Davies (Qu.).   Camb.
—— Cato Major, &c., engl.   S. Parker (*Bras.*).   *Oxon.*
Xenophon Cyropaed.   T. Hutchinson (*Linc.*).   *Oxon.*
   ———— and Anabasis.   T. Hutchinson (*Linc.*).   4to.   *Oxon.*
   ———— Oeconomics, engl. Ri. Bradley (prof. Camb.).   Lond.
   ———— Journey of Cyrus, engl.   *Oxon.*
Physico-Theologia.   W. Derham (*Trin.*).   Lond.
Catalogue of Oxford Graduates, 1603—1726.   *Oxon.*
Principles of Philos. of Expansive and Contractive Forces.   Ro. Green
   (Clare).   Camb.
Vegetable Staticks.   Ste. Hales (Benet.).   Lond.
Historiae Plantarum Succulent. decas 5ta.   Ri. Bradley (prof. Camb.).   4to.
1728 De Bened. Patriarchae Jacob conjectt.   G. Hooper (*Ch. Ch.*).   4to.   *Oxon.*
Novatian.   J. Jackson (Jes.).   Lond.
Antiquitates Asiaticae.   Edm. Chishull (*Corpus*).   Bowyer.   Lond.
Aristotelis Poetica, editio 2do Goulstoniana.   Camb.
   ———— Rhetorica, var.   ? W. Beattie (Magd.).   Camb.
Cicero De Finibus.   J. Davies (Qu.).   Camb.
Dionys. Halicarn.   Ja. Upton (King's).   Bowyer.   Lond.
Q. Horatius Flaccus (an edition of Bentley's).   Amst.
Plato Parmenides.   J. W. Thomson.   *Oxon.*
Statii Silv.   Jer. Markland (Pet.).   Bowyer.   Lond.
Foundation of Moral Goodness.   J. Balguy (Joh.).
Annals of University Coll.   W. Smith.   Newcastle.
System of Opticks.   Ro. Smith (Trin.).
Optice Newtoni.   S. Clarke (Caius).   Lond.
1729 Common Prayer.   *Oxon*   8vo. and 12mo.
Antiquities of Constantinople.   J. Ball (*Corpus*).   Bowyer.   Lond.
Aeschylus Choë.; Soph. and Eurip. Electra Westmonast.   *Oxon.*
Ciceronis Orationes.   Delphin.   Camb.
Homer.   Vol. I.   S. Clarke, sen. (Caius).   4 vols.   4to.
Isocrates, var.   Vol. I. (see 1749).   W. Battie (King's).   Camb.
Plutarchi Vitae (1723—9).   Aug^{ne}. Bryan (Trin.).   5 vols. 4to.   Lond.
Sophocles engl.   G. Adams (Joh.).   Bowyer.   Lond.
Instit. Logicae.   J. Wallis (Emm. and Qu. and *Oxon.*).   *Oxon.*
De Laude Univ. Oxon. Metrice.   Ed. T. Hearne (*Edm. H.*).   *Oxon.*
Parecbolae Statut. Univ. Oxon.   *Oxon.*
Ambr. Bonwicke (Joh.), A Pattern for Young Students.   Lond.
1730 Aelius Aristides.   3 vols. 4to.   *Oxon.*
Cicero De Divinatione var.   ⎫
—— Tusculan. Disp.   ⎬ J. Davies (Qu.).   Camb.
—— Philosophica.   ⎭

Longinus. J. Hudson (*Qu.*, *Univ.* and *S. Mary H.*). Ed. 2. *Oxon.*
Lucian. N. Kent (King's). Camb.
Sallust (Minelli)'. 24mo. *Oxon.*
Xenophon Cyropaedia. T. Hutchinson (*Linc.*). Lond.
Vindiciae Antiquit. Acad. Oxon. T. Cai. Ed. Hearne. 2 vols. *Oxon.*
Keill's Oxf. Astron. Lectures. Edm. Halley (*Qu.*). Bowyer. Lond.
Cambridge Lectures on Materia Medica. Prof. Ri. Bradley. Bowyer.
Musick Speeches by J. Taylor (Joh.)
Scripture Chronology. A. Bedford (*Bras.*).
Articuli XXXIX. E. Welchman (*Mert.*). Ed. 5. *Oxon.*
A System of Ecclesiastical Law. Ri. Grey (*Linc.*).
A New Institute of Imperial or Civil Law. T. Wood (*New C.*). Ed. 4.
Bowyer. Lond.
1731 Cicero's Dialogues (s. a. 1727) tr. S. Parker (*Bras.*). 4to. *Oxon.*
Demosthenes Select Oratt. var. R. Mounteney, Cambr. *Oxon.*
Horatii Carmina. G. Wade (Chr.). Bowyer. Lond.
Thucydides. Jos. Wasse (Qu.) and Duker. 2 vols. fol. *Amst.*
Observationes Miscellaneae (Dutch Philol. Journ.) transl. J. Jortin (Jes.),
&c. (Camb.)
Conic Sections. L. Trevigar. Camb.
Eternal and Immutable Morality. Ra. Cudworth (Emm., Clare and Chr.).
Tertullian adv. Praxean. Camb.
Euclid. *Oxon.*
On Moral Obligation. T. Johnson (King's and Magd.). Camb.
Origin of Evil. W. King (T. C. D.). Engl. Edm. Law (Joh., Chr. and
Pet.). 4to.
1732 Apparatus ad Ling. Graec. G. Thompson, assisted by Prof. Pilgrim
(Trin.). Bowyer. Lond.
Cicero De Oratore. Z. Pearce (Trin.). 2 ed. Camb.
—— De Nat. Deor. J. Davies (Qu.). Camb.
—— Offices. trs. T. Cockman (*Univ.*). Ed. 8. Bowyer. Lond.
Homeri Ilias. Vol. 2. S. Clarke (Caius).
Gemmae Antiquae. G. Ogle (? Sid.). Paris (see 1741).
Livy. Mich. Maittaire (*Ch. Ch.*). 6 vols.
Longinus. Z. Pearce (Trin.).
Marmora Oxoniensia. Ed. 2. Mich. Maittaire (*Ch. Ch.*). Fol. Bowyer.
Harmonia Mensurarum. Rog. Cotes (Trin.). 4to. Camb.
Hortus Elthamensis. J. J. Sherard Dillenius (Joh.).
Oratio Woodwardiana. Conyers Middleton (Trin.). Bowyer. Lond.
Origin of Evil. W. King (T. C. D.). Engl. Edm. Law (Joh., Chr. and
Pet.). Ed. 2. 2 vols. Lond.
Observationes in Comment. Gr. Demosth. Ulpiano v. adscriptae. J. Chap-
man (King's).
Oxonia Depicta. W. Williams.. Fol.
Quaestiones Philosophicae in Usum Juvent. Acad. T. Johnson (King's
and Magd.). Camb.
Thucydides (Duker).
1733 Indices III. ad Cyrillum. T. Hearne (*Edm.*). *Oxon.*
Appendix ad Marmora Oxoniensia. Bowyer. Lond.
Bacon Opus Majus. S. Jebb (Pet.). Fol. Bowyer. Lond.
Bellus Homo et Academicus, &c. Bowyer. Lond.
Cicero Nat. Deor. Ed. 3. J. and Ri. Davies (Qu.). Camb.
Epist. Critica. Jer. Markland and Fr. Hare (Horace emended). Camb.
1734 Some Thoughts concerning...studying Divinity. W. Wotton (Joh.).
Anacreon. Josh. Barnes (Emm.). Lond.
Pandect and Parergon. J. Ayliffe (*New C.*). 2 vols. Fol.
Poematia. V. Bourne (Trin.). Westmon.
Historia Plantarum Succulent. Ri. Bradley (prof.). Reprint.
Mathematical Lectures. Is. Barrow (Trin.). Bowyer. Lond.
Oratio Woodwardiana. C. Mason (Trin.). 4to. Camb.
Inquiry into the Ideas of Space. J. Clarke, E. Law, &c.

1735 Bibliotheca Biblica.   S. Parker.   5 vols. 4to.   *Oxon.*
   Tho. à Kempis' Christian Pattern.   J. Wesley (*Ch. Ch.*, *Linc.*).
   Ro. Stephani Thesaurus Ling. Lat.   Augmented and emended by Edm.
      Law (Joh., Chr., Pet.), J. Taylor (Joh.), T. Johnson (King's, Magd.),
      and Sandys Hutchinson (bibl. Trin.).
   The Scholar's Instructor, Hebrew Grammar.   Isr. Lyons.   Camb.
   Ant. Blackwall De Praestantia Classic. Auct. trs.   G. H. Ayrer.   *Lipsiae.*
   Usefulness of Mathematical Learning.   Is. Barrow.   Tr. J. Kirkby (Joh.).
   Enquiry into the Life and Writings of Homer.   Ant. Blackwall (Emm.).
   Josephus, transl.   W. Whiston [Clare].   Bowyer.   Lond.
   Origin of Evil.   W. King (T. C. D.).   Engl.   Camb.
   Puffendorf De Off. Hominis et Civis.   Johnson.   Camb.
   Quaestiones Philosophicae.   T. Johnson (King's and Magd.)   Camb. Ed. 2.
   Xenophon Anabasis.   T. Hutchinson (*Linc.*).   4to.   Agesilaus. 8vo. *Oxon.*
   Catoptricks, &c.   D. Gregory (*Ch. Ch.*).   Reflecting Telescopes, &c.   J. T.
      Desaguliers (*Ch. Ch.*, *Hart. H.*).   Lond.
   Critical Remarks on Capt. Gulliver's Travels.   R. Bentley (Trin.).   Camb.
1736 S. Scripturae Versio Metrica.   J. Burton (*Corpus*).   *Oxon.*
   Dissertationes et Conjectt. in Librum Jobi.   S. Wesley (*Exon.*).   Bowyer.
   Solomon de Mundi Vanitate.   Mat. Prior (Joh.), W. Dobson (? *New C.*).
      4to.   *Oxon.*
   Psalmi Hebr. Lat.   Fr. Hare (King's).   Lond.
   Cicero Academica.   J. Davies (Qu.).   Camb.
   Lysias.   Jer. Markland (Pet.).   Lond.
   Newton's Fluxions.   J. Colson (Sid. and Emm.)
   Praelectiones Poeticae.   Jos. Trapp (*Wadh.*).   2 vols.   Lond.
   Catalogue of Oxford Graduates.   *Oxon.*
1737 Graecae Linguae Dialecti.   Mich. Maittaire (*Ch. Ch.*).   Ed. 2.   Lond.
   Hesiod.   T. Robinson (*Linc.*, *Mert.*).   4to.   *Oxon.*
   Xenophon Cyr.   T. Hutchinson (*Linc.*).   4to.   *Oxon.*
   La Secchia of Tasso.   2 pts.   1 vol.   *Oxon.*
   On the Sacrament.   D. Waterland (Magd.).
   Poems.   W. Shenstone (*Pemb.*).   *Oxon.*
   Concilia.   D. Wilkins (Camb.).   4 vols.
   New Theory of the Earth.   W. Whiston (Clare).   Camb.
1738 Catalogus Interpp. S. Script. Bodl.   Ro. Fysher (*Ch. Ch.*).   2 vols. fol. *Oxon.*
   Census habitus nascente Christo.   J. Reinoldius (? King's, and *Oxon.*).   *Oxon.*
   Cicero Disp. Tusc. em. Bentl.   J. Davies (Qu.).   Ed. 4.   Camb.
   Lingua Etruriae.   J. Swinton (*Ch. Ch.*).   *Oxon.*
   The Scholar's Instructor, Hebrew Grammar.   Isr. Lyons.   Ed. 2.   Camb.
   Bodleian Catalogue.   *Oxon.*
   Travels in Barbary.   T. Shaw (*Qu.* and *Edm. Hall*).
   Hydrostatical and Pneumatical Lectures.   Rog. Cotes (Trin.).   Bowyer.
   Complete System of Opticks.   Ro. Smith (Trin.).   2 vols. Bowyer. Lond.
1739 Discourse on Anc. and Mod. Learning, from MS. of Jos. Addison (*Magd.*).
   De antiq. et util. Ling. Arabicae.   T. Hunt (*Ch. Ch.*, *Hart H.*).   *Oxon.*
   Epictetus.   Ja. Upton (*Exon.*).   Lond.
   Epictetus, Cebes and Theophrastus.   Jos. Simpson (*Qu.*).   *Oxon.*
   Lysias.   J. Taylor (Joh.), Jer. Markland (Pet.).   Bowyer.   Lond.
   Manilius.   R. Bentley (Joh., Trin. and *Wadh.*).   4to.   Lond.
   Pomponius Mela.   J. Reynolds (King's).   4to. ed. 3.   Lond.
   Tryphiodorus Troja.   J. Merrick.   *Oxon.*
   Origin of Evil.   W. King (T. C. D.).   Engl. ed. 3.   Edm. Law (Joh., Chr.
      and Pet.).   Camb.
   Astronomy of the Moon and Tables of the Moon's Motions.   R. Dun-
      thorne (Pemb. Lodge).   Camb.
1740 Historiae Litterariae.   Ed. 2.   Vol. 1.   W. Cave (Joh.) and H. Wharton
      (Caius).   *Oxon.*
   Anacreon.   Mich. Maittaire (*Ch. Ch.*).   Ed. 2.   Lond.
   Epictetus, Cebes, Prodicus and Theophr.   Jos. Simpson (*Qu.*).   *Oxon.*
   Refl. on Logick in the Schools.   E. Bentham (*Ch. Ch.*, *Corpus*, *Oriel*). *Oxon.*

Lysias. J. Taylor (Joh.). Camb.
Maximi Tyrii Dissertt. J. Davies (Qu.), Jer. Markland (Pet.). Bowyer.
On Antique Painting. G. Turnbull (? *Exon.*). Lond.
Historia Muscorum. J. J. Sherard Dillenius (Joh.)
N. Sanderson's (Chr.) Palpable Arith. and Algebra. J. Colson (Sid. and Emm.). 4to. Camb.
1741 Callimachus Theognis, Galen of Pergamos, &c. T. Bentley (Trin.). Lond.
Cicero De Finibus, var. J. Davies (Qu.). Ed. 2. Camb.
—— De Divinatione. J. Davies (Qu.). Ed. 3. Camb.
—— De Legibus, &c. Camb.
Epistola. Ja. Tunstal (Joh.) ad Middletonum, c. dissert. de aetate Ciceronis de Legibus. J. Chapman (King's and *Oxon.*). Camb.
Defence of the Antient Greek Chronology, and Enquiry into the Origin of the Greek Language. S. Squire (Joh.). Camb.
Carmina Quadragesimalia. Vol. i. ed. 2. C. Este (*Ch. Ch.*). Lond.
Epictetus and Arrian. Ja. Upton (*Exon.*). 2 vols. Lond.
Gemmae Antiquae. G. Ogle (? Sid.). Ed. 2. Lond.
Plutarchi Apophthegmata Regum. Mich. Maittaire (*Ch. Ch.*). Lond.
Tryphiodorus, var. tr. Ja. Merrick (*Trin.*). Oxon.
Virgil's Georgicks, engl. J. Martyn (Emm.). 4to.
Xenophon Memorab. Gr. Lat. Bolton Simpson (*Qu.*). Oxon.
Elements of Algebra. N. Saunderson (*Chr.*). With memoir. 2 vols. 4to.
Logicae Artis Compendium. R. Sanderson (*Linc.*). Oxon.
Quaestiones Philosophicae. T. Johnson (King's and Magd.). Camb. Ed. 3.
Expence of Univ. Education Reduced. Ri. Newton (*Ch. Ch., Hart. H.*). ed. 4 (ed. 1. 1727). *Oxon.*
1742 Nov. Test. Graec. J. Gambold. 12mo. *Oxon.*
Anacreon, gr. lat. Camb.
Cicero and Brutus. Conyers Middleton (Trin.). Lond.
Commentarius ad Legem Xviralem, &c. J. Taylor (Joh.), R. Bentley (Joh., Trin. and *Wadh.*), &c. Camb.
De Graecis Illustribus. Hum. Hody (*Wadh.*). Bowyer. Lond.
Observations upon Liberal Education. G. Turnbull (? *Exon.*). Lond.
Philo Judaeus. T. Mangey (Joh.). Bowyer. Lond.
Poetry Lectures in Schol. Philos. Oxon. Jos. Trapp (*Wadh.*). Bowyer.
Astronomy. Roger Long (Pemb.). 4to. Camb.
1743 Cave Historia Literaria. 2 vols. fol. *Oxon.* (s. a. 1740.)
Demosthenes in Midiam and Lycurgus c. Leocr. J. Taylor (Joh.). Camb.
Junii Etymologicon. E. Lye (*Hart. H.*). Fol. *Oxon.*
Marmor Sandvicense et De inope Debitore dissecando. J. Taylor (Joh.). Camb.
Ordo Institutionum Physicarum. T. Rutherford (Joh.).
1744 Cicero De Nat. Deor. var. Ed. 2. Camb.
De aetate Ciceronis De Legibus. J. Chapman (King's and *Oxon.*). Camb.
On the Genuineness of Cicero's Epp. ad Brutum, Ja. Tunstall (Joh.), against Middleton, and On the Numerals of the Legions. J. Chapman (King's and *Oxon.*). Bowyer. Lond. Cf. 1741.
Jurisprudentia Philologica. R. Eden (*Linc., Univ.*). 4to. *Oxon.*
Antiquities near Bishopsgate. J. Woodward, M.D., *Oxon.* (Ed. 1. 1712.)
Marmor Estonianum in agro Northampt. J. Nixon (? King's). Lond.
Plutarch Vitae Parallelae Demosth. Ciceron. gr. lat. P. Barton. (?) *Oxon.*
Plutarch De Iside et Osiride. S. Squire (Joh.). Camb.
Nature and Obligations of Virtue. T. Rutherford (Joh.).
Genuineness of Clarendon's Hist. J. Burton (*Corpus*). Oxon.
Shakespeare. ed. Sir T. Hanmer (*Ch. Ch.*). 6 vols. 4to. *Oxon.*
Harmonics. R. Smith (Trin.). Camb.
Astronomic Doubts. P. Parsons (Sid.). Camb.
1745 Cicero De Officiis. Z. Pearce (Trin.).
—— De Legibus, var. J. Davies (Qu.). Ed. 2.
—— De Oratore, var. Lond.

Remarks on the Epistles of Cicero and Brutus, and four Orations. Jer.
    Markland (Pet.). Bowyer. Lond.
Dissertations of Bentley exam^d. C. Boyle (*Ch. Ch.*).
Ethices Compendium. 12mo. *Oxon.*
Langbaenii Ethices Compendium et Methodus Arg. Aristot. J. Hudson
    (*Qu., Univ., S. Mary H.*). 24mo. *Oxon.*
Xenophon's Anab. T. Hutchinson (? *Linc.*). Ed. 2. *Oxon.*
Miscellanea Critica. R. Dawes (Emm.). Camb.
Moral Philosophy. E. Bentham (*Ch. Ch., Corpus, Oriel*). *Oxon.*
Platonis Dialogi v. var. Nat. Forster (*Corpus*). *Oxon.*
Mithridatium et Theriaca. W. Heberden (Joh.). 2 vols. Lond.
Enquiry into Anglo-Saxon Government. S. Squire (Joh.).
1746 Specimen of an Ed. of Aeschylus. Ant. Askew (Emm.). Lug. Bat.
Ciceronis Quaestt. Acad. var. Camb.
De Priscis Rom. litteris. J. Swinton (*Ch. Ch.*). *Oxon.*
Sophocles Tragg. VII. T. Johnson. Bowyer. Lond.
Thucydidis, Platonis Lysiae, Orationes Funebres. *Oxon.*
————, Engl. Notes. E. Bentham (*Ch. Ch., Corpus, Oriel*). *Oxon.*
Virgil's Georgicks. J. Martyn (Emm.). Lond.
Pope's Ode on S. Caecilia's Day, lat. Chr. Smart (Pemb.). 4to. Camb.
Two Letters to M. Folkes. G. Costard (*Wadh.*).
Appendix Liviana. N. Forster (*Corpus*). *Oxon.*
1747 Calasio's Hebrew Concordance. W. Romaine (*Hert.* and *Ch. Ch.*) and
    E. R. Mores (*Qu.*). 4 vols. 4to. Lond.
Demosthenis Selectae Orationes. Ri. Mounteney (King's). Bowyer. Lond.
Demosth. Aesch. Deinarch, &c. J. Taylor (Joh.). 3 vols. Camb.
Polymetis. Jos. Spence (*New Coll.*). Fol.
Travels in Turkey and back. E. Chishull (*Corpus*). Ed. Ri. Mead, M.D.
Xenophon Cyropaedia. T. Hutchinson (? *Linc.*). Ed. 4. Lond.
Euclid. J. Keill (*Ball.*). Ed. 4. *Oxon.*
Historia Astronomiae. Ra. Heathcote (Jes.). Camb.
Observations on Job. G. Costard (*Wadh.*). *Oxon.*
On S. John ch. VI. R. Hutchins (*All S., Linc.*). *Oxon.*
Euclides. *Oxon.*
Rules and Statutes for Hertford College. Ri. Newton (*Ch. Ch., Hert.*).
    Oxon.
Isis. W. Mason (Joh., Pemb.).
Triumph of Isis. T. Warton (*Trin.*).
1748 Aristarchus. T. Bowles (*Oxon.*).
Bion and Moschus, var. J. Heskin (*Ch. Ch.*). *Oxon.*
Carmina Quadragesimalia, vol. II. A. Parsons (*Ch. Ch.*).
Demosthenes and Aeschines. J. Taylor (Joh.) (no vol. I.) (*Ch. Ch.*) *Oxon.*
System of Natural Philos. T. Rutherforth (Joh.). Camb.
Harmonia Trigonometrica. H. Owen (Jes.).
De Patrum Auctoritate. J. Bear (? *Exon.*). *Oxon.*
De Doctorum Auctoritate. C. Whiting (*Trin., Oriel*). *Oxon.*
De Usu Dialectt. Orientalium. T. Hunt (*Hart H., Ch. Ch.*). 4to. *Oxon.*
Astronomy among the Antients. G. Costard (*Wadh.*). *Oxon.*
Letter to a Young Gentleman. E. Bentham (*Corpus, Oriel*). *Oxon.* (and
    1749.)
Epistolae II. E. Bentham (*Corpus, Oriel*). *Oxon.*
Nomina Nobilium, sub Edv. III°. G. R. Mores (*Qu.*). 4to. (and 1749.)
1749 Cicero Ad Familiares. J. Ross (Joh.). Camb.
Isocrates. W. Battie (King's). Vol. 2. See 1729. Bowyer. Lond.
Pindar, &c., engl. verse. Gil. West (*Ch. Ch.*). Lond.
Virgil's Bucolicks, engl. J. Martyn (Emm.). 4to. Lond.
Xenophon Memorabilia, var. Bolton Simpson (*Qu.*). Ed. 2. *Oxon.*
Harmonics. Ro. Smith (Trin.). Camb.
Tabulae Astronomicae. Edm. Halley (*Qu.*). 4to. Lond.
Observations on Man. D. Hartley (Jes.). 2 vols.
Josephus' Account of Christ. N. Forster (*Corpus*). *Oxon.*

Journey from Aleppo to Jerusalem, Easter, 1697. H. Maundrell (*Exon.*).
 ed. 7. *Oxon.*
Poetae Eleg. and Lyr. Minores.
Xenophon's Memorabilia, var. Bolton Simpson (*Qu.*). *Oxon.*
1750 Biblia Hebraica sine punctis. N. Foster (*Corpus*). 2 vols. 4to. *Oxon.*
Evangeliorum V. Gothica. E. Lye (*Hart H.*) *Oxon.*
New Testament. 12mo. T. Baskett (also 1763). *Oxon.*
Catalogue of the Bodleian Coins. F. Wise (*Trin.*). *Oxon.*
Homer Odyssea. *Oxon.*
Metilia...e numis vet. et Inscriptiones Citieae accedit De Numis Samarit.
 et Phoeniciis. J. Swinton (*Ch. Ch.*). *Oxon.*
On the Roman Senate. T. Chapman (Magd.). Camb.
Virgil. G. Sandby (*Mert.*).
Xenophon Oeconomicus, gr. lat. *Oxon.*
Elogium Jacci Etonensis. E. Bentham (*Ch. Ch., Corpus, Oriel*). *Oxon.*
Notae in Terentium. J. Graevius (Devent., Utr.). *Oxon.*
Persian-Arab.-Engl. Dictionary. J. Richardson. *Oxon.*
Delineation of Universal Law. Fettip. Bellers. *Oxon.*
Turnus and Drances. W. Beare (*Corpus*). *Oxon.*
Artis Logicae Compendium. H. Aldrich (*Ch. Ch.*). *Oxon.*
Οἶνος κρίθινος. S. Rolleston (*Or., Mert.*). 4to. *Oxon.*
De Tabe Glandulari et Aqua Marina. Ri. Russell (M.D. Camb.). *Oxon.*
 also 1753.
Essay on Collateral Consanguinity. W. Blackstone (*Pemb., All S., Qu.,*
 New C.). *Oxon.*
Several Cambridge Pamphlets, 1750—52, are noted in Wordsworth's Univ.
 Life, pp. 613—632.
The Student or Oxford (and Cambridge) Monthly Miscellany. Ri. Raw-
 linson (*Joh.*), T. Warton (*Trin.*), S. Johnson (*Pemb.*), B. Thornton
 and G. Colman (*Ch. Ch.*), and Chr. Smart (Pemb. Hall). 2 vols.
 1750—51.
1751 Elihu, Inquiry on Job. W. Hodges (*Oriel*).
Some Conjectures on a Coin found at Eltham in Kent. C. Clarke (*Ball.*).
Horace ad Augustum et ad Pisones. Ri. Hurd (Emm.). Bowyer. Lond.
Dissertatio de Oriuna Carausi Uxore. C. Clarke (*Ball.*). Lond.
In Pindari Pyth. I. ? W. Barford (Qu.). Camb.
Terence. G. Sandby (*Mert.*).
The Theology and Philos. in Cic. Somn. Scip. explained (anti-newtonian).
 G. Horne (*Magd.*). Lond.
Grammatica Hebraea sine punctis. G. Wilmot (? *Worc.*). *Oxon.*
Originals Phys. and Theol. B. Holloway (*Linc.*). 2 vols. *Oxon.*
Pindar's Isthmian Odes in engl. v. 4to. *Oxon.*
Modius Salium. Ant. Wood (*Mert.*). *Oxon.*
Dryden's Alexander's Feast. lat. J. Hughes (*?*). 4to. *Oxon.*
Argument from Prophecy. J. Rotheram (*Qu.*). *Oxon.* also 1754.
Interpretation of 'Elohim.' W. Hodges (? *Oriel*). 4to. *Oxon.*
1752 M. Antoninus. T. Gataker (Joh., Sid.). Camb.
Inscriptt. Gr. Lat. Numism. Ptolemaeorum. Ri. Pococke (*Corpus*). Fol.
Hist. gr. et lat. Litt. et Vita Homeri. J. Reynolds (King's, *Oxon*). Eton.
Elfrida. W. Mason (Joh. and Pemb.).
Translations in Verse. T. Tyrwhitt (*Qu., Mert.*). Lond.
Astronomical Tables. Edm. Halley (*Qu.*). 4to. Lond.
Aristotle's De Virt. et Vitiis. S. Fawconer (*Mert.*). *Oxon.*
Plato's Dialogues. N. Forster (*Corpus*). *Oxon.*
Memoirs of Learned Ladies. G. Ballard. 4to. *Oxon.*
1753 State of the Hebrew Text. B. Kennicott (*Wadh., Ex.* and *Ch. Ch.*). *Oxon.*
De S. Poesi Hebraeorum. Ro. Lowth (*New C.*). *Oxon.*
Enquiry into Anglo-Saxon Government. S. Squire (Joh.).
Horace. Ri. Hurd (Emm.). Ed. 2. (See 1751.)
Ruins of Palmyra or Tadmor. Ro. Wood. Lond.
Progymnastica Hellenica. R. Hingeston (Pemb.). Camb.

Virgil. Jos. Warton (*Oriel*) and Chr. Pitt (*New C.*).
'Fair...State of Case betw. Newton and Hutchinson.' G. Horne (*Magd.*).
III. Quaestiones [de baptism.] in Vesp. Comit. H. Savage (*Bras.*). 4to. *Oxon.*
Letter and Spirit. B. Holloway (*Linc.*). *Oxon.*
Theological works of J. Potter (*Univ., Linc.*). 3 vols. *Oxon.*
Λόγοι ἐπιτάφιοι (see 1746, 1768), gr. lat., notis angll. E. Bentham (*Corpus, Oriel*). *Oxon.*
Virgidemiarum Satires. Jos. Hall (Emm.). ed. *Oxon.*
1754 Homer. S. Clarke (Caius). Ed. 2. 4 vols. Lond.
Institutes of Natural Law. T. Rutherford (Joh.).
Theophrastus, Gr. Lat., engl. notes. Ri. Newton (*Hart H.*). *Oxon.*
Dissertation on Greek Accents. H. Gally (Benet.). Lond.
The Sacred Hebrew (against Hunt). B. Holloway (*Linc.*). *Oxon.*
De Ling. Graecae Institutionibus (from Iter Surriense, Lond. 1752). J. Burton (*Ch. Ch.*, M.D. Rheims). *Oxon.*
Xenophon's Opuscula. Bolton Simpson (*Qu.*). *Oxon.*
Antiquities of Cornwall. W. Borlase (*Exon.*). *Oxon.*
Several Pamphlets relating to *Exeter* College. 1754—5.
1755 Aeschines and Demosthenes De Corona, engl. Portal.
Greek Accents. H. Gally (Benet.). Ed. 2. Lond.
———————— Roger Long (Pemb.). *Oxon.*
Phaedrus Fables, Lat. Eng. Camb.
English Dictionary. S. Johnson (*Pemb.*).
W. King and the 'Society of Informers.'
Justin Martyr c. Tryphon. trs. H. Brown (*Linc.*). 2 vols. *Oxon.*
Advice to a Young Student. D. Waterland (Magd. Camb.). 2nd ed. *Oxon.*
Sale Catalogue of Library of Roger Bouchier (*Glo. H.*). *Oxon.*
On Logick. E. Bentham (*Corpus, Oriel*). *Oxon.* also 1740.
De Aqua Marina. J. Speed (*Joh.*). *Oxon.*
Μελετήματα. J. Burton (*Ch. Ch.*, M.D. Rheims). *Oxon.*
1756 Euripides Hippolytus. S. Musgrave (*Corpus, Univ.*). *Oxon.*
Justinian, engl. G. Harris (*Oriel*). 4to. Lond.
Institutes of Natural Law. T. Rutherford (Joh.).
Ordo Instit. Physicarum in privatis Lectionibus. T. Rutherford. Ed. 2. 4to. Camb.
Compendium Anatomico-Medicum. C. Collignon (Trin.).
Apology for the Hutchinsonians. G. Hodges (*Ch. Ch.*). *Oxon.*
Reply to Huddesford on Delegates of the Press. Ben. Buckler (*Or., All S.*). 4to. *Oxon.*
Ben Jonson's Works. 7 vols. *Oxon.*
Letter to Univ. of Camb. on a late Resignation (D. of Newcastle's). *Oxon.* and Lond.
Observations on the Island of Scilly. W. Borlase (*Exon.*). 4to. *Oxon.*
1757 Demosthenes and Aeschines. Vol. 3. J. Taylor (Joh.). Camb.
Horace, with notes, 2 vols. Ri. Hurd (Emm.). Camb.
Travels in Barbary and the Levant. T. Shaw (*prof. Gr. Qu.* and *Edm. H.*). Ed. 2. Bowyer. Lond.
On a Parthian Coin. J. Swinton (*Ch. Ch.*). Lond.
The Scholar's Instructor, Hebrew Grammar. Isr. Lyons. Ed. 3. Camb.
Poems. W. Thompson. *Oxon.*
Sacerdos Paroecialis. J. Burton (*Corpus*). *Oxon.*
Works of bp. G. Hooper (*Ch. Ch.*). fol. *Oxon.*
Comment. in Plutarchi Demosth. and Cic. P. Barton (? *New C.*). *Oxon.*
1758 Dio. Halicarn. (preface and Gk. Accents). E. Spelman.
Imitations of Horace. T. Nevile (Emm., Jes.). Bowyer. Lond.
De Literarum Graec. Institutione. J. Burton (*Corpus*). *Oxon.*
Pentalogia (Greek Plays). J. Burton (*Corpus*). *Oxon.*
Discourse on the Study of Law. W. Blackstone (*Pemb., All S.*, Qu. and *New Inn*). 4to. *Oxon.*
Menelai Sphaerica. E. Halley (*Qu.*), G. Costard (*Wadh.*). *Oxon.*

Origin of Evil. W. King (T. C. D.) eng. Edm. Law (Joh., Chr., Pet.).
    Camb.
Plan of Chemistry Lectures. J. Hadley (Qu.). Camb.
The Negative Sign in Algebra. F. Maseres (Clare).
Tracts by W. Hawkins (*Pemb.*). 3 vols. *Oxon.*
Praelectiones Poeticae. W. Hawkins (*Pemb.*). *Oxon.*
Poems by W. Hawkins (*Pemb.*). *Oxon.*
Poems by W. Thompson (*Qu.*) *Oxon.*
Homer's Iliad. *Oxon.*
Nat. Hist. of Cornwall. W. Borlase (*Exon.*). fol. *Oxon.*
Analysis of Laws. W. Blackstone (*Pemb., All S., Qu., New C.*). ed. 3.
    Oxon.
First Inhabitants and Language of Europe. F. Wise (*Trin.*). *Oxon.*
1759 State of the Hebrew Text of O. T. B. Kennicott (*Wadh., Ex.* and *Ch. Ch.*).
    2 ed. *Oxon.*
Aristotle Rhetorica (from the Camb. ed. of 1728). *Oxon.*
Xenophon Memorabilia. Bolton Simpson (*Qu.*). Ed. 3. *Oxon.*
Clarendon's History. 7 vols. *Oxon.*
Elegiaca Graeca. *Oxon.*
General State of Education, to Dr Hales. Ri. Davies, M.D. (Qu.)
Treatise on Fluxions. Isr. Lyons, junior (Camb.). Bowyer. Lond.
Harmonicks. R. Smith (Trin.). Ed. 2. Camb.
Tablet of Cebes. T. Powys (*Joh.*). *Oxon.*
Poetae Elegiaci et Lyrici. Ri. Chandler (*Magd.*). *Oxon.*
Cicero De Amicit. &c. T. Tooly (*Joh.*).
Xenophon's Memorabilia. *Oxon.*
Law of Descent in Fee Simple, 8vo ; Charters (the Great and Forest). 4to.
Analysis of Laws of England. W. Blackstone (*Pemb., All S., Qu., New I.*).
    Oxon.
Autobiography of E. Hyde Earl of Clarendon (*Magd. H.*). Fol. and 3
    vols. 8vo. *Oxon.*
1760 Aristotle Poetica. ? Ri. Chandler (? *Magd.*). *Oxon.*
Cicero Orationes. Delphin. Camb.
Life of Erasmus. J. Jortin (Jes.). Lond.
Lithophylacii Brit. Iconographia. E. Lhuyd (*Jes.*). *Oxon.*
Lucan, typis Hor. Walpole (King's). Strawberry Hill.
Emendationes in Suidam. Jonath. Toup (*Exon.* and Pemb., Camb.).
    Bowyer. Lond.
Theocritus Bion and Moschus. T. Martin (*Ball.*). Lond.
Harmonicks. Ro. Smith (Trin.).
Observations on Waring's 'Misc. Analyt.'. W. S. Powell (Joh.). Bowyer.
    Lond.
G. Horne v. Kennicott on the Hebrew Text. *Oxon.*
Hist. Relig. Persarum. T. Hyde (*King's, Qu.*). ed. 2. G. Costard. 4to.
    Oxon.
Advice to a Young Man of Quality. Camb.
1761 Account of Collation of Hebrew MSS. i. B. Kennicott (*Wadh., Ex.* and
    Ch. Ch.).
Life of Clarendon. *Oxon.*
Catalogue of Oxford Graduates. *Oxon.*
Codex Juris Eccles. Anglicani. E. Gibson (Qu.). Ed. 2. 2 vols. Fol.
    Oxon.
Justinian, engl. G. Harris (*Oriel*). Ed. 2. 4to. Lond.
Calendar of Flora. B. Stillingfleet (Trin.).
Harmonics. R. Smith (Trin.). Ed. 3.
Pomponius Mela. J. Reynolds (King's). 4to. Ed. 4. Eton.
Ornaments of Parish Churches (St Margaret, Westmr.). T. Wilson (*Ch.
    Ch.*). *Oxon.*
Catalogue of Ant. Wood's MSS. W. Huddesford (*Trin.*). *Oxon.*
1762 Acc[t] of Collat[n] of Hebrew MSS. ii. B. Kennicott (*Wadh., Ex.* and *Ch. Ch.*).
Essay on Natural Philosophy. W. Jones. *Oxon.*

Thesaurus Graecae Poeseos. T. Morell (King's). 4to. Eton.
Prologomena in Libr. V. T. Poeticos. T. Edwards (Clare). Camb.
Notae et Lectiones ad Aeschylum, Sophoclem, et Euripidem. Ben. Heath.
    (*Oxon.*). *Oxon.*
Exercitationes in Euripidem. S. Musgrave (*Corpus, Univ.*). Lug. Bat.
On the Different Nature of Accent and Quantity. J. Foster (King's).
Medit. Algebr. ed. 1. Misc. Analyt. de Aequationibus &c. E. Waring
    (Magd.). Camb.
Henochismus. Jos. Hall (Emm.). 12mo. *Oxon.*
Pliny's Panegyr. Lipsius (Traj. ad Rhen.). 12mo. *Oxon.*
Proposals for Theophrastus for the benefit of Hertf. Coll. Ri. Newton
    (*Ch. Ch., Hert.*).
A Companion to the Guide or a Guide to the Companion. T. Warton
    (*Trin.*). *Oxon.*
1763 Account of Collation of Hebr. MSS. iii. B. Kennicott. (*Wadh., Ex.* and
    Ch. Ch.).
Greek Testament. Baskerville. 4to. and 8vo. *Oxon.*
Accent and Quantity, Dissertation ii. H. Gally (Benet.). Lond.
————————— Ed. 2. J. Foster (King's). Eton.
Apologia pro Medicina Empirica. S. Musgrave. 4to. Lug. Bat.
Euripides Supplices. Jer. Markland (Pet.). Bowyer. Lond.
Horace (an edition of Bentley's). 2 vols. Lips.
Juvenal and Persius. G. Sandby (*Mert.*). *Oxon.*
Marmora Oxoniensia. R. Chandler (*Magd.*). Fol. *Oxon.*
Plantae et Herbationes Cantabr. T. Martyn (Emm. and Sid.)
Fasciculus Plantarum c. Cantabr. Isr. Lyons. Bowyer. Lond.
Harmonics. R. Smith (Trin.). Ed. 4.
Poems on Sacred Subjects. Ja. Merrick (*Trin.*). *Oxon.*
Jacob and·Moses to the xii. D. Durell (*Pemb., Hert.*). 4to. *Oxon.*
In R. Lowth. Praelectt. D. Michaelis (Gott.). 2 vols. *Oxon.*
Chronol. Annals of the War, 1755—62. W. Dobson (? *New C.*). *Oxon.*
1764 An enquiry into structure of Human Body. C. Collignon (Trin.). Camb.
De Studiis Theol. Praelect. E. Bentham (*Ch. Ch., Corpus, Oriel*).
    Oxon.
De Rebus Gestis Ricardi Regis in Palaestina, Abulpharagii. P. Ja. Bruns
    (*Oxon.* and *Helmstadt*) *Oxon.* See 1780.
Accentus Redivivi. W. Primatt (Sid.). Camb.
The Human Rational Soul. Z. Langton (*Magd. H.*). *Oxon.*
Hist. and Chronol. of Bacchus, Heracles, &c. F. Wise (*Trin.*). 4to. *Oxon.*
Life of Card. Pole. T. Phillips (S. J.). 4to. *Oxon.*
State of the R. Thames. J. Burton (*Corpus*). *Oxon.*
Astronomy. S. Bamfield (of Honiton). *Oxon.*
The Oxford Sausage. Edited by T. Warton (*Trin.*). 12mo. *Oxon.*
1765 Platonis Dialogi v., Gr. Lat. N. Forster (*Corpus*). *Oxon.*
Excerpta quaedam e Newton. Princip., G. Wollaston (Sid.). J. Jebb,
    Ro. Thorp (Pet.). 4to. Camb.
Stemmata Chiceleana. B. Buckler. 4to. *Oxon.* (Suppl. 1775.)
Ro. Lowth v. Warburton.
1766 Directions to Young Students in Divinity. H. Owen (*Jes.*).
Cephalae Anthol. Gr. J. J. Reiske (Leips.) *Oxon.*
On Phillips' Hist. of Reg. Pole. Tim. Neve (*Corpus*). *Oxon.*
Observations and Conj. on Shakespeare. T. Tyrwhitt (*Qu., Mert.*). *Oxon.*
Proceedings and Debates, 1620—21, fr. *Queen's* Coll. MS. T. Tyrwhitt
    (*Qu., Mert.*). 2 vols. *Oxon.*
On Jurisprudence (introd. to Lectures). T. Bever (*Or., All S.*). *Oxon.*
1767 Critica Hebraea (Dict. Hebr.-Engl.). Julius Bate (Joh.). Bowyer. Lond.
Account of Collation of Hebrew MSS. vii. B. Kennicott (*Wadh.,* &c.).
Six Assemblies...of Learned Arabians. Leo. Chappelow (Joh.). Camb.
Syntagma Dissertationum. T. Hyde (King's, and *Qu. Oxon.*). ed. Greg.
    Sharpe (Aberd.). 2 vols. 4to. *Oxon.*
Clarendon State Papers. *Oxon.*

Epistola Critica ad Episc. Glocestr.   Jonathan Toup   (*Exon.*, Pemb. Camb.).   Bowyer.   Lond.
Statius Thebaid, Engl.   W. L. Lewis (*Pemb.*).   2 vols.   *Oxon.*
Virgil Georgics, Engl.   T. Nevile (Emm. and Jes.).   Camb.
History of Astronomy.   G. Costard (*Wadh.*).
Improvement of Roads.   H. Homer (*Magd.*).   *Oxon.*
1768 Account of Hebrew MSS. VIII.   B. Kennicott (*Wadh., Ex., Ch. Ch.*).
Justin Martyr Dialog.   C. Ashton (Qu. and Jes.).   ed. F. Keller (Jes.). Camb.
Aristophanes Plutus.   Eton.   *Oxon.* and Camb.
Ciceronis Opuscula.
Euripides Iphigeniae.   Jer. Markland (Pet.).   Bowyer.   Lond.
Elementa Rhetorica [Cicero and Quintilian].
Orationes Funebres, c. notis angl.   [E. Bentham, *Ch. Ch., Corpus, Oriel*]   *Oxon.*   (See 1746, 1753, 1776, 1780.   Cf. 1775.)
On Virgil.   E. Holdsworth (*Magd.*).   Bowyer.   Lond.
The Commentaries.   W. Blackstone (*Pemb., All S., Qu.* and *New Inn*).   4 vols.   *Oxon.*
Institutiones Metallurgicae.   Ri. Watson (Trin.).
Bp. Hall's Enoch. trs.   H. Brown (*Linc.*)   *Oxon.*
Leland's Itiner.   9 vols. ed. 3.   *Oxon.*
Plutarchi Apophthegmata.   Steph. Pemberton (*Worc., Or.*).   *Oxon.*
Corpus Statut. Acad. Oxon.   4to.   *Oxon.*
Whole Doctrine of Parallaxes (transit of Venus and Mercury).   *Oxon.*
1769 Holy Bible.   Refs. revised by B. Blayney (*Worc.* and *Hertf.*).   *Oxon.*
An Enquiry into the Septuagint.   H. Owen (*Jes.*)
Demosthenes De Cor. and Fals. Leg. Gr. Lat. var.   J. Taylor (Joh.).   2 vols.   Camb.
Ionian Antiquities.   Ri. Chandler (*Magd.*).   Lond.
Cambridge Astronomical Observations.   W. Ludlam (Joh.).   Lond.
Imitations of Juvenal and Persius.   T. Nevile (Jes.).   Bowyer.   Lond.
Medical and Moral Tracts.   C. Collignon (Trin.).
John the Baptist.   G. Horne (*Univ., Magd.*).   *Oxon.*   Also 1777.
Des. Jacotius. De Philos. Doctr. ex Cicerone.   Ed. 2.   *Oxon.*
Euripidis Hippolytus.   F. H. Egerton (*Ch. Ch., All S.*).   4to.   *Oxon.*
1770 Collected Accounts of Collation of Hebrew MSS.   B. Kennicott (*Wadh., Ex.* and *Ch. Ch.*).
Litania et Ordo Caenae Domin.   *Oxon.*   Common Prayer.   Fol.
Historiae sive Synopsis Conchyliorum, auct.   Martin Lister (Joh., Camb. and *Oxon.*), 'ed. altera' [? tertia].   W. Huddesford (*Trin.*).   Fol.   *Oxon.*
Elementa Logicae.   J. Napleton.   *Oxon.*
Extracts from Hippocrates.   T. Okes.   Camb.
Registrum Privil. Univ. Oxon.   4to.   *Oxon.*
Theocritus.   T. Warton (*Trin.*) [Jonathan Toup. (*Exon.* and Pemb. H.), and Ja. Saintamand (*Linc.*)].   2 Vols.   4to.   *Oxon.*
Meditationes Algebraicae.   E. Waring (Magd.).   ed. 2.   4to.   Camb.
De Relig. Sonnitic. arab.   J. Ury.   4to.   *Oxon.*
Apollarius Pergaeus.   S. Horsley (Trin. H., *Ch. Ch.*).   2 vols.   4to.   *Oxon.*
Homer.   5 vols.   *Oxon.*
Leland's Itinerary.   9 vols. in 5. ed. 3.   *Oxon.*
Commentaries.   W. Blackstone (*Pemb., All S., Qu., New I.*).   4 vols.   *Oxon.*
Oratio Harveiana.   Swithin Adee (*Corpus*).   *Oxon.*
Warm Bathing in Palsies.   Rice Charleton (*Qu.*).   *Oxon.*
De Descensu Gravium.   Roger Cotes (Trin.).   4to.   Camb.
The Mechanic Powers.   C. Morgan (Clare).   Camb.
1771 Catalogus Librorum in Biblioth. Aul. D. Cath. Cant.   C. Prescot(Cath.).   4to.
Study of Divinity, with Heads.   E. Bentham (*Ch. Ch., Corpus, Oriel*).   *Oxon.*
Demosthenis Orationes Selectae.   R. Mounteney (Qu.).   Ed. 5.

Euripides Iphigeniae. Jer. Markland (Pet.). Bowyer. **Lond.**
Clavis Homerica. S. Patrick (?). Bowyer. **Lond.**
Plato Dialogi III. W. Etwall (*Magd.*). *Oxon.*
An Enquiry into the Structure of the Body. C. Collignon (Trin.) Ed. 2.
  Camb.
Artis Logicae Compendium. *Oxon.*
Catalogus Horti Botanici Cantabr. T. Martyn (Emm. and Sid.). Camb.
Hadley's Quadrant, with Supplement. W. Ludlam (Joh.). Lond.
? Plut..? Opusc. Misc. J. Burton (*Corpus*). *Oxon.*
Epist. Turc. ; Narr. Persicae. J. Uri. *Oxon.*
Tracts by Sir W. Blackstone (*Pemb. All S., Qu., New I.*) Ed. 3. 4to.
  Oxon.
Shakespeare's Works. 6 vols. Sir T. Hanmer (*Ch. Ch.*). *Oxon.*
Specimen of the Lusiad trs. W. J. Mickle (Edinb.). *Oxon.*
Pamphlets on Subscription. By J. Jebb (Pet.), &c. Camb.
——— on Annual Examination. By J. Jebb, Powell, &c. Camb.
1772 Hist. Univ., Oxon. Sir J. Peshall. *Oxon.*
Asseri Alfred. Fr. Wise (*Trin.*).
Indices in Longinum, Eunapium et Hieroclem, cura R. Robinson.
  Oxon.
Anglo-Saxon and Gothic Dictionary. E. Lye (*Hert.*), O. Manning (Qu.).
Leges Saxonicae. O. Manning (Qu.).
Longinus, Gr. Lat. R. Robinson. *Oxon.*
Xenophon Memorabilia, var. Bolton Simpson (*Qu.*). Ed. 4. *Oxon.*
Institute of the Laws of England. T. Wood (*New Coll.*). Ed. 10.
Poems. Sir W. Jones (*Univ.*). *Oxon.*
Catalogus Horti Botan. Cant. T. Martyn (Emm. and Sid.). Ed. 2. Camb.
Catalogue of Oxford Graduates. J. Chalmers (*Joh.*)
Proprietates Algebr. Curvarum. E. Waring (Magd.). 4to. Camb.
On the Power of the Wedge. W. Ludlam (Joh.). Lond.
Hagiographa. D. Durell (*Pemb., Hert.*). 4to. *Oxon.*
Animadversions on Baker's Chronicle. T. Blount. *Oxon.*
Lives of Leland, Hearne and Wood. 2 vols. *Oxon.*
The Oxford Sausage. Ed. 2 [T. Warton, &c.]. 12mo. *Oxon.*
Notae in Tragg. Graec. B. Heath (*Univ.*). 4to. *Oxon.*
Platonis v. Dial. N. Forster (*Corpus*). Ed. 3. *Oxon.*
Xenophon Cyrop. T. Hutchinson (? *Linc.*). ed. *Oxon.*
——— Expeditio Cyri. *Oxon.*
1773 Antiquities of Herculaneum. Vol. I., Engl. T. Martyn and J. Lettice
  (Sid.). Bowyer. Lond.
Letters concerning Homer the Sleeper in Horace, &c. Kenrick Prescot
  (Cath.). 4to. Camb.
Introd. to Logic. E. Bentham (*Ch. Ch.*, &c.).
Fragmenta II. Plutarchi. T. Tyrwhitt (*Qu., Mert.*). Lond.
Xenophon, the Socratic System. E. Edwards (? *Jes.*). *Oxon.*
Considerations on the Exercises for Degrees. *Oxon.*
1774 Critica Sacra, Hebr. H. Owen (*Jes.*).
A New System or Analysis of Anc. Mythology. Vols. I. II. Jacob Bryant
  (King's).
Demosthenes and Aeschines. J. Taylor (Joh.). 4to. Camb.
History of English Poetry, Vol. I. T. Warton (*Trin.*). *Oxon.*
Inscriptiones Antiquae in Asia M. &c. Ri. Chandler (*Magd.*). Fol. *Oxon.*
Selecta Poemata Anglorum. E. Popham (*Oriel*). Bath.
Analysis of Roman Civil Law. S. Hallifax (Jes. and Trin. H.).
Reflexions and Heads of Divinity. E. Bentham (*Corpus, Or.*). *Oxon.*
Vindication of the Liturgy. G. Bingham (*Ch. Ch., All S.*). *Oxon.*
Leland's Collectanea. T. Hearne (*Edm. H.*). 6 vols. *Oxon.*
Considerations on Residence required. *Oxon.*
Faringdon Hill. H. J. Pye (*Magd.*). 2 vols. *Oxon.* (Also 1778.)
1775 On the Gospels. Jos. Trapp (*Wadh.*). *Oxon.*
De Utilitate Lingu. Arab. Jos. White (*Wadh.*). *Oxon.*

Travels in Asia Minor. Ri. Chandler (*Magd.*). Lond. 2 vols. 4to. *Oxon.*
Lexicon Aegypt, Lat. Lacroze, Scholtz and Woide. *Oxon.*
E. Spelman on Greek Accents. G. W. Lemon (Norwich). Ed. Jacob
    Bryant (King's). 4to. Lond.
On the Genius of Homer. Ed. 2. Ro. Wood.
A New System of Mythology. Vol. I. Ed. 2. Jacob Bryant (King's).
ποικίλη ἱστορία ex Aeliano, Polyaeno, Aristot., Max. Tyrio &c., and Orationes
    Funebres. Ja. Upton (King's). Eton.
Pomponius Mela. J. Reynolds (King's). 4to. Ed. 5. Eton.
Electa ex Ovidio et Tibullo. Eton.
———— Ovidii Metamorph. Eton.
Elements of Nat. Hist. [Mammalia]. T. Martyn (Emm. and Sid.).
    Camb.
Book of Proverbs. T. Hunt (*Ch. Ch., Hertf.*). *Oxon.*
Beauties of Homer. W. Holwell (*Ch. Ch.*). *Oxon.*
Elegia (Gray's) lat. verse. Gil. Wakefield [Jes.]. Camb.
Praelectiones Poeticae. Ro. Lowth (*New C.*). *Oxon.*
De Rhythmis Graecorum. W. Cleaver (*Magd., Bras.*). 12mo. *Oxon.*
The Lusiad trs. W. J. Mickle (Edinb.). *Oxon.*
Commentaries. Sir W. Blackstone (*Pemb., All S., Qu., New I.*). 4 vols.
    Oxon.
1776 Vetus Testamentum Hebraicum. B. Kennicott (*Wadh., Exon.* and *Ch.*
    Ch.). Vol. I.
Commentary on the Psalms. G. Horne (*Univ.* and *Magd.*). 2 vols. 4to.
    Fol. *Oxon.*
De Babrio. T. Tyrwhitt (*Qu.* and *Mert.*). Bowyer. Lond.
Cicero De Officiis, Engl. T. Cockman (*Univ.*). 12mo. ed. 9. Camb.
Poemata et in Horatium Observationes. G. Wakefield [Jes.]. Camb.
Travels in Greece. Ri. Chandler (*Magd.*). Lond.
Vindiciae Flavianae. Jacob Bryant (King's). 2 vols.
Xenophon Anabasis, Engl. E. Spelman. Camb.
Meditationes Analyticae. E. Waring (*Magd.*). 4to. (1773—5). Camb.
De Util. Ling. Arabicae. J. White (*Wadh.*). *Oxon.*
Luciani Quomodo Hist. Conscr. F. W. Rioally (T. C. D., *Hertf.*). *Oxon.*
Sophoclis Oed. Tyr., eng. T. Francklin (Trin.). Camb.
Funebres Orationes. lat. E. Bentham (*Ch. Ch., Corpus, Oriel*). Camb.
Elementa Logices. J. Napleton (*Bras.*). *Oxon.*
Netherby, a Poem. T. Maurice. *Oxon.*
1777 Commentary on the Gospels and Acts, with new transl. 1 Cor. Z. Pearce
    (Trin.). J. Derby. Lond.
Apollonius Rhodius. J. Shaw. Ja. Saintamand. (*Linc.*). 2 vols. 4to.
    Oxon.
Phalaris with a Latin version of Bentley's Dissertation and Boyle's notes.
    J. D. a'Lennep and Valckenaer. Groningae.
————Dissertation. R. Bentley (Joh. and Trin.). Lond.
Cicero De Officiis. Z. Pearce (Trin.). Ed. 3.
Decretum Lacedaemoniorum. W. Cleaver (*Magd., Bras.*). *Oxon.*
Epistola ad J. D. Michaelis. B. Kennicott (*Wadh., Ex.* and *Ch. Ch.*). *Oxon.*
Xenophon Anabasis. T. Hutchinson (? *Linc.*). Ed. 3. 1st Camb. ed.
Nov. Test. Vers. Syriaca Philoxen. J. White (*Wadh.*). 4to. *Oxon.*
Grammat. Aegypt., Scholtz et Woide. *Oxon.*
John the Baptist. G. Horne (*Univ., Magd. Coll.*). *Oxon.*
Persian-Arab.-Engl. Dictionary. J. Richardson. *Oxon.*
Collectio Sententiarum in usum Juvent. J. Bennet. Camb.
Juvenal trs. Camb.
Persius trs. T. Sheridan (D.D., T. C. D.). ed. 3. Camb.
Xenophon's Anabasis engl. E. Spelman. Ed. 3. 2 vols. Camb.
Letter to Adam Smith on Hume. G. Horne (*Univ., Magd.*). *Oxon.*
William of Wykeham. R. Lowth (*New C.*). Ed. 3. *Oxon.*
Locke's Common Place Book improved by a Gentleman of Camb. Univ.
    Fol. and 4to. Camb.

1778 Euripides. S. Musgrave (*Corpus, Univ.*). 4 vols. 4to. *Oxon.*
Longinus. Jonathan Toup (*Exon.* and Pemb. Camb.) and D. Ruhnken. 4to. and 8vo. *Oxon.*
Observationes in Tragoedias Burtoni 'Pentalogia' complexas. T. Burgess (*Corpus*).
Albucasis de Chirurgia, Arab, Lat., J. Channing (*Ch. Ch.*). Oxon.
Elementary part of Smith's Optics (Trin.). T. Kipling (Joh.).
1779 Apollonius Rhodius, J. Shaw (*Magd.*). Ed. 2. 2 vols. 8vo. *Oxon.*
Homeri Ilias, S. Clarke (Caius). Ed. nova. Lond.
Burtoni Pentalogia. Ed. 2. T. Burgess (*Corpus*).
Theocritus, T. Edwards (Clare). Camb.
On Versions of Scripture, &c. Jos. White (*Wadh.*). *Oxon.*
Locke's Essay abridged. 12mo. Camb.
Analysis of Roman Civil Law, S. Hallifax (Jes. and Trin. H.).
IV. Evang. MSS. Ridl. 2 vols. 4to. *Oxon.*
On the Gospels, &c. T. Townson (*Ch. Ch., Magd.*). 4to and 8vo. *Oxon.*
Dissertation on Language, Literature and Manners of Eastern Nations. J. Richardson. *Oxon.*
Alfred and Six Sonnets. R. Holmes (*New C., Ch. Ch.*). 4to. *Oxon.*
Commentaries. W. Blackstone (*Pemb., All S., Qu., New I.*). 4 vols. *Oxon.*
Institutes of National Law, Grotius. T. Rutherford (Joh.). Ed. 2. Camb.
On the last II chapters of Gibbon. Ja. Chelsum (*Ch. Ch.*). *Oxon.*
Fluxions. Isr. Lyons, jun. Camb.
1780 Biblia Hebraica, B. Kennicott (*Wadh. Ex.*). Vol. II., fol. *Oxon.*
Aristotelis Poetica, var. T. Winstanley (*Hert.*) *Oxon.*
———— ——— engl. Theod. Goulston (*Mert.*). *Oxon.*
Aristophanes' Frogs engl. C. Dunster (*Oriel, Trin.*). *Oxon.*
Caesar Oudendorp. *Oxon.*
G. Abulpharagius de R. Gestis Ric. Regis. P. J. Bruns (*Oxon.*). *Oxon.*
Homer. J. A. Ernesti (*Leips.*). *Oxon.*
J. Wall's Medical Tracts. Mart. Wall (*New C.*). *Oxon.*
Locke's Essay, with abstract. Camb.
Index Homericus. W. Seber. *Oxon.*
Institutes of Timour. Jos. White (*Wadh.*) *Oxon.*
Orationes Crewianae. W. Crowe (*New C.*). *Oxon.*
Orationes Funebres, engl. E. Bentham (*Ch. Ch., Corpus, Oriel*). Camb.
Xenophon Memorabilia, var. Bolton Simpson (*Qu.*). Ed. 5. *Oxon.*
On Newton's 2nd Law of Motion. W. Ludlam (Joh.). Lond.
1781 Collectanea Curiosa. J. Gutch (*All S.*). *Oxon.*
Linguae Hebraicae Studium. G. Jubb (*Ch. Ch.*). 4to. *Oxon.*
Enchiridion. T. Walgrave (? *Linc., Magd.*). *Oxon.*
Dio. Halicarn. E. R. Mores (*Qu.*). *Oxon.*
Miscellanea Critica. Ri. Dawes (Emm.). Ed. 2. T. Burgess (*Corpus*). *Oxon.*
Mason's Caractacus in Greek verse. H. G. Glasse. *Oxon.*
Orphica De Lapidibus. T. Tyrwhitt (*Qu.* and *Mert.*). Lond.
Euclid I—VI. Examined by W. Austin (*Wadh.*). *Oxon.*
Euclid. J. Williamson (? *Alb., Hertf.*). *Oxon.*
Xenophon Cyropaedia. T. Hutchinson (? *Linc.*). Camb.
Chemical Lectures. Ri. Watson (Trin.).
Conic Sections. S. Vince (Caius). Camb.
1782 N. T. Quotations compared with Hebr. LXX. J. Randolph (*Ch. Ch.*). *Oxon.*
On the Study of Antiquities. T. Burgess (*Corpus*). Ed. 2. *Oxon.*
The XIX Tragedies and Fragments of Euripides, engl. Mich. Wodhul (*Bras.*). 4 vols.
De Graecae Ling. Studio praelect. J. Randolph (*Ch. Ch.*).
Introd. to writing Greek for Winchester. G. Is. Huntingford (*New C.*). 2 parts. *Oxon.*
Syllabus of Lectures. Martin Wall (*New C.*). *Oxon.*
Homeri Odyssea, Gr. Lat. Ed. 2. *Oxon.*
Chemical Lectures. Ri. Watson (Trin.).

Experiments on Mercury. Ja. Price (? *Magd. H.*). *Oxon.*
Heads of Lectures on Botany, Nat. Hist. and Fossils. T. Martyn (Emm. and Sid.).
Meditationes Algebraicae. E. Waring (Magd.) Ed. 3.
1783 Praxis [latin exercises]. H. Bright (*New C.*). *Oxon.*
Preacher's Assistant. J. Cooke. 2 vols. *Oxon.*
Progress of Refinement, a poem. H. J. Pye (*Magd.*). 4to. *Oxon.*
Cicero. J. T. Oliveti (*S. J.*). 10 vols. *Oxon.*
In Strabonem conjecturae. T. Tyrwhitt (*Qu.* and *Mert.*). Lond.
Gemmarum Antiquarum Delectus. Jacob Bryant (King's).
Blackstone's Commentaries. Ri. Burn (*Qu.*). 4 vols. *Oxon.*
Dissertations in Chemistry and Medicine. Mart. Wall (*New C.*). *Oxon.*
De Graecae Ling. Studio praelect. J. Randolph (*Ch. Ch.*). 4to. *Oxon.*
A Fair Statement on Celibacy. Camb.
1784 Analysis of Greek Metres. J. B. Seale (Chr.). Camb.
Jeremiah and Lamentations, tr. B. Blayney (*Worc.* and *Hert.*). 4to. *Oxon.*
View of our Saviour's Ministry and Mission. T. Randolph (*Corpus*). *Oxon.*
Manners and Government of the Greeks, De Mably, tr. Chamberland. *Oxon.*
Cure of Apoplexies and Palsies. B. Chandler. Camb.
Plato Euthydemus et Gorgias. Martin Jos. Routh (*Magd.*). *Oxon.*
Plan of Education. G. Croft (*Univ.*). Wolverhampton.
Letters on Infidelity. G. Horne (*Univ.* and *Magd.*). 8vo. and 12mo. *Oxon.*
Rectilinear Motion. G. Atwood (Trin.). Camb.
Analysis of Lectures on Nat. Philos. G. Atwood (Trin.).
Astronomy. Roger Long (Pemb.). 2 vols. Camb.
Meditationes Analyticae, E. Waring (Magd.). Ed. 2. 4to. Camb.
1785 Aristotle Poetica. W. Cooke (King's). Camb.
Greek Metres. J. B. Seale (Chr.). Camb.
Roman Law. A. C. Schomberg. *Oxon.*
Xenophon Anab. var. T. Hutchinson (? *Linc.*), R. Porson (Trin.). Camb.
—— Memorabilia. E. Edwards and H. Owen (*Jes.*). *Oxon.*
Moral and Political Philosophy. W. Paley (Chr.). Lond.
Flora Cantabrigiensis. R. Relhan (Trin.). Camb.
Rousseau's Letters on Botany. T. Martyn (Emm. and Sid.).
Rudiments on Mathematics. W. Ludlam (Joh.). Lond.
System of Mechanics and Hydrostatics. T. Parkinson (Chr.). 2 vols. 4to. Camb.
Prize Essays on Gambling, Duelling and Suicide. Ri. Hey (Sid., Magd.). Camb.
1786 Euripides Hippolytus. Honble F. H. Egerton (*Ch. Ch.*, *All S.*). *Oxon.*
Shakespeare. Jos. Rann (*Trin.*). *Oxon.*
Diversions of Purley. J. Horne [Tooke] (Joh.).
History of Oxford. A. Wood (*Mert.*) J. Gutch (*All S.*). 2 vols. 4to. *Oxon.*
Maritime Laws of Rhodes. A. C. Schomberg. *Oxon.*
Clinical Observations on Opium. Mart. Wall. *Oxon.*
Chemical Lectures. R. Watson (Trin.).
Florae Cantabrigiensis I. R. Relhan (Trin.). Lond.
1787 Catalogue of Oriental MSS. Oxon. J. Uri. fol. *Oxon.*
Historical Account of Textus Roffensis with mem. of the Elstobs and J. Johnson. S. Pegge (Joh.).
Heads of Botanical lectures. · R. Relhan (Trin.). Camb.
Rudiments of Mathematics. W. Ludlam (Joh). Lond.
1788 Conspectus Critt. Observationum in Scripturas, Gr. and Lat. T. Burgess (*Corpus*).
The Proverbs from the Hebrew. Ber. Hodgson (*Ch. Ch.*, *Hert.*). 4to. *Oxon.*
Initia Homerica. T. Burgess (*Corpus*).
Longinus. Jonathan Toup (*Exon.* and Pemb., Camb.). 4to. *Oxon.*

Sententiae Philosophorum e cod. Leidensi Vossiano. T. Burgess (*Corpus*).
12mo.

Milton's Samson Agonistes in Greek Verse. J. H. Glasse (*Ch. Ch.*). *Oxon.*

Virgil Georgicon. Gil. Wakefield (Jes.). Camb.

Xenophon Anabasis. T. Hutchinson, &c. Memorab. B. Simpson. *Oxon.*

Antiquarian Tracts. F. Wise (*Trin.*). 2 vols. *Oxon.*

Italian Selections transl. by Camb. gentlemen. Ag. Isola. Camb.

XXXVIII Botanical Plates. T. Martyn (Emm. and Sid.).

Considerations on the Oaths and Discipline. By a Member of the Senate.
Camb.

Remarks on Enormous Expence in Cambridge.

1789 Aristotle's Poetics. T. Twining (Sid.). 4to. *Oxon.*

Analysis of Greek Metres. J. B. Seale (Chr.). Camb.

Ariosto. Orlando Furioso. Ag. Isola. (Camb.).

Elementa Architecturae Civilis. H. Aldrich (*Ch. Ch.*). P. Smyth. *Oxon.*

Sallust. H. Homer (Emm.).

Silvae Criticae I. Gil. Wakefield (Jes.). Camb.

Elements of Jurisprudence. Ri. Woodeson (*Magd.*).

General Astronomical Catalogue. F. Wollaston (Sid.). Lond.

Bibliotheca Classica. J. Lempriere (*Pemb.*).

1790 Pentateuchus Hebr. Samarit. charact. Hebr. B. Blayney. (*Worc.* and
Hert.). *Oxon.*

Ecclesiastes, from the Hebrew. Bern. Hodgson (*Ch. Ch., Hert.*). *Oxon.*

Marmorum Oxon. Inscrr. Graecae. W. Roberts (? Pemb. H., *Mert.*). *Oxon.*

Sophocles Oedipus, engl. G. S. Clarke (Trin.). *Oxon.*

Emendationes in Suidam et Hesych., &c. Jonathan Toup (*Exon.* and
Pemb. Camb.). T. Tyrwhitt (*Qu.* and *Mert.*). R. Porson (Trin.)
4 vols. *Oxon.*

Tacitus. H. Homer (Emm.).

On Practical Astronomy. S. Vince (Cai. and Sid.). Camb. and Lond.

Treatise on Gaming. C. Moore (Trin.)

1791 A List of Books for the Clergy dio. Chester. W. Cleaver (*Magd., Bras.*).
Oxon.

Demosthenis Orr. selectae. Ri. Mounteney (King's). Eton.

Marmorum Oxon. Inscriptiones. W. Roberts (? Pemb. H., *Mert.*). *Oxon.*

Plutarch de Educ. Liberorum. T. Edwards (Clare, ? Jes.). Camb.

Shakespeare's Plays. Jos. Rann (*Trin.*). 6 vols. *Oxon.*

Tryphiodorus. T. Northmore, F. S. A. *Oxon.*

1792 The Book of Daniel Translated. T. Wintle. 4to. *Oxon.*

A List of Books, &c. Ed. 2 with Dodwell's. W. Cleaver (*Magd., Br.*).
Oxon.

Enchiridion Theologicum (tracts). J. Randolph (*Ch. Ch.*). 5 vols. *Oxon.*

Archimedes. J. Torelli (Padua). Fol. *Oxon.*

Aristotle's Poetics gr. lat. T. Tyrwhitt (*Qu., Mert.*). *Oxon.*

Maured Allatafet...Annales Aegypt. J. D. Carlyle (Chr. and Qu.).

Flora Rustica. T. Martyn (Emm. and Sid.). Vol. 1. Lond.

Gravinae Opuscula. T. Burgess (*Corpus*).

Horace. Combe. 2 vols. Lond.

Musei Oxon. fasc. 1. T. Burgess (*Corpus*).

Strictures on the Discipline, Cambridge. [W. Heberden (Joh.)]. Lond.

Tour from Oxford to Newcastle on Tyne in the Long Vacation. J. Briggs
(*S. Mary H.*). *Oxon.*

Herodotus, trs. with notes. Vol. 1. J. Lempriere (*Pemb.*).

1793 Articuli XXXIX. E. Welchman. *Oxon.*

Works of Ri. Hooker (*Corpus*). 3 vols. *Oxon.*

Flora Cantabrigiensis III., R. Relhan (*Trin.*). Lond.

Silva Critica iv. &c. quibus accedunt Hymni Orphici tres. Gil. Wakefield
[Jes.]. Lond.

Systematic View of the Laws of England. Ri. Woodeson (*Magd.*). 3 vols.

Plan of Lectures on Natural Philosophy. S. Vince (Caius and Sid.).
Lond.

Sectiones Conicae. A. Robertson (? *Ch. Ch.*). 4to. *Oxon.*
Universal Meridian Dial. F. Wollaston (Sid.). 4to.
Peace and Union. W. Frend (Jes.).
Alma Mater. T. Castley (Jes.). Camb.
On Kipling's Preface. T. Edwards (Trin. H.)
1794 Holy Bible. *Oxon.*
    The Ch. of England Man's Companion, or a Rational Illustration of the
        Book of Common Prayer, by C. Wheatley (*Joh.*) [ed. 1. 1710]. *Oxon.*
    An Attempt to render the daily reading of the Psalms more intelligible to
        the unlearned. F. Travell (? *Exon.*). *Oxon.*
    Aristotelis Poetica, var. T. Tyrwhitt (*Qu.* and *Mert.*), T. Burgess (*Corpus*)
        and bp. J. Randolph (*Ch. Ch.*). 4to and 8vo. *Oxon.*
    Horace. Gil. Wakefield [Jes.]. Lond.
    Flora Oxoniensis. J. Sibthorp (*Linc.* and *Univ.*).
    Flora Rustica. T. Martyn (Emm. and Sid.). 4 vols. Lond.
    Horti Botanici Catalogus. Camb.
    Catalogue of Oxford Graduates. J. Gutch (*All Souls*). *Oxon.*
    Parecbolae Statutorum. *Oxon.*
    Tragoediarum Graec. Delectus. Gil. Wakefield [Jes.]. Lond.
    Short Treatise on Conic Sections. T. Newton (Jes.). Camb.
    Letter on Celibacy of Fellows. Camb.
1795 Notitia Librorum Hebr. Gr. Lat. saecl. xv., et Aldin. *Oxon.*
    Bion and Moschus. Gil. Wakefield [Jes.]. 8vo. and 12mo. Lond.
    Chaucer modernized by W. Lipscomb (*Corpus*). 3 vols. *Oxon.*
    Translations from Petrarch, Metastasio, &c. T. Le Mesurier (*New C.*).
        Oxon.
    Plutarchi Moralia. Dan. Wyttenbach. 5 or 7 vols. 4to.; 13 or 15 8vo.
        Oxon.
    Virgil, Heyne. 2 vols. *Oxon.*
    ———— Phin. Pett (*Ch. Ch.*). *Oxon.*
    Analysis of Paley's Moral and Polit. Philos. ed. C. V. De Grice (Trin.).
        Camb.
    Analysis of Roman Civil Law. S. Hallifax (Jes. and Trin. Hall).
    Elements of Algebra I. Ja. Wood (Joh.). Camb.
    Fluxions. S. Vince (Caius and Sid.). Camb.
1796 Novum Testament. Vulgatae Edit. *Oxon.*
    Job transl. J. Garden. *Oxon.*
    XXXIX Articles. Gil. Burnet (Aberd.). *Oxon.*
    Specimens of Arabic Poetry. J. D. Carlyle (Chr. and Qu.).
    Cambridge University Calendar. Camb.
    On the Cheltenham Waters. J. Smith. *Oxon.*
    Dissertation concerning the War of Troy. Jacob Bryant (King's).
    Euripidis Hippolytus. Hon. F. H. Egerton (*Ch. Ch.*, *All S.*). 4to. *Oxon.*
    Lucretius. Gil. Wakefield [Jes.]. 3 vol. 4to. Lond.
    On the Prosodies of Greek and Latin. [S. Horsley (Trin. Hall)]. Lond.
    Virgil. Gil. Wakefield [Jes.]. 12mo. Lond.
    W. Blackstone's Commentaries. ed. E. Christian (Joh.). Lond.
    Syllabus of Locke's Essay. 12mo. Camb.
    Chronological Tables from Solomon to Alexander the Great. J. Falconer.
        4to. *Oxon.*
    Arithmetic and Algebra. T. Manning (Caius).
    Principles of Algebra. W. Frend [Jes.].
    Hydrostatics. S. Vince (Caius and Sid.).
    Principles of Mechanics. Ja. Wood (Joh.). Camb.
1797 Biblia Graeca. Ro. Holmes (*New C.* and *Ch. Ch.*). fol. Vol. 1. *Oxon.*
    Jeremiah, Lamentations, with Daniel. B. Blayney (*Worc.* and *Hert.*). 4to.
        Oxon.
    Zechariah, transl. B. Blayney (*Worc.* and *Hert.*). 4to. *Oxon.*
    Zechariah, ch. ii. T. Wintle (*Joh.*). *Oxon.*
    On the Creed. J. Pearson (King's and Trin. Camb.). ed. *Oxon.*
    Origines Sacrae. E. Stillingfleet (Joh. Camb.). 2 vols. *Oxon.*

Aeschylus typis quos vocant homeric's. [R. Porson (Trin.)]. Foulis. Glasg.
Euripidis Hecuba. Ri. Porson (Trin.). Lond.
In Eur. Hec. Diatribe Extemporalis. Gil. Wakefield [Jes.]. Lond.
Homeri Odyssea. . 2 vols. *Oxon.*
Musei Oxon. fasc. ii. T. Burgess (*Corpus*). *Oxon.*
Voyage of Hanno. T. Falconer (*Corpus*). *Oxon.*
Introd. Lecture on Chemistry. R. Bourne (*Worc.*). *Oxon.*
Syllabus of Lectures on the Laws of England. E. Christian (Joh.). Lond.
On Plants, &c. Analogy between Animal and Vegetable Kingdoms. Ro.
  Hooper (? *Pemb.*). *Oxon.*
Complete Analysis of Adam Smith's Wealth of Nations. Jer. Joyce. Camb.
Cambridge University Calendar.
Astronomy. Vol. 1. S. Vince (Caius and Sid.). 4to. Camb.
Astron. Observations at Greenwich 1750—62. Ja. Bradley (*Ball.*). 2 vols.
  fol. *Oxon.*
1798 Vet. Testamentum Graec. vol. 1. Ro. Holmes (*New C., Ch. Ch.*). *Oxon.*
Greek Testament, vol. i. (Gospels). J. White (*Wadh.*). *Oxon.*
Method of Settling Canonical Authority of N. T. Jer. Jones (nonconf.).
  Oxon.
T. Tyrwhitti Conjecturae in Aesch. Eurip. and Aristoph. ed. 1. T. Bur-
  gess (*Corpus*).
Aristotelis Πέπλος sive Epitaphia. T. Burgess (*Corpus*).
Euripidis Orestes. R. Porson (Trin.). Lond.
Demosthenis Olynth. ii, iii; Philipp. ii. Jer. Wolf, &c. *Oxon.*
Chaucer's Canterbury Tales. ed. T. Tyrwhitt (*Qu., Mert.*). ed. 2. 2 vols.
  4to. *Oxon.*
Saxon and English illustrative of each other. S. Henshall (*Bras.*).
Interview with the Jeshoo Lama. Capt. S. Turner. 12mo. *Oxon.*
Algebra, vol. ii. T. Manning (Caius). Lond.
Elements of Optics. Ja. Wood (Joh.). Camb.
Greenwich Observations. J. Bradley (*Ball.*). N. Bliss. vol. 1, fol. *Oxon.*
Reflections on the Caelibacy of Fellows. Camb.
1799 Act. Apost. and Epistt. versio Syr. Philoxen. J. White (*Wadh.*). vol. 1.
  4to. *Oxon.*
Appendix ad N. T. e cod. Alexandr. C. G. Woide (Haffn., *Oxon.*). ed. H.
  Ford (*Ch. Ch., Magd. H.*). fol. *Oxon.*
Diatessaron. J. White (*Wadh.*). *Oxon.*
Horae Biblicae. C. Butler (Douay). *Oxon.*
History of the Interpr. of Prophecy. H. Kett (*Trin.*). *Oxon.*
Common Prayer with Psalms in Metre. *Oxon.*
Antonini Iter Brit., ed. T. Reynolds (*Linc.* and Camb.). 4to.
Euripidis Phoenissae. R. Porson (Trin.). Lond.
Molière. 2 vols. *Oxon.*
Cambridge University Calendar.
Principles of Algebra. W. Frend [Jes.]
Principles of Astronomy. S. Vince (Caius and Sid.).
The Sizar: a Rhapsody. 12mo. Camb.
1800 Abollatiph Hist. Aegypt. Jos. White (*Wadh.*). *Oxon.*
Dict. Graec. H. Hoogeveen (Leyd.). 4to. Camb.
Homer. Grenville. *Oxon.*
Livy. H. Homer (Emm.). *Oxon.*
Sophocles, S. Musgrave (*Corpus, Univ.*). *Oxon.*
Cambridge University Calendar.
Fasciculus Astronomicus. F. Wollaston (Sid.). Lond.
Latitude of the N. Hemisphere. J. Stephens (Joh.). Camb.
Principles of Fluxions .... ⎞ S. Vince (Caius and
Principles of Hydrostatics .... ⎟ Sid.). Camb.
Plane and Spherical Trigonometry and Logarithms... ⎠

INDEX.

₊ *Names, &c.,* in *italics* refer to the University of *Oxford.*

Under the names of the Colleges or Halls it has not been thought necessary to give a reference to each page on which any alumnus is mentioned, though this has been done in some instances; the use of the brackets in this Index and in the foregoing List of Publications will enable any one to compile such a list without much labour if it be thought worth the while.